The private sector plays a pivotal role in fighting corruption worldwide. Transparency International's *Global Corruption Report 2009* documents in unique detail the many corruption risks for businesses, ranging from small entrepreneurs in Sub-Saharan Africa to multinationals from Europe and North America. More than 75 experts examine the scale, scope and devastating consequences of a wide range of corruption issues, including bribery and policy capture, corporate fraud, cartels, corruption in supply chains and transnational transactions, emerging challenges for carbon trading markets, sovereign wealth funds and growing economic centres, such as Brazil, China and India.

The Global Corruption Report 2009 also discusses the most promising tools to tackle corruption in business, identifies pressing areas for reform and outlines how companies, governments, investors, consumers and other stakeholders can contribute to raising corporate integrity and meeting the challenges that corruption poses to sustainable economic growth and development.

Transparency International (TI) is the global civil society organisation leading the fight against corruption. Through more than ninety chapters worldwide and an international secretariat in Berlin, Germany, TI raises awareness of the damaging effects of corruption and works with partners in government, business and civil society to develop and implement effective measures to tackle it. For more information go to www.transparency.org.

Global Corruption Report 2009

Corruption and the Private Sector

TRANSPARENCY INTERNATIONAL
the global coalition against corruption

CAMBRIDGE
UNIVERSITY PRESS

ERNST & YOUNG
Quality In Everything We Do

CAMBRIDGE UNIVERSITY PRESS

Cambridge, New York, Melbourne, Madrid, Cape Town, Singapore, São Paulo, Delhi

Cambridge University Press
The Edinburgh Building, Cambridge CB2 8RU, UK

Published in the United States of America by Cambridge University Press, New York

www.cambridge.org
Information on this title: www.cambridge.org/9780521132404

First published 2009

Printed in the United Kingdom at the University Press, Cambridge

A catalogue record for this publication is available from the British Library

ISBN 978-0-521-13240-4
ISSN 1749-3161

Cambridge University Press has no responsibility for the persistence or
accuracy of URLs for external or third-party internet websites referred to
in this book, and does not guarantee that any content on such
websites is, or will remain, accurate or appropriate.

Edited by Dieter Zinnbauer, Rebecca Dobson and Krina Despota

Every effort has been made to verify the accuracy of the information contained in this report, including
allegations. All information was believed to be correct as of January 2009. Nevertheless, Transparency
International cannot guarantee the accuracy and the completeness of the contents. Nor can Transparency
International accept responsibility for the consequences of its use for other purposes or in other contents.
Contributions to the *Global Corruption Report 2009* by authors external to Transparency International do not
necessarily reflect the view of Transparency International or its national chapters.

Contents

Part one: Corruption and the private sector

Part two: Country reports

Part three: Research

Illustrations

Boxes

Contributors

- Dante Mendes Aldrighi – University of São Paulo
- Noémi Alexa – TI Hungary
- Victor Alistar – TI Romania
- Léopold Ambassa – TI Cameroon
- Amare Aregawi – Transparency Ethiopia (TI Ethiopia)
- Federico Arenoso – Poder Ciudadano (TI Argentina)
- Julieta Arias – Poder Ciudadano (TI Argentina)
- Vitus A. Azeem – Ghana Integrity Initiative (TI Ghana)
- Vénant Bacinoni – ABUCO (Consumers' Association of Burundi)
- Alma Rocío Balcázar – Transparencia por Colombia (TI Colombia)
- Ayesha Barenblat – Business for Social Responsibility
- María Batch – Poder Ciudadano (TI Argentina)
- Frédéric Boehm – Deutsche Gesellschaft für Technische Zusammenarbeit
- Deborah A. Bräutigam – American University, Washington, DC
- John Bray – Control Risks
- Jørund Buen – Point Carbon
- Elaine Burns – TI
- María del Pilar Callizo – Transparencia Paraguay
- Manuel Calvagno – Poder Ciudadano (TI Argentina)
- Indira Carr – University of Surrey
- Marcelo Cerna – Chile Transparente (TI Chile)
- John C. Coffee, Jr. – Columbia University
- Julien Coll – TI France
- Susan Côté-Freeman – TI
- Alvaro Cuervo-Cazurra – University of South Carolina
- Mercedes De Freitas – Transparencia Venezuela (TI Venezuela)
- Clara Delavallade – University Paris 1 Panthéon Sorbonne
- Gillian Dell – TI
- Luz Ángela Díaz – Transparencia por Colombia (TI Colombia)
- Sarah Dix – National Research Institute, Papua New Guinea
- Rebecca Dobson – TI
- Apostolos Dousias – TI Greece
- Alexander Dyck – University of Toronto
- Badri El Meouchi – Lebanese Transparency Association (TI Lebanon)
- Georges Enderle – University of Notre Dame
- Santeri Eriksson – Transparency Finland (TI Finland)
- Dolores Español – TI Philippines
- Rob Evans – *The Guardian*
- Gretta Fenner – Basel Institute on Governance
- Cristie Ford – University of British Columbia
- Carla Gasser – TI Switzerland
- Khalil Gebara – Lebanese Transparency Association (TI Lebanon)
- Alphonse Gelu – National Research Institute, Papua New Guinea

- Lynne Ghossein – Lebanese Transparency Association (TI Lebanon)
- Syed Adil Gilani – TI Pakistan
- Ana Carolina González Espinosa – Transparencia por Colombia (TI Colombia)
- Kristóf Gosztonyi – Control Risks
- Johann Graf Lambsdorff – University of Passau
- Grupo Cívico Ética y Transparencia (TI Nicaragua)
- Guo Yong – Anti Corruption and Governance Research Center, Tsinghua University
- Pierre Habbard – Trade Union Advisory Committee
- Gavin Hayman – Global Witness
- Ben W. Heineman, Jr. – Harvard University
- David Hess – Ross School of Business, University of Michigan
- Hans-Christoph Hirt – Hermes Equity Ownership Services
- Robin Hodess – TI
- Varuzhan Hoktanyan – TI Anti-corruption Center (TI Armenia)
- Georg Huber-Grabenwarter – Deutsche Gesellschaft für Technische Zusammenarbeit
- Christian Humborg – TI Germany
- Howell E. Jackson – Harvard University
- María Celeste Jara – Transparencia Paraguay
- Fernando Jiménez – University of Murcia and TI Spain
- Paul Kananura – TI Rwanda
- Sung-Goo Kang – TI South Korea
- Muel Kaptein – Erasmus University, the Netherlands
- Vikramaditya Khanna – University of Michigan
- Alan Knight – AccountAbility
- Chandrashekhar Krishnan – TI UK
- Mazvita Debra Kubwalo – TI Zimbabwe
- Jomo Kwame Sundaram – United Nations
- Huguette Labelle – TI
- Oscar Lanza – Committee for the Defence of Consumer Rights, Bolivia
- Aileen Laus – TI Philippines
- Emmanuelle Lavallée – DIAL, Paris
- Daniel Lebègue – TI France
- Gregore Pio Lopez – East Asian Bureau for Economic Research, Australia
- Alina Lungu – TI Romania
- Tanvir Mahmud – TI Bangladesh
- Narayen Manandhar – TI Nepal
- Aleksandra Martinović – TI Bosnia and Herzegovina
- Pradeep S. Mehta – CUTS International, India
- Udai Mehta – CUTS International, India
- Bettina Meier – TI Sri Lanka
- Kamal Mesbahi – TI Morocco
- Axel Michaelowa – Perspectives GmbH
- Nebojša Milanović – TI Bosnia and Herzegovina
- David Miller – University of Strathclyde
- Siddhartha Mitra – CUTS International, India
- Apollinaire Mupiganyi – TI Rwanda

- Sergej Muravjov – TI Lithuania
- N. R. Narayana Murthy – Infosys
- Florentina Nastase – TI Romania
- John Nellis – International Analytics
- Rocío Noriega – Chile Transparente (TI Chile)
- Léopold Nzeusseu – TI Cameroon
- Osita Nnamani Ogbu – TI Nigeria
- Elewechi Okike – University of Sunderland
- Juanita Olaya – Consultant
- Josefina Palma – Poder Ciudadano (TI Argentina)
- Elena Panfilova – TI Russia
- Sol Picciotto – Lancaster University
- Janelle Plummer – World Bank
- Mark Pyman – TI UK
- Tara Rangarajan – Business for Social Responsibility
- Juanita Riaño – TI
- Mark J. Roe – Harvard University
- Segundo Romero – TI Philippines
- Susan Rose-Ackerman – Yale University
- François Roubaud – DIAL, Paris
- Varina Suleiman – Poder Ciudadano (TI Argentina)
- Susanne Tam – TI Israel
- TI Austria
- TI Cameroon
- TI India
- TI Indonesia
- TI Kenya
- TI Malaysia
- TI Nepal
- TI Poland
- TI Russia
- TI UK
- TI USA
- Trinidad and Tobago Transparency Institute (TI Trinidad and Tobago)
- Toru Umeda – TI Japan
- Oscar Vallés – Universidad Metropolitana, Venezuela
- Shirley van Buiren – TI Germany
- Frank Vogl – TI
- Natalya Volchkova – Center for Economic and Financial Research, Moscow
- Jennifer Walmsley – Hermes Equity Ownership Services
- Sebastian Wolf – TI Germany
- Eyasu Yimer – Transparency Ethiopia (TI Ethiopia)
- Iftekhar Zaman – TI Bangladesh
- Luigi Zingales – University of Chicago
- Dieter Zinnbauer – TI
- Michèle Zirari – TI Morocco

Preface

Huguette Labelle, Chair of Transparency International

Supporting and encouraging business to do its part in tackling corruption has been a global priority for Transparency International (TI) since its inception. Our approach is firmly anchored in the belief that sustainable progress towards a world free of corruption requires a systematic and constructive engagement with the demand for and supply of corruption and the incentive systems that shape them both.

To name just a few examples, we have developed – often in close cooperation with partners in the private sector and civil society – a number of widely used tools and templates that assist business in establishing anti-corruption systems or that enhance the integrity and transparency of public tendering processes. Likewise, many of our diagnostic and research activities aim to identify corruption risks that are a particular challenge for business and to measure the progress that is being made in addressing them.

TI's choice of corruption and the private sector as the focus of its *Global Corruption Report 2009* is an extension of these efforts. The report provides a platform for combining reflections on practical experience with rigorous analysis and a forward-looking perspective on the reform of policy and practice. After fifteen years working with the private sector, and on issues of the supply side of corruption, we felt it was an opportune time to take stock of progress and suggest new and constructive ways ahead.

Few issues are more cross-cutting and more relevant to a wide array of corruption challenges than the question of how business around the world can ensure that it performs to the highest standards of integrity and does not become a party to or facilitator of corrupt transactions. As the *Global Corruption Report 2009* shows clearly, making business, markets and globalisation work, and making them work to the benefit of all, requires concerted and continuing efforts by business, governments and civil society to root out corruption in the commercial sector.

The window of opportunity for taking decisive action has rarely been more favourable. The financial crisis that began to shake the world economy in 2008 has reminded us that opacity, insufficient regulatory oversight and conflicts of interest in some parts of the economy can bring the entire system to the brink of collapse. The crisis has imbued business, policy-makers and communities with a sense of urgency and an unprecedented readiness to examine whether the structures and mechanisms to govern our global economy are adequate to meet the challenges of the twenty-first century.

A raft of reform proposals are already on the table. Greater transparency features among them. Indeed, many of the suggested ways forward echo the policy recommendations made by the *Global Corruption Report 2009* and align with TI's long-standing demands for more, and more effective, disclosure, alongside increased accountability on the part of markets, market players and the institutions entrusted with regulating them.

It is encouraging that this discussion is being taken forward under the umbrella of the G20 – a larger group of governments, as it includes major developing countries, than the familiar industrialised G8 grouping. Opening this dialogue on the future architecture for the global economic system to a broader range of stakeholders, including civil society, is imperative. The global dimension of the crisis, which reminds us all how interwoven economies are in both the developed and developing worlds, aptly reminds us that only a truly inclusive and cooperative approach across countries and stakeholders will succeed in making real progress in curbing corruption, raising standards of transparency and accountability, and restoring the public trust that is so essential for economies to work and communities to prosper. The private sector has always been a part of the corruption equation, but we are encouraged that the demands of our time mean that it can also be a key driver of the integrity revolution – a revolution that will secure greater sustainability in markets and more economic opportunities for all.

Foreword 1
Tackling corruption in business: profitable and feasible

N. R. Narayana Murthy[1]

Growing a successful and sustainable business requires at least three things: an uncompromising devotion to developing products and services that contribute real value and allow clients to achieve their goals in the most effective and efficient way; passionate leadership that attracts and inspires the best of the class to join this venture; and an unwavering commitment to act as a responsible player in the community, nurturing the public trust and support on which all businesses ultimately depend.

Corruption erodes each of these pillars of business success: it means cutting corners and shirking honest competition rather than producing real, competitive value for clients; it means compromising corporate and individual integrity, deterring and demotivating the brightest and most innovative entrepreneurs and scientists from signing on; and it means consenting to, and propping up, a business environment in which complicity is for sale, entrusted public power is routinely abused for the sake of private gain, and public trust in the beneficial partnership between business and society is gradually undone.

Infosys, the company that I founded with little more than US$250 in seed capital, has always taken a strong and principled position to resist the temptation of corruption. We passionately believed that our commitment to both customers and communities meant that illegal short cuts were never an option. We were confident that our values would prevail and, indeed, help us excel in the marketplace. Our hopes proved justified. Today Infosys is one of the largest, most respected and most trusted players in the global information technology and services arena. Far from disadvantaging us, our anti-corruption stance has been a driver for sustainable growth and performance. With it we have earned the trust of local and international business partners and fended off opportunistic overtures to rig the game. These standards continue to attract the most talented and value-oriented workforce to Infosys, proving to the business community and broader society that an open, accountable business environment, personal integrity and hard work are the indispensable ingredients that create a dynamic economy, expediting both economic and social development.

It is with this experience in mind that I warmly welcome Transparency International's *Global Corruption Report 2009*. It delivers the timely and compelling message that business can, and must, stand up to corruption. To do so on a global scale is a daunting challenge; but it is the vigorous pursuit of this challenge that leads to trust, leads to growth, leads to success. For business. For society.

---

1 N. R. Narayana Murthy is chairman and chief mentor of Infosys Technologies Limited.

Foreword 2
The role of the private sector in fighting corruption: essential for meeting local and global governance challenges

Jomo Kwame Sundaram[1]

The level of corruption in the private sector remains disturbingly high. It is not uncommon for domestic firms and multinationals to pay bribes in order to secure public procurement contracts, nor unusual to learn of powerful corporate entities exerting undue pressure so as to capture institutions and influence regulations to elicit favourable investment conditions.

Such practices are all too often encouraged by or met with cooperation from civil servants, many of whom may be underpaid and hence struggling to make ends meet, or corrupt political leaders who use politics to make money that they may claim they need to advance their political ends or to pay for political support. Some who amass huge fortunes while in office may smuggle these assets out of their countries into secret personal bank accounts abroad.

We know only too well that corporate corruption significantly diminishes or threatens the dynamism and growth that comes with fair competition.

All the same, the harm that corruption inflicts does not confine itself to undermining healthy competition or paralysing economic growth. Some of the most important public policy challenges that we face today will be tackled only when business fully assumes its due responsibilities, which need to be complemented by effective regulation.

Climate change, for example, will require huge investments, resource transfers and the ingenuity of business leaders to refashion their strategies in a sustainable manner. Greed and a short-sighted defence of anachronistic business models provide two of the most significant obstacles to addressing global warming in an equitable, effective and timely manner. Entrepreneurial vision, business integrity and corporate responsibility can, and must, play a central role in this context.

Fragile states present another challenge. These countries are the backdrops of unimaginable human suffering and regional insecurity. Often they contain large military forces and formidable wealth in natural resources. In this context, extractive industries and the defence sector must play a central role in ensuring that corruption has no place in business dealings and that revenue streams and public expenditures alike remain transparent – a precondition for public accountability.

---

1 Jomo Kwame Sundaram is the assistant secretary general for economic development in the United Nations (UN) Department of Economic and Social Affairs.

Stamping out corruption and strengthening corporate integrity is a challenging agenda, but one with ample opportunities for engagement.

One important strategy is to establish and implement firmly the national and international normative frameworks against corruption. At the domestic level, most countries already have anti-corruption laws and policies in place. Unfortunately, these are often rendered ineffective by uneven or weak enforcement and implementation. The comparable framework at the international level is the United Nations Convention against Corruption, which entered into force in 2005 and needs now to be embraced fully by signatory countries.

The active involvement of the business community is a second strategy in the fight against corruption. The UN Global Compact's tenth principle against corruption underlines the shared responsibility and willingness of the private sector to play its part in eliminating corruption. This reflects the ongoing development of rules of corporate social responsibility (CSR), which are prompting companies to integrate anti-corruption measures as a means of protecting their reputations. Today a growing number of investment managers are looking closely at internal controls related to business ethics and corporate integrity as evidence of good business practices and sound management.

A third strategy asks us to utilise fully the countervailing forces of civil society and public opinion to fight corruption in the corporate sector. Civil society can help the state to design appropriate strategies, enrol the participation of citizens and enterprises in implementing anti-corruption measures and maintain social pressure for continued political commitment to tackle corruption.

The bottom line is clear: we need to deal with corruption in the private sector creatively, at all levels, and through different channels of intervention and regulation. Furthermore, we need to encourage the private sector towards voluntary initiatives that promote CSR. By identifying priorities for action and innovative approaches for engagement, Transparency International's *Global Corruption Report 2009* demonstrates that all stakeholders can play their part in enhancing the transparency and accountability of businesses and help them fulfil their vital role in meeting the global public policy challenges of our time.

Acknowledgements

The *Global Corruption Report 2009* relies on the concerted efforts of more than 200 individuals, none more essential than the book's authors, whose professional knowledge and personal insights gave shape and substance to the report.

Transparency International's national chapters continue to be a driving force behind the report, developing informed country-level accounts of corruption, and leading national advocacy activities concerning the book's thematic focus. Our colleagues at the TI Secretariat and our friends in the wider TI movement have similarly supported the project with their intellectual input and enthusiasm.

Jermyn Brooks, Elaine Burns, Susan Côté-Freeman, Birgit Errath and Peter Wilkinson form the backbone of Transparency International's private sector team and have been instrumental in developing the report from its earliest stages.

The thematic section of the book has benefited enormously from input and inspiration by a group of distinguished experts who graciously served on the report's Editorial Advisory Panel: Soji Apampa, Jeremy Baskin, Peter von Blomberg, Jermyn Brooks, Arun Duggal, Eileen Kohl Kaufman, Georg Kell, Michael Klein, Sergei Litovchenko, Frank Vogl and Ricardo Young.

The members of Transparency International's Index Advisory Committee supported our call for research, harnessing their knowledge and contacts to provide us with cutting-edge contributions. These individuals are Jeremy Baskin, Julius Court, Steven Finkel, Johann Graf Lambsdorff, Daniel Kaufmann, Jocelyn Kuper, Emmanuelle Lavallée, Mireille Razafindrakoto, Richard Rose, Susan Rose-Ackerman, François Roubaud, Shang-Jin Wei and Walter Zucchini.

We are indebted to our external editors. Mark Worth provided essential research and revisions, Sarah Repucci cast a careful eye over the country reports, and copy-editor Mike Richardson dotted our 'i's, crossed our 't's. As ever, we are grateful to Robin Hodess for her sharp editorial oversight and unflagging optimism.

We would like to express our sincere thanks to Daniel Dunlavey, Mainda Kiwelu, Finola O'Sullivan, Tim Ryder and Richard Woodham at Cambridge University Press for their continued flexibility and professionalism.

Also meriting mention are the many individuals around the world whose various skills and insights were vital for the success of the report, including Andrew Aeria, Aimee Ansari, Ari-Veikko Anttiroiko, Antonio Argandoña, Aida Arutyunova, Nicole Ball, Joanne Bauer, Adriana Begeer, Predrag Bejakovic, Ron Berenbeim, János Bertók, Bernhard Bodenstorfer, Matthew Brown, Jennie Burnet, Nadine Bushell, Andrés Cañizález, Emilio J. Cárdenas, Richard L.

Cassin, A. Didrick Castberg, Pavel Castka, Rajesh Chakrabarti, Raj Chari, Simon Chesterman, Juscelino F. Colares, John Connor, George Dallas, Orit Dayagi-Epstein, Eva Dienel, Bradford Dillman, Phyllis Dininio, Simeon Djankov, Arkan El Seblani, Abel Escribà-Folch, Tamirace Fakhoury Muehlbacher, Eduardo Flores-Trejo, Alessandra Fontana, Elizabeth Fuller, Olga Ghazaryan, Audra K. Grant, Jing Gu, Doug Guthrie, Jennifer Hanley-Giersch, Jayn Harding, Nicole M. Healy, Peter Henning, Clement M. Henry, Joss Heywood, Paul Heywood, Karen Hussman, P. C. Ioakimidis, Sorin Ionita, Stéphane Jaggers, David T. Johnson, Michael Johnston, Sony Kapoor, Tamás Kende, George Kegoro, Charles Kenny, Feisal Khan, Harvey F. Kline, Edwin Kok, Magda Lanuza, Peter Lewis, Karina Litvack, Robert B. Lloyd, Joan Lofgren, Stephen Ma, Darren McCauley, William Megginson, Samuli Miettinen, Joseph Mullen, Faris Natour, Bill O'Neill, Juanita Olaya, Manuel Orozco, Diane Osgood, Werner Pascha, Orlando J. Pérez, Sylwia Plaza, Heiko Pleines, Samuel D. Porteous, Gabriella Quimson, Karthik Ramanna, Douglas Rediker, Jean-Daniel Rinaudo, Sorin Dan Sandor, Beatrice Schlee, David Seddon, Kirsten Sehnbruch, Prem Sikka, Ajit Singh, Craig Smith, Tina Søreide, Wolfgang Sterk, Rotimi Suberu, Celia Szusterman, Susanne Tam, Nicolas van de Walle, Spencer Weber Waller, Jonathan Webb, Brian Woodall and Sappho Xenakis.

Fact-checkers Christofer Berg, Ariana Mendoza, Holly Nazar, Leila Peacock, Myroslava Purska, Talía La Rosa, Shelagh Roxburgh, Jessica Saltz, Berit Schlumbohm, Juho Siltanen, Katherine Stecher and Paulina González Tiburcio deserve thanks for combing through Web archives and digging up documents in pursuit of small truths.

As in years past we have relied on the law firm Covington and Burling, which generously provided pro-bono libel advice. On this year's team was Brandon Almond, Stephen Anthony, Enrique Armijo, Sarah Chasnovitz, Jason Criss, Simon Frankel, Eric Hellerman, Gregory Lipper, Eve Pogoriler, Brent Powell, Rob Sherman, Lindsey Tonsager and Steve Weiswasser.

Finally, we wish to acknowledge the generous financial support provided by the many donors to Transparency International's core activities, of which the *Global Corruption Report* is a key component. We would like to extend a special thank you to Ernst & Young for its significant support as a platinum-level funding partner, as well as the European Investment Bank as a silver-level funding partner of the *Global Corruption Report 2009*.

Dieter Zinnbauer, Rebecca Dobson, Krina Despota and Tobias Bock,
Editors

Executive summary

Transparency International

It may be that in no other time in history have entrepreneurship, private economic activity and markets been more important and intertwined with the economic prosperity, political stability and environmental sustainability of societies than they are at present. The financial crisis and the economic turmoil that this crisis has triggered have thrown this insight into sharp relief.

The private sector can be a source of dynamic innovation and growth. Nonetheless, as Transparency International's *Global Corruption Report 2009* clearly demonstrates, it can also fail to live up to its potential, if corruption goes unchecked, and turn into a destructive force that undermines fair competition, stifles economic growth and political development and ultimately undercuts its own existence.

Despite prominent corruption scandals and the lack of transparency and accountability that has been shown to lie at the root of the financial crisis, there has been encouraging and real progress towards stronger corporate integrity. Corporate performance in the fight against corruption often does not yet match corporate commitments, however. Crucial corruption risks, as well as loopholes in transparency, accountability and oversight, persist across all industries and all countries. Dynamic markets continue to produce new and subtle corruption challenges.

After a first broad wave of anti-corruption activism and corporate social responsibility (CSR) activities, business worldwide now has a *clearer responsibility, more profound self-interest and greater potential* to assume a vital role in the fight against corruption. This is a key message of the *Global Corruption Report 2009*, which brings together more than eighty recognised experts, practitioners and scholars to present the most comprehensive analysis to date of corruption and remedies for the business sector in all world regions.

The lesson from the analysis is clear: more of the same simply will not do. A step change in strategy and action is required to ensure that corruption in the business sector is tackled effectively.

- *Business* needs to recognise that corruption risks start with bribery and go beyond, requiring an integrated approach to corporate integrity and corporate citizenship.
- *Governments* need to take advantage of a new generation of innovative tools and thereby put much more emphasis on regulatory capabilities, actual enforcement and international cooperation.
- *Civil society* needs to become fully aware of how corruption in business is at the core of many other social, developmental and environmental challenges, and must forge much broader and more effective partnerships to support corporate integrity.
- *Stakeholders* – from business owners, executives and workers to auditors, investors,

regulators and anti-corruption activists – have to acknowledge that corporate integrity is a multi-stakeholder effort that requires collective action across sectors, borders and institutional boundaries.

Descriptions of a growing and complex problem

The evidence presented by the *Global Corruption Report 2009* is conclusive and troublesome: corruption is a central and growing challenge for business and society, from informal vendors in the least developed countries to multinational companies in industrialised ones, for citizens, communities and nations, all over the world.

Bribery and corruption in the value chain are a persistent challenge and more destructive than previously understood

Business continues to play a very exposed role as the supplier of corrupt payments to civil servants, members of government and political parties. Kickbacks may be actively solicited, extorted or offered proactively. Irrespective of the degree of coercion involved, the fact remains that bribery fosters a culture of impunity and repeat corruption, undermines the functioning of public institutions and fuels a public perception that governments and bureaucracies are up for sale to the highest bidder.

The scale and scope of bribery in business is staggering. Nearly two in five polled business executives have been asked to pay a bribe when dealing with public institutions. Half estimated that corruption raised project costs by at least 10 per cent. One in five claimed to have lost business because of bribes by a competitor. More than a third felt that corruption is getting worse.

The consequences are dramatic. In developing and transition countries alone, corrupt politicians and government officials receive bribes believed to total between US$20 and 40 billion annually – the equivalent of some 20 to 40 per cent of official development assistance. The cost is measurable in more than money. When corruption allows reckless companies to disregard the law, the consequences range from water shortages in Spain, exploitative work conditions in China or illegal logging in Indonesia to unsafe medicines in Nigeria and poorly constructed buildings in Turkey that collapse with deadly consequences. Even facilitation payments – the many, often small payments made by companies to 'get things done' – are found to be harmful, as they are funnelled up through the system and help nurture and sustain corrupt bureaucracies, political parties and governments.

The corruption challenge is much broader, more complex and more subtle than paying bribes

The *Global Corruption Report 2009* examines corruption in the private sector in a comprehensive way and finds that corrupt payments to public officials are only one part of the problem.

- **Nepotism and corruption in private business interactions are two issues that require much more attention**

Almost a half of the executives from the Organisation for Economic Co-operation and Development (OECD) countries who were polled reported that *personal and familiar relationships* are used to win public contracts in the non-OECD countries they do business in, pointing to corruption challenges that are more difficult to police and legislate for than direct corrupt payments.

In addition, senior executives cite corruption *within* the private sector more frequently as an obstacle to their business operations than infrastructure issues or the functioning of the judiciary. This issue so far has received very limited attention.

- **Corruption inside the enterprise is a widespread threat to sustainable performance and accountability**

Corruption not only affects business relationships but poses a considerable risk inside an enterprise. This report documents many cases of managers, majority shareholders and other actors inside corporations who abuse their entrusted powers for personal gain, to the detriment of owners, investors, employees and society at large. *Executives*, for example, may focus opportunistically on securing generous payouts to themselves, rather than on long-term profitability and sustainability – a phenomenon that has been identified as an important factor in the current financial crisis. *Majority owners* may try to leverage their influence on corporate strategy to expropriate smaller shareholders through 'self-dealing' and similar practices. The benefits of majority control are estimated to exceed 30 per cent of equity value in countries such as Austria, Italy, Mexico and Turkey. They amount to as much as 60 per cent or so of equity value in the Czech Republic and Brazil, raising serious concerns about checks on the powers of these actors.

The report underlines the fact that these and other types of corruption inside an enterprise are common in many countries, indicating serious shortcomings in internal checks and balances. In the long run, corruption compromises the core ability of companies to deliver value for all their stakeholders and act as responsible corporate citizens.

- **Corruption in the marketplace undermines fair competition, fair prices and efficiency worldwide**

Price-fixing cartels and other collusion schemes can cause serious harm to consumers, markets and the world economy. The *Global Corruption Report 2009* presents compelling evidence that a new and potent wave of globalised cartel activity has been sweeping through the world since the 1980s, often implicating well-known brand names and hitting developing countries particularly hard. Key market sectors worldwide have been corrupted, from food and vitamins to infrastructure projects, from anti-malaria medicines to the most sophisticated high-tech products and consumer services.

Experts believe that only between one in three or one in six cartels is exposed, yet even the cases that have come to light attest to a problem of enormous scale. More than 283 private international cartels that came to light between 1990 and 2005 caused direct economic losses to consumers through overcharges totalling some US$300 billion. In just one year, 1997, developing countries imported US$54.7 billion of goods from a sample of nineteen industries that participated in price-fixing conspiracies. Estimates suggest that direct economic losses due to overcharges by international cartel activities alone could match or even exceed the total volume of development aid given to developing countries.

- **Corruption risks in corporate lobbying can turn legitimate participation into undue influence and put the legitimacy of governments and business itself at risk**

Businesses are entitled to be heard in the democratic decision-making process, and lobbying conveys important information and opinion to political representatives and public officials. There is a risk, however, that powerful private sector players capture policies and governments and profoundly thwart democratic decisions, posing a significant threat to accountable and inclusive governance everywhere.

The *Global Corruption Report 2009* presents evidence of persistently close linkages between business and governments in developing and industrialised countries alike, multiple conflicts of interest and the growing risks of disproportionate influence on the part of corporate lobbying. Case studies from Bangladesh, Germany, Malaysia and Trinidad and Tobago all document a precariously close nexus between private business and public institutions. In the United Kingdom, politically connected firms are estimated to account for almost 40 per cent of market capitalisation – a level that rises to a staggering 80 per cent in Russia. In addition, the scale and rapid growth of lobbying raises serious concerns about equal visibility and the right to get heard for citizens who cannot afford to hire lobbyists. In Brussels an estimated 2,500 lobbying organisations with 15,000 lobbyists vie for influence on EU policy-making. In the United States, lobbying expenditures by companies have risen sharply and, at state level, lobbying expenditures average US$200,000 per legislator, while five lobbyists vie for the attention of each lawmaker.

- **The business case for fighting corruption has never been stronger**

At the level of the individual firm, corruption raises costs and introduces uncertainties, reputational risks and vulnerability to extortion. It makes access to capital more expensive, depresses company valuations and corrodes staff morale. In the broader market environment, corruption undermines fair competition, leads to lost business opportunities and nurtures corrupt bureaucracies. Corruption in and by business hollows out the very basis on which its own existence and success depends: the functioning and sound governance of markets. Corrupt practices invalidate the social licence to operate, breaking the legitimacy and trust that business depends upon in society.

Strong internal governance and corporate integrity are found to pay 'integrity dividends', dispelling the claim that companies can ill afford to abstain from corrupt practices without spoiling their business prospects. Companies with anti-corruption programmes and ethical guidelines are found to suffer up to 50 per cent fewer incidents of corruption, and to be less likely to lose business opportunities than companies without such programmes. Companies with superior performance as corporate citizens are shown not only to match but often to outperform their peers. Better corporate governance in companies located in emerging economies is associated with better performance and market valuation.

Lessons in strengthening corporate integrity

The *Global Corruption Report 2009* takes stock of the achievements of a first generation of CSR and anti-corruption efforts and draws a number of important conclusions.

- **Corruption risks for business are interlinked and mutually reinforcing, and must not therefore be tackled in isolation**

The *Global Corruption Report 2009* emphasises that the policy debate must be extended from core bribery issues to broader types of corrupt business practice. All forms of corruption take advantage of shortcomings in transparency, internal governance and oversight. Each fosters covert organisational practices and an opportunistic climate that make it difficult to root out individual incidences of corruption. For example, condemning bribery as illegal, or even morally wrong, will not work if practices seen as equally illegal and harmful, such as price-fixing, are condoned.

- **Progress is discernible, but many shortcomings remain**

More companies than ever have adopted business codes and report on their environmental and social performance. Governments in some countries have stepped up their efforts to tackle corporate corruption, leading to high-level prosecutions, such as that against the German company Siemens, thereby providing a much more credible deterrent to corrupt behaviour. Civil society groups have contributed to these moves, taking a keen interest in stronger corporate disclosure and commitments to the community.

The persistent and growing corruption risks described earlier underline the fact that current efforts are not sufficient, however. This report lists several key shortcomings. Internal checks and balances are far from fully effective. Almost one in three companies in a large international survey told of incidences of asset misappropriation and more than one in ten reported being affected by accounting fraud during a four-year period, while senior and middle management were found to be involved in a half of all cases of economic crime.

- **Awareness, training and monitoring need to be fully supported by all stakeholders**

In France, Germany, the United Kingdom and the United States, all major foreign investors and exporters and more than 80 per cent of surveyed executives admitted to 'not being familiar at all' with one of the most important legal frameworks in global business, the OECD Convention on Combating Bribery of Foreign Public Officials in International Business Transactions. Only a third or so of companies surveyed by other polls in the construction and power sector – industries with high corruption risks – had training programmes for executives on how to avoid corruption.

Monitoring progress and verifying corporate disclosure is not widespread either. Almost 90 per cent of the top 200 businesses worldwide have adopted business codes, but fewer than half report that they monitor compliance. Although more than 3,000 companies have published CSR reports in 2007, fewer than a third were verified through independent assurance.

- **Legal frameworks for tackling corruption must pay more attention to business-specific issues**

The country report section in the *Global Corruption Report 2009* indicates that many countries have passed or updated anti-corruption laws or established new anti-corruption agencies. At the same time, rules that deal specifically with some of the most prevalent corruption risks for business are still evolving and far from widely adopted. Stronger sanctions for the suppliers of corruption, better coverage of incidences of private-to-private bribery, influence-peddling and the use of intermediaries, as well as the criminal liability of companies and a clear approach to facilitation payments, are major areas of continuing concern in many countries. Establishing an effective review mechanism for the United Nations Convention against Corruption is an important task in this regard at international level, in order to track progress and speed up the strengthening of legal frameworks at country level.

- **Efforts for stronger corporate integrity need to address new players and new markets**

Countries such as Brazil, China and India already boast some of the world's largest markets, and their companies play an increasingly active and important role in global business. As this report documents, encouraging efforts are under way to update many aspects of regulatory and governance standards in these countries. Nevertheless, these efforts need to be deepened and extended beyond the 'first in class' companies. Firms from India, China and Brazil are regarded by their peers as among the most corrupt when doing business abroad.

Market solutions to public policy challenges also raise the risk of new arenas for corrupt practices. Corruption risks in new markets need to be addressed proactively. A rapidly growing market for trade in carbon emissions is an integral part of the global answer to climate change, but it faces serious transparency and accountability issues. Sovereign wealth funds have emerged as powerful actors in the investment arena. As managers of significant portions of nations' public wealth, they should live up to particularly high standards of public transparency and accountability. Many fail to do so.

- **A rethink in strategy and stronger action must take place to take sustainable corporate integrity to the next level**

Closing loopholes, strengthening compliance and bringing new players into the fold are important factors for progress. By themselves, though, they will not suffice. A threefold shift in strategy and action is required to address corruption in the sector more effectively.

First, this report clearly highlights the fact that many more stakeholders must join business executives and regulators in tackling corruption in business. These allies include owners, investors and workers, financial intermediaries and auditors and, in the broader business environment, the media, citizens as consumers and – last but not least – civil society. Taken together, they constitute *corporate integrity systems*, providing a web of vital checks, balances and incentives that make corporate integrity sound and sustainable. The report highlights the impact made by all these actors, but also underlines the fact that their contributions are put at risk by conflicts of interests, a lack of whistleblower protection, insufficient disclosure and reporting and other obstacles, all of which need to receive more attention in the policy debate.

Second, the focus of attention has to go beyond setting rules and pledging commitment to issues of implementation, monitoring and accountability for results to be achieved. Commitments, codes and laws matter, but they are only as good as their verifiable enforcement.

Third, collective action and collaboration need to be better recognised as essential principles in addressing corruption challenges in business. Collective action by companies can stimulate learning, contain the costly fragmentation and proliferation of reporting and compliance standards, protect against free-riding and create peer pressures that are instrumental to rooting out bribery in competition for contracts. Joint pressure allows investors and consumers to bundle their influence in holding business to account. More cooperation among small and medium enterprises enables them to pool their resource and defences against corruption, while more collaboration among national regulators can help close transnational loopholes.

Corporate corruption and the global financial and economic crisis: a closely linked policy agenda

Only over time will the full picture of the eventual scale of the global financial crisis and the economic downturn in 2009 emerge. One key insight, however, is already reflected in several contributions to the *Global Corruption Report 2009*: many of the conditions enabling the crisis are closely linked to corruption risks for business. These conditions include serious shortcomings in corporate integrity systems, such as conflicts of interest entangling key gatekeepers; insufficient transparency and accountability on the part of important markets, market players and oversight mechanisms; and serious lapses in corporate due diligence, governance and integrity.

The crisis also illustrates the hazardous implications of corporate strategies that seek to exploit weak regulation and disclosure standards in some pockets of the global economy. Similar strategies and the structures they generate can also blunt the ability to tackle transnational corruption. They can be abused to establish slush funds for large-scale bribery, while hindering the recovery of public assets stolen by corrupt rulers.

With regard to public oversight and supervision, the crisis has focused attention on the failings of regulators, related shortcomings in resources and staffing, and serious problems in international cooperation – issues that the *Global Corruption Report 2009* also identifies as concerns for the effective prevention and punishment of corruption in business.

All these interlinkages highlight one message: building fully effective corporate integrity systems is not just a question of tackling corruption in business. It is also important for financial and economic stability and the ongoing reforms of the global financial architecture, thereby lending additional urgency and momentum to this task.

Actions for sustainable corporate integrity

The *Global Corruption Report 2009* translates all these insights into a number of concrete policy proposals.

Recommended actions for business

1   Report on key aspects of corporate citizenship

Businesses have made great progress in communicating their corporate responsibility activities and environmental performance to the public. They need to match these efforts by reporting on other equally important elements of corporate citizenship:

- their anti-corruption and compliance activities, as the basic safeguards for respecting laws and regulations;
- their lobbying and political finance activities, so that their investors, workers and customers, and the wider public understand how some of the most powerful organisations in their country define their political interests and make their voices heard in the democratic arena; and
- their revenues and payments to governments for each country they do business in, so that local communities can fully understand how companies contribute to and benefit from the public good.

2   Make all commitments binding, verifiable and open to monitors of compliance

The independent monitoring and verification of compliance with the various codes and commitments that an increasing number of businesses are undertaking to strengthen their corporate integrity is essential, both for maximum effectiveness and public credibility. There is a great opportunity for top performers to lead by example and turn promises into credible performance.

3   Do not go it alone but, where possible, support existing standards and collective action frameworks

A growing commitment to disclosure and reporting can easily lead to a cacophony of individual information streams that are difficult to compile, compare and understand by investors and the larger public. In order to turn disclosure into meaningful transparency, business should adopt, support and actively engage in the development of related standards, such as the Global Reporting Initiative. Additionally, businesses should join and actively promulgate collective action frameworks for corporate integrity, which exist for anything from individual tendering processes and sectors to supply chain integrity, or multi-stakeholder action in key development areas from extractive industries to health and construction.

Recommended actions for governments and regulators

4   Put stronger emphasis on enforcing rules, the resources required and the measurement and performance of enforcement

Enforcement matters, but the resources devoted to it and the outputs achieved vary widely between countries and are difficult to monitor and compare. Governments and regulators need to make enforcement efficiency and effectiveness more transparent and accountable. They need to pay more attention to ensuring that adequate resources for regulators and enforcement activities are made available. In addition, those responsible for public oversight should report more fully on the money and staffing devoted to different types of enforcement action and the 'outputs' they produce, in terms of investigations, cases brought, fines and other sanctions imposed.

5   Use and further refine innovative tools for smart regulation and enforcement

Some countries have successfully experimented with a host of more flexible regulatory tools, which reach beyond rigid command and control approaches to rework incentives more strategically. Tools such as mandatory disclosure, blacklisting, deferred prosecution agreements and compliance monitors can be adopted and adapted by regulators and enforcement agencies in many more countries.

6   Strengthen international cooperation between regulators and make it truly global

Addressing corruption in global business requires a global approach, involving cooperation across borders for anti-corruption agencies, the competition and tax authorities and financial market regulators. The financial crisis provides a potent reminder that blind spots with regard to transparency and oversight can destabilise the entire global economy. Governments should seize the momentum for reform in terms of stronger cooperation between regulators and enforcement agencies – for all countries, markets and market actors.

Recommended actions for civil society

7   Make corporate integrity and anti-corruption assessments an integral part of monitoring initiatives on corporate social responsibility and performance

A business that cannot control corruption and thus ensure compliance with laws and regulations cannot live up to its commitments on social, environmental or other corporate citizenship issues. Assessments of corporate anti-corruption efforts need to be mainstreamed into the many metrics and initiatives to assess supply chain integrity, environmental performance, sustainability and responsible corporate citizenship more broadly.

8   Advocate for the development, widespread adoption and sound legal protection of complaints and whistleblower systems for employees in the private sector

Employees are found to play a pivotal role in ensuring corporate integrity. They can provide an early warning system for shortcomings in supply chain integrity, corporate governance structures and business culture or for corrupt business practices. They are also found to be the single most important source of public disclosure of corporate fraud after self-reporting by companies. Empowering workers to become drivers for corporate integrity requires strong provisions for legal protection, as well as sincere commitments by companies to establish effective complaints and whistleblower systems and align human resource management with incentives for ethical behaviour. Business watchdog groups and labour unions can encourage companies and legislators alike to create such an enabling environment.

9   Forge broader coalitions for corporate integrity and ensure that citizens and their interests are taken fully into account

Corporate integrity and anti-corruption compliance are common concerns for owners, investors, consumers, employees and non-governmental organisations working on many different public policy issues. This provides excellent opportunities for all these groups to work more closely together to monitor and advocate for corporate integrity.

Stronger linkages should also be established with the research community. Much important empirical work on corporate corruption and regulation is undertaken by business or law schools. The insights gained are often shared only among small groups of experts, even though they could provide important inputs to civil-society-based policy and advocacy efforts.

Finally, civil society coalitions that straddle borders, link grass-roots campaigners to policy experts and adopt a focus that is independent of national governments or business play an essential role as a third force, ensuring that citizens and their interests are given due weight and oversight in policy-making. Such civil society groups can act as independent watchdogs. They can serve as an important channel for citizens to engage with business and business-related governance frameworks. Finally, civil society coalitions can act as credible catalysts of multi-stakeholder action on a large number of issues related to corruption in the private sector, giving voice and creating capacity for citizens to influence the rules of the game for companies, markets and society. Only strong civil society participation can build the societal consensus that is necessary to tackle corruption in all its forms.

Part one
Corruption and the private sector

1   Introducing corruption and the private sector

The opening contribution for the thematic section of the Global Corruption Report 2009 *provides an overview of the scale, diversity and pervasiveness of corruption risks for business. It maps in detail the persistent nature of bribery as a core corruption risk, discusses interlinkages between corruption in the private sector and the financial and economic crisis, presents the business case for tackling corruption in the private sector and previews the key tools, mechanisms and stakeholders that have a role to play in this context. Georges Enderle adds to this overview by highlighting the moral responsibility of business to play a leading role in the fight against corruption.*

The scale and challenge of private sector corruption
Transparency International

The private sector plays a pivotal and expanding role in improving the well-being of societies, communities and individuals. It can help produce the economic wealth that lifts people out of poverty and expands access to health care, education and other vital public services. It can create economic opportunities to fulfil the aspirations of the young, the poor, the disenfranchised and all people intent on staking out their individual path to continuing improvement and a prosperous future for their families. It can generate ideas, innovation and efficiency in the use of resources, to help meet the environmental challenges of our times.

The private sector can also fail on all these counts, however. It can enrich a few at the cost of the many. It can recklessly overexploit the environment and obstruct innovation. It can disenfranchise, destabilise society and foster corruption, whether in communities, markets, governments or international relations, ultimately undermining the prerequisites for its own existence.

Corruption risks in the business sector and success in controlling them are crucial determinants of whether businesses and markets can live up to their productive, contributory role, or succumb to their destructive potential.

The scale and pervasiveness of corruption risks for business

Corruption is not a marginal issue but a central concern for business – in developing, emerging and industrialised countries alike. It affects multinationals in the United States and Europe. It touches manufacturing powerhouses in China, information technology service providers in India, farmers in Latin America and extractive industries in Africa, central Asia and the Middle East. It is an issue for large-scale conglomerates, family-owned businesses and individual entrepreneurs. In developing and transition countries alone, corrupt politicians and government officials receive bribes believed to total some US$20 to 40 billion annually – the equivalent of around 20 to 40 per cent of official development assistance. Moreover, the problem appears to be growing.

Many actors in the business sector are entrusted with powers that are vulnerable to abuse for private gain, to the detriment of other stakeholders and society more broadly. Executives and board directors are empowered to steer companies and manage risks in the interest of sustainable profitability for shareholders and stakeholders alike. Purchase managers oversee large budgets to source inputs for the enterprise. Human resource managers are entrusted with hiring staff. Labour representatives are entrusted by workers to represent their interests to management. Investment firms handle the savings and pensions of citizens and are expected to manage these investments responsibly. Accountants, auditors and rating agencies are entrusted by regulators and investors to verify and assess critical information and risks reported by companies.

Bribing public officials to win public contracts, circumvent regulations or speed up services is a central and persistent concern. Evidence of the prevalence of bribery provides a worrying example. In a survey of more than 2,700 business executives in twenty-six countries conducted by Transparency International in 2008, almost two in five respondents claimed that they had been requested to pay a bribe in the previous year when seeking attention from a series of institutions that provide vital services for business, such as customs and tax revenue authorities, the judiciary, the police, registry and permit offices or providers of basic services.[1] In a different survey, of more than 1,000 executives, almost one in five claimed to have lost business due to a competitor paying bribes, and more than a third felt that corruption was getting worse.[2]

In many places the problem is even more pronounced. In countries such as Egypt, India, Indonesia, Morocco, Nigeria and Pakistan, more than 60 per cent of the business executives polled in the TI survey reported having been solicited for bribe payments from the key institutions listed above.[3] In Colombia, more than a half of the companies interviewed in that country's first comprehensive survey on business and corruption described bribery as a viable strategy to trump the competition.[4] In Brazil more than 40 per cent, and in Hong Kong as many as two-thirds, of businesses believed that they lost opportunities on account of corruption by competitors within a one-year time frame.[5]

---

1 TI, *2008 Bribe Payers Index* (Berlin: TI, 2008).
2 Ernst & Young, *Corruption or Compliance: Weighing the Costs: Tenth Global Fraud Study* (London: Ernst & Young , 2008).
3 TI, 2008.
4 See article starting on page 221.
5 Control Risks and Simmons & Simmons, *Facing up to Corruption 2007: A Practical Business Guide* (London: Control Risks, 2007).

No sector or industry is unaffected by corruption, although some are hit harder than others. More than a half of all companies interviewed in the construction sector and the oil, gas and mining sector complained that bribery by competitors had deprived them of business opportunities in a five-year time frame.[6] In a different survey, more than a half of all the polled executives operating in the energy, mineral resources and telecommunications sectors reported having been asked for bribes in a one-year time frame.[7]

The overall impact of corrupt business practices, which allow companies to operate beyond the reach of the law, may be visible and imminent – such as water scarcity in Spain,[8] exploitative work conditions in China,[9] illegal logging in Indonesia,[10] unsafe medicines in Nigeria[11] and poorly constructed buildings that collapse with deadly consequences in Turkey.[12] Many other adverse effects are more hidden, but no less harmful, such as inflated costs for a public contract, a biased judicial ruling or the nurturing of a kleptocratic political class that plunders the public wealth of a country. Even small payments made to 'get things done' are harmful, as they are funnelled up through the system and help sustain corrupt bureaucracies, parties and governments.[13]

What business has to gain from the fight against corruption

The business case for countering corruption is clear. A half of international business managers estimate that corruption increases project costs by at least 10 per cent – in some cases more than 25 per cent.[14] In addition to direct financial costs and lost business opportunities, there are substantial damages to brand, staff morale and external business and government relations. Stronger enforcement of anti-bribery rules in some jurisdictions has significantly upped the ante, making stiff prison sentences and penalties in the tens of millions of US dollars increasingly likely.[15]

Corporate compliance and responsible citizenship also pays direct rewards. Higher-quality internal governance opens access to lower-cost capital and can raise company valuations and result in better performance. Responsible corporate citizenship also offers opportunities for brand differentiation and marketing that can increase sales in industries sensitive to consumer perceptions.[16] Contrary to common belief, a commitment to clean business also seems to boost rather than harm immediate business prospects. Companies with anti-corruption programmes

---

6 Control Risks and Simmons & Simmons, 2007.
7 TI, 2008.
8 TI, *Global Corruption Report 2008* (Cambridge: Cambridge University Press, 2008).
9 *International Herald Tribune* (US), 5 January 2008.
10 B. Setiono, *Corruption and Forest Revenues in Papua*, U4 Brief no. 18 (Bergen: Chr. Michelsen Institute, 2008).
11 TI, *Global Corruption Report 2006* (London: Pluto Press, 2006).
12 TI, *Global Corruption Report 2005* (London: Pluto Press, 2005).
13 See article starting on page 116.
14 Control Risks and Simmons & Simmons, 2007.
15 See article starting on page 238.
16 B. Lev, C. Petrovits and S. Radhakrishnan, *Is Doing Good Good for You? Yes, Charitable Contributions Enhance Revenue Growth*, working paper (New York: New York University, 2006).

and ethical guidelines were found to suffer up to 50 per cent fewer incidents of corruption, and were less likely to lose business opportunities than companies without such programmes.[17]

The corruption challenge for business does not stop with countering bribery, however. It extends to the broader challenges of doing business in a more complex and more globally competitive climate, in which new forms of corruption are taking hold and provide an additional threat to a competitive, sustainable business environment.

Corporate corruption and the global financial crisis

The dramatic consequences of the global financial and economic crisis were unfolding at the time of writing this report. Only over time will the full picture of the eventual scale, consequences and causes of the crisis develop.

The broad message is already clear, however: the conditions enabling the crisis to build and unfold include structural shortcomings in corporate integrity systems, such as conflicts of interests entangling key gatekeepers; insufficient transparency and accountability on the part of important markets, market players and oversight mechanisms; and widespread lapses in corporate due diligence, governance and integrity.

Persistent conflicts of interest for a vital layer of financial gatekeepers, such as auditors, accountants and rating agencies, have been identified as a major issue for corporate integrity and an important factor in the financial crisis.

Executive remuneration and its misalignment with long-term performance have encouraged excessive risk-taking that prepared the ground for the crisis. It is a major focus of reform efforts.

The crisis has also brought into sharp relief the new nature of the interdependence in the international financial system and the hazardous implications of corporate strategies that seek to exploit weak regulation, taxation and disclosure standards in some pockets of the global banking system. Such manoeuvres have created highly opaque and leveraged financial risks that have wiped out investors' confidence and brought the international credit markets to their knees.

There has long been concern about financial offshore structures whose lack of transparency, regulatory oversight and cooperation facilitate capital flight and tax evasion while hindering the recovery of public assets stolen by corrupt rulers. These structures have also been abused to establish and hide slush funds for large-scale bribery.

In the wake of the financial crisis, the leaders of the European Union have demanded that '[n]o financial institution, no market segment and no jurisdiction must escape proportionate and adequate regulation or at least oversight'.[18] This represents a promising commitment to

---

17 PricewaterhouseCoopers, *Economic Crime: People, Culture and Controls: The Fourth Biennial Global Economic Crime Survey* (London: PricewaterhouseCoopers, 2007).
18 Council of the European Union, 'Agreed Language: Global Financial Crisis: European Council Conclusions of the Informal Meeting of Heads of State or Government', Brussels, 7 November 2008.

reform, but there needs to be improvement in the transparency and accountability of key stakeholders in this setting.

Closely related, the crisis has also focused attention on the failings of public regulators. Overhauling and strengthening regulatory oversight has been put high on the agenda, as the leaders of the world's twenty most powerful countries resolved at their first major meeting on reforming the financial system: 'We pledge to strengthen our regulatory regimes, prudential oversight, and risk management [and] commit to transparent assessment of our national regulatory systems.' Much remains to be done, both with regard to regulatory frameworks and ensuring that adequate resources for enforcement are available to translate such promises into action.

The global financial crisis has not only added new urgency to addressing corruption risks in the business sector and strengthening corporate integrity systems. It has also provided a much-needed impetus for real reform.

Beyond bribery: a more comprehensive look at corruption risks for the business sector

Corruption is defined by Transparency International as 'the abuse of entrusted power for private gain'. For business, this means more than the perceived need to bribe public officials.

Corruption risks inside the enterprise include, among many others, corporate fraud, manipulating accounts and insider trading. Corruption in dealing with customers and suppliers can take the classic form of kickbacks to public officials, but it also includes, for example, the bribing of purchase officers to win business at other companies' expense (commercial bribery). In the wider market environment, entrusted power can be abused to collude with competitors or form cartels, hurting markets and consumers. At the societal level, corporate power can be abused to dodge laws and regulatory oversight, or exercise undue influence on regulations and policy-making, with implications for foreign direct investment, global supply chain integrity and transnational taxation.

All these corruption risks are interrelated, and at times mutually reinforcing, in at least two important ways.

- *At the motivational level.* Corruption in any of these business spheres fosters a culture of moral ambivalence and reckless opportunism that undermines the overall commitment to integrity and opens the door for other corrupt acts. When high-level executives award themselves extraordinary pay packages, lower-level managers may be tempted to sweeten their own pay package by soliciting bribes from suppliers. When top managers take steps to corner the market by forming illegal cartels, lower-level managers may feel encouraged, or even pressured, to close these important deals with the help of kickbacks – all in the spirit of boosting company profits at any price.
- *At the organisational level.* The very strategies and mechanisms used to circumvent internal or external controls and cover up a specific corrupt activity can also provide the

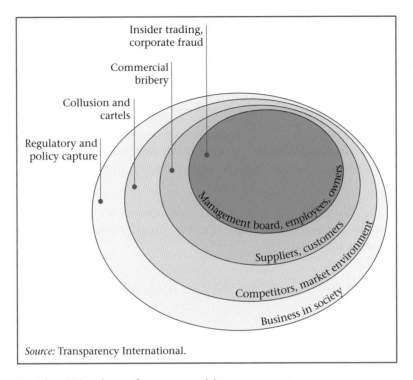

Figure 1: Corruption risks within spheres of corporate activity

infrastructure for other corrupt acts. For example, slush funds set up to bribe purchasing managers can be retooled to pay off politicians. Likewise, financial structures that leverage secrecy and weak regulation to win business, such as tax avoidance at the borderline of legality, can be abused to launder the proceeds of corruption, conceal financial risks or manipulate earnings. All this puts the stability of companies, investments and even markets generally more at risk.

Companies are entrusted by society with a social licence to operate. This requires them to act as responsible corporate citizens and manage what are often enormous economic resources, as well as their social, environmental and political impact, with integrity, accountability and according to the letter and spirit of the law.

Addressing corruption risks sustainably: towards a comprehensive corporate integrity system

Efforts to tackle corruption risks in the business sector and strengthen corporate integrity have traditionally focused on two main elements: the commitment and the compliance systems of *companies*; and the rules, regulations and enforcement of *governments*. Understanding these two dimensions and sets of interests is critical to preventing and addressing private sector corruption. In terms of companies, for instance, there already exist a variety of internal mechanisms to curb corruption, from corporate ethics, codes of conduct and corporate

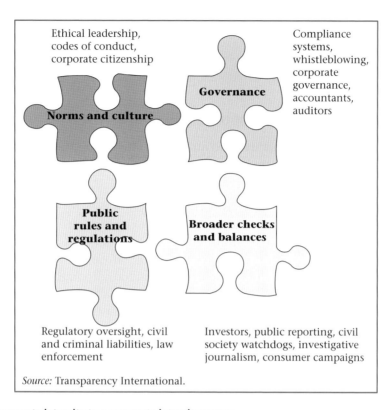

Source: Transparency International.

Figure 2: From corporate integrity to a corporate integrity system

governance mechanisms, including whistleblower protection, to reporting and the growing role of investors in incentivising corporate integrity.

At the same time, a number of other stakeholders are also critical in the fight to stop the supply of bribery and corruption from the private sector. These include key gatekeepers (auditors, accountants, rating agencies) and banks, as well as the media, consumer organisations and other civil society watchdogs. Together, these anti-corruption stakeholders comprise a broader corporate integrity system.

The mechanisms used to strengthen corporate integrity are mutually reinforcing and complement each other in a variety of ways. Corporate compliance systems, for example, are more widespread in places where the threat of sanctions and effective enforcement is more prevalent.[19] Self-disclosure and consistent public reporting can enable investors and consumers to reward top performers and provide further incentives for laggards to improve their governance and corporate citizenship commitments. Whistleblowers provide valuable information for internal investigations and investigative journalism.

---

19 OECD, *Mid-term Study of Phase 2 Reports: Application of the Convention on Combating Bribery of Foreign Public Officials in International Business Transactions* (Paris: OECD, 2006).

Sustainable and effective corporate integrity depends on a finely woven web of checks and balances. The better each individual stakeholder fulfils its role in such a corporate integrity system the easier it is for others to do the same, and the more likely corruption in the business sector will be discouraged and prevented – or, at least, detected and sanctioned.

How the Global Corruption Report 2009 is organised

The chapters that follow provide a detailed analysis of the corruption risks for business and systematically examine the key elements, tools and stakeholders involved in corporate integrity systems.

Chapter 2 presents the diagnostic analysis of core corruption risks for business. Following the different spheres of corruption presented in figure 1, it examines corruption inside the enterprise and discusses risks with regard to interactions with suppliers and customers. Moving into the broader market environment, the chapter then looks at cartels and collusion in market competition, and it concludes by discussing issues of undue corporate influence and the risk of policy and regulatory capture in relations between business and governments. For a better understanding of emerging corruption risks, the chapter also covers new forms of corporate lobbying and issues in carbon offset trading, a new and rapidly growing market at the heart of the global response to climate change.

Chapter 3 extends the analysis of corruption risks to key issues in a global economic perspective. It explores specific challenges for corporate integrity in developing economies that may be characterised by weak governance systems, a large informal sector, major privatisation programmes and, in many countries, a reliance on natural resources and extractive industries as a major source of economic wealth. The chapter also looks at a set of transnational issues, including corruption in the context of foreign direct investments, global supply chains and transfer pricing.

Chapter 4 moves from the diagnosis of corruption dynamics to a discussion of the remedies, in the framework of a comprehensive corporate integrity system, as outlined in figure 2. It starts with an exploration of internal mechanisms, from corporate ethics, codes of conduct and corporate governance mechanisms to reporting and the growing role of investors in incentivising corporate integrity. Given the centrality of employees in fraud detection, particular attention is paid to whistleblowing mechanisms, while an account by institutional investors highlights how share ownership can be leveraged for corporate integrity.

Chapter 5 completes the analysis and examines key elements of the broader corporate integrity system. It reviews the growing toolbox of laws and rules against corporate corruption, discusses enforcement issues and presents a set of innovative approaches to make rules and enforcement more effective. Other contributions in this chapter examine the role of key gatekeepers and banks, as well as the media, consumer organisations and other civil society watchdogs.

Beyond profits and rules: the moral case for business to fight corruption globally

Georges Enderle[1]

It has become popular to make the 'business case' for corporations to promote good ends and fight diseases and other evils. Building a 'moral case' for business to do good and avoid harm has been shied away from, however. Why this reluctance? Perhaps it is because business is seen by many as being value-free, or because the moral case itself is considered weak and vague, without the adequate support of laws and market forces.

From an ethics perspective, such explanations are not satisfactory. Business as an organisation has a clear twofold moral responsibility to engage in the global fight against corruption by setting a positive example through its own conduct, while contributing to the public good of working towards a corruption-free market. Together, these aims reinforce each other.

Perhaps the most frequently expressed objection to these moral responsibilities of business builds on the abundantly quoted, yet often misinterpreted, view of Milton Friedman that 'the business of business is business'. Even Friedman concedes, however, that this should apply only as long as the corporation 'stays within the rules of the game, which is to say, engages in open and free competition, without deception and fraud'.[2] Hence, an accurate reading of Friedman's stockholder (shareholder) model does not claim that profit maximisation trumps 'the rules of the game' by allowing for hidden and coerced competition, deception and fraud. Corruption clearly violates these rules of the game.

Looked at broadly, however, Friedman's view does contain several flaws. He claims that only individual persons (for instance, corporate executives) can bear moral responsibility. Corporations are neither moral nor immoral and thus cannot be morally committed nor held responsible for their behaviour in an ethical sense. Consequently, there is no place for the ethics of business organisations. This view has been widely rejected, however. As one expert has put it: 'In today's society, the doctrine of corporate amorality is no longer tenable.'[3] Corporations set and promulgate objectives and aspirations, rules, norms and operational principles, all of which generate a distinctive organisational culture that influences employees and their sense of what behaviour is expected to achieve the corporate objectives beyond making a profit.

Such a distinctive corporate culture is nurtured and lives on well beyond the involvement of a specific chief executive officer (CEO) that may have laid the foundations for it.

1 Georges Enderle is Professor of International Business Ethics at the University of Notre Dame, Indiana.
2 M. Friedman, 'The Social Responsibility of Business is to Increase Its Profits', *New York Times Sunday Magazine*, 13 September 1970.
3 L. S Paine, *Value Shift: Why Companies Must Merge Social and Financial Imperatives to Achieve Superior Performance* (New York: McGraw-Hill, 2003).

Many jurisdictions already acknowledge such a corporate morality. The United States, for example, has introduced a legal liability of companies – not just individuals, for a weak ethical culture – when employees commit offences, including bribery, and act both within the scope of their duty and in the interest of the firm. Australia holds corporations responsible when a corporate culture has existed that encouraged, tolerated or led to an offence.[4]

Friedman also holds the belief that demanding more from corporations than merely doing business and paying taxes would be 'fundamentally subversive', and he denies any moral responsibility on the part of corporations to contribute to the public good. It is difficult to follow this line of reasoning. The size and social, economic and environmental impact of business, as well as its political influence, dwarf most other collective entities and institutions in a country. This extraordinary economic and social clout wielded by the corporate citizenry constitutes an obligation to contribute to the public good. This is particularly the case when many of the public goods in question, such as fair market competition, sustainable resource use and predictable regulations, are part of the very foundations on which businesses depend and thrive.

Additionally, the rules of the game with which Friedman demands compliance have not kept pace with the forces of globalisation and economic innovation, as the most recent series of financial crises that began in 2007 has shown. The results are rule uncertainties, loopholes and enforcement voids. Along with better rules, only moral responsibility can fill this gap. A moral commitment to the spirit of rules and the ethical principles that underpin them, not just narrow compliance with the letter of the law, is required.

Corporations are not simply cogs in the machine of the global economy, nor merely bundles of contracts. They are moral actors, with some, albeit limited, spaces of freedom. As far as their freedoms extend, corporations bear moral responsibility.

Being moral is not easy. Very often corporations face difficult situations that challenge their efforts to set a good example of corruption-free behaviour. Here two evolving principles may help, which draw on assessing responsibilities for human rights violations. The degree of corporate responsibility is determined by the extent of the company's sphere of influence and its degree of complicity.[5]

As 'good citizens', corporations have to make a moral commitment that shapes their entire organisation, from their mission and objectives to their structures, policies and cultures, and down to their daily performances, evaluations and reporting. This moral commitment must be consistent and made transparent to the public. Without the commitment of the major players in global business, the fair rules of the game will never be effective.

---

4 OECD, *Corruption. A Glossary of International Standards in Criminal Law* (Paris: OECD, 2008).
5 United Nations Human Rights Council, *Business and Human Rights: Mapping International Standards of Responsibility and Accountability for Corporate Acts*, Document A/HRC/4/035 (New York: UN, 2007); United Nations Human Rights Council, *Protect, Respect and Remedy: A Framework for Business and Human Rights*, Document A/HRC/8/5 (New York: UN, 2008).

2 Understanding the dynamics: examining the different types of business corruption

The contributions in this chapter present the diagnostic analysis of core corruption risks for business and economies. Dante Mendes Aldrighi discusses corruption inside the enterprise with a focus on how majority shareholders, executives and labour representatives can abuse the power they are entrusted with for private gain. David Hess examines corruption in transactions with suppliers and clients and identifies private-to-private corruption as an important area that has so far received very limited attention. Pradeep S. Mehta focuses in his contribution on corruption risks in the market environment, when competitors form cartels to rig fair competition. He draws on a wide range of evidence to show that a new wave of international cartel activity is undermining fair competition and hitting developing countries particularly hard. Dieter Zinnbauer looks at corruption risks in business–government relations and discusses how to avoid legitimate lobbying turning into undue corporate influence.

A set of shorter contributions complements the analysis. Elaine Burns discusses the specific corruption challenges for small and medium enterprises, suggesting more collective action as a promising way forward. David Miller examines corruption risks in connection with new forms of lobbying that aim to influence public opinion subtly rather than target policy-makers directly. Finally, Jørund Buen and Axel Michaelowa provide an inside perspective on transparency and accountability issues in the new and rapidly growing market for carbon credits that has been set up as part of the global policy response to climate change.

Corruption inside the enterprise: corporate fraud and conflicts of interest
Dante Mendes Aldrighi[1]

It is not only when dealing with customers and suppliers that companies face corruption risks. Corruption can also take place inside the enterprise and critically undermine corporate performance. Companies are not monolithic entities. In a sense, they are 'joint ventures' bringing together owners, investors, staff and management, all with different roles, responsibilities and interests. Therefore specific entitlements are defined, negotiated, aligned and protected through a multitude of legal and contractual rights, responsibilities and codified procedures, according to which a company is directed and controlled. Nevertheless, such a

---

1 Dante Mendes Aldrighi is Professor of Economics at the University of São Paulo, Brazil.

system of corporate governance is susceptible to abuses of entrusted power for private gain – as corruption is commonly defined – in many ways.

Managers are vested with the power to run the day-to-day operations of a company, but they may focus opportunistically more on short-term profits that influence their bonuses than on long-term profitability. Majority owners may try to leverage their influence on corporate strategy to expropriate smaller shareholders. Labour representatives may be tempted to collude with management in exchange for generous expense allowances rather than representing employees' interests.

These are just a few examples that highlight the challenges that arise when corporate stakeholders with differing interests opportunistically exploit their power or informational advantage to further their own aims at the expense of the overall corporate venture. These major internal corruption risks come into focus when set against the backdrop of a changing corporate culture that provides a fertile ground for corporate fraud.

A changing business environment

Despite remarkable improvements in corporate governance since the 1980s, the scale and scope of corporate fraud and conflicts of interest continue to be vast, for several reasons.

First, deregulation and globalisation in product and financial markets, coupled with falling communication and information costs, have made it easier to conceal information, manipulate financial accounts and divert assets and funds.

Second, fierce competition and an ever stronger focus on shareholder value and short-term profitability have put heightened pressure on management to set ambitious targets for financial results, link compensation to short-term performance and follow highly risky strategies, such as daring acquisitions and transactions involving hard-to-control, complex financing mechanisms.[2] This has spurred innovations in financing and accounting practices, such as off-balance-sheet financing, special purpose entities and special investment vehicles, which allow companies to segregate a given transaction's risks, assets and liabilities from their own balance sheets. These strategies can be used to embellish financial statements, conceal liquidity risks and liabilities, and undertake highly leveraged and complex transactions.

In light of these far-reaching structural changes, what are the main internal corruption risks and types of conflicts of interest that affect the modern corporation?

The rapid growth in executives' compensation: failing oversight and risky incentives

Since the 1980s chief executive officer pay has sharply increased in the United States and Europe. Among large US firms, the ratio of average CEO income to the average worker's wage

---

2 J. Coffee, 'What Caused Enron? A Capsule of Social and Economic History of the 1990s', in P. Cornelius and B. Kogut (eds.), *Corporate Governance and Capital Flows in a Global Economy* (New York: Oxford University Press, 2003).

jumped from forty-two in 1982 to 531 in 2000.[3] The average compensation for the top five executives at US-based Standard & Poor's (S&P) 500 companies alone more than doubled between 1993 and 2003, to more than US$20 million per year.[4]

The immense growth in executive remuneration is partly due to boards of directors ceding to executives' interests rather than exerting independent oversight on management in the interest of shareholders. Collegiality, loyalty and friendship play a role in these excessively close relationships. In many countries, CEOs sit on each other's boards, creating a dense network of interlocking directorships. Mutual benefits further discourage critical distance. CEOs have the power to reward directors, and dissenting directors may impair their prospects for being renominated to a lucrative board position.[5]

The financial crisis that began in 2007 exposed the scale of the failure of boards to impose stronger controls, even at times of crisis. Executives continued to receive generous bonuses or severance packages when it had already become clear that their risky investment strategies had pushed their companies to the brink of bankruptcy and would have to be supported by tax money. The insurance giant AIG even continued to line up generous severance packages and expense accounts after it had had to be saved from collapse with public money.[6]

When executives award themselves massive compensation packages without adequate oversight they divert company resources into their own pockets, and set an example of greed likely to permeate the culture of the company. Where to draw the line between appropriate compensation and excess is an open question, but the sums involved are certainly far from trivial. Between 1993 and 2003 packages for only the top five executives of all publicly held companies in the United States totalled US$350 billion, absorbing 6.6 per cent of net income during this period.[7]

The increasing use of stock options to reward CEOs has contributed to this explosion in executive remuneration. Equity-based pay was welcomed as a means to align the interests of management more closely with overall corporate performance. It has been found to distort the incentives for managers to tweak short-term profits and earnings reports, however, with a view to affecting market expectations and thus the firm's share price. Stock options were an important device used by Enron to perpetrate fraud. At one point, stock options accounted for almost 13 per cent of Enron's total voting capital, providing a strong incentive for their owners to manipulate earnings and revenues.[8] As two prominent experts observe, equity-based pay is often not so much an incentive device as a somewhat covert mechanism for self-dealing.[9]

3 J. Tirole, *The Theory of Corporate Finance* (Princeton, NJ: Princeton University Press, 2006).
4 L. Bebchuk and Y. Grinstein, 'The Growth of Executive Pay', *Oxford Review of Economic Policy*, vol. 21, no. 2 (2005).
5 L. Bebchuk and J. Fried, *Pay without Performance: The Unfulfilled Promise of Executive Compensation* (Cambridge, MA: Harvard University Press, 2004).
6 *International Herald Tribune* (US), 17 October 2008; 22 October 2008.
7 L. Bebchuk and Y. Grinstein, 2005.
8 P. Healy and K. Palepu, 'The Fall of Enron', *Journal of Economic Perspectives*, vol. 17, no. 2 (2003).
9 A. Shleifer and R. Vishny, 'A Survey of Corporate Governance', *Journal of Finance*, vol. 52, no. 2 (1997).

Even if compensation levels and techniques are considered appropriate, the misalignment between pay and long-term performance that ensues creates some troubling incentives. Between 2000 and 2004 a sample of sixty poorly performing US companies lost a total of US$769 billion in market value, while their top managers earned more than US$12 billion.[10] Such misalignment encourages a narrow focus for CEOs on short-term profits and extreme risk-taking, both of which contributed to the 2007/8 financial meltdown, when highly speculative and leveraged transactions unravelled and led many financial institutions into bankruptcy.

Corporate ownership: controlling shareholders and minority shareholders' expropriation

A key problem of corporate governance around the world is protecting the interests of often dispersed and weak minority shareholders from opportunistic activities by strong managers and powerful block owners. This phenomenon, often referred to as 'self-dealing', is also known as 'tunnelling' or 'the private benefits of control'.

This risk of self-dealing is particularly high when share ownership is concentrated in the hands of powerful owners and the protection of minority shareholders is weak. Both are common characteristics of, but by no means confined to, emerging economies. Across Asia, for example, there is little protection of minority shareholders, and small investors find it difficult to enforce their rights.[11] At the same time, ownership in Asia and Latin America is highly concentrated. In six key economies in Latin America the single largest shareholder owns on average more than 50 per cent of a company.[12] Powerful shareholders can further expand their influence on corporate decisions through pyramid schemes of ownership, allowing majority owners to accumulate more voting rights than their capital share permits. In Brazil, half the public companies were owned through pyramid schemes as of 2002.[13]

Transfer pricing is one of the principal strategies for powerful shareholders to extract private gains at the expense of minority owners. It entails the under- or overpricing of transactions with companies directly or indirectly owned by controlling shareholders or senior executives, and thus makes it possible to transfer cash flow and assets to these companies under the guise of regular business operations.[14]

Although such incidences of self-dealing are difficult to detect and measure, compelling evidence suggests that they pose a major problem worldwide. A survey of more than 390 companies in thirty-nine countries finds that the overall private benefits of holding a controlling stake in a company amount on average to a remarkable 14 per cent of firm equity value. In Austria, Italy,

---

10 S. Davis, J. Lukomnik and D. Pitt-Watson, *The New Capitalists: How Citizen Investors are Reshaping the Corporate Agenda* (Boston: Harvard Business School Press, 2006).

11 OECD, *Enforcement of Corporate Governance in Asia. The Unfinished Agenda* (Paris: OECD, 2008).

12 OECD, *White Paper on Corporate Governance in Latin America* (Paris: OECD, 2003).

13 D. Aldrighi and R. Mazzer Neto, 'Evidências sobre as Estruturas de Propriedade de Capital e de Voto das Empresas de Capital Aberto no Brasil', *Revista Brasileira de Economia*, vol. 61, no. 2 (2007).

14 For more problems with transfer pricing, see article starting on page 70.

Mexico and Turkey these benefits of control exceed a mean of 30 per cent of equity value, reaching as high as 58 and 65 per cent of firm value in the Czech Republic and Brazil, respectively.

Part of these value premiums may be related to the psychological benefit of being in control. The benefits of private control are found to be significantly lower in countries where tax provisions are more strongly enforced, however, thus leaving less discretion for transfer pricing. This strongly indicates that transfer pricing plays a significant role in diverting company profits to controlling shareholders.[15]

Subverting shareholder value: collusion between workers' representatives and executives

Corporate governance is not only about the relationship between managers, owners and investors. Workers also have a legitimate stake in corporate performance and governance, for at least three reasons. First, workers' performance and commitment are essential contributors to corporate success. Second, employees can provide important additional checks and balances for corporate governance. Finally, and perhaps most importantly, their job and company-specific qualifications, skills and experience tie workers' personal economic well-being to the success and failure of the company as much as, or even more than, investors and owners, who may find it easier to switch their investments to other ventures. The view of a company as a nexus of relationships among different types of stakeholders, rather than a narrow shareholder venture, is supported by leading scholars such as Jean Tirole and Luigi Zingales, and it is reflected in the corporate governance frameworks of several countries.[16]

Crucial as the role is that workers play in any given company, the integrity of their union representatives in corporate governance can be undermined if they are wooed by personal perks to support managers' decisions. This is a particularly salient risk in Germany, where co-determination laws ensure that a half of large firms' supervisory boards are comprised of workers' representatives and require the consultation of union leaders on major company decisions.

Consider the case of Volkswagen's (VW) labour leader, Klaus Volkert, who was sentenced to thirty-three months in prison in February 2008 for receiving €2 million in bribes from VW executives in exchange for supporting managers' decisions. The case was part of a broader investigation into claims that VW managers had bought the support of union representatives with secret bonuses, luxury holidays, clothing, jewellery and fake consulting fees.[17]

This type of corrupt manipulation does not appear to be isolated. Ongoing court proceedings suggest that the labour union Arbeitsgemeinschaft Unabhängiger Betriebsräte (AUB) has been financially supported and at times systematically groomed by large German companies, including

---

15 A. Dyck and L. Zingales, 'Private Benefits of Control: An International Comparison', *Journal of Finance*, vol. 59, no. 2 (2004).

16 J. Stiglitz, 'Credit Markets and the Control of Capital', *Journal of Money, Credit, and Banking*, vol. 17, no. 2 (1985).

17 *Financial Times* (UK), 17 January 2007.

Siemens and the grocery giant Aldi Nord. AUB exhibited particularly management-friendly conduct when it opposed the demands of established German labour unions. Prosecutors have accused Siemens of covertly transferring millions of euros to AUB, which company management considered a 'child of Siemens'.[18]

The conflicts of interests and corruption risks caused by such illicit payments, and the havoc they wreak on independent labour representation and corporate governance more broadly, are apparent. Business leaders, trade unions and policy-makers have yet to recognise these problems fully, though. The cases against Volkswagen and Siemens may be no more than the tip of the iceberg.

Corruption inside the enterprise: a concern for all

Conflicts of interest and the abuse of entrusted power for private gain can take many forms inside a company. The cases described here are only illustrative of the problem. Many other forms of corporate fraud have been identified and widely documented.

Ownership changes caused by mergers and acquisitions present ample opportunities for insiders to act on their preferential information to the detriment of other investors. Investment bankers have been found to buy shares in unusual numbers and at unusual times in companies targeted for mergers while their colleagues were advising the acquirers in the deal, raising the strong possibility of unconstrained and illegal flows of inside information.[19] Similarly, stark conflicts of interest can arise for management when private equity groups buy out publicly listed companies and negotiate the deals with the very same executives who will report to them after the takeover.[20]

The scale and scope of these internal corporate corruption risks cannot be underestimated, although concrete statistics can only be approximated because many cases may not be publicly disclosed. In a 2007 survey of more than 5,400 companies in forty countries, almost one-third reported having suffered asset misappropriation, and 12 per cent indicated that they were affected by accounting fraud during a four-year period.[21]

All these types of corruption may occur mainly inside a company, but it is important to understand that their negative impacts are felt much more broadly. Buying off labour representatives or self-dealing in the form of transfer pricing demonstrates not only a disregard for the legitimate interests of minority owners and employees, but also a readiness to manipulate tax payments and collude with suppliers and clients, creating a slippery slope, both morally and practically, to related corrupt practices such as tax fraud, collusion and commercial bribery.

---

18 *Sueddeutsche Zeitung* (Germany), 15 August 2008; 24 September 2008; see article starting on page 331.
19 M. Maremont and S. Craig, 'Trading in Deal Stocks Triggers Look at Banks', *Wall Street Journal* (US), 14 January 2008.
20 B. Gordon, *The State of Responsible Business: Global Corporate Response to Environmental, Social and Governance (ESG) Challenges* (London: Ethical Investment Research Services, 2007).
21 PricewaterhouseCoopers, *Economic Crime: People, Culture and Controls: The 4th Biennial Global Economic Crime Survey* (London: PricewaterhouseCoopers, 2007).

Similarly, excessive remuneration or collusion between labour representatives and management constitute lapses in individual integrity and expressions of greed by key company officials who are supposed to provide ethical leadership. In this context, it is particularly distressing that more than a quarter of economic fraud cases have been found to involve senior management and another quarter to be perpetrated by middle management. Research shows that a decline in working morale was experienced as a significant collateral damage from this fraud perpetrated by management in a half of all affected companies.[22]

Cases of corporate fraud at the executive level also indicate that fundamental checks and balances of corporate governance are failing or have been actively manipulated. This also has serious repercussions for the capability of companies to act as responsible corporate citizens. The very same corporate checks and balances that are circumvented, manipulated or morally compromised by internal fraud also form the internal governance fundaments that ensure that corporate commitments and responsibilities are effectively implemented.

In essence, internal corporate fraud is an indicator of and catalyst for flaws and shortcomings in how companies are governed and controlled. It is the thin end of the wedge, which prises open the space for corporate corruption in other areas. Strengthening corporate governance systems is a key step in strengthening corporate integrity more broadly.[23]

---

22 PricewaterhouseCoopers, 2007.
23 Chapter 4 describes some of the most important steps that can be taken in this regard. See article starting on page 81.

Corruption in the value chain: private-to-private and private-to-public corruption
David Hess[1]

> There is an expectation that you have to increase the amount of the invoice between 10 and 50%, sometimes more, and give the extra to the decision maker. They call it 'surfacturation' or overbilling in English. . . The shock came not from the expected public sector corruption but from the corruption in the private sector, including – especially – multinationals.
>
> *Diary of an African Entrepreneur*[2]

People typically think of bribery by companies as illicit payments to government officials to win public contracts or receive government services. This type of private-to-public bribery is just a small segment of the corruption risks that companies face along their entire value chain, however.

---

1 David Hess is a Professor of Law at the Ross School of Business, University of Michigan.
2 'Private Sector Corruption . . . Win/Win?' *Diary of an African Entrepreneur*, 8 November 2006; http://africanentrepreneur.blogspot.com/2006/11/insideousness-of-private-sector.html.

The many faces of corruption in the value chain

From sourcing inputs, to value-adding in-house operations to the final sale and distribution to the customer (together commonly referred to as the value chain), individuals who work for private companies and negotiate contracts with suppliers, subcontractors, staff members or clients on behalf of their company have many opportunities to participate in corrupt payments. In what is often called 'commercial bribery', or, more broadly, 'private-to-private corruption', the bribe receiver accepts corrupt payments or other favours, in return for making deals that may not be in his or her employer's best interests.[3]

In the United States, for example, several managers at Honda granted new automobile dealership contracts from the late 1970s to 1992 allegedly on the basis of the willingness of potential dealers to pay bribes – in the form of cash and gifts[4,5] – as opposed to selecting those dealers who would best perform for the company. A class-action lawsuit culminated in 1,800 dealers receiving US$330 million in damages from Honda.[6]

Honda dealers claimed that they could not get the cars they needed because they did not bribe Honda.[7] Among them was a Pennsylvania couple who said that they had lost their dealership because they did not pay bribes. The couple sued Honda and a competing dealer, saying that, because they had refused to offer kickbacks, they received the least saleable cars, lost US$15 million between 1985 and 1989 and eventually lost their business. While their competitor received the latest best-selling models, the couple was told that the cars were unavailable. Honda told them to renovate their dealership, but, when they could not repay the US$3 million they had taken out to fund the project, they were forced to sell their business.[8] An owner of a Honda dealership in North Carolina also sued Honda and a competing car dealer, accusing them of damaging his business. 'There's a feeling of hurt that this actually happened,' the dealer said. 'The automobile business is a very competitive business. We expect fair and equal treatment.'[9]

Such practices cause significant harm to society by distorting the marketplace. Corrupt Honda sales managers may have distorted the competitive market for potential dealers, to the detriment of their company and more efficient dealers who otherwise would have landed contracts. Such private-to-private corruption is not confined to supply chains or distribution networks, but affects all business operations.

Starting with the initial stages of forming a company, including hiring employees and securing financing, there is a potential for corruption. From casino workers in the United States to nurses in Bahrain, the hiring process can be corrupted by recruiters and their agents requiring

---

3 A. Argandoña, 'Private-to-private Corruption', *Journal of Business Ethics*, vol. 47, no. 3 (2003).
4 *United States* v. *Josleyn*, 99 F.3d 1182, 1996.
5 *New York Times* (US), 6 April 1995.
6 Associated Press (US), 31 October 1998.
7 *Washington Post* (US), 5 December 1996.
8 Knight Ridder/Tribune Business News (US), 27 October 1995.
9 Knight Ridder/Tribune Business News (US), 12 September 1995.

applicants to pay kickbacks to land jobs.[10] To obtain capital, a bank employee could be bribed to give the company a loan on favourable terms. Recently, for example, a senior account manager at Royal Bank of Canada was accused of accepting C$362,000 (US$300,000) in bribes from a now defunct metal supply company in exchange for approving loans, increasing the company's multimillion-dollar credit line and preparing fraudulent financial statements.[11] This is not an isolated case of corruption in obtaining banking services. As more than a third of companies indicated in a survey in 1999, they consider corruption in bank lending as a major, modest or minor obstacle for their operations.[12]

Corruption risks also abound in transactions with suppliers and subcontractors. Managers who control the purse strings for what often amount to multimillion dollar supply or outsourcing budgets that can make or break entire businesses are likely targets of corruption. Purchasing agents may be tempted to select suppliers based on bribes rather than on quality and cost. In South Korea, for example, the chief executive of one of the largest telecommunications groups had to step down in 2008 following allegations over kickbacks from equipment suppliers in return for contracts.[13] Even competitive bidding processes are vulnerable. For instance, using a sealed auction process in procurement creates strong incentives for suppliers to pay bribes to obtain undisclosed information from the corporation about the contract or information about competitors' bids.[14]

Sales and distribution, the transactions with the public and business clients, present a final set of corruption challenges that mirrors the corruption risks in the supply chain. Now a company's own sales managers, such as the Honda car dealers, may be tempted to grease the palms of their counterparts in procurement departments in order to make sales targets and win lucrative business.

If a corporation expands internationally, the risks of corruption in relationships with suppliers, customers and service providers can increase dramatically. Companies without local market knowledge or business contacts often have to hire local agents or form joint ventures with local companies. Unless carefully selected and monitored, however, these local actors may go on to pay bribes to get the results they were hired to achieve, in effect leading to an outsourcing of corruption.

An underestimated phenomenon

Understanding the impact of commercial bribery on markets is a matter of growing importance, on account of such trends as the increasing privatisation and outsourcing of government

10 Associated Press (US), 21 June 2008; *Trade Arabia* (Bahrain), 8 October 2008.
11 *Toronto Star* (Canada), 20 October 2008.
12 T. Beck, A. Demirgüç-Kunt and R. Levine, *Bank Supervision and Corruption in Lending*, Working Paper no. 11498 (Cambridge, MA: National Bureau of Economic Research, 2005).
13 *International Herald Tribune* (US), 5 November 2008.
14 J. Andvig, 'Corruption in the North Sea Oil Industry: Issues and Assessments', *Crime, Law, and Social Change*, vol. 28, no. 4 (1995).

services, the liberalisation of markets in many countries and the increasing size of the private sector compared to the public sector.[15]

Corruption in the value chain can penetrate all aspects of business operations. What all corrupt acts have in common is that they harm at least one party to the transaction, since an agent is induced to favour an inferior supplier or service provider, hire a less qualified employee, suspend due diligence in providing services, etc. In the long run, however, all market participants, and society more broadly, are affected. Paying bribes increases uncertainty and the costs of doing business for all. It fosters a culture and practice of dishonesty and moral decay that opens the door to other types of corporate wrongdoing. Perhaps most importantly, it hollows out the fundamental principles of doing business, of fair competition and merit-based selection, which are prerequisites for markets to deliver innovation, efficiency, productivity gains and growth. In essence, corruption in the value chain – private-to-private and private-to-public – poses a fundamental threat to the trust in and functioning of market economies.

As the International Chamber of Commerce says: 'Fighting private-to-private corruption will be a key element of worldwide efforts to create a level playing field for all market participants, to build public and private sector trust in the rule of law and to lower trans-border transaction costs.'[16]

Limited awareness and regulation

Though it constitutes perhaps the largest component of corruption in the value chain and has adverse consequences for the working of markets and economies, private-to-private corruption so far has received surprisingly limited attention from lawmakers.

At the international level, various instruments treat private-to-private corruption differently. The Organisation for Economic Co-operation and Development's (OECD's) anti-bribery convention addresses only the bribing of public officials.[17] The United Nations Convention against Corruption requires countries solely to 'consider' criminalising commercial bribery.[18] Only the Council of Europe's Criminal Law Convention on Corruption requires countries to prohibit private sector bribery.[19]

At the national level, commercial corruption is dealt with in different ways. Even if a country does not have a law specifically addressing commercial bribery as a form of corruption, other

---

15 P. Webb, 'The United Nations Convention against Corruption', *Journal of International Economic Law*, vol. 8, no.1 (2005); G. Heine, 'Comparative Analysis', in G. Heine, B. Huber and T. Rose (eds.), *Private Commercial Bribery: A Comparison of National and Supranational Legal Structures* (Paris: International Chamber of Commerce, 2003); A. Argandoña, 2003.

16 International Chamber of Commerce, *Memorandum to the OECD Working Group on Bribery in International Business Transactions* (Paris: International Chamber of Commerce, 2006).

17 Convention on Combating Bribery of Foreign Public Officials in International Business Transactions, Working Group on Bribery in International Business Transactions (Paris: OECD, 1997).

18 'Bribery in the Private Sector', United Nations Convention against Corruption, article 21 (New York: UN, 2003).

19 Criminal Law Convention on Corruption, Council of Europe, articles 7 and 8 (Strasbourg: Council of Europe, 1999).

laws may be available to punish such actions.[20] These laws can be based on different theories for regulating behaviour, including breach of fiduciary duties to the company owner, breach of trust to an employer, or restriction of free competition.[21] This patchwork of available rules comes with different standards for evidence collection and culpability, however, failing to provide a coherent basis for tackling private-to-private corruption.

Overall, private-to-private corruption is an area in need of further exploration. At a minimum, a dialogue is necessary on the policy goals behind prohibiting private sector bribery, which will influence the nature of any anti-bribery laws that nations may enact.

Invoking legislation on competition and fraud in the absence of direct prohibitions on private-to-private corruption may leave loopholes and fail to produce the dissuasive effect commensurate to the overall social harm of corruption. It also fails to resolve a state of moral and practical ambivalence that hinders consistent corporate compliance and the fight against corruption in public procurement. On the one hand, sales managers are legally prohibited from bribing public clients. On the other, the very same practices fall into a legal grey zone and may even be legal when it comes to private clients, so long as such activities do not directly defraud their own company or directly harm market competition. Building effective compliance programmes on such an ambivalent basis for what is allowed and what is not is very difficult.

There also needs to be a better understanding of the scale and focus of private commercial bribery. One problem is that corporations are often reluctant to pursue actions publicly against commercial bribery because of the potential for a negative impact on their reputation. Instead, corporations try to handle the situation internally.[22] As a result, statistics are extremely difficult to come by.

One exception is Transparency International's 2008 Bribe Payers Survey, which interviewed more than 2,700 business executives in twenty-six major countries receiving foreign direct investment. One respondent in four indicated that corruption within the private sector impedes the operation and growth of his or her business, thus making private-to-private corruption a more widely reported obstacle than infrastructure issues or the functioning of the judiciary.[23]

In South Korea, which cracked down on private-to-private corruption in the wake of the 1997 financial crisis, more than 7,000 cases were investigated between 1998 and 1999.[24] This is likely to be only the tip of the iceberg in private-to-private corruption. Even these anecdotal figures, however, underline the fact that the focus on tackling bribery in the business sector needs to be extended from public procurement to cover the entire business value chain, from relations with suppliers and subcontractors to transactions with service providers, distributors and clients.

---

20 For an overview of the laws of thirteen OECD countries that address private-to-private bribery, see G. Heine, B. Huber and T. Rose (eds.), 2003.
21 Ibid. See also F. A. Gevurtz, 'Commercial Bribery and the Sherman Act: The Case for Per Se Illegality', *University of Miami Law Review*, vol. 42 (1987).
22 A. Argandoña, 2003.
23 TI, '2008 Bribe Payers Survey' (Berlin: TI, 2008).
24 B.-S. Cho, 'Korea', in G. Heine, B. Huber and T. Rose (eds.), 2003.

Small and medium enterprises: challenges in combating corruption
Elaine Burns[1]

Small and medium enterprises (SMEs) are of huge importance to the global economy, representing over 95 per cent of businesses worldwide and even more than 99 per cent of the business sector in countries such as Belgium, Greece, Italy and South Korea.[2] Operating, as many do, in difficult developing markets and supporting major industries as crucial links in their supply chains, SMEs are vulnerable to the threat of corruption. As a European Bank for Reconstruction and Development (EBRD)/World Bank survey has revealed, more than 70 per cent of SMEs perceive corruption as an impediment to their business, compared to around 60 per cent of large companies.[3]

What can an SME do to avoid bribery when a customs official demands a bribe in order to allow the import of a perishable product? Where can a supplier get help when the buyer for a major retailer expects 'encouragement' when awarding contracts? Assisting SMEs to resist corruption is an essential component of any comprehensive anti-corruption initiative and can prevent them from becoming the weakest link.

SMEs can be as small as a sole trader or a family business of twenty, but they can also reach the size of a company with several hundred employees. Each of these categories of SME, however, whatever its size or structure, faces four main challenges, albeit to varying extents.

- It is possible that the culture of bribery may be so much a part of the business scene that SMEs are under pressure to submit or fail. In some contexts bribery may be seen as just another business device, a necessary short cut that would be an overwhelming challenge to the company to counter. A business run on bribery is not only acting illegally, however, but also exposing itself to penalties. Such vulnerabilities can further increase the pressure on SMEs to succumb to the demands of corruption.
- SMEs may often not recognise or understand the complexities or grey areas of corruption. There may be uncertainty as to when a gift or entertainment is intended as inducement; when a donation to a political party or charity might be used as a bribe; and what the consequences of undetected conflicts of interest could be. An OECD analysis of some major export countries, for example, reports that even when SMEs represented the majority of exporting businesses they still tended to be poorly informed about anti-bribery laws.[4]
- Limited resources are also a major challenge. The amount of people, time and money

---

1 Elaine Burns works with the private sector team of Transparency International.
2 OECD, *Mid-term Study of Phase 2 Reports: Application of the Convention on Combating Bribery of Foreign Public Officials in International Business Transactions* (Paris: OECD, 2006).
3 EBRD and World Bank, 'Business Environment and Enterprise Performance Survey (BEEPS) data set', 2000; question: 'How problematic are obstacles in the business environment in the following areas? Corruption.'
4 OECD, 2006.

needed to create anti-bribery programmes will generally be more restricted than in larger organisations, but there is already considerable pressure on many SMEs just to make enough profit to survive, let alone find additional resources to resist corruption.

- SMEs have little support when dealing with extortion – demands for money, goods or services – and as a result they are often unable to offer much resistance. While there may be good intentions and good practice among many SMEs, there are few networks of support for such organisations and little consistency in anti-bribery measures.

In order to meet the specific challenges above, SMEs need to be made aware of the clear margins of corruption, be provided with knowledge on how to resist it and be supported in doing so. As an incentive to resist bribery, businesses need to understand the damage that it causes – such as loss of control and reputation and potential penalties and convictions – as well as recognise that the money paid in bribes has a direct impact on the economic viability of companies, by eating away at the bottom line. Furthermore, as the wider business environment becomes more aware of the risks involved in corruption, SMEs need to catch up: a reputation for integrity and anti-bribery activism is becoming increasingly important in making companies attractive to financial institutions and in the selection processes for becoming part of supply chains for larger companies.

As such, it is essential that SMEs begin tackling the issue of corruption in a concerted and coordinated fashion. In order to do this, they will need support from governments, primarily through the committed enforcement of anti-bribery legislation, and also from government procurement agencies, which can establish integrity pacts for bidders and contractors as agreements on transparency and accountability prior to entering into contracts with SMEs. Incentives from banks, such as a favourable interest rate for businesses that have implemented anti-bribery plans, could also encourage SMEs to invest in anti-corruption initiatives. Importantly, assistance from large companies, which can use their experience in supporting their suppliers through training and resources, would help SMEs prepare for bribery situations. There is also assistance being offered by civil society. Transparency International has recently developed a tool for use by SMEs that sets out clear guidance and gives practical examples of the issues involved and how to set up an anti-bribery programme.[5]

Bribery can also be resisted in imaginative, cost-effective ways. In some countries, SMEs have formed cooperatives in order to fight corruption through mutual support and by developing their own collective anti-corruption plans. When one voice may be insubstantial or ineffective, many are strong. In another initiative, sponsored by the Danish International Development Agency through the Confederation of Tanzanian Industries, SMEs in Tanzania fought back against fraudulent tax demands by referring them to a dedicated phone number manned by a small staff who deluged callers with questions concerning the demands, requiring names, reference numbers, department heads and telephone numbers, until the scam eventually stopped, drowned out by the detail.[6] With all this activity, the OECD statement

---

5 Available in a number of languages, at Business Principles for Countering Bribery: Small and Medium Enterprise (SME) edition; www.transparency.org/tools.

6 Interview by author.

in its Anti-Bribery Convention, that 'corruption is no longer business as usual', is starting to become more convincing, even in the complex environment in which SMEs work.[7]

---

7 See for example United Nations Office on Drugs and Crime, 'Small Business Development and Corruption', discussion paper (draft) (Vienna: UNODC, 2006).

Corruption in market competition: collusion and cartels
Pradeep S. Mehta[1]

> A recent and dramatic development in cartel prosecutions has been the discovery of very large cartels that operated internationally; some of them were worldwide in scope. Their participants were multinational companies headquartered in different countries.
>
> OECD, 2003[2]

Cartels are viewed as 'the supreme evil of antitrust'.[3] Cartels and other collusion schemes can gain enormous anticompetitive rents that wreak havoc on consumers and the world economy. No product or service is immune. Price-fixing and collusion schemes have been found to penetrate markets from food and vitamins to the most arcane chemical compounds, from industrial inputs and infrastructure projects to the most sophisticated high-tech information technology (IT) and health products, as well as consumer services.

By one estimate, a first wave of cartels in international trade in the 1920s and 1930s accounted for 40 per cent of world merchandise trade and prompted anti-cartel action in key trading countries.[4] After more than fifty years of relatively low visibility and low prosecution rates, a new and at least equally pernicious and potent wave of globalised cartel activity has been sweeping through the world since the 1980s, riding on ever cheaper international communication and the globalisation of economic production networks.

More than 283 private international cartels that were discovered between 1990 and 2005 chalked up aggregate sales of some US$1.2 trillion and caused direct economic losses to consumers through overcharges of US$300 billion. In the early 2000s about thirty-five such cartels were being discovered each year, and worldwide corporate penalties totalled about US$2 billion per year.[5]

---

1 The author is the secretary general of Consumer Unity & Trust Society (CUTS) International, Jaipur, and co-chairman of the International Network of Civil Society Organisations on Competition. Siddhartha Mitra and Udai Mehta of CUTS International contributed to this article.

2 OECD, *Hard Core Cartels: Recent Progress and Challenges Ahead* (Paris: OECD, 2003).

3 *Verizon Communications Inc.* v. *Law Offices of Curtis V. Trinko*, 540 U.S. 398 (2004).

4 C. D. Edwards, *Economic and Political Aspects of International Cartels* (New York: Arno Press, 1976).

5 J. M. Connor and C. G. Helmers, *Statistics on Modern Private International Cartels, 1990–2005*, Working Paper no. 06-11 (West Lafayette, IN: Department of Agricultural Economics, Purdue University, 2006); see also J. Chowdhury, *Private International Cartels: An Overview*, Briefing Paper no. 5 (Jaipur: CUTS Centre for Competition, Investment & Regulation, 2006).

The nexus between cartels and corruption

Cartels and collusion schemes are both illegal and immoral, just like bribery – the more classic type of corruption. Bribery and cartel formation often employ similar strategies of deceit and cover-ups, such as off-budget slush funds, hidden communication links or the use of go-betweens. They also nurture and feed on the same corporate climate of moral ambiguity and reckless opportunism that undermines corporate integrity standards and respect for the law more broadly.

It is not surprising, therefore, that price-fixing and bribery often go hand in hand in the case of bid-rigging, and manipulating public procurement and tendering processes. A review of more than 230 cartel cases found that almost a third were related to bid-rigging.[6] Many companies tend to delicately layer unfair and anticompetitive behaviour. Similarly, corporate bribery facilitates and smoothes the functioning of cartels.

In India, for example, a review of several multimillion-dollar, World-Bank-funded projects in the health sector found multiple incidences of possible fraud, corruption and collusion of suppliers. As part of a US\$114 million anti-malaria project in India, four European chemical companies were alleged to have formed a cartel in 1999 to submit identical bids to supply pyrethroid insecticides, equally divide the contracts among themselves, inflate prices and limit competition from companies submitting lower bids.[7] Figure 3 shows the market shares during and after the suspected collusion.

Bribery and cartel formation also harness very similar mechanisms for disguising their activities and they thrive on the same corporate culture of ruthless opportunism. Fighting one without dealing with the other would leave intact the very disregard for the law and the very organisational mechanisms for working around it that abet cartels and bribery alike. Thus a starting point for a successful antitrust enforcement strategy is a comprehensive approach for curbing corporate white-collar crimes and offences. Only a holistic, uncompromising approach to anti-corruption and anti-collusion compliance is likely to yield sustainable and credible improvements in corporate integrity.

Wiping out the development aid dividend

Developing countries are particularly vulnerable. Relatively weak antitrust laws and enforcement capabilities seem to invite more intense price-fixing activities, by both domestic and international cartels.[8] International cartels are found to have significantly higher overcharges in Latin America and Asia than in North America and the European Union.[9]

---

6 J. M. Connor and Y. Bolotova, 'Cartel Overcharges: Survey and Meta-Analysis', *International Journal of Industrial Organization*, vol. 24, no. 6 (2006).

7 M. Voith, 'Collusion Alleged among Pyrethroid Makers', *Chemical & Engineering News*, 24 January 2008.

8 D. D. Sokol, 'Monopolists without Borders: The Institutional Challenge of International Antitrust in a Global Gilded Age', *Berkeley Business Law Journal*, vol. 4 (2007); D. D. Sokol, 'What Do We Really Know about Export Cartels and What Is the Appropriate Solution?', *Journal of Competition Law and Economics*, vol. 4, no. 3 (2008).

9 J. M. Connor and Y. Bolotova, 2006.

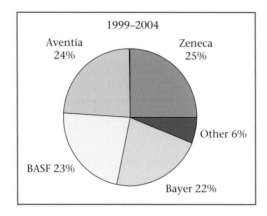

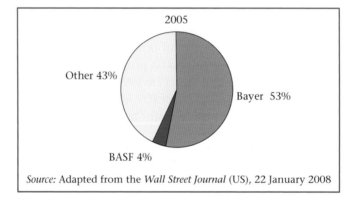

Figure 3: Share of pyrethroid contracts won

The consequences are devastating. In 1997 alone developing countries imported US$54.7 billion of goods from a sample of nineteen industries participating in price-fixing conspiracies. These imports accounted for 5.2 per cent of total imports and 1.2 per cent of GDP in these countries. Even with a very conservative estimate of a 10 per cent price increase through over-charging, these nineteen cartels caused direct economic losses to the countries, equivalent to 15 per cent of the foreign aid they received.[10]

This is only the tip of the iceberg. Experts estimate that as few as between one in three and one in six cartel cases is being detected[11] and that average overcharge rates may actually be closer to 30 per cent.[12] This means that direct economic losses due to overcharges by international

---

10 M. Levenstein, L. Oswald and V. Suslow, *International Price-fixing Cartels and Developing Countries: A Discussion of Effects and Policy Remedies*, Working Paper no. 53 (Amherst, MA: Political Economy Research Institute, University of Massachusetts, 2003).

11 OECD, 2003.

12 M. Levenstein, L. Oswald and V. Suslow, 2003; J. M. Connor and Y. Bolotova, 2006.

cartel activities alone could match or even exceed the total volume of development aid given to developing countries. Price increases have ranged from 10 per cent for thermal fax paper, to 35 per cent for vitamins to 100 percent for stainless steel.[13]

These overcharges also stifle longer-term development opportunities. They raise the prices of vital inputs for fledgling local industries and make it more difficult for them to compete internationally. They drain public budgets for essential infrastructure and health projects, impeding social development. Moreover, they make basic food items and essential health services even less affordable to the millions of poor households that live on less than US$1.25 per day.[14]

Comprehensive and aggressive antitrust enforcement is a must, as price-fixing and overcharging, bid-rigging and the carving up of geographic markets and customer groups through collusion affect countries across the globe at very different stages of development.

Tools for effective enforcement

Limited awareness about the scale, scope and pernicious impact of cartels has meant that, until very recently, only a handful of industrialised countries, including the United States, Canada and some EU countries, have pursued real efforts to tackle cartels. Even in these countries enforcement has waxed and waned considerably. Fortunately, the last decade has seen a remarkable awakening of anti-cartel action in several countries. Countries such as Brazil, Japan and South Korea have stepped up their cartel prosecution activities.[15] China's new anti-monopoly law entered into force in August 2008,[16] and India is expected to follow suit with a stronger competition law in 2009.[17]

Meanwhile, the legal framework and toolbox for fighting cartels is growing and becoming more refined. In addition to the core deterrents of civil liability and administrative fines (typically up to 10 per cent of sales value), new enforcement measures include the following carrots and sticks.

Higher public fines and compensation for private damages

Penalties imposed on cartel participants have risen significantly over the past decade, with fines of tens or even hundreds of millions of dollars becoming increasingly common.[18] The highest fine to date for a single firm was meted out by the European Union in 2007, when it

---

13 Y. Yu, 'The Impact of Private International Cartels on Developing Countries', Honors thesis, Stanford University, CA, 2003.
14 US$1.25 per day is the official poverty line defined by the World Bank; see http://go.worldbank.org/K7LWQUT9L0.
15 D. D. Sokol, 2007; *Financial Times* (UK), 10 June 2008.
16 *Financial Times* (UK), 28 July 2008.
17 See article starting on page 258.
18 J. M. Connor and C. G. Helmers, 2006.

fined ThyssenKrupp of Germany nearly €480 million for working with three other companies to rig the elevator and escalator market in four EU countries.[19,20]

In order to strengthen deterrence and enforcement, several jurisdictions have also made it easier for private parties affected by cartels to sue cartel participants for damages and compensation, though this tactic is still mainly confined to the United States.[21]

Criminal penalties

Strong antitrust sanctions against companies are not as efficient a deterrent as criminal sanctions against individuals. So far, however, running a cartel constitutes a crime punishable by imprisonment and/or fines in only a few countries, including France, Germany, Ireland, Japan, the United Kingdom and the United States. More countries are now adopting this strategy.

Leniency for early defectors

A partial or even full suspension of fines for those who report cartel activities to the authorities has proved to be an extremely successful instrument in revealing and prosecuting cartels. At the EU level, for example, a 2002 leniency programme for cartel defectors that included full amnesty to the first and most cooperative defectors led to an upsurge in disclosures and fines. The programme enabled the European Commission to take nineteen actions involving more than 100 companies for a total of nearly €3 billion (US$3.12 billion) in fines in 2002 and 2003 alone.[22]

Disclosure: rewards for individual informers

Monetary incentives may also be used to encourage disclosure. The UK Office of Fair Trading offers whistleblowers up to £100,000 for providing information on cartels.[23] In the United States, the False Claims Act, which provides financial incentives to whistleblowers, has been used extensively to attack fraud in procurement.[24]

Leniency can also be effective. The US Department of Justice has proactively approached companies suspected to be part of cartels to lay out clearly the advantages of leniency programmes for defectors.

---

19 International Competition Network, *Setting of Fines for Cartels in ICN Jurisdictions, Report to the 7th ICN Annual Conference, Kyoto, April 2008* (Luxembourg: Office for Official Publications of the European Communities, 2008).
20 BBC News (UK), 21 February 2007.
21 OECD, 2003.
22 C. Aubert, P. Rey and W. Kovacic, 'The Impact of Leniency and Whistle-blowing Programs on Cartels', *International Journal of Industrial Organization*, vol. 24, no. 6 (2006).
23 Reuters (UK), 29 February 2008.
24 C. Aubert, P. Rey and W. Kovacic, 2006.

Anti-cartel coalitions in procurement

Integrity pacts, conceived and promoted by Transparency International, provide a framework for national governments and potential suppliers to make explicit commitments to honest conduct when bidding for public tenders, and to instil a mutual sense of trust that no one will resort to bribery or bid-rigging.

Sending signals to investors and consumers: ethical blacklisting

In a different form of blacklisting, the Norwegian Competition Authority has begun to remove companies convicted of violating competition regulations from listings on ethical investment indices and funds. With these ethical funds and indices increasing investor awareness of ethical issues, such blacklisting is sending out a strong message about the unacceptability of anti-competitive crime.[25] Naming and shaming can also be taken further. Under Brazil's competition law, cartel operators can be ordered to pay for a summary of their offences to be published in a newspaper.[26]

The way forward

On a positive note, the close links between corruption and cartels offers opportunities for mutual learning about innovative enforcement strategies. The great success of whistleblower programmes and the lessons learnt on how to design them can inform similar efforts with regard to corruption and vice versa. The potential synergies go well beyond mutual learning, however. When bribery and price-fixing coincide, as in the area of public procurement, competition authorities and anti-corruption authorities may find it useful to expand their cooperation and information-sharing. Exposing firms colluding to bribe their way through a public tender process may hint at the possibility of a more systematic collusion in the broader market. Likewise, the revelation of cartels in a specific industry may prompt the authorities to review public tenders for the same products for potential bid-rigging and explore the possibility of claiming compensation for cartel-related damages.

Last but not least, these synergies and the pooling of resources also apply to civil society groups and their research and advocacy activities. Consumer organisations have been leading research and advocacy efforts for better antitrust regimes. Good governance advocates have long built expertise and raised awareness on tackling corruption and strengthening public and corporate integrity.

More enforcement capabilities, stronger legal frameworks with substantial fines and criminal liabilities, and the more effective use of refined incentive mechanisms such as leniency and transparency initiatives are of common concern to trust-busters and corruption fighters alike. International organisations, civil society groups and national governments should devise concerted actions to solve the complex and interlinked problems of corporate bribe-paying

25 'Blacklisting May Strengthen the Fight against Cartels', Norwegian Competition Authority, 15 May 2008.
26 International Competition Network, 2008.

and international cartels. It is high time to compare notes on the pernicious symbiosis of corruption and cartels and work together more closely to strengthen corporate integrity in a comprehensive manner.

Despite the surge and expansion of anti-cartel enforcement, the fight is only beginning. Worldwide, median cartel penalties are estimated to recoup only about 20 per cent of direct overcharges.[27] High-profile cases of cartels, very often involving the most respectable brand names in business, continue to hit the headlines around the world.[28] Likewise, recidivism remains high, as 170 companies that participated in cartels between 1990 and 2005 have been found to be repeat offenders.[29] All this indicates that deterrence is still not effective, and a sense of impunity prevails even in the most advanced economies.

In addition, cartels are increasingly operating globally, while many developing countries can barely muster the resources and determination to fight entrenched local cartels, not to mention the price-fixing of imports. All this is compounded by irresponsible 'beggar-my-neighbour' behaviour: as recently as 2005 the regulatory frameworks of at least fifty-one, mainly OECD, countries were still found to tolerate, explicitly or implicitly, export cartels that engaged in price-fixing outside their own countries.[30] This makes stronger international cooperation and a further strengthening of anti-cartel efforts around the world a priority, to make markets work better, create development opportunities and strengthen overall corporate integrity.

27 J. M. Connor and C. G. Helmers, 2006.
28 For example, *The Economist* (UK), 1 May 2008.
29 J. M. Connor and C. G. Helmers, 2006.
30 M. Levenstein and V. Suslow, 'The Changing International Status of Export Cartels', *American University International Law Review*, vol. 20, no. 4 (2005).

Corrupting the rules of the game: from legitimate lobbying to capturing regulations and policies
Dieter Zinnbauer[1]

Lobbying includes all activities carried out to influence the policy- and decision-making processes of governmental or other similar institutions. The lobbyists who carry out these activities work in a variety of organisations, such as public affairs consultancies, law firms, non-governmental organisations (NGOs), think tanks, corporate lobby units ('in-house representatives') or trade associations.[2]

In principle, lobbying conveys information and opinion to political representatives and public officials. It is not, therefore, a morally dubious or illegitimate activity *per se* but an important

1 Dieter Zinnbauer is editor-in-chief of the *Global Corruption Report*.
2 For a useful definition of lobbying, see, for example, European Commission, *Green Paper: European Transparency Initiative* (Brussels: European Commission, 2006).

element of the democratic discussion and decision-making process. This also pertains to corporate lobbying. Businesses, as collective endeavours by citizens, are, as much as any other association of interests, entitled to be heard in the democratic decision-making process.

Very serious issues have arisen about the disproportionate influence of corporate lobbying, however. Companies whose turnover dwarfs the national income of entire countries command a level of financial firepower that it is impossible for any other voice to match in the competition for political visibility and persuasion.

Companies do not hesitate to make lavish use of their resources. In the United States, lobbying expenses have almost doubled over the last decade, reaching US$2.8 billion in 2007 and swelling the ranks of lobbyists to a record 16,000 in 2008.[3] In Brussels an estimated 2,500 lobbying organisations with 15,000 lobbyists vie for influence on EU policy-making.[4] Among interest groups that have permanent offices in Brussels, about two-thirds represent commercial interests, 10 per cent business/labour associations, 10 per cent regional and international organisations, 10 per cent NGOs and 1 per cent think tanks.[5]

Numbers such as these and stories of influence-trading around the world fuel suspicions of corporate hijacking or the 'capture' of lawmakers and government officials. The consequence is a cynical and, in the longer term, corrosive mistrust of politics and democracy. TI's Global Corruption Barometer 2007, an annual survey of more than 60,000 households in over sixty countries, bears sad testament to this trend: parliaments and political parties are invariably perceived to be the two most corrupt institutions in society.[6]

Concerns about undue corporate influence on public affairs can be broken down into four main categories.

Direct political corruption and influence-peddling

Even in the most laissez-faire regimes, lawmakers and senior civil servants make decisions on a wide range of issues of immense material importance to the business sector. Risks of political corruption are high when the enormous economic value of such a political mandate meets with low public salaries, uncertain tenure, campaign finance needs or simply individual greed. Trading political influence for money or personal gain is illegal almost everywhere yet it is still a problem. It ranges from individual acts of gift-giving or bribery, to sway a particular vote or regulatory decision, to intricate institutionalised systems of political patronage and cronyism in which public and private actors join hands to appropriate portions of a country's wealth.[7]

---

3 Based on opensecrets.org, the lobbying database maintained by the Center for Responsive Politics.
4 Committee on Constitutional Affairs, European Parliament, *Draft Report on the Development of the Framework for the Activities of Interest Representatives (Lobbyists) in the European Institutions* (Brussels: European Commission, 2008).
5 W. Lehmann and L. Bosche, *Lobbying in the European Union: Current Rules and Practices,* Working Paper no. 04-2003 (Brussels: Directorate-General for Research, European Commission, 2003).
6 TI, Global Corruption Barometer 2007.
7 For a description of rent-seeking and crony capitalism, see E. Gomez and K. S. Jomo, *Malaysia's Political Economy: Politics, Patronage and Profits* (Cambridge: Cambridge University Press, 1999). See article starting on page 295.

Conflicts of interest between government officials and business sectors

Even when pertinent laws are effective and political decisions are officially not for sale, a close nexus between politics and business may still give corporate interests disproportionate influence. Politicians or their families may have direct financial stakes in the industries they are supposed to regulate, or set their sights on lucrative private sector posts when they leave office. National elites often attend the same selective schools and move easily between public bureaucracies and corporate postings during their professional careers (the 'revolving door' phenomenon), cultivating strong interpersonal ties. In the United Kingdom, for example, politically connected firms are estimated to account for almost 40 per cent of market capitalisation – a number that rises to a staggering 80 per cent in Russia.[8]

Nothing of this is illegal per se. A robust exchange of expertise and talent can raise the quality of regulation and decision-making. If personal ties are too densely interwoven and financial interests are too closely aligned, however, the chances are slim that all stakeholders' views or the public interest will be carefully considered. In the US state of Texas, up to seventy former state legislators lobby their former colleagues. In Germany the federal audit commission (Bundesrechnungshof) has raised concerns that, since 2004, an estimated 300 people on company or business association payrolls have been seconded to ministries and have often worked closely with rule-making processes involving their former corporate employers.[9] Empirical evidence suggests that such connections pay off. A study of US companies listed on the S&P 500 index finds that companies with board members connected to the Republican Party realised abnormal gains in their stock market values after the 2000 congressional and presidential elections, which were won by the Republicans, while companies with connections to the opposition Democratic Party decreased in value.[10] Moreover, 50 per cent of executives from OECD countries reported that personal and familiar relationships are used to win public contracts in non-OECD countries.[11]

Unequal access to policy-makers and decision-making processes

Even leaving personal and financial interlinkages aside, the sheer scale, growth and cost of the lobbying industry makes a level playing field appear all but impossible. At the US state level, lobbying expenditures average some US$200,000 per legislator, and five lobbyists vie for the attention of each lawmaker (ten in California and Florida, twenty-four in New York).[12] It is hard to imagine that less endowed and less organised interests can compete equitably for the scarce attention of politicians and public officials.

---

8 M. Faccio, 'Politically Connected Firms', *American Economic Review*, vol. 96, no. 1 (2006).
9 *Financial Times* (UK), 7 April 2008. See article starting on page 331.
10 E. Goldman, J. Rocholl and J. So, 'Do Politically Connected Boards Affect Firm Value?', *Review of Financial Studies*, forthcoming (2009).
11 TI, '2008 Bribe Payers Survey' (Berlin: TI, 2008).
12 See L. Rush, 'Influence: A Booming Business. Record $1.3 Billion Spent to Lobby State Government', *Center for Public Integrity*, 20 December 2007, as well as http://projects.publicintegrity.org/hiredguns/chart.aspx?act=lobtoleg for the lobbyists to legislators ratio 2006.

Globalisation has made establishing equal voices and representation even more challenging. More and more policies that affect communities are being shaped by international and supranational institutions in faraway places such as Geneva, Brussels and Washington. Tracking policy developments and lobbying delegates on this international summit circuit can turn into a costly and time-consuming endeavour that is feasible only for well-resourced special interests.

Integrity and the balance of information and representation

Lobbying does more than target decision-makers and decision-making processes directly. Linking up with broader public relations strategies, corporate lobbying is increasingly moving upstream to shape public opinion and debate on specific policy issues in more subtle ways. Corporate interests can, of course, legitimately produce information for and participate in the public debate and help make the democratic discourse as informed and inclusive as possible. The unrivalled resources that businesses can muster for this engagement, as well as a range of sophisticated strategies employed to sway public opinion by influencing science, the media and civil society, raise serious concerns, however.[12]

What can be done? Ensuring integrity in corporate lobbying

Preventing undue corporate influence on political affairs and policy-making is as important as it is difficult. Professional interaction and personal ties cannot be 'regulated away'. Undue influence can be exerted in a myriad of ways, many very subtle, that are difficult to trace and even more difficult to link to specific benefits. Keeping undue corporate influence in check, therefore, cannot rely solely on outlawing specific activities. It requires putting in place a broad range of carrots and sticks, as well as checks and balances that provide strong incentives for all involved to play by the rules. The best mix and first priorities of policy provisions will depend on the specific nexus between business and politics in a particular country, the characteristics of the policy-making process, the state of development of the lobbying industry and the agility of the media, science and civil society sectors. Measures relate to four principal stakeholder groups:

- public office-holders as the ultimate lobbying targets;
- the media, civil society and science as information providers and brokers;
- lobbyists as the agents that carry out lobbying activities; and
- businesses as the principals that commission lobbying.

The recipient side: political representatives and public office-holders

Many established provisions for good governance are aimed directly at preventing undue influence on democratic decision-making. They include campaign and political party finance laws and the criminalisation of bribing public officials and influence-peddling. Many

---

13 See article starting on page 39.

countries have enacted such provisions, but enforcement remains patchy. Loopholes and workarounds continue to be exploited even in the most advanced regulations, requiring continuous refinements.[14]

Transparency initiatives are relatively new additions to this toolbox and provide essential checks when enforcement is otherwise poor. Provisions such as asset disclosure by public officials, open hearings and consultative rule-making processes, all backed up by strong access to information, enable citizens, watchdog groups and the media to track and engage with political decision-making better.

Revolving-door provisions established in the United States, France and Latvia, for example,[15] further help defuse conflicts of interest. They typically require 'cooling-off' periods before civil servants or legislators can lobby their former colleagues or join the industries that they were previously entrusted with overseeing.

The information brokers: media, civil society and science

Ensuring that the media are free, fair and inclusive in the context of commercial pressures rests on strong provisions for freedom of expression and low entry barriers. The policy response to lobbying that masquerades as journalism can include requirements for the strict disclosure of funding sources and a clear distinction between content and commercial messages. Media diversity should be encouraged through subsidies for alternative media, access to bandwidth and channels, and continuing support for the independent public service media. A thriving media sphere requires a thousand flowers to bloom.

Protecting the integrity and critical contribution of science rests on the full disclosure of research funding, continuing public funding for critical research, robust peer review and an unwavering commitment by the scientific community to integrity and the principles of scientific inquiry.

Similarly, ensuring the integrity and authenticity of interventions by civil society in the public debate rests on the full disclosure of funding and policy purpose.

The agents of influence: regulating the lobby industry

Lobbying firms are frequently part of larger transnational communication conglomerates that maintain representations in important economies around the world. Until recently the lobbying industry has enjoyed very limited special oversight or regulation, despite its growth, global expansion and close interaction with the processes of policy-making. For over a century the United States was the only country that regulated lobbyists. By 1991 Australia, Canada and Germany had followed suit, and as of this writing several other countries had enacted

---

14 See, for example, the high-profile 2006 scandal in the United States involving lobbyist Jack Abramoff, which prompted refined lobbying regulation in the Honest Leadership and Open Government Act of 2007.

15 Group of States against Corruption (GRECO), *Rules and Guidelines regarding Revolving Doors/Pantouflage* (Strasbourg: GRECO, 2007).

rules for lobbyists or were in the process of doing so.[16] The European Commission initiated a consultation process on regulating lobbyists in 2005 and opened a voluntary lobbyist registry in mid-2008. A surge of interest by think tanks and civil society organisations (CSOs) in making lobbying more accountable and transparent further testifies to the salience of these issues.[17]

In addition to codes of conduct and specific prohibitions on illicit lobbying activities, mandatory lobbying registries are a central plank for making lobbying activities more transparent and accountable. The obligations of 'meaningful disclosure' require lobbyists to provide their names, clients, issue areas, targets, techniques and financial information. While disclosure will vary between political systems and require continuous fine-tuning and strong enforcement, such a comprehensive lobby transparency initiative is not an untested, unrealistic demand. Every element of disclosure mentioned here is already being implemented in one of the vanguard countries moving to enhance transparency.

The US example clearly demonstrates the impact of such transparency systems. Several CSOs, such as the Center for Public Integrity and the Center for Responsive Politics, use these lobby registers to undertake detailed analyses of corporate lobbying. Citizens, the media and other NGOs can easily trace the flows of corporate money in campaign financing and lobbying with user-friendly online databases.

In order to enable and facilitate such vital analysis, freedom of information and disclosure provisions must specify conducive reporting formats (standardised, open access to raw data), in particular with regard to electronic filing and the online presentation of the information.[18]

Viewed globally, lobbying regulation is still in its infancy. While Canada, the US federal government and almost all US states have instituted rules for lobbying, so far only a few other countries have made attempts to follow suit. Rules drawn up in Germany and for the European Parliament, for example, are judged to be significantly less strict and comprehensive than those in much of North America.[19]

The most straightforward, yet missing link in lobbying integrity: corporations

Efforts to curb undue corporate influence are being increasingly expanded from a focus on lobby targets to the activities of lobbyists. Efforts to make lobbying more transparent and accountable have so far paid rather limited attention to what is arguably the most important factor in the equation, however: corporations themselves.

---

16 OECD, *Lobbyists, Governments and Public Trust: Building A Legislative Framework for Enhancing Transparency and Accountability in Lobbying* (Paris: OECD, 2008).

17 See, for example, the Alliance for Lobbying Transparency & Ethics Regulation, a coalition of more than 160 groups advocating lobbying reform at the European level: www.alter-eu.org/.

18 For more specific requirements for electronic information disclosure, see D. Zinnbauer, *With the Internet and Information Disclosure towards a New Quality in Democratic Governance: A Policy Agenda and Ways to Take It Forward*, Research Memo no. 4 (New York: Social Science Research Council, 2004).

19 R. Chari, G. Murphy and J. Hogan, 'Regulating Lobbyists: A Comparative Analysis of the United States, Canada, Germany and the European Union', *Political Quarterly*, vol. 78, no. 3 (2007).

Corporate money has fuelled the expansion of the lobbying industry, and at the same time companies have also ramped up their in-house lobbying capabilities. The number of corporate–government relations offices in Washington grew from just one in 1920 to 175 in 1968, and by 2005 had risen to more than 600.[20] Disclosure by lobbyists and government officials – if effective, comprehensive and accessible – can enable civil society to construct some pieces of the lobbying puzzle. Companies themselves are uniquely positioned to account and take responsibility for all their lobbying activities, however, but are rarely taken to task to disclose such information.

Even more surprisingly, lobbying activities, and, where applicable, political contributions, are of central strategic interest and potentially material importance for corporations, but are rarely subject to internal corporate oversight. By 2008 only about one-third of S&P 100 companies required board oversight of political spending.[21] The result is that corporate actors may engage in public policy-making without sufficient consultation, accountability and robust checks on whether the lobbying is consistent with shareholders' long-term goals and interests.[22]

The public disclosure of lobbying activities is in most cases very limited. With millions of dollars being spent, lobbying has become an essential component of corporate identity, citizenship and responsibility. Reporting falls far below other, well-established disclosure practices and requirements for environmental and social impact, however.

Pressure to make corporations themselves more accountable and transparent with regard to their lobbying activities is gradually building from different directions.

- *Internally*: in a 2008 survey of 255 US corporate board members, more than three-quarters of the respondents supported the suggestion that corporations should have to disclose payments to trade associations and other tax-exempt organisations used for political purposes.[23]
- *By shareholders*: shareholders proposed more than fifty requests for reporting on corporate political donations and underlying policies during the 2008 US proxy season, and those put up for a vote received record levels of support (on average 26 per cent).[24]
- *By civil society and think tanks*: several civil society initiatives seek to strengthen corporate disclosure and oversight on political finance and, more recently, lobbying activities. The Global Reporting Initiative, for example, provides widely used guidelines for sustainability reporting and offers a detailed template for reporting on public policy positions and participation. Likewise, the OECD has recognised voluntary corporate disclosure of participation in public policy development and lobbying as 'emerging good practices in corporate governance'.[25]

---

20 R. Repetto, *Best Practice in Internal Oversight of Lobbying Practice*, Working Paper no. 200601 (New Haven, CT: Yale Center for Environmental Law and Policy, 2006).

21 Center for Political Accountability, 'Political Disclosure Tops 50 Companies', 28 May 2008.

22 R. Repetto, 2006.

23 Mason-Dixon Polling and Research, 'Corporate Political Spending: A Survey of American Directors', 4–15 February 2008.

24 RiskMetrics Group, *2008 Proxy Season Preview: Social Service* (New York: RiskMetrics Group, 2008); L. Reed Walton, 'Postseason Review: Social Proposals', RiskMetrics Group, 5 August 2008.

25 OECD, 2008.

Old and new shores for responsible lobbying

Ensuring that economic power does not translate into disproportionate and undue influence on political decision-making is a fundamental challenge that accompanies countries through all stages of development. Failure to curb undue influence lays the foundations for a kleptocratic state, stunted economic and political development, and, perhaps most perniciously, a citizenry that loses trust in a fair democratic bargain, with dramatic consequences for the viability of the entire political and economic system.

A more refined and comprehensive system of checks and balances notwithstanding, the buck ultimately stops at corporate actors themselves. Corporations have arguably been slow to recognise that transparency and fairness in lobbying are core features of twenty-first-century corporate citizenship. Laws, regulations, transparency and watchdog groups are essential to reduce and mitigate risks, but they continuously have to play catch-up and cannot supplant a corporate commitment to fair and transparent engagement in public policy-making. Public pressure is increasing, and the templates for good practice are in place. It is time for more companies in more countries to step up to the plate.

Corporate lobbying's new frontier: from influencing policy-making to shaping public debate
David Miller[1]

To obtain a more subtle and sustained impact, lobbying groups are increasingly targeting wider public debates on policy issues in the hope of framing specific issues, promoting the evidence that underpins their messages and building public support for a certain company or industry. Sponsoring dubious scientific research, manipulating media coverage and creating 'astroturf' organisations are among the strategies being employed to achieve these goals.

Shaping science

Shaping the focus and presentation of scientific research can be a key conduit for influencing public debate. With many universities cash-strapped and tasked to move towards industry-relevant research agendas, corporations are playing an increasingly important role in funding science, endowing academic chairs and sponsoring think tanks and research outlets. Some companies pay scientists to attend international conferences and arrange for public relations (PR) firms to ghostwrite journal articles 'authored' by scientists.[2]

---

1 David Miller is Professor of Sociology at the University of Strathclyde, United Kingdom.
2 S. Krimsky, *Science in the Private Interest* (New York: Rowman and Littlefield, 2003); D. Michaels, *Doubt is Their Product: How Industry's Assault on Science Threatens Your Health* (Oxford: Oxford University Press, 2008); L. Soley, *Leasing the Ivory Tower: The Corporate Takeover of Academia* (Boston: South End Press, 1995).

In such an environment, there are real risks that critical scholarship will remain underfunded and that inopportune findings will not be given their due visibility. The tobacco industry, for example, successfully muddied the waters about the health effects of tobacco for thirty years.[3] Similarly, Exxon gave nearly US$16 million between 1998 and 2005 to research institutes and policy groups that questioned global warming, prompting the United Kingdom's Royal Society to call on Exxon to stop this practice.[4]

Managing the media message

Worries about the loss of editorial independence and media diversity, both essential pillars of free democratic debate, have long accompanied the evolution of the conventional media into a more commercialised and concentrated sector. It is not uncommon for large business conglomerates to own major television, cable and radio networks, newspapers, magazines, movie studios and internet sites, or to be major advertising clients for these media outlets. This raises questions about conflicts of interest that are difficult to ignore.

A new concern arises from the fact that the media have become important resources in lobbying campaigns. One US PR and lobbying firm calls this phenomenon 'journo-lobbying'.[5] A pioneering example is Tech Central Station (TCS), which appears at first glance to be a kind of think-tank-cum-internet-magazine. Look a little deeper, and it is apparent that TCS has 'increasingly taken aggressive positions on one side or another of intra-industry debates', and was actually published until 2006 by a prominent Washington public affairs firm.[6]

Such shrewd initiatives and the sheer scale of the lobbying sector makes it difficult even for professional journalists, not to mention the citizenry, to distinguish sponsored from independent information. In Germany, an estimated 30,000 to 50,000 PR workers provide input to and compete for public attention with 48,000 journalists.[7]

Landscaping the grassroots

Strategies to influence science and the media are complemented by the establishment of fake citizen groups – so-called 'astroturf' organisations. These appear to be genuine charitable organisations set up by or in the interests of ordinary citizens. In reality, though, they are often the brainchild of lobbying firms and their corporate sponsors. Astroturf groups work to inhibit or encourage particular policy changes by conjuring up the impression of a groundswell of public enthusiasm about a specific issue.

3 C. Mooney, 'The Manufacture of Uncertainty', *American Prospect,* 28 March 2008.
4 *Guardian* (UK), 20 September 2006; Union of Concerned Scientists, *Smoke, Mirrors & Hot Air* (Cambridge, MA: Union of Concerned Scientists, 2007).
5 D. Miller and W. Dinan, 'Journalism, Public Relations, and Spin', in K. Wahl-Jorgensen and T. Hanitzsch (eds.), *The Handbook of Journalism Studies* (New York: Routledge, 2008).
6 N. Confessore, 'Meet the Press: How James Glassman Reinvented Journalism – as Lobbying', *Washington Monthly,* December 2003.
7 Netzwerk Recherche, *Kritischer Wirtschaftsjournalismus: Analysen und Argumente, Tipps und Tricks* (Hamburg: Netzwerk Recherche, 2007).

Myriad 'patient groups', for example, are working in the apparent interests of patients and their relatives. One such organisation, the pan-European Cancer United, was believed to be closely linked to Swiss-based Roche, a leading maker of cancer drugs. According to news reports, Roche helped fund the group and the research for the principal study on which it is based, had a senior company executive on its board and a PR firm served as Cancer United's secretariat.[8]

With such strategies, companies can populate the information environment with seemingly independent organisations and generate the impression of public support and authenticity, when both may actually be lacking.

Critical scientific analysis, independent media and authentic representation in public debates are prerequisites for a thriving democratic discourse. They help citizens as much as policy-makers to understand and form opinions about issues. Corporations and their lobbying agents are important participants in this discourse. If they are found to create and exploit dependencies, conflicts of interests and inauthentic representations systematically, however, they breach the rules of democratic fairness. In the long run they also undermine the legitimacy of the very public stage on which they argue their case.

---

8 *Guardian* (UK), 18 October 2006. Roche denied that the Cancer United campaign was about marketing for Roche.

View from the inside – Markets for carbon credits to fight climate change: addressing corruption risks proactively
Jørund Buen[1] and Axel Michaelowa[2]

A general scientific consensus has established a relationship between the accumulation of greenhouse gases in the atmosphere and global warming. In response, more than 180 countries have ratified the Kyoto Protocol, which caps greenhouse gas emissions in industrialised countries at around 5 per cent below their 1990 levels.

Kyoto contains several important market mechanisms that are intended to ensure that the required cuts can be made most effectively and efficiently. One of them is the Clean Development Mechanism (CDM), whereby the private and public sectors can invest in emission reduction projects in developing countries and receive related emission reduction credits, which are tradable in so-called 'compliance markets' and can be bought by emitters to offset their own emissions. Similarly, under Kyoto's Joint Implementation (JI) scheme,

---

1 Jørund Buen is a senior partner at Point Carbon, a research and consulting firm with headquarters in Oslo.

2 Axel Michaelowa is a senior founding partner at Perspectives GmbH, a research and consulting firm based in Zurich and Hamburg, that provides project review and management services related to the Clean Development Mechanism.

investors from one industrialised country can engage in an emission reduction project in another industrialised country and use the credits they obtain through this to meet their own compliance targets.

Some doubt the general viability of these mechanisms and fear that they distract from the more fundamental structural policy changes that are needed to tackle climate change. Carbon trading is here to stay, however, and is expected to grow considerably in the near future. It is certainly not the only answer to climate change, but an integral element of the overall solution.

International carbon markets have grown almost exponentially since their inception in the late 1990s. By 2007 2.7 billion tonnes of carbon-dioxide-equivalent emissions with a total value of €40 billion had been traded globally, of which about one-third were CDM- and JI-related offsets.[3] The future size of these markets depends on whether policy-makers agree on further reductions after the Kyoto Protocol expires in 2012, as well the level of US participation. Even in a low-growth scenario, the market will probably be several times larger than it is today. In a high-growth scenario, it may grow by a factor of almost thirty by 2020.[4]

New markets – new risks of corruption?

Theoretically, the nature of carbon markets might present a number of corruption risks, but most of them have been addressed by the regulatory design of the compliance markets under Kyoto.[5] One potential challenge is that carbon markets deal with intangible assets (carbon offsets). Compared to markets for tangible objects with apparent physical characteristics – apples, for example – the quality and veracity of carbon intangibles are potentially difficult to verify 'on the spot' by the purchaser in markets in which certificates and not products with physical characteristics change hands. The tracking of certificates through registries, as well as the independent verification of emission reductions that give rise to certificates, are therefore key elements in regulated carbon credit markets, and have been fully implemented in the Kyoto Protocol compliance market.

The only open flank of the compliance markets is the check of the general eligibility of a project under the project-based mechanisms CDM and JI. Offsets are valid and make an effective contribution to reducing carbon emissions only if they are awarded for projects that would not otherwise have taken place. This *additionality* criterion is difficult to ascertain and can provide scope for manipulation. Here there is an ongoing 'cat and mouse' game between project developers, who try to get projects that would have happened anyway approved as *additional*, and the regulators, who have developed detailed rules to prevent such projects from qualifying under the mechanisms. In broader perspective, this underlines the fact that carbon markets are political constructs in which products, values

---

3 K. Røine, E. Tvinnereim and H. Hasselknippe (eds.), *Carbon 2008: Post-2012 Is Now* (Oslo: Point Carbon, 2008).
4 *Carbon Market Analyst* (Norway), 21 May 2008.
5 Some of these conceptual ideas have been presented by J. Werksman, of the World Resources Institute, at the thirteenth International Anti-Corruption Conference (IACC), Athens, 30 October 2008.

and their distribution are critically shaped by rules and regulations, which as a consequence become the focus of intense lobbying, some of which might degenerate into corruption. Against this backdrop, it is quite striking that published allegations and evidence about corruption in the carbon market are still very rare.[6] The following sections discuss some of the key challenges in more detail.

Additionality in practice

Carbon credits are awarded to CDM and JI projects if they can prove that they face prohibitive barriers, or that another way of producing the same service or product would be more profitable and thus would have been chosen instead of the less carbon-emitting method. In most cases, the cited obstacles are real, and the claim that the low-carbon alternative is not profitable *enough* to go forward without revenues from carbon offsets is correct. It is very difficult to be absolutely sure, however. As a result, a number of commentators claim that CDM and JI projects are not always leading to real emission reductions,[7] and some even link this directly to corruption.[8]

Project developers seeking carbon credits need to make detailed documentation publicly available for stakeholder comments, resulting in a high degree of transparency that is likely to deter corruption. One of the authors personally witnessed a corruption attempt in India, however, where a project developer on whose project the author had submitted a critical public comment proposed a 'fee' to write a positive report.

The need to prove additionality has probably tempted some project developers to forge documents in order to qualify for the CDM. Indeed, the CDM executive board has recently referred to 'incidents of attempts of falsification of documents by project participants'.[9]

Market players in India say that CDM project developers frequently backdate documents in order to show that they considered the CDM before they started the project. Another tactic is manipulating rate of return calculations to make it appear that CDM revenue would push the project above a certain profitability level that determines execution. Moreover, CDM consultants in India have on at least a couple of occasions copied and pasted stakeholder consultations carried out for one project into documentation for other projects.[10] To prevent such behaviour, British CDM authorities require project developers

---

6 See K. Holliday, 'Clean and transparent', Energy Risk; available at www.energyrisk.com/public/showPage. html?page=834295.

7 A. Michaelowa and K. Umamaheswaran, *Additionality and Sustainable Development Issues Regarding CDM Projects in Energy Efficiency Sector*, Discussion Paper no. 346 (Hamburg: Hamburg Institute of International Economics, 2006); L. Schneider, *Is the CDM Fulfilling Its Environmental and Sustainable Development Objectives?* (Berlin: Öko-Institut, 2007); M. W. Wara and D. G. Victor, *A Realistic Policy on International Carbon Offsets*, Working Paper no. 74 (Stanford, CA: Program on Energy and Sustainable Development, Stanford University, 2008).

8 *Guardian* (UK), 21 May 2008.

9 CDM Accreditation Panel, *Twenty-sixth Progress Report of the CDM Accreditation Panel* (New York: CDM Accreditation Panel, 2008).

10 Point Carbon, *Consulting Firms Deny Wrongdoing in Drafting Indian PDDs* (Oslo: Point Carbon, 2005); A. Michaelowa, 'Experiences in Evaluation of PDDs, Validation and Verification Reports', paper presented at Austrian JI/CDM workshop, Vienna, 26 January 2007.

to sign a declaration certifying that their information is correct, and hold them criminally liable if fraud is discovered.

Corruption risks for certifying agencies

In order to obtain carbon credits, project buyers need host- and investor-country approval, validation of the project documentation by an accredited third party, international UN approval and third-party verification of project operations compared to the plan. The 'street-level' staff in some of these organisations are not paid particularly well, and can be inexperienced, due to the rapid development of the market.

Project approval by host countries is, arguably, the stage most vulnerable to corruption. Although kickbacks to officials have not been reported, a Russian agency reportedly asked for direct monetary payments.[11] In South-east Asian countries, it is fairly common for developers to invite the authorities to workshops (with attractive *per diems*) before submitting projects for approval. In China, it is not uncommon for project developers to invite experts reviewing their projects to dinner. On the other hand, the Indonesian Designated National Authority has an elaborate ethics code that aims at preventing corruption.[12]

Ambivalent incentives and revolving doors for expert consultants

Ensuring the integrity of the expert consultants involved can also be a challenge. In China, consultant fees are capped, and these experts cannot take a share of carbon credits as payment. The unintended consequence seems to be that consultants charge separate, undisclosed fees to both the seller and the buyer of the same project. In the United Kingdom, buyers are barred from making such payments.[13]

Assessing CDM projects requires detailed technical competence and an intimate understanding of the CDM. Because very few people fulfil these criteria, potential conflicts of interest have been very difficult to avoid. Several project consultants also conduct expert project reviews for the CDM's executive board. In addition, consultants assess project baseline and monitoring methodologies, and theoretically could block methodologies submitted by their competitors. To our knowledge, there are no quarantine rules preventing executive board members from entering the private sector as lobbyists, and at least two members were hired by companies submitting projects after their terms on the board had expired.

11 A. Korppoo, 'JI Projects in Russian Energy Sector', paper presented at St Petersburg, 30 September 2005.
12 Government of Indonesia, 'Code of Conducts (2007)', available at dna-cdm.menlh.go.id/en/about/?pg=ethic.
13 L. Mortimer, 'Overly Protective?', in Environmental Finance, *Global Carbon 2008* (London: Environmental Finance, 2008).

Strengthening governance for improving the markets for carbon credits

Corruption risks in markets for carbon credits could be reduced by making procedures more standardised and transparent. More specifically, this could include:

- not awarding carbon credits to projects if they are not submitted for UN approval within a limited time period after investment decisions are made;
- selecting members for the UN bodies approving carbon projects based on professional competence rather than geographical representation, granting them legal immunity and requiring them to state their current and previous roles and potential conflicts of interest in detail in a publicly available document;
- where feasible, making summaries of the contents of discussions relating to the approval of CDM (as well as relevant JI) projects publicly available; and
- restricting situations in which former regulators work for private companies, and perhaps vice versa.

A host of additional corruption risks

Discussions, both under the auspices of the UN and in many individual countries, are under way on how to design the post-Kyoto carbon market, after the protocol expires in 2012. One lesson to draw from the experience with carbon markets so far is that particular attention should be paid to new market segments for which data are limited or additionality criteria are particularly difficult to prove. These could include credits for avoided deforestation, carbon capture and storage, aviation and marine transport.

The sale of governments' Kyoto units presents another accountability challenge. Since former Soviet bloc countries were allocated Kyoto allowances based on their economic activity before the 1990 collapse, they have many surplus allowances to sell. If these countries fulfil a number of (relatively strict) criteria they can implement JI[14] projects, for which no international third-party checking or UN approval is needed. In principle, they can thereby transfer some of their surplus allowances to buyers via JI. Revenues from such sales could be significant – in the billions of euros in the cases of Russia and Ukraine. It is not clear which government organisations in these countries have the authority to sell the surplus and how transparently and accountably such transfers of public wealth will be carried out.

A final area of concern is the voluntary carbon credit market, in which companies and individuals without formal compliance obligations can buy offsets to compensate for their carbon footprint. While standards have been developed for such markets and most players act responsibly, a lack of regulation poses the risk of fraud – for example, the selling of one and the same emissions reduction to several customers.

---

14 So-called 'Track 1' JI projects.

3 The international dimension: corruption in a globalising and diverse economy

The contributions in this chapter extend the analysis to key issues in a global economic perspective. *Georg Huber-Grabenwarter and Frédéric Boehm explore specific challenges for corporate integrity in developing economies that may be characterised by weak governance systems and a large informal sector. Gavin Hayman adds to this analysis by outlining corruption risks in the extractive industries, which are of particular importance for many developing countries as they are home to large stocks of natural resources. Transparency International examines whether and to what extent foreign direct investment and global supply chains make a contribution to enhancing corporate integrity across the world. Ayesha Barenblat and Tara Rangarajan expand this discussion and propose some promising ways to strengthen the integrity of supply chains, while Deborah A. Bräutigam broaches the question of whether China's rise as an important global investor bodes ill or well for tackling corruption in business.*

Sol Piciotto in his contribution looks at the important issue of transfer pricing, and directs attention to corruption risks that arise when companies operate globally while their taxes are to be determined and paid at country level. Finally, John Nellis discusses corruption in the context of privatisation programmes, which continue to play an important role in many economies around the world.

Laying the foundations for sound and sustainable development: strengthening corporate integrity in weak governance zones
Georg Huber-Grabenwarter and Frédéric Boehm[1]

Strengthening corporate integrity in least developed countries with limited basic governance structures in place poses a set of distinctive challenges. For businesses, aligning corporate activities with company values and principles of corporate integrity is more difficult when the institutional environment is weak and inefficient. For governments, strengthening the rule of law and sectoral integrity is particularly taxing when a large portion of economic activity takes place in the informal sector. For donors, corruption in the business sector is a cross-cutting concern for aid programming.

---

1 Georg Huber-Grabenwarter and Frédéric Boehm are project staff at the Deutsche Gesellschaft für Technische Zusammenarbeit (GTZ). The ideas expressed constitute the personal opinion of the authors and do not necessarily comprise the position of the organisations associated with them.

Building and asserting corporate integrity when the rules are weak

About 900 million people live in so-called 'weak governance' zones, particularly in sub-Saharan Africa, where governments struggle to provide essential services and to assume their responsibilities with regard to public administration and human rights.[2] Doing business in countries with weak institutions and possibly high levels of corruption poses enormous challenges to the integrity of domestic and foreign businesses alike.

When local rules are incomplete, ill enforced or blatantly manipulated, simply playing by those rules is not sufficient. When laws and their enforcement fail to place reasonable boundaries on corporate behaviour, companies need to ensure that their actions do not undermine the protection and fulfilment of human rights and general principles of responsible business conduct. A lack of basic legal guidance therefore mandates more due diligence and individual responsibility for businesses, both domestic and foreign.

Weak institutions not only fail to provide guidance for responsible corporate behaviour, they also tend actively to undermine it. Weak institutions very often mean that property rights are poorly protected, contracts are difficult to enforce and companies are faced with arbitrary and excessive regulations (red tape).

As a result, companies may be tempted to use bribery and other corrupt practices as a political 'risk insurance' to protect investments. Similarly, they may be lured to manipulate rules in their favour, avoid the enforcement of regulations, gain lucrative contracts or resource extraction permits, or simply to cut through red tape and administrative hold-ups.

Resorting to corruption in weak institutional settings undermines the very business opportunities companies seek to exploit or protect, however, in addition to creating significant reputational and material risks for foreign companies. The willingness to bribe makes unaccountable rule-making, arbitrary rule enforcement, hold-ups and extortion lucrative propositions for corrupt office-holders, and thereby reinforces the very system it is trying to overcome. Using corrupt means to outflank competitors further amplifies market uncertainty, by destroying fair competition and predictable regulation, with adverse implications for the cost of capital and business planning. Resorting to high-level influence-peddling and patronage to protect investments ties the future of a business venture to the often uncertain fate of a specific political power broker. In Indonesia, for example, the valuation of firms connected to the late President Suharto fluctuated significantly in line with rumours about his health, and firms that had staked their future on ties to Suharto continued to under-perform after regime change.[3]

What can companies do to protect their corporate integrity in such a challenging environment and act as positive agents of change?

---

2 OECD, *Risk Awareness Tool for Multinational Enterprises in Weak Governance Zones* (Paris: OECD, 2006).
3 R. Fisman, 'Estimating the Value of Political Connections', *American Economic Review*, vol. 91, no. 4 (2001); F. Oberholzer-Gee and C. Leuz, 'Political Relationships, Global Financing and Corporate Transparency: Evidence from Indonesia', *Journal of Financial Economics*, vol. 81, no. 2 (2003).

First, awareness and preparedness are important. Mapping the risks specific to a company's operations and developing a tailored compliance and anti-corruption training programme should ensure clear ground rules and operating procedures on how to respond to demands for corrupt payments. A variety of tools and templates are at hand to help companies craft business strategies and compliance programmes for institutionally weak environments.[4]

Second, clean business requires clean business partners. Extra-managerial care and due diligence in vetting business associates, contractors and agents are a prerequisite to avoid the outsourcing of corruption.[5] Screening out unreliable partners and establishing deeper, long-term relationships with trusted ones, known as relational contracting, can help enforce contracts even when formal institutions are still weak and corrupt.[6]

Companies can also join and lend support to initiatives that seek to mitigate problems of collective action and instil trust in fair competition and the integrity of public contract awards. The Extractive Industries Transparency Initiative commits business and host governments in more than twenty countries to enhanced transparency in revenue-sharing arrangements. Sectoral agreements and integrity pacts demand explicit no-bribery commitments from competing companies and public sector clients. Such agreements raise the costs and consequences of non-compliance. Once they reach a critical mass of buy-in, they can make it very difficult for non-signatories to stand on the sidelines.[7]

Finally, foreign companies can also help strengthen business integrity in a host country without unduly interfering with domestic political affairs by extending support to business associations or chambers of commerce that pledge to promulgate corporate integrity.[8]

As the rise of Infosys in India shows, asserting corporate integrity in a high-corruption environment is both feasible and good business. Infosys has grown from a small software company in 1981 to a multinational information technology service provider while steering clear of corruption in a setting infamous for red tape and high corruption risks.[9]

The complex role of the informal sector

Many developing nations are characterised by well-established informal sectors.[10] While exact definitions vary, the informal sector or shadow economy usually refers to economic activity

---

4 OECD, *Investments in Weak Governance Zones. Summary of Consultations* (Paris: OECD, 2005).

5 J. Bray, 'The Use of Intermediaries', in J. G. Lambsdorff, M. Taube and M. Schramm (eds.), *The New Institutional Economics of Corruption* (London and New York: Routledge, 2005).

6 D. Rodrik, 'Second-best Institutions', *American Economic Review, Papers and Proceedings*, May 2008.

7 For an example in Colombia, see V. Lencina, L. Polzinetti and A. R. Balcázar, 'Pipe Manufacturers in Colombia and Argentina Take the Anti-corruption Pledge', in TI, *Global Corruption Report 2008* (Cambridge: Cambridge University Press, 2008).

8 M. Weimer, *Anti-corruption and the Role of Chambers of Commerce and Business Associations*, U4 Brief no. 12 (Bergen: Chr. Michelsen Institute, 2007).

9 R. Abdelal, R. DiTella and P. Kothanandaraman, *Infosys in India: Building a Software Giant in a Corrupt Environment*, Case Study no. 9-707-030 (Boston: Harvard Business School, 2007).

10 F. Schneider, 'Shadow Economies and Corruption all over the World: New Estimates for 145 Countries', *Economics: The Open-Access, Open-Assessment E-Journal*, vol. 1, no. 2007-9 (2007).

that is not illegal *per se* but carried out at least partly below the radar of official statistics and regulations.[11]

The size, economic importance and persistence of the informal economy in developing countries is particularly striking. For 2005 it was estimated that the shadow economy (excluding household production) equalled almost a third of the official GDP across Asia. In Africa and Latin America this share amounts to more than 40 per cent, and it reaches well over 50 per cent in countries as diverse as Azerbaijan, Bolivia, Cambodia, Georgia, Nigeria, Peru, Tanzania and Thailand. Strong growth of the formal economy has hardly put a dent into these numbers. In addition to providing income and employment to many on the lower rungs of the economic ladder, the informal sector often complements formal economic activities and serves vital bridging functions in sectors such as waste management and water provision.[12]

Tackling corruption and strengthening business integrity when large parts of important economic activity are carried out outside officially regulated structures is vexing for governments, especially since the relationship between corruption and the informal sector is ambivalent. Corruption nurtures informality. Excessive regulation and the entry points for corruption that it provides further exacerbate arbitrariness in regulation and entry costs and drives economic activity into informality. At the same time, the lack of legal protection and the desire to dodge regulations makes the informal sector a particularly easy prey for extortion and solicitation of bribes by corrupt officials, thereby helping to sustain petty corruption among tax collectors, local police, environmental inspectors and other officials. Where the informal sector competes with formal businesses, this also may encourage others to follow suit in order to reduce regulatory burdens and compete on an equal footing.[13]

Several strategies can help break these vicious circles.

- Reducing red tape, which has been significantly related to higher corruption and larger unofficial economies,[14] can make the switch to formality easier. The burden of red tape is as well documented as it is striking. In countries such as Botswana, Brazil, Indonesia and Venezuela, registering a business takes more than seventy-five days. The overall procedure costs more than the average per capita income in countries such as Angola, Bolivia, Cambodia, Cameroon, Malawi, Nicaragua and Uganda, putting formal status well beyond the means of many informal entrepreneurs.[15] Improvements are feasible and can be effective. After reducing the minimum capital requirements for companies, Georgia and Saudi Arabia saw registrations increase by 55 and 81 per cent, respectively.[16] Egypt undertook sweeping reforms in 2006 and 2007, reducing minimum capital requirements for a new

---

11 Please note that some definitions of the informal sector may include elements of illegal activities – an approach not adopted for the purpose of this article.
12 See TI, 2008.
13 E. Lavallée, 'Corruption, Concurrence et Développement: Une Analyse Econométrique à l'Echelle des Entreprises', *European Journal of Development Research*, vol.19, no. 2 (2007).
14 S. Djankov, R. La Porta, F. Lopez-de-Silanes and A. Shleifer, 'The Regulation of Entry', *Quarterly Journal of Economics*, vol. 117, no. 1 (2002). For a classic study, see H. De Soto, *The Other Path* (New York: I. B. Tauris, 1989).
15 World Bank, *Doing Business 2009* (Washington, DC: World Bank, 2008).
16 World Bank, 2008.

business by 98 per cent, cutting the start-up times and costs for new businesses in half and significantly reducing property registration fees. After cutting the time required to establish a business from fifty-eight to twenty-seven days, Mexico saw the number of registered businesses rise by nearly 6 per cent.[17] Improving knowledge on how to register, and supporting informal business in these processes may thus help in reducing corruption. For example, after Ghana began facilitating and promoting registration, entrepreneurs reported being exposed to less corruption.[18]

- Enhancing access to capital, social insurance schemes, formal training and self-organisation can help informal workers and businesses regularise more of their business relations and reduce their vulnerability to extortion and bribe-paying. In many countries microfinance schemes have already brought credit and saving services to the rural and urban poor, long shunned by conventional banks.[19] In Malawi, workers from the informal economy can obtain formal qualifications for their skills and receive further vocational training in areas ranging from carpentry and tailoring to bricklaying, electrical installation and motor vehicle repair.[20] In India, the Self-Employed Women's Association (SEWA) has successfully organised informal workers and helped them enforce their basic rights since 1971. SEWA has grown to more than 400,000 members and the model is being copied in other countries.[21]

- Recognising and facilitating the informal sector's contributions to the formal economy and public service provision can improve precarious working conditions and reduce exposure to abuse. Countries such as Ghana, Senegal and Vietnam have licensed or are considering licensing informal water vendors, and have established guidelines for tanker operators and independent entrepreneurs.[22] Another example is informal waste-pickers, who assume a vital role for waste collection and recycling in many urban areas in developing countries such as Egypt and India. Solid waste management schemes can foster these activities by registering informal waste-pickers, designating waste transfer points and clarifying interaction with formal procedures.[23]

Taken together, these strategies can bring more informal economic activities into the legal fold, reduce exposure to extortion and other forms of corruption, and strengthen access to legal recourse in cases of abuse. These steps can ensure that informality and corruption do not feed on each other and taint prospects for tackling corruption in the broader economy.

---

17 World Bank, *Doing Business 2008* (Washington, DC: World Bank, 2007).

18 A. Darkwa-Amanor, 'Corruption, Registration of MSMEs, and Their Linkages: New Evidence and Recommendations from Ghana', paper presented at the Africa Regional Consultative Conference, Accra, Ghana, 5 November 2007.

19 M. Pagura and M. Kirsten, 'Formal–informal financial linkages: lessons from developing countries', *Small Enterprise Development*, vol. 17, no.1 (2006).

20 J. Chafa, 'Informal Sector Programmes in Teveta', paper presented at 'Training for Survival and Development in Southern Africa' seminar, Oslo, 15 November 2002.

21 M. A. Chen, N. Mirani and M. Parikh, *Self-employed Women. A Profile of SEWA's Membership* (Oxford: Oxford University Press, 2006); E. Crowley, S. Baas, P. Termine and G. Dionne, 'Organizations of the Poor: Conditions for Success', paper prepared for the International Conference on Membership-Based Organizations of the Poor, Ahmedabad, India, 17–21 January 2005.

22 TI, 2008.

23 K. Sandhu, 'Role of Informal Solid Waste Management Sector and Possibilities of Integration: The Case of Amritsar City, India', paper presented at International Conference on Sustainable Sanitation, Dongsheng, China, 28 August 2007.

Activities of donors on private sector corruption in developing countries

By the 1970s donors had recognised private sector development as a major engine for both economic growth and poverty reduction. Corruption remained an untouchable issue, however.[24] It was only in the 1990s that donors acknowledged corruption's tremendous negative consequences for the investment climate in developing countries and began to tackle corruption, mostly through public sector reforms.

While the private sector was understood primarily as a 'partner and an important driver'[25] for these reforms, donors also acknowledged that companies are not just victims of corrupt public officials but, rather, often actively resort to corrupt practices in order to gain contracts, or influence or evade laws and regulations. As a result, donors realised that tackling private sector corruption and strengthening corporate integrity are prerequisites for sound and sustainable development.

Today both bilateral and multilateral donors, as well as export credit agencies, are placing a stronger focus on fighting corruption not only in the public but also in the private sector. Initiatives to tackle the supply side of corruption include: (1) anti-corruption measures in donor operations; (2) support for home country and international anti-corruption instruments; (3) cooperation with the private sector to strengthen corporate integrity; and (4) helping developing countries establish sound investment climates.

Anti-corruption provisions in donor operations

Almost all donors today have integrated anti-corruption clauses into their agreements with project partners and contractors. Corruption awareness and reporting obligations for donor staff have been found wanting for several donors,[26] however, and facilitation payments are still regarded as permissible by some donor agencies.[27] Sanctions in cases of breach of such agreements include revoking contracts, penalties or debarment from future contracts. The World Bank, for example, established such a debarment system in 1996 and continues to refine it, for instance with provisions for voluntary disclosure and the use of independent compliance monitors.[28]

---

24 See W. Easterly, *The Elusive Quest for Growth* (Cambridge, MA/London: MIT Press, 2001).
25 H. Mathisen and M. Weimer, *Assessing Donor Anti-corruption Initiatives in Support of Private Sector Development: A Mapping Study* (Bergen: Chr. Michelsen Institute, 2007).
26 OECD, *Mid-term Study of Phase 2 Reports: Application of the Convention on Combating Bribery of Foreign Public Officials in International Business Transactions* (Paris: OECD, 2006).
27 This mirrors a comparably reluctant approach to criminalising facilitation payments in several donor countries. See article starting on page 116.
28 S. Williams, 'The Debarment of Corrupt Contractors from World Bank-financed Contracts', *Public Contract Law Journal,* vol. 36, no. 3 (2007).

Other mechanisms established to monitor compliance include hotlines (e.g. at DANIDA, the Danish public donor),[29] ombudspersons (e.g. at Germany's GTZ) and the World Bank's Department of Institutional Integrity, which investigates allegations of fraud, corruption and staff misconduct in bank operations.

Export credit agencies (ECAs) can also make a major contribution to incentivise corporate integrity. They underwrite an estimated 10 per cent of global exports by large industrialised countries and provide loans that exceed the lending of multilateral development banks.[30] ECAs can help tackle corruption in foreign investment projects by including strong due diligence and anti-corruption measures in their guarantee and loan schemes. In order to get a guarantee from the Norwegian Export Credit Agency (*Garanti-Instituttet for Eksport Kreditt*), for example, companies must sign a statement declaring that they will refrain from any illegal bribes.

The 2006 OECD recommendations to deter bribery in officially supported export credits provide an updated guiding framework for good anti-corruption practices. The challenge is to ensure more widespread and effective implementation of many important provisions, such as the requirement for the applying exporters to disclose the use of agents and commission fees, and to induce the ECAs of non-OECD countries to adopt the same principles.[31]

Addressing the global supply side of corruption

Ring-fencing donor projects is not enough. For a sustained impact on corporate integrity in developing countries, donors must address the global supply side of corruption. A major step forward is the OECD's Principles of Donor Action in Anti-Corruption.[32] Principle 2 provides a clear mandate for donors to address proactively the supply side of corruption, stating: 'Donors recognise that corruption is a two-way street [and that] action is needed in donor countries to bear down on corrupt practices by home-based companies doing business internationally.'

In this context, donors aim at influencing national and international processes and instruments that address the supply side of corruption. At the national level, the GTZ and BMZ (Federal Ministry for Economic Cooperation and Development), for example, are currently engaging in a reform of the German National Contact Point that monitors the OECD Guidelines for Multinational Enterprises.

At the international level, donors support the further development of private sector anti-corruption instruments, such as the OECD Anti-Bribery Convention and the UN Convention against Corruption (UNCAC).

29 Ministry of Foreign Affairs of Denmark, *Help Us to Fight Corruption* (Copenhagen: Ministry of Foreign Affairs of Denmark, 2005).

30 'Exporting Corruption: How Rich Country Export Credit Agencies Facilitate Corruption in the Global South', An interview with The Corner House, *Multinational Monitor*, vol. 27, no. 3 (2006).

31 OECD, *OECD Council Recommendation on Bribery and Officially Supported Export Credits* (Paris: OECD, 2006); OECD, *Export Credits and Bribery* (Paris: OECD, 2008); S. Hawley, *Experience and Practice of Combating Bribery in Officially Supported Export Credits* (Sturminster Newton, UK: Corner House, 2006).

32 The principles are annexed to the *Policy Paper and Principles on Anti-Corruption: Setting an Agenda for Collective Action* (Paris: OECD, 2007) elaborated by the OECD–DAC–GOVNET Anti-Corruption Task Team.

Cooperating with the private sector in fighting corruption

Donors are also working directly with the private sector to address corruption risks. Initiatives include:[33]

- sector-specific initiatives that bring together governments, industry and civil society to raise transparency and accountability in key economic development sectors, beginning with extractive industries in 2002 and followed by health, construction and development aid;[34] and
- the donor-supported Business Anti-Corruption Portal, an online database that provides information and resources to help small and medium enterprises avoid corruption when operating in developing countries.

Helping developing countries establish sound investment climates

Donors' key strategy to fight private sector corruption is fostering a sound investment climate and supporting good governance in developing countries through institutional reforms and administrative capacity-building. This includes assistance in drafting policies and regulatory frameworks, enhancing the integrity of the judiciary and state bureaucracies and incorporating a business climate perspective in national development plans and poverty reduction strategies.[35] The World Bank, for example, has spent US$3.8 billion, or more than 15 per cent of total group lending, on supporting governance and the rule of law.[36]

As an analysis of more than 400 private sector anti-corruption projects by major donors shows, most of these initiatives target corruption implicitly.[37] In addition, most efforts to support sound investment climates focus rather narrowly on curbing corruption that affects day-to-day business operations, but otherwise give rather short shrift to high-level corruption at the business–government nexus that can lead to policy or state capture. Measures to tackle such higher-level corruption more directly, such as transparency initiatives for political decision-making and political party-financing reforms, go beyond a narrow focus on economic affairs. Diplomatic considerations and concerns about overstepping their mandate make many official donors hesitant to engage too explicitly in this area.

Solutions depend on a broad base

Strengthening corporate integrity in developing countries requires commitment and action by a large band of stakeholders. Corporations need to step up their due diligence and compliance efforts, especially in institutionally weak environments that are particularly vulnerable to

---

33 J. Brüggemann, *Preventing Corruption in Government-to-Business Interaction*, working paper (Eschborn, Germany: GTZ, 2007).

34 Extractive Industries Transparency Initiative (see article starting on page 54), Construction Sector Transparency Initiative (COST), Medicines Transparency Alliance (MeTA) and International Aid Transparency Initiative.

35 H. Mathisen and M. Weimer, 2007.

36 World Bank, *Improving Development Outcomes: Fiscal Year 2007 Annual Integrity Report* (Washington, DC: World Bank, 2007).

37 H. Mathisen and M. Weimer, 2007.

corruption. Governments need to help the informal economy and ensure that it becomes a positive force in fostering business integrity.

Donors can also play their part. Ensuring effective anti-corruption compliance in their own programming means leading by example, setting important integrity incentives for local as well as international contractors. Working with governments and the private sector to address corruption risks proactively in key industries and sectors helps build and expand islands of integrity in the broader economy. Importantly, these strategies can unfold their full potential only if there is support for overall good governance reforms to raise regulatory quality and institutional accountability, and efforts to tackle corruption in international trade continue apace. Finally, for maximum efficacy, donors should place more emphasis on grand corruption and encourage new and increasingly important donors from non-OECD countries to join all these efforts.

Corruption and bribery in the extractive industries
Gavin Hayman[1]

The recent commodities boom created an unprecedented transfer of wealth from rich nations that consume natural resources to poorer countries that produce them. In 2006 exports of oil and minerals from Africa were worth roughly US$249 billion, nearly eight times the value of exported farm products (US$32 billion) and nearly six times the value of international aid (US$43 billion).[2] A similar story is apparent in much of the rest of the developing world.

If used properly, this money could be one of the best chances in a generation to lift many of the world's poorest and most dispossessed citizens out of poverty. History shows, however, that countries relying on oil and mining revenues tend, with surprisingly few exceptions, to be poor, badly run and prone to violent instability: the infamous 'resource curse' is now a well-documented phenomenon. To give just one example: from 1970 to 2000 the Nigerian government received over US$300 billion from oil sales while the percentage of citizens living in extreme poverty (on less than US$1 per day) increased from 36 per cent to around 70 per cent.[3]

The mechanisms behind the curse

The political structures that accrete around resource-rich 'bonanza' economies rarely bring about the social and cultural changes that lead to long-term investment in social development. Governments typically depend on taxes to run their affairs and have to justify to their citizens

---

1 Gavin Hayman is campaigns director at Global Witness.
2 World Trade Organization, *International Trade Statistics 2007* (Geneva: WTO, 2007); OECD, 'Query Wizard for International Development Statistics' (online database).
3 X. Sala-i-Martin and A. Subramanian, *Addressing the Natural Resource Curse: An Illustration from Nigeria*, Working Paper no. WP/03/139 (Washington, DC: IMF, 2003).

how much and how they spend the money they appropriate from them. In countries rich in natural resources, this principal accountability relation is broken. Governments can rely on natural resource revenues to fund their activities and focus their efforts on controlling these resource rents. The end result is 'crony capitalism', widespread patronage takes the place of meritocracy in government. The state becomes less of a rational manager of resources and behaves more like a 'protection racket'.

A recent example demonstrates how corruption is at the core of this pernicious system. In 2003 one of the largest ever foreign corruption investigations in US legal history uncovered what is alleged to be a major international corruption scandal that, in the words of an indictment by US prosecutors, 'defrauded the Government of Kazakhstan of funds to which it was entitled from oil transactions and defrauded the people of Kazakhstan of the right to the honest services of their elected and appointed officials'.[4]

The alleged scheme was based on the Kazakh president and oil minister demanding that international oil companies pay fees to a middleman. This arrangement, the indictment alleges, helped the middleman to skim money from the deals and send some US$78 million in gifts and kickbacks to the Kazakh president and others through dozens of overseas bank accounts in Switzerland, Liechtenstein and the British Virgin Islands.[5] One 'gift' was matching 'his and hers' snowmobiles for the president and his wife.[6] The case has yet to go to trial.

A lacklustre response

The international response to corruption in oil and mining has generally been weak and fragmented, not least because of geopolitical competition for influence and access to vital natural resources. Governments and companies alike have been slow to recognise that the short-term benefits of indulging in corruption, or turning a blind eye to it, are far outweighed by the damage.

Although foreign bribery has been criminalised in the OECD countries – especially in its conventional manifestation of a businessman providing a 'suitcase full of cash' in return for largesse – new forms of interaction to win contracts and enjoy special advantages have arisen that are equally corrosive to the governance of the country concerned, but that may avoid prosecution under the laws of OECD member states.

These mostly involve sophisticated 'current pay-off and deferred gift' structures, in which a company enters into some sort of business relationship with state officials or their friends and relatives. These relationships can be structured to provide benefits to the official and his or her networks in lieu of direct bribe payments. Untangling such relationships is

4 United States Attorney Southern District of New York, Indictment against James H. Giffen. For further information, see United States Attorney Southern District of New York, press release, 2 April 2003.
5 Global Witness, *Time for Transparency. Coming Clean on Oil, Mining and Gas Revenues* (Washington, DC: Global Witness, 2004).
6 Ibid.

made doubly difficult by the hugely complex nature of many extractive investment agreements.[7]

In addition, the enforcement record of some OECD members is poor: the United Kingdom is a case in point. There has been only one successful prosecution for foreign bribery, ever, and the BAe Systems affair has left the impression that, if an inquiry were seen to threaten major commercial and strategic interests, the government would intervene to stop it. Some other OECD members, such as Switzerland, have been gradually improving the oversight of their home companies' behaviour abroad, but have been poor at recognising their domestic role as launderers of corrupt money flowing through the international system.

Collective action for more transparency

One promising new initiative, however, has been the Extractive Industries Transparency Initiative (EITI), which makes public the flow of revenue to governments from oil and mining companies. This information is secret in many countries, preventing citizens from asking their governments how the money has been used. EITI breaks new ground, by bringing together governments, the private sector and civil society groups from around the world. Some twenty-three countries are now candidates, implementing EITI, and about ten or so have published some sort of public report on their revenues.[8]

EITI also has shortcomings. It does not cover the allocation of oil and mining concessions, issues of money-laundering or the tracking of revenues once they reach government budgets, to ensure that the money is spent properly. The voluntary character of EITI also means that those likely to be the worst offenders are not compelled to take part.

A key challenge for the future is how to expand initiatives such as the EITI into a more comprehensive road map that will help countries to manage their natural resource revenues better and more fairly, starting from the award of concessions through to the drawing up of transparent public budgets. Such efforts would need the support of the wider international community, which means a diplomatic push to involve China and India too.

Another important development is the effort by the Publish What You Pay campaign[9] to ensure that securities markets require resource extraction companies to report publicly all payments made to foreign governments on a country-by-country basis, and that international accounting standards require the disclosure of such payments by companies in their financial statements. Various items of legislation or rule-making on this are pending. If passed, they will ensure better information about the international business dealings of countries that are not prepared to be more open by other means.

Lastly, we need to address the role of the global financial system in laundering stolen wealth; compare, for example, the seriousness with which banks pursue terrorist financing

---

7 T. H. Moran, *Combating Corrupt Payments in Foreign Investment Concessions: Closing the Loopholes, Extending the Tools* (Washington, DC: Center for Global Development, 2008).
8 As of November 2008. See www.eitransparency.org for the latest list.
9 Global Witness is a member of this campaign.

to that with which they pursue the proceeds of corruption. There is little point pouring aid into poor countries when equal amounts in stolen public money can flow straight out into banks and tax havens.

The transfer of natural resource wealth to poor countries offers an unprecedented opportunity for development. If the international community does not respond to it in a coherent and concerted way, however, we risk a chaotic scramble for resources, just as unedifying as that which took place in the colonial era, with corruption leaving the citizens of the affected countries as poor as, or poorer than, they were thirty years ago.

Foreign direct investment and global supply chains: do they spread or dilute corporate integrity?
Transparency International

Are foreign investment and the broader phenomenon of globalisation a force for good or bad? Do they help spread or undermine corporate integrity? No other questions have been as polarising and defining for political world views for such a long time, and they are questions whose answers have proved to be just as elusive and inconclusive. One thing for certain is that global interdependence is deepening, and it is here to stay.

The challenge is to map the specific features and implications of globalisation for a particular policy issue and devise strategies to manage it for the benefits of all. The impact of economic globalisation on corporate integrity and good governance around the world is one such issue, and, arguably, one of the most important. It is central to formulating trade policies and plotting a viable trajectory for political as well as economic development.

Two opposing claims drive the debate. On the one hand, foreign direct investment (FDI) and trade have been expected to bring advanced standards and practices of corporate governance and corporate responsibility to emerging economies with weaker governance frameworks. On the other hand, the practices of outsourcing and offshoring associated with globalisation are suspected to circumvent the very same standards for responsible corporate citizenship, and are believed to exploit and even aggravate weak and corrupt regulatory environments. Which scenario is closer to the truth? What do we know about the relationship between economic integration and corruption? Here are three insights.

(1) As global production networks continue to expand, deepen and involve new actors, the duty of major players to act with integrity and a sense of global responsibility is also growing

Global FDI reached an all-time peak of more than US$1.8 trillion in 2007. Flows into developing and least developed countries have also continued to grow sharply, reaching a record

US$500 billion and US$13 billion, respectively. All world regions posted record inflows, which in Africa and Latin America were driven mainly by booming demand for natural resources and other commodities.[1]

Likewise, cross-border mergers and acquisitions have also reached record highs. By 2007 the number of transnational corporations (TNCs) had grown to around 79,000. They are estimated to control some 790,000 foreign affiliates around the world, accounting for 11 per cent of global GDP, sales worth US$31 trillion and a workforce of more than 80 million people.[2]

The largest TNCs continue to grow and expand their economic footprints. At the same time, new players have begun to enter the scene. The 100 largest TNCs from developing countries posted growth rates of more than 20 per cent between 2005 and 2006 alone. By 2006 they controlled more than US$570 billion worth of foreign assets, led mainly by investors from China, South Korea, Brazil and Mexico.[3]

Direct ownership and growing economic footprints translate into direct accountability for enforcing corporate standards of integrity and responsible citizenship across subsidiaries around the globe. Even when cross-border business takes the form of outsourcing and trade rather than foreign ownership, however, corporate integrity does not stop at the factory door.

Global supply chains have grown ever more complex, integrated and concentrated. Producers in many key industries, from chemicals and pharmaceuticals to electric machinery, radio, TV, computing and medical equipment, source more than 30 per cent of their inputs from outside their countries.[4] The shift towards manufacturing in developing countries, in particular to Asia, continues unabated, and the trend is even more pronounced for key consumer goods. Asian production alone by now accounts for a half of world trade in clothing.[5]

These globalised supply chains are rarely networks among equals. A relatively small number of branded retailers, manufacturers and, increasingly, clients for offshore services from industrialised countries typically establish and lead far-flung global supply networks, with thousands of highly competitive input providers. Just-in-time-production, the flexible customisation of products and the need for reliable quality with sourced inputs and services require the global supply chain leaders to establish close relationships with their suppliers and get deeply involved in organisational, training and planning aspects.

Wal-Mart, for example, the world's largest retailer with sales of around US$375 billion in 2007,[6] maintains a global supply network of some 6,000 factories, more than 80 per cent of which are in China. In 2003 Wal-Mart spent US$15 billion on Chinese-made products, accounting for nearly one-eighth of all Chinese exports to the United States. If Wal-Mart were

---

1 United Nations Conference on Trade and Development (UNCTAD), *World Investment Report 2008: Transnational Corporations and the Infrastructure Challenge* (Geneva: UNCTAD, 2008).
2 Ibid.
3 Ibid.
4 World Trade Organization (WTO), *World Trade Report 2008: Trade in a Globalizing World* (Geneva: WTO, 2008).
5 WTO, 2008.
6 'Wal-Mart Reports Record Fourth Quarter Sales and Earnings', Wal-Mart Stores Inc., 19 February 2008.

a separate nation, it would rank as China's fifth largest export market, ahead of Germany and the United Kingdom.[7]

This leverage, created by dominant businesses' deep involvement in production processes, means that the responsibility of supply chain leaders to uphold standards of corporate integrity and responsible conduct also applies to the wider supply chain. Consumer boycotts and fair trade initiatives have already put enormous pressure on well-known branded retailers to live up to these responsibilities and guarantee ethical conduct across their supply networks. Other supply chain leaders outside the public spotlight of well-known consumer brands face the same moral responsibility to make their commitment to corporate integrity congruent with their spheres of influence throughout their global networks of suppliers.

(2) Corruption is bad for attracting foreign direct investment and maximising its contribution to sustainable development

Corruption makes it difficult to garner benefits from FDI. In a large survey conducted in 2008 by Transparency International, almost a half (45 per cent) of the multinational companies from OECD countries that were interviewed reported that personal and familiar relationships rather than competitive bidding are frequently used to win public contracts in the non-OECD countries where they operate.[8] In a different study, more than a third of international business managers estimated that corruption increases international project costs by more than 10 per cent, while one-sixth believed that corruption inflates costs by more than a quarter.[9]

The resulting deterrent effect of corruption on foreign investment is palpable. In a survey of more than 390 senior business executives, almost 45 per cent said that they had decided against entering a market or pursuing a business opportunity because of corruption risks.[10] Controlling for other factors that influence investment decisions, an increase in the corruption level from that of Singapore to Mexico has the same deterrent effect on foreign investment as a tax increase of more than twenty percentage points. An analysis of almost 5,000 cross-border mergers and takeovers shows that high corruption environments depress the valuation of domestic firms significantly, making them less attractive to investors.[11]

Corruption also discourages the most coveted future-orientated investors: knowledge-based and high-technology industries. High levels of corruption shift ownership structures towards joint ventures and short-term management contracts with local partners that can help navigate

---

7 G. Gereffi, *The New Offshoring of Jobs and Global Development* (Geneva: International Labour Organization, 2006).

8 TI, '2008 Bribe Payers Survey' (Berlin: TI, 2008).

9 Control Risks and Simmons & Simmons, *Facing up to Corruption 2007: A Practical Business Guide* (London: Control Risks, 2007).

10 PricewaterhouseCoopers, *Confronting Corruption: The Business Case for an Effective Anti-corruption Programme* (London: PricewaterhouseCoopers, 2008).

11 S.-J. Wei, 'How Taxing Is Corruption on International Investors?', *Review of Economics and Statistics*, vol. 82, no. 1 (2000); U. Weitzel and S. Berns, 'Cross-border Takeovers, Corruption, and Related Aspects of Governance', *Journal of International Business Studies*, vol. 37, no. 6 (2006).

the more challenging corrupt political terrain. Innovative high-tech companies are less likely to enter such relationships, since they are eager to protect their innovations and expertise.[12]

Finally, a lack of transparent governance also leads to less long-term and development-orientated portfolio investments, as it makes such funds more prone to sudden withdrawals in times of crisis. During the Asian and Russian financial crises of the late 1990s, for example, emerging market funds withdrew more strongly from countries that were less transparent.[13]

(3) Increased foreign direct investment and trade are not automatically benign; companies can and must do a lot more to live up to their responsibilities in host countries

The negative impact of corruption on foreign investment does not mean, however, that more FDI inevitably promotes good governance and helps reduce corruption.

In countries with weak and/or non-democratic structures, FDI appears to magnify the problems of state capture and procurement bribery.[14] It is unlikely to serve automatically as a beacon for better corporate governance, and the evidence available suggests that currently it does not export higher non-wage-related working standards abroad. In countries with more advanced governance structures, the outcome is more positive, as FDI has been found to support improvements in corporate and public governance.[15]

Many believe that strategic choice rather than coercion is behind this amplifying effect. As World Bank researchers have observed, 'FDI firms undertake those forms of corruption that suit their comparative advantages, generating substantial gains for them and challenging the premise that they are coerced.'[16] The use of local agents with essential connections and superior knowledge of the local marketplace is widespread, and sometimes even legally mandated, but it is problematic from a corruption perspective. The bribing of local business partners can be 'outsourced' to these agents, conveniently hidden in excessive service fees, thereby diluting legal and moral culpability for the corrupt act. One survey found that about three-quarters of managers from countries including the United States, United Kingdom and Germany believed that companies from their countries 'regularly' or 'occasionally' used intermediaries to circumvent anti-corruption laws.[17]

---

12 B. S. Javorcik and S.-J. Wei, *Corruption and Composition of Foreign Direct Investment: Firm-level Evidence*, Working Paper no. 7969 (Cambridge, MA: National Bureau of Economic Research [NBER], 2000).

13 R. G. Gelos and S.-J. Wei, *Transparency and International Investor Behavior*, Working Paper no. 9260 (Cambridge, MA: NBER, 2002).

14 J. S. Hellman, G. Jones and D. Kaufmann, 'Far From Home: Do Foreign Investors Import Higher Standards of Governance in Transition Economies?', draft paper, August 2002; P. M. Pinto and B. Zhu, *Fortune or Evil? The Effect of Inward Foreign Direct Investment on Corruption*, Salztman Working Paper no. 10 (New York: Columbia University, 2008).

15 B. Kogut and M. Macpherson, 'Direct Investment and Corporate Governance', in P. Cornelius and B. Kogut (eds.), *Corporate Governance and Capital Flows in a Global Economy* (Oxford: Oxford University Press, 2003); OECD, *Policy Brief: The Social Impact of Foreign Direct Investment* (Paris: OECD, 2008).

16 J. S. Hellman, G. Jones and D. Kaufmann, 2002.

17 Control Risks and Simmons & Simmons, *International Business Attitudes to Corruption: Survey 2006* (London: Control Risks, 2006).

Foreign investors and supply chain leaders acknowledge this corruption challenge and have begun to strengthen their compliance efforts. Much remains to be done, however, not only by new players on the international economic scene but also by the established and most advanced multinationals.

Ignorance about the illegality of foreign bribery continues to be widespread and persistent, while anti-corruption provisions and training remain inadequate. According to Transparency International's 2008 Bribe Payers Survey, nearly 75 per cent of more than 2,700 interviewed executives were not familiar with the OECD Convention on Combating Bribery of Foreign Public Officials in International Business Transactions. In France, Germany, the United Kingdom and the United States, more than 80 per cent of surveyed executives admitted to 'not being familiar at all' with this legal framework. In Brazil, a new and growing player in FDI, this number reached 77 per cent.[18]

Similarly, a 2006 survey of 350 senior business executives in companies with foreign operations revealed the following.

- In Hong Kong, Germany, France and Brazil, fewer than half the surveyed companies reported having a specific procedure for vetting agents and suppliers before entering into a relationship with them.[19]
- Only a quarter to a third of companies in the construction, power and retail sectors had training programmes for executives on how to avoid corruption. In the information and communication technology, pharmaceutical, oil, gas, mining and defence sectors, fewer than 45 per cent of companies provided such training.[20]

A similar pattern of poor performance with regard to ensuring corporate integrity and compliance across supply chains emerges from an analysis of 280 companies with high or medium risk of exposure to potential labour rights violations in their international supply chains. Fewer than 30 per cent of companies from North America, Australia and New Zealand were found to have even basic systems for communicating, reporting and monitoring labour rights standards across their supply networks. In Europe, only slightly more than a half of companies appeared to have any kind of system in place, while in Japan and other parts of Asia this was the case for fewer than 10 per cent of companies.[21]

Frameworks for action: making global efforts work in the local setting

All this indicates that companies, both from industrialised and emerging economies, need to do much more to live up to their responsibilities as good corporate citizens on the global scene and make foreign business engagement a definite, positive force for stronger corporate integrity and good governance.

---

18 TI, 2008.
19 Control Risks and Simmons & Simmons, 2006.
20 Ibid.
21 B. Gordon, *The State of Responsible Business: Global Corporate Response to Environmental, Social and Governance (ESG) Challenges* (London: Ethical Investment Research Services, 2007).

A number of initiatives have sprung up over the last decade that facilitate such an engagement.

- At the international level, the United Nations Global Compact provides a guiding policy framework and an information-sharing platform for companies to help them align their global operations with established human rights, labour, environmental and anti-corruption norms. By 2008 more than 4,700 companies and stakeholders had signed up and committed to reporting on their performance. Although this high participation rate and explicit recognition of corporate responsibilities beyond compliance with local laws is encouraging, the important next step will be to monitor corporations effectively and hold them to account for their commitments.[22]

- Linking home-country and local host-country accountability, the OECD Guidelines for Multinational Enterprises formulate the expectations of mainly OECD and some supporting countries with regard to the responsible conduct of business abroad, including supply chain and anti-corruption issues. Governments are required to set up national contact points to facilitate adherence to these voluntary standards. These offices are increasingly being recognised as an important mechanism by which civil society can bring specific concerns about corporate conduct in host countries to public attention, and have them assessed and discussed in the home jurisdiction of the multinational corporation.[23]

- At the local level, a wide range of reporting and certification initiatives provide businesses with the opportunity to enhance transparency and integrity throughout their supply chains.[24] These tools have more recently been supplemented by innovative new frameworks for collective action, such as the Extractive Industries Transparency Initiative[25] and a strategic approach to enhancing public policy frameworks, ownership and worker participation at local level.[26]

The growing toolkit for supply chain integrity is encouraging and bodes well for making FDI and international supply chains a positive force for good governance, human rights and corporate integrity. The remaining challenges are many, however. Voluntary initiatives need to develop mechanisms for enforcement, independent assurance and monitoring in order to strengthen their legitimacy and effectiveness. Collective action needs to become more inclusive. Small and medium-sized companies and more multinational companies from emerging economies, which play an increasingly important role in foreign investment and global supply chains, need to be encouraged to make use of these integrity tools and join related initiatives for collective action.[27]

---

22 See www.unglobalcompact.org/; for a discussion of monitoring and enforcement challenges, see www.global compactcritics.net/.

23 See article starting on page 331.

24 See article starting on page 99.

25 See article starting on page 54.

26 See article starting on page 63.

27 Global Compact membership and compliance, for example, is concentrated in western Europe, while non-financial reporting by companies in emerging economies is found to be rather limited; see M. Palenberg, W. Reinicke and J. M. Witte, *Trends in Non-financial Reporting*, Research Paper no. 6 (Berlin: Global Public Policy Institute, 2006) and J. Bremer, 'How Global is the Global Compact?', *Business Ethics: A European Review*, vol. 17, no. 3 (2008).

The intensification of the global competition for fossil fuels, food and many other natural resources provides enormous opportunities for many developing countries to gain greater benefits from trade, investment and integration in global supply chains. At the same time, this race for resources presents a huge stress test for business integrity overseas, making more effective and inclusive collective commitments to responsible investment and supply chain management an urgent task.

Strengthening compliance and integrity in the supply chain: what comes next?

Ayesha Barenblat and Tara Rangarajan[1]

I firmly believe that a company that cheats on overtime and on the age of its labour, that dumps its scraps and chemicals in our rivers, that does not pay its taxes or honour its contracts will ultimately cheat on the quality of its products. And cheating on the quality of products is the same as cheating on customers.

Wal-Mart CEO Lee Scott, October 2008

Sustainability in supply chains: from sticks to carrots, partnerships and ownership

Fifteen years ago efforts to ensure supply chain integrity focused on labour and environmental issues, and relied mainly on risk mitigation and social audits as tools to assess such risks. This approach turned out not to be enough. Monitoring and the threat of sanctions alone were not effective in safeguarding compliance and integrity across supply chains.

Today, leading companies have moved beyond this narrow control-based approach. They are increasingly taking a hard look at how their own purchasing practices may have an impact on factory conditions and the sustainability of supply chains in a broader sense, including compliance with all applicable laws, not least those related to a country's anti-corruption stance. At the same time, these companies also seek to instil greater 'ownership' for improving conditions with the factories themselves.

Translating these lessons and new approaches into a strategic framework, Business for Social Responsibility, in partnership with some of its most innovative member companies, has identified four key pillars that must work in concert with one another to make supply chains effective and sustainable:

---

1 Ayesha Barenblat is a manager in Advisory Services at Business for Social Responsibility (BSR). Tara Rangarajan is the managing director of Advisory Services at BSR.

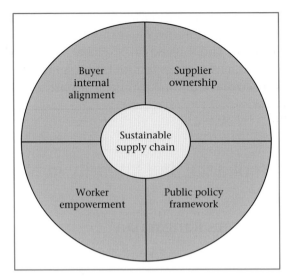

Figure 4: The four key pillars of the Business for Social Responsibility framework

- the internal alignment between the commercial and social objectives of buyers;
- the supplier ownership of labour and environmental conditions;
- the empowerment of workers to be informed and participating constituents; and
- public policy frameworks that foster public–private dialogue, partnerships and local solutions.[2]

Internal alignment requires that companies place sustainability on an equal footing with commercial objectives and organise their supply chain management accordingly. At a global textile retailer, for example, the firm's sustainable supply chain team helps to ensure sustainability integration and buy-in across the organisation. The company has also charged its senior vice-president in the sourcing unit with ensuring that suppliers deliver the products according to ethical standards.

In addition to this organisational alignment, buyers are paying considerable attention to changing the 'comply or die' model for suppliers and adjusting commercial incentives accordingly. That system, which led suppliers to falsify information and focus on beating the system, has been replaced by a more effective approach that emphasises a mutual commitment between brands and suppliers to identify and address the root causes of social and environmental challenges.

Towards partnerships and local ownership of supply chain integrity

Tackling the next generation of supply chain issues requires buyers and suppliers to begin operating as partners. A stronger sense of commitment by suppliers to good working and

---

2 BSR, *Beyond Monitoring: A New Vision for Sustainable Supply Chains* (San Francisco: BSR, 2007).

Box 1 Making compliance feasible rather than walking away

A multinational coffee chain purchased a bulk product from a supplier that in turn sourced the product from a third-party manufacturer. Through the factory assessment process, the coffee chain learnt that the third-party manufacturer was not paying workers the minimum wage and was exceeding acceptable overtime limits. The chain informed the supplier that no more orders would be placed until the situation improved. Rather than terminating the relationship, though, the chain asked whether the price it paid was sufficient to guarantee the minimum wage. When the supplier said it was not high enough a new price was set that would allow the minimum wage to be paid and other compliance issues to be remedied.

environmental conditions can be achieved through a basic bargain: suppliers assume greater responsibility in exchange for buyers providing greater security for business relations.

There is also a need for more information-sharing and dialogue, so as to create holistic, long-term solutions that truly improve the lives of vulnerable workers and our fragile environment.

Initially, many large buyers may seek to go it alone and set compliance standards for their own suppliers. This could lead to a confusing and costly proliferation of standards and compliance expectations for suppliers while forgoing the opportunity for a more systematic learning about good practices.

A good example of how buyers and suppliers are working together to help overcome these shortcomings is BSR's Apparel, Mills, and Sundries Working Group. Buyers and sellers have created one set of labour, health and safety, and environmental principles, and they have agreed on one audit with an emphasis on continuous improvement.

Empowering workers

It is broadly recognised today that the conventional reliance only on top-down auditing systems is flawed and needs to be supplemented by additional checks and balances. Empowering the workers most directly affected by lapses in corporate integrity to raise their concerns and actively participate in creating sound working conditions is key in this context.

Box 2 Engaging workers in supply chain integrity

Project Kaleidoscope is a multi-stakeholder effort of global corporations, organisations dedicated to advancing international labour issues, and a group of socially responsible investors. Participants have been working on a new approach to improve working conditions through a pilot project in ten factories in southern China. The focus is on moving beyond audit checklists to soliciting regular worker feedback, which has helped build trust and strengthen the overall worker–management relationship. In addition, suppliers were asked to provide regular performance data, which indicated the need for more robust management systems. The result has been a more proactive problem-solving attitude on the part of participating suppliers.

Supporting an enabling public policy framework

Buyer-initiated integrity initiatives for supply chains have arisen in response to the ineffective public enforcement of labour and environmental regulations in many developing countries. There is a growing recognition, however, that such private initiatives need to work in tandem with and support efforts to strengthen public policy frameworks. This has opened a wide array of new strategic engagement opportunities for supply chain leaders, including:

- support for a level playing field, by advocating for the recognition of integrity principles in international trade agreements;
- working with home governments to promote sustainable supply chains through appropriate design of procurement rules and aid programmes; and
- initiating a dialogue with suppliers, buyers and local governments on how to improve capabilities for local public enforcement.

A promising drive towards improvement

Credibility, transparency and a continuing commitment to improvement are the important principles needed to underpin this innovative approach to supply chain sustainability. There are reasons to be optimistic that standard-setting suppliers are moving in the right direction. Speaking in 2008 to leading advocacy groups, government officials and thousands of his company's top suppliers, Wal-Mart CEO Lee Scott announced far-reaching changes to the company's supply chain policies, including the following.

- *Certification:* A new supplier agreement requiring factories to certify compliance with local laws and regulations as well as 'rigorous' social and environmental standards. The agreement will be phased in by Chinese suppliers in 2009 and expanded to suppliers around the world by 2011.
- *Transparency:* By 2009 Wal-Mart will require all direct import suppliers, plus all suppliers of private label and non-branded products, to provide the name and location of every factory where their products are made.
- *Raising the bar:* By 2012 all direct suppliers will be required to source 95 per cent of their products from factories that receive the highest environmental and social ratings.[3]

Time will tell if these intentions can be effectively translated into activities on the ground. What is particularly significant, however, is that these commitments link supply chain sustainability to the core of the company's business model and business success – a recognition that no supply chain leader will be able to ignore any longer.

---

3 Wal-Mart Stores Inc., 'Wal-Mart Announces Global Responsibility Sourcing Initiative at China Summit', press release, 22 October 2008.

When China goes shopping abroad: new pressure for corporate integrity?

Deborah A. Bräutigam[1]

Chinese businesses have gone global – in a big way. Multibillion-dollar investments by Chinese companies in Angola (oil), South Africa (banking) and the Democratic Republic of Congo (minerals) have made headlines, but these are just the tip of the iceberg. Forty-nine Chinese contractors are listed among the world's top 225 firms, carrying out major construction projects from Dubai to Timbuktu.[2]

Turnover for Chinese companies involved in large construction projects overseas rose from US\$8.4 billion in 2000 to US\$40.6 billion in 2007.[3] China's telecommunications multi-nationals Huawei and ZTE have won dozens of major contracts with governments in the developing world. Manufacturers of consumer durables and pharmaceuticals have built factories in Nigeria, Pakistan and Tanzania. A portion of the country's enormous foreign currency reserves is channelled through the China Development Bank and the Export-Import (Exim) Bank of China, which help companies win business overseas. In 2007 alone the Exim Bank disbursed almost US\$26 billion, making it among the world's largest export credit agencies.[4]

The corruption challenge that comes with this international expansion is imminent. Contracts involving construction, natural resources and land are areas in which the tempta-tion for kickbacks and corrupt deals are ever-present.[5] This is true around the globe, but all the more so in the weak and conflict-prone states in which much recent Chinese business activity has taken place.

Tightening domestic rules

China's government has moved in recent years to clarify, tighten and enforce domestic anti-corruption laws and address widespread public disgust after a wave of bribery and embezzlement scandals. This has resulted in a series of high-profile prosecutions and con-victions.[6] China's own criminal laws on bribery still contain many grey areas, however.

---

1 Deborah Bräutigam is Professor of International Development at the American University, Washington, DC.

2 P. Reina and G. J. Tulacz, 'The Top 225 International Contractors', *Engineering News-Record*, 13 August 2008.

3 Ministry of Foreign Economic Relations and Trade, *Almanac of China's Foreign Economic Relations and Trade* (Beijing: China Economic Publishing House, 2001); Ministry of Commerce, *China Commerce Yearbook 2008* (Beijing: China Commerce and Trade Press, 2008).

4 China Export-Import Bank, *Annual Report 2007* (Beijing: China Commerce and Trade Press, 2007).

5 More than 2,700 senior business executives from twenty-six countries polled in Transparency International's Bribe Payers Survey 2008 identified these sectors as particularly vulnerable to bribery. See article starting on page 402 and TI, *2008 Bribe Payers Index* (Berlin: TI, 2008).

6 *Caijing Magazine* (China), 24 September 2007.

Giving a bribe to a foreign official in China and bribing a foreign official overseas, for example, are not specifically criminalised, and the definition of what comprises a bribe is vague. China also lacks penalties for accounting practices that cover up kickbacks and bribes, and generous 'commissions' are still permitted as legitimate business expenses.[7]

The overseas corruption challenge

China's official pronouncements and practices are mixed when it comes to condemning bribery by its corporations overseas. On the one hand, while meeting with a large group of Chinese entrepreneurs in Africa in 2006, Premier Wen Jiabao laid down clear expectations: 'Our enterprises must conform to international rules when running businesses, must be open and transparent, should go through a bidding process for the big projects, forbid inappropriate deals and reject corruption and kickbacks.'[8] Wen's foremost concern was that corruption could sidestep healthy competition and condone products and work of inferior quality, inflicting long-term damage on China's commercial and political interests. In addition, China's Ministry of Commerce has promised to blacklist for at least two years companies implicated in bribery or collusion in the tendering for materials and equipment under China's foreign aid programme.[9]

On the other hand, the Exim Bank, which channels a large share of China's foreign aid as well as export credits, may still not have wholeheartedly adopted Wen Jiabao's call for transparency and may still not be fully averse to funding contracts awarded under the kind of no-bid arrangements Wen Jiabao warned against. When queried in 2007 about his bank's policies on transparency, Exim Bank president Li Ruogu commented: 'In China, we have a saying: "If the water is too clear, you don't catch any fish."'[10] In 2007 a political scandal broke in the Philippines over allegations of kickbacks connected to a contract awarded to Chinese telecoms firm ZTE and backed by a preferential export credit from the Exim Bank.[11]

To address corruption concerns, the Exim Bank is working to reduce embezzlement risks by not disbursing loans in some countries to the borrowing government itself but, rather, by keeping funds in a Chinese account under the country's name. Payments to Chinese companies that supply goods or build infrastructure are made directly from that account, after being authorised by the borrowing country. Additionally, Exim Bank loans for large infrastructure packages are sometimes repaid in oil or other natural resources. These practices make loans more secure, while also helping to ensure that receipts from natural resource exports are actually used for development.

---

7 *Caijing Magazine* (China), 19 September 2007; T. Ming. 'Jiejian haiwai jingyan, Jianquan fan shangye huiluo fagui' ['Learn from Overseas Experience, Improve Anti-commercial Bribery Laws and Regulations'], *Guoji Jingjifa Wang* [*International Economic Law*], 31 October 2006; *China Daily*, 20 October 2007.
8 *Nanfang Zhoumo* [*Nanfang Weekend*] (China), 2 November 2006.
9 Ministry of Commerce, 'Interim Measures for the Administration of Foreign Assistance Material Projects,' Decree no. 5, 1 September 2006.
10 Comment at the Center for Strategic and International Studies, Washington, DC, April 2007.
11 *Caijing Magazine* (China), 21 September 2007; *Philippines Today*, 16 February 2008.

Corporate conduct

Chinese companies are increasingly aware that adopting responsible business practices can be important for their international reputations. TI's 2008 Bribe Payers Index ranked Chinese companies twenty-first out of the twenty-two countries surveyed for their perceived propensity to bribe overseas.[12] At the same time, more than 180 Chinese companies, including Huawei, PetroChina and China Railway Engineering Corporation, have signed the UN Global Compact. Some, such as Huawei, have developed corporate codes of practice regarding corruption. Becoming a publicly listed company may further encourage this. In 2008 ZTE was sanctioned by Norway's national cellular operator Telenor for breaching its code of conduct in a business tender. ZTE admitted the breach but said it was the work of a rogue employee, commenting: 'ZTE has a very clear Code of Conduct and, as a listed company, our employees have to adhere to the highest business standards.'[13] As in other places, the increased exposure of corrupt practices is not always a sign of more corruption, but could be an indicator that control systems are functioning properly. It is then important, if and how such cases are sanctioned.

Promising legal reforms

Legal changes now under way may boost efforts to combat bribery by Chinese firms outside the country. China was a sponsor, and has signed and ratified, the UN Convention against Corruption (UNCAC), which stipulates that bribery overseas be made a crime. Chinese officials have repeatedly said that China will modify its laws to comply with all the convention's obligations.[14] In September 2007 China set up the National Corruption Prevention Bureau, tasked to improve international cooperation against corruption and fulfil China's responsibilities as an UNCAC signatory. The agency was not made autonomous, however. In June 2008 the Communist Party's Central Committee included the prohibition of commercial bribery overseas in its five-year anti-corruption work plan.[15]

Bad role models

China's reform efforts are taking place amid a new wave of bribery scandals involving well-known Western firms in China. In 2006 a Beijing consulting firm, Anbound, reported that 64 per cent of the nearly 100,000 corruption scandals investigated by China's government over the previous ten years had involved foreign companies.[16] China seems to have started up the steep road of reining in corporate corruption, but, with bad role models from the wealthy world so close at hand, we should not be surprised if these reforms proceed

---

12 TI, 2008, and see article starting on page 402.
13 Telecompaper.com (Netherlands), 14 October 2008.
14 Li Jinzhang, vice minister of foreign affairs, statement at the First Conference of the State Parties to the UN Convention against Corruption, Amman, Jordan, 10 December 2006; *Caijing Magazine* (China), 25 July 2007.
15 Central Committee of the Chinese Communist Party, 'Work Proposal of Establishing and Improving the Anti-corruption System 2008–2012', June 2008.
16 *People's Daily* (China), 17 November 2006.

slowly. The urgency of the challenge is clear, however. China's growing appetite for entrepreneurial risk-taking and its increasingly pivotal role in expanding foreign direct investment and trade to developing countries need to be matched by a strong commitment to anti-corruption standards when doing business abroad.

Risky interstices: transfer pricing and global tax management
Sol Picciotto[1]

Transfer pricing : a challenge for companies and the tax authorities

The term *transfer pricing* refers to the pricing of assets, products and services, usually when they are transferred between different units within a company. The term is also often used pejoratively, however, to mean the mispricing of cross-border transactions for an illegitimate purpose.

Under current accounting and taxation regimes, transfer pricing is an inevitable task for transnational corporations (TNCs) with branches or affiliates in many countries. Indeed, it is estimated that intra-firm flows of goods account for perhaps 40 to 50 per cent of world trade, although for OECD countries for which data is available the proportion varies widely, between 15 and 60 per cent.[2] Many other transfer payments within TNCs are made for services and finance. In addition, TNCs often dominate international supply chains, which, although they involve entities under different ownership, also provide flexibility in pricing transfers.[3] These enormous internal flows offer substantial opportunities to adjust prices to gain advantage for the firm. In particular, the prices used can have a significant impact on declared profits, and thus tax liability, in different jurisdictions.

The darker side and grey areas of transfer pricing

Transfer mispricing may be deliberate and at times fraudulent. The purposes may include reducing tax liability or import duties, evading currency controls and concealing the origins of funds transferred abroad, especially funds derived from criminal activity or corruption. When plastic buckets change hands for almost US$1,000 apiece, while a bulldozer is sold for a bargain US$1,700, it is clear that such egregious mispricing may be deliberate and fraudulent, involving collusion between exporters and importers.[4]

---

1 Sol Picciotto is an Emeritus Professor of Law at Lancaster University Law School.
2 OECD, *Measuring Globalisation: OECD Economic Globalisation Indicators* (Paris: OECD, 2005).
3 Ibid.
4 S. Pak and J. Zdanowicz, *US Trade with the World: An Estimate of 2001 Lost US Federal Income Tax Revenues Due to Over-invoiced Imports and Under-invoiced Exports*, working paper (Miami: Center for International Business Education and Research, Florida International University, 2005).

The complexity and often arbitrary nature of transfer pricing by TNCs also make it very difficult to know or prove that deliberate mispricing has taken place, however. Sometimes quite small and defensible adjustments to internal pricing can make a considerable difference to the profits a firm declares in different jurisdictions. This involves a legal grey zone.

The scale and scope of transfer mispricing are extremely difficult to establish, but the evidence suggests that it is being practised at levels that raise serious doubts about responsible tax management. Estimates based on trade databases of abnormal price deviations show likely levels of income-shifting due to under- and over-invoicing between the United States and other countries. These indicate mispricing generally ranging from 2 to 10 per cent of trade volumes, amounting to billions of dollars per year.[5] This contributes to a situation in which more than 60 per cent of US corporations reported no annual tax liabilities in any given year between 1998 and 2005.[6]

Europe faces similar issues. A detailed analysis of transfer pricing in Europe found many nations appear to gain revenues from intra-European profit-shifting by multinationals, largely at the expense of Germany.[7]

How to set the right price?

What is the norm for pricing between related parties operating within an integrated firm? Companies and tax authorities have long grappled with this problem, especially in relation to taxing income and profit. For corporate groups operating within a single tax jurisdiction, the usual approach is to require consolidated accounts, which simply eliminate intra-firm transactions and include as income the proceeds of sales only once made outside the group. This is obviously difficult for a single tax authority to apply to a TNC, and in the early twentieth century national tax authorities were given powers to adjust the accounts of companies within their jurisdiction to counteract any 'diversion' of profits to their foreign affiliates. Conflicting adjustments by different national authorities created a danger of international double taxation, however. This led to the adoption of internationally agreed principles for the allocation of income, to be embodied in bilateral tax treaties.[8]

The basic criterion for transfer pricing has been agreed to be the 'arm's-length' principle – that is to say, the price for equivalent transactions between independent entities, based on separate accounting by separate legal entities. This is inappropriate in principle, however, since TNCs by nature are globally integrated and derive much of their competitive advantage from

---

5 M. E. de Boyrie, S. Pak and J. Zdanowicz, 'Money Laundering and Income Tax Evasion: The Determination of Optimal Audits and Inspections to Detect Abnormal Prices in International Trade', *Journal of Financial Crime*, vol. 12, no. 2 (2004).

6 US Government Accountability Office (GAO), *Comparison of the Reported Tax Liabilities of Foreign and US-controlled Corporations, 1998–2005* (Washington, DC: GAO, 2008).

7 H. Huizinga and L. Laeven, *International Profit Shifting within European Multinationals*, Discussion Paper no. 6048 (London: Centre for Economic Policy Research, 2007).

8 S. Picciotto, *International Business Taxation* (London: Weidenfeld, 1992); M. B. Carroll, *Global Perspectives of an International Tax Lawyer* (Hicksville, NY: Exposition Press, 1978).

internal synergies and economies of scale and scope. This is especially so in today's knowledge economy, in which much added value depends on intangibles generated in the firm as a whole.

Although the OECD's Committee on Fiscal Affairs continues to maintain that separate accounts based on the arm's-length pricing of transactions should be the primary transfer pricing method, it has been obliged to accept alternatives based on allocating the overall profit earned according to the contribution made by each affiliate – an approach that is now often used.[9]

As a result, transfer pricing rules now applied by tax authorities are both complex and arbitrary. They result in frequent disputes, often involving negotiations between different authorities, to try to resolve double taxation resulting from inconsistent allocations that pose considerable problems for companies. Such cases may involve many millions of dollars and drag on for many years. In one notable transfer pricing case, the pharmaceutical company GlaxoSmithKline was assessed for US$5.2 billion in back taxes and interest by the US Internal Revenue Service in 2004 related to profits from its anti-ulcer drug Zantac. Glaxo claimed that this was arbitrary and appealed, arguing for a refund of US$1 billion. The dispute was finally settled for US$3.4 billion.[10]

Though extreme, the Glaxo case is far from unique, especially in globally integrated and knowledge-based industries such as pharmaceuticals. Conflicts emerge not only between firms and tax authorities but also between different tax authorities, since relatively small differences in transfer prices may affect the allocation of significant proportions of the tax base.

Inconsistent transfer-pricing adjustments between different national authorities are said to account for 80 per cent of bilateral double taxation disputes, although this cannot be verified, since the 'competent authority' procedure is secret and issues can take many years to resolve. To deal with this, the United States has introduced a procedure for advanced pricing agreements (APAs), which has also been adopted by other OECD countries. While this can provide firms with some certainty, it does not resolve the problems of arbitrariness or secrecy, as they are essentially private deals with each firm. Indeed, Glaxo's complaint of unfairness in the case above was based on a comparison with the treatment given by the US tax authorities in an APA with its then rival SmithKline. Glaxo discovered this differential treatment only after its merger with SmithKline in 2001.

A global challenge that hits developing countries particularly hard

In a survey of 850 multinational enterprises in twenty-four countries in 2007, a half said that they had undergone a transfer pricing examination since 2003, and a quarter said that

---

9 Intergovernmental Working Group of Experts on International Standards of Accounting and Reporting, *Transfer Pricing Regulations and Transnational Corporation Practices: Guidance for Developing Countries* (Geneva: UN Conference on Trade and Development [UNCTAD], 1997).

10 M. A. Sullivan, 'With Billions at Stake, Glaxo Puts US APA Program on Trial', *Tax Notes International*, vol. 34 (2004); *The Economist* (UK), 31 January 2004; *Wall Street Journal* (Eastern edition), 12 September 2006.

the examination had led to adjustments. In addition, 87 per cent of respondents said they consider transfer pricing a risk issue in relation to their financial statements.[11]

Transfer pricing is not confined to a particular sector but plays an important role in all industries, from natural resource extraction and forestry to high-tech goods and services. Two-thirds of oil and gas multinationals considered transfer pricing issues as absolutely critical or very important. About a half of pharmaceuticals and telecommunications multinationals regarded transfer pricing as the largest risk issue for their financial statements.[12]

The scale and scope of transfer pricing, which may also involve transactions via tax havens for maximum tax avoidance, makes it an important issue for industrialised and developing countries alike. The former seek to protect their tax base and prevent legitimate tax competition between countries from becoming an unfair race to the bottom of special tax breaks, as well as ever lower corporate tax rates, such as those offered by international tax havens and offshore centres.

Developing countries face the additional challenge of ensuring that transfer pricing does not support capital flight or erode their revenues from what is, quite often, their single most important source of income: natural resources. In Papua New Guinea, transfer pricing on timber sales is estimated to cost the government tens of millions of dollars a year, and concerns about manipulative transfer pricing with regard to timber, other natural resources and a wide range of other trade transactions involving developing countries have been documented in many other parts of the world.[13]

Moreover, the tax authorities in developing countries are challenged to muster the expertise and resources to prevent transfer pricing abuses. As of this writing, only about forty countries are believed to have established some form of specific transfer pricing regulations.[14] Although in industrialised countries such as Australia and Denmark a half of multinational companies say they were challenged by the authorities when they adjusted their transfer prices, no such extra scrutiny was reported in Argentina, Brazil, India or Mexico.[15] As a result, the potential for abusive transfer pricing has emerged as an important concern on the international agenda for securing adequate financing for development.[16]

Two ideas for reform

The indeterminate or arbitrary criteria related to transfer pricing inevitably create opportunities and temptations for firms to adjust prices to gain tax advantages. Such practices may

---

11 Ernst & Young, *Precision under Pressure, Global Transfer Pricing Survey 2007–2008* (London: Ernst & Young, 2008).
12 Ibid.
13 *The Australian*, 19 July 2006; Bloomberg (US), 30 July 2008; I. Bannon and P. Collier, *Natural Resources and Violent Conflict: Options and Actions* (Washington, DC: World Bank, 2003); M. Grote, 'Tax Aspects of Domestic Resource Mobilisation: A Discussion of Enduring and Emerging Issues', presentation at UN Financing for Development and International Fund for Agricultural Development conference, Rome, 5 September 2007.
14 Ernst & Young, 2008.
15 Ibid.
16 See UNCTAD, *Draft Accra Accord* (Geneva: UNCTAD, 2008).

often be abusive. Both tax authorities and firms could do much to establish a better basis for preventing such abuse.

A common base for tax assessment

The tax authorities should reorientate their approach to transfer pricing by abandoning the chimera of the arm's-length principle. A new approach advocated by many specialists is a unitary or consolidated basis for the tax assessment of TNCs, with an allocation of the tax base based on formula apportionment.[17] This would sidestep the problem of transfer pricing by simply eliminating from the accounts internal transfers within the firm. It would also help to tackle other thorny problems of international tax avoidance related to intermediary entities formed in convenient jurisdictions or tax havens. This concept poses its own problems, however, especially the need for an international agreement on the formula for apportionment. This would not be easy to resolve, since much is at stake. Nevertheless, these issues should be faced and resolved openly, rather than having them shrouded in a fog of technical detail, imprecision and uncertainty, as under the present system.

Such solutions offer win-win opportunities. Firms and tax authorities alike would benefit from reduced compliance costs. This would be especially helpful for developing countries that lack the resources to operate complex anti-avoidance rules or check transfer prices. Greater effectiveness would mean higher revenues, which would provide the opportunity to reduce marginal corporate tax rates further.

Transparency of tax payments as an integral part of corporate citizenship

Firms should adopt clear and open guidelines for tax compliance, including a high degree of transparency about the amount of tax they actually pay broken down by jurisdiction. At present, companies usually report only a global figure, which is often misleading, because provisions made for tax are shown while the actual amounts paid in the end are often lower due to deferral. A promising approach that could serve as a template for disclosing how much tax companies pay, and how much tax governments receive, has been developed by the Extractive Industries Transparency Initiative and endorsed by the G8 group of developed countries.[18]

Furthermore, corporate codes of conduct should include a clear commitment to comply with both the letter and the spirit of tax rules, and reject overly aggressive tax planning and avoidance schemes. Surprisingly, such a commitment is ignored in most corporate codes of conduct. The Tax Justice Network's Code of Conduct for Taxation, which has basic principles applicable to both revenue authorities and firms, could provide a useful template.

As companies increasingly acknowledge their role as corporate citizens, they are reporting more information on their social and environmental impact. Tax payments, as the most direct and

---

17 K. A. Clausing and R. S. Avi-Yonah, *Reforming Corporate Taxation in a Global Economy: A Proposal to Adopt Formulary Apportionment* (Washington, DC: Brookings Institution, 2007).
18 See article starting on page 54.

fundamental way that companies contribute to society, should be central to a company's public disclosure. More transparency about tax payments is also a prerequisite for an informed debate on the fairness of specific tax management and transfer-pricing schemes. Opinions on what is considered appropriate will inevitably vary, but an informed debate as to whether a company is living up to its most fundamental commitments to society is essential and legitimate.

Such a combined constructive approach could establish a stronger basis of trust between the tax authorities and the private sector, which would greatly improve tax compliance and help strengthen the confidence of citizens in the legitimacy of taxation.

Where public and private merge: privatisation and corruption

John Nellis[1]

Brazil, May 2003: Brazilian officials alleged collusion between American investors AES and Enron in the 1998 sale of an electricity utility in São Paulo. The authorities claimed that the two agreed in advance that AES would be the only bidder. In return, Enron would be given a contract to build a generation plant. The *Financial Times* reported that the AES representative came to the final meeting with two envelopes, the first containing a bid for US$1.78 billion, the second for US$2.28 billion. Once it was clear that Enron was not going to submit an offer, the lower bid was tendered. The Brazilian government investigated. All the parties denied any illegality. In 2007 collusion charges were dismissed for lack of evidence. That Enron (which underwent bankruptcy and dissolution in 2001) never built a power plant was a factor in the decision to drop the case.[2]

Worldwide, more than 100,000 large enterprises and firms have been privatised since 1980, along with an equal or larger number of small businesses.[3] Sales revenues are in the neighbourhood of US$700 billion. The total value of privatised assets is actually much higher than indicated by sales revenues, since many of the firms have literally been given away, particularly in former communist countries.

Ex post assessments conclude that privatisation generally results in declining production costs and increased returns to owners.[4] Efficiency and financial gains following privatisation have

---

1 John Nellis is a principal in the research and consulting firm International Analytics.
2 *Financial Times* (UK), 21 May 2003; see also 'AES in Latin America', at www.aes-latinamerica.com/tom-tribone-aes-enron/.
3 F. Schneider, *Privatization in Austria and Other EU Countries: Some Theoretical Reasons and First Results about the Privitization Proceeds* (Munich: CESifo, 2003).
4 W. L. Megginson and J. M. Netter, 'From State to Market: A Survey of Empirical Studies on Privatization', *Journal of Economic Literature*, vol. 39, no. 2 (2001).

been frequent and sizeable enough to impress many economists, financial analysts, finance ministers and international financial institutions.

Performance improvements stir technicians, but concerns about privatisation's unequal distributive effects have provoked criticisms. The complaint is that privatisation rewards the foreign, the wealthy, the agile and the corrupt at the expense of the local, the poor, the non-connected and the honest.[5] Opponents have made their points skilfully: privatisation has become the most widely criticised and popularly disliked of all economic liberalisation policies.

Rather than debating the merits of privatisation, the present task is to discuss the commonly asserted but little analysed linkage between privatisation and corruption. There is plenty of smoke around privatisation and how it fosters corruption, but determining if there is fire – and, if so, its nature, extent and how to put it out – is a complex matter.

Underachievement in Russia and eastern Europe

Privatisation has increased inequality, at least in the short run and particularly in former communist countries. Russia is the prime example. Despite a distribution of shares in privatised firms to the general public, as much as 90 percent of the prime assets were accumulated by a tiny group of entrepreneurs. Other countries using such a 'voucher privatisation' distribution scheme, such as the Czech Republic, Romania and the Ukraine, experienced similar if somewhat less dramatic results.

Methods of transferring ownership have varied. In Russia, former managers of state-owned firms transformed themselves into new owners and then persuaded or pressured worker-shareholders to support them, arguing that this would be a better arrangement than dealing with unknown, perhaps foreign, capitalists. In other cases, private Russian banks received shares in key firms as collateral for loans to the state that were never repaid, resulting in banks becoming owners of major assets for a relative pittance. Russia's Uneximbank obtained 38 per cent of the shares in Norilsk Nickel, a firm with reportedly US$2 billion in profits, in return for a US$170 million loan.[6] In the Czech Republic, investment fund managers accumulated vouchers and then 'tunnelled' resources by transferring decent assets to subsidiaries they personally owned or controlled, leaving the citizens to own liabilities in 'shell' companies.[7] Variations on these themes have occurred in most former communist countries, and also, belatedly, in China. In all instances, former members of the communist administrative *nomenklatura* transformed themselves into a property-owning bourgeoisie.

In retrospect, it can be seen that privatisation in 'transition' states was vastly oversold. Citizens were misled, and the expectations and promises of domestic reformers and international

---

5 S. Kahn and E. Minnich, *The Fox in the Henhouse: How Privatization Threatens Democracy* (San Francisco: Berrett-Koehler, 2005).

6 J. Nellis, 'The World Bank, Privatization, and Enterprise Reform in Transition Economies', *Transition Newsletter*, vol. 13, no. 1 (2002).

7 D. Ellerman, *Voucher Privatization with Investment Funds: An Institutional Analysis*, Policy Reseach Working Paper no. 1924 (Washington, DC: World Bank, 1998).

supporters alike were not met. These actions were seldom outright illegal, however, in the chaotic post-communist legal/institutional framework. Moreover, a large percentage of the privatised assets ended up in the hands of people who arguably made better use of them than the former state managers. These firms eventually contributed to recovery, growth and – through taxation – government revenues. Analysts of a *realpolitik* bent have thus concluded that privatisation in former socialist economies, while messy and unfair, was unavoidable, ultimately beneficial and superior to the only likely alternative: continued stagnation.[8]

Fifteen years on, however, most in the former Soviet states regard the privatisation exercise as having been unjust and fraudulent; they also regard it as largely over. Few think it worthwhile to try to correct or undo the process.

Some renationalisation has subsequently taken place in the incredibly lucrative Russian gas and oil sectors. This process appears to have been just as unfair as the original privatisations. In 2004, for example, the main assets of once private Yukos Oil were transferred by means of a rather dubious legal process 'at a minimal cost' to state-owned Rosneft. At least one very valuable Yukos unit was sold for a low price, which the then President Vladimir Putin's own economic adviser termed 'the scam of the year'.[9] Yukos head Mikhail Khodorkovsky, Russia's richest person at the time, and several other top Yukos executives were tried and jailed for tax evasion.

Other renationalisation efforts have occurred in Slovakia, which reassumed control of several strategic industries and halted all large-scale privatisation plans, and in Estonia, which renationalised Estonian Railways in early 2007. Additionally, Lithuania and Poland have prevented the privatisation of firms deemed to be of national strategic importance.[10]

What can we learn?

Several lessons can be learnt from these and other privatisation schemes. First, the idea that private ownership could occur in an efficient and equitable manner in the absence of the legal and policy frameworks that underpin the functioning of markets was naive or worse. Furthermore, corruption risks are greater in poor countries.

Privatisation-related corruption rises as the value of the privatised company increases and as the selling country's overall income level declines. The best explanation is that a country's income level correlates closely with its level of institutional development – with low levels weakening or eliminating both the internal and the external monitoring of administrative and investor behaviour. One small, easily hidden act can reward officials with multiples of

---

8 D. Kaufmann and P. Siegelbaum, 'Privatization and Corruption in Transitional Economies', *Journal of International Affairs*, vol. 50, no. 2 (1997); A. Aslund, 'US–Russia Economic Relationship: Implications of the Yukos Affair', testimony before the House Subcommittee on Domestic and International Monetary Policy, Trade and Technology, Washington, DC, 17 October 2007; A. Shleifer and D. Treisman, *Without a Map: Political Tactics and Economic Reform in Russia* (Cambridge, MA: MIT Press, 2000).

9 A. Aslund, 2007.

10 UNCTAD, *World Investment Report 2008: Transnational Corporations and the Infrastructure Challenge* (Geneva: UNCTAD, 2008).

their regular salary. With relatively small payments to government officials or other bidders, investors can eliminate a competitor, obtain a monopoly position or favourable policy stance, win a contract or bend bidding qualifications.

For example, after winning the competition to take over Tanzania Telecommunications Company Limited (TTCL), the investing consortium entered into further negotiations with the government. Two major changes to the original bid document were made, cutting the final price in half and awarding the consortium a 'management assistance fee' of 3.5 per cent of monthly gross turnover. Presumably the other bidders were unaware that these additional arrangements could be negotiated, yet the bidding was not reopened. Though corruption was not proved, the consistent lack of clarity gives great cause for concern and feeds the misgivings of opponents.[11]

This hardly means that transparency can or should be ignored. Worldwide, privatisation has tended to win the economic battles while losing the political wars. The public perception that deals were corrupt has been the primary determinant of the political outcome. Numerous water privatisation efforts have failed recently in Latin America, Africa, Asia and the United States, following opposition from public interest groups claiming not only that deals with multinational contractors were not transparent, but that rates rose unreasonably and the promised service improvements were not carried out. The most high-profile reversal came in 2000 in Cochabamba, Bolivia, where the privatised water utility was returned to public control.

While not sufficient for economic success, transparency is essential for privatisation to be viewed as politically legitimate. The most effective way to combat corruption in privatisation is by increasing the flow of information to the public, not simply on transactions but also on the financial and operational performance of state-owned firms prior to sale. Thus, standard legal procedures promoting transparency, such as those in competitive bidding and procurement manuals of international financial institutions, are helpful and worth promoting.

Another lesson is that both venality and suspicion thrive on opaquness and ignorance. All the same, transparency is important but not a cure-all. Transparent sales procedures alone do not guarantee technically good privatisation outcomes. For example, Senegal's government followed all recommended transparency procedures in the 1999 sale of part of its electricity firm. The government repurchased the shares eighteen months later, however, following disputes over investments and tariffs, lack of service improvements and arguments between the two private shareholders. A second privatisation attempt, again using good transparency practices, also failed to produce an acceptable bidder.[12]

It is essential to go deeper than this, however, and address the previously used or abused financial management systems applied in state-owned enterprises (SOEs). In many settings, basic operational and financial data on firm performance has been not produced, not sent to

---

11 Tanzanian Presidential Commission to Review Infrastructure Privatisation, unpublished report of consultants on the privatisation of TTCL, 2005.
12 Boston Institute for Developing Economies (BIDE), 'Impact of Privatization in Africa: Synthesis of Eight Cases' [unpublished report submitted to the World Bank] (Bethesda, MD: BIDE, 2006).

supervisors, not tabulated in supervising bodies or not acted upon. Some governments there-fore have not been precisely aware of what they were selling, and buyers were not sure of what they were getting. The resulting uncertainty creates an informational vacuum in which delay, renegotiation and corruption can flourish.

Efforts by governments and their advisers to achieve SOE reform must be renewed and redou-bled. A first step is the independent accounting and auditing of SOEs consistent with generally accepted accounting principles. Also needed are financial reporting and management systems that allow treasury officials to measure the fiscal and macroeconomic impact of SOE actions. Having open sales procedures can help sooth public suspicion and mistrust, as was done in Bolivia, which opened all privatisation bids live on television, and in Slovakia, which invited independent observers to vet a transaction.

Information discovered through these procedures can assist all parties. First, reformers become armed with information on the past costs of poor SOE performance and the future costs of continued inaction. Second, potential investors have a clearer picture of what is on the market, allowing them to make more precise offers and rely less on post-sale manoeu-vring. Third, the press and public are aided in their quest to find out what is being proposed and who benefits.

The ultimate factor, though, is giving voice to local actors as well as external observers – an authoritative mechanism to confront decision-makers with information and hold them accountable. Weak or absent voice and empowerment in much of the world's poorer areas constitute a prime reason privatisation has been criticised, even when financial and efficiency accomplishments were unquestioned. Again, there is a close correlation between a country's income level and the extent and efficacy of these factors.

Signs of progress are appearing. In 2006 Tanzania's government contracted with a US firm to build and operate a power plant. Much of the negotiation was carried out in secret. The plant did not go online on schedule and the costs to Tanzania were very high. Having had dramatically bad experiences with two previous private generating contracts, citizens and MPs expressed concern and an acute desire to know more. In November 2007 parliament formed a committee to investigate the tendering process. Three months later the commit-tee issued a detailed report that alleges, *inter alia*, that high-ranking officials influenced the decision to retain the US firm, overriding the objections of technicians. The prime minister, the energy and minerals minister and a former energy and minerals minister serving in a different post all resigned – an unprecedented event in Tanzania, and a rare one in Africa as a whole.[13]

A simple yet important lesson is that method matters. Privatisation by selling shares on a stock exchange offers more transparency and broad dispersion of ownership, and thereby fewer

---

13 'Report of the Select Committee formed by the Parliament of the United Republic of Tanzania on 13 November 2007 to Investigate the Tendering Process for Emergency Power Supply which Awarded the Tender to Richmond Development Company LLC of Houston, Texas, USA, in 2006', Parliament of Tanzania, 2007.

opportunities for corruption than other methods. Kenya used public offerings to sell off significant portions of the national airline, the main electric utility and a mobile phone company. All three sales have been regarded as comparatively clean by internal and external observers alike.[14]

When capital markets are not sufficiently developed for this approach auctioning can be another good method, as was used in Serbia and Poland to divest small and medium enterprises. Open competition among bidders on the public auction floor greatly reduces the likelihood of corrupt dealings. A few countries have also successfully used an open tender process to obtain offers from competing bidders for larger firms.[15]

Finally, open, robust competition is key. Few bidders means a greater chance for corruption, through a greater need for confidential negotiations with selling agents, poor information flow and more complex sales contracts. These complicating conditions apply in many if not most large privatisations in developing and transition countries, particularly in the high-value infrastructure and financial sectors.

14 Y. A. Debrah and O. K. Toroitich, 'The Making of an African Success Story: The Privatization of Kenya Airways', *Thunderbird International Business Review*, vol. 47, no. 2 (2005).

15 I. Goldberg and J. Nellis, 'Methods and Institutions – How Do They Matter?: Lessons from Privatization and Restructuring in the Post-socialist Transition', in I. W. Lieberman and D. J. Kopf (eds.), *Privatization in Transition Economies: The Ongoing Story* (New York: Elsevier, 2008).

4 Tackling corruption effectively: from corporate commitment to accountability

The contributions in this chapter focus on the major tools and mechanisms that support corporate integrity. Ben W. Heineman, Jr., highlights the fact that ethical leadership is essential for building a culture of integrity. Muel Kaptein reviews the spread and effectiveness of business codes of conduct, while Dante Mendes Aldrighi discusses good practices and innovations for internal corporate governance. Moving to broader drivers for corporate integrity, Alan Knight traces the evolution of management and reporting standards and Dieter Zinnbauer explores how owners and investors can leverage their influence to enhance corporate compliance and anti-corruption efforts.

Supplementary contributions shed further light on the state of corporate governance in India (Vikramaditya Khanna), the experience of institutional investors in engaging with companies on corporate integrity issues (Hans-Christoph Hirt and Jennifer Walmsley) and the transparency of sovereign wealth funds, as well as their potential to become drivers of corporate integrity (Pierre Habbard).

View from the inside – Robust anti-corruption programmes in a high-performance with high integrity global company
Ben W. Heineman, Jr.[1]

Powerful corporate efforts to combat corruption – the prevention of private and public sector bribery, extortion and misappropriation – can occur only when a company has a strong commitment from its board of directors and CEO to attain the two foundational goals of global capitalism: the fusion of high performance with high integrity.

'High performance' means: strong, sustained economic growth; the provision of superior goods and services; the creation of durable benefits for shareholders and other stakeholders; and a sound balance between risk-taking and risk management.

'High integrity' has three elements: robust adherence to the spirit and letter of formal rules, legal and financial; the voluntary adoption of global ethical standards that bind the company and its employees; and an employee commitment to core values of honesty, candour, fairness, trustworthiness and reliability.

---

1 Ben W. Heineman, Jr., is GE's former senior vice-president for law and public affairs and a distinguished senior fellow at Harvard Law School and at the Belfer Center for Science and International Affairs at Harvard's Kennedy School of Government.

The fundamental task of the CEO is to create the 'performance with integrity' culture – both to avoid catastrophic integrity misses and to create affirmative benefits inside the company, in the marketplace and in the broader global society. That culture entails shared principles (values, policies and attitudes) and shared practices (norms, systems and processes). Although it must, in the first instance, include some elements of deterrence (violation of norms will lead to punishment), it must also, at the end of the day, be affirmative (people want to do the right thing – because leaders make this a real company imperative). Critically, this culture of fundamental integrity must be uniform and global: it should apply in every nation and must not be bent by corrupt local practices, *even if it means losing business in the short run*. Companies such as BP and Siemens have faced major problems because they failed to have such a strong global culture, on plant safety in BP's case and against bribery in Siemens' case.

Based on my nearly twenty years of experience trying to help create a corporate culture of integrity at one of the world's largest companies, I have identified eight core principles that are important for business leaders intent on fusing high performance with high integrity:[2]

- committed and consistent leadership that makes performance with integrity the foundation of the corporation;
- managing performance with integrity as a business process by building the integrity infrastructure (risk assessment and risk abatement to prevent, detect and respond) into business operations;
- adopting global ethical standards beyond what the law requires (e.g. no bribery in either public or private sectors anywhere);
- using early warning systems to stay ahead of global trends and expectations;
- fostering employee awareness, knowledge and commitment through stimulating, systematic education and training;
- giving employees voice through ombuds systems that treat concerns professionally, fairly and promptly and prohibit retaliation;
- recognising that the top staff leaders – the chief financial officer, General Counsel and human resources leader – must be both partners to the business leadership and, ultimately, guardians of the corporation; and
- designing compensation systems so that top business leadership are paid not just for performance, but for performance *with* integrity.

Without robust implementation of these principles and associated practices, the critical uniform global high performance with high integrity culture will not exist – and the 'tone at the top' rhetoric from the board and business leadership will be just so much eyewash.

Only when a corporation has this comprehensive, systematic (and complex) commitment to high performance with high integrity can the company's anti-corruption programme be effective. Let there be no misunderstanding: *that programme must take root in this broader corporate effort and culture.* This is so because anti-bribery programmes require intense, good-faith

---

2 For an elaboration of this argument, see B. W. Heineman, Jr., *High Performance with High Integrity* (Cambridge, MA: Harvard Business School Press, 2008).

implementation. Direct cash payments to officials are forbidden, but improper payments take many other, even more clandestine forms: the use of third parties; gifts and entertainment; reimbursement of travel and living 'expenses'; 'charitable and political' contributions; and the improper use of partners, suppliers and investors connected to decision-makers. These practices may also be legitimate, though, and decisions by a transnational corporation of what is proper and improper can be fact-bound. A strong anti-corruption programme requires a strong cultural commitment to do the right thing; clear guidelines and presumptions (no gifts over a nominal amount); and strong, centralised processes to ensure that hard cases are decided on the right side of the line.

For example, third parties pose one of the most dangerous problems: the agents, consultants, sales representatives and distributors who stand between the company and the customer – and who can be conduits for illicit payments. A good risk abatement process requires written specification at the outset defining the commercial context and the specific need. Senior management should approve this specification so that accountability is clearly fixed. Then there must be real due diligence relating both to the party's resources and expertise (what did their financials look like?; who worked for them?; what was their expertise in the industry?; what was their formal business documentation?) and to its reputation (involving both interviews and public record checks). A written contract must contain key terms: for example, the specification of work; a fee within a reasonable range (1–2 per cent, not 10–15 per cent); structured payments for deliverables; the exclusion of unknown subcontractors; audit rights; and termination rights. In addition, company employees must be given 'red flag' training, which would lead to reports up the 'integrity infrastructure', if questions arise.

Nevertheless, these systems and processes for vetting third parties and implementing express contracts can have real meaning and impact only if a company's employees are imbued with the imperatives of performance with integrity; and such a commitment takes us back to the broader proposition. A pervasive high performance with high integrity culture – and the adoption and implementation of core principles and practices – are the necessary conditions for a potent corporate anti-corruption programme.

The living business code: improving corporate integrity and reducing corruption from the inside
Muel Kaptein[1]

Recent corporate scandals and the resulting calls among various stakeholders for enhanced private sector accountability have led to a sharp increase in the implementation of business

---

1 Muel Kaptein is Professor of Business Ethics at RSM Erasmus University, the Netherlands, and director at KPMG Forensic & Integrity.

codes of ethics, particularly among the world's largest corporations. While many codes look good on paper, however, they can become living documents only if they are deeply embedded in the daily routine of a company.

Ethical leadership is key for this, as well as monitoring by internal and external supervisory institutions.

Business codes are everywhere

Nowadays, many companies have a business code of ethics, a document developed for and by a company to guide the behaviour of managers and employees. In 2007 86 per cent of Fortune Global 200 companies had a business code, an increase of 51 per cent from 2000[2] (see figure 5). Among these companies, all North American firms had a business code, while 52 per cent of Asian companies and 80 per cent of European companies had a code.

At the national level, codes are, for example, on the books in about three-quarters of the largest 1,000 companies in South Africa, the 800 largest companies in India and the largest 100 companies in the Netherlands. In the United States, 57 per cent of companies with a workforce of at least 200 people have a code.[3]

Why do companies develop a code?

Companies have cited many reasons for developing codes of ethics, which signifies their flexibility and broad utility. The most important reason among Fortune Global 200 companies is

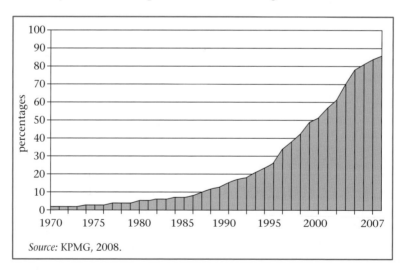

Source: KPMG, 2008.

Figure 5: Increase in business codes among Fortune Global 200 companies, 1970–2007

---

2 KPMG, *Business Codes of the Global 200: Their Prevalence, Content and Embedding* (London: KPMG, 2008).
3 M. Kaptein, *The Living Code: Embedding Ethics into the Corporate DNA* (Sheffield: Greenleaf, 2008).

to comply with legal obligations. This reflects the strong emphasis on compliance measures, particularly in the United States, where the Sarbanes–Oxley Act, Federal Sentencing Guidelines and the Foreign Corrupt Practices Act (FCPA) have led to fundamental changes in corporate governance. The increase also reflects new guidance in a variety of highly regulated industries, plus trade-group-sponsored codes, stock exchange rules and national corporate governance codes.

Other significant drivers of code development include:

- limiting liability in the event of accidents;
- limiting government initiatives to create new legislation;
- creating a positive, shared company culture;
- protecting and enhancing a company's reputation; and
- improving staff behaviour and corporate social responsibility.

What's inside: the content of a code

Codes range in size from a single page to up to eighty pages. Their content also differs. Among Fortune Global 200 firms, 63 per cent of codes address corruption and bribery. Specific company codes vary, but the bulk contain provisions addressing most of the following issues: conflicts of interest; complying with applicable laws and regulations; financial records and other internal information; confidentiality; accepting gifts and bribes; reporting violations; fair competition; insider trading; and discrimination.

Whereas some companies include a monetary limit on gifts and entertainment offered or accepted, others have more open-ended terms, such as 'as long as it does not eliminate com-petition', 'as long as it does not contravene local culture' and 'as long as we can explain our behaviour to others and face ourselves in the mirror'. While some companies make reference to anti-corruption legislation such as the United States' FCPA, others cite their responsibility and desire to be an open, honest and reliable company maintaining fair relationships with stakeholders.

An effective code should be:

- *comprehensive*, addressing issues that stakeholders expect the company to respond to and giving guidance on dilemmas that managers and employees confront;
- *morally justifiable*, so that it is able to withstand moral scrutiny and be consistent with national laws and regulations, with generally accepted codes for businesses, industry organisations and sectors, and with stakeholders' legitimate expectations;
- *authentic*, tailor-made and exuding the spirit of the company and expressing the company's identity; and
- *feasible*, being manageable, realisable and practicable.[4]

---

4 M. Kaptein, 2008.

Embedding a code

A code is a dead letter if it is not distributed or if, after distribution, it disappears into the desk drawer or shredder. In brief: 'A code is nothing, coding is everything.' A code's importance lies in how it is introduced, implemented, internalised and institutionalised. This coding process can be much more important than the code itself.

Coding starts with the way companies develop their code. It is important to involve internal and external stakeholders in determining the code's content. Actual and potential dilemmas faced by managers and employers can be collected, through workshops, questionnaires, interviews and round-table meetings. These stories can be used as building blocks for writing a code, creating a sense of ownership among stakeholders and helping to make a code unique.

Truly embedding a code means that all the managers and employees:

- know and understand what is expected of them;
- feel inspired and motivated to comply with the code; and
- are able to comply with the code.

To achieve this, companies embed a living code by:

- communicating the code periodically;
- training managers and employees to implement the code;
- using role-modelling by managers to propagate the code in their words and deeds;
- creating a culture in which dilemmas can be raised and discussed;
- establishing monitoring systems that can detect code violations in a timely manner;
- punishing code violators if necessary and learning from violations; and
- rewarding people who go above and beyond the code.

Many instruments are available to embed a code, ranging from hotlines and whistleblower procedures, to compliance monitoring and ethics committees (see figure 6).

Are codes effective?

In view of the growing use of business codes, as well as the increasing accountability pressures from governments, NGOs and other stakeholders, the question arises as to whether codes actually work. A recent summary of related scientific studies yields mixed results. About half the scientific studies found that codes are effective or slightly effective, a third found that they are not effective and 14 per cent found that they are sometimes effective and sometimes ineffective. One study found that business codes could be counterproductive when employees perceive them as window-dressing.[5]

Most of these studies relate a code to one or more outcomes. What they ignore is the content of the code and how the code is embedded in the company. Given the diversity of code

---

5 M. Kaptein and M. Schwartz, 'The Effectiveness of Business Codes: A Critical Examination of Existing Studies and the Development of an Integrated Research Model', *Journal of Business Ethics*, vol. 77, no. 2 (2008).

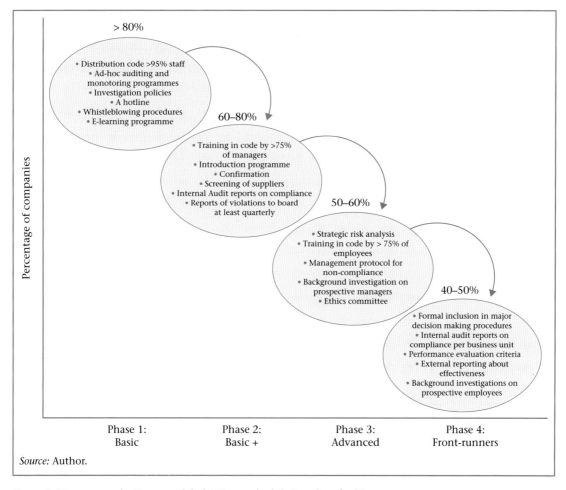

> 80%

• Distribution code >95% staff
• Ad-hoc auditing and
monotoring programmes
• Investigation policies
• A hotline
• Whistleblowing procedures
• E-learning programme

60–80%

• Training in code by >75%
of managers
• Introduction programme
• Confirmation
• Screening of suppliers
• Internal Audit reports on compliance
• Reports of violations to board
at least quarterly

50–60%

• Strategic risk analysis
• Training in code by > 75% of
employees
• Management protocol for
non-compliance
• Background investigation on
prospective managers
• Ethics committee

40–50%

• Formal inclusion in major
decision making procedures
• Internal audit reports on
compliance per business unit
• Performance evaluation criteria
• External reporting about
effectiveness
• Background investigations on
prospective employees

Percentage of companies

| Phase 1: | Phase 2: | Phase 3: | Phase 4: |
| Basic | Basic + | Advanced | Front-runners |

Source: Author.

Figure 6: Measures at the Fortune Global 200 to embed their codes of ethics

content and the ways they are embedded, the studies' mixed findings are not surprising. To understand the effectiveness of codes better and to improve their effectiveness, attention should be paid to their content and how they are embedded. This can be summarised with the simple formula:

$$\text{Effectiveness of code} = \text{Content} \times \text{Embedding}$$

Challenges

Companies face a range of challenges in improving the effectiveness of their codes, including the following.

● Developing a code tailored to a company's particular situation that reflects its strategy, identity and dilemmas.

- Avoiding implementing a code in a limited, standardised and uninspiring way, such as by using e-learning modules instead of in-depth discussions.
- Monitoring compliance with each aspect of the code, which is currently performed by less than a half of the Fortune Global 200 companies, and which can be aided by internal audit departments and external reporting on code implementation and compliance. External parties will increasingly demand that organisations demonstrate that their code is a living document. This also offers opportunities to companies to distinguish themselves.
- Shifting the focus from the existence of a code to its content and how it is embedded. Stakeholders should be more lenient in criticising a company if legal violations occur despite the presence of a living code that follows best content and implementation practices.

In conclusion, a code can be an effective tool, but as Neville Cooper, founder of London's Institute of Business Ethics, remarks, 'A code of ethics cannot make people or companies ethical. But nor can hammers and saws produce furniture. In both cases they are necessary tools, which need intelligent design and use.'[6]

---

6 N. Cooper, *Developing a Code of Business Ethics* (London: Institute of Business Ethics, 1990).

From conflict to alignment of interests: structuring internal corporate governance to minimise corruption risks

Dante Mendes Aldrighi[1]

Because the executives and controlling shareholders of publicly traded companies possess great discretionary powers, they are in the position to maximise private benefits at the expense of minority shareholders and other stakeholders, opening the door to corporate fraud and corruption. Chapter 2 has highlighted some key challenges for corporate governance. This contribution focuses on remedies and discusses good practices in corporate governance and some promising areas for reform.

How good corporate governance matters for companies and economies

Lapses in corporate governance expose companies to material risks that threaten their financial stability, increasing the vulnerability of financial systems and the broader economy. Empirical research has shown that sound governance can reduce the cost of capital and

---

1 Dante Mendes Aldrighi is Professor of Economics at the University of São Paulo, Brazil.

provide incentives for all players to behave in the interest of the firm. For example, an analysis of more than 1,500 companies found an investment portfolio focusing on the best-governed companies would have outperformed the market by more than 8 per cent.[2] Positive impacts at the macroeconomic level are also evident. A study focusing on companies from forty countries shows that corporate governance improvements significantly enhanced GDP growth, productivity and the investment-to-GDP ratio.[3]

Good corporate governance is also of increasing importance to the stability of pension systems around the world. Reforms of private and public pension schemes have taken place on all continents, linking pension payouts more closely to the stability and performance of financial markets and publicly listed companies.[4]

Recent developments in corporate governance

Over the last decade corporate governance has been high on the agenda for strengthening corporate integrity in industrialised and, increasingly, in emerging countries. The stunning corporate governance failures in east Asia in 1997/8 and the United States in 2001/2 spurred tighter regulations to curb managerial opportunism and inefficiencies, prevent corporate fraud and protect minority shareholders. The US Sarbanes–Oxley Act of 2002 is considered a seminal piece of legislation in this regard. The law provides for a wide array of corporate governance reforms, including stronger liability for management in case of corporate fraud, extended reporting and disclosure requirements, additional checks and balances through more independent audit committees, and clearer responsibilities and liabilities for accountants and auditors to improve the accuracy of financial information.

Since Sarbanes–Oxley was passed, pressure has been brought to bear on companies in many countries to separate the jobs of CEO and chairman, and to include more non-executive and independent members on boards to tackle conflicts of interest related to internal controls, financial reporting and executive nomination and compensation.

As a result of these and other efforts, the quality of corporate governance has improved in many countries. The United States is widely believed to lead the way. In a sample of more than 7,500 companies in twenty-three developed countries, only 8 per cent of non-US companies exhibited better corporate governance characteristics than comparable US companies.[5] Among developing regions, Asia, with the exception of China, is the most dynamic area with regard to corporate governance reform. Latin America has also experienced some improvements,

---

2 P. A. Gompers, J. Ishii and A. Metrick, 'Corporate Governance and Equity Prices', *Quarterly Journal of Economics*, vol. 118, no. 1 (2003). For more evidence, see Hermes, *Corporate Governance and Performance: The Missing Links* (London: Hermes, 2007).

3 G. De Nicolo, L. Laeven and K. Ueda, *Corporate Governance Quality: Trends and Real Effects*, Working Paper no. 06/293 (Washington, DC: IMF, 2006).

4 See, for example, OECD, *White Paper on Corporate Governance in Latin America* (Paris: OECD, 2003).

5 R. Aggarwal, I. Erel, R. Stulz and R. Williamson, *Do US Firms Have the Best Corporate Governance?*, Working Paper no. 145/2007 (Brussels: European Corporate Governance Institute, 2007).

though from a smaller base and by a smaller margin than in Asia.[6] Still, much remains to be done. The financial crisis that began in 2007 has highlighted both persistent and new challenges regarding executive remuneration, risk management and conflicts of interest. Even in the most advanced countries, corporate governance is an unfinished agenda that needs to adapt continuously to financial innovations and transforming economies.

Good practice in corporate governance, for example, needs to be extended to the family- and state-owned companies that make up large portions of many countries' economies. Developing private mechanisms, aimed at empowering minority shareholders and other stakeholders to assert their interests and hold management accountable, is lagging behind public checks and balances. Similarly, there is a gap between corporate governance rules on the books and their effective enforcement, which depends critically on resources, information disclosure and the efficacy of the court system.[7]

Key elements of good corporate governance

There is no single best model for corporate governance, since the most effective implementation depends on ownership structures, financial market development and the legal environment of a specific country. A set of key principles and good practices can be discerned, however.

Broadly speaking, corporate governance mechanisms include incentive-based contracts, regulation and laws, competition and monitoring. Monitoring is provided by large shareholders, boards of directors and banks, as well as information-based services such as audit firms, rating agencies and investment analysts. The roles and responsibilities of these external monitors are described elsewhere in this book.[8] The focus here is on four key *internal* building blocks for corporate governance that lay the foundation for companies to be managed in the interest of all stakeholders, and in accordance with laws and public commitments.

(1) Aligning incentives for executives with corporate interests in an accountable manner

Aligning executive compensation with performance is important not only for preventing managers from unduly appropriating company resources, but also for setting the proper incentives for them to focus on sustainable profitability and adequate risk management.

It is important to use performance-based compensation carefully and make the process of setting executive remuneration as transparent and accountable as possible. To do this, more information must be disclosed, and shareholders must be given a stronger voice in the process. Neither step has been fully implemented, even in the most advanced corporate governance regimes.

---

6 De Nicolo, L. Laeven and K. Ueda, 2006.

7 For more on the enforcement gap in eastern Europe, see E. Berglöf and A. Pajuste, 'Emerging Owners, Eclipsing Markets? Corporate Governance in Central and Eastern Europe', in P. Cornelius and B. Kogut (eds.), *Corporate Governance and Capital Flows in a Global Economy* (Oxford: Oxford University Press, 2003).

8 See articles starting on pages 116 and 131.

Table 1: Disclosure policies for executive remuneration in selected European countries

Current disclosure		Country	Anticipated future disclosure
Individual disclosure Detailed pay policy	HIGH	UK Ireland Netherlands France	More information required on the link between pay and performance, and a focus on peer groups
	MEDIUM	Sweden Germany Switzerland Italy Norway	Pressure to disclose information on individual board members rather than just the CEO/ highest paid executive, with more information on remuneration policies
Aggregate disclosure Limited pay policy	LOW	Finland Spain Portugal Denmark	Pressure to provide individual disclosure and increased information on remuneration policies

Source: 'Executive Compensation Disclosure in Europe', *Executive Remuneration Perspective*, no. 3 (2007).

US rules adopted in 2006 set an example and require that pay disclosure needs to be dis-aggregated per director, all cash and non-cash benefits be listed and the determination of remuneration packages be explained and compared with peer groups. In Europe, the European Commission has reinvigorated its call for better disclosure in the wake of the financial crisis, as disclosure standards vary across the European Union (see table 1).

Disclosure in other regions has an even a longer way to go, as the situation of major Asian countries illustrates (see table 2).

Giving shareholders a stronger voice in deciding executive pay has been pioneered in the United Kingdom. The 'Say on Pay' initiative was introduced in 2002 to provide shareholders with an advisory vote on executive compensation. The programme is widely credited with forcing company boards to explain and justify in much more detail how pay packages are determined. Similar provisions have since been adopted in Australia, the Netherlands, Norway and Sweden, and they could become part of the standard toolbox of corporate governance.[9]

(2) Making boards more independent and effective

The job of the board of directors is to define a company's strategy and major policies. They are charged with appointing, monitoring and, if necessary, dismissing managers, overseeing executive compensation, ensuring the reliability of financial accounts and ensuring the effectiveness of internal controls and external audits, as well as compliance with laws and regulations. Board members should be accountable to shareholders and honour their fiduciary

9 S. Davis, *Does 'Say on Pay' Work? Lessons on Making CEO Compensation Accountable*, Policy Briefing no. 1 (New Haven, CT: Yale School of Management, 2007).

Table 2: Executive remuneration policies in Asia

	Do laws or regulations require disclosing how a director's compensation was reviewed and evaluated?	Is compensation linked to the director's performance?
Bangladesh	No	No
China	No	Yes
Hong Kong	Yes	No
India	Yes	No
Indonesia	Yes	Yes
Malaysia	No, but it is recommended by the Malaysian Corporate Governance Code	Yes
Pakistan	No	No
Philippines	No	No
Singapore	No, but it is recommended by the Code of Corporate Governance	Not mandatory but recommended
South Korea	No	Not mandatory but recommended
Taiwan	Yes	Yes
Thailand	No	Yes
Vietnam	No	No

Source: Adapted from OECD, *Asia: Overview of Corporate Governance Frameworks in 2007* (Paris: OECD, 2007).

relationship with them. As the main internal governance mechanism, directors should be the first line of resistance against managerial opportunism.

As described in chapter 2, however, loyalty and friendship, reciprocal benefits (as when a CEO nominates a director) and time and information constraints can make it difficult for boards to fulfil their oversight roles effectively and accountably.[10] This is even more the case when the CEO also serves as board chairman. Supporting the claim that executives are inclined to capture boards, two observers remarked that 'a true performance disaster is required before boards actually act'.[11]

Boards that are neither too small nor too large to fulfil their duties and include a sufficient number of competent, independent directors who actively participate in audit and compensation committees are essential for sound corporate governance. Government regulations and corporate guidelines are mixed on these issues, however, even where standards of corporate governance are most advanced. In the United States, publicly traded companies are required to have a majority of independent members on their boards. In the European Union, the

---

10 See article starting on page 13.
11 A. Shleifer and R. Vishny, 'A Survey of Corporate Governance', *Journal of Finance*, vol. 52, no. 2 (1997).

Table 3: Independent directors and corporate governance in the Middle East and north Africa

Are there recommended proportions of independent board members?	
Algeria	Yes, voluntary
Bahrain	Yes, voluntary
Egypt	No
Jordan	No
Kuwait	No
Morocco	Yes, voluntary
Oman	No
Qatar	No
Tunisia	Yes, voluntary
United Arab Emirates	No

Source: Adapted from OECD, *Advancing the Corporate Governance Agenda in the Middle East and North Africa: A Survey of Legal and Institutional Frameworks* (Paris: OECD, 2005).

European Commission has expressed concerns that regulations on board composition and the definition of independence itself vary widely across member states. '[Managers] may still be able to have a major influence on their own remuneration and control over the company's accounts may be insufficient,' the commission said in 2007. 'The costs for the company and risk of abuse may remain high.'[12]

Creating a stronger role for independent directors is an issue everywhere. In the fledgling corporate governance frameworks in the Middle East and north Africa, requirements were still largely absent or purely voluntary as of 2005 (see table 3).

In Latin America, empirical evidence shows some encouraging developments. A remarkable 91 per cent of the directors of the largest 100 companies traded on the Brazilian exchange BOVESPA (*Bolsa de Valores de São Paulo*) were outside directors as of 2006.[13] In Chile, Colombia, Mexico and Peru, more than a half of all directors were considered independent as of 2002.[14]

A stronger role for independent directors is an important, but not the only, element needed for effective corporate governance, especially when independent directors are nominated by a controlling shareholder. Additional measures with regard to strengthening board independence and accountability should include stronger liability of directors for negligence

---

12 European Commission, *Report on the Application by the Member States of the EU of the Commission Recommendation on the Role of Non-executive or Supervisory Directors of Listed Companies and on the Committees of the (Supervisory) Board*, staff working document (Brussels: European Commission, 2007).
13 Research by the author. Friendship or kinship ties may still limit formal independence.
14 OECD, 2003.

and innovative approaches, such as holding committee and board meetings without the presence of executives. This has proved very popular in the United States, where the share of firms whose board of directors met without their CEO jumped from 41 per cent in 2002 to 93 per cent in 2004.[15]

(3) Recognising the role of whistleblowers

Employees are the single most important group of actors capable of detecting corporate fraud, and as such they represent an extraordinarily important pillar in the system of checks and balances that comprise corporate governance. According to an analysis of publicly reported cases of corporate fraud in large US companies between 1996 and 2004, employees exposed nearly a fifth of the cases – more than any other players, including regulators, auditors and the media.[16] A survey of companies and the way they themselves detect internal corporate fraud confirms the importance of employees in this context. Here companies reported that almost one-third of fraud cases were revealed by whistleblowers and internal tip-offs.[17] Recognising the important role of employees, companies are increasingly integrating hotlines and whistleblower protection into their compliance and fraud detection programmes, and typically regard them as effective (see figure 7).

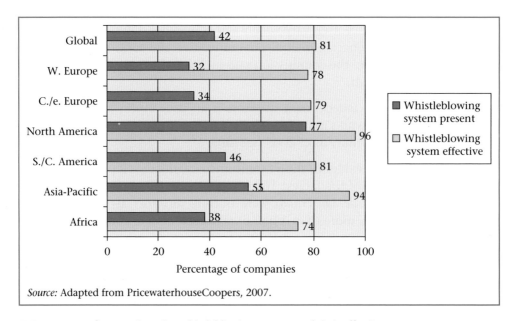

Source: Adapted from PricewaterhouseCoopers, 2007.

Figure 7: Percentage of companies using whistleblowing systems and their effectiveness

15 *The Economist* (UK), 11 November 2004.
16 A. Dyck, A. Morse and L. Zingales, *Who Blows the Whistle on Corporate Fraud?*, Working Paper no. 618 (Chicago: Center for Research in Security Prices, University of Chicago, 2007).
17 PricewaterhouseCoopers, *Economic Crime: People, Culture and Controls: The 4th Biennial Global Economic Crime Survey* (London: PricewaterhouseCoopers, 2007).

Table 4: Whistleblower laws for private sector employees in Asia	
Does the legal and regulatory framework provide whistleblower protection?	
Bangladesh	No
China	No
Hong Kong	No
India	No statutory provision but listed companies are highly encouraged
Indonesia	Protection only for criminal witnesses or victims
Malaysia	Yes
Pakistan	No
Philippines	No
Singapore	Protection for auditors
South Korea	Yes
Taiwan	Yes (Witness Protection Act)
Thailand	No (but the draft Securities and Exchange Act would provide protection for employees who report to the regulator or support its investigation)

Source: Adapted from OECD, 2007.

In Europe and Africa, however, only about one-third of companies had adopted whistleblowing systems as of 2007. Moreover, even in the leading region of North America, still more than a quarter of companies lack this important mechanism.

In terms of the legal protection of whistleblowers in the private sector, regulations are extremely fragmented. As of 2007 only New Zealand, South Africa and the United Kingdom had passed comprehensive whistleblower protection to cover both the public and private sectors. Japan has a whistleblower law that applies to the private sector. The United States' Sarbanes–Oxley Act requires whistleblower protection for publicly listed companies. Other countries recognise and protect whistleblowing with regard to environmental, labour, bribery, accounting and auditing issues, but do not provide comprehensive protection for corporate wrongdoing in general (see table 4).[18]

The United States also provides an interesting example of how to make whistleblowing more effective. Under the False Claims Act, employees who expose fraud against the government can receive awards ranging from 15 to 30 per cent of the recovered losses. Concerns that such financial reward may lead to opportunistic overuse of whistleblowing were not borne out by reality. Whistleblowing on corporate fraud in the United States has been found to be most salient in the health sector, and triggered fewer lawsuits that were eventually dismissed as

18 D. Banisar, *Whistleblowing: International Standards and Developments* (Mexico City: Instituto de Investigaciones Sociales, Universidad Nacional Autónoma de México, 2006); K. Drew, *Whistle Blowing and Corruption: An Initial and Comparative Review* (London: Public Services International Research Unit, University of Greenwich, 2003).

frivolous than was the case in other industries in which other fraud detection mechanisms played a greater role.[19]

(4) A mechanism for governance self-selection: the innovative approach of BOVESPA

In the late 1990s the Brazilian stock exchange BOVESPA was mired in appalling conditions, with many public companies going private, small numbers of initial public offerings (IPOs) and issuances of new shares, a shrinking trading volume, low market capitalisation of companies, and major Brazilian companies listing their shares on the New York Stock Exchange.

Probably acknowledging the insurmountable political economy hurdles to adopting legislation protecting minority shareholders' rights, BOVESPA launched new listing segments in 2001 called Special Corporate Governance Levels and Novo Mercado. Companies listed under these segments voluntarily agree and confirm by contract to adopt higher corporate governance standards than those required by law. This mechanism of certification allows companies to self-select their respective governance quality, fitting the rising demand for better governance from domestic and foreign investors, as well as facilitating Brazilian companies' access to global capital markets. This private-led innovation has been credited with increasing the number of IPOs and new share issues. Notably, foreign investors have purchased an overwhelming portion of the public offerings, particularly IPOs.[20]

This example carries an encouraging message for other developing countries: companies that take the initiative and upgrade their internal corporate governance mechanisms are rewarded by the market and can compensate for shortcomings in the broader institutional environment that deter investors and business partners. A World Bank study of more than 370 firms in fourteen emerging markets finds that firm-level corporate governance has a significant impact on performance and market valuation, and makes an even bigger impact in countries with a weak legal environment.[21]

This highlights once more the fact that internal corporate governance matters. Though interlinked with the broader regulatory and legal environment, it can act as an important driver of reform for higher corporate integrity and better business performance, even when laws and institutions are weak.

---

19 A. Dyck, A. Morse and L. Zingales, 2007.
20 See D. M. Aldrighi, 'Especulações sobre o Mercado de Capitais no Brasil', paper presented at a seminar at the University of São Paulo; available at www.econ.fea.usp.br/seculo_xxi/arquivos/30_05_aldrighi.pdf.
21 L. F. Klapper and I. Love, *Corporate Governance, Investor Protection and Performance in Emerging Markets*, Policy Research Working Paper no. 2818 (Washington, DC: World Bank, 2002).

New centres of economic power: new challenges and priorities for fighting corruption? Corporate governance and corporate integrity in India

Vikramaditya Khanna[1]

All eyes are on India, with recent annual GDP growth rates topping 8 per cent, an ever-burgeoning middle class and remarkable demographics (one-third of the population is under fifteen). India is now the world's fourth largest economy in terms of purchasing power parity,[2] and, though still facing obstacles such as poor infrastructure and corruption, India's overall outlook is very positive.[3] Partly as a result of this economic success, foreign investment is pouring into the country. Until the onset of the financial crisis that began in 2007 this had led to a nearly unprecedented boom in India's stock markets, which has yet to be matched by any of the world's other major emerging economies.

Attracting investor interest in Indian firms has not always been easy. When the country's liberalisation began in 1991, Indian corporate governance was considered dysfunctional by global standards, with weak boards, inconsistent disclosure, frequent insider expropriation and endemic corruption.[4] Stock scandals of the late 1980s and early 1990s further weakened India's essentially moribund stock markets.

Prospects improved in the mid-1990s, when Indian firms began searching for capital to expand into competitive spaces created by the government's withdrawal from certain sectors (such as telecommunications) and to finance the growth of outsourcing. Given the poor state of the domestic stock markets, however, industry could not expect domestic investment alone to provide the necessary capital. Foreign capital was needed, and this required improved corporate governance.

In 1998 the Confederation of Indian Industry (CII) – a large industry trade association – put forward a voluntary governance code based on international best practices to help enhance governance and assure investors that the practices of the past were history.[5] The code's key recommendations included more independence for boards, audit committees with greater independence and financial expertise, the certification of key results and processes by executives, and enhanced disclosure. Because only a handful of large firms adopted this

---

1 The author is a Professor of Law at the University of Michigan Law School.

2 Central Intelligence Agency (CIA), *The 2008 World Factbook* (Washington, DC: CIA, 2008); World Bank, *India Country Overview 2007* (Washington, DC: World Bank, 2007).

3 Y. Huang and T. Khanna, 'Can India Overtake China?', *Foreign Policy*, July–August 2003.

4 O. Goswami, 'India: The Tide Rises Gradually', in C. P. Oman, *Corporate Governance in Development*, Working Paper no. 180 (Paris: OECD Development Centre, 2001).

5 D. Dharmapala and V. Khanna, *The Anatomy of Corporate Governance Reform in Emerging Markets: The Case of India*, Working Paper no. 84 (Ann Arbor: University of Michigan Law School, 2008); O. Goswami, 2001.

voluntary code, however, a more sustained effort was needed to generate widespread governance improvements and attract greater foreign investment.

The CII and other groups lobbied the Securities and Exchange Board of India (SEBI), which responded in 2000 by devising clause 49 of the stock exchange Listing Agreement. This clause was very similar to the CII code and the United States' Sarbanes–Oxley Act, which was enacted just two years later. Clause 49 was followed by attempts to reform the laws that regulate corporate governance. These reforms, if instituted, could signal important changes in the way business is conducted in India.

Governance improvements could reduce corruption by enhancing disclosure and making corporate boards more independent, which would make it more difficult for companies to use slush funds to bribe officials. In general, stronger governance would reduce the tolerance shown towards corrupt behaviour, as people who demand efficient and ethical behaviour in the private sector would not tolerate endemic corruption in government. The promise of better corporate governance is therefore important to the broader fight against corruption in India. Whether this promise will come to fruition depends on the degree to which the market embraces these reforms, and on compliance and enforcement levels.

Answers to these questions are beginning to emerge. Recent research finds that India's governance reforms and severe sanctions for violations have caused the value of firms to rise.[6] Furthermore, a survey found that Indian firms were generally complying with clause 49's major provisions, although there was room for improvement. Whether better governance will spread beyond these firms into the general Indian economy remains to be seen. Overall, corporate governance practices seem to be changing for the better, though many firms are still not complying or are only providing 'paper compliance'.[7]

High-profile corporate fraud at Satyam, one of India's largest outsourcing companies, that came to light in January 2009, provides a potent reminder that additional reforms are needed.[8] The greater disclosure and regulation of transactions with related parties, such as executives or major shareholders, executive compensation and annual reports would be useful, as would enhanced shareholder voting, performance evaluation of executives and the assurance that companies' compliance programmes address corruption and bribery.

Moreover, a potentially critical element in ensuring better governance and less corruption is stronger enforcement. No enforcement actions under clause 49 were brought until September 2007, when SEBI reportedly began taking action against eighteen government-owned corporations (public sector undertakings, or PSUs), including several prestigious

6 D. Dharmapala and V. Khanna, *Corporate Governance, Enforcement, and Firm Value: Evidence from India*, Olin Working Paper no. 08-005 (Ann Arbor: University of Michigan Law School, 2008); B. S. Black and V. Khanna, 'Can Corporate Governance Reforms Increase Firm Market Values? Event Study Evidence from India', *Journal of Empirical Legal Studies*, vol. 4, no. 4 (2007).
7 N. Balasubramanian, B. Black and V. Khanna, *Firm-level Corporate Governance in Emerging Markets: A Case Study of India*, Olin Working Paper no. 08-011 (Ann Arbor: University of Michigan Law School, 2008).
8 *International Herald Tribune* (US), 11 January 2009.

firms. These actions, stemming from information in quarterly reports filed by stock exchanges, relate to non-compliance with board composition rules.[9] The results of SEBI's actions and the response to the Satyam fraud are very likely to have a sizeable impact on perceptions of enforcement in India.

---

9 D. Dharmapala and V. Khanna, 2008; A. Rukhaiyar, 'Navratnas Join Listing Rule Violators', *Economic Times* (India), 13 September 2007.

From voluntary commitments to responsible conduct: making codes and standards effective and credible
Alan Knight[1]

Company-specific codes of conduct, as described earlier in chapter 4, articulate and underpin a company's own ethical commitment and compliance approach tailored to its specific structure, activities and place of operations.[2] More general industry codes and standards can support and complement these efforts. They provide a template for adopting and effectively communicating key good practices and commitments, and often come with ready-made mechanisms for certification and assurance. The huge potential of standards to drive and promulgate corporate integrity and compliance is not fully recognised, however. Standards are too often associated solely with arcane technical specifications, for anything from paper, to wristwatches to food.

A widening horizon: from technical specifications to corporate responsibility – from rules to principles

Such a view ignores the rapid evolution of standards that has taken place over the last forty years. A growing number of new standards have moved beyond technical specifications to include organisational systems, processes and performance requirements. At the same time, standards have shifted from prescribing detailed rules to setting broader principles that allow for more tailored and flexible adherence. As this new generation of standards and codes development has matured it has begun to be applied to a wider range of issues. During the last fifteen years standards and codes have been increasingly used to cover social and ethical issues: livelihoods, equality, human rights, governance or corruption.

---

1 Alan Knight is head of standards at AccountAbility, an international not-for-profit organisation that develops tools and standards for accountability issues.
2 See article starting on page 83.

At the same time, established standards producers, such as the International Organization for Standardization (ISO), a non-governmental umbrella for national standards bodies from more than 150 countries that has so far published more than 17,000 international standards, have been joined by a multitude of new standards initiatives promoted by the business sector, NGOs, foundations or international organisations. It is estimated that there are now more than 400 standards, codes, frameworks and sets of principles that address corporate sustainability and responsibility issues. As a result, standards no longer simply ensure that products are compatible and that production processes can be coordinated; they have become vital tools to identify, manage and communicate to a broad range of stakeholders the performance associated with corporate qualities, commitments and impacts. These new stakeholders include consumers in a globalised economy, who demand to know that corporations are behaving in an ethically responsible manner.

Some key standards related to corporate integrity

The following widely used standards demonstrate the breadth and diversity of standards relating to corporate sustainability and integrity. Some focus on the quality of management processes or seek to make reporting frameworks better and more comparable. Others encourage compliance with broad human rights principles, seek to ensure sound workplace conditions or focus on a specific sectoral sustainability issue.

- *ISO 9000, 14000 and 26000*: classic standards for corporate quality management (ISO 9000), environmental management (ISO 14001) and soon corporate social responsibility (CSR) (ISO 26000 is expected for 2010), covering a wide range of good management requirements from record-keeping and environmental policy formulation to impact monitoring, reporting and stakeholder engagement.
- *Forest Stewardship Council (FSC)*: forest management certification is a leading global standard for timber that has been grown and harvested according to principles of responsible forest management.
- *SA8000*: a widely used social accountability standard that focuses on making workplace conditions compliant with international labour conventions and human rights principles.
- *UN Global Compact (UNGC)*: the largest global corporate citizenship initiative, it encourages businesses worldwide to align their operations with ten principles of responsible and sustainable corporate conduct.
- *Global Reporting Initiative G3 Guidelines (GRI G3)*: widely used reporting guidelines for companies to make their reporting on environmental, social and other corporate responsibility issues comprehensive, consistent and comparable.
- *AA1000 Assurance Standard (AA1000AS)*: a standard that provides the requirements for evaluating the extent to which an organisation is accountable to its stakeholders.

A 2003 survey of 107 multinational enterprises shows that these and other voluntary standards are seeping into the corporate establishment. Respondents said that the standards that are most influential to their business include: ISO 14000 (46 per cent), Global Reporting Initiative (36 per cent), World Business Council for Sustainable Development (35 per cent), International Labour Organization conventions (35 per cent), UN Global Compact (33 per cent), OECD

Guidelines for Multinational Enterprises (22 per cent), Ethical Trading Initiative (17 per cent), Social Accountability International's SA 8000 (17 per cent); and AccountAbility's Assurance Standard AA1000 (10 per cent).[3]

Driving and demonstrating corporate performance in emerging economies

The diffusion of ISO standards in many developing countries is particularly striking. By December 2007 more than 950,000 certificates in 175 countries for quality management according to ISO 9001 and more than 150,000 certificates in 148 countries for environmental management according to ISO 14001 had been issued.[4]

With more than 200,000 certifications, China is by far the top country for ISO 9001, and India is the fifth largest adopter with some 46,000 certificates. Both are well ahead of key industrialised countries such as Germany (around 45,000), the United States (36,000) or the United Kingdom (35,000). China is also the world's top adopter of environmental management standards under ISO 14000, with over 30,000 certificates.[5] This and related studies demonstrate that ISO certification is an important tool for emerging economies, to communicate the quality of management and environmental performance to business partners and the public abroad and to gain entry into global supply chains.[6] To the extent that they increasingly cover issues of corporate compliance and accountability, such standards can therefore serve as important drivers for corporate integrity in developing country economies.[7]

Factors for success – and failure

The power of a standard to drive corporate integrity and responsibility depends on two things: its reach and its potential for impact.

Achieving reach: facilitating recognition, reducing certification costs

Ensuring the wide adoption of standards is a considerable challenge. The last fifteen years have seen a huge proliferation of standards, and more are being developed every year by a large variety of initiatives. Standards that are not widely adopted by their target groups lose their benchmarking appeal, public visibility and potential for impact. At the same time,

---

3 J. Berman and T. Webb, *Race to the Top: Attracting and Enabling Global Sustainable Business* (Washington, DC: World Bank, 2003).

4 ISO, *The ISO Survey of Certifications 2007* (Geneva: ISO, 2008).

5 Ibid.

6 See, for example, A. A. King, M. J. Lenox and A. Terlaak, 'The Strategic Use of Decentralized Institutions: Exploring Certification with the ISO 14001 Management Standard', *Academy of Management Journal*, vol. 48, no. 6 (2005); M. Grajek, *Diffusion of ISO 9000 Standards and International Trade*, Working Paper no. SP II 2004-16 (Berlin: Social Science Research Center Berlin [WZB], 2004).

7 Studies show that ISO 9000 spreads 'upstream' through supply chains. See C. J. Corbett, 'Global Diffusion of ISO 9000 Certification through Supply Chains', *Manufacturing and Service Operations Management*, vol. 8, no. 4 (2005).

the proliferation of standards means that companies, particularly smaller ones with limited resources, ask themselves which standards they should adopt – or whether they should comply with one at all.

It is one thing to develop a good standard; it is quite another thing to get organisations to use it. Unless a good standard can be scaled up it will not achieve its potential for impact. While the ISO, as an international organisation with more than 150 national member bodies, has the means to promulgate its standards widely, other smaller and less well-resourced groups face a stiffer challenge. There needs to be a way to recognise good standards and accept them internationally to send clear signals to the marketplace. This will help to reduce the proliferation of new standards and make it easier for organisations to decide to use a standard.

Costs for certification can be another barrier to scaling up. Estimates range from less than US$50,000 for small firms to greater than US$200,000 for larger firms.[8] Governments can play a role to promote adoption. Singapore and Pakistan, for example, have subsidised training related to the adoption of environmental and labour standards.[9]

Potential for impact: performance, credibility and independent verification

The potential for a standard to have impact depends on a number of things: (1) an emphasis on performance and outcomes, including performance benchmarks; (2) the flexibility to drive innovation (it is accepted that principle-based rather than rule-based standards are more flexible and drive innovation rather than conformance to minimum requirements); (3) legitimacy in the marketplace, provided by a full multi-stakeholder process for the development of the standards; and (4) an assurance process that is inclusive and that evaluates, judges and provides conclusions on performance issues as well as systems and data.

Performance, outcomes and the flexibility to reward innovation

An emphasis on performance and outcomes, and not just the systems that 'should' enable performance, is important. The widely diffused ISO management system standards focus on specifying the quality of management processes, such as environmental management, rather than specific outcomes, such as emissions or resource use. In addition, they can only encourage compliance with minimum requirements rather than reward innovative, top-of-the-class performance. A case study of mining companies in Peru that adopted the ISO 14001 standard, for example, found that the mandated audits helped discover environmental problems, which were addressed by end-of-pipe technologies, however, rather than by the preferable alternative of cleaner production techniques.[10] Likewise, case evidence from China suggests that the surge in ISO 14001 certifications motivates few, if any, improvements in environmental performance

---

8 R. Watkins and E. Gutzwiller, 'Buying into ISO 14001', *Occupational Health & Safety*, vol. 68, no. 2 (1999).
9 A. Chatterji and M. Toffel, *Shamed and Able: How Firms Respond to Information Disclosure*, Working Paper no. 08-05 (Boston: Harvard Business School, 2007).
10 S. A. Mongrut and S. Valdivia, 'Cleaner Production Techniques in the Peruvian Mining Sector Based on ISO 14001 Audits', *Icfai Journal of Environmental Economics*, vol. 5, no. 1 (2007).

beyond the bottom line of environmental regulations. This also highlights the fact that these types of standards act as complements to environmental regulation rather than replacing it.[11]

Inclusive credibility

Today corporate sustainability and integrity standards are driven by the need not only to improve performance, but also to provide a way for organisations to demonstrate commitment, performance and accountability to external stakeholders – from business partners to consumers, from communities to social or environmental watchdog groups. In order to achieve credibility and legitimacy with all these stakeholders, a standard and its supporting assurance mechanism needs to be developed in an open and inclusive multi-stakeholder process. The Amsterdam-based Global Reporting Initiative continues to refine its G3 reporting guidelines in this way, and AccountAbility of London uses the same approach for its AA1000 standards. This process of standards development is itself becoming more standardised. ISEAL, the International Social and Environmental Accreditation and Labelling Alliance, is an association of international standards developers that produces best practices for designing and implementing social and environmental standards and the associated assurance. Stakeholders need to be engaged at all points – from standard and code development, to organisational strategy development and implementation to public disclosure and assurance.

Certification and assurance: independence matters

Mechanisms for certification or assurance are key to making a standard credible and to monitoring compliance and performance. The credibility of these certification and assurance mechanisms is equally important. Many schemes allow for self-declaration, by which the people who have implemented the standard or code evaluate their own performance and assert that they have done it correctly. Sometimes they have the support of a second party, such as an internal audit group. The preferred route is independent, third-party certification or assurance, in which the provider must demonstrate its qualifications to provide the service and declare its independence from the organisation it is evaluating.

The self-reporting mechanism of the voluntary UN Global Compact has been challenged on exactly this basis. Many CSR reports also fail to avail themselves of the credibility bonus that comes with independent assurance. Of the almost 3,000 corporate social responsibility reports published in 2007, only about 30 per cent had independent assurance.[12] Independently assured reports come out on top by a significant margin in all major assessments of reporting credibility and quality.[13]

Table 5 and figure 8 compare the key voluntary standards described earlier with regard to their reach and potential for impact.

---

11 H. Yin and C. Ma, 'A Hope for a Greener China', *International Marketing Review* (forthcoming 2009).

12 CorporateRegister.com, *Assure View: The CSR Assurance Statement Report* (London: CorporateRegister.com, 2008).

13 Examples include Chartered Certified Accountants' Awards for Sustainability Reporting and the *Global Reporters Survey of Corporate Sustainability Reporting*, published by the United Nations Environment Programme, SustainAbility and Standard & Poor's.

Table 5: Selected standards in comparative perspective

Reach – based on 2008 data published on the website of each initiative[14]	FSC (10,500)	SA8000 (1,780)	ISO 14001 (130,000)	UNGC (5,600)	GRI G3 (1,000)	AA1000AS (300)
Impact[15] scores (maximum 5 [best] per criterion):						
Systems + performance	5	5	3	3	5	4
Rules or principles	5	3	3	5	5	5
Independent judgment (certification /assurance)	3	3	3	1	3	5
Multi-stakeholder	5	5	3	4	5	5
Total potential for impact	18	16	12	13	18	19

Source: Author.

In sum, the surge in standards development and diffusion has the potential to serve as an important driver for more corporate integrity around the world. A growing number of standards that address aspects of corporate responsibility and sustainability provide both strong encouragement and a continuously enhanced range of templates for companies to strengthen their social and environmental performance and communicate their commitments to external stakeholders. The broad adoption of open and inclusive standard development processes, more pressure for independent assurance and certification, and more harmonisation, mutual recognition and coordinated standard design will ensure that current and future standards fulfil their potential to drive corporate integrity.

---

14 One organisation may have one or many certificates, depending on how the standard is organised, so numbers for 'Reach' are difficult to compare.

15 The focus here is on the conditions that create the potential for impact. Four assumptions guide the analysis of potential impact:

(1) performance is of primary importance, as, although systems are good, they must be supported by performance benchmarks;

(2) principles are better than rules, since they are more flexible and drive innovation rather than conformance to minimum requirements;

(3) assurance that evaluates, judges and provides conclusions is better than certification that simply applies a pass/fail response to criteria; and

(4) a full multi-stakeholder process for the development of the standards provides higher legitimacy.

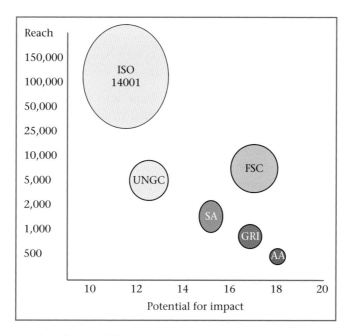

Figure 8: Key standards: reach and potential impact

The role of investors in strengthening corporate integrity and responsibility
Dieter Zinnbauer[1]

Responsible investing, the concept of considering environmental, social and governance criteria in the strategy and management of financial investments, is not a new phenomenon.

In the middle of the eighteenth century religious movements such as the Methodists and Quakers applied ethical guidelines to their financial dealings in the emerging modern capitalist economy. From the 1960s and 1970s onwards the anti-war, anti-apartheid and environmental movements have helped broaden the responsible investment (RI)[2] agenda and deepen its use as a tool for progressive politics. Since the 1990s the principle that citizens and corporations should take broader responsibility for the social, environmental and ethical implications

---

1 Dieter Zinnbauer is editor-in-chief of the *Global Corruption Report*.
2 This article uses the newer term, 'responsible investment', as compared to the older term of 'socially responsible investment' (SRI), which refers to the same concept.

of their consumption, production and investment activities has gained further momentum. This recent trend has been fuelled by a variety of factors, including human rights, global trade, climate change, weapons manufacturing and workplace issues such as sweatshops and child labour.

Investment, in its forward-looking function to shape and underwrite economic activities, assumes a particularly strategic role in aligning market structures and behaviour with societal values. At the same time, mainstream investors increasingly realise the material importance of many environmental, social and governance (ESG) criteria for sustainable business success. Superior environmental performance is associated with future competitive advantages in the context of rising energy prices and more stringent regulations. A proactive approach to social responsibilities is more and more valued for consumer loyalty and brand protection, while sound governance practices are increasingly recognised as indicators of effective risk and overall sound corporate management.

Empirically, such a direct causal link is difficult to prove, on account of the large array of intervening factors. A large number of studies point to a mutually reinforcing relationship between corporate social performance and corporate financial performance, however, and indicate that RI-oriented investment portfolios deliver returns that either match or outperform conventional portfolios.[3]

As a result, responsible investment has developed into a sizeable market force and continues to grow at a strong pace. The United States and Europe, the latter led by the United Kingdom, the Netherlands and Nordic countries, are the major centres of RI activity. Together they account for 92 per cent of the global RI market of approximately €5 trillion. A total of US$2.71 trillion, roughly 11 per cent of all assets under professional management, were estimated to be involved in RI in the United States at the end of 2007. In Europe, RI-related assets had more than doubled between 2005 and 2007, reaching €2.65 trillion, or 17.5 per cent of all managed assets.[4]

Tools of the trade

Ethical investors seek to influence corporations through three major strategies. The most straightforward way is to exclude companies from investment portfolios that violate specific ethical criteria (negative screening) or focus investments only on the top-performing companies in a specific category or industry (positive selection). In the US market alone, more than 250 funds offer portfolios based on such positive and negative screening techniques. More than US$2 trillion of assets are invested in screened portfolios, directing considerable resources into responsible investments.[5]

---

3 C. Juravle and A. Lewis, 'Identifying Impediments to SRI in Europe: A Review of the Practitioner and Academic Literature', *Business Ethics: A European Review*, vol. 17, no. 3 (2008).

4 Eurosif, *European SRI Study 2008* (Paris: Eurosif, 2008); Social Investment Forum, *2007 Report on Socially Responsible Investing Trends in the United States* (Washington, DC: Social Investment Forum, 2008).

5 Social Investment Forum, 2008.

Seeking informal private meetings with companies to encourage them to improve their ESG performance is a second RI strategy popular with large institutional investors in Europe.[6]

Finally, shareholder resolutions and proxy voting are used to pressure companies to recognise ESG concerns more substantively. These high-profile techniques, often used by large US and UK investors, have had positive impacts on company performance as well as corporate policies.[7] Institutional investors in the United States controlling almost US$740 billion in 2007 co-sponsored 367 resolutions on ESG issues in 2006.[8]

Both investment screening and engagement are aided by a growing number of indices and ratings that seek to assess the performance of companies on ESG issues. Two major indices of particular importance for bribery and corruption issues are as follows.

- The FTSE4Good index, formed by the *Financial Times* and London Stock Exchange, which screens companies based on globally recognised corporate responsibility standards, including environmental performance, stakeholder relationships, human rights and supply chain management. In 2006 it added a 'countering bribery' set of criteria, based on the Business Principles for Countering Bribery developed by TI and Social Accountability International.
- The Dow Jones Sustainability Index, which examines the content, implementation and reporting of codes of conduct and anti-corruption/bribery provisions, also drawing on the Business Principles for Countering Bribery.

The road ahead for responsible investment

Despite impressive growth rates and a growing track record of influence, responsible investment is far from fully utilising its potential to incentivise responsible corporate behaviour and compliance.

Integrating environmental, social and governance considerations into conventional investment models and valuation is key to mainstreaming RI, but it remains a big challenge even in Europe, the leading region for ethical investment. A focus on short-term financial results, rather than longer-term performance, and a narrow view by many conventional analysts of what is of material importance to profitability are major impediments to stronger integration.[9]

Achieving global reach is another concern. As yet only 8 per cent of the global RI market is outside Europe and the United States. Asia is gradually coming on board, but it is growing from a low base. Japan saw the launch of its first RI fund in 1999 and its first RI stock index in

---

6 See article starting on page 110.
7 B. Buchanan and T. Yang, 'A Comparative Analysis of Shareholder Activism in the US and UK: Evidence from Shareholder Proposals', paper prepared for the 2008 Financial Management Association International annual meeting, Dallas, 8–11 October 2008.
8 Social Investment Forum, 2008.
9 C. Juravle and A. Lewis, 2008.

2003.[10] In India the first stock index for ESG issues was established in 2008.[11] In South Korea shareholder activism emerged in 1997 and is still considered to be in a nascent stage.[12]

Policy intervention can provide an important stimulus to the uptake of RI by helping savers understand better how ethically their money is invested and by facilitating reporting by companies on their ESG performance. Several European countries, including the United Kingdom, Germany and Belgium, require pension funds to disclose their RI policies.[13] France has made social and environmental reporting compulsory for companies.[14] Again, the challenge is to get these useful disclosure obligations required in more countries and for more asset classes.

Spreading responsible investing beyond conventional investment portfolios to other investment forms is also imperative. Even institutional investors committed to RI are slow in incorporating ESG criteria into fixed-income investments.[15] Some private equity funds, and even some hedge funds, already offer responsible investment options, but without more transparency regarding their investment policies the public pressure for stronger integration of ESG principles is likely to remain low.[16] Sovereign wealth funds that administer the public wealth of their citizens may have a specific fiduciary duty to reflect broad social ethical preference in their investment strategies, but with some few notable exceptions they leave the public in the dark concerning their investment policies.[17]

ESG measurement and reporting practices are also an important area for improvement. More awareness and transparency in connection with the specifics of responsible investment policies is essential to distinguish RI funds that simply screen out tobacco companies from those that practice sophisticated analysis and engagement with regard to a comprehensive set of ESG issues.

With respect to the availability of ESG information, a pan-European survey of analysts indicates that the sustainability reporting of companies has improved, but is still viewed as unsatisfactory.[18] At the same time, companies complain about the lack of standardisation and transparency of ESG questionnaires. A first set of academic studies on ESG rating systems highlights the fact that even the most widely used ESG indices and specialised corporate governance ratings are often unable to predict future failings of companies with regard to key governance issues.[19]

---

10 E. Adachi, 'SRI in Japan', paper presented at the World Business Council for Sustainable Development conference 'SRI in Taiwan', Taipei, 24 October 2003.

11 Principles for Responsible Investment (PRI), *PRI Report on Progress 2008* (New York: PRI, 2008).

12 J. Kim and J. Kim, 'Shareholder Activism in Korea: A Review of How PSPD Has Used Legal Measures to Strengthen Korean Corporate Governance', *Journal of Korean Law*, vol. 1, no. 1 (2001).

13 Eurosif, 2008.

14 C. Juravle and A. Lewis, 2008.

15 PRI, 2008.

16 J. Dobris, *SRI: Shibboleth or Canard (Socially Responsible Investing, That Is)*, Legal Studies Research Paper no. 121 (Davis: University of California-Davis, 2007).

17 See article starting on page 112.

18 C. Juravle and A. Lewis, 2008.

19 A. Chatterji and D. Levine, *Imitate or Differentiate? Evaluating the Validity of Corporate Social Responsibility Ratings*, Working Paper no. 37 (Berkeley: Center for Responsible Business, University of California-Berkeley, 2008).

Collective action has emerged as a promising approach to addressing some of these challenges. By May 2008 more than 360 asset owners, investment managers and RI service providers had signed up to the UN-sponsored Principles for Responsible Investment initiative. Launched in 2005, the initiative commits signatories to a shared set of principles for practising and promulgating responsible investment. It also offers a collaboration platform for collective efforts to refine ESG research methodologies, joint engagement with companies to improve ESG performance and outreach efforts to extend RI to emerging and developing nations.[20]

RI in the context of global policy challenges

The financial crisis that began to unfold in 2007 presents both challenges and opportunities for responsible investment. The growing appreciation of transparency, accountability and the long-term prospects of financial investment are closely aligned with RI core principles and could spur growing demand for such investment strategies. Polled in late 2008 about their plans for asset allocations, a quarter of European and North American pension fund managers indicated that they intend to increase the proportion of RI investments.[21] At the same time, the financial crisis may prompt RI investors to pay more attention to the governance elements of the ESG criteria and consider transparency and accountability even more strongly in their screenings.[22]

Climate change is another global policy challenge of importance to RI. Tackling global warming will require channelling resources to the most climate-responsible companies, which in turn depends critically on functioning sustainability reporting and an ESG-orientated investment system.

Very importantly, the governance dimension of ESG in this context is not an optional addendum to environmental reporting but a cross-cutting precondition for turning the private sector's green or social ambitions into sound and responsible corporate performance.

The issue of climate change also highlights the fact that responsible investment is more than just an important mechanism for converting the ethical principles that societies have chosen for themselves into the blueprint for future economic activities. It is also an essential tool to help markets respond to pressing global challenges and ensure the sustainability and long-term profitability of economic activity. This means that RI is in the strong interest of everyone – the ethically motivated saver as well as the financial investor.

---

20 PRI, 2008.
21 *Financial Times* (UK), 10 November 2008.
22 Ethical Corporation, 'Financial Crisis: Social Investment – Crunch Time for Ethical Investing', 28 October 2008, see www.ethicalcorp.com/content.asp?ContentID=6159.

View from the inside – How investors can boost anti-corruption efforts

Hans-Christoph Hirt and Jennifer Walmsley[1]

The position of investors in advocating a no-bribery policy for companies is, potentially, a tricky one. Does it make sense to rail against kickbacks when such payments help companies win contracts and thus generate better returns for investors? Far from being a misappropriation of shareholder money, slipping a sweetener under the table to secure the outcome of a competitive tender could well be regarded as a profitable use of funds, and, indeed, the only way to do business in some areas of the world.

Unfortunately, it is not quite that simple. While bribes may often go undetected, the outcome is invariably the destruction of value, both at the level of individual companies and at the macroeconomic level in the markets in which bribery is tolerated.

From the perspective of an investor with widely diversified assets, bribery can reduce returns across his or her portfolios because the actions of one corrupt company can damage the business of competitors unable to win contracts in a fair competition. For companies, the repercussions can be far-reaching. Once malfeasance comes to light, the result will almost certainly be expensive and time-consuming investigations, dismissals of implicated individuals, fines or even prison sentences. A company found guilty of corruption will find its social licence to operate badly damaged and its future business prospects jeopardised or even eliminated. Capital-raising will become more expensive. Its attractiveness as an employer is also likely to be severely impeded, at a time when corporate ethics have never been so critical in the job market.

Companies with a culture of turning a blind eye to kickbacks are also far more likely to tolerate other illegal behaviours. If controls around bribery and corruption are lax, what other value-destroying activities are going unpunished? Companies doing business in countries with relatively low standards of transparency must make it clear to all employees and suppliers that lower standards in business integrity are not an option. Hermes Equity Ownership Services certainly sees the existence, and, more importantly, the effective enforcement, of comprehensive transparency and anti-corruption policies and practices as key indicators of management integrity and trustworthiness.

For all these reasons, it is important for long-term investors to protect clients' investments by engaging with companies in which the risks of bribery and corruption do not appear to be well managed. Here is an example.

---

1 Hans-Christoph Hirt is a director and Jennifer Walmsley is an associate director at Hermes Equity Ownership Services, an institutional investment company with more than £35 billion under management.

Following media reports about inappropriate businesses practices and a number of compliance-related lawsuits, Hermes began a process of intensive engagement with the company that was implicated in these reports. The company, which is involved in a range of sectors including defence and security systems, adopted a code of conduct covering compliance and set up an ethics committee to monitor its implementation. Nevertheless, the press has continued to report regularly on compliance issues and a number of pending lawsuits. While the company can argue that it has never been found guilty of any charges and its practices have changed since the cases were filed, the frequency, sources and substantiation of the allegations are of continued concern.

After several discussions it became clear that Hermes would need to escalate its engagement in order to effect further change. Initially the company's chairman adopted very much the same line as other company representatives. Hermes explained that past and present allegations of misconduct and the company's continuing significant exposure to corruption risks required further measures to reassure investors.

Hermes then recommended that the company implement an external validation of its systems and procedures and, alongside this, take steps to improve its communication with the market. The company agreed to a set of concrete measures, including a forensic audit carried out by a specialised firm and better reporting on how the systems and procedures work in practice and on how the company monitors their effectiveness.

Hermes also offered to assist the company in communicating to the market the positive steps it has taken, and is continuing its engagement to ensure that the company puts the proposals into practice.

Such activities are part of a growing tide of investor interest in preventing bribery and corruption at the companies in which they invest. For example, the International Corporate Governance Network, an umbrella organisation for institutional investors with more than US$10 trillion under management, is developing anti-corruption principles that will provide investors with a framework to undertake engagements such as those described here.[2]

---

2 See www.icgn.org.

Sovereign wealth funds: a challenge for governance and transparency

Pierre Habbard[1]

The rapid growth of sovereign wealth funds (SWFs) in the past five years has changed the landscape of global asset ownership and established a number of emerging economies as significant players in global financial markets. SWFs are comprised of assets that governments keep separate from their regular budgeting and asset management processes. The major SWFs in the Middle East, Norway, Russia and a few regional funds are based largely on revenues from oil and other natural resources. China's SWF draws mainly on foreign exchange earnings from its huge trade surplus. Others, such as Singapore's Temasek Holdings, reinvest budget surpluses or privatisation proceeds. Of the estimated US$3 trillion under SWF management, an estimated US$2.2 trillion is managed by just seven funds – those in the United Arab Emirates, Norway, Singapore, Kuwait and China.[2] Total SWF investments are expected to grow to up to US$10 to 15 trillion by 2015.[3]

As with the recent boom in alternative investment assets – hedge funds and private equity – the global economic muscle of SWFs, in combination with their lightly regulated nature, if not outright opacity, has raised a series of public concerns, including:

- on the home country side, that public wealth and savings are not managed in a transparent and accountable manner and that investments are not made in line with basic ethical principles of the country; and
- on the recipient's side, that sovereign wealth funds are misused as levers for politics, that they present conflicts of interest for governments that act both as investors and regulators, and that SWFs could be a poorly understood source of financial instability alongside hedge funds and other lightly regulated investments.

Transparency and accountability issues

Little is known about most SWFs' investment policies, governance structures and accountability mechanisms. Only Norway and Alaska release audited financial reports to the public. In the case of the Kuwait Investment Authority (KIA), disclosure to the public of the funds' assets is actually prohibited by law, and until June 2007 the KIA would not even reveal the total value of its holdings.[4]

---

1 Pierre Habbard is senior policy advisor at the Trade Union Advisory Committee to the OECD, Paris.
2 C. Ervin, 'Should Sovereign Wealth Funds Be Treated Differently than Other Investors? An OECD Project Has Set Out to Answer This Question', *OECD Observer*, no. 267 (May–June 2008).
3 R. M. Kimmitt, 'Public Footprints in Private Markets: Sovereign Wealth Funds and the World Economy', *Foreign Affairs*, vol. 87, no. 1 (2008).
4 E. M. Truman, *Sovereign Wealth Funds: The Need for Greater Transparency and Accountability*, Policy Brief no. PB07-6 (Washington, DC: Peterson Institute for International Economics, 2007).

Part of the problem is the ad hoc nature of SWF regulations, which in many instances exempt SWFs from regulations that apply to other institutional investors. This situation raises questions about potential conflicts of interest between a government's regulatory and supervisory duties and its SWF ownership functions. Along these lines, the US Securities and Exchange Commission expressed concerns that the much-needed cooperation with the SEC's overseas counterparts could be at risk when investigating a SWF's investment behaviour.[5] Accountability is also an issue. A study of twenty large SWFs found that more than one-fifth were not accountable to the legislature and only 16 per cent were audited by the legislature.[6]

Some SWFs have released their codes of ethics – including Singapore's Temasek Holdings and Government Investment Corporation, Kuwait's KIA and the United States' Alaska Permanent Fund. None of the top fifteen SWFs have developed compliance programmes for their ethical codes, however, with the notable exception of Norway.[7]

The Norwegian Government Pension Fund – Global is the second largest pension fund in the world, with assets of around US$400 billion, and it sets standards for transparency and accountability by releasing extensive information on its investment strategy, its quarterly results and its stock and bond holdings of individual countries and corporations. Few other SWFs match these practices.

Norway's SWF is also leading the way in investing the wealth of the citizenry in line with ethical investment principles. For example, it is among the signatories of the UN Principles for Responsible Investment,[8] and divested from sixteen companies for breach of its ethical guidelines, including a violation of core labour standards as defined by the International Labour Organization (ILO).[9]

Raising standards collectively

Much work remains to be done in the area of the SWF governance and transparency, on both the home- and host-country sides.

In May 2008 the OECD Ministerial Council emphasised that SWF home countries and SWFs themselves can enhance confidence by strengthening transparency and governance.[10] The council further supported the IMF's ongoing work on best governance practices.[11] In October

---

5 Christopher Cox, chairman US Securities and Exchange Commission (SEC), 'The Rise of Sovereign Business', speech, Washington, DC, 5 December 2007.
6 International Working Group of Sovereign Wealth Funds, *Sovereign Wealth Funds: Current Institutional and Operational Practices* (Washington, DC: IMF, 2008).
7 OECD, *The Relevance of the OECD Guidelines for Corporate Governance of State Owned Enterprises to the Governance of State Owned Investment Vehicles*, unpublished working paper (Paris: OECD, 2008).
8 See www.unpri.org.
9 S. Chesterman, 'The Turn to Ethics: Disinvestment from Multinational Corporations for Human Rights Violations – The Case of Norway's Sovereign Wealth Fund', *American University International Law Review*, vol. 23 (2008).
10 'Declaration on Sovereign Wealth Funds and Recipient Country Policies', OECD, Meeting of the Council at Ministerial Level, Paris, 5 June 2008.
11 'IMF Intensifies Work on Sovereign Wealth Funds', *IMF Survey Magazine*, 4 March 2008.

2008 the IMF-led International Working Group of Sovereign Wealth Funds presented twenty-four voluntary guidelines known as the 'Santiago Principles'. The principles' guiding purpose is to install transparent and sound governance structures.[12] No independent enforcement or monitoring mechanism is foreseen to ensure effective compliance with the guidelines, however. Importantly, the text that was agreed by the IMF falls short of disclosure and governance standards as laid down in OECD guidance agreements that are relevant to SWFs, namely the Principles of Corporate Governance, the Guidelines for the Corporate Governance of State-Owned Enterprises and the Guidelines for Multinational Enterprises.

The policy dialogue on SWFs does not come easily. Suspicions of ulterior motives seem to abound in every corner. Because the vast majority of SWFs are hosted by non-OECD countries, the apparent North–South dimension of the discussions does not help. The Trade Union Advisory Committee (TUAC) to the OECD has warned the OECD against the risk of double-standard treatment of SWFs, in contrast to other classes of investors.[13] Indeed, many of the corporate governance and market integrity issues raised by SWFs are common to other lightly regulated investment funds, including hedge funds and private equity. At the same time, any reforms should keep in mind the fact that SWFs are entrusted with the current and future wealth of their citizens, their pension savings, foreign exchange earnings or natural resource revenues. Full public transparency and the strongest standards of public accountability are therefore essential. Citizens have the right to know that their wealth and savings are being managed properly and prudently.

---

12 See www.iwg-swf.org/.
13 TUAC, *OECD Investment Committee Consultation on Sovereign Wealth Funds, 13 December 2007: Comments by the TUAC* (Paris: TUAC, 2007).

Shedding more light on the transparency and accountability of sovereign wealth funds: ranking exercises

Transparency International

A systematic comparison of sovereign wealth funds (SWFs) with regard to important accountability features is an important step in identifying areas for improvement and encouraging collective learning. To this end, a comprehensive scoreboard has been developed at the Peterson Institute for International Economics that assesses the governance structures and behaviour of SWFs.

Rank	Country and fund	Structure	Governance	Accountability, transparency	Behaviour	Total
	Table 6: Sovereign wealth fund scoreboard: leaders and laggards					
1	United States (Alaska) Alaska Permanent Fund	100	80	100	83	94
2	Norway Government Pension Fund – Global	94	100	100	67	92
3	United States (Wyoming) Permanent Mineral Trust Fund	100	90	82	100	91
4	United States (New Mexico) Severance Tax Permanent Fund	100	50	86	100	86
5	Timor-Leste Petroleum Fund for Timor-Leste	100	40	96	50	80
6	Azerbaijan State Oil Fund of the Republic of Azerbaijan	88	60	89	50	77
	. . .					
29	Sudan Oil Revenue Stabilization Account	56	0	14	0	20
30	Brunei Darussalam Brunei Investment Agency	31	0	25	0	18
31	United Arab Emirates (Abu Dhabi) Mubadala Development Company	44	10	7	0	15
32	United Arab Emirates (Dubai) Istithmar World	38	10	7	0	14
33	Qatar Qatar Investment Authority	34	0	2	0	9
34	United Arab Emirates (Abu Dhabi) Abu Dhabi Investment Authority and Council	25	0	4	8	9

Source: Adapted from E. Truman, *A Blueprint for Sovereign Wealth Fund Best Practices*, Policy Brief no. PB08-03 (Washington, DC: Peterson Institute for International Economics, 2008).

Note: Scores are per cent of maximum possible points.

5 Towards a comprehensive business integrity system: checks and balances in the business environment

Indira Carr provides a global overview of legal frameworks for anti-corruption activity and discusses key principles that are of relevance to corruption risks for business. Two supplementary contributions move the analysis from laws to their enforcement. Transparency International examines the extent of resources available to regulatory agencies in different countries and Cristie Ford discusses some innovative tools that promise to make enforcement activities more efficient and effective.

Several other stakeholders in the broader business environment can make important contributions to ensure corporate integrity. Transparency International examines the extent to which auditors, accountants and rating agencies are effective in this respect while Gretta Fenner draws attention to the pivotal role of banks and other financial intermediaries in the fight against corruption. Oscar Lanza traces various contributions by the consumer movement to hold companies to account and Frank Vogl provides a self-critical account of the achievements of civil society groups in advocating for enhanced corporate integrity. Supplementary contributions further deepen some important aspects of the analysis. Elewechi Okike highlights the difficult working conditions faced by accountants and auditors in a country such as Nigeria. Rob Evans recalls the challenges he faced as a journalist when researching a major corruption case in the United Kingdom and Mark Pyman describes some successful multi-stakeholder activities to enhance integrity in the defence industry.

The public rules for private enterprise: corporate anti-corruption legislation in comparative and international perspective
Indira Carr[1]

For many years developing and developed nations alike have had some form of legislation on the books to deal with corruption in its various guises, from bribes and the misappropriation of public funds to the funding of political parties. The laws across jurisdictions were by no means comprehensive, harmonised or thoroughly enforced, however. Furthermore, no national legislation has outlawed the private sector bribing of foreign public officials.

1 Indira Carr is Professor of Law at the University of Surrey, United Kingdom, and Principal Investigator on the UK Art & Humanities Research Council (AHRC) funded project 'Corruption in International Business: Limitations of Law'. Support from the AHRC for funding this project is gratefully acknowledged.

Only in the past decade have regional and international institutions such as the OECD, UN and African Union responded to the call to fight the 'cancer of corruption' with conventions intended to harmonise anti-corruption laws across jurisdictions.

The impetus for this came from a number of directions. The United States lobbied intensely following a 1976 Securities and Exchange Commission study that found that illegal payments by US corporations to foreign public officials and politicians were widespread.[2] Based on this evidence, the United States passed the Foreign Corrupt Practices Act in 1977, which criminalised the bribing of foreign public officials by businesses within its jurisdiction. Further momentum came from international institutions such as the World Bank, which was concerned about high levels of corruption in development programming, and from NGOs committed to fighting corruption, such as Transparency International.

Regional and international anti-corruption conventions

There are currently five major international anti-corruption conventions. In chronological order of when they entered into force, they are:

- Inter-American Convention against Corruption (IACAC), Organisation of American States, March 1997;
- Convention on Combating Bribery of Foreign Public Officials in International Business Transactions, OECD, February 1999;
- Criminal Law Convention on Corruption, Council of Europe (COE), July 2002;
- Convention against Corruption (UNCAC), UN, December 2005; and
- Convention on Preventing and Combating Corruption, African Union (AU), August 2006.

All these conventions other than the OECD's go beyond the classic cases of corruption and bribery by including a wide range of offences, such as the embezzlement of public and private funds, trading in influence, illicit enrichment and abuse of functions (see table 7). Not all conventions are public-sector-centred, as some also address corruption in the private sector, such as the African Union's convention and the UNCAC.

The OECD convention, which has thirty-seven signatories representing most of the main countries involved in trade and investment, has convincingly laid down rules of engagement for private enterprises that deal with foreign public officials in the context of international business. The convention has made a notable impact on the corporate sector, as it has spurred a reassessment of business ethical codes. Additionally, robust monitoring by the OECD's Anti-Bribery Working Group has brought the goal of harmonisation closer, though differences remain due to flexibility in the convention. Table 7 summarises the main scope of these five conventions.

Where do anti-corruption frameworks draw the line between legitimate competitive behaviour and corrupt acts by businesses? The following sections provide an overview of the scope, main

---

2 'Report of the Securities and Exchange Commission on Questionable and Illegal Corporate Payments and Practices', report to the US Senate Committee on Banking, Housing and Urban Affairs, 1976.

Table 7: Offences and related provisions in regional and international anti-corruption conventions

Offences and related provisions	IACAC	OECD	COE	AU convention	UNCAC
Active bribery of domestic public official	✓		✓	✓	✓
Active bribery of foreign public official	✓	✓[3]	✓		✓
Bribery of members of foreign public assemblies; officials of international organisations; members of international parliamentary assemblies; judges and officials of international courts		✓	✓		✓
Active bribery in private sector			✓	✓	✓[4]
Passive bribery in private sector			✓	✓	✓[5]
Illicit enrichment	✓			✓	✓[6]
Diversion of monies, securities, property, etc. for purposes unrelated to those for which they were intended by public official for own/third-party benefit	✓			✓	✓
Omission/act in discharge of duties by public official for illicitly obtaining benefit for himself/third party	✓			✓	✓
Trading in influence			✓	✓	✓
Fraudulent use/concealment of property derived through corruption offences	✓			✓	✓
Transparency in funding of political parties				✓	
Accounting offences		✓	✓		
Corporate liability		✓	✓	✓	✓
Bank secrecy	✓		✓	✓	✓
Laundering of proceeds		✓	✓	✓	✓

Source: Author.

---

3 Restricted to the conduct of international business.
4 Optional.
5 Optional.
6 Optional.

principles and sanctions that the evolving norms of anti-bribery laws and regulations establish to tackle the supply side of corruption, providing the boundaries for legal business behaviour.[7]

What not to do: corruption means much more than the greasing of palms of government officials and civil servants

A concise legal definition of bribery is difficult to establish, and most legal frameworks enumerate a range of behaviours regarded as illegal. On the bribe-payers' side (active bribery), the standard approach is to prohibit 'the promising, offering or giving of a bribe', which highlights the fact that even attempting to bribe is punishable and neither agreement nor awareness by the recipient is required. Nor is the corrupt act confined to payments of money. The OECD convention, for example, construes it as *any* undue advantage, irrespective of value, results, perception of local custom, tolerance or alleged necessity.[8]

Likewise, the beneficiaries of such an undue advantage need not only be domestic civil servants or government officials. Evolving international norms cast a wider net and also cover parliamentarians, public agencies, enterprises and service providers, as well as foreign public officials and international organisations. Granting an undue advantage is also increasingly considered illegal when the recipients are friends, family members or other people in the environment of the public officials with the potential of influencing his or her decisions.[9]

Outsourcing corruption through the use of intermediaries: a disappearing loophole

The UN, OECD and Council of Europe conventions all cover indirect forms of bribery, in which a briber gives or offers a bribe to an official through an intermediary. Such bribes could be made through an agent, financial institution or company. Many countries, however, have been relatively slow to incorporate bribery through intermediaries into their anti-corruption laws – particularly in explicit terms.

Among those that have taken steps forward, Hungary has formally included both intermediaries and third-party beneficiaries in its criminal code. This was confirmed when the Supreme Court held an intermediary liable for influence-trafficking for accepting a bribe to help a person obtain a driver's licence.[10] Iceland and the Netherlands are among the countries whose criminal laws do not expressly mention bribes made through intermediaries, but whose authorities say that the existing laws are broad enough to include intermediaries.[11] In the United States, foreign subsidiaries of domestic companies previously excluded from the FCPA can now be brought in as 'agents' susceptible to investigation and prosecution.[12]

---

7 OECD, *Corruption: A Glossary of International Standards in Criminal Law* (Paris: OECD, 2008).

8 See OECD convention, commentaries nos. 7 and 8.

9 Some qualifications may apply and provide loopholes, such as requiring knowledge by the public officials or a direct link between the bribe and the favour granted in return.

10 OECD, *Hungary: Phase 2* (Paris: OECD, 2005).

11 OECD, *The Netherlands: Phase 2* (Paris: OECD, 2006); *Iceland: Phase 2* (Paris: OECD, 2003).

12 *Mondaq Business Briefing* (UK), 6 May 2008.

Just paying to get things done? The diminishing tolerance for facilitation payments

The treatment of payments made to obtain routine services from public officials who provide these services as part of their customary duties (facilitation payments) is one of the most controversial issues in anti-bribery legislation.

The UNCAC does not include an explicit distinction between bribes and facilitation payments but leaves the door open for such a practice in domestic law. The OECD convention does distinguish between the two types of payments, though it does not classify facilitation payments as illegal.[13] This justification could well be pragmatic, since in many parts of the world such payments are seen as a necessary part of conducting business. The practice introduces a double standard and creates ample scope for abuse, however, because there is no upper limit on facilitation payments.

Different countries treat facilitation payments differently. Some countries, such as France, do not recognise this distinction at all. The same is true for the United Kingdom and Japan, but official guidance in these countries suggests that facilitation payments may not be prosecuted.[14] Others, including Canada, South Korea, the United States and Australia, recognise the distinction by including a facilitation payment defence. Neither Australia nor the United States sets upper limits for facilitation payments.

Such a legal distinction between legitimate facilitation payments and illegal corruption is problematic and heavily contested, for several reasons. First, the distinction between facilitation payments and bribes is precariously open to interpretation. Does a civil servant who expedites a specific service against payments simply execute a routine task, or does he or she help the bribe-payer jump the queue to the disadvantage of other, less well-placed applicants? Such uncertainty translates into moral ambiguity, and creates room for abuse and liberal interpretation that could encourage companies to take risks in the mistaken belief that the facilitation payment defence would protect them from prosecution.

On the recipient's side, lower-level public officials are encouraged to delay or deny services in order to extract facilitation payments. In a broader perspective, this promotes a culture and perception of corruption among public service providers that erodes trust in fair and accountable public institutions. Equally importantly, facilitation payments and the extra income they provide can give rise to an intricate and cascading system of corruption in the awarding of public sector jobs.

As the *Global Corruption Report 2008* demonstrates, lower-level officials in India's water sector were found to be buying their positions and recouping these 'investments' by extracting extra payments from the clients they were supposed to serve. Similarly, higher-level officials have to share with their superiors some of the rents they extract from selling jobs and turning a blind eye to corrupt behaviour on the ground.[15] As a result, many small payments of 'tea money', as facilitation payments are sometimes euphemistically called, are funnelled upwards through

---

13 See OECD convention, paragraph 1, commentary no. 9.
14 For the United Kingdom, see 'Advice & Support: Preparing to Trade', UK Trade and Investment; for Japan, see 'Guidelines to Prevent Bribery of Foreign Public Officials', Ministry of Economy, Trade and Industry, 2004.
15 See TI, *Global Corruption Report 2008* (Cambridge: Cambridge University Press, 2008).

the political system, promulgating a corrupt bureaucracy in which jobs go to the highest bidder and integrity is discouraged.

In sum, the impact of facilitation payments is far from trivial, making a legal distinction between legal and illegal bribes highly questionable, and arguing for its elimination.

Fines for bribery as calculable business risks? A growing and deepening toolbox of sanctions

International standards require *effective, proportionate and dissuasive sanctions* for bribery offences and require the confiscation of the bribe and any proceeds derived from it. As a result, companies implicated in bribery offences are typically confronted with a range of sanctions, from administrative fines and civil liabilities to criminal sentences. Individual employees found guilty of bribing foreign public officials face a maximum prison sentence of five years in many OECD countries. Companies may be subject to sanctions including large fines, debarment from future contracts, disgorgement of profits from corrupt activities and compensation to third parties for damages caused.

The following excerpt from the 2007 annual report of a US company whose former CEO had pleaded guilty to violating the FCPA gives a sense of the range of sanctions and related consequences that businesses face.

Box 3 Facing up to the consequences of bribery: a real-world case

A person or entity found in violation of the FCPA could be subject to fines, civil penalties of up to $500,000 per violation, . . . disgorgement . . . and injunctive relief. Criminal penalties could range up to the greater of $2 million per violation or twice the gross pecuniary gain or loss from the violation, which could be substantially greater than $2 million per violation. It is possible that . . . there have been multiple violations, which could lead to multiple fines.

Other potential consequences could be significant and include suspension or debarment of our ability to contract with governmental agencies of the United States and of foreign countries. [. . .] Suspension or debarment from the government contracts business would have a material adverse effect on our business, results of operations, and cash flow.

These investigations could also result in (1) third-party claims against us, which may include claims for . . . damages, (2) damage to our business or reputation, (3) loss of, or adverse effect on, cash flow, assets, goodwill, results of operations, business, prospects, profits or business value, (4) adverse consequences on our ability to obtain or continue financing for current or future projects.

[. . .]

Continuing negative publicity arising out of these investigations could also result in our inability to bid successfully for governmental contracts and adversely affect our prospects in the commercial marketplace. In addition, we could incur costs and expenses for any monitor required by or agreed to with a governmental authority to review our continued compliance with FCPA law.

Source: Adapted from the FCPA blog, 5 September 2008.

Translating international norms into national rules: some areas of progress and concern

International norms gradually find their way into national anti-corruption legislation. The African Union convention has made a noticeable impact on African nations alongside the UNCAC. A number of countries with major investment potential have amended their anti-corruption legislation, including Nigeria, South Africa, Tanzania and Uganda. In the Americas, the Organisation of American States' Inter-American Convention against Corruption has provided some impetus towards harmonising anti-corruption laws, and an implementation follow-up scheme promises more pressure for reform.

Much still needs to be done, however. Many anti-bribery laws in developing countries are still in a nascent stage. Across the world, bribe-takers typically face stricter rules and harsher punishment than bribe-givers. More attention to tightening the rules on the supply side of corruption has therefore been a continuing concern.[16]

Much more needs to be done in industrialised countries as well. An assessment of thirty-four countries that are party to the OECD convention highlights some of the typical shortcomings in national anti-corruption laws with regard to the supply side of bribery (see table 8).

Brazil, Russia, India and China, the so-called 'BRIC countries' that represent emerging economic powerhouses with international reach, are particularly important for the promulgation of international anti-corruption norms. Their track record for adopting international instruments leaves ample room for improvement, though. Brazil has ratified both the OECD convention and the UNCAC, whilst China and Russia have ratified only the UNCAC and India has yet to ratify any.

Finally, it is worth stating that the best rules on the books are useless when they are not enforced. As the next article explains, this is a primary area of concern.[17]

Table 8: Shortcomings in OECD country anti-corruption legislation			
Statutory limitations very short	Penalties too low	No or ineffective criminal liability for legal persons	Inadequate definition of foreign bribery
Austria, France, Italy, Spain	Australia, Ireland, Italy, South Korea	Argentina, Czech Republic, Germany, Greece, Poland, Slovakia, Sweden, United Kingdom	Canada, Chile, Ireland, Spain

Source: Adapted from TI, *Progress Report 2008: OECD Anti-Bribery Convention* (Berlin: TI, 2008).

---

16 Asian Development Bank (ADB) and OECD, *Anti-corruption Policies in Asia and the Pacific: Progress in Legal and Institutional Reform in 25 Countries* (Manila: ADB/OECD, 2006).

17 See articles starting on pages 123 and 127.

From rules to enforcement: regulators' resources and enforcement action

Transparency International

Any law, regulation or policy is only as good as its enforcement. Perhaps this fact is so obvious, though, that it often seems to be overlooked. Both the analysis of governance systems and the related advocacy efforts are typically focused on putting in place the appropriate rules and regulations that should apply to businesses and markets. Governance is often assumed to be 'good' when all the right rules are in place and the reporting lines of regulatory agencies guarantee truly independent oversight. Good laws and institutions do not automatically translate into adequate oversight and enforcement, however.

The enforcement of rules in the private sector is no different. Monitoring complex, intertwined and fast-moving markets and business operations that transcend jurisdictions, innovate continuously and have grown to unprecedented scale is extremely time- and resource-consuming. Investigating and prosecuting white-collar crime requires specialised knowledge, tenacity and time, with the outcome often far from certain. In the United States alone, the combined budget of financial regulatory agencies as of 2002 exceeded US$5.6 billion, with staffing levels of more than 43,000 employees.[1]

Making business regulation and market oversight work is therefore as much a matter of the right rules and mechanisms as it is about available resources for enforcement, as well as the political will to bring these resources to bear on priority issues.[2] The more limited the resources the larger the gap between rules on the books and their monitoring and enforcement.

Resource constraints translate into enforcement shortcomings

The global financial crisis that began to unfold in 2007 has brought the issue of resource constraints in enforcement to the forefront.

The US Federal Bureau of Investigation (FBI) warned as early as 2004 that rising mortgage fraud posed a considerable threat to the stability of financial institutions. Despite repeated requests for more staff, the FBI's white-collar crime investigation unit shrunk by more than a third between 2001 and 2008, as resources were dramatically reallocated to fighting terrorism. As a consequence, the number of cases related to financial institution fraud had all but halved by 2007 compared to 2000.[3]

---

1 H. Jackson, *Variation in the Intensity of Financial Regulation: Preliminary Evidence and Potential Implications*, Discussion Paper no. 521 (Boston: Harvard Law School, 2005).
2 For a rare glimpse into the internal rules for case selection that a regulator applies, see the US Securities and Exchange Commission's first ever published enforcement manual: SEC Enforcement Division, 'Enforcement Manual', Office of the Chief Counsel, October 2008.
3 *New York Times* (US), 18 October 2008.

Some hope on the anti-corruption front

A laudable exception to this trend in the United States is the enforcement of anti-bribery legislation, which, having long languished, has picked up steam in the last few years. Staff resources devoted to enforcing the Foreign Corrupt Practices Act, the United States' corner-stone legislation for prosecuting the bribery of foreign officials by US companies, have been expanded while enforcement has been stepped up significantly.[4]

This strong focus on the enforcement of foreign bribery laws is only partly mirrored at the international level. A half of the thirty-seven countries that are parties to the 1997 OECD Convention on Combating Bribery of Foreign Public Officials in International Business Transactions still have no significant enforcement activity. Although prosecutions have picked up in some countries, such as France, Germany, Sweden and Switzerland, G8 countries Canada, Japan and the United Kingdom have carried out little or no enforcement.[5]

The broader picture: international regulatory resources to counter corporate fraud

Only very recently have studies of business regulation systematically begun to shed more light on the resources that regulators in different countries have at their disposal, and how they are used to tackle white-collar-crime. Three key messages emerge.

Even after adjusting for population and market size, the disparities in resource allocation for enforcement between different countries are quite dramatic

An international comparison of staffing levels and the budgets of securities regulators shows not only that emerging economies lag considerably behind in enforcement resources but also that several countries with advanced regulatory systems, such as France, Germany and Japan, devote only a fraction of the resources to enforcement that the United States or United Kingdom do.[6]

Such enforcement disparities are particularly troubling in a globally interconnected economy, where the impacts of enforcement failures may generate serious ripple effects across the world economy.

---

4 See article starting on page 238.
5 See article starting on page 426.
6 H. Jackson and M. Roe, *Public and Private Enforcement of Securities Laws: Resource-based Evidence*, Working Paper no. 08-28 (Boston: Harvard Law School, 2008). For a summary of the study, see article starting on page 431.

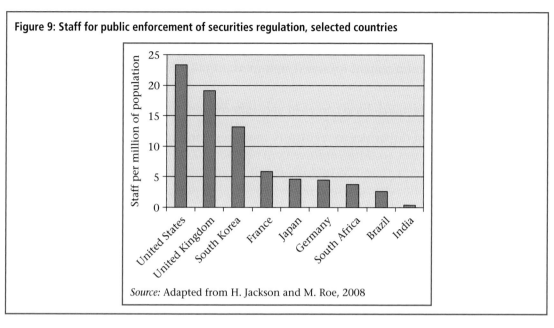

Figure 9: Staff for public enforcement of securities regulation, selected countries

Source: Adapted from H. Jackson and M. Roe, 2008

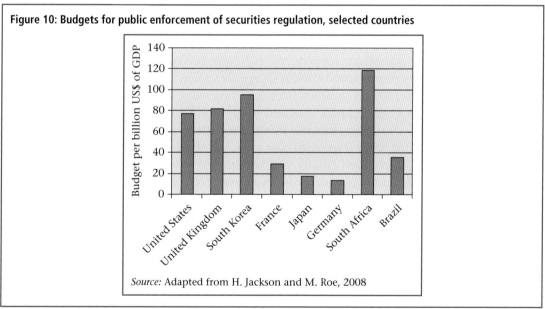

Figure 10: Budgets for public enforcement of securities regulation, selected countries

Source: Adapted from H. Jackson and M. Roe, 2008

Public enforcement matters: devoting more resources to enforcement means better-performing markets

International comparisons find a clear and significant link between better-endowed and -staffed enforcement agencies and superior performance of stock markets in terms of market capitalisation, trading volumes, numbers of domestic firms and initial public offerings.

This finding casts serious doubt on previous analyses that had questioned the efficacy of enforcement by comparing rules with market outcomes without considering the important factor of enforcement intensity. Bringing enforcement into the analysis provides compelling evidence that public enforcement is indeed an important pillar for market regulation.[7]

Even a rather similar resource base can yield very different enforcement action

It is not surprising that disparities in regulatory resources translate into disparities in enforcement. In the United States, securities enforcement between 2000 and 2002 averaged some 5,000 actions, sanctions of more than US$1.8 billion and about 400 years of prison terms annually. This is around eighty times the caseload of the lesser-endowed German regulator.

Similar resources can also lead to different enforcement intensity, however. Although budgetary and staffing resources for the US and UK securities regulators are not markedly different relative to market size, the annual monetary sanctions imposed by the US regulator are ten times larger than in the United Kingdom.[8]

This may have to do with political will, efficiencies and policy choices about whether to emphasise prevention or prosecution. In any case, this much-needed analysis of enforcement outputs provides important benchmarks and indicators for assessing the performance of regulatory agencies and the policy-makers who determine their budgets and enforcement priorities.

Taken together, these insights into regulatory capabilities and outputs have several important ramifications. First, they place capacity and resource allocation issues at the centre of the need for better market regulation and business oversight. Second, they highlight the fact that the analysis of actual enforcement capabilities and output must be an integral part of assessing the functioning of governance systems and holding regulators and policy-makers to account. Looking at rules and laws is an important first step, but the extent to which they are actually enforced is vitally important. Finally, the heightened awareness of regulatory resource constraints and enforcement intensity prompts an important debate as to which innovative enforcement techniques at hand can make limited resources go further. Some of the most promising innovations in this regard are discussed in the following article.

---

7 H. Jackson and M. Roe, 2008.
8 This ratio is already adjusted for differences in market capitalisation; the ratio for the difference in absolute terms is thirty to one. See J. C. Coffee Jr., *Law and the Market: The Impact of Enforcement*, Working Paper no. 304 (New York: Columbia Law School, 2007).

Smart enforcement: trends and innovations for monitoring, investigating and prosecuting corporate corruption

Cristie Ford[1]

Recent experience has shown that the traditional tools of criminal and civil enforcement historically applied to individual wrongdoers and violent criminals are poorly suited to institutional and white-collar crimes. Prosecuting individuals only, while certainly justified in many cases, does not address deeper organisational issues. Organisational norms, culture and practices are often deeply complicit in organisational misfeasance. Likewise, enforcement action, especially with regard to sophisticated white-collar crime, is often very expensive, complex and protracted, making it an instrument of last resort.

A new generation of civil and criminal enforcement speaks directly to organisational structures. These new approaches and tools seek to realign incentives better in order to meet the goals of the law. They also strategically harness the business and reputational forces that are at least as important as deterrent sanctions in motivating companies to obey the law. This article identifies three such trends.

Beyond prosecution: compliance, structural reform and deferred prosecution agreements

These innovative enforcement approaches look beyond enforcement instruments and focus on creating an environment conducive to compliance. Along these lines, scholars have reminded us of four commonsensical but critical points.

First, people and organisations are inclined to obey laws they think are legitimate, credible and fair.[2] A regulator (at least, a civil-side one) that communicates effectively, and acts fairly and predictably – and that is perceived to behave this way – may be able to avoid even having to bring some downstream enforcement actions.

Second, reputational and social contexts matter. Suppliers, consumers, investors, trade associations and peers are all part of a network that applies pressure on corporations that can be leveraged to keep them onside.[3]

Third, the most severe enforcement methods should be deployed against the small group of actors not adequately motivated by personal responsibility, reputation and cheaper

---

1 Cristie Ford is an Assistant Professor and Co-Director of the National Centre for Business Law at the University of British Columbia, Canada.
2 T. Tyler, *Why People Obey the Law* (New Haven, CT: Yale University Press, 1990).
3 N. Gunningham, R. Kagan and D. Thornton, *Shades of Green: Business, Regulation, and Environment* (Stanford, CA: Stanford University Press, 2003).

regulatory methods such as compliance audits, disclosure obligations and publicity.[4] All these factors counsel restraint when it comes to expectations about what enforcement alone can achieve.

Finally, the responsibility for internal compliance ultimately lies with corporate management. A regulator is in a poor position to figure out the precise mix of internal drivers, structures and incentives required to keep any particular company law-abiding. Managers, not regulators, are accountable for identifying and addressing the risks associated with their businesses.[5] The US Sarbanes–Oxley Act provisions requiring chief executive officers and chief financial officers to certify the effectiveness of their companies' disclosure controls and procedures brought this point home.

The 2004 amendments to the US sentencing guidelines,[6] as well as recent changes to US Securities and Exchange Commission (Framework for Cooperation) and Department of Justice policy,[7] use different approaches to encourage compliance. These 'credit for compliance' provisions offer organisations in trouble the prospect of reduced or even no sanctions if they demonstrate that they have effective compliance policies and procedures in place to detect and prevent internal violations of the law.

Other enforcement initiatives use the acute enforcement event to spur companies to improve their compliance policies and procedures. Civil and criminal regulators have been increasingly using deferred and non-prosecution agreements (DPAs and NPAs) and their civil counterpart, the so-called 'reform undertaking'. This is the case especially in the United States in connection with securities and Foreign Corrupt Practices Act violations,[8] and also in Australia, Canada and the United Kingdom.

Under a DPA, NPA or reform undertaking, a firm enters into a settlement agreement with regulators that typically requires it to end its wrongful practices and implement an improved compliance programme, and often to hire an independent monitor to oversee reforms. The flexibility of these programmes makes them suitable platforms for many innovative remedies to deter misconduct and address the underlying causes. They also help minimise the risk of 'cosmetic' and 'paper' compliance programmes while helping to develop a body of best practices on how compliance improvements can be achieved. Between 2002 and 2005 US prosecutors used twice as many DPAs and NPAs as in the previous ten years.[9]

---

4 I. Ayres and J. Braithwaite, *Responsive Regulation: Transcending the Deregulation Debate* (New York: Oxford University Press, 1991).

5 C. Coglianese and D. Lazer, 'Management-Based Regulation: Prescribing Private Management to Achieve Public Goals', *Law & Society Review*, vol. 37 (2003).

6 The US *Sentencing Guidelines Manual* requires corporations to 'promote an organizational culture that encourages ethical conduct and a commitment to compliance with the law'.

7 See memorandum from Paul J. McNulty, deputy US attorney general, to heads of department components, United States attorneys, subject: 'Principles of Federal Prosecution of Business Organizations', 12 December 2006.

8 For a comprehensive list of recent agreements in the United States, see http://judiciary.house.gov/issues/issues_deferredprosecution.html.

9 *Corporate Crime Reporter* (US), 28 December 2005.

Monitorships

The regulation of corporate compliance entered a new phase with the development of corporate monitorships. Many recent DPAs and reform undertakings now require a corporation seeking to reach a settlement to retain, at its own expense, an independent third-party monitor or consultant. The monitor's role is to engage closely with the company over a period ranging from a few months to a few years, identifying compliance failures and the reasons for underlying violations, and reporting back to regulators with findings and recommendations.[10]

Monitorships are best suited to cases in which corrupt practices arise from insidious organisational cultural issues, and when such practices seem to persist despite other sanctioning efforts. Small-scale or isolated problems do not justify the significant cost of a monitorship. On the other end of the spectrum, traditional sanctions remain appropriate for the very worst actors. Even there, however, a monitorship can help address deep problems while imposing less collateral damage on other stakeholders than would the 'corporate death penalty' of criminal prosecution.[11] In the United States, compliance monitors were appointed in thirty-five cases in 2007, up from twenty a year earlier.[12]

Monitorships have several advantages. They go beyond merely encouraging compliance, working to structure the process through deadlines, deliverables and accountability measures to help key actors overcome institutional inertia. Embedding the monitorship process within an enforcement action also keeps the organisation's feet to the fire, and makes the consequences of shirking responsibilities clear and immediate. In addition, a well-chosen monitor brings vital expertise and an outside perspective that can be more effective in working through persistent cultural problems.

In order to be effective at this level, practice needs to align with theory. Third-party monitors must have the necessary compliance expertise and not just be former prosecutors, as seems to be a major trend in the United States. There must be meaningful follow-up and accountability – for example, through a regulatory compliance arm that incorporates the monitor's recommendations into future compliance audits. Monitors must also have the support to take their role seriously in the face of organisational and perhaps even regulatory pressure that could lead them to interpret their mandate narrowly, keep expenses down and write a positive report.[13]

---

10 T. L. Dickinson and V. Khanna, 'The Corporate Monitor: The New Corporate Czar?', *Michigan Law Review*, vol. 105 (2007).

11 C. Ford and D. Hess, 'Can Corporate Monitorships Improve Corporate Compliance?', *Journal of Corporate Law Studies*, vol. 34, no. 3 (forthcoming 2009).

12 Shearman & Sterling, *Recent Trends and Patterns in FCPA Enforcement* (London: Shearman & Sterling, 2008).

13 C. Ford and D. Hess, 2009.

Partial blackouts

A less common but thought-provoking option to enhance the enforcement toolbox is a 'partial blackout'. Depending on the nature of a corporate entity and the extent of its malfeasance, it may be possible simply to 'black out' a corrupted component while the organisation as a whole confronts its compliance problems. Under a partial blackout, certain business lines or units of a corporation are mandatorily suspended for a period of time.[14]

A partial blackout is less interventionist than a corporate monitorship. It assumes that a corporation can identify and solve its own problems. Partial blackouts can be very effective in providing the motivation for this, and in dispelling the notion that a corporation can simply buy its way out of a problem. In addition, the uncertainty and stigma associated with a partial blackout can have a broad impact not only on the corporation's overall bottom line but also on its relationships with business partners, customers, lenders and investors. This puts pressure directly on management to address and resolve compliance problems.[15]

Smarter enforcement to catalyse corporate integrity

Conventional enforcement is generally an acute, isolated event in the larger life of a corporation. With regard to compliance, enforcement serves the purpose of concentrating the mind on a problem. On the other hand, an enforcement action is very unlikely to create or foster a real culture of compliance. The spectre of sanctions can be useful, but people obey the law for reasons that have at least as much to do with reputation, credibility, business relationships and personal values. Enforcement is more likely to be effective when it leverages the full range of regulatory, social and reputational factors that actually drive corporate culture and action.

When it comes to corporate corruption, what does it mean to have the tools truly match the goals? Corporate corruption is rarely just a matter of individual bad apples, though most of the time there will be an individual element along with the institutional one. One must also respond at the organisational level to the forces that made the wrongdoing possible. Sometimes this is a matter of ensuring that appropriate compliance structures are in place, as a DPA or reform undertaking can do. Sometimes it is a matter of increasing management's accountability and sense of urgency, as the partial blackout can do. Sometimes the pressure of internal culture is such that nothing short of the close intervention of a monitorship will stand a chance of forcing real change. The latest generation of enforcement officials recognises that they cannot force meaningful internal change on an organisation, but through tools like these they may be in a good position to catalyse and support it.

---

14 See, e.g., In the Matter of Ernst & Young LLP, File no. 3-10933. Ernst & Young was prohibited from taking on any new audit clients for a period of six months.

15 US Internal Revenue Service, 'KPMG to Pay $456 Million for Criminal Violations', press release, 29 August 2005. Partial blackouts can be combined with traditional sanctions. In 2005 auditing firm KPMG entered into a deferred prosecution agreement that included permanently terminating two tax practices, appointing an independent monitor, developing a compliance and ethics programme and paying US$456 million in fines, restitution and penalties.

The flexibility that these new enforcement tools offer must be used carefully and account-ably, so that they do not dilute the deterring effect of criminal sanctions and invite strategic horse-trading, or even collusive deals between defendants and prosecuting authorities. This is a steep agenda even for well-resourced and independent enforcement agencies, and may still be out of reach in many countries.

Gatekeeping corporate integrity: the role of accountants, auditors and rating agencies
Transparency International

> Let's hope we are all wealthy and retired by the time this house of cards falters.
> Anonymous e-mail by a rating analyst, December 2006[1]

A wide range of players – including accountants, analysts, auditors and rating agencies – produce and verify crucial information about companies. They analyse their financial situations, compliance with laws, risks, prospects and corporate strategy. The proper functioning of markets and economies depends critically on this information and these informational gate-keepers, as do management, investors, creditors, regulators, the media and the wider public.

Unfortunately, repeated waves of corporate scandals in the United States, Japan, Europe and elsewhere have highlighted the corruption risks related to these gatekeepers, which have the potential to compromise corporate integrity and dramatically destabilise markets.[2] To under-stand these risks, it is important first to explore the roles and failings of these players.

The role of accountants and auditors

During the 1990s earnings restatements of public companies increased, widening the gap between reported earnings and financial realities.[3] Between 1997 and 2002 approximately 10 per cent of all publicly listed companies in the United States restated their financial statements at least once.[4] This poor performance of accountants and auditors may be partly explained by increasing financial complexity and risk-taking; but it is also linked to accounting

---

1 *Los Angeles Times* (US), 9 July 2008.
2 For Japan, see Y. Fuchita, 'Financial Gatekeepers in Japan', in R. Litan and Y. Fuchita (eds.), *Financial Gatekeepers: Can They Protect Investors?* (Washington, DC: Brookings Institution Press, 2006); for Europe, see S. Di Castri and F. Benedetto, *There Is Something about Parmalat (On Directors and Gatekeepers)*, working paper, 2005 (available at SSRN: http://ssrn.com/abstract=896940); for Asia, see OECD, *Enforcement of Corporate Governance in Asia: The Unfinished Agenda* (Paris: OECD, 2008).
3 B. Lev, 'Corporate Earnings: Fact and Fiction', *Journal of Economic Perspectives*, vol. 17, no. 2 (2003).
4 J. C. Coffee Jr., *Gatekeeper Failure and Reform: The Challenges of Fashioning Relevant Reforms*, Working Paper no. 237 (New York: Columbia Law School, 2003).

manipulation, exemplified most prominently by the accounting irregularities at the collapsed US energy giant Enron, which also spelt the demise of its auditor, Arthur Andersen. Together with a series of other exposed accounting frauds, this contributed to a dramatic stock market meltdown.

The role of analysts

Industry analysts contributed to the stock market bubble of the late 1990s by issuing overly optimistic 'buy' recommendations for many new technology stocks. The ratio of analysts' 'buy' to 'sell' recommendations in 1999 and 2000 was found to be as high as 100 to one, while many analysts expressed serious doubts in private about companies they recommended in public. Sixteen out of seventeen analysts that tracked Enron, for example, maintained a 'buy' or 'strong buy' virtually up until the time it filed for bankruptcy.[5]

The role of rating agencies

The dramatic financial crisis that has engulfed the world since mid-June 2007 was triggered by US$3.2 trillion of Wall Street-backed loans to homebuyers with bad credit and undocumented incomes. These extremely risky loans were packaged and repackaged into highly complex investment pools that eventually ended up as 'toxic waste' on the balance sheets of banks, fatally undermining trust in banks and financial markets, with devastating consequences.

Rating agencies played a crucial role in this. They made packaging and dispersing bad loans possible in the first place by awarding very favourable, low-risk investment grades to financial products in which bad loans were hidden. Often, the awarding of the lowest possible risk rating put these extremely risky products on a par with rock-solid government bonds. By mid-2008 the two dominant rating agencies, Moody's and Standard & Poor's, downgraded an estimated 90 and 84 per cent respectively of all these investment products, including more than three-quarters of those originally given premium ratings.[6]

Multiple conflicts of interest

These dramatic errors in judgment by auditors, analysts and rating agencies may have been partly due to the unprecedented complexity of financial relations and the infectious belief that off-balance sheet holdings (as with Enron), high-tech markets and repackaged housing loans somehow constituted unprecedented innovations that transcended normal market rules.

More importantly, however, all three groups face a structural risk of corruption at the root of the problem. They are paid by the very clients on whose information disclosure they are meant to pass an independent judgment.

---

5 J. C. Coffee Jr., *Understanding Enron: It's about the Gatekeepers, Stupid*, Working Paper no. 207 (New York: Columbia Law School, 2002).

6 E. B. Smith, 'Race to Bottom at Moody's, S&P Secured Subprime's Boom, Bust', Bloomberg, 25 September 2008.

Auditors are paid by their audit clients. Before the late 1990s few large companies bought significant consulting services from their auditors. By 2002, however, auditors were estimated to receive three times more in consulting fees than in auditing fees, with the latter often considered a 'loss-leader' to help open the door for consulting opportunities.[7]

At an investment firm, analysts assess the prospects of companies and issue purchase recommendations, while their colleagues in the investment arm of the same firm provide consulting services to the analysed client or sell their stocks in initial public offerings. Investment analysis was an add-on service cross-subsidised by the more lucrative investment banking activities. As a consequence, analysts at times publicly recommended the purchase of stocks they derided privately as 'powder keg' or 'piece of junk'.[8]

Rating agencies are paid mainly by the companies whose products they rate. Although they provide some of their ratings for free, such services are considered loss-leaders that help gain media visibility and stimulate demand for follow-up services.[9] Ironically, rating the complex repackaged sub-prime mortgages at the heart of the global financial crisis has proved particularly lucrative. The top two rating agencies, Moody's and Standard & Poor's, are believed to have earned as much as three times more from grading these complex instruments than normal corporate bonds, while earning large advisory fees for helping the same group of clients structure related products. Senior executives warned of the 'threat of losing deals' and argued not to 'kill the golden goose', while analysts expressed concerns that the models did not capture the risks and complained in one incident that a particular deal 'could be structured by cows and we would rate it'.[10]

Addressing the conflicts

It is impossible to avoid conflicts of interests in fast-paced and complex international financial markets, in which the same highly specialised expertise is required to advise and audit/assess or rate companies and only a small number of firms have the global reach and reputation that many of their clients demand. A number of measures have been taken in the United States, however, that are increasingly being adopted in other countries to mitigate the conflicts of interests.

For analysts, these measures include a stronger organisational separation – a so-called 'Chinese wall' – between analysts and investment banking services, explicit disclosure of conflicts of interest and mandatory use of independent analyst services in some contexts. For auditors, limitations on consulting services and rules about selecting and rotating auditing partners have been introduced. As a result, three out of the 'big four' accounting firms sold off their consultancy divisions after the Enron scandal. For rating agencies, new rules requiring more

7 *New York Times* (US), 13 May 2002.
8 *USA Today*, 14 April 2002.
9 Autorité des marchés financiers (AMF), *AMF 2006 Report on Rating Agencies*, Part II, *Fund Management Rating*, (Paris: AMF, 2007).
10 E. B. Smith, 2008; Securities and Exchange Commission, *Summary Report of Issues Identified in the Commission Staff's Examinations of Select Credit Rating Agencies* (Washington, DC: SEC, 2008).

internal control, as well as greater transparency in rating procedures and the meaning of ratings, were being considered at the time of writing.

The wall has become porous again

Despite these efforts, mitigating conflicts of interest is an unfinished agenda. In the area of stock analysis, the ratio of 'buy' to 'sell' recommendations has again become peculiarly unbalanced, with six times more 'buy' recommendations being registered in February 2007 than 'sell' ones. As one former investment bank analyst confirms, the conflicts are still simmering: 'No one is explicitly saying anything to you as an analyst, but if you're helping to bring in a banking deal, everyone knows it, and your bonus will reflect it, and your job will be secure. That's the way it goes, that's what pays the bills. Banks have put in new Chinese wall restrictions, but at the end of the day, it's still going to be hard for analysts to say something negative about a banking client.'[11]

Accounting firms once again have significantly expanded their consulting activities. By late 2007 the 'big four' accounting providers had re-entered the United Kingdom's top ten consultancy fee earners.[12] At the same time, traditional auditing services are increasingly viewed as a commodity, making it ever more difficult for firms to earn sufficient margins from this activity alone.

Investigations into the mortgage lending collapse also attest to the persistence of potential conflicts of interests in auditing. One auditor cited the need to keep its client happy as a reason for softening its findings.[13]

Meanwhile, new areas of concern have emerged. Insurance and mutual funds are allowed to offer investment advice to US pension-holders on how to manage their portfolios, while at the same time offering products that may be part of these very same portfolios.[14] In addition, stock exchanges in many other countries have been much slower in addressing conflicts of interests. India's regulator proposed Chinese-wall-like rules for analysts only in 2008,[15] and China's Shenzhen Stock Exchange finally urged the authorities in 2007 to introduce measures to reduce conflicts of interest and stock manipulation.[16]

All this strongly suggests that gatekeepers, whose independence is essential, continue to be exposed to potential conflicts of interest, old and new.

---

11 C. O'Leary, 'Cracks in the Chinese Wall: Four Years after SEC Settlement, Is Street Research Withering in the Shadows?', *Investment Dealer's Digest*, 5 March 2007.
12 *Financial Times* (UK), 19 November 2007.
13 R. Nelsestuen, 'Lessons from the Dark Side of the Credit Crunch: For Auditors and Clients, the Credit Crunch Reaffirms that Risk Management Can Never Be Delegated', *Bank Accounting & Finance*, vol. 21, no. 5 (2008).
14 *Wall Street Journal* (US), 3 December 2007.
15 *Indian Express*, 1 April 2008.
16 *Shanghai Daily* (China), 28 April 2007.

Stepping up reforms

Existing safeguards need to be strengthened and new ones explored. Consolidating and simplifying a patchwork regulatory environment can be helpful in countries such as the United States. Industry self-regulation is also important, but it requires credible and effective mechanisms for monitoring and enforcing codes and standards. Such mechanisms are still in short supply, in particular for rating agencies and enforcement in emerging economies.[17]

Proportionate liability for gatekeepers and their errors or omissions in judgment is another area requiring further progress. Rating agencies, for example, for quite some time have sought to stave off more responsibility for their ratings by depicting them as mere opinions ('the world's shortest editorial') – a defence even more difficult to uphold against the backdrop of their contribution to the financial crisis.[18]

Most importantly, a fresh discussion on alternative funding models to shore up the independence of gatekeeper services is in order. Investors could pool resources to fund bond ratings and more independent analysis. Auditors could be incentivised with bonus payments for fraud detection.[19] Public money may be better spent in stimulating demand for independent market research and ratings and in supporting independent oversight and standard-setting processes for gatekeepers, rather than propping up collapsing markets when controls have failed.

Reforms in many countries also need to consider the pivotal role that many gatekeepers play in ensuring corporate compliance with anti-corruption and anti-money laundering (AML) provisions. Elaborate schemes for kickbacks, bribes or money-laundering are often supported by corporate slush funds and complex financial transactions that auditors and accountants are best positioned to detect. [20]

The OECD Anti-Bribery Convention, for example, requires sanctions for accounting violations related to bribing foreign public officials to be 'effective, proportionate and dissuasive'.[21] A progress report in 2006 identified a lack of clear legal obligations in many countries for auditors and accountants to report suspicions of crimes to the authorities, however. In addition, the report faulted several countries, including Australia, France, Italy and South Korea, for insufficient and ineffective sanctions such as low maximum fines and suspended sentences, and countries such as Belgium, Hungary, Luxembourg and Slovakia for weak enforcement.[22]

Clarified legal obligations and accountability, less financial dependence on clients and credible enforcement of industry codes and conducts are key measures to help gatekeepers fulfil their essential roles. Ultimately, though, no system of checks and balances can guard fully against

---

17 See article starting on page 136.
18 D. J. Grais and K. D. Katsiris, 'Not "The World's Shortest Editorial"', *Bloomberg Law Reports*, November 2007.
19 L. A. Cunningham, 'Book Review of Gatekeepers: The Professions and Corporate Governance by John C. Coffee, Jr', *British Accounting Review*, vol. 40, no. 87 (2008).
20 OECD, *Mid-term Study of Phase 2 Reports* (Paris: OECD, 2006).
21 OECD, *Convention on Combating Bribery of Foreign Public Officials in International Business Transactions* (Paris: OECD, 1997).
22 OECD, 2006.

all potential manipulations of and by highly specialised information professionals operating in an immensely complex corporate environment. Sticking to the letter of disclosure rules, while material information is hidden elsewhere, is not sufficient. Neither is lip service to a corporate code without a credible support for transparent reporting and independent enforcement. Professional and personal integrity are indispensable to ensure that gatekeepers use the privileged knowledge and informational power with which they are entrusted in accordance with their responsibilities to clients, owners, investors and society.

Seeding corporate integrity: the challenges to accounting and auditing in Nigeria

Elewechi Okike[1]

Widespread corruption in almost all spheres of public and private endeavours has made achieving an adequate level of accountability in Nigeria a major problem. The situation has degenerated to the point that bribery and other forms of corruption are referred to as the 'Nigerian factor'.[2] Members of Nigeria's auditing profession have at times fallen into this trap, bedevilling the nation's economy. Their independence in doubt, accountants have been involved in cases of negligence, incompetence, collusion and fraud. Before 1990 Nigeria did not formally regulate the auditing profession, and the country lacked a professional code and standard of auditing practice.[3]

Keen to address these problems, the government has embarked on an anti-corruption campaign aimed at restoring foreign investors' confidence in Nigeria's capital markets and improving the operation of the securities system. The success of the campaign hinges in large part on enhancing the integrity and transparency of financial reporting by accountants and auditors.

Over the years, auditors in Nigeria have faced various challenges and shortcomings in discharging their duties. When the Companies and Allied Matters Act was enacted in 1990 it contained provisions suggesting that the public had lost confidence in auditors – such as a requirement that their reports be countersigned by members of the legal profession.

Two questions come to mind when examining the issue of corruption and its relationship to the accounting profession. Is it the duty of accountants and auditors to expose corruption? And how can accountants and auditors free themselves from corruption in a highly corrupt environment?

---

1 Elewechi Okike is Principal Lecturer in Accounting at the University of Sunderland, United Kingdom.
2 R. S. O. Wallace, 'Growing Pains of an Indigenous Accountancy Profession: The Nigerian Experience', *Accounting, Business and Financial History*, vol. 2, no. 1 (1992).
3 E. N. M. Okike, 'Management of Crisis: The Response of the Auditing Profession in Nigeria to the Challenge to Its Legitimacy', *Accounting, Auditing & Accountability Journal*, vol. 17, no. 5 (2004).

Although accountants have the duty to maintain the confidentiality of client information, situations arise in which legal or professional requirements could override that responsibility, and in which accountants might be obliged to report their findings and suspicions to the authorities. Depending on the legal protection offered to accountants and auditors who expose corruption, however, whistleblowers can suffer legal problems, the loss of a job or client, a damaged reputation and, in the most extreme circumstances, loss of life.[4]

This scenario best depicts the situation in which accountants and auditors in Nigeria have found themselves. On the one hand, they have the uphill task of dealing with corruption, and on the other hand there is the issue of personal safety. Some auditors have been assassinated after unearthing fraud in their client companies. These include the 1989 murders of two auditors, an accountant and a secretary involved with the uncovering of fraud in Guinness (Nigeria) plc.[5]

Additionally, cultural factors often influence auditors' relationships. Cultural demands – such as displaying respect for elders and loyalty to family, village or tribe – have and will continue to have telling effects on auditors' independence and professionalism. The obligation to respect elders probably makes it difficult for a young Nigerian accountant to seek an explanation from an elderly person for a statement that the younger person knows is questionable.[6]

With Nigeria lacking professional guidance for auditors, numerous cases of non-compliance with international auditing standards and professional codes of ethics have been observed, including:

- auditors preparing the same financial statements they audited;
- auditors not applying rigorous procedures;
- quality control arrangements existing only in big multinational firms;
- a lack of access to quality practice-oriented manuals; and
- a lack of auditing skills in a computer information systems environment.[7]

Times are changing in Nigeria – and so is the auditing profession. Chief J. O. Omidiora, former president of the Institute of Chartered Accountants of Nigeria (ICAN), has acknowledged that auditors are aware of changes in the economy and their growing responsibility to the nation: 'As a Professional Body, the Institute regards itself as partners in progress with the Government in the task of Nation building. Members of the profession . . . feel especially challenged by the developments in the economy and as such consider [themselves] obliged to . . . the task of returning the economy to the path of sustained growth and viability.'[8]

---

4 J. Gruner, 'Is It the Professional Duty of an Accountant to Expose Corruption?', *The Nigerian Accountant*, vol. 32, no. 2 (1999).
5 R. S. O. Wallace, 1992.
6 Ibid.
7 E. N. M. Okike, 'Corporate Governance in Nigeria: The Status Quo', *Corporate Governance: An International Review*, vol. 15, no. 2 (2007).
8 *The Nigerian Accountant*, vol. 21, no. 1 (1988).

The Institute of Chartered Accountants of Nigeria has an established code of ethics to guide the conduct of its members, as well as an investigatory panel to monitor and probe allegations of wrongdoing. ICAN investigated fifty cases between 1992 and 1995, and has revoked the licences and memberships of erring members. ICAN has also issued planning and performance guidelines that set out basic audit principles, the infrastructure requirements of an audit, the pre-engagement basics of an audit, procedures for audit planning and quality control methods.[9]

The accounting profession in Nigeria must continue to monitor developments in the external and internal reporting environments and respond adequately. The complexity of the Nigerian economy will demand that auditors are appropriately equipped to address the various aspects of financial and economic management. If members of the profession are unable to do this, their relevance, especially as professionals, may be called into question again.

---

9 Ibid.

Financial institutions and the fight against corruption
Gretta Fenner[1]

As most forms of corruption usually involve a financial transaction between one person or institution and another, many corrupt dealings eventually involve banks or other financial intermediaries. In most cases this involvement will be involuntary and unknowing. The fact remains, however, that financial intermediaries are highly exposed to and potentially directly involved in corruption. Most if not all of their services are at risk, be it private banking, trade financing or investment banking.

As a consequence, banks have a great responsibility as well as much potential to combat corruption, and the related legal, economic and reputational threats are becoming increasingly recognised within the financial industry. Banks' exposure to corruption risks was thrown into sharp relief by the case of late Nigerian ruler Sani Abacha, who is alleged to have spirited several billion dollars of stolen assets out of his country. By 2008 more than US$1.2 billion had been repatriated from accounts in a number of countries, including Belgium, Liechtenstein, Luxembourg, Switzerland and the United Kingdom (including the crown dependency of Jersey).[2] In 2000 this and similar episodes motivated the launch of the Wolfsberg Group's anti-money laundering (AML) initiative, a self-regulatory project led by eleven global banks.[3]

---

1 Gretta Fenner was until July 2008 executive director of the Basel Institute on Governance, Switzerland.
2 See the International Centre for Asset Recovery; www.assetrecovery.org.
3 M. Pieth and G. Aiolfi, 'The Private Sector Becomes Active: The Wolfsberg Process', in A. Clark and P. Burrell (eds.), *A Practitioner's Guide to International Money Laundering Law and Regulation* (London: City & Financial Publishing, 2003).

The specific role of financial institutions and their capacity to combat corruption has been less the focus of research and policy-making than in other business sectors, however, and thus it is not well understood by either the industry or the public.

Public opinion tends to overestimate the capacity of financial intermediaries, particularly their ability to detect corrupt money flows. At the same time, financial intermediaries seem to have a tendency to underestimate their exposure to direct corruption, the related legal and reputation risks, and the potential of being indirectly abused to facilitate corrupt payments. Unfortunately, they also remain unaware of the full potential of some of their well-tested AML instruments.

Risks and remedies

When financial institutions are involved in corruption it usually happens in one of two ways: Either the financial institution itself or an employee directly commits an act of corruption by bribing or by accepting bribes (employee risk); or the financial institution is (mis-)used by one of its clients to disguise the corrupt origin of funds or to commit tax fraud (client risk).

It is critical to understand that financial institutions as legal persons, their employees and their managers can all be held legally liable for corruption and abetting tax fraud. It is therefore of vital interest for any financial intermediary to implement recommended reform measures to the fullest extent possible.

Active and passive bribery: an underestimated risk profile

When it comes to the active and passive bribery associated with employee risk, the financial sector is usually not mentioned among the most exposed industries, such as construction and the extractive industries. Nonetheless, certain risk factors are likely to increase potential exposure, such as the countries where an institution operates, the quality of the institution's compliance system and general business culture, and the sectors and types of actors with which it interacts. Dealings with particularly corruption-exposed sectors and institutions – such as political parties, legislatures, the police, the judiciary, and public procurement, taxation and public licensing agencies – would dramatically increase an institution's risk exposure and thus warrant a particularly stringent compliance system.

Such a heightened exposure to corruption is not a remote possibility. Foreign banks significantly expanded their global presence in the 1990s, including in many countries perceived to harbour relatively high risks of corruption.[4] Corruption in lending operations is considered a higher risk than commonly assumed.[5] Likewise, in a survey of more than 2,700 businesspeople in twenty-six countries in 2008, almost 10 per cent of the bank managers

---

4 P. Cornelius, 'Foreign Bank Ownership and Corporate Governance in Emerging-Market Economies', in P. Cornelius and B. Kogut (eds.), *Corporate Governance and Capital Flows in a Global Economy* (New York: Oxford University Press, 2003).
5 See article starting on page 19.

interviewed believed that their colleagues and competitors were involved in the bribery of public officials.[6]

Remedies: risk-specific compliance systems

Given this risk profile, financial institutions are as obliged as any other private sector player to equip themselves with a comprehensive internal anti-bribery compliance system. Such a system will have the added value of putting the bank one step ahead of law enforcement when it comes to detecting corruption cases. A proactive approach of this type can make it easier to obtain some leniency from law enforcement and can help retain the trust of clients, staff and the general public. International frameworks such as the World Economic Forum's Partnering Against Corruption Initiative and the Business Principles for Countering Bribery developed by Transparency International and Social Accountability International provide useful guidance and can form the basis for an industry- and institution-specific risk-mapping. Once the outline of an anti-bribery system has been established, a financial institution should carefully analyse geographic-, as well as industry- and institution-specific, risks.

To prevent the typical operational risks, banks are well advised to pay particular attention to policies on gifts and entertainment, and the handling of intermediaries and agents, both those acting on behalf of the financial institution and the institution's clients. Furthermore, kickbacks may be of particular importance for private and retail banking, while conflicts of interest and procurement are a special concern for investment banking and trade financing. Additionally, insurance providers and retail banks should be particularly watchful of political and charitable contributions, and facilitation payments.

The risk of facilitating corruption and other dubious activities

With respect to the risk of being (mis-)used to participate in money laundering and other criminal acts, the financial industry's exposure is unique compared to other industries. Complex financial transactions that cross multiple jurisdictions can protect the proceeds of criminal activities from seizure by the authorities, while covering up their origin and reintroducing them into the formal economy.

Similarly, such transactions can be structured to help hide assets from the tax authorities or to obscure losses, risks or outright fraud in corporate accounts. A US Senate Subcommittee report released in July 2008, for example, accused the Swiss bank UBS of helping 19,000 US citizens to hide US$18 billion in undeclared accounts from the US tax authorities.[7] J.P. Morgan Chase and Citigroup were ordered to pay a combined US$236 million to investors who had lost money in Enron for their role in helping the company conceal the true scale of its debt.[8]

---

6 TI, '2008 Bribe Payers Survey' (Berlin: TI, 2008).
7 US Senate Permanent Subcommittee on Investigations, *Tax Haven Banks and U.S. Tax Compliance* (Washington, DC: Permanent Subcommittee on Investigations, 2008).
8 *International Herald Tribune* (US), 30 July 2003.

Banks can also be abused to channel bribes or to fund illegal or terrorist activities discretely. In one notable example, a trust in Liechtenstein and a bank in the Bahamas, both of which the United Nations linked to al Qaeda, were alleged to be embroiled in the oil-for-food scandal.[9]

Although notoriously difficult to estimate, the sums involved are thought to be significant. The overall cross-border flow of proceeds from criminal activities, corruption and tax evasion is estimated to range from several hundred billion dollars to US$1.5 trillion.[10]

Banks and other financial intermediaries therefore play a pivotal role in preventing and sanctioning money-laundering and corruption. They can also help tackle tax and financial corporate fraud.

Consequently, law enforcement and international standard-setting bodies such as the Financial Action Task Force on Money Laundering (FATF) and the Basel Committee on Banking Supervision exert considerable pressure on countries to establish effective and comprehensive remedial strategies for financial intermediaries. Initially concerned with money-laundering related to organised crime and drug-trafficking, international efforts began focusing on corruption as a predicative offence for money-laundering when the OECD Anti-Bribery Convention entered into force in 1999. Finally, in 2003, the FATF followed suit. The Abacha scandal and other highly publicised money-laundering cases that were alleged to involve the proceeds of corruption and related crimes have directed the attention of public standard setters and financial institutions alike to the close linkages between corruption and money-laundering.[11]

A triple link to bribery: underwriting, catalysing and concealing bribes

Typically, a financial institution could be (mis-)used as a vehicle for corruption by a corporate customer who places funds in a bank, often in offshore locations, to pay bribes. These slush funds have been found to be plentiful in recent large-scale corruption cases.

Box 4 Global bribery risks and the global banking system: some recent examples

In large corporations with complex financial structures, slush funds and their use can be very difficult to detect, even for accountants and auditors, and for the banks that host these accounts.

- Siemens, the German engineering conglomerate, allegedly used a web of accounts and shell companies in Liechtenstein and other locations to channel and conceal some of the estimated US$1.6 billion in bribe payments it made around the world.[12]

---

9 *National Review* (US), 18 April 2004.
10 R. Baker and J. Nordin, 'Dirty Money: What the Underworld Understands that Economists Do Not', *Economists' Voice*, vol. 4, no. 1 (2007); J. Smith, M. Pieth and G. Jorge, *The Recovery of Stolen Assets*, U4 Brief no. 2007-02 (Bergen: Chr. Michelsen Institute, 2007); World Bank and United Nations, *Stolen Asset Recovery (StAR) Initiative: Challenges, Opportunities, and Action Plan* (Washington, DC: World Bank, 2007).
11 For examples of corruption-related international money laundering cases, see www.assetrecovery.org.
12 *Businessweek* (Europe), 14 March 2007; Bundesgerichtshof, Judgment of 29 August 2008 – 2 StR 587/07.

Box 4 (continued)

- A subsidiary of Halliburton, the US energy contractor formerly run by the previous US vice-president, Dick Cheney, is believed to have used offshore arrangements in Gibraltar for tens of millions of dollars in bribe payments to win a contract in Nigeria.[13]

- BAe Systems, a UK military contractor, allegedly routed questionable payments of £7 million (US$10.5 million) through the offshore banking centre of Jersey.[14]

- Alstom, the French engineering group, is alleged by Swiss prosecutors to have used Switzerland and Panama as transit points for payments to Zambia. Investigations into Alstom are ongoing and the company has denied any wrongdoing.[15]

In addition, a client may misuse banks to spirit the proceeds from corruption or ill-gotten gains out of the country, using seemingly normal but complex layers of transactions to conceal the funds' origin.

The stakes are high. Proceeds from corruption are believed to amount to US$20 to 40 billion in developing and transition countries – the equivalent of 20 to 40 per cent of official development assistance.[16] The Abacha scandal and other episodes of rulers allegedly looting public wealth further demonstrate the risks that banks face.

Finally, banks may be misused as financiers of corrupt business operations, such as business projects won through corrupt means or corrupt payments made during the execution phase. Again, this raises significant reputational and material risks for banks. When corruption is exposed, contracts can be revoked and fines can be imposed that put repayments at risk or raise liability issues for the lender.

Remedies: broadening existing screening mechanisms

Financial institutions usually argue that it is exceedingly difficult for them to detect business relationships and transactions related to corruption. They also claim, however, to be effective in detecting funds from other illegal origins with their anti-money laundering systems. It is worth exploring, therefore, how existing AML systems can be used and enhanced so that banks can better detect and distinguish patterns of illicit transactions related to corruption, along with patterns related to other crimes they screen.

Acknowledging this potential, the Wolfsberg Group's 2007 Statement against Corruption identifies typical red flags for corruption-related activities, and the characteristics of clients and transactions that should raise suspicions of corruption. A typical risk situation involves a public official who has a large amount of money transferred into his or her account by an

---

13 *Harper's* (US), 30 September 2008.
14 *Guardian* (UK), 8 June 2006.
15 *Wall Street Journal Asia*, 12 November 2008.
16 World Bank and United Nations, 2007.

agent or intermediary in the oil and gas sector. Additional red flags include funds transferred from an offshore financial centre, or through a shell company or another corporate vehicle typically used to obscure the origin of funds. Any of these indicators should naturally trigger an enhanced due diligence process.

Refining existing screening systems to include more red flags that focus on the typical characteristics of corruption is well within the reach of any financial institution. At a minimum, the red flags identified by the Wolfsberg Group should be included in a financial institution's AML system.

Current challenges

Politically exposed persons

AML systems also need to be strengthened and expanded more broadly, including their capacity to deal with politically exposed persons (PEPs). PEPs are individuals who are active and visible in the political arena or who hold high public office, and thus are highly exposed to corruption risks. As a consequence, they represent a special risk for financial institutions, including in reputational terms, given that they are often in the public spotlight. Dealing with PEPs requires special due diligence measures on the part of banks to verify the identity and information provided by clients and to identify potentially suspicious transactions they may be involved in.

The devil is in the details, however. Defining who should be classified as a PEP, and thus require extra scrutiny, is far from clear and continues to engage the anti-corruption community. How senior would a public official have to be? Should the label apply only to heads of state and Cabinet ministers, or to members of parliament as well? Should a PEP's family, close friends and business partners also be screened?

Even the UN Convention against Corruption fails to reflect on PEPs in great detail, and guidance provided by the Financial Action Task Force on Money Laundering is similarly unspecific. A significant improvement is expected from the Third EU Money Laundering Directive, which provides a detailed definition of a PEP, as well as the enhanced due diligence measures that banks must follow when dealing with PEPs. The directive could make a considerable contribution in the fight against corruption, as well as to efforts to recover stolen assets – another highly prominent topic on the anti-corruption agenda.

Recovering stolen assets

Whenever stolen assets are seized and attempts are made to return them to the victimised country, the involved financial institutions find themselves in the spotlight of public outrage and in close association with the alleged crime. The reputational damage to the financial institution, to the financial centre where it is located and, more broadly, to its home country is increasingly recognised within the industry. Public attention on this topic has never been greater.

As of September 2007 Switzerland had returned an estimated Fr1.6 billion (US$1.3 billion) to countries such as Brazil, Chile, France, Italy, Jordan, Kazakhstan, Russia, Ukraine and the United States. The most prominent cases include those of Marcos (the return of assets to the Philippines), Abacha (Nigeria) and Montesinos (Peru). Such laudable exceptions aside, success in asset recovery is still minimal. A multiple of the assets returned so far is still suspected to remain hidden in many of the world's financial centres, and by no means have all the concerned jurisdictions been equally responsive to this challenge.

A large portion of the responsibility for changing this situation lies with the governments of the countries in which the banks are domiciled. They need to ensure that their laws and enforcement practices adhere to the highest standards, such as those of the FATF, the European Union, the Basel Committee on Banking Supervision and the UN Office on Drugs and Crime. Governments need to abolish the typical hurdles that hamper asset recovery, such as unreasonably high legal thresholds, lengthy procedures and overly formalistic requirements for granting judicial assistance to victim states and repatriating the stolen funds.[17]

Because the UN Convention against Corruption addresses many of these challenges, significant improvements in this area should be expected in the coming years, as more countries implement the convention. This should result in a dramatic increase in the funds actually being repatriated.

A stronger commitment to the benefit of all

Financial institutions are not mere bystanders in this corruption challenge. At a minimum, they will need to prove that they adhere strictly to new rules and standards implemented in line with international frameworks. Ideally, financial institutions should contribute constructively to the dialogue at the domestic level, by lobbying their governments to observe these international standards stringently and by working with governments to define the implementing measures financial institutions may need to take. They should also contribute to dialogues at the international level.

Unfortunately, the financial community so far has not taken a very active or outspoken position in these arenas. For instance, the virtual absence of the private sector in general, and the financial industry in particular, from the two Conferences of State Parties to the UNCAC and the fact that more than a half of the banking executives in a large survey in 2008 indicated that they were not familiar with the UNCAC framework must be interpreted as a clear lack of interest.[18] Another 2008 poll of financial services and investment management executives further corroborates this suspicion. Almost a quarter of the respondents said that their companies did not have a monitoring system for suspicious transactions, while another third were not aware of whether their companies had one.[19]

---

17 For an in-depth analysis of the challenges governments and law enforcement face in recovering stolen assets, see
    M. Pieth (ed.), *Recovering Stolen Assets* (Berne: Peter Lang, 2008).
18 TI, '2008 Bribe Payers Survey' (Berlin: TI, 2008).
19 *PR Newswire* (US), 23 July 2008.

It is to be hoped that the financial crisis that erupted in 2008 will provide the impetus for stronger commitments. The crisis has prompted a strong and growing call for financial centres and institutions to adopt transparency, accountability and integrity standards commensurate with their essential role in safeguarding the stability and integrity of a globally interconnected economy. Helping to tackle corruption and fraud should be part and parcel of such a commitment by the banking sector everywhere.

Leveraging consumer power for corporate integrity
Oscar Lanza[1]

Corporations today have achieved such immense economic prowess that some rival or exceed the financial power of many countries. The revenue of the top five multinational companies is two and a half times as large as the combined gross domestic product of the world's fifty poorest countries measured by per capita income.[2] Of the world's 100 leading economic entities, fifty-one are companies and forty-nine are countries. The top 200 businesses in the world represent more than a quarter of global economic activity, and their total sales surpass the GDP of the entire planet, excluding the nine most industrialised countries.[3]

Although the growing power and influence of corporations ought to correspond to improvements in corporate social responsibility (CSR), all too often this has not been the case. Corporate failures have compelled citizens to self-organise as consumers and users of products and services, pooling their strength to demand improved product safety and quality, and stronger CSR. Consumer advocacy groups of various types have been formed in virtually every country in the world. The modern consumer movement has become one of the strongest forces for fostering enhanced corporate transparency, accountability and integrity.

The evolution of consumer activism

Since 1960 Consumers International (CI) has been one of the key driving forces behind this steadily growing movement. CI's global federation of more than 220 associate organisations in 115 countries has helped protect and strengthen consumer rights throughout the world, acting as a singular authoritative and independent voice for consumers. CI works on

---

1 Oscar Lanza is a Professor of Public Health at Universidad Mayor de San Andres de La Paz (Bolivia) and coordinator of the Committee for the Defence of Consumer Rights (Accion Internacional por la Salud/Comité de Defensa de los Derechos de los Consumidores: AIS-CODEDCO) in Bolivia.
2 Calculations based on IMF, 'World Economic Outlook Database', October 2008 edition (Washington, DC: IMF, 2008); CNN Money, 'Fortune Global 500 Annual Ranking', 21 July 2008; see http://money.cnn.com/magazines/fortune/global500/2008/.
3 S. Anderson and J. Cavanagh, *The Top 200: The Rise of Global Corporate Power* (Washington, DC: Institute for Policy Studies, 2000).

a wide range of issues, from food safety and sustainable consumption to antitrust and drug marketing.[4]

Two years after CI was founded, US President John F. Kennedy acknowledged the nascent role and potential breadth of the consumer movement: 'Consumers by definition include us all. They are the largest economic group, affecting and affected by almost every public and private economic decision. Yet they are the only important group . . . whose views are often not heard.'[5]

Kennedy declared four basic consumer entitlements, which have evolved into a more comprehensive set of eight widely accepted principles.

- The right to the satisfaction of basic needs – including food, clothing, shelter, health care, education, public utilities, water and sanitation.
- The right to safety – protection from hazardous products, production processes and services.
- The right to be informed – with the facts necessary to make informed choices and provide protection from dishonest advertising and labelling.
- The right to choose – from quality-assured products and services offered at competitive prices.
- The right to be heard – so that consumers are represented in government policy-making and in product and service development.
- The right to redress – guaranteeing compensation for misrepresentation, shoddy goods or unsatisfactory services.
- The right to consumer education – the knowledge and skills to make confident choices and provide awareness of basic consumer rights.
- The right to a healthy environment – living and working in an environment non-threatening to present and future generations.

Consumers' rights received international recognition on 9 April 1985, when the UN General Assembly adopted guidelines for consumer protection following a decade-long lobbying and advocacy battle. This elevated the rights of consumers to a position of legitimacy and international recognition in industrialised and developing countries alike.[6] The guidelines are now reflected in legislation and consumer protection laws in most parts of the world, and in many places they have led to increased respect for the basic rights of consumers.

The consumer movement seeks to further these rights. In industrialised countries, the movement has concentrated on monitoring business conduct and educating citizens, with the objective of discouraging and punishing business practices detrimental to the interests of consumers and society, and promoting consumer activities that reward businesses for responsible behaviour.[7]

---

4 See www.consumersinternational.org.
5 J. F. Kennedy, 'Special Message to the Congress on Protecting the Consumer Interest', Washington, DC, 15 March 1962.
6 See www.consumersinternational.org/Templates/Internal.asp?NodeID=97460.
7 J. Vargas Niello, 'Responsabilidad Social Empresarial (RES) desde la Perspectiva de los Consumidores' (Santiago: UN, 2006).

In other regions, such as Latin America, the government and civil society have not yet developed sufficient actions to compel corporations to act responsibly with regard to ethics, the environment, finance and society. Nonetheless, some encouraging headway has been achieved. The UN's guidelines and their incorporation into the legislation of many Latin American countries have reinforced consumer rights and granted significant institutional support to consumers.[8] Bolivia remains an exception, however, being the only country in the Americas lacking a consumer protection law.

Consumer practices to strengthen corporate integrity

Commercial practices, advertising and marketing should be governed by ethical standards, laws and regulations, as well as measures of safety, security and quality to ensure that products and services meet the legal obligations related to consumer health and safety. To this end, businesses should provide reliable information pertaining to the contents of their products, as well as instructions for their proper use, maintenance, storage and disposal. Processes to resolve conflicts with consumers in a fair and timely manner and that avoid expensive or undue inconvenience also need to be introduced.[9]

In addition, companies should refrain from statements or practices that are misleading, fraudulent or unfair. Consumer privacy ought to be respected and private information protected. When necessary, companies should collaborate with the authorities to prevent any risks to health and public safety that might arise from their products.[10]

In pursuit of these goals, consumers seeking to restrict unethical practices have undertaken many transformative campaigns.

Product safety and the precautionary principle

In 2000, following a global consumer and public interest campaign, 122 countries agreed on a UN-sponsored treaty banning twelve persistent organic pollutants known as the 'dirty dozen', including DDT and PCBs.[11] This and other public health victories have led to a change in consciousness about how potential threats should be assessed. Whereas the authorities have most commonly asked for scientific proof that a product is harmful to humans or the environment, consumer activists and progressive-minded policy-makers are increasingly adopting the precautionary principle, saying: 'Until we know whether this product is safe for people and the environment, it should be kept off the market.' The former approach, which emphasises proof of harm, is more common in the United States, while the latter, which stresses precaution, is more common in the European Union.

8 Ibid.
9 M. Sánchez, 'La Responsabilidad Social Empresarial y los Consumidores', *CIRIEC-España*, no. 53 (2005).
10 Ibid.
11 *New York Times* (US), 20 April 2001.

Consumer boycotts in action

One of the largest boycotts ever undertaken was the campaign to pressure corporations operating in apartheid-era South Africa to divest from the country, which also led to protests at
universities with investments in these companies. Some 200 companies had left the country
by the time Nelson Mandela called for the boycott to end in 1993, contributing to the down-
fall of the apartheid system.[12]

Among the many major boycotts targeting specific companies, consumers stopped buying
General Electric (GE) light bulbs, refrigerators and other products in the 1980s and 1990s to
protest at GE's role in nuclear weapons production. McDonald's has been boycotted for using
styrofoam and other environmentally unsustainable packaging materials, and for buying
meat from factory-style farms with poor environmental and animal welfare practices. Wal-
Mart has been boycotted for buying products made in sweatshops. Nestlé was boycotted by
consumers wanting the company to stop selling its infant formula in developing countries.
All these campaigns have achieved at least a portion of their goals.[13]

Responsible marketing

Successful campaigns against the tobacco industry are among the innumerable consumer
actions contributing to the prevention of unethical practices and furthering the cause of
social justice – not to mention the prevention of hundreds of thousands of deaths every year.
Consumer groups have succeeded in placing severe restrictions on cigarette advertising and
forcing tobacco companies to pay for public service campaigns. Florida's 'Truth' advertising
campaign helped cut teenage smoking rates significantly after just two years in action.[14] Such
initiatives constitute a powerful set of tools to strengthen corporate ethics and integrity.

As citizens acquire greater awareness of global problems and their own rights, they are exerting
ever greater pressure to persuade the private sector to operate in a responsible manner. In a
global market increasingly dominated by multinational companies, the consumer movement
is now more essential than ever to guaranteeing a safe and sustainable future.

A change in strategy may be needed to maximise the effectiveness of consumer-based
anti-corruption efforts, however. Traditional consumer organisations, such as Consumers
International, tend to work against unseemly corporate practices by taking on particular
policy issues, industries and companies. Broader anti-corruption measures have generally not
been the purview of such groups. Adding such a role deserves further exploration.

---

12 R. E. Edgar (ed.), *Sanctioning Apartheid* (Trenton, NJ: Africa World Press, 1990).
13 *New York Times* (US), 13 June 1991; *Oregon Daily Emerald* (US), 18 February 2002; *Multinational Monitor* (US),
    December 1990; Knight Ridder/Tribune Business News (US), 16 December 2002; *New York Times* (US), 5 October
    1988.
14 *Business Wire* (US), 21 March 2001.

NGOs and corporate integrity: the tempo of effective action accelerates

Frank Vogl[1]

There is no evidence that corporate bribe-paying to secure contracts and unfair advantage over competitors has declined in the dozen years since thirty-seven countries agreed the OECD Convention on Combating Bribery of Foreign Public Officials in International Business Transactions (the OECD Anti-Bribery Convention) in 1997. Indeed, given the dramatic expansion since then in international trade, foreign direct investment and other forms of global capital flows, it is probable that such malfeasance has increased. This is the realistic setting within which the impact of increased activities by non-governmental organisations to curb business corruption needs to be assessed.

NGOs have racked up many impressive results investigating and exposing corrupt practices at some giant companies and in major industries. They have taken large numbers of actions that have threatened, and indeed often undermined, the comforting veil of secrecy that cloaks the payment of bribes by companies to governmental officials.

NGO achievements in making life tougher for corporations determined to use kickbacks to clinch deals are significant, but there are shortcomings as well. The balance sheet of NGO activism to thwart corruption and bribery by business is a mixed one at best.

Making progress

In its quest to speak truth to power, for instance, Global Witness[2] in the United Kingdom took to task those associated with the trade in 'blood diamonds' – stones that are produced in areas controlled by rebel forces that are opposed to internationally recognised governments, and pioneered research into the opaque and shady relationships between natural resource firms and the governments to which they make payments. No less significant, to take another example, has been the work of the Center for Public Integrity[3] in the United States, which has documented in dozens of studies the often ethically challenged ties between US enterprises, their Washington-based lobbyists and powerful politicians.

Perhaps even more impressive, although less of a headline-catcher, has been the mounting success of NGOs in forging constructive multi-stakeholder institutions that enable them to sit at the table with business and government and promote accountability, new ethics codes and anti-corruption monitoring mechanisms. For example, the Extractive Industries Transparency

---

1 Frank Vogl is a co-founder of Transparency International and a director of Vogl Communications, Inc.
2 See www.globalwitness.org.
3 See www.publicintegrity.org.

Initiative (EITI)[4] in natural resources, the United Nations Global Compact[5] in corporate social responsibility and the Partnering Against Corruption Initiative (PACI)[6] in business ethics codes have all been driven by NGOs seeking to convince business and government alike to raise corporate ethics voluntarily.

More subtly, many NGOs have pursued research into many aspects of corporate activity, bringing to light cases of inadequate transparency (often implying that transactions that are kept secret may involve corrupt practices), or they have highlighted the key lessons learnt from actual business experiences. Studies, for example, over the last eighteen months by Transparency International[7] into the revenue transparency of major oil and gas companies, and by Oxfam[8] into mining in Central America, are significant. Studies such as these, just as the exposés produced by Global Witness, the Center for Public Integrity and numerous others, often fuel journalistic investigations and publicity that promote public debate, and sometimes important legislation. The TI study, combined with similar work on energy enterprises by Global Witness, contributed to efforts by the Publish What You Pay[9] NGO coalition to secure support for legislative initiatives in the US House of Representatives in the late summer of 2008.

NGOs have also taken advantage of high-profile situations to push the anti-corruption agenda, with considerable success. For instance, the remarkable revelations of far-reaching arms corruption on the part of the Indian government in 2001 by the Tehelka[10] internet group of journalists was, over time, to contribute to efforts by NGOs to promote significant domestic reforms in arms procurement. In 2007 and 2008, to take quite a different example, two NGO coalitions in the United Kingdom, the Campaign Against Arms Trade (CAAT) and the Corner House, challenged relentlessly the decision by the UK government to quash investigations into alleged bribe-paying by defence contractor BAe Systems to Saudi Arabian officials. By keeping the story on the media's radar screen these NGOs won a series of court victories, and pressure rose on the government to review its approaches. Even though the UK courts finally sided with the original government action, the work of the NGOs contributed significantly to exposing the problems and, more importantly, to pressuring the company's board of directors to call upon former high court judge Lord Woolf of Barnes to lead an internal investigation. His findings and reform recommendations have established key new benchmarks for UK corporate behaviour, particularly in the defence sector.[11]

In addition, NGOs have actively challenged the arguments so often made by too many globe-trotting business executives that, in much of the world, the culture of corruption and rigged

---

4 See eitransparency.org.
5 See www.unglobalcompact.org.
6 See www.weforum.org/en/initiatives/paci.
7 TI, *2008 Report on Revenue Transparency of Oil and Gas Companies* (Berlin: TI, 2008).
8 Oxfam America, 'Metals Mining and Sustainable Development in Central America: An Assessment of Benefits and Costs', July 2008.
9 See www.publishwhatyoupay.org.
10 See CNN news story on the Indian scandal at archives.cnn.com/2001/WORLD/asiapcf/south/03/15/naji.debrief.
11 See www.caat.org.uk and www.thecornerhouse.org.uk. The report by Lord Woolf of Barnes in mid-2008 can be found at www.ethicsworld.org/corporategovernance/PDF%20links/Woolf_report_2008.pdf.

public procurement bidding is so entrenched that firms have no choice other than to go along and play the game. Unmasking the dirty deals and prominently promoting legal actions can start to turn the tide.

Only public pressure, driven to a degree by NGOs, for example, has forced multilateral aid agencies to start blacklisting firms. At the same time, the use of 'integrity pacts' and the establishment of what former TI chairman Peter Eigen has called 'islands of integrity' have demonstrated that appropriate conditions can be established in major public contracts to secure clean and transparent bidding.

The above examples are just a few of hundreds of NGO actions in recent years that have played a role in gradually bringing about greater public acknowledgement of the need to pursue improved transparency and accountability with regard to prominent multinational corporations.[12]

This has been possible only because, as NGOs focus more sharply on business behaviour, they also work to strengthen the important institutional capacities needed to secure meaningful pressure on business. From media education programmes in Mongolia, to access to information projects in Argentina, to building support for whistleblower protection in Nigeria[13] and scores of similar initiatives across the world, key frameworks are being constructed. Together with many NGO projects in the area of judicial reform and capacity-building, the frameworks create levels of awareness as well as potential for the exposure of corrupt acts and penalties for the guilty.

Shortcomings

Although it is difficult to overstate the scale of activity and progress pursued by NGOs, the challenge remains vast. The extent of the trade and competitive distortions in global commerce resulting from business corruption is huge, as is the waste and inefficiency associated with private sector contracting in public procurement.

Unquestionably, there are shortcomings in NGO anti-corruption work vis-à-vis business. None is probably more serious than action to secure meaningful law enforcement. At the moment, corrupt businesspeople in most countries have little to fear even when their crimes are exposed. Even in those few countries where corrupt firms have been brought to justice, implicated top executives have rarely faced imprisonment. NGOs have failed, by and large, to heed the insight of Professor Robert Klitgaard, who, on addressing the founding conference of Transparency International in Berlin in May 1993, emphasised the need to 'fry a few big fish'. Klitgaard has frequently written: 'When there is a culture of engaging in corrupt acts with impunity, the way to begin breaking it up is for a number of major corrupt figures to be convicted and punished.'[14]

---

12 This is indicated both by the greater participation of companies seeking to implement the Global Reporting Initiative (GRI) social responsibility standards and the willingness of more than 4,000 companies to join the UN Global Compact and agree to enhance public communications on their corporate citizenship programmes.

13 For more information on these projects, see the Partnership for Transparency Fund at www.partnershipfortransparency.info/Completed+Projects.html.

14 For example, see R. Klitgaard, 'International Cooperation against Corruption', *Finance and Development*, vol. 35, no. 1 (1998).

NGOs do not organise enough marches and public demonstrations, nor high-profile media events or TV-directed campaigns, to decry the monstrous failure of governments to 'walk the talk' when it comes to investigating, prosecuting and punishing corrupt companies and their leaders. The international NGO movement was largely silent when, for example, South Korean President and former Hyundai executive Cheong Wa Dae announced[15] a sweeping amnesty for seventy-four prominent convicted corporate executives. He said the move would help encourage the business community to redouble its efforts to revive the economy. Pardoned tycoons included Hyundai Motor chairman Chung Mong-koo, SK Energy chairman Chey Tae-won and Hanwha Group chairman Kim Seung-youn.

Taking another example, there was not so much as a murmur of protest when, in 2005, no effort was made by the US authorities to prosecute Philip Condit, then the chief executive officer of the Boeing Company. Boeing had allegedly been discovered stealing documents from rival Lockheed Martin Corporation to secure US Defense Department contracts, and it was caught having secretly recruited one of the Pentagon's top procurement officers.[16] The company agreed to an unprecedented record fine of US$615 million to settle charges against it by the US justice authorities, but Condit faced no charges.[17]

Transparency International has periodically reported on the failures of most signatory governments to enforce the OECD Anti-Bribery Convention, but these reports have not triggered major international NGO protest campaigns.

Another shortcoming relates to developing countries and much of eastern Europe, where it is more politically difficult than in OECD-member countries – indeed, dangerous – for NGOs to campaign publicly against corrupt enterprises and call for tough enforcement of anti-corruption laws. In most of these countries, laws and regulations to protect minority shareholder rights in publicly quoted companies are rarely enforced, and access to business information for such shareholders, let alone for NGOs, is difficult.

Moreover, even in the rapidly advancing emerging economies, let alone the less economically prosperous nations, corporate governance regulation as it relates to transparency and accountability is very weak when it comes to the vast majority of enterprises that are not quoted on the stock exchanges; here the NGOs often consider themselves to have even less access and less opportunity to effect change. The promotion of voluntary business ethics standards by some NGOs is worthy, but it is not likely to be very effective in countries in which governments lack the will or the capacity to enforce domestic laws that make business bribe-paying illegal, or that even seek to enforce fairly minimum public information reporting by firms.

Finally, an additional shortcoming relates to NGO participation in multi-stakeholder organisations such as EITI, the UN Global Compact and PACI. So far, NGOs have been cautious in

---

15 *Korean Times*, 12 August 2008.
16 US Department of Justice, Release no. 03-95, 25 June 2003; *New York Times* (US), 4 February 2005.
17 See www.boeing.com/news/releases/2006/q2/060515a_nr.html.

pushing business and government hard to reform, and businesses engaged in these forums have made only modest concessions. In some cases, companies have improved public reporting, but have then tended to oppose external independent verification of their anti-bribery claims. Furthermore, while businesses have declared their opposition to bribing foreign government officials, many nevertheless continue to use loopholes, such as facilitation payments, to suborn foreign officials.

The organisers of these forums counsel the NGOs to be patient and to work quietly to build the institutions and modus operandi so that they can gradually and consistently make advances.

The road ahead

The shortcomings that are noted above are understandable as pragmatic realities in a rapidly changing world in which NGOs engaged in anti-corruption work are still, for the most part, very young and, compared to major corporations, massively underfunded. These realities make the achievements of NGOs in influencing improvements in corporate behaviour over the last decade or so all the more impressive.

What we have learnt since the founding of Transparency International in 1993 is that there is enormous public concern about the corrupt relationships that exist so widely in almost all countries between top tycoons and top politicians. We have also learnt that the greatest weapon in the NGO armoury is public communications. The ability of NGOs to strengthen their investigative skills, to campaign forcefully and publicly in protest at business corruption and to use the internet to inform the world's most influential press rapidly of new episodes of corporate malfeasance can combine to leave businesses with nowhere to hide.

Indeed, if such NGO skills in this area can continue to develop, and if at the same time there is more law enforcement, more emphasis on corporate corruption by NGOs in emerging economies and more effective NGO use of the multi-stakeholder forums, then, in time, unethical corporate executives may finally have something to fear when they pursue their corrupt ways.

View from the inside – Shining the light on corporate wrongdoing: the role of business journalism

Rob Evans[1]

Investigating corruption is difficult. Prosecutors find it hard, as do journalists. The corrupt go to great lengths to conceal their wrongdoing. There are any number of tax havens and front companies they can exploit to hide their loot. Reporters can and do uncover corruption, however, and this is often the first step towards a prosecution.

Reporters' greatest allies are whistleblowers: they are often the true heroes and heroines of journalism. It is they who have the courage to leak vital information, often putting their jobs – and even their lives – at risk. What they can tell reporters is invaluable, however, and their stories expose some of the most serious corruption cases. Whistleblowers know what is actually going on, because they are inside the system and have had a ringside seat to the wrongdoing. They are the ones with the crucial information to destroy the public denials issued by the corrupt. They can pinpoint exactly who has received illicit payments, how much has been paid out and by what route.

My experience of working with David Leigh on the *Guardian* investigation that led to the exposure of the BAe Systems scandal in the United Kingdom is illustrative of the challenges that journalists face in investigating corruption. The articles we wrote prompted the Serious Fraud Office (SFO) to launch an investigation into allegations that BAe Systems, the United Kingdom's biggest arms company, had paid bribes to win contracts from Saudi Arabia and other governments. Tony Blair's government eventually stepped in and stopped the SFO from completing its investigation into the allegations in December 2006.[2]

Many of the people who contributed to the reports can never be identified, although two whistleblowers have already been named. They show how well-placed sources can provide inside information that can propel an investigation forward. Often investigations into corruption run into the sand after a while because journalists have no new information for further articles.

The investigation into BAe System's payments began in late 2002. Over three days in June 2003 the *Guardian* published articles into alleged bribery in the Czech Republic, India, Qatar and South Africa.[3] A few weeks later whistleblower Edward Cunningham contacted the *Guardian* with new allegations of a slush fund that BAe Systems was using to bribe

---

1 Rob Evans is an investigative reporter for the *Guardian* newspaper in the United Kingdom. Along with his colleague David Leigh, he uncovered the British Aerospace (BAe) Systems scandal that earned international renown when the Serious Fraud Office (SFO) discontinued its investigation into alleged corruption between BAe Systems and the Saudi Arabian government.
2 *Guardian* (UK), 15 December 2006.
3 *Guardian* (UK), 12 June 2003; 13 June 2003; 14 June 2003.

and 'sweeten' Saudi officials connected to a huge arms contract.[4] Cunningham spoke out because he was appalled by what he had seen. Those articles in September 2003 reported that BAe Systems was allegedly providing prostitutes, sports cars, yachts, first-class plane tickets and other inducements.

The *Guardian* continued to publish articles about BAe Systems, prompting another whistle-blower to come forward. Peter Gardiner had worked in a more senior role in the slush fund than Cunningham. He was able to provide more detailed evidence showing how the extent of the alleged corruption was far bigger than previously thought.[5] In May 2004 the *Guardian* published allegations of how BAe Systems had paid £17 million in benefits and cash to the key Saudi politician in charge of purchasing arms from the United Kingdom. Documents listed every Saudi official alleged to have received benefits from BAe Systems, which included luxury London houses.[6] This new evidence persuaded the SFO to launch its investigation into the deals. Without Cunningham or Gardiner, there probably would have been no investigation at all, and the *Guardian* would not have been able to publish its articles.

During our investigation we faced a number of challenges. One of the most acute was the difficulty in penetrating the banking system to find out how BAe Systems had made its allegedly corrupt payments. The money flowed from the United Kingdom to the tax haven of the British Virgin Islands to Switzerland and onwards – to the Czech Republic, Romania, Qatar, Tanzania, South Africa and Chile. As the allegations concerning BAe Systems' bribery around the globe proliferated, more and more prosecutors abroad were drawn into investigating them. Unlike reporters, these prosecutors possess the powers to serve legal papers on banks and companies ordering them to release information. As the number of investigations expanded around the world, so did the leaks, and slowly a picture of the payments began to emerge. We were working with reporters in other countries who were better placed to find out what was going on in the investigations in their countries and share information with us.

We also needed to avoid being sued. This is one of the hazards when you are writing unflattering articles about a big corporation with deep pockets. We were able to take advantage of a legal ruling, called the Reynolds defence, which allows reporters to air allegations of wrongdoing that are in the public interest provided you act in a responsible manner. One of the requirements is to give the accused ample time to respond to the allegations and to include his or her response properly in the article. We found that BAe Systems never wanted to say much, however; it seems clear that the company took a decision early on in the saga not to respond in detail and, instead, simply to issue a blanket denial. It appears that the company did not want to sue us, since a public trial would reveal all sorts of sensitive and embarrassing secrets. Reporters investigating corruption would be helped if the law gave them a strong defence against being sued, however.

If policy-makers are looking to help journalists uncover corruption, one of the most effective ways would be to strengthen the protection afforded to whistleblowers. Employees who have

---

4 *Guardian* (UK), 11 September 2003; 12 September 2003.
5 Guardian website (video), 6 June 2007.
6 *Guardian* (UK), 4 May 2004.

become concerned about alleged wrongdoing and want to inform the outside world are often worried about the consequences. They need to feel that they will be listened to and protected afterwards. In the United Kingdom, for instance, the government has passed into law the Public Interest Disclosure Act 1998. This law gives a whistleblower a shield against dismissal and victimisation, provided the information being disclosed is in the public interest.[7]

Policy-makers seeking to stamp out corruption should also put in place a strong freedom of information act. Such an act is useful to reporters. It is unlikely to reveal the details of the alleged corruption, as police investigators often remain able to prevent the release of documents they have seized from the alleged perpetrators. The act has another value, however: documents released under the act can often show what else a company alleged to be involved in corruption has been up to. This gives a more rounded picture of the company. For example, the *Guardian* published an article in 2005 about a UK firm that was accused of corruption and overcharging in the Philippines. During our investigation, we obtained documents under the Freedom of Information Act 2000 showing how the firm had told the UK government that the accusations were baseless.[8]

Journalists aiming to expose corruption also need to be persistent. They need time to dig around – to go and see people who may have information, to look through archives, read long reports to retrieve vital pieces of information buried deep within them, and so forth. Often reporters are prevented from doing this, however, as the media owners are far more interested in celebrity stories, or their next set of profits. For many editors, exposing the dry details of how improper payments have been laundered through bank accounts is, quite simply, less exciting than Britney Spears' latest antics. Many people believe that reporters are now being given less time to investigate stories over an extended period. This is a problem that afflicts reporters in developed countries, and it is even more so for journalists in developing countries.

7 Public Concern at Work; see www.pcaw.co.uk/individuals/individuals.htm.
8 *Guardian* (UK), 20 December 2005.

Tackling corruption risks in the defence sector: an example for collective action
Mark Pyman[1]

The defence sector has historically been secretive, prone to corruption and dangerous to probe. In many countries it still is. All the same, there is now some openness to change apparent in

1 Mark Pyman is project leader of TI UK's Defence Project.

many governments, and a readiness on the part of defence companies to act collaboratively in addressing the corruption risks involved.

One of the most prominent areas of corruption in the defence industry, and, arguably, the most important to tackle first is corruption in the procurement of defence equipment.[2] This involves large amounts of money, as well as highly technical expertise for determining the most appropriate purchases, testing the skills of even the most experienced procurement officers in sophisticated defence economies, such as the United States. Furthermore, procurement in defence is more veiled than in other sectors, as issues of national security can be used to uphold barriers to information about the details of contracts and purchases. This traditional climate of secrecy makes it easy for corrupt officials to avoid transparency and public accountability.[3]

Other procurement concerns include the trend towards non-competitive sourcing[4] and the use of 'offsets', which are obligations on bidding companies to invest in other businesses in the country as a condition of being awarded the contract. Although banned by World Trade Organization regulations in other industries, offset requirements are ballooning in defence; now they are usually more than 100 per cent of the value of the main contract. These represent an uncontrolled and dangerous area of corruption risk.[5]

A collective action approach

Transparency International, through its UK defence team, is leading a major project – 'Defence Against Corruption' (DAC) – to catalyse global efforts to combat corruption in the defence sector. The DAC team is working with multiple parties – defence companies (e.g. Lockheed Martin, Raytheon, BAe Systems, Rolls Royce, EADS, Thales, Saab), NATO, the World Bank – and with some fifteen nations (e.g. Colombia, Poland, Latvia) to develop practical tools and pilot them in real defence sector situations. The DAC team's work complements national work on defence in other TI chapters, notably South Korea, India and Colombia.

The DAC team has convened meetings of most of the major European and US defence companies, under the chairmanship of the former NATO secretary general Lord Robertson, to catalyse such action. In a major first step, all thirty European defence industry associations that are members of the AeroSpace and Defence Industries Association of Europe (ASD) agreed in 2008 to a common set of anti-bribery standards.[6] It is anticipated that this will

---

2 Other risks involve inappropriate defence policies, (which is often due to defence lobbying), opaque budgeting and off-budget sources of extra defence revenue.
3 The ease of extracting money corruptly from defence, largely because of the secrecy, also means that there is a spillover of the infrastructure of corruption – the lawyers, agents, bankers, middlemen – from defence into other areas of government.
4 TI UK, 'Offsets and Corruption Risk', paper presented at Global Industrial Cooperation Conference, Seville, 12 May, 2008; TI UK, *The Extent of Single Sourcing and Attendant Corruption Risk in Defence Procurement: A First Look*, working paper (London: TI UK, 2006; final paper to be published in *Journal of Defence and Peace Economics*).
5 TI UK, 2008; 2006.
6 ASD Common Industry Standards, available at www.sbac.co.uk/community/dms/download.asp?txtPageLinkDoc PK=11260.

be followed by a truly global set of minimum anti-bribery standards for international arms transfers.

The DAC team has developed a well-known civil society oversight tool, the 'Defence Integrity Pact', into a version specifically applicable to defence procurement. This tool enables independent insight into the technical requirements of the proposed contract, and entails independent monitoring of the procurement as it unfolds. Real application experience has been gained through large fast jet procurement in Colombia[7] and aircraft procurement in Poland.[8] The feedback was that both had made a positive impact.

A second tool for engaging civil society in defence procurement at the national level is through 'roundtable' events. Roundtables are public forums at which the corruption risks in major forthcoming defence procurements are discussed openly by interested parties. They benefit defence sector stakeholders by raising the level of awareness of corruption risks, through media coverage of the event and through the scrutiny – often for the first time – of senior defence officials. TI Croatia hosted one such roundtable event in Zagreb in 2007, under the patronage of the president, regarding a large purchase of armoured vehicles.[9] TI Croatia and the DAC team facilitated the event, with attendance from senior defence officials, defence companies and representatives from the media, academia and civil society. Well covered by the media, it was seen as a success, leading to further interest within the Ministry of Defence and a follow-up workshop on best practices.

To have an impact on defence corruption, however, we need more than just tools. The cornerstone of such work is ensuring that there are experienced people and institutions able to deal with such issues in both government and civil society. Through the DAC project, NATO, national defence colleges and think tanks are working on building this capacity by developing anti-corruption training courses and workshops to exchange knowledge and experience. NATO, for example, is now piloting a five-day course for defence officials. This initiative was trialled for defence officials from a wide variety of countries during 2008, with courses held in the United Kingdom, Germany and Bosnia.

On the defence company side, defence associations are now publishing guides to good compliance programmes, running courses for small defence companies and organising workshops on setting up compliance programmes.[10] This progress would have been unthinkable even five years ago. It has been made possible because, today, there are civil society teams with defence expertise focusing on practical, constructive measures. Most importantly, civil society has

---

7 Transparencia por Colombia and TI UK, *An Independent Review of the Procurement of Military Items and the Use of Integrity Pacts in Those Contracts* (Bogotá: Transparencia por Colombia/TI UK, 2006).

8 TI UK, 'Building Integrity and Reducing Corruption Risk in Defense Establishments', *NATO Connections*, vol. 8, no. 2 (2008); TI UK, *Report to TI Poland on the Acquisition of VIP Aircraft for the Polish Ministry of National Defence* (London: TI UK, 2006).

9 TI UK, 'Building Integrity', 2008.

10 For example, the Defense Industry Initiative on Business Ethics and Conduct in the United States (www.dii.org/) and the Defence Manufacturers Association in the United Kingdom (www.the-dma.org.uk/).

made progress in making the subject of corruption a real issue for discussion within defence ministries. While defence ministers are only too aware of the inadequacy of corruptly bought equipment and the waste of money involved, there have been no practical initiatives to demonstrate that the subject can be tackled effectively until now.

The DAC project demonstrates that civil society can act as a powerful means of assisting the defence sector's anti-corruption reform through a strategy of positive engagement. An encouraging way forward would be for national organisations to build their own defence integrity expertise, and to use the DAC team to provide credible international back-up for their own defence anti-corruption campaigns.

Part two
Country reports

6 Country perspectives on corruption and the private sector

Introduction
Rebecca Dobson[1]

The *Global Corruption Report 2009* presents perhaps the most comprehensive and multifaceted selection of case studies from around the world on corruption risks and anti-corruption measures in the private sector. Transparency International's global movement of national chapters have contributed forty-six detailed perspectives, representing all regions and levels of economic development.

The contributions cover events in 2007 and 2008 and provide a country-specific approach to a sector that increasingly transcends national boundaries. As such, the case studies highlight not only the similarity of major corruption risks that echo throughout the world, but also the interdependence of states often linked primarily through trade and commerce. The collection as a whole illustrates how difficult it is to talk about national economies without considering how they interact with the global economy; the same goes for corruption in this sector and, consequently, efforts to combat it.

Bribery – national and international

Of all the international conventions that promote anti-corruption, the OECD Anti-Bribery Convention is arguably the most relevant to an internationally operating private sector. Seventeen of the countries that are featured in this report have accepted or ratified the convention, but the emphasis in our contributors' analysis is of a convention with uneven implementation.[2] The vulnerability of the convention is aptly illustrated by the United Kingdom's BAe Systems case. Our reports on both the United Kingdom and France show how the House of Lords' endorsement of the UK government's halting of the investigation into transnational bribery has not only jeopardised the effectiveness of anti-bribery efforts in the United Kingdom, but may also have an impact abroad, as the perceived immunity of UK companies is likely to distort the level playing field of international competition.

---

1 Rebecca Dobson is the contributing editor to the *Global Corruption Report*.
2 As of December 2008 thirty-seven countries had ratified the OECD Convention on Combating Bribery of Foreign Public Officials in International Business Transactions (the OECD Anti-Bribery Convention).

Bribes are often the focus of scandals involving companies vying for lucrative government contracts. The corruption involved in the procurement process features in eighteen of the reports. In Ghana, for example, many contractors and suppliers report making unofficial payments in order to secure contracts; in some instances it appears that this money enters the political sphere and finances political party interests. The cases highlighted in the report on the Philippines illustrate the increased corruption risks when dealing with public procurement funded by foreign investment. In many cases, it seems, the government was unable to impose caps on the costs of project bids, paving the way for inflated bids that allowed ample margin for providing bribes in order to win contracts.

The international dimension of the Siemens scandal, which involved systematic bribery in order to win business, is remarkable, and the reports from Germany, Greece and Israel document some of the local and transnational implications. The extensive investigations conducted by the company as well as by national authorities have implicated both private and public actors all over the world. The Greek case is notable, in that one of the implicated bodies, the state-owned telecommunications company, has brought a case against Siemens in a Munich court, claiming damages for Siemens' unlawful actions. This has the potential to set an interesting precedent, as it is the first foreign company to make such claims against Siemens in a German court.

Public–private relationships: undue influence and decision-making

The impact of undue influence and the dangers of revolving doors are highlighted in many of the reports. A case in Bangladesh indicates that government decisions have been unduly influenced by telecommunications companies, resulting in the government failing to legalise the use of VoIP (Voice over Internet Protocol) operations by private cellphone operators. In Papua New Guinea, the effects of lobbying alongside other forms of corruption to influence decisions on forestry and logging have had a significant impact on the sustainability of the industry.

The means of distorting public and private sector decision-making for private gain are further exacerbated when businesspeople and politicians have dual roles. As members of the government or civil service *and* the business community, they can face significant conflicts of interest, heightening the risks of improper influence on decision-making in all spheres. The reports from Malaysia and Trinidad and Tobago underline these risks. In Malaysia, the complex interwoven network of individuals with vested interests involved in the Port Klang free zone development is illustrative. With wrangling over the project encompassing both private businesspeople and the politically powerful, the project is alleged to have resulted in huge losses to the public purse to the tune of approximately US$1.3 billion.

Enhancing corporate integrity: reforms and strategies

Although the country reports provide ample examples of corruption scandals and paint a picture of a private sector grappling with corruption risks in all its forms, there is also considerable hope for reform. The potential for improvement is twofold, both from the top down in terms of government regulation and from the bottom up in terms of proactive self-regulatory measures taken by business.

There is evidence of a swathe of new legislation in all regions aimed at tackling private sector corruption, from the establishment of new anti-corruption agencies to the provision of whistleblower protection. What is clear from all the reports, however, is that, while legislation is an important foundation, the political will to fight corruption and the effective implementation of laws are essential in ensuring that reforms are effective.

The role of regulation is a key issue highlighted across the range of reports. Public sector regulators can clearly be effective and in some cases have significant influence even outside their own borders. The US Department of Justice and the US Securities and Exchange Commission (SEC) have both been instrumental in stepping up efforts to place sanctions on foreign bribery. The SEC's reach is not limited to US companies, however, and this report provides examples of foreign companies that have incurred severe fines for corrupt dealings. Regulators elsewhere have also been successful. In Chile, the securities and insurance regulator has ruled on a series of corporate actions that threatened to undermine the stability of the stock market. In the United Kingdom, however, the actions of the Serious Fraud Office in relation to the BAe Systems scandal have raised questions over regulators' powers and independence when serious political interests are at play.

Private sector initiatives and collective action by companies are also documented in several reports, demonstrating the way in which a variety of stakeholders, such as investors or financial intermediaries, can set positive incentives. The Israel report illustrates how stock exchange indices that use corporate responsibility as indicators can engage companies in strengthening corporate integrity by integrating corruption as a consideration in investment decision-making. The Colombo Stock Exchange in Sri Lanka has developed mandatory corporate governance standards for all companies listed on the exchange, and the Spanish sustainability index, the FTSE4Good IBEX, founded in April 2008, requires companies to take steps to counter bribery to qualify for inclusion. The Lebanon report highlights a proactive initiative in the banking sector to improve corporate citizenship. In this case, one of the leading banks has taken the initiative to develop codes on corporate social responsibility that are meant to be integrated into the working culture of the bank.

Business and its role in fighting corruption – at home and across borders

The 2009 country reports illustrate a whole range of subjects related to a myriad of actors in the private sector: from issues related to bribery overseas to the obstacles faced by small and medium enterprises. The overarching message, however, is that both the private and public sectors have a role to play in ensuring that corruption is identified, investigated and confronted. Moreover, the implications of an increasing global economic interdependence make it imperative that countries and companies work together and cooperate across borders in order to be able to tackle corruption risks most effectively.

6.1 Africa and the Middle East

Burundi

Corruption Perceptions Index 2008: 1.9 (158th out of 180 countries)

Conventions

African Union Convention on Preventing and Combating Corruption (signed December 2003; ratified January 2005)

UN Convention against Corruption (acceded March 2006)

UN Convention against Transnational Organized Crime (signed December 2000; not yet ratified)

Legal and institutional changes

- On 4 February 2008 a new law on the public procurement code, Law no. 1/01, was passed. Until recently, public procurement had been regulated by a May 1990 decree (Law no. 1/015). The new law will come into effect after eight months, bringing with it principles of freedom of access to the contracting process, the equal treatment of candidates and transparent procedures. This gives hope that corruption, now very common in public procurement, will be noticeably reduced in the coming years. The law imposes these procedures on contracting authorities in the context of procurement procedures for public services of any value.

- The Special Anti-corruption Brigade (Law no. 1/27) was created on 3 August 2006. It was not implemented until 2007 and 2008, however, by Ministerial Order no. 214/CAB/05 of 21 February 2007 on the appointment of Anti-corruption Brigade officers, and Ministerial Order no. 214/CAB/2008 of 5 July 2007 on the appointment of Special Anti-corruption Brigade officers. The brigade should cover the entire domestic territory through regional offices. The officers ensure that cases of corruption and related offences filed at the regional level are followed up. These cases are then transferred to the general prosecutor at the Anti-corruption Court for criminal prosecution. The officers are auxiliary to the justice system.

- On 13 December 2006 the Anti-corruption Court was created by Law no. 1/36. Its establishment (equipment and staff) began immediately, and it was operational by 5 February 2007. The number of cases heard by the court has been steadily increasing since June 2007.

- The State General Inspectorate is the supreme institution for the inspection and control of all public services. It was created on 27 September 2006 by Order no. 100/277, though it was not set up until 1 July 2007, when state inspectors were recruited through a competitive examination. The State General Inspectorate deals with corruption only as a secondary matter. Article 80 of the order provides that 'in cases where embezzlement, fraudulent management or other misappropriation are recorded, the final inspection reports of the State General Inspectorate should be systematically transferred to the Office of the Public Prosecutor for legal proceedings'.

- Local good governance committees are being set up either by the government or civil society to monitor corruption in the field, and to produce reports for the relevant entities. Recently, acts of corruption have been systematically denounced in these areas and their number has begun to decrease. The Consumers Association of Burundi has its own local good governance committees established in three provinces: Muramvya, Kayanza and Ngozi. Others have been established by the Ministry of Good Governance and by the Anti-corruption and Economic Malpractice Observatory.

Corruption in Burundi's private sector: the part played by tax and customs

Corruption clearly exists in Burundi's private sector, where it is often connected to corrupt practices in the public sector. Two points at which the public and private sector are intimately linked are tax collection and the payment of customs at the border.

Tax services are a cornerstone of the country's development. The system is rife with corruption and bribery, however. Private businesses with a high turnover report lower figures by bribing tax officers in order to pay minimal taxes. In addition, they may pay bribes to ensure that their tax return is dealt with and to avoid the fines they would otherwise have to pay.[1] According to the May 2008 *Diagnostic Study on Governance and Corruption in Burundi*,[2] 90 per cent of entrepreneurs think paying bribes is standard practice, and a number of them have admitted to being the victim of bribes for:

- reducing tax payments (11 per cent), with an average annual payment of BIF 1,667,500 (US$1,667);
- pushing forward a file in the tax services (14 per cent), with an average payment of BIF 184,702 (US$185); and
- avoiding a fine (16 per cent), with an average annual payment of BIF 217,717 (US$218).

Customs revenue is an important source of income for the government, but this revenue is put in jeopardy by corruption, and, accordingly, customs officers are thriving at the expense of the Treasury. A majority of survey respondents cite customs as one of the least honest services in the country.[3] Business leaders report paying bribes to customs services in order to speed up procedures, pay reduced duties and bypass regulations.

The study has amply demonstrated that deficiencies in customs legislation have caused the quality of this public service to deteriorate and that there has been a cost to the Treasury arising from embezzlement and mismanagement. The report presents the experiences of businesses and NGOs that have had contact with the customs services. A large majority of such businesses (79 per cent) stated that the customs system is corrupt, and 68 per cent considered corruption a major obstacle to private sector development.[4]

Embezzlement and bribes: the case of the Bujumbura–Rumonge road

Burundi is starting to recover from a civil war that plunged it into despair for fifteen years. The entire socio-economic infrastructure was in ruins, and now it needs to be rebuilt or rehabilitated. This is the challenge facing the current government. A February 2008 report by the Observatory for the Fight against Corruption

---

1 Government of Burundi, *Etude diagnostique sur la gouvernance et la corruption au Burundi* (Bujumbura: Government of Burundi, 2008).
2 Ibid.
3 Ibid.
4 Ibid.

and Economic Embezzlement gave some idea of the extent of embezzlement, stating that in 2006 and 2007 more than BIF 200 billion (US$200 million) had disappeared from state finances.[5]

Corruption risks are particularly high in the construction industry, as reconstruction tends to absorb vast sums of capital. The most telling example concerns the reconstruction of the main road between Bujumbura and Rumonge.

Emugeco, on the face of it an unqualified Rwandan company, was awarded the contract for rebuilding the road.[6] The person responsible for procurement contracts at the time was Hussein Radjabu, chairman of the *Conseil national pour la défense de la democratie/Forces pour la défense de la democratie* (CNDD-FDD), the party then in power.[7] There were allegations, however, that before the company started work it had given a cheque for BIF 10 million (US$8,500) to Mathias Basabose, treasurer of the CNDD-FDD. The cheque was drawn from Bujumbura's Finalease Bank.[8] At a press conference on 11 April 2006 Radjabu 'unleashed a violent attack against his former friend . . . accusing him, among other misdeeds, of having pocketed large sums of money in connection with . . . the rehabilitation of the road link'.[9] Basabose denied the claims, despite the fact that it was 'an open secret' that, in total, some BIF 120 million had been paid by the bidder to the party's treasury.[10]

Ultimately, the cheque was returned to the issuer. The government cancelled the contract with Emugeco, accusing it of several breaches. The contract was awarded to a Chinese company for completion. The controversy continued between Basabose and Radjabu, however, as each accused the other of corruption.[11] The case is currently before the Supreme Court.

While Burundi is struggling to recover from its years of strife and rebuild its infrastructure, shortcomings in the law of public contracting and the immoral behaviour of some in power are undermining these efforts. That this case has come to light, and that those involved are being held to account, are encouraging developments, as they weaken the current system that enables corruption to flourish.

The oil sector and corruption

The oil industry is very sensitive, as oil plays an essential role in Burundi's development and acts as a driving force for other sectors. Private interests control 100 per cent of oil exploitation, and they must deal with public services, thus leading to a high risk of corruption.

A scandal involving the oil industry that broke in 2007 had serious implications, including an impact on the country's economic condition, the withholding of donor funds and Burundi's derailment from the Heavily Indebted Poor Countries programme, resulting in the postponement of essential debt relief.[12]

The scandal involved the transfer of an amount equivalent to 1.6 per cent of Burundi's GDP to one oil company, Interpetrol.[13] The payments were made between July 1996 and December 2006 as compensation for implicit interest/

---

5 AllAfrica.com (Mauritius), 2 February 2008.

6 Ibid.

7 R. Lemarchand, *Burundi's Endangered Transition*, Working Paper no. 3 (Berne: Swiss Peace Foundation, 2006).

8 TI Burundi has a copy of this cheque.

9 Lemarchand, 2006.

10 Ibid.

11 Such allegations were levelled over the radio stations in Burundi, and they are also discussed in R. Lemarchand, 2006.

12 Global Insight Same-day Analysis (US), 4 February 2008.

13 Ibid.

exchange rate subsidies and unpaid customs debts.[14] Interpetrol actually received compensation of US$21 million, a substantially larger amount than what was lost due to exchange rates. The unwarranted payments were made as a result of dubious transactions that implicated the former governor of the Bank of Burundi and the minister of finance.[15] The minister, Denise Sinankwa, fled abroad, while bank governor Isaac Bizimana was arrested in August 2007 under a warrant issued by the attorney general relating to the theft of more than BIF 23 billion.[16]

According to an audit report, conducted with World Bank support, the oil sector owes the Burundi government US$38 million, equivalent to 3.8 per cent of GDP.[17] An audit report by Eura Audit International in February 2008 sets the amount Interpetrol owes to the state at BIF 32.3 billion (US$27 million).[18]

There is corruption in the Burundi oil sector for two fundamental reasons. First, it is monopolised by two large companies, Engen Petroleum and Interpetrol. Second, the legislation pertaining to the sector is unstable, going through periodic change with respect to the regulation of importation and the commercialisation of the product. Three presidential decrees have successively governed the sector since 1988, starting with Decree 100/160 of 30 September 1988, under which the sector appeared to be regulated well and functioning normally. Following this, however, the decree was modified on 7 November 1996 by Decree 100/072, which was signed while the country was under embargo by neighbouring countries. This formalised the disorganisation of the sector in the face of the embargo and allowed the importation and com-

mercialisation of oil by any means, as long as the product was available. Finally, order was restored with the 25 June 2008 Decree 100/110. Although this order is unambiguous, much will depend on the law's enforcement. If Burundi wants to fight corruption in this capacity it will succeed; otherwise the sector will remain as it is.

Vénant Bacinoni (ABUCO [Consumers' Association of Burundi])

Additional reading

Eura Audit International, *Audit Report on the Debts between the State of Burundi and the Oil Sector* (Paris: Eura Audit International, 2008).

Government of Burundi, *Etude diagnostique sur la gouvernance et la corruption au Burundi* (Bujumbura: Government of Burundi, 2008).

M. Masabo, *L'action citoyenne pour la promotion des droits de l'homme par la lutte contre la corruption* (Bujumbura: ABUCO, 2007).

Country Review of Legal and Practical Challenges to the Domestication of the Anticorruption Conventions in Burundi (Bujumbura: TI, 2006).

Nathan Associates, *Fighting Corruption and Restoring Accountability in Burundi* (Arlington, VA: Nathan Associates, 2006).

J. Nimubona, *Revue synthétique et critique de publication sur les questions de gouvernance et de corruption au Burundi* (Bujumbura: Observatoire de l'Action Gouvernementale, 2008).

J. Nimubona and C. Sebudandi, 'Le phénomène de la corruption au Burundi: Révolte silencieuse et résignation', USAID International Alert, February 2008.

World Bank, *Burundi Governance Diagnostics* (Washington, DC: World Bank, 2008).

---

14 Eura Audit International, *Audit Report on the Debts between the State of Burundi and the Oil Sector* (Paris: Eura Audit International, 2008).

15 Global Insight Same-day Analysis (US), 4 February 2008.

16 *Sapa AFP* (South Africa), 4 August 2007; AfricaNews.com (Netherlands), 6 August 2007; BBC News (UK), 4 August 2007.

17 Government of Burundi, 'Letter of Intent, Memorandum of Economic and Financial Policies, and Technical Memorandum of Understanding [to IMF]', 24 June 2008.

18 Eura Audit International, 2008.

Cameroon

Corruption Perceptions Index 2008: 2.3 (141st out of 180 countries)

Conventions

African Union Convention on Preventing and Combating Corruption (signed June 2008)

UN Convention against Corruption (signed December 2003; ratified February 2006)

UN Convention against Transnational Organized Crime (signed December 2000; ratified February 2006)

Legal and institutional changes

- In 2007 and 2008 the legal environment for curbing corruption in Cameroon did not undergo any significant change. This was despite President Paul Biya's communication, at the first meeting of newly appointed Cabinet ministers in 2007, that his three priorities for action were boosting economic growth, improving the population's living conditions and fighting corruption. In his end-of-year address to the nation,[1] Biya underlined the depth of his commitment by stating, 'The time has come for action. We must shake off inertia, remove obstacles, set goals and deadlines… and meet these targets.' Although such statements are encouraging, words are not enough. Laws need to be implemented and be made effective if Cameroon's efforts to adopt anti-corruption measures are to be successful.[2]

Current state of private sector corruption in Cameroon

Corruption in Cameroon is a perceived problem, and supported by Transparency International's Corruption Perceptions Index and Global Corruption Barometer.[3] Corruption, like any other form of widespread social phenomenon, is built on networks and interactions. Treating it in isolation is therefore ineffective, and as such it should be approached in a systemic way, looking not only at cases of corruption but also the reforms under way to identify weaknesses in the fight against it.

In April 2002 Law 2002/04 on the Investment Charter provided a reference for defining the boundaries of the private sector. The law specifies that companies should play by the rules of fair competition and be free from corruption. They must also allow business ethics to triumph and ethical standards to be enforced

---

1   *Cameroon Tribune,* 2 January 2008.

2   Previous to the reporting period there had been some developments in the form of implementing the National Anti-corruption Commission. See TI, *Global Corruption Report 2008* (Cambridge: Cambridge University Press, 2008).

3   In TI's Corruption Perceptions Index 2008, Cameroon scored 2.3 out of a possible 10 in terms of perceived freedom from corruption, and the Global Corruption Barometer 2007 listed it in the top quintile as a country most affected by bribery.

Table 9: Comparison of the level of obstacles for doing business: rank among 181 countries

Stage of business life	Cameroon		Ghana		Canada	
Year	2008	2007	2008	2007	2008	2007
Doing business	154	154	87	109	7	7

Source: World Bank, 2008.

in their specific trade, maintaining loyal collaboration with the government and its institutions to ensure the success of the national economic policy. Whether or not companies adhere to these standards, however, is another matter.

The World Bank has made concerted efforts to explain and measure governance in the private sector through its report *Doing Business 2008*.[4] The indicators in the report provide a comparison of the relative ease or difficulty of completing administrative procedures for doing business in 2007 and 2008 (see table 9). Efficient administrative systems can discourage corruption by creating fewer incentives than in countries where it is particularly difficult to navigate bureaucracy when doing business.

The figures in table 9 show the countries' rankings out of 181 economies in terms of ease of doing business. In comparison to Canada, it is considerably more difficult to do business in Cameroon. Moreover, in comparison to another west African country, Ghana appears to have shown improvement in the World Bank report while Cameroon has not. These figures support the president's assessment that Cameroon is suffering inertia in promoting reforms that could assist in anti-corruption initiatives.

The situation of Cameroon's private sector

The following data, from a 2006 survey by the Economics and Survey Research Centre (*Centre de Recherche et d'Etudes en Economie et Sondage* – CRETES), provides a starting point for understanding the causes of corruption.[5] When ranked against twenty institutions, the private sector comes fifth from the bottom in terms of perceived levels of corruption – behind religious institutions, NGOs, civil registry services and the media (religious institutions having the lowest levels).[6] The survey also indicates the eight major corrupt practices identified by the respondents (see table 10).

Respondents reported that all these are pervasive practices, although influencing procurement is seen as by far the most widespread. Before looking at how these practices are distributed between different sectors, however, it is important to examine the cost of corruption and where this money appears to end up.

The study examines the entire private sector by looking at 835 businesses. Of these, 536 declared their turnover, totalling CFA449.7 billion (US$1.08 billion), or an average turnover of CFA839 million (US$2 million). The primary finding is that corruption has high costs for

4 World Bank, *Doing Business 2008* (Washington, DC: World Bank, 2008).

5 CRETES and TI, *Enquête nationale 2006 auprès des entreprises sur la corruption au Cameroun: Rapport final* (Yaoundé: CRETES/TI, 2007).

6 The survey asked for participants' personal estimations and beliefs.

Table 10: Acceptability of corrupt practices in the private sector[7]

Rank / Practice		Index
1	Interference in awarding of public contracts in order to qualify	0.91
2	Seeking confidential information to win a public contract	0.88
3	Influencing a police investigation	0.88
4	Speeding up a service that is normally part of one's work	0.86
5	Obtaining a position without the required qualifications	0.83
6	Facilitating/accelerating administrative procedures	0.80
7	Obtaining special favours	0.78
8	Changing the location of a project for one's own benefit	0.65

Source: CRETES and TI, 2007.

private sector companies, representing 1 per cent of their turnover or about CFA4.5 billion (US$10.8 million). Corruption also has a negative impact on the competitiveness and level of development of these businesses, as well as on the various stakeholders who depend on them.

Bribe money within each sector goes to a variety of recipients (see table 11). It is clear that, across sectors, the most prevalent form of corruption involves bribing the police. This is particularly the case in the industrial sector, commercial sector, goods and services, and financial and property services. Furthermore, across different sectors there is considerable variation in the numbers of respondents to the questionnaire. It is debatable whether this is indicative of levels of transparency in the sector, but it is interesting to note that stakeholders in certain industries, such as the extractive industries, systematically refused to answer questions related to corruption.

Moreover, according to the survey, individuals resort to corrupt practices for a number of major reasons (see table 12). This list provides an indication of the challenges and issues that need

to be dealt with in Cameroon, according to the respondents.

Moving forward: lessons to be learnt

This information provides an overall perspective on corruption in Cameroon in relation to the private sector's interaction with the government. This is a starting point from which lessons can be learnt, particularly considering President Biya's statement that Cameroon is facing inaction and inertia in its efforts against corruption.

In relation to the issues raised by private sector stakeholders in table 12, the most important factors that encourage corruption are impunity and lack of sanctions, inertia and inaction on the part of the administration, the desire for personal enrichment, lack of transparency and low wages. The government has responded with various measures to deal with these challenges.

In relation to impunity and lack of sanctions, an acceleration of legal proceedings has led to high-level government dignitaries being charged and imprisoned. The cases, dealt with under

---

7 A score of 0 indicates quite acceptable, 1 indicates not at all acceptable.

Table 11: Prevalence of corrupt practices according to the reason for giving a gift or bribe in the course of paying local taxes, by sector

Type of industry	Access to a public service	Facilitating administrative procedures	Bribing the police	Seeking special favours	No answer	Total
Extractive industries	0.0	0.0	0.0	0.0	100.0	100.0
Industrial	8.3	16.7	33.3	20.8	20.8	100.0
Construction and public works	0.0	100.0	0.0	0.0	0.0	100.0
Commercial sector	2.1	27.7	38.3	17.0	14.9	100.0
Goods and services	7.4	29.6	40.7	14.8	7.4	100.0
Financial and property services	0.0	0.0	66.7	33.3	0.0	100.0
Health and social welfare	0.0	50.0	0.0	0.0	50.0	100.0
Total average	4.7	26.4	36.8	17.0	15.1	100.0

Source: CRETES and TI, 2007.

Table 12: Classification of the causes of corruption in public sectors/services

Rank	Cause of corruption	Index
1	Lack of sanctions or impunity	0.93
2	Inertia and inaction	0.86
3	Desire for personal enrichment	0.84
4	Lack of transparency	0.81
5	Lack of motivation due to the drop in purchasing power	0.81
6	Arbitrary career promotion	0.79
7	Abuse of power by public officials	0.78
8	Poor functioning of the administration	0.78
9	Lack of clear rules and standards of conduct	0.66
10	Pressure from superiors/high-ranking persons	0.57
11	Excessive patronage and tutelage	0.53
12	Everyone else does it	0.44

Source: CRETES and TI, 2007.

the code name *'Opération Epervier'* (see *Global Corruption Report 2008*), include the following.

- In April 2008 former economy and finance minister Polycarpe Abah Abah was charged with embezzlement and complicity in the embezzlement of government funds invested with *Crédit Foncier du Cameroun*.[8] The case also implicated numerous civil servants and private sector suppliers.
- Former public health minister Urbain Olanguena Awono was charged with embezzlement.[9] The case implicated many other senior officials.
- Cameroon Industrial Shipyard CEO Zacchaeus Forjindam was charged with embezzlement[10] and complicity in the embezzlement of CFA969.2 million (over US$2 million) and placed under committal order on 8 May 2008;[11]
- The Albatros Case,[12] which concerned the purchase of a presidential plane, illustrated how senior officials were charged with colluding with the judicial police.

Meanwhile, pending court proceedings have accelerated. The former CEO of FEICOM (Special Council Support Fund for Mutual Assistance) received a custodial sentence of about twenty years, while other executives were caught and jailed.[13] In the case of the Autonomous Port, several executives received prison sentences averaging fifteen years, with the general manager Alphonse Siyam Siwe receiving thirty years, related to the embezzlement of about CFA38 billion in public funds.[14]

More cases should follow. About twenty cases are currently being considered, according to a statement by the deputy prime minister and justice minister during the National Assembly's last plenary session in March 2008.[15] Overall, efforts are being made to fight corruption by breaking the cycle of impunity, thus bringing about more equity and credibility in the justice system.

Despite these recent scandals and the relative success of *Opération Epervier*, it is too early to affirm that there has been real progress. Although a new criminal procedure code entered into force in January 2007, it is not yet fully implemented. Furthermore, the number of trials is relatively low: of the twenty announced cases, only four have proceeded to the courts, and these have not yet reached the Supreme Court.

Impunity and sanctions alone cannot be the solution. A holistic approach to fighting corruption is needed. In terms of inertia and inaction on the part of the administration, less progress has been made. Despite this, the 2008 Order 2008/13 established the National Decentralisation Council, which may offer the beginnings of a solution to countless administrative procedures and difficulty in accessing public services by private sector stakeholders. Moreover, there have been moves to look at personal enrichment issues. Efforts have reportedly been made to use intermediaries to repatriate funds that have been hidden abroad.[16] While there has been no success so far, it is the wish of most Cameroonians that this be pursued.

---

8 *Cameroon Tribune*, 11 April 2008; PostNewsLine.com (Cameroon), 4 April 2008.
9 PostNewsLine.com (Cameroon), 4 April 2008.
10 *Cameroon Tribune*, 9 May 2008.
11 Ibid.
12 *La Nouvelle Expression* (Cameroon), 19 August 2008; PostNewsLine.com (Cameroon), 15 August 2008.
13 Africa Presse (Cameroon), 1 November 2008.
14 Reuters (UK), 13 December 2007.
15 See www.camer.be/index1.php?art=1741.
16 In its 28 May 2008, no. 73, edition, the weekly magazine *Repères* (France) published the headline: 'Funds Invested Abroad: Multimillionaires Beware! French Lawyer Jacques Vergès May Help the State of Cameroon to Repatriate Funds Invested in Foreign Banks by Senior State Officials'. See www.camer.be/index1.php?art=2208.

Lack of transparency is an issue that has been affected by activities in other areas. For example, governmental communication has increased and arrests of high-profile figures on corruption charges have featured heavily in the media. Debates on transparency and corruption issues on Cameroon's radio and television channels, and their subsequent press coverage, have increased transparency in some areas.[17]

Finally, low wages in Cameroon, which have reduced the motivation to fight corruption, require the government to improve the welfare of Cameroonian people and businesses. Repeated increases in the price of petrol and staple products have weakened the population's purchasing power. As a result, the president has taken a range of directly enforceable measures to address this matter.[18] In March 2008 basic wages and housing allowances for the public sector and military personnel rose 15 and 20 per cent, respectively.[19] According to finance minister Essimi Menye, the overall payroll has increased by CFA8 billion per month (over US$19 million). There has also been tax exemption on basic consumer products, such as rice, fish, corn, flour and cooking oil, as well as a decrease in customs duties on clinker, a product used for making cement.[20]

While these measures address major challenges that are linked either directly or indirectly to private sector corruption, they are recent and potentially short-term fixes to an entrenched problem. Furthermore, while they may be effective in terms of relations between the private and public sectors, they do not necessarily address private-to-private corruption.

In conclusion, Cameroon's predicament is a matter of governance that requires an all-encompassing and systemic approach. While the legal and institutional system may be adequate, the problem lies in its enforcement and implementation. After a ten-year delay in implementation, however, the National Competition Commission began launching its activities in 2007.[21] With this commission in place there will be more hope for tackling anti-competitive behaviour such as collusion, price-fixing and bid-rigging.[22] From the priorities presented by President Biya, only the aspect of impunity seems to have been launched; the other priorities are yet to be tackled, betraying the lack of a systemic approach to corruption.

Léonard Ambassa and Léopold Nzeusseu (TI Cameroon)

Additional reading

L. Ayisi, *Corruption et gouvernance* (Yaoundé: University Press of Yaoundé, 2003).

F. E. Boulaga and V. S. Zinga, *La lutte contre la corruption: Impossible est-il camerounais?* (Yaoundé: Friedrich Ebert Foundation, 2002).

C. A. Eyene, *Stratégie de corruption et de détournement des fonds publics comme logique de coup d'état* (Yaoundé: Edition Saint-Paul, 2006).

P. T. Nwell, *De la corruption au Cameroun* (Yaoundé: Gerddes-Cameroon/Friedrich Ebert Foundation, 2001).

P. N. Penda, *Les parrains de la corruption* (Yaoundé: Editions CLE, 2006).

TI Cameroon: www.ti-cameroon.org.

---

17 See various debates in Cameroon on CRTV (public radio and TV), Canal 2 (private TV), STV (private TV) and independent FM radio (Magic FM, Siantou, Radio Reine). CRTV, 'Elections Were Transparent', 28 October 2008. The Canal 2 director was questioned by the police after reporting the Albatros Case; see http://en.afrik.com/article13774.html. So was the editor-in-chief of STV; ibid. Magic FM was closed in February 2008; ibid.
18 These measures were announced in a press release on 7 March 2008 following a Cabinet meeting.
19 It should be noted that these wages shrank by a drastic 50 per cent after the CFA franc was devalued in 1993 following an unprecedented banking crisis.
20 See www.enoh-meyomesse.blogspot.com/2008/03/252-milliards-de-dficit-budgtaire-la.html.
21 This will assist in the implementation of the Competition Act 1998.
22 See www.globalcompetitionforum.org/africa.htm#Cameroon.

Ethiopia

Corruption Perceptions Index 2008: 2.6 (126th out of 180 countries)

Conventions

African Union Convention on Preventing and Combating Corruption (signed June 2004; ratified
    September 2007)
UN Convention against Corruption (signed December 2003; ratified November 2007)
UN Convention against Transnational Organized Crime (signed December 2000; ratified July 2007)

Legal and institutional changes

- The Federal Ethics and Anti-corruption
  Commission (FEAC) grew in staff size and
  activity in 2007. Established by proclamation in 2001, the FEAC is charged with
  investigating and prosecuting allegations of
  corruption involving federal offices or federal
  funds. It also oversees a system of ethics
  officers placed within government agencies
  and directs a public education campaign.
  The commission is currently taking a multi-
  stakeholder approach, working closely in its
  anti-corruption struggle with civil society
  organisations (CSOs) such as Transparency
  Ethiopia and international organisations
  such as the World Bank. In its most recent
  nine-month report to parliament, covering
  the period July 2007 to March 2008, the
  FEAC reports receiving some 2,500 tips from
  the public, of which 984 were within its
  jurisdiction. Of these, sixty were eventually
  prosecuted, along with 120 cases still pending
  from the previous year.[1] Although the FEAC
  has prosecuted some high-profile cases, there

are still concerns that the commission is not
fully independent.[2]

- Ethiopia signed the African Union Convention
  on Preventing and Combating Corruption
  in 2004 and the UN Convention against
  Corruption in 2003, but it was only on 18
  September 2007 and 26 November 2007,
  respectively, that the federal parliament ratified the two accords. Their ratification has
  the potential to bring added pressure on the
  government to strengthen its anti-corruption
  mechanisms, but in the year since ratification
  no new relevant legislation has been passed.
  As legal experts from the FEAC explain, nonetheless, the inclusion of some articles in different legal codes, such as the Civil and Criminal
  Code, is cited as evidence of the strong side of
  Ethiopian law with respect to the ratified anti-
  corruption conventions, and this was also
  used as justification for the late ratification of
  the conventions.

- In May 2008 the Ministry of Justice proposed
  a draft law to create an administrative and
  regulatory framework for charities, societies
  and other NGOs. The draft has caused enor-

---

1 FEAC, *Nine-month Report of the Federal Ethics and Anti-Corruption Commission to the FDRE House of Peoples'
    Representatives (July 2007–March 2008)* (Addis Ababa: FEAC, 2008).
2 See the Ethiopia Country Profile on the Business Anti-Corruption Portal; last accessed 28 January 2009.

mous concern amongst civil society organisations, donor agencies and foreign embassies. It would prohibit international NGOs and most local NGOs from operating in key sectors, facilitate thorough government monitoring of internal organisational activities and probably prompt many international organisations to withdraw from the country.[3] The largest umbrella of NGOs in Ethiopia, the Christian Relief & Development Association (CRDA), held a preparatory meeting among its members to raise concerns with the prime minister regarding the draft proclamation law. The member NGOs came up with four core points to be addressed in the dialogue with the premier: recognising the CSO community's role as the third sector; the need to adopt a comprehensive national policy for the sector; creating an enabling working environment and conducive operative system for the sector; and issuing enabling CSO legislation for the sector.[4] The response from the prime minister underlined that these were 'firm positions of the government that will not change'. Significantly, foreign agencies will not be able to engage in any political matters, including human rights issues, unless they are working on a case-by-case basis; local NGOs whose budgets are funded by more than 10 per cent from foreign sources will also be excluded from political matters; and foreign NGOs will be regulated through administrative procedures rather than through prolonged court proceedings.[5] While there have been concerns relating to the operation of some CSOs with regard to fund management and resource utilisation, they are not to the extent that justifies the enactment of such a law. If passed, this law will have a detrimental effect on Ethiopia's already weak civil society. In June 2008 discussions about the law among government, civil society and international partners were ongoing.

- On 1 July 2008 the federal parliament enacted the Mass Media and Freedom of Information Law. The law was debated at length before it was enacted.[6] According to independent media groups and international press watchdogs, the endorsed law is seen as contravening freedom of expression and international human rights.[7] During parliamentary discussion, opposition parties were gravely concerned, and some called the law 'draconian'.[8] Other parliamentarians also criticised the law, saying that 'to impound the press material before distribution is tantamount to censorship'.[9] In June 2004 London-based NGO Article 19 commented on the then draft Ethiopian Proclamation on the Freedom of the Press, which had been released by the Ministry of Information in May that year. Article 19 said: 'Such measures constitute the worst form of prior censorship, a restraint on freedom of expression which has historically been open to abuse and must be regarded with extreme suspicion.'[10] For any anti-corruption struggle to be fruitful, independent and flourishing media are of paramount importance.

Corruption and the private sector

Ethiopia's economy has grown considerably over the last five years.[11] The current government, which came to power in 1991, has made

---

3 *A Week in the Horn* (Ethiopia), 18 July 2008.

4 CRDA, *Documents on FDRE Charities and Societies Draft Proclamation* (Addis Ababa: CRDA, 2008).

5 Ibid.

6 *A Week in the Horn* (Ethiopia), 2008.

7 *Daily Monitor* (Ethiopia), 4 July 2008.

8 Ibid.

9 Ibid.

10 Article 19, 'Briefing Note on the Draft Ethiopian Proclamation to Provide for the Freedom of Press' (London: Article 19, 2004).

11 World Bank, *Doing Business 2009: Country Profile for Ethiopia* (Washington, DC: World Bank, 2008).

significant progress in building the legislative and institutional framework needed to control and guide this boom. The rapidity of the growth and the increase in sums of money at stake, however, have enhanced opportunities and incentives for corruption. Although the private sector has grown rapidly during this period, a significant number of businesses continue to operate outside the formal sector. According to the Central Statistical Agency, the urban informal sector in Ethiopia comprised 997,379 people in 2003, with an initial capital of US$4 billion.[12]

Banking

The National Bank of Ethiopia (NBE), the central bank, is the major buyer of the gold that is panned in parts of rural Ethiopia. The bank holds the gold in reserve or sells it on the international market. Individual sellers and middlemen have their gold inspected and verified by chemists at the Geological Survey of Ethiopia (GSE) and then take their certified product in sealed boxes to the NBE.

In early 2008 some of the NBE's gold that was ready to be exported was discovered to be gold-plated iron bars.[13] The discovery prompted an extensive investigation, which eventually revealed a complicated system of corruption and fraud involving officials at both the bank and the GSE. Gold-plated iron or steel bars were being sold to the NBE by buying certificates from corrupt GSE staff, who allegedly used forged documents or paid off bank staff.[14] The scheme had been in operation since at least early 2005, and in 2006 a single dealer had been paid approximately US$3 million for the 239 kg of fake gold

he had sold to the NBE. The following year he received more than US$3 million for 223 kg of fake gold.[15] The cases are now being brought to court. According to the FEAC, thirty-nine suspects have been prosecuted to date, including NBE officials, GSE technicians, businesspeople and police officers.[16]

The fraud has been widely publicised and the public are keen to see the outcomes of the investigation. This immense case of fraud is associated with the nation's very critical economic situation, due to the bank's supervisory and oversight role in relation to other banks in the country.

While the scandal dominated the headlines and threatened the NBE's finances, there were also reports of petty corruption within the banks. In one case, a client of a Commercial Bank of Ethiopia branch paid off a bank employee to transfer sums illegally into the client's account.[17] Another case involved the alleged granting of an improper credit guarantee bond contract signed between the managers of two banks that provided a standby letter of credit amounting to more than US$6 million on behalf of a company called Addis Industrial PLC.[18]

Land distribution and administration

The government owns all land in Ethiopia; there is no private ownership. With land values increasing in Addis Ababa, incentives for corruption in the allocation of land, which is provided to individuals and investors on long-term leases, have grown significantly, and there are increasing reports of collusion between private sector players and government officials.

---

12 Central Statistical Agency, 'Report on Urban Informal Sector Sample Survey, January 2003' (Addis Ababa: Central Statistical Agency, 2004).
13 *Ethics* (quarterly newsletter of the Federal Ethics and Anti-corruption Commission), vol. 7, no. 4 (June 2008).
14 *The Reporter* (Ethiopia), 15 March 2008.
15 Ibid.
16 *Ethics*, vol. 7, no. 4 (June 2008); see also Ethiopian News Agency, 16 April 2008.
17 See www.feac.gov.et/web_collection/news.htm.
18 Ibid.

In July 2007 the FEAC released a study in which it examined five of Addis Ababa's ten sub-cities.[19] It concludes that acquiring land in the city without bribing city officials had become virtually impossible. It also finds that ambiguities in the legal code and relevant regulations enabled corrupt officials to exploit these loopholes to their own personal benefit. According to the study, the land administration system's major problems are an absence of efficient systems; a lack of trained and sufficient numbers of employees to provide efficient and effective services; a lack of clarity in the proclamation, rules and regulations prepared for leasing land; and an absence of codes of conduct.[20] The report documents cases in which land was awarded to individuals on the basis of bribes or forged bank statements.

There have been frequent reports of corruption cases being pursued against land developers. In the first nine months of the fiscal year the FEAC reports prosecuting forty-one cases involving land distribution.[21] The commission also reports that its investigations led to the confiscation of 575,531 square metres of land with an estimated value of US$118.6 million.[22]

In line with the study's findings, and the experience of most Addis Ababa residents, land administration and land management need to have clear guidelines, employ a code of conduct and adopt a citizens' charter. Although amending the current rules and regulations is a priority, building the capacity of land administration employees is key. A supervisory body is also needed to provide checks and balances on complaints raised by citizens. Above all, the government's will to bring suspects to court is paramount in the fight against corruption in the sector.

Amare Aregawi and Eyasu Yimer (Transparency Ethiopia), Janelle Plummer (World Bank)

Additional reading

Ethics, vol. 7, nos. 1, 3 and 4 (September 2007, March 2008 and June 2008).

FEAC, *Annual Report of the Federal Ethics and Anti-corruption Commission* (Addis Ababa: FEAC, 2008).

Nine-month Report of the Federal Ethics and Anti-corruption Commission to the FDRE House of Peoples' Representatives (July 2007–March 2008) (Addis Ababa: FEAC, 2008).

Federal Negarit Gazeta 'Proclamation no.434/ 2005: The Revised Proclamation to Provide for Special Procedure and Rules of Evidence on Anti-corruption', *Federal Negarit Gazeta*, year 11, no. 19 (February 2005).

Reporter, The, 'The Gold Scam', *The Reporter* (15 March 2008).

World Bank, *Doing Business in Ethiopia* (Washington, DC: World Bank, 2008).

Transparency Ethiopia: www.transparency ethiopia.org.

19 Ibid.
20 *Ethics*, vol. 7, no. 3 (March, 2008).
21 FEAC, 2008.
22 *Ethics*, vol. 7, no. 3 (March 2008).

Ghana

Corruption Perceptions Index 2008: 3.9 (67th out of 180 countries)

Conventions

African Union Convention on Preventing and Combating Corruption (signed October 2003; ratified June 2007)

UN Convention against Corruption (signed December 2004; ratified June 2007)

Legal and institutional changes

- In October 2007 the Public Accounts Committee (PAC) of parliament opened its deliberations to the Ghanaian public for the first time. The PAC's discussions were attended by the public and even broadcast live on radio and television. Audit reports revealed cases in which ministries and agencies failed to award contracts using procurement procedures spelt out in the Public Procurement Act 2003.[1] The public meetings put pressure on the government to act on the audit reports. Ghana's attorney general, who doubles as the minister of justice, announced that a committee would be formed within the ministry to investigate and prosecute implicated officials.[2] The attorney general also announced that the government would develop an anti-corruption policy for the private sector to address gaps in laws and regulatory institutions while promoting cooperation between law enforcement agencies and private entities.[3]
- In January 2008 Ghana's parliament enacted a new law, the Anti-Money Laundering Act 2008 (Act 749), which makes it an offence to convert, conceal, disguise or transfer property from the proceeds of unlawful activity or the origin of such property, or acquire, use or take possession of such property. To ensure that the law will be enforced, a new institution, the Financial Intelligence Centre (FIC), is to be established. The FIC will process, analyse, disseminate and interpret information it discloses or obtains, and inform, advise and cooperate with relevant agencies. Enforcing the law would enhance existing transparency and accountability laws, such as the Whistleblower Act 2006 (Act 720). The FIC's work would also facilitate investigations by the police, the Commission on Human Rights and Administrative Justice (CHRAJ) and the Serious Fraud Office.
- Despite President John Kufuor's declaration of zero tolerance for corruption in 2001, subsequent legislation designed to improve transparency and reduce corruption, and anti-corruption programmes by CHRAJ and civil society, many still believe that graft and corruption remain widespread and political patronage systems remain deeply rooted.

---

1 GBC News (Ghana), 13 May 2008.
2 *The Statesman* (Ghana), 20 March 2008.
3 *Ghanaian Times*, 12 June 2008.

Corruption in public procurement and contracting and the private sector

According to newspaper reports, public complaints and a survey by the Center for Democratic Development (CDD-Ghana),[4] many businesses, especially suppliers and contractors seeking to supply goods and services to the government, have had to make unofficial payments as a condition to secure contracts. As a result, the Public Procurement Act 2003 (PPA) (Act 663) was enacted to harmonise various guidelines for public procurement, bringing them into line with international standards and helping to curb corruption.

Despite the passage of the PPA, there are still issues of implementation, capacity and resources that affect the transparency of award procedures. It appears that anti-corruption legislation, such as the Public Office Holders (Declaration of Assets and Disqualification) Act 1998 and the Whistleblower Act 2006, have not been effective mechanisms for fighting corruption, such as monitoring the assets, incomes and lifestyles of public officers who may benefit from underhand deals.[5] The assets declaration legislation is not being enforced because there are no provisions to verify the declarations and no public disclosure requirement. The Whistleblower Act is quite new, and citizens need to build confidence in the implementing agencies, as potential whistleblowers fear victimisation and are not sure their reports will be acted upon.

In its 2006 review of Ghana's public financial management, the World Bank praises Ghana

for developing its public procurement system and its commitment to monitoring the law.[6] Ghana appears to have a strong legislative and regulatory framework for public procurement, but the more practical components, such as integrity, transparency, institutional and management capacity, and operation of the markets, are not so highly commended.[7] Public procurement represents between 50 and 80 per cent of the national budget and about 14 per cent of GDP.[8]

The Public Procurement Authority claims that corrupt practices by public procurement officials have been reduced considerably because of the potential for punitive measures. The private sector is not excluded from sanctions. For example, any supplier, contractor or consultant who attempts to influence a procurement process or the administration of a contract by any unfair method will be subject to sanctions, including debarment from government contracts for five years and any other remedies the courts may seek.[9] While it is likely that this is taking effect, there is no concrete evidence of its impact as yet.[10]

In September 2007 Yendi district chief executive Alhaji Mohammed Habib Tijani claimed that contracts he had allegedly taken for himself were awarded and executed on behalf of the ruling party, using borrowed documents of private companies to generate funds for the party. Tijani alleged that some of the projects cost between C270 million (US$27,000) and C300 million (US$30,000).[11]

---

4 World Bank and CDD-Ghana, *The Ghana Governance and Corruption Survey: Evidence from Households, Enterprises and Public Officials* (Accra: World Bank/CDD-Ghana, 2000).
5 Business Anti-Corruption Portal, 'Ghana Country Profile'; last accessed 28 January 2009.
6 World Bank, *Ghana: 2006 External Review of Public Financial Management*, Report no. 36384-GH, vol. I (Washington, DC: World Bank, 2006).
7 *The Statesman* (Ghana), 20 August 2007.
8 'Ghana small traders shy away from contracts', *Procurement News*, no. 22 (May 2008).
9 Public Procurement Board, 'Manuals - Public Procurement Act, 2003 (Act 663)', 2006.
10 Department for International Development (DfID), *Ghana Poverty Reduction Budget Support 2006–2008* (London: DfID, 2008).
11 *The Enquirer* (Ghana), vol. 5, no. 168 (2007).

In Ghana's procurement system the political heads of the local authorities, including the district chief executives (DCEs), chair tender board committees. This particular DCE, Tijani, was compelled to make these revelations to defend himself against allegations that he had diverted all the contracts in the assembly to his own construction company.[12] Other firms that allegedly benefited from special consideration in contract awards were the Sulbas and Barikase Construction Companies, both of which are allegedly affiliated with the ruling party.[13] These claims corroborate the allegations of the ex-chairman of the New Patriotic Party, Haruna Esseku, in connection with how government contracts were being awarded.[14]

Such allegations that some DCEs may be acting improperly are both alarming and worrisome. When procurement is managed in such a fashion, there is a genuine risk that companies may, with impunity, fail to do the work or do substandard work, and still be paid or inflate costs. In some cases, the political head and project supervisors may also exploit this situation for their personal gain. Moreover, when parties obtain funds fraudulently they are likely to spend frivolously, including buying votes from poor citizens who need money for basic social services. In addition, corrupt and sometimes unqualified people who can buy votes with stolen money get elected to positions of trust and continue to plunder state resources. This leads to general dissatisfaction and a lack of trust in local governance systems.

Concerns with tax administration and the private sector

Most Ghanaians are not familiar with tax laws, a fact that has often led taxpayers in the private sector to complain about corruption and extortion by tax officials. A 2003 CDD-Ghana study reports that corruption, evasion, abuse and misapplication of exemption laws are serious problems in the tax collection system.[15] A Ghana Integrity Initiative survey and the Global Corruption Barometer 2007 place the revenue agencies among Ghana's most corrupt service providers.[16]

Furthermore, writers and analysts have reported various problems, such as tax evasion, corruption, abuse of discretion, misapplication of exemption laws, political interference and low levels of capacity among tax collection agencies.[17] The embezzlement of tax proceeds by tax officials and agents has also been reported by the auditor general.[18] Such corruption can cost the government billions of cedis in lost revenue, through the pocketing of stolen tax proceeds and the underassessment of taxes and payments by citizens. In situations in which the impact falls on the taxpayer, there is an extra cost to the private sector in the form of excessive payments and reduced profits, which can discourage investment in the country.

In July 2007 the IRS set up a Revenue Mobilization Task Force to collect taxes from defaulters, with the mandate to recover the huge debts by issuing demand notices and final notices to defaulters who have failed to honour their tax

---

12 Ibid.
13 Ibid.
14 Ibid.
15 B. Agyeman-Duah, *Curbing Corruption and Improving Economic Governance: The Case of Ghana* (Accra: CDD-Ghana, 2003).
16 Ghana Integrity Initiative, '"Voice of the People" Survey, 2005' (Accra: Ghana Integrity Initiative, 2005); TI, Global Corruption Barometer, 2007.
17 V. A. Azeem, *Taxation in Ghana Made Simple* (Accra: Integrated Social Development Centre, 2002).
18 S. Akrofi-Quarco, *Reporters' Notebook: Ghana* (Washington, DC: Global Integrity, 2006).

obligations.[19] A newspaper reported, however, 'underhand dealings and deliberate cover-ups of a massive tax evasion by high-ranking officials' of the IRS, as revealed in an audit report.[20]

Similarly, the government in August 2007 set up a four-member committee to probe bribery allegations levelled against Customs, Excise and Preventive Service officers by members of the public.[21] One of the committee's tasks was to review the agency's systems, procedures, processes, and rules and regulations. Witnesses claimed that cars were being cleared from the port without payment of import duties, because of the connivance of customs and port security officers. Furthermore, even though computers had been installed to curb corruption in the clearance of goods, people were still able to clear goods without paying taxes, as these and the management systems were not being utilised.[22]

When goods are cleared without going through automated systems, customs officials can use or misuse their discretion to determine duties in return for a kickback. In some cases, private sector actors who refuse to cooperate tend to suffer, as they can be overcharged to meet revenue targets.

Problems in tax and customs administration deprives the government of much-needed revenue, in an aid-dependent country that has also been declared a heavily indebted poor country (HIPC). Resources for development and running public institutions, including high-quality health care and education, are drastically reduced if revenues find their way into private pockets. The private sector also suffers from issues, as it increases the cost of doing business, particularly if companies are finally caught and forced to pay the appropriate taxes in addition to irretrievable bribes. When the cost of doing business is high, potential investors may be scared away and economic growth may suffer as a result.

Recommendations

Fighting corruption at the nexus of private and public entities requires a radical change in the government's commitment to addressing problems. Prompt investigations of alleged corruption cases and harsh sanctions for violators constitute one solution, but this approach can be successful only when the political leadership adopts a strong anti-corruption stance.

What is needed is an enabling legal environment for key stakeholders to operate smoothly, including legislation to enable citizens to access information, report cases of corruption and enable accountability institutions to investigate credible reports of alleged corruption cases and prosecute violators. The Freedom of Information Bill, pending since the 1990s, should be enacted into law. Moreover, the Assets Declaration Law (Act 550) needs to be amended, and the relevant regulations currently before the attorney general laid before parliament for approval, to make the law an effective anti-corruption tool. The CHRAJ guidelines on conflict of interest for public officials need to be institutionalised and/or made into law to help curb corruption.

Ghanaians themselves must also recognise their duty to ensure that anti-corruption laws are enforced, that cases of corruption are reported and that the government is pressured to prosecute such cases. Transparency must be injected into Ghana's public system. Adequate information about systems and procedures must be widely disseminated to give citizens access to

---

19 *The Enquirer* (Ghana), 19–23 July 2007.
20 *Ghanaian Chronicle*, 16 April 2008.
21 *The Statesman* (Ghana), 1 August 2007.
22 *Daily Graphic* (Ghana), 5 September 2007.

goods and services as a right, rather than favours from corrupt officials who demand payment in return.

Vitus A. Azeem (Ghana Integrity Initiative)

Additional reading

Business Anti-Corruption Portal, 'Ghana Country Profile'; available at www.business-anti-corruption.com/normal.asp?pageid=82.

CDD-Ghana, 'CDD Issues Statement on PAC Hearings', 6 November 2007.

Economist Intelligence Unit, *Country Report Ghana* (London: Economist Intelligence Unit, 2008).

Ghana Integrity Initiative, '"Voice of the People Survey", 2005' (Accra: Ghana Integrity Initiative, 2005).

F. Kaufmann, P. Madelung, J. Spatz and M. Wegmann, *Business Climate Surveys: Experiences from Ghana, Mozambique, and South Africa* (Bergen: CHR Michelsen Institute, 2008).

World Bank, *Ghana: 2006 External Review of Public Financial Management*, Report no. 36384-GH, vol. I (Washington, DC: World Bank, 2006).

World Bank and CDD-Ghana, *The Ghana Governance and Corruption Survey: Evidence from Households, Enterprises and Public Officials* (Accra: World Bank/CDD-Ghana, 2000).

World Bank and International Finance Corporation (IFC), *Doing Business 2008* (Washington, DC: World Bank/IFC, 2007).

Ghana Integrity Initiative: www.tighana.org.

Kenya

Corruption Perceptions Index 2008: 2.1 (147th out of 180 countries)

Conventions

African Union Convention on Preventing and Combating Corruption (signed December 2003; ratified February 2007)

UN Convention against Corruption (signed December 2003; ratified December 2003)

UN Convention against Transnational Organized Crime (acceded June 2004)

Legal and institutional changes

- The Media Act 2007 was passed in October 2007. It provides for the establishment of the Media Council of Kenya and the Media Advisory Board and enables self-regulation of the media. Intended to be independent from the government, political parties or any nominating authority, the council has a core function to mediate the relationship between media and government. By attempting to build on media independence, the law has the potential to improve corruption reporting, while enhancing the autonomy of the media from political partisans and reducing activities in political advocacy. There remain concerns, however, that competent determination of claims may not be maintained if the Media Council finds itself either denuded of resources or if the resources it has are derived from the media industry, leading to possibilities and/or perceptions of bias.

- The Statute Law (Miscellaneous Amendment) Bill, agreed on 11 October 2007, vests the Kenya Anti-Corruption Commission (KACC) with powers akin to those of the police, including the power to arrest and detain suspects and seize fraudulently obtained property.
- The Licensing Laws (Repeal and Amendment) Bill, agreed on 11 October 2007, proposes amendments to fifteen acts and is intended to fine-tune the business-licensing regime in Kenya. Over 140 different licences that were previously essential have been abolished altogether. According to the Kenya Bribery Indices, excessive regulatory requirements such as licensing create widespread opportunities for bribery in the attempt to avoid compliance.
- The Political Parties Act, agreed on 20 October 2007, seeks to monitor and regulate political party financing and internal party management. It represents an excellent opportunity for monitoring compliance.
- The Supplies Practitioners Management Bill 2007 regulates the training, licensing and practice of supplies practitioners. It addresses loopholes in the Public Procurement and Disposal Act 2005 by, *inter alia*, restricting public procurement practice to procurement professionals.
- The Constituencies Development Fund (Amendment) Bill 2007 amends the Constituencies Development Fund Act 2003 by, *inter alia*, expanding the scope of spending to cover the purchase of machinery and equipment, environmental programmes and student bursaries. Although the prior restriction of

spending to infrastructure projects made it easier to cost-verify, the current amendments may now provide greater scope for concealment and/or the diversion of funds.

- The Constitution of Kenya (Amendment) and National Accord Reconciliation Bills, both agreed on 18 March 2008, created a coalition government between the Orange Democratic Party and the Party of National Unity and, notably, established the positions of prime minister and two deputies. While the arrangement can be said to have prevented a continued and total breakdown of law and order in the immediate term, it has perhaps inadvertently culminated in the absence of an effective opposition. This severely compromises parliament's oversight role over the executive. Currently, all MPs save for one, Cyrus Jirongo, the MP for Lugari, belong to parties affiliated to the ruling coalition. The possibility that civil service jobs are to be allocated following party loyalties greatly affects independence from political influences and complicates the oversight role of parliament.[1]
- The Ministry of Lands published the final draft of a National Land Policy on 14 August 2007. The document acknowledges land as a politically sensitive and culturally complex issue and is intended to regulate human settlement, clarify the broad agenda of land ownership and encourage the sustainable and equitable use of land. The main issues addressed by the policy are: land tenure reform, establishing 'secure and formalised property rights in land for all Kenyans'; and property redistribution, relating to 'access to land by the landless and disadvantaged groups'. Significantly, the provision of 'redress to those who were dispossessed of their land as a result of past discriminatory laws or practices will go some way in combating the corruption that has always engulfed transactions involving land'.[2]

1 *The Standard* (Kenya), 21 April 2008.
2 See www.kenyalandalliance.or.ke, 'Draft National Land Policy: A Call to Debate and Critique its Policy and Provisions'.

- On 6 February 2007[3] the government established civilian committees at the district level under the National Anti-Corruption Campaign Steering Committee to monitor devolved funds, including the Constituency Development Fund, the Local Authority Transfer Fund, secondary school bursaries, Youth Enterprise Funds, the Road Maintenance Levy Fund and HIV/AIDS funds.[4] The initiative aims to provide formal structures at the grassroots level that link communities with other public bodies in the collection and dissemination of information, and it is currently being piloted in nine districts. It is intended that whistleblowers will be able to report to the committees.
- The Judicial Citizen Dialogue Card (CDC) initiative, launched in July 2007, provides the public with an avenue for complaints and feedback on the judiciary. Submitted information will be posted on a transparency and accountability window and forwarded to Court Users Committees, piloted in various districts. A judicial Peer Review Mechanism enables the formulation of minimum standards of professional conduct.
- In June 2007 a presidential decree established a Public Complaints Standing Committee, geared towards enhancing accountability in public institutions. The body, akin to an ombudsman, is mandated to receive and process complaints against public officials.
- In May 2008 the government launched a multisectoral task force to formulate a framework for the implementation of the Witness Protection Act 2006. Established under section 4 of the act, the task force is required to develop a programme that will protect vulnerable witnesses.

The corporate governance crisis in Kenya's financial sector

On 13 October 2008[5] the Capital Markets Authority intervened in the management of Discount Securities Ltd, a stockbroker with the Nairobi Stock Exchange, and appointed an auditing firm, KPMG, to investigate allegations of a weak financial base and poor corporate governance. Following these developments, the National Social Security Fund (NSSF) lost, or is likely to lose, Sh1.4 billion (approximately US$19 million) belonging to desperately poor retirees invested through the stockbroker.[6]

Such losses are not new. In 2003 Euro Bank collapsed with Sh256 million (US$3.37 million) of NSSF contributors' money.[7] The funds had allegedly been invested in Euro Bank through Shah Munge and Partners stockbrokers.[8] It later turned out that Munge was one of the directors of Euro Bank.[9] Munge has since been acquitted of charges relating to the case.[10] In 1993 Mugoya Construction secured a contract to construct NSSF's Embakasi housing project, despite being one of the highest bidders.[11] Although NSSF had already estimated the cost of the project to be a mind-boggling Sh11 billion (US$160 million), Mugoya was still given an extra Sh2 billion (US$29 million) when he asked for more funds.[12]

The issues in Kenya's financial sector seem aligned to the peccadilloes of multi-party

---

3 See www.naccsc.go.ke.
4 See the presidential speech on the launch of the District Oversight Committees at the National Anti-Corruption Steering Committee website: www.naccsc.go.ke.
5 *Business Daily* (Kenya), 14 October 2008.
6 *The Standard* (Kenya), 17 October 2008.
7 BBC News (UK), 27 February 2003; see also www.clarionkenya.org/documents/corruption8.pdf.
8 *Business Daily* (Kenya), 21 August 2007.
9 BBC News (UK), 27 February 2003.
10 *Daily Nation* (Kenya), 19 September 2008.
11 *Business Daily* (Kenya), 3 August 2007.
12 Ibid.

elections. Following the 1992 general and presidential elections at least six banks, mainly associated with Asian business people, were put under statutory management, with disastrous consequences for their largely poor depositors and creditors. After the 1997 elections one of the country's largest banks, the National Bank of Kenya (NBK), teetered on the brink of liquidation before the NSSF and the government injected capital. Had the largest bank in the country, Kenya Commercial Bank, not been better capitalised than NBK it would have suffered a similar fate.[13]

What ails Kenya's financial sector is poor sectoral and corporate governance, resulting in weaknesses that make pensioners, creditors, employees and depositors extremely vulnerable. These weaknesses include ineffective laws, poor financial sector oversight, a base sector culture and overbearing political and executive corruption.

There are no effective laws in Kenya that criminalise the laundering of the proceeds of drug trade, illegal arms dealings and other crimes. Money-laundering rarely adds value to the country, as Kenya is only a conduit of value to other locations. Money-laundering also entrenches political corruption, as criminals fund political processes. The alleged Charterhouse Bank scam, involving money-laundering and tax evasion, was exposed by whistleblowers in 2004.[14] Investigators believe that the cost of the tax evasion and money-laundering that took place through the bank was equivalent to 10 per cent of Kenya's national income. The auditors' opinion was that the scale of the scandal 'threatens the stability of the Kenyan economy'.[15]

According to claims made in parliament by the shadow minister of finance, Billow Kerrow, on 21 June 2006, Charterhouse Bank was part of a network of businesses involved in money-laundering and tax evasion activities relating to about Sh18 billion. The shadow minister further claimed that Andrew Mulei had been suspended as the governor of the central bank for seeking to close down the bank. Mulei had earlier been suspended on allegations of abuse of office.[16] The bank was put under statutory management on 23 June 2006.[17]

Another issue is Kenya's failure to pass the Access to Information Bill; as a result, pensioners are unable to scrutinise the NSSF's handling of their money. In addition, the laws that guide the licensing of financial institutions are grossly inadequate in protecting customers and depositors in banking, pension, insurance, securities and foreign exchange institutions.

Kenya's financial sector culture has been consistently serpentine, thereby eliminating prospects for the sector's effective self-regulation. News reports on the stockbroker firm Mwangi Thuo and Partners' collapse in April 2007, following alleged 'fraudulent dealings of its directors and staff, weak capital position and the sale of investors' shares without their consent', claim that investigations implicated both directors of the firm in drawing on clients' money for personal use.[18] In addition, Nyaga Stockbrokers was put under statutory management by the Capital Markets Authority in March 2008, jeopardising Sh800 million of clients' money.[19]

Company directors are suspected of indulging in insider trading and political corruption

---

13 News from Africa, March 2003.
14 BBC News (UK), 7 November 2006.
15 Ibid.
16 *Daily Nation* (Kenya), 22 June 2006.
17 See Central Bank of Kenya press release, 23 June 2006.
18 *Business Daily* (Kenya), 29 April 2008.
19 Ibid.

with abandon. Reports around the collapse of the Uchumi supermarkets in June 2006 raised suspicions of insider trading by some directors. According to news reports, just before the public pronouncement was made huge sums of shares were sold off. Terry Davidson, who was the chief executive officer of Kenya Commercial Bank, a creditor for Uchumi, was arraigned in court on 27 August 2008 and charged with insider trading.[20] Similarly, national broadsheets reported that Chris Kirubi, a major Kenyan industrialist and a former director of Uchumi, was also charged with the offence of conspiracy to defraud the supermarket of Sh147 million.[21] Good governance demands that sector players are seen to be responsible in the conduct of their business – demonstrating their integrity in providing value to customers, adopting ethical employment practices and showing commitment to communities.

Despite its admirable infrastructure, Kenya has one of the lowest rates of foreign direct investment in the region. The direct costs of corruption (such as bribery for a banking licence) remain a deterrent to potential investors in the financial sector. Corruption is a major impediment both for existing businesses and those seeking to establish new businesses. According to *The Global Competitiveness Report 2007–2008*, corruption remains the largest obstacle in doing business.[22] Further, the capacity of public institutions to facilitate corporate performance is ranked as weak, with a score of 3.5 on a scale of 1 to 7.[23]

At present there is a somewhat pointless debate about Kenya's constitutional review and the effectiveness of oversight institutions such as the central bank. The fundamental problem that mostly causes poor governance in Kenya is singular: excessive power within the presidency. If power were devolved from the presidency, Kenyans would no longer clamour for federalism, which would be risky (a multiplication of corruption centres) and needless. The judiciary and parliament would have the power to redress any resource and services imbalance that any future president would attempt. Oversight institutions such as the CMA, the central bank and the Kenya Anti-Corruption Commission would be effective in ensuring good corporate governance without undue influence from an overbearing executive. The executive powers greatly compromise the effectiveness of the oversight institutions. The KACC, for example, a supposedly independent institution, has to depend on the attorney general's decision as to which cases to prosecute. The Kenyan constitution grants the attorney general sole prosecutorial powers. When the holder of this office is a presidential appointee, the president's influence on prosecution is not hard to see. The central bank's independence came to the spotlight this year with claims of corruption by a former deputy governor, Jacinta Mwatela. Mwatela claimed that her redeployment to the Ministry of Northern Kenya was a cover-up in connection with corruption surrounding the award of a currency printing tender to the De la Rue company.[24]

Short of this devolution of power, all attempts to govern Kenya's financial sector effectively will routinely be rendered futile by the executive. In August 2008 the attorney general (who is part of the executive) withdrew a case involving a former Euro Bank employee, Peter Fernandez, whom the KACC had accused of wrongdoing within the bank.[25] If excessive presidential

---

20　*The Standard* (Kenya), 23 August 2008; *The Nation* (Kenya), 27 August 2008.

21　*Daily Nation* (Kenya), 27 August 2008; according to *Business Daily Africa* (Kenya), 2 January 2009, the cases of Davidson and Kirubi were both due to be heard in March 2009.

22　World Economic Forum, *The Global Competitiveness Report 2007–2008*, (Geneva: World Economic Forum, 2008).

23　Ibid.

24　*The Standard* (Kenya), 17 September 2008.

25　*Daily Nation* (Kenya), 19 September 2008.

power is reclaimed and returned to the judiciary, justice will be served.

TI Kenya

Additional reading

Coalition for Accountable Party Financing [CAPF], *Campaign Finance and Corruption: A Monitoring Report on the Campaign Finance on the General Elections* (Nairobi: CAPF, 2008).

P. K. Kidombo, *The Architecture of Corruption in Kenya* (Nairobi: Sino Printers and Publishers, 2007).

D. M. Muia, *An Assessment of Roles and Responsibilities of Central and Local Government in the Management of Public Finances in Kenya*, Discussion Paper no 103/2008 (Nairobi: Institute of Policy Analysis and Research, 2008).

TI Kenya, *Kenya Bribery Index 2008* (Nairobi: TI Kenya, 2008).

P. Wanyande, M. Omosa and C. Ludeki (eds.), *Governance and Transition Politics in Kenya* (Nairobi: University of Nairobi Press, 2007).

TI Kenya: www.tikenya.org.

Lebanon

Corruption Perceptions Index 2008: 3.0 (102nd out of 180 countries)

Conventions

UN Convention against Corruption (acceded April 2009)

UN Convention against Transnational Organized Crime (signed December 2001; ratified October 2005)

Legal and institutional changes

- As a consequence of political stalemate, from December 2006 to May 2008 the Lebanese parliament was unable to convene on a regular basis, let alone enact laws. As such, there were few legal and institutional changes in relation to corruption in this period.

- In September 2007 Banque du Liban, the central bank of Lebanon issued a decision aimed at regulating corporate governance in Lebanese Islamic banks.[1] The decision states that banks should use the framework of internal regulations relating to corporate governance according to internationally recognised rules; create special corporate governance

---

1 Decision no. 9725.

units, independent from the management of each bank and excluded from all executive prerogatives; adopt an investment strategy taking into consideration all risks; and create an administrative unit with a mission consisting of auditing, evaluating and pursuing the compliance of the banks' operations.[2]

- A new draft of the competition law was adopted by the Council of Ministers in October 2007, and submitted to parliament on 24 November 2007.[3] The draft law includes the creation of an independent national competition council with a specific mandate. 'The Competition Council's competences will apply to both private and public undertakings. Lebanon intends to develop a mechanism to exchange information on the total amount and distribution of state aid granted, so as to ensure transparency.'[4] Since 1967 monopolies have been legal and, as such, competition in Lebanon has decreased.[5] The Lebanese government's Paris III reform programme has been intended to work towards ratifying a modern competition law and removing state protection including exclusive agency rights, which could reduce monopoly power and prices. This law is the realisation of this aim.
- In January 2006 the International Finance Corporation (IFC) signed an agreement with Lebanon's Ministry of Economy and Trade (MoET) aiming to simplify business registration procedures by reducing the cost and time of business registration. In September 2007 an agreement between the MoET, the Ministry of Finance, the Ministry of Justice and LibanPost

was signed with the support of the IFC so as to facilitate business registration procedures. In this regard, a 'Guide to Business Registration in Lebanon' was developed, and LibanPost will serve as a one-stop shop for business registration in the country.[6]

- The Lebanese Transparency Association has updated the 2001 draft law on access to information and is currently discussing with the legal committee in the Lebanese parliament the new updated draft law.
- As an initial step in improving public administration and reducing corruption risks, the Ministry of Finance signed a Memorandum of Understanding with the Lebanese Transparency Association (LTA) in October 2007.[7] The project involves drafting a code of conduct and focuses on access to information.

Lebanon and the private sector

The economic system in Lebanon has always been distinct from its neighbouring countries, as it enjoys an open and free economy that relies on services, mainly tourism and banking. In 2007 the share of the services sector totalled 75.9 per cent of GDP.[8] Despite its size, however, the Lebanese economy is still dominated by small and medium enterprises (SMEs) and family-owned enterprises (FOEs). According to a survey on corporate governance in Lebanon, 95 per cent of the 298 companies surveyed in the Greater Beirut Area were SMEs, and 58 per cent were FOEs.[9]

---

2 Badri and Salim El Meouchi Law Firm, 'Lebanon', in Getting the Deal Through, *Corporate Governance 2008* (London: Getting the Deal Through, Law Business Research Ltd, 2008).

3 International Conference for Support to Lebanon – Paris III, Fifth Progress Report, 31 March 2008.

4 See http://ec.europa.eu/world/enp/pdf/progress2008/sec08_397_en.pdf.

5 This is the result of Legislative Decree 34 on commercial representation introduced in 1967.

6 See www.economy.gov.lb/MOET/English/Navigation/News/BusinessRegistrationGuide.htm.

7 Commission Staff Working Document: Accompanying the Communication from the Commission to the Council and the European Parliament 'Implementation of the European Neighbourhood Policy in 2007' Progress Report Lebanon 2008. Partners in Transparency: Memorandum of Understanding between the Ministry of Finance and the Lebanese Transparency Association, signed 25 October 2007.

8 See www.cia.gov/library/publications/the-world-factbook/geos/le.html#Econ.

9 LTA, 'Corporate Governance Survey 2004' (Beirut: LTA, 2004); available at www.lcgtf.org.

In 2006 the Foreign Investment Advisory Service (FIAS) surveyed more than 450 enterprises from all sectors. The study finds that corruption is the main obstacle to investment.[10] Although the Penal Code of Lebanon stipulates that it is a criminal act to give or accept a bribe, and its penalty is imprisonment for up to three years, 60 per cent of the Lebanese firms surveyed reported nonetheless that 'they must give gifts or informal payments to public officials to get things done, and these gifts impose an annual tax equivalent to 5% of sales'.

While the Lebanese private sector has shown resilience during the past years of political instability, it continues to face many challenges. Despite its free and open nature, the private sector still experiences high fixed costs, difficult access to credit facilities, complicated and bureaucratic procedures and a weak regulatory framework. The World Bank *Doing Business 2008* report ranked Lebanon eighty-fifth among 178 countries in the world and seventh among seventeen countries in the Middle East and north Africa region with respect to the ease of doing business.

Addressing procurement inefficiencies

Public procurement is a vulnerable process in Lebanon. The Global Integrity report on Lebanon in 2006 states that the cost of corruption annually in the Lebanese economy was estimated at about US$1 billion in 2000.[11] This was corroborated in 2001 when a UN-commissioned report noted that, of the total project expenditures by the state, only 2.4 per cent was awarded by the state Administration for Tenders, indicating that the remainder had gone to those willing to pay the highest bribes.[12] While this information

is outdated, its findings are not. The situation has not changed and the public procurement law is still awaiting the Council of Ministers' endorsement.[13]

The inefficiencies in the public procurement process, which allow these corrupt acts to take place, are the result of a public procurement law that is more than forty years old.[14] The rules apply to the majority of goods procured by the state from the private sector and demand compliance by all institutions apart from the army and the internal security service. There are safeguards included in the law, which require a public tender for any project costing over LL800,000 (US$500). Furthermore, procurement contracts that are financed by the Lebanese government are announced in the national press as well as the *Official Gazette*, which affords some level of transparency. Procurements that are financed by foreign entities must conform to the rules of the entity concerned, however, which, depending on the financier, could either mean more or less transparency and accountability.

In terms of winning contracts, bids should be treated equally, although there is a clause that allows Lebanese companies to be given preference in cases where their bid is no more than 10 per cent higher than the lowest bid presented by a foreign company. Since 1959 the Public Procurement Directorate has been responsible for organising the procurement process and approving contracts above LL75 million (US$50,000). It works under the supervision of the Council of Ministers. Contracts undertaken by the Council for Development and Reconstruction (CDR), and by the army and security forces, are exempt from this process, as well as those below the threshold amount, which are managed by the

---

10 The study was carried out for the Ministry of Economy and Trade, but was not published.
11 M. Al-Azar, 'Lebanon: Reporters Notebook' (Washington, DC: Global Integrity, 2006).
12 Ibid.
13 International Conference for Support to Lebanon – Paris III, Seventh Progress Report, 30 September 2008.
14 Global Integrity, 'Lebanon Integrity Indicators Scorecard, 2007 Assessment'. The rules regarding public procurement are outlined in the Public Accounting Law (PAL) of 1963.

ministries and pubic entities concerned. The CDR applies international standards of procurement, however, based mainly on those of the World Bank. As such, its decisions are made public and the bidder is not informed ahead of time. Nonetheless, experience has shown that the resources are lacking for implementing fair and transparent procurement processes under these conditions, leading to increased opportunities for abuse.

There has been an awareness of the need for reform in the public procurement law for some time. A proposal was submitted to parliament in 2000, but it was never approved. According to an IMF report in 2005, however 'while it contained important reform measures it did not reflect a fundamental overhaul of the law as suggested in the 2004 report on Public Expenditure Management'.[15]

Despite these setbacks, a new public procurement law was drafted by the Lebanese government and finalised in September 2007. It has yet to be approved by parliament, however, as, due to the political crisis, parliament did not convene between December 2007 and May 2008. The new procurement law seeks to harmonise the organisation of tenders and requires the creation of a regulatory body to ensure the proper implementation of the law.[16]

A further development in terms of improving the system of government tenders to the private sector is the introduction by the Office of the Minister of State for Administrative Reform (OMSAR) of a system for e-procurement. The idea was first mooted, and a strategy drafted, in December 2002. In January 2008, however, OMSAR published an e-government strategy for Lebanon.[17] One aspect of the government's new

e-governance is the preparation of a strategy for e-procurement, meaning that the government would manage tenders for government procurements online. In terms of anti-corruption measures, this can be seen to have advantages, as it is fully public information and it involves less interaction between the bidders and the government officials managing the tender. The aims of the new e-procurement, in the words of the strategy, are to create a 'more effective government, better and easier procedures for the private sector [and] greater transparency in purchasing'.

Corporate governance as a tool to fight corruption in the private sector

Systemic corruption ultimately diminishes the attractiveness of the Lebanese economy to foreign investors and undermines the sustainability of Lebanese businesses and their ability to survive in a highly competitive global economy. As such, it is in the interests of both the government and the private sector to address corruption and develop a culture of corporate governance and accountability.

Accountable corporate governance is a new concept in Lebanon, and is undoubtedly complicated by regulatory and legal obstacles that do not allow for the application of certain corporate governance principles. Lebanese law, for example, stipulates that a shareholder who has owned shares in a company for more than two years automatically has double voting rights. As a result, new shareholders, and thus new investment, are deterred because the rights attached to each new share are less than those attached to shares previously issued. In addition, shareholders who own less than 49.9 per cent of the shares do not have the authority to nominate

---

15 IMF, *Lebanon: Report on Observance of Standards and Codes – Fiscal Transparency Module*, Country Report no. 05/158 (Washington, DC: IMF, 2005), p. 8.

16 See ec.europa.eu/world/enp/pdf/progress2008/sec08_397_en.pdf.

17 See http://msib.omsar.gov.lb/Cultures/en-US/Publications/Strategies/EGov_Strategy08.htm.

board members. Lebanese law does not provide for the adoption of mechanisms of cumulative voting for the protection of minority shareholders, as it violates the principle of one share, one vote.[18] Thus, minority shareholders are not adequately represented on boards of directors. Both of these shortcomings do little to protect the rights of new or minority shareholders, and they run counter to the principles of corporate governance, which advocate accountability, responsibility, disclosure and fairness. Moreover, Lebanese law does not allow for the separation of the functions of chairman and general manager (the chairman is responsible for all operations – i.e. he can appoint a general manager – but it is the chairman who will be held accountable under law).[19] This, in turn, does not allow for the creation of truly accountable officers within a corporation.

There are developments afoot, however, and improvements are being made at least in the banking sector, which is by far the most prominent and powerful sector in the economy.

The Banking Control Commission has been focusing on the urgent challenge of preparing Lebanese banks for fulfilling the requirements of Basel II. In this context, there has been an emphasis on developing a culture of appropriate internal audit practices and risk management. The governor of the central bank has been pushing for the implementation of corporate governance and Basel II as a means to promote transparency in the banking sector. While the regulatory framework for banks in Lebanon is robust, it has been interesting to observe how the banks themselves have taken voluntary initiatives to apply appropriate standards of good governance. An excellent example is the initiative by Banque Audi, the first bank in Lebanon to apply corporate governance standards.[20] Other banks are now starting to show some interest in corporate governance principles, but at the time of writing Banque Audi is the only one that has taken the initiative.

Lynne Ghossein, Khalil Gebara and Badri El Meouchi (Lebanese Transparency Association)

---

18 See www.ifc.org/ifcext/cgf.nsf/AttachmentsByTitle/MENA2_LTA_LCGTF/$FILE/LTA+&+LCGTF+Pres.Amman.12.12.2006.pp.
19 Ibid.
20 What follows is derived from an interview with Mr Farid Lahoud, the corporate secretary of Banque Audi (since 2005). Interview conducted on 3 June 2008.

Box 5 Extract of an interview with Mr Farid Lahoud, Banque Audi

Where did the drive to carry out the 2005 Corporate Governance (CG) assessment come from?

The bank started by carrying out a Corporate Governance (CG) assessment in 2005, with the support of the International Finance Corporation (IFC) and Nestor Advisors (NeAd). The drive to carry out the assessment came from awareness at the level of the board of directors and the executive management. Beyond the importance of CG for investors, regulators, rating agencies and researchers, it was seen by the board and the management as an essential contributor to the bank's perpetuation and as a value generator at a time when the bank was embarking on an expansion strategy and was in the process of raising capital.

Box 5 (continued)

Out of the recommendations of the assessment, were some recommendations problematic? Were you faced with any obstacles for their implementation? If yes, how did you overcome them?

Over the past few years the bank has progressed significantly, and still has further challenges to overcome. It is aiming at moving as close as possible to best practice, and this process of introducing a new culture requires time, where every step forward needs support and ratification. For example, when the bank was developing its code of ethics and conduct, it would have been easy to apply a code available on the internet. But the bank chose to design its own code, reflecting its own values and culture. It took significant coordination efforts and months of work, during which the code was circulated to a large population in the bank, who commented on it before it was adopted.

The bank did face obstacles in implementing CG but these obstacles were easier to overcome through continued commitment from the top. One of the main problems the bank initially faced was to set enough time aside for the board and the executive management to put the CG framework in place – especially that board members' time has always been among the scarcest of resources. Furthermore, the governance framework had to be reviewed and accepted by shareholders and the executive management, while ensuring that it addressed the concerns of relevant stakeholders (an exercise that sometimes led to diverging points of view). The bank was assisted by the IFC, who assessed the existing governance framework and offered recommendations, and a consultancy firm (Nestor Advisors) assisted the bank in the implementation phase.

Is Basel II going to be an issue for the banking sector in Lebanon? And for your bank?

The CG practices in Basel II are challenging and difficult to implement, particularly at the level of the composition of the board. If we want to have independent board members, the pool of candidates is limited in Lebanon, so we have to look overseas. For large banks, it makes sense since they already have branches overseas, but for small banks it is challenging to apply good rules of CG. Nonetheless, the Basel II requirements are a target, and banks have to work towards fulfilling these requirements.

Additional reading

K. Gebara, *Reconstruction Survey: The Political Economy of Corruption in Post-war Lebanon* (London: Tiri, 2007).
   'The Role of the Lebanese Parliament in Fighting Corruption', presentation at seminar 'Programme on Governance in the Arab Region', Beirut, 24 July 2007.

R. Leenders, 'Nobody Having Too Much to Answer for: Laissez-faire, Networks and Postwar Reconstruction in Lebanon', in S. Heydemann (ed.), *Networks of Privilege in the Middle East: The Politics of Economic Reform Revisited* (New York: Palgrave Macmillan, 2004).

Lebanese Transparency Association: www.transparency-lebanon.org.

Morocco

Corruption Perceptions Index 2008: 3.5 (80th out of 180 countries)

Conventions

UN Convention against Corruption (signed December 2003; ratified May 2007)

UN Convention against Transnational Organized Crime (signed December 2000; ratified September 2002)

Legal and institutional changes

- On 17 April 2007 a law on money-laundering was enacted.[1] It defines money-laundering as 'concealing and altering goods originating from a number of restrictively enumerated offences including corruption, extortion, influence peddling and misappropriation of public and private property'. This law also provides for the formation of the Moroccan Financial Intelligence Unit (UTRF), a major mechanism under the authority of the prime minister's office. The UTRF will consist of representatives of Bank Al-Maghrib (Morocco's central bank), magistrates, bankers and accountants, among others. With broad powers, it will be able to track and police financial crimes related to terrorism or money-laundering. The law also addresses income and asset declarations, which will be implemented by institutions such as the revenue court and a commission within the Supreme Court. Certain categories of people are not yet included in the legal provisions, such as ministers, prefects, ambassadors and advisers to heads of state. Informally, it has been said that a similar law will be published for these groups subsequent to the publication of the asset declaration law. Regrettably, the money-laundering law does not include tax offences, under-the-table payments and bribes, which can occur in real estate transactions. It is likely that implementing these measures will take some time, considering the usual delays in implementing anti-corruption initiatives.

- Morocco has also seen delays in implementing the UN Convention against Corruption. Despite having signed the UNCAC in 2003, it was ratified only on 9 May 2007 and published on 17 January 2008. While the ratification is a commendable effort in itself, dealing with corruption is not useful unless real decisions are made to fight it in the long term. Although it might be argued that deficiencies in the formulation of anti-corruption laws account for their lack of effectiveness, anti-corruption is not the only area where the law is not properly enforced. It is, therefore, much more likely to be an entrenched issue related to lawmaking and respect for the rule of law in Morocco. Furthermore, many of the institutions in charge of financial controls are generally ineffective, such as the auditor general, inspector general, ministers and the revenue court. For example, while there is an obligation to audit all public contracts

---

1 *Official Gazette*, 3 May 2007, p. 602.

over DH 5 million (US$700,000), audits are often not done.[2] When audits are carried out, sometimes they are not followed up. Such failings in the institutions and structures surrounding the judicial system mean that, even where laws are passed, they are difficult to implement.

Public procurement: intimate relationships between the public and private sectors

In Morocco, corruption in the private sector is intimately linked to its relationship with the public sector. A lack of transparency, a lack of competition, collusion of public and private sector officials in selection processes, and inefficient public procedures all help determine the outcomes of public procurement.[3] As such, it is a real governance problem, as a lack of transparency and poor management of systems can lead to corruption, inflated transaction costs and substandard products or quality of work. These costs are generally borne by the community and taxpayers.

Several studies corroborate the tight correlation between a lack of transparency and the development of corruption. For instance, integrity studies carried out by Transparency Morocco show that only 7 per cent of companies say they have attempted to act when faced with a situation involving corruption. This passive attitude is associated with a 'feeling of powerlessness'. Companies are not at all certain

they would be vindicated for their actions, and some even feared 'creating problems for themselves'.[4]

The lack of transparency in public procurement has been estimated to cost an amount equivalent to approximately 0.5 per cent of GDP[5] in the Middle East and north Africa region. Applied to Morocco, this implies an annual loss of some US$3.6 billion (based on a GDP of US$74 billion in 2007). This is a considerable proportion of the approximately DH 100 billion (US$13.8 billion) spent annually on public procurement in Morocco. As such, greater transparency and increased competition in the public procurement process would surely have an impact on the country's annual growth rate.

In July 2007 Transparency Morocco opened a National Corruption Monitoring Centre. One of its functions is to collect and analyse news items related to corruption and poor governance.[6] Bulletins in *Transparency News*[7] listed over 1,500 items related to corruption, the embezzlement of public funds, special privileges and patronage between July 2007 and April 2008. The private sector is deeply mired in all these issues, which explains the opacity of its ties with public administration.

Some efforts have been made to improve public procurement, however. On 5 February 2007 Decree 2-06-388 set out the terms and conditions for awarding public contracts as well as certain rules relating to their management and

---

2 Le décret des marchés publics, 1998.
3 See A. Akesbi, 'La corruption endémique au Maroc: béquille de l'économie de rente', paper presented at the International Colloquium of the Association of Moroccan Economists, Rabat, 6 June 2008; K. Mesbahi, 'Transparence versus corruption dans les marchés publics', *Critique Economique*, no. 21, Winter 2008; *Economia*, no. 3, September 2008.
4 Transparency Morocco, 'Summary Report of National Survey Results' (Rabat: Transparency Morocco, 2003).
5 World Bank, *Pour une meilleure gouvernance dans les pays du MENA* (Washington, DC: World Bank, 2004).
6 See www.transparencymaroc.ma.
7 The first issue focused on the general election of September 2007, and the second on the justice system. A third issue will be published in June 2008 on the topic of land and real estate, and a fourth will deal with local governance. See www.transparencymaroc.ma.

supervision.[8] This reform was introduced nine years after the previous law had been published, in 1998. In theory, it improves the system by putting greater responsibility in the hands of certifying officers and granting them increased freedom and flexibility, so as to achieve effective reforms. The decree aims, *inter alia*, to strengthen the rules promoting free and broad competition among bidders, establish transparency in the system, adopt a principle of equal treatment for all bidders (including equal access to adequate information), strengthen the rules of administrative ethics, introduce measures to reduce possible fraud and corruption, and establish legal remedies for dispute settlement. While the discretionary powers of the administration are reduced, they are nonetheless still inscribed in the current law.

The new decree could still be improved, especially in terms of making it more precise by adding complementary provisions or establishing procedures that would make mere statements of principle more concrete. Although it needs to be emphasised that this decree represents an important step, such progress can be gauged only by the effectiveness of the laws currently in force. Rather than discuss all cases, the construction sector serves as a revealing example.

The construction industry: deconstructing corruption brick by brick

In May 2002 Transparency International's Bribe Payers Index on exporting countries noted that 'the most blatant corruption could be found in public works, construction, armaments and defence'. At the time, Morocco was included in the sample of fifteen 'emerging market countries'. On presenting this report, TI founder Peter Eigen declared, 'Our new survey leaves no doubt that large numbers of multinational corporations from the richest nations are pursuing a criminal course to win contracts.' It must be recognised that little has changed since then. In many countries, the building and construction industry is a source of many corrupt practices. Morocco is no exception.

The current extent of corruption in the construction sector is acknowledged by all stakeholders. Building and construction involve more than 300 professions, entailing a large bureaucracy. The longer the chain the more likely it is to include weak links. Indeed, according to an architect reported in *TelQuel*, 'The procedure for obtaining a building permit is so long and complicated that project managers have no choice but to resort to corrupt practices to speed up their project.'[9] Such bypassing of rules, regulations and procedures can have disastrous effects.

On 17 January 2008 a building under construction collapsed in Kenitra (30km from Rabat), killing eighteen people and injuring twenty-six others. It appeared that, while all the necessary prior studies had been conducted, the collapse was due either to unstable soil or the use of non-compliant concrete. Said Sekkat, a member of the National Federation of Property Developers, argued, 'The problem lies mainly in building in the absence of any control.'[10] The government and city authorities were struck with panic because of the scale of the damage – and even more so because of the reaction of the king, who the same day ordered an inquiry to determine who was responsible. On 21 January the minister of housing held a meeting with stakeholders in the real estate industry to carry out an industry-wide assessment. He told them that 'the government will not spare any effort' to shed light on the accident. Unfortunately, as is often

8 See www.marchespublics.gov.ma.
9 *TelQuel* (Morocco), 2 February 2008.
10 Ibid.

the case, the judicial system did not get to the root of the problem. Weak legislation appeared to be a key problem. Although six people were interviewed related to the incident, the hearing was made under the provisions of article 769 of Dahir Bonds and Contracts, which relates to the responsibilities of architects, engineers and contractors in the event of a collapse. The law only provides for fines as punishment, however, and there are no standards for construction.[11]

This and other examples are only the tip of the iceberg. The building sector is criss-crossed by a great variety of channels for corruption, including authorisation for land parcelling and building, lenient occupancy permits, inadequate architectural plans, frequent and questionable exceptions made to development plans (such as hazardous extra height for buildings) and deficient compliance and quality control, upstream as well as downstream.

A ray of light: increased transparency led by the private sector

Several stakeholders, particularly domestic economic agents, are calling for increased transparency in government calls for tenders, as well as in concessions and the outsourcing of public services. It is a positive step that the Moroccan private sector is beginning to address these issues publicly and understand how dangerous corruption can be for business.

On 21 May 2008, during the Construction and Public Works (BTP) forum, the BTP Integrity and Social Responsibility Pact was signed between construction industry professionals, the Ministry of Housing, the Ministry of Transport and contractors. Three principles were put forward: fighting corruption, the environment, and quality and performance. The deputy director of

the National Federation for Building and Public Works (FNBTP) declared that 'a corruption risk map for public procurement will be drawn so as to identify affected areas'. As DH 70 billion of public procurement funds are spent annually on supplies, works and services, the FNBTP official argued that saving 5 per cent of this sum through corruption prevention would equal DH 3.5 billion in investment.[12]

A few such initiatives have been taken up by the General Confederation of Moroccan Entrepreneurs (CGEM).[13]

- A new anti-corruption committee was set up in 2006 to focus on four priorities: training, awareness-raising, relations with public authorities and developing sector-specific priorities.
- As a joint initiative by the private sector (represented by CGEM) and the public authorities, the Moroccan Code of Good Practice for Corporate Governance was adopted in 2008. It is based on the principles of good management, transparency and the promotion of ethics. The code is also in line with international benchmarks and the OECD's good governance principles, while being adapted to the local context. Provisions are made for follow-up and monitoring procedures.
- A Corruption Risk Map, stemming from CGEM's Anti-corruption Committee, consists of a map of corruption risks in the awarding and execution of electricity procurement contracts. As corruption is not simply a technical problem but, rather, the result of non-transparent management, the risk map will help illuminate how and where risks exist in order to fight corruption more effectively.

The reputedly pro-business daily newspaper *L'Economiste* reacted to these initiatives in its

---

11 *TelQuel* (Morocco), 2 February 2008.
12 *L'Economiste* (Morocco), 24 May 2008.
13 See www.cgem.ma.

19 May 2008 edition: 'The code of good practice for corporate governance led by CGEM is having difficulty making its mark. . . Explanatory work and awareness-raising are needed. It would seem that most SMEs [small and medium enterprises] are reluctant to use safety and transparency regulation, and even large corporations still have a hard time making radical changes.'[14]

Although the effectiveness of CGEM efforts may be questioned, the most important point is that the private sector is beginning to understand the dangers that a system of widespread corruption can produce for competitiveness in an increasingly open economy.

Kamal Mesbahi and Michèle Zirari (TI Morocco)

Additional reading

A. Akesbi, 'La corruption endémique au Maroc: béquille de l'économie de rente', paper presented at the International Colloquium of the Association of Moroccan Economists, Rabat, 6 June 2008.

K. Mesbahi, 'Transparence versus corruption dans les marchés publics', *Critique Economique*, no. 21, Winter 2008.

K. Mesbahi and A. Debbagh, 'Lutte contre la corruption et transparence dans la gestion publique: essai d'évaluation de l'action du gouvernement d'alternance', *Critique Economique*, no. 8, Summer/Autumn 2002.

Transparency News, 'La nébuleuse du foncier et de l'immobilier', *Transparency News*, no. 3, August 2008; available at www.transparency-maroc.ma.

M. Zirari, *L'implementation de l'UNCAC au Maroc* (Rabat: Transparency Maroc, 2007).

Transparency Maroc: www.transparencymaroc.org.

---

14 *L'Economiste* (Morocco), 19 May 2008.

Nigeria

Corruption Perceptions Index 2008: 2.7 (121st out of 180 countries)

Conventions

African Union Convention on Preventing and Combating Corruption (signed December 2003; ratified September 2006)

UN Convention against Corruption (signed December 2003; ratified December 2004)

UN Convention against Transnational Organized Crime (signed December 2000; ratified June 2001)

Legal and institutional changes

- Upon taking office on 29 May 2007, President Umaru Yar'Adua pronounced that fighting corruption would be on his seven-point agenda. To this effect, new legislation aimed at preventing corruption has been enacted since he assumed office.
- The Nigeria Extractive Industries Transparency Initiative Act 2007 was passed on 28 May 2007. The act aims to facilitate transparency in the extractive industries, which account for more than 80 per cent of Nigeria's foreign earnings. The oil, gas and mining sector will now be audited annually according to international standards, and violations will be punished with fines, loss of licences and, when individuals are found guilty, criminal sanctions.[1] Based on the act's provisions, the National Stakeholders Working Group of the Nigeria Extractive Industries Transparency Initiative was formed.
- Passed on 17 May 2007, the Public Procurement Act 2007 aims to ensure more transparency in procurement and increases the fines for corruption and abuse of public funding. The new Bureau for Public Procurement, which replaces the Budget Monitoring and Price Intelligence Unit, will now vet all government procurement contracts. Unlike its predecessor, the bureau will not report to the president but, instead, to the National Council on Public Procurement. The bureau can also refer cases to the law enforcement agencies if offences are uncovered.[2]
- In July 2007 the Fiscal Responsibility Act 2007 was enacted into law with the aim to 'redirect governments at all levels to imbue a fiscal behaviour that will promote prudence and sound financial management in the system'. In short, the law provides guidelines for planning budgets, as well as executing and reporting them. Although some argue that the act will interfere with Nigeria's fiscal federalism,[3] there seems to be little dispute over its potential to improve budgeting and, in turn, reduce opportunities for corruption.

---

1 Nigeria Extractive Industries Transparency Initiative, 'NEITI Bill Signed into Law', 30 May 2007.
2 Nigeria Budget Monitoring Project, 'Beware, That Business Proposal Could Procure a Jail Term for You'; see www.budgetmonitoringng.org.
3 Nigeria Budget Monitoring Project, 'Fiscal Responsibility Bill: Rising Hopes in the Horizon'; see www.budgetmonitoringng.org.

- The Investments and Securities Act 2007 came into force on 25 June 2007, replacing the 1999 act. The new act reconstituted the Investment and Securities Tribunal, which demonstrated success in its first few months in operation by resolving over 100 cases in May 2007. Small or non-contentious cases that do not warrant the resources of the tribunal can be referred to its Alternative Dispute Resolution Centre.[4]
- Following the outcry over malpractice in the 2007 general election, the president created an Electoral Reform Committee. As of October 2008 the committee had already received memoranda from members of the public and held public sittings. The committee submitted its report to the president in December 2008. There are concerns, however, that while the committee's purview is broad its recommendations will not be implemented.[5]
- The Central Bank of Nigeria (CBN) restructured the financial sector in 2005, introducing a policy of consolidation that reduced the number of banks from eighty-nine to twenty-five. The policy was fully implemented by 2007. The CBN also issued a regulation in 2004 requiring banks to raise their capital base from N2 billion to N25 billion, leading to the merger of many banks that could not meet the requirement individually. Others that could not meet it were wound up.
- At the seventh National Economic Crime Seminar in Abuja in September 2008 the executive chairman of the Economic and Financial Crimes Commission (EFCC), Farida Waziri, called on Nigerians to support the proposed asset forfeiture bill.[6]
- The Freedom of Information Bill suffered a setback in 2008, when the Senate Committee

on Information introduced a new section 2 to the bill that reads as follows: 'Every citizen . . . has a legally enforceable right to, and shall, on application be given access to, any information or record under the control of a government or public institution or private company performing public functions, provided the disclosure of such information or release of such record(s) shall not compromise national security and the applicant shall have satisfied a State or Federal High Court of the need for the disclosure of such information or release of such record(s).'[7] Furthermore, section 31(2) of the draft bill, dealing with whistleblowers' protection, was deleted by the Senate Committee.[8] The controversy generated by these amendments, which will no doubt have an effect on its efficacy, has stalled further action on the bill.

Corruption in the banking sector

Nigeria's banking sector has a long history of corruption, which was partly responsible for the collapse of many banks in the 1990s and losses to many depositors and stakeholders. The failures were a result of fraud committed by bank owners and managers, who had: granted unsecured loans, resulting in high levels of bad debt and a loss of liquidity; failed to maintain a strong capital base; granted unsecured loans to friends and bank owners or managers; and, in some cases, embezzled funds outright.[9]

It was against this backdrop that the law was amended, and the Failed Banks (Recovery of Debts) and Financial Malpractices in Banks Decree 1994[10] was enacted. Under this law, a

---

4 The Investments and Securities Act, 2007.
5 BBC News (UK), 23 August 2007.
6 *Vanguard* (Nigeria), 19 September 2008.
7 *Guardian* (Nigeria), 30 September 2008.
8 Ibid.
9 *Vanguard* (Nigeria), 19 November 2007; *Nigerian Tribune*, 1 April 2008.
10 Laws made by the Federal Military Government are called 'decrees'. Under a democratic dispensation, the laws made by the National Assembly are called 'acts'.

number of cases were brought to court in 2008. Although none of these cases has reached a conclusion, they still serve to illustrate a few important points. Their successful conclusion would show the law's ability to bring corrupt individuals to justice, but the persistent number of abuses, even after the collapse in the 1990s, raises the question as to whether there is currently adequate oversight in the system.

On 11 July 2008 the former managing director of Triumph Bank, Francis Atoju, and three others were brought before a Federal High Court in Lagos on charges of corruption filed by the Economic and Financial Crimes Commission.[11] They were alleged to have granted unauthorised loans of about N600 million (US$5.2 million) to customers of the bank while in office.[12] Accused along with Atoju was Jude Idigbe and his company, Lushann Enternit Energy Limited, and Road Marks Nigeria Limited, allegedly owned by Atoju.

Atoju, Idigbe and Lushann were accused of conspiring in May 2001 to make an unlawful and unauthorised grant of an overdraft facility of US$1.4 million to Idigbe and Lushann. The charge further stated that Atoju, as Triumph Bank's managing director and Road Marks' CEO, conspired in August 2003 to grant unlawfully an unauthorised overdraft facility of N418 million (US$3.61 million)[13] to Road Marks. These actions were considered to violate the bank's rules and regulations and thereby constitute a violation of the Failed Banks Act 1994.[14] As of June 2008 the charges were still pending in court.

Another intriguing case, involving three managing directors of the Wema Bank plc, hit the head-lines at the end of 2007, resulting in a protracted and complex chain of events that had still not been resolved by September 2008. After a complicated shuffling of managing directors, Adebisi Omoyeni took the reins. He then proceeded, in January 2008, to suspend former managing director Chief Samuel Adegbite, who by this time had become chairman of Wema Securities and Finance, a subsidiary of the bank.[15] Following allegations of fraudulent practices in the subsidiary's management, Adegbite, along with Wema Holdings' managing director Lekan Are, were invited for questioning by the Independent and Corrupt Practices Commission (ICPC) in April 2008.[16]

While investigations were ongoing allegations were soon levelled at Omoyeni himself, leading the Nigeria Deposit Insurance Corporation (NDIC) to examine the bank's books at the behest of the central bank. The NDIC complained, however, that Omoyeni was not allowing 'unfettered access to the books and records of the bank in a manner that was tantamount to obstructing their duty'. As a result, Omoyeni was requested by the central bank to leave Wema Bank until the special examination was completed.[17]

The central bank's deputy governor, Tunde Lemo, also a former Wema Bank managing director, was the next official to enter the fray. In reaction to his suspension, Omoyeni accused Lemo of colluding with the NDIC to 'kill Wema Bank', 'reduce the bank's shareholders funds' and then 'buy over the bank at a ridiculously cheap price'.[18] In a letter to the president on 21 January, he requested that the bank be examined by neutral parties from the NDIC.

---

11 *Guardian* (Nigeria), 12 July 2008.
12 Ibid.
13 Ibid.
14 Section 23(4) of the Failed Banks Act no. 18 of 1994. Ibid.; offence contrary to 23(4) of the Failed Banks (Recovery of Debt) and Financial Malpractices in Banks Act no. 18 of 1994 and punishable under section 20(1)(a) of the act.
15 AllAfrica.com, 15 March 2008.
16 *Daily Independent* (Nigeria), 9 April 2008; www.businessdayonline.com/national/7413.html.
17 *Sunday Tribune* (Nigeria), 16 March 2008.
18 Ibid.

Further allegations were brought against Lemo related to his stewardship of the bank during his term as director. He was accused of having knowingly deceived the regulatory authorities and the general public by declaring a profit of N3.1 billion (US$26.6 million), when the actual profit was N891million (US$7.65 million).[19] It was also alleged that he had furnished false reports related to non-performing loans he had granted, and that he had concealed a debt of N8.1 billion (US$69.8 million) from the regulatory authorities through fictitious payments from debtor-customers using cheques purchased from other banks.[20] In April 2008 he was requested to appear before the ICPC, and he was questioned on 21 April after twice failing to appear before the commission.[21]

Following the NDIC's investigation, Omoyeni was accused of a number of misdemeanours, including breach of prudent banking guidelines, abuse of the loans administration procedure and contract award processes, and making upfront payments of N450 million (US$3.9 million) in housing grants to himself for five years at N90 million per year.[22] Toyin Onifade, head of finance, was also ordered to go on leave, as he was alleged to have profited from the illegal sale of Wema Terrace in Ikoyi Lagos through the allocation of property worth N47 million.[23]

Discussions commenced in August between the parties, and an agreement was reached that allowed Omoyeni to be reinstated in his post, subject to certain conditions. Despite failing to fulfil these conditions, including dropping the cases initiated by him in relation to the other former managing directors,[24] Omoyeni resumed his post on 2 September. He was accompanied by police, and proceeded to dismiss staff and reverse many of the decisions made during his eight-month absence. As a consequence, Omoyeni was again arrested on 4 September and dismissed from the bank.

The above stories show the lack of efficiency and effectiveness on the part of the bank regulatory authorities in the country. The situation is compounded by the slowness of the investigation and prosecution processes in Nigeria. Indeed, the chairman of the EFCC, Mrs Farida Waziri, had, in December 2008, lamented that the courts were frustrating the anti-corruption war in Nigeria.[25]

Osita Nnamani Ogbu (TI Nigeria)

Additional reading

F. Asogwah and P. Okoli, *Economic Crimes and National Development* (Enugu: Institute for Development Studies, University of Nigeria, 2008).

I. Ayua and B. Owasanoye, *Problems of Corruption in Nigeria* (Lagos: Nigerian Institute of Advanced Legal Studies, 2002).

F. Mzamber Waziri, *Advance Fee Fraud, National Security and the Law* (Ibadan: African Book Builders, 2005).

O. N. Ogbu, 'Combating Corruption in Nigeria: A Critical Appraisal of the Laws, the Institutions and the Political Will', *Annual Survey of International & Comparative Law*, vol. 14 (2008).

E. Onyekpere and J. Essiet, *Critical Issues in Public Expenditure Management* (Abuja: Budget Transparency Network, 2006).

---

19 *Daily Independent* (Nigeria), 9 April 2008.
20 Ibid.
21 *Nigerian Tribune*, 22 April 2008.
22 *The News* (Nigeria), 11 February 2008.
23 Ibid.
24 Vanguard Online (Nigeria), 7 September 2008.
25 *Guardian* (Nigeria), 10 December 2008.

Rwanda

Corruption Perceptions Index 2008: 3.0 (102nd out of 180 countries)

Conventions

African Union Convention on Preventing and Combating Corruption (signed December 2003; ratified June 2004)

UN Convention against Corruption (signed November 2004; ratified October 2006)

UN Convention against Transnational Organized Crime (signed December 2000; ratified September 2003)

Legal and institutional changes

- On 30 December 2007 Law 63/2007 established the Rwanda Public Procurement Authority (RPPA) and laid out its organisation, functions and responsibilities. The new agency will replace the National Tender Board (NTB).[1] According to an RPPA official,[2] the objective of the reorganisation is to allow greater flexibility in the public procurement system, in order to increase the level of accountability to the public. The law also makes it easier for economic agents to lodge an appeal with another institution when irregularities linked to corruption are suspected of having taken place within a public contract procedure. Accordingly, an independent Public Procurement Appeals Commission has been set up with the power to review RPPA decisions if they are contrary to the law on procurement contracts. The appeals commission is made up of five

members – two from the government and three from civil society, with the latter's inclusion raising hopes that the commission's decisions will be more credible. Before being replaced, the National Tender Board had been both judge and party in cases of objections related to tenders.[3]

- On 15 January 2008 Ministerial Order 001/08/10/min was issued to regulate public procurement and calls for tender. The order provides a legal framework on standards for calls for tender, to prevent biased wording that favours one or more parties to a public contract.

- Recommendations were made during a retreat of Rwandan political leaders held under the direction of President Paul Kagame between 24 and 28 February 2008 at the Akagera Hotel. The recommendations included a demand that national integrity institutions without a code of conduct adopt one as soon as possible. The Private Sector Secretariat and Rwanda

---

1 *Official Gazette*, 20 February 2008.
2 Interview with Kayiranga Rukumbi Bernard, director of the RPPA's unit of research and legal affairs.
3 Decision no.12/IRP/2008 IRP, on the appeal against the results of the technical evaluation of the market concerning consultants' services for the inspection and supervision of the construction work for the Nyabarongo hydroelectric power plant (27.5MW). Plaintiff: RSW International Inc.; against: RPPA.

Public Procurement Authority are aiming to set up their own codes by the end of 2008.[4]

- Since January 2008 performance contracts (known as *imihigo*[5]) have been instituted in Rwandan households, committing each family to fight corruption in its daily activities. The president initiated the idea for such contracts in July 2006 in connection with decentralised local districts.[6]

Some hope of improvement in public procurement?

Figures from 1 June 2007 to 30 May 2008 published by the Office of the Public Prosecutor provide a general overview of corruption and embezzlement cases currently under legal proceedings in Rwanda.[7] During this period 502 such cases were brought to the office's attention. Among these, 269 were subject to prosecution, forty were closed and 213 received court judgments, including prison sentences.[8]

The work of the Public Procurement Appeals Committee is a good indicator of the scale of the problem in public procurement. Although the committee has been operational only since July 2007, forty-six complaints concerning irregularities in the awarding of public contracts were submitted from 1 August 2007 to 15 May 2008.[9] Actions taken by the committee include:[10]

- cancelling a contract and launching a new call for tenders;

- cancelling a decision made by the public authorities and granting a contract to the aggrieved bidder; and
- compensating an aggrieved bidder when the public contract had already been signed and could no longer be cancelled due to financial losses the government would incur.

In thirteen cases in which legal action was taken, the public authorities' decision was cancelled and the plaintiff won the case. In fifteen cases the public authorities' decision was upheld. The other cases did not comply with the appeals procedure and were not considered by the committee. This does not mean, however, that parties have been cleared of the charge of dubious practices.

Forms of corruption associated with public procurement often involve non-compliance with procedures, such as dividing tenders into smaller units to allow contracts to be awarded by private agreement and thus bypass public calls for bids, and collusion, whereby a public official on the contract award committee gives preferential treatment to an economic agent.[11]

Corruption in micro-finance institutions

Following years of conflict and unrest in Rwanda, and the consequent poverty of Rwandan society, micro-finance institutions (MFIs) were set up in response to the critical need for access to financial services by low-income Rwandans. In an MFI, individuals deposit funds into cooperative

---

4 Interviews with Ruzindana Clément, director of the department of services enterprises, Private Sector Federation, and Kayiranga Rukumbi Bernard.
5 The word *imihigo* comes from the verb *guhiga*, which means 'to compete'. In this context, it means to determine the level at which each family combats corruption daily and compare their achievements.
6 See www.minaloc.gov.rw.
7 Document put at the disposal of Transparency Rwanda by the inspector general, Jules Marius Ntete, Office of the Public Prosecutor.
8 Office of the Public Prosecutor, Rfce M. Ruberwa, prosecutor in charge of corruption offences.
9 Interview with and documents from Ruganintwali Pascal, chairperson of the Appeals Committee of the public procurement market.
10 Other information on Appeals Committee decisions is available at www.ntb.gov.rw.
11 Results of investigations by the Office of the Ombudsman and reported at a workshop organised by Transparency Rwanda, 25 July 2008.

arrangements that receive a provisional banking licence from the National Bank of Rwanda, the central bank. Their share capital amounted to F.Rw. 150 million (US$272,000).[12]

In 2006, after only three years of activity, many MFIs became insolvent and were unable to meet their obligations to investors. At this point the government intervened and disbursed F.Rw. 3 billion (US$5.44 million) to compensate those who had lost their deposits. Because the government was not able to cover the full cost of the deposits, efforts have begun to recover money from the institutions' owners. The MFIs that were forced to close down include Gasabo, Intambwe, Igisubizo, Ongera, Urumuri, Urugero, Gwiza, Umbumwe-Iwacu and Iwacu.[13] In May 2008 two of these institutions were placed under judicial supervision: Gasabo, which is currently in judicial liquidation, and Urunana, which is under supervision for likely financial adjustment.

Two relevant issues have arisen in relation to MFIs. On the one hand, it has been alleged that depositors' cash was misappropriated, with those implicated including former MPs and a pastor.[14] On the other, loans in some cases have been obtained illegally and never serviced. According to Deputy Prosecutor General Alphonse Hitiyaremye, the pastors often 'lack professional guidance' when doing business to raise money for their churches. Many MFIs have collapsed, and investigations have been initiated. By April 2008 the Prosecutor General's Office had arrested fifteen people accused of causing 'huge losses' to MFIs.[15] In June 2008 it was reported that prosecutors were searching for at least forty suspects, with another thirty-five having already been arrested and charged.[16]

The auditor directly involved in some of these cases, Anastase Sebudandi, claimed that the MFI bankruptcies had been caused by mismanagement and lack of supervision. Some MFIs were run by people with no experience of the credit business. Nepotism was practised, whereby family members were granted credit without providing guarantees. In addition, poor oversight allowed managers to become involved in financial embezzlement.[17]

As is all too often the case, it was the poor who were affected by the wrongdoing. While few institutional measures have been taken to deter such practices, the authorities have concentrated on prosecuting and convicting those responsible, as well as attempting to recover funds.

One way to curb corrupt practices in Rwanda's private sector would be strengthening and rigorously enforcing the legal framework. As reported in the magazine of Transparency Rwanda, there are always discrepancies between the penalties and fines that are imposed and the amounts diverted or given as bribes. In many cases, those who commit serious crimes do not get the appropriate punishment.[18]

Observers hope that the Rwandese leadership's firm rejection of the status quo will raise public awareness, so that corruption is no longer tolerated in the private sector. Its financial costs are too heavy a burden for the community as a whole, as well as for the individual citizens of Rwanda.

Apollinaire Mupiganyi and Paul Kananura (TI Rwanda)

---

12 Interview with Sebudandi Anastase, the auditor of some MFIs placed under judicial supervision.
13 *New Times* (Rwanda), 16 April 2008.
14 *New Times* (Rwanda), 8 June 2008.
15 *New Times* (Rwanda), 16 April 2008.
16 *New Times* (Rwanda), 8 June 2008.
17 Analysis of auditor Anastase Sebudandi.
18 Supreme Court, *Report of the Year 2007* (Kigali: Supreme Court, 2007).

Additional reading

Conseil de Concertation des Organisations d'Appui aux Initiatives de Base (CCOAIB), *Réflexion et analyse sur la contribution au rétablissement des valeurs morales humaines: approche des collectifs dans la lutte contre la corruption* (Kigali: CCOAIB, 2002).

Districts and Kigali City Association (RALGA), *Duhagurukire kurwanya ruswa mu nzego z'ibanze mu Rwanda (Stand up to fight corruption in local administration in Rwanda)* (Kigali: RALGA, 2008).

Ministry of Local Government (MINALOC), 'Stratégie rwandaise et plan d'action pour la prévention et la lutte contre la corruption' (summary of the workshop held 12–13 August) (Kigali: MINALOC, 2004).

Rwanda Feedback Consultation, World Bank Group, seminar workshop 'Governance and Anti-corruption Strategy', 15–16 January 2007, Kigali.

Transparency Rwanda, 'Etude et proposition d'un projet de prévention, lutte et répression de la corruption dans la magistrature rwandaise' (Kigali: Transparency Rwanda, 2007).

'Etude du Système National d'Intégrité' (Kigali: Transparency Rwanda, 2008).

The Transparent Magazine, August–September 2008.

Zimbabwe

Corruption Perceptions Index 2008: 1.8 (166th out of 180 countries)

Conventions

African Union Convention on Preventing and Combating Corruption (signed November 2003; ratified December 2006)

SADC Protocol against Corruption (signed August 2001; ratified October 2004)

UN Convention against Corruption (signed February 2004; ratified March 2007)

UN Convention against Transnational Organized Crime (signed December 2000; ratified December 2007)

Legal and institutional changes

- In December 2007 the Public Order and Security Act was amended to restrict the right to freedom of expression, a right enshrined in the constitution. The amendment states, for example, that appeals against bans on public marches are no longer decided by the executive but by a magistrate's court. The independence of magistrate's courts is questionable, as they have been accused by various civil society organisations of deliberately misinterpreting the law to support police bans on marches. There is now a general ban on demonstrations outside parliament, the courts and other public institutions. Additionally, the act requires more detailed information to be submitted before a meeting or demonstration can be held, including the names of the convener and deputy convener. This allows the authorities to arrest and charge individuals, whereas previously they could charge only organisations as a whole. While the amendment does not see any change in the overall restrictive framework of the act,[1] it does not advance the cause for basic freedoms such as the right to freedom of expression, assembly and association.[2] Civil society organisations still have to send a letter of notice to the police if they want to have public meetings, demonstrations and marches, and the police still have the power to ban, stop or postpone them.

- In March 2008 the Indigenization and Economic Empowerment Bill was signed into law, empowering the government to take control of foreign- and white-owned businesses. The act has the adverse effect of deterring both foreign and domestic investment, as well as eroding property rights with the risk of nationalising business. (Similarly, the Land Acquisition Act of 1992 and the Land Reform and Resettlement Programme Phase 2 of 1998 saw the compulsory acquisition of land owned by commercial farmers and subsequent violent land invasions.)[3] The move came just three weeks before presidential and parliamentary elections, and was widely

viewed as a vote-buying exercise.[4] It is also feared that the likely beneficiaries will be Zimbabwe's elite security forces, politburo members of the ruling Zimbabwe African National Union – Patriotic Front (ZANU–PF) party, and their family members.[5] This move has the potential to cripple yet further the industrial sector, which is already operating at less than 30 per cent of its capacity.[6] It therefore has the effect of enhancing corruption, by encouraging the private sector to support key government officials to avoid losses. Furthermore, those who benefit from such a system will remain beholden to government patrons. Because ZANU–PF is part of a state patronage system, the confiscation of land and the takeover of business will help keep it running.[7]

Informal outlaws: the informal sector's impact on the effectiveness of anti-corruption laws

The Zimbabwean private sector largely comprises companies registered under the Companies Act 1996, chapter 24:03. Other minor players are partnerships and cooperatives.[8] There are multiple interpretations of what is ethical in the business sector, leading to a number of laws that seek to ensure that businesses are responsible and accountable, and practice sound corporate governance.[9] The main law that governs the private sector is the Prevention of Corruption

---

1 Media Institute of Southern Africa (MISA) Zimbabwe, 'African Media Barometer Zimbabwe 2008' (Harare: MISA Zimbabwe, 2007).

2 MISA Zimbabwe, 'Statement on AIPPA, BSA, POSA Amendments', ZimOnline, 19 December 2007.

3 Interview with Cliff Dube, trade and economics specialist, Confederation of Zimbabwe Industries.

4 See www.timesonline.co.uk/tol/news/world/africa/article3517151.ecen; 'Mugabe approves Zimbabwe nationalization law', Reuters (UK), 9 March 2008.

5 TI Zimbabwe observation following analysis of statements by civil society organisations and members of the private sector following passage of the bill.

6 See www.timesonline.co.uk/tol/news/world/africa/article3517151.ecen.

7 TI Zimbabwe observation and analysis.

8 TI Zimbabwe, 'A Comparative Study of National Integrity Systems Studies in 5 Southern African Countries' (Harare: TI Zimbabwe, 2007).

9 Code of Ethics Survey, commissioned by TI Zimbabwe on behalf of the Business Forum against Corruption (BFAC), carried out by Dr Shepherd Bhero.

Act 2004. This law covers both the private and public sectors, and as well as defining corruption it provides a framework for establishing the existence of corruption and any remedial action. It is supported by other laws, such as the Banking Acts 1999 and 2001, the Insurance Act 1996, the Financial Law Act 2007 and the Anti-Monopolies and Anti-Money Laundering Act 2004, which were enacted to monitor the operations of the respective players in these sectors.[10] Despite this legislation, anecdotal evidence gathered by TI Zimbabwe through workshops and news reports suggests that corruption in Zimbabwe has become endemic.[11] In the past few years the private sector has been plagued by reports of rising corruption and related offences, such as fraud, insider dealing (trading), unscrupulous accounting methods and extortion.

This crisis is exacerbated by the state of the economy, which is characterised by a still rising inflation rate that stands at present at around 1.7 million per cent, fuelling a thriving parallel market and currency speculation.

Evidence[12] suggests that the large amounts of money traded in the parallel market increase opportunities for money-laundering, particularly when it involves players in the informal sector, whose activities remain largely unregulated. Industry and commerce have shrunk, raising questions about how effectively current laws can curb corruption if the bulk of industrial and commercial activities are largely informal. Although the rise of the informal private sector may be a rational solution to the crushing of the formal private sector, the lack of protection from breaches of contracts fosters yet more corruption.[13]

This has no doubt led to corrupt practices that have a tremendously damaging impact on Zimbabwe's social and economic development. Moreover, the relatively low percentage of formal private sector companies, estimated at 10 per cent,[14] means that there is so much cross-pollination of illicit and corrupt activities between the informal and formal sectors that even formal businesses regulated by the law can make their corrupt activities very difficult to detect.[15]

Survival corruption: playing the game in the Zimbabwean context

The attitude towards corruption has become a major challenge to the economic recovery of Zimbabwe, as small-scale risks in the form of bribery, fraud and extortion interfere with the private sector's ability to access foreign direct investment. Corruption also interferes with commerce, increases costs, slows growth and makes the future difficult to predict.[16]

Good corporate governance is undermined, as corruption is perceived as a low-risk, high-profit activity, particularly amid the country's current extreme economic difficulties.[17] The term 'survival corruption' has been aptly coined to explain how, under such circumstances, corrupt acts can be regarded as a means of survival, and therefore become normalised.

Survival corruption is a consequence of the Zimbabwean government's introduction of draconian laws and the enforcement of controls on products such as basic commodities. In July 2007 businesses were ordered by presidential decree to restore prices to 18 June 2007 levels,

---

10 TI Zimbabwe, 2007.
11 *Independent* (UK), 15 September 2004; http://allafrica.com/stories/200801290332.
12 Gathered by TI Zimbabwe through workshops.
13 *Independent* (UK), 15 September 2004.
14 Zimbabwesituation.com, 'Fact Sheet: Zimbabwean Crisis', 27 March 2008.
15 TI Zimbabwe observation and analysis.
16 TI Zimbabwe, 'A Journal of Investigative Journalism Focusing on Corruption in Zimbabwe' (Harare: TI Zimbabwe, 2005).
17 TI Zimbabwe observation and analysis.

effectively slashing them by about 50 per cent after a surge in inflation. This led businesses to downsize their operations and strategise with the informal market to survive. It further pushed formal activities into the parallel market, where there is no regulation, worsening the scourge of corruption.

By the end of 2007 most major companies were operating at below 30 per cent of their capacity, with some down to 15 per cent. This led to a shortage of basic commodities, as the parallel market absorbed the activities that businesses could no longer sustain and offered commodities at astronomical prices. By August 2007 more than 12,000 executives, businesspeople and managers had been arrested and fined for defying the decree and exceeding the price controls. This figure rose to 28,000 two months later, worsening shortages and boosting the black market countrywide. Many businesses could no longer afford to keep operating and were forced to close down. This further exacerbated the extraordinarily high unemployment rate of about 85 per cent, with people losing their jobs and being naturally absorbed by the unregulated informal sector.[18]

The shortages did not end with commodities but hit the financial sector as well. Terrible cash shortages resulted in hundreds of people sleeping in bank queues to withdraw small amounts of money over the 2007 Christmas season. Such experiences, coupled with restrictions such as cash controls that limit cash withdrawals from banking institutions, have contributed to the emergence of middlemen in the parallel market.[19] The middlemen facilitate the attainment of goods and services unofficially, for example by obtaining cash above the maximum amounts allowed by banks. The cost of this service fluctuates depending on supply

and demand pressures. This has not only created opportunities for corruption but has increased the cost of living beyond the reach of the poor, who now make up approximately 90 per cent of the population.[20]

As businesses struggle to survive, often resorting to the informal sector and flouting regulations in order to keep afloat, the business community probably has neither the inclination nor the resources to make a stand against corruption. Added to this, public officials mandated with enforcing corruption-related laws in the private sector lack credibility, and the judicial system is so formal, bureaucratic and time-consuming that it often works as a disincentive to reporting crimes. As a result, it is easier to take part in acts of corruption or turn a blind eye when they occur.

Private sector accountability: inseparable from the state

Zimbabwe has serious deficiencies in relation to holding its private sector accountable. Currently, the only way the government appears able to control the sector is through retributive action such as the 'price blitz' – enforcing compulsorily reduced prices for basic commodities. Furthermore, a TI Zimbabwe study has revealed that the business sector evades accountability, and, other than the requirement to publish financial statements, they are not held accountable. The report further argues that the lack of stringent requirements for accountability has led to unscrupulous business transactions going unnoticed for long periods of time, inflicting irreversible damage.[21]

Nevertheless, many companies operating in the formal sector are concerned with organisational and industrial integrity, and have formed insti-

---

18 Zimbabwesituation.com, 2008.
19 TI Zimbabwe observation.
20 Zimbabwesituation.com, 2008.
21 TI Zimbabwe, 2007.

tutional codes of conduct and ethics. Since the 2003/4 banking crisis, banking institutions are now required to have a code of ethics. One finding of the Code of Ethics Survey conducted by the Business Forum against Corruption (BFAC) is that, while the concept of a code of ethics is generally understood, its salient features, utility and purpose are not implicit. As a result, the implementation of codes is not very successful.[22]

TI Zimbabwe formed the BFAC in October 2006 in collaboration with a broad cross-section of the private sector. This group of private sector organisations and individual businesses seeks to drive a coordinated business response in the fight against corruption. The broad representation includes the financial, hospitality, tourism and leisure, and motor industries, as well as professional bodies.

In 2007 the BFAC identified a need to develop tools to build a value system in the private sector. As a first step, the BFAC commissioned a consultant to conduct the Code of Ethics Survey to analyse the codes of ethics already in existence. The survey was completed in July 2008. The second stage will be to harmonise different codes into a generic code of ethics that can broadly govern the entire private sector, thus raising the bar on ethical business standards. The code will be designed to incorporate strong anti-corruption provisions.

Although certain portions of the private sector have acknowledged the prevalence of corruption and its cost to business, the government needs to be similarly engaged. Enacting laws that undermine the private sector and push formal business into the unregulated informal sector will only encourage corruption, while ensuring that, rather than focusing on long-term transparency and accountability, companies are equipped only to consider short-term profiteering and, ultimately, engage in survival corruption. As such, it is clear that private sector corruption is highly dependent on government security and stability. While corruption in the sector should be condemned, the solution lies not only in implementing voluntary corporate codes of conduct but, essentially, in the accountability, legitimacy and credibility of laws and law enforcement.[23]

Mazvita Debra Kubwalo (TI Zimbabwe)

Additional reading

Business Monitor International, *The Zimbabwe Business Forecast Report* (London: Business Monitor International, 2007); available at www.businessmonitor.com/businessforecasts/zimbabwe.html.

M. Mawere, 'Financial Sector Central to Africa's Growth', in *Conversations with Mawere*, 12 October 2006; http://africanhopes.blogspot.com/2008/01/financial-sector-central-to-africas.html.

Pazambuka News, 'Corruption'; www.pambazuka.org/en/category/corruption.

TI Zimbabwe, *A Journal of Investigative Journalism Focusing on Corruption in Zimbabwe* (Harare: TI Zimbabwe, 2005).

  A Comparative Study of National Integrity Systems Studies in 5 Southern African Countries (Harare: TI Zimbabwe, 2007).

  Code of Ethics Survey (Harare: TI Zimbabwe, 2008).

---

22 Code of Ethics Survey.
23 TI Zimbabwe, 2007.

6.2 Americas

Argentina

Corruption Perceptions Index 2008: 2.9 (109th out of 180 countries)

Conventions

OAS Inter-American Convention against Corruption (signed March 1996; ratified August 1997)

OECD Convention on Combating Bribery of Foreign Public Officials (signed December 1997; ratified February 2001)

UN Convention against Corruption (signed December 2003; ratified August 2006)

UN Convention against Transnational Organized Crime (signed December 2000; ratified November 2002)

Legal and institutional changes

• In September 2007, based on an appeal submitted by Fundación Poder Ciudadano, the Judicial Council made the financial declaration forms of judges and civil servants in the judiciary accessible to the public by Resolution 581/07. Two months later the council acknowledged with Resolution 734/07 that requesting judges' statements entailed a cumbersome bureaucratic process that ran contrary to the principles of transparency and the citizen's right to public information. The council therefore resolved to allow citizens to access the declarations of judges without first initiating an administrative process. Following the resolution, one member of the judiciary tried to obtain protection against having his declaration form released, on the grounds that the disclosure violated his right to personal data protection. Though his petition was initially successful, the Federal Appeals Court for Administrative Matters soon ruled that the individual's declaration should be made available.

• Under Resolution 30/2007, the Supreme Court agreed to call public hearings whenever at least three out of seven judges agree to the process. The court outlined three forms that the hearings could take: an informative hearing would examine the features of a case; a conciliatory hearing would seek to mediate a solution; and an organisational hearing would make decisions to improve the procedural management of a case. The Supreme Court believes that public hearings will test the efficiency, transparency and objectivity of the administration of justice, while enhancing citizens' knowledge of judicial processes.

• Law number 26.376, passed in May 2008, introduced serious obstacles to the appointment of highly qualified judges. Whereas qualifications for new judges are generally determined by an examination of the candidate by the Judicial Council, the new law deems that no examination will be necessary for acting judges. Should a position become available in jurisdictions where there is no sufficiently competent judge, acting judges will be appointed by the president, giving wide discretionary powers to the executive branch. Because the new law makes no provisions for the term limits of acting judges, it becomes increasingly likely that underqualified acting judges will hold powerful positions for indefinite periods of time. As most acting judges are vying for permanent positions, executive appointment may compel acting judges to rule in ways that please the president.

On the wrong track: lack of transparency in government contracting for the 'bullet train'

In 1992, under the presidency of Carlos Menem and aided by loans from the World Bank,[1] the State Reform Law paved the way for the privatisation of Ferrocarriles Argentinos, the national railroad system. Ten years later 8,500 kilometres remained of the previous 35,000 kilometres of tracks,[2] running at the slow speed of 90 to 120 kilometres per hour.[3] Today, millions of citizens suffer the negative consequences of these changes, which have led to a lack of investment and planning, the closure of branch lines and increasingly deficient services by operators, particularly in Greater Buenos Aires.[4] With

dilapidated carriages and abandoned stations characterising much of Argentina's current rail system,[5] many citizens now look with scepticism on the government's plan to build a high-speed railway linking the cities of Buenos Aires, Rosario and Córdoba.

The 'bullet train', estimated to cost approximately US$4 billion,[6] has raised numerous legal, financial and technical concerns. If the project becomes a reality, Argentina will increase its external debt to build a train that competes with air transportation, targeted to a public that differs significantly – in numbers and socio-economic status – from those who use the Buenos Aires Metropolitan Area's current rail system on a daily basis.[7] According to information provided by the National Transport Regulation Commission, the Metropolitan Railroad Network transported approximately 407 million passengers in 2007,[8] while predictions indicate that the bullet train will transport 4.5 million people per year[9] – just over 1 per cent of the previous figure.

With no immediate plan in place to improve suburban lines,[10] many question the rationale for undertaking an ambitious enterprise at the expense of more urgent public transport needs and social welfare in general.[11] The tendering process has also been scrutinised.[12] The process left central matters, such as an environmental impact study, in the hands of bidders while the

---

1 Inter Press Service (Italy), 25 June 2004.
2 Ibid.
3 For further information, see N. Dassen, 'Por un Sistema Ferroviario para Todos: La Construcción del Tren Bala y la Búsqueda de la Unión Ciudadana contra la Consumación de la Insensatez' (Buenos Aires: Poder Ciudadano, Plataforma ¿Megaciudad?, 2008).
4 Inter Press Service (Italy), 30 May 2008; Greater Buenos Aires is generally understood as the city of Buenos Aires as well as adjacent municipalities in the province of Buenos Aires.
5 Ibid.
6 N. Dassen, 2008.
7 DERF (Argentina), 18 March 2008.
8 Comisión Nacional de Regulación del Transporte, 'Estadísticas: FFCC Trenes y Subtes,' 2007; available at www.cnrt.gov.ar.
9 N. Dassen, 2008.
10 Inter Press Service (Italy), 30 May 2008.
11 N. Dassen, 2008.
12 DERF (Argentina), 18 March 2008; *Clarín* (Argentina), 30 April 2008; Perfil.com (Argentina), 29 April 2008.

route design, ticket prices and final costs of the project remain uncertain.[13] These frustrations were exacerbated by the government's decision in 2008 to grant the tender for the bullet train to a consortium headed by the French company Alstom.[14] The company is currently under investigation in France and Switzerland for allegedly making improper payments of US$200 million[15] to secure contracts for Brazil's Itá hydroelectric plant, for São Paulo's subway expansion and for other major works in Venezuela, Singapore and Indonesia.[16] The Mexican government has also penalised Alstom with suspension from its State Registry of Contractors,[17] and in 2007 the European Commission's antitrust authority fined Alstom €65 million for price-fixing with competitors.[18]

Attempts on the part of civil society to gather more information on the bullet train bid have been unsuccessful. In May 2008 Poder Ciudadano submitted a public information request to the secretary for transport,[19] asking for access to the file containing the general application for the bullet train in order to examine the development of the bidding and award process. The undersecretary of rail transport replied that the file would be released following the approval of the financing agreement.

Following a second request, the undersecretary erroneously invoked an exception included in the regulations of access to public information, which states that information can be withheld if it threatens to undermine the economic system.[20] When Poder Ciudadano was finally allowed to access to the file, in October 2008, the organisation was not allowed to see any documents relating to the financing of the project.

In developing its transportation policy, the national government has failed on multiple fronts. It was reluctant to include citizen participation in railway development plans, disregarded the dubious record of the company it contracted and was hesitant to provide public information on the bidding process. These failures suggest that citizens still face many obstacles to exerting their right to information – a necessary condition for the development of a genuinely participatory citizenry, capable of monitoring contracting processes and public affairs more generally.

Cooked books: Argentina's government reported to meddle with the official inflation rate

In the months leading up to Cristina Fernández de Kirchner's 2007 presidential win, news sources suggested that her husband, then-president Néstor Kirchner, had meddled with economic indicators to keep inflation favourably low.[21] Employees of the national statistics institute (Instituto Nacional de Estadísticas y Censos, or INDEC) spent much of the summer

---

13   Resolution of 17 June 2007, signed by the secretary of transport.
14   elEconomista.es (Spain), 2 May 2008.
15   See chiletren.mforos.com/1045568/7536286-alstom-investigado-en-suiza-y-francia-sobornos-en-contratos/.
16   *La Nación* (Argentina), 6 May 2008, 7 May 2008; *Clarín* (Argentina), 6 July 2008.
17   *Crítica* (Argentina), 13 May 2008; see also 'Mexico: Follow-Up Report on the Implementation of the Phase 2 Recommendations'; available at www.oecd.org/dataoecd/39/39/38376307.pdf.
18   *Economic Times* (India), 25 January 2007.
19   The request was submitted in the framework of Decree 1172/2003 of Access to Public Information.
20   Note that SSTF 1140/2008 from the undersecretary of rail transport specifically stated: 'Decree 1172/2003 establishes exceptions to access to information, in cases where the latter is expressly classified as reserved information, in view of the risk, among other issues, of undermining the correct functioning of the financial system. In view of the above and having informed in due time that the financing agreement is under approval process, the requested information will be available for review, after being approved.'
21   *Clarín* (Argentina), 11 July 2007.

on strike in protest at the government's intervention in their work and the replacement of senior INDEC officials with less qualified personnel.[22] In July 2007 eight INDEC employees who worked on inflation statistics presented a letter stating that the new methods and procedures for collecting data and calculating inflation were arbitrary and inconsistent. The results, they said, did not reflect reality.[23] News sources later stated that at least fourteen INDEC employees had been reassigned from the statistics office to the Economy Ministry following their testimony against the government's manipulation of INDEC data.[24]

Despite suggestions that Fernández de Kirchner's government would work to restore public trust in INDEC by removing controversial officials,[25] the opposite proved true. Shortly after President Fernández de Kirchner took office, the Greater Buenos Aires consumer price index, considered to be a reliable gauge of inflation, was officially deemed to have risen by 8.5 per cent in 2007. Frustrated INDEC employees contested these findings, estimating instead that inflation actually stood at over 20 per cent for that year.[26] Half a year into Fernández de Kirchner's term, such disparities between official and independent estimates remained. In May 2008 analysts estimated that the real rate of inflation was at least two or three times the official rate.[27]

The unrealistic alteration of official inflation figures carries far-reaching consequences. By underestimating cost-of-living indicators, governments can manage to keep official poverty rates down. In mid-May 2008 INDEC announced that the incidence of poverty had decreased to 20.6 per cent, down almost three percentage points from early 2007.[28] This figure clashed with other estimates drawn from universities, private consultancies and social organisations, which found that poverty levels approached 30 per cent during the same period.[29] Deflated inflation rates also have the effect of lowering Argentina's US$129 billion debt,[30] some 40 per cent of which is made up of bonds that are linked to the inflation rate.[31]

While critics stop short of suggesting that manipulation of the inflation rate is illegal, the behaviour nevertheless raises serious doubts among Argentinians and international observers. In early 2008 the International Monetary Fund (IMF) sent a letter to INDEC requesting an explanation of its methodology.[32] Later that year the IMF included INDEC's statistics in its October 2008 *World Economic Outlook* report only after making clear that analysts doubted the official rate.[33] The World Bank likewise suggested that the INDEC figures were problematic and pushed the government to restore public confidence in the statistics institute.[34] The reluctance of the Fernández de Kirchner administration to come clean on its statistical methods may also be contributing to the president's plummeting approval ratings. In May 2008 positive opinions of Fernández de Kirchner fell to 26 per cent,

---

22 *La Nación* (Argentina), 13 June 2007; 24 August 2007.
23 *La Nación* (Argentina), 5 July 2007.
24 Dow Jones International News (US), 30 January 2008; Bolsonweb.com (Argentina), 5 December 2007.
25 Economist Intelligence Unit (UK), 15 October 2007.
26 Dow Jones International News (US), 30 January 2008.
27 *Latin American Economic and Business Report* (UK), 29 May 2008; *El País* (Spain), 23 May 2008.
28 Agencia EFE (Spain), 22 May 2008.
29 *El País* (Spain), 23 May 2008; Agencia EFE (Spain), 22 May 2008.
30 Soitu.es (Spain), 20 September 2008.
31 Reuters (UK), 18 September 2008.
32 Dow Jones International News (US), 10 April 2008.
33 Reuters (UK), 18 September 2008; IMF, *World Economic Outlook* (Washington, DC: IMF, 2008).
34 *Clarín* (Argentina), 27 September 2008.

down from 54 per cent at the beginning of the year.[35]

Argentinians remain defiant of the official inflation rate. Although the INDEC rate hovered under 10 per cent in 2008, private sector salaries were renegotiated with 20 per cent increases.[36] Even the government implicitly acknowledged the real rate of inflation by granting wage increases of over 19 per cent to union workers.[37]

Despite local and international criticism, Fernández de Kirchner has kept steadfast in defence of the new INDEC methodology and data. As late as September 2008 she maintained that the INDEC data 'responds to a new model of economic development',[38] and suggested that 'the conditions [for high] inflation do not exist'.[39] Although her administration invited legislators to meet with INDEC officials to discuss the inflation data, at the time of writing the government had not publically released any information that would reveal how the inflation rate is determined.[40]

As early as 2007 a local civil rights organisation requested an emergency judicial action to prevent the government from appealing against a court order to make information about INDEC publicly available.[41] Despite further judicial orders to reveal the methodology used to calculate inflation and to disclose the reasons for adopting the new measurements, however, the government remains silent.

Federico Arenoso, Julieta Arias, María Batch,
Manuel Calvagno, Josefina Palma and Varina
Suleiman (Poder Ciudadano/TI Argentina)

Additional reading

J. Arias and M. Calvagno, *Estrategias de transparencia y lucha contra la corrupción en el sector privado* (Buenos Aires: Poder Ciudadano, 2008).

H. Mairal, *Las raíces legales de la corrupción – O de cómo el derecho público fomenta la corrupción en lugar de combatirla* (Buenos Aires: Cuadernos RPA, Ediciones RAP, 2008).

Poder Ciudadano: www.poderciudadano.org.

---

35 Europa Press (Spain), 23 May 2008; *The Economist* (UK), 12 June 2008.
36 SEL Consultores, 'Newsletter sobre la situación social y laboral de la Argentina', Buenos Aires, April 2008.
37 *Clarín* (Argentina), 21 February 2008.
38 NoticiasFinancieras (US), 26 September 2008.
39 *Latinnews Daily* (UK), 26 September 2008.
40 Dow Jones International News (US), 1 October 2008.
41 NoticiasFinancieras (US), 21 August 2008.

Chile

Corruption Perceptions Index 2008: 6.9 (23rd out of 180 countries)

Conventions

OAS Inter-American Convention against Corruption (signed March 1996; ratified September 1998)

OECD Convention on Combating Bribery of Foreign Public Officials (signed December 1997; ratified April 2001)

UN Convention against Corruption (signed December 2003; ratified September 2006)

UN Convention against Transnational Organized Crime (signed December 2000; ratified November 2004)

Legal and institutional changes

- In May 2007 legislation was presented before Congress to modify several articles related to the criminal liability of legal persons[1] connected to money laundering.[2] Under the proposed modifications, legal persons would be held criminally responsible for money-laundering activities undertaken by a company board of directors, or a member of the board, managers or anyone positioned to make decisions independently concerning the company. Even if violations cannot be linked to a specific actor within an organisation, the legal person can still be found liable. The bill stipulates that the legal liability of a natural person is 'independent, compatible, and ... complementary' to the liability of the legal person.[3] If passed, the new legislation would give judges the right to fine companies for up to 50 per cent of the amount laundered, prohibit the company from performing specified risk-related activities or dissolve the company.

- Of the eight pro-transparency bills presented by President Michelle Bachelet in 2006 (see *Global Corruption Report 2008*), the whistle-blower protection act published in July 2007 is the first to become law.[4] The legislation protects whistleblowers against disciplinary action during the course of an investigation, but in comparison to international law it lacks real warranties to protect employees who report irregularities or breaches of integrity. The law's reach is limited, failing to protect private sector whistleblowers or whistleblowers at state-owned or state-controlled companies.[5]

- The access to information bill, also among the eight transparency bills presented by President Bachelet, came into force in August 2008. This

---

1 A 'legal person' is understood as a group of people whom the law considers a single composite person for the purposes of legal transactions – for example, corporations, political parties and unions.
2 Modification of Law 19.913 of 2007; see http://sil.congreso.cl/pags/index.html, bulletin 5046-07.
3 Modification of Law 19.913 of 2007.
4 Law 20.205 of 2007.
5 OECD, *Chile: Phase 2. Report on the Application of the Convention on Combating Bribery of Foreign Public Officials in International Business Transactions* (Paris: OECD, 2007).

legislation guarantees citizens access to public information and creates an autonomous body to control and enforce this public right (see *Global Corruption Report 2008*).

- A lobbying bill, which would have established a registry of professional lobbyists, was passed by Congress in April 2008. Although the legislation was among the original eight bills presented by Bachelet in 2006, she vetoed the bill after finding it to be incomplete. Among the changes stipulated by her veto was the requirement that oversight of the lobby registry belongs to the president's Transparency Council rather than the Ministry of Justice. While the original bill obliged lobbyists to disclose their visits to public officials, the presidential veto required that public officials also disclose all visits from lobbyists as well as the topics discussed in these meetings. Moreover, while the original bill referred only to professional lobbyists, the presidential veto expanded the definition of a lobbyist to anyone who professionally or habitually performs a lobbying function.[6] With this change, non-governmental organisations and think tanks that lobby in a non-professional capacity will nevertheless have to register their meetings with state administrators or members of the national assembly. Because some articles of the veto were rejected in the House, the veto has been suspended, and the government proposed a new bill to Congress on 5 November 2008.[7]

Chile takes another look at corporate governance standards

In June 2007 KPMG published its first survey of private sector fraud in Chile, which found that one out of three Chilean companies experienced corporate fraud. The survey collected the opinions of company presidents, general managers and financial managers from 600 national and multinational companies that operate in almost all sectors of the Chilean economy. Respondents claimed that their businesses were most affected by conflicts of interest, fraud in personal expense declarations, and the theft of money and company materials. Forty-six per cent of those surveyed believed fraud would increase in the next five years and 44 per cent responded that it would remain the same.[8]

Recognising the risks of corporate fraud and the value of corporate governance for the country's economy, the government submitted a bill in September 2007 that attempts to bring Chilean corporate governance practices up to par with international standards.[9] The bill demands greater leadership from company boards of directors, mandating them to develop and implement a set of internal guidelines that enhance company transparency and establish greater levels of public disclosure. Each company board would be required to develop regulations that outline the circumstances under which directors, managers and principal executives may buy or sell – directly or indirectly – shares in the company. The board would also be responsible for ensuring the disclosure of any information related to key financial or organisational changes on the same day that they occur.

To protect against insider deals and improve the supervisory capacity of the Chilean securities and insurance regulator (Superintendencia de Valores y Seguros, or SVS), shareholders that obtain control of over 10 per cent of a company's stock as a result of a transaction would be required to provide transaction details to the SVS on the same day that the transaction took place.

---

6 The veto defines 'habitually' as eight lobbying activities regarding the same topic in a given month or fifteen lobbying actions within a quarter. For details, see http://sil.congreso.cl/pags/index.html, bulletin 3407-07.

7 See http://sil.congreso.cl/pags/index.html, bulletin 3407-07.

8 KPMG, 'Primera encuesta de Fraude Corporativo en Chile, 2007'; see www.kpmg.ch/library/publikationen_studien/19125.asp.

9 See http://sil.congreso.cl/pags/index.html, bulletin 5301-05.

Under the new legislation, directors and executives of the company would be obliged to inform the SVS of shares they own in the company in which they work or in companies belonging to the same business group. To identify possible conflicts of interest, directors and executives would have to inform the SVS when they buy or sell stock from their company's main suppliers, clients or competitors. To allow shareholders and investors to make informed market decisions, the proposal requires each company to disclose its legal, economic and financial information to potential investors and shareholders via the SVS and the company website, should it have one.

In addition to promoting disclosure, the proposal also seeks to protect against insider trading. It is currently illegal in Chile to purchase shares on the basis of privileged information. The initiative would expand this regulation, also making it illegal to sell shares when the seller possesses confidential information related to the company in question.

Unfortunately, the proposal makes no mention of the need for the legal protection of private sector whistleblowers. Although this could be guaranteed in each company's unique code of ethics, many argue that whistleblower protection must be regulated by law, as self-regulation alone cannot guarantee safety for those who speak out against corporate corruption. Despite this setback, the bill can be expected to have a far-reaching impact if it is enacted. In addition to standardising the responsibilities of company boards and establishing good governance mechanisms in Chilean companies, the proposal would enhance the SVS's monitoring capacity by providing it with a constant flow of market information. Nonetheless, however promising these mechanisms might appear, they will be

effective only if the information that companies supply to the SVS is timely and of high quality. The success of the proposed reforms would also depend on companies making an honest effort to implement thorough and committed codes of conduct that include training, monitoring and control mechanisms. Success also requires the political will to ensure that Chilean regulatory bodies are equipped with the resources to properly monitor and enforce the law. Currently the bill is the subject of an ongoing discussion in the House of Representatives; though it is expected that it will be approved in 2009.

Insider trading catches up with Chilean business

Illustrating the need for tighter corporate governance standards, two high-profile cases emerged in 2007 and 2008 that highlighted the market's continued vulnerability to insider trading. In the summer of 2008 Chile's SVS found that three individuals violated confidentiality rules relating to a merger attempt by Chilean retail giant Falabella and the leading supermarket conglomerate D&S.[10] The SVS charged an additional five people with using privileged information in relation to the attempted merger.[11]

The SVS determined that, during the course of merger negotiations in May 2007, a D&S director, as well as a D&S external communications consultant and a member of Falabella's controlling group, all conveyed confidential information regarding the merger negotiations to familial or professional contacts. The traders were discovered when the regulator noticed that among the investors were individuals who did 'not habitually participate in the stock market' or who made investments concentrated on D&S stock, and who purchased shares in unusually large amounts.[12]

---

10 SVS, 'SVS Publishes Sanctions for the Use of Privileged Information in the Purchase of Shares and Violation of Confidentiality', press release, 17 July 2008.
11 Ibid.
12 Ibid.

Of the five individuals who were fined for using privileged information, three were found to have received information from the D&S director. The combined total of their fines surpassed US$2 million, with additional requirements that the three return earnings amounting to a further US$2 million.[13] Announcing the fines, the head of the SVS emphasised that strong sanctions against insider trading were necessary to maintain investor confidence in the Santiago stock market.[14]

A second incident involving the potential misuse of insider information centres on Sebastian Piñera, one of Chile's richest citizens and Michelle Bachelet's opponent in the 2006 presidential election. In July 2006, just months after joining the board of directors of Chile's LAN Airlines, and just one day before the company announced its first-half earnings, Piñera purchased 3 million shares in LAN, amounting to almost 1 per cent of the company's outstanding shares.[15]

The ensuing SVS investigation revealed that Piñera had purchased the shares directly after LAN's board of directors had approved financial statements indicating that company profits had increased by 31 per cent in the first half of the year.[16] Shares jumped when the financial statements were made public the following day, leaving Piñera with a US$700,000 windfall.[17] Although Piñera's purchase of stocks appeared to be motivated by revelations at the board meeting,

the SVS came to believe that he had made the purchase prior to learning of LAN's performance, and noted that his order fitted within an established purchasing pattern. Not all observers agreed with the SVS decision, however, and they questioned the ethics of the purchase.[18]

In July 2007, in what proved to be a contentious ruling for both Piñera's supporters and detractors, the SVS charged Piñera for allowing the purchase to move ahead even after he had gained privileged information concerning the company.[19]

The SVS's strict interpretation of the law was questioned,[20] including by Piñera, who denounced the findings as politically motivated, though he declined to appeal against the decision.[21] In spite of the ruling, Piñera, a candidate for the presidency in 2009, appears not to have suffered politically from the incident. Though his financial activities were open to scrutiny from opponents in Congress, his approval ratings did not diminish.[22]

Like the D&S case, the use of insider information carried consequences for LAN. Following the SVS ruling, Piñera announced his resignation from the company's board, citing his desire to distance his political identity from his business endeavours. Despite this decision, Piñera still held over 25 per cent of LAN's shares in mid-2008.[23]

13 See www.latercera.cl/contenido/26_31373_9.shtml.
14 SVS, 2008.
15 Associated Press (US), 6 July 2007.
16 Cooperativa.cl (Chile), 12 January 2007; SVS, 'Resolución Exenta no. 306: Aplica Sanción de Multa al Señor Sebastián Piñera Echeñique', 6 July 2007.
17 *Global Insight* (UK), 9 July 2007.
18 *Latin American Weekly Report* (UK), 12 July 2007.
19 Specifically, Piñera was found to be in violation of article 165 of Law 18.045. For detailed information, see SVS, 6 July 2007.
20 *Qué Pasa* (Chile), available at http://icarito.tercera.cl/medio/articulo/0,0,38039290_101111578_247676675,00.html.
21 Associated Press (US), 6 July 2007.
22 See www.jorgeinsunza.cl/content/view/65020/Intervenci_n_Caso_LAN_Pi_era.html; *Brazil & Southern Cone Report* (UK), 23 August 2007.
23 *El Mercurio* (Chile), 29 July 2008.

Though D&S, Falabella and LAN seem to have experienced only minor setbacks from the incidents, the long-term credibility of the Santiago stock market may be less resilient. Insider trading enables large shareholders to enrich themselves at the expense of smaller investors. Over time this drives up the cost of capital, deters investors, fuels speculation and contributes to stock market volatility. While SVS is taking measures to prevent these problems, Chile should nevertheless improve corporate governance and regulatory oversight in order to strengthen the country's international business reputation.

Marcelo Cerna and Rocío Noriega (TI Chile)

Additional reading

M. Amar, *Uso de Información privilegiada: La Relación entre Empresa y Política en el Debate*, Serie Estudios no. 4/2007 (Santiago: Biblioteca del Congreso Nacional, 2007).

Information regarding corporate governance in Chile: www.gobiernodelaempresa.cl.

KPMG, *Primera encuesta de fraude corporativo en Chile, 2007* (Santiago: KPMG, 2007).

F. Lefort, 'La Estructura de Gobierno Corporativo de las Empresas Chilenas', PowerPoint presentation, Centro para el Gobierno de la Empresa, Chile, 2006; available at www.gobiernodelaempresa.cl/files/cge/act/conf/FLefort_DFinanciero_2006.pdf.

TI Chile: www.chiletransparente.cl.

Colombia

Corruption Perceptions Index 2008: 3.8 (70th out of 180 countries)

Conventions

OAS Inter-American Convention against Corruption (signed March 1996; ratified November 1998)
UN Convention against Corruption (signed December 2003; ratified October 2006)
UN Convention against Transnational Organized Crime (signed December 2000; ratified August 2004)

Legal and institutional changes

- Law 1150 of July 2007 introduced significant reforms to the public procurement law of 1993.[1] Procurement regulations now apply to previously exempt bodies such as cooperatives, public universities and associations of departmental[2] or municipal governments, all of which had previously been used by other public bodies to skirt procurement requirements.[3]

---

1 Reform of Law 80 of 1993; Law 1150 of 2007.
2 Colombia is comprised of thirty-two departments, each of which in turn is composed of a number of municipalities.
3 For example, see, 'La Gran Constructora', *Semana* (Colombia), 29 May 2005.

Addressing concerns that time-consuming tendering procedures inadvertently encourage low-profile direct procurement, the law introduces streamlined purchasing processes for some widely used goods. The reforms also mandate a system to enable the entire procurement process to be conducted electronically, increasing transparency while lowering costs. Despite these improvements, concerns linger about the lack of visibility in direct procurement, the possibility that bias will influence tender decisions, and the extent to which the law must be followed when procurement funding comes from multilateral lending agencies or international aid organisations.[4]

- In response to scandals concerning the misuse of regionally distributed national taxes,[5] Decree 028 of 2008 creates a Special Administrative Unit at the National Planning Department (DNP). The unit will be responsible for monitoring the departmental and municipal distribution of federal funds, and evaluating administrative, tax, budgeting and contracting processes at the local level. Should any department or municipality improperly alter the destination of resources or fail to provide complete budgets and documentation, the unit will have the power to suspend payments to the body or arrange for the temporary takeover of its responsibilities. There are concerns that the new unit duplicates the oversight efforts of other national offices and regulatory agencies, and there are doubts whether the DNP can effectively monitor thirty-two departments and more than 1,000 municipalities.

Pipe manufacturers take on a public procuring body

Facing declining public trust caused by a lack of industry transparency and allegations of unjustified overpricing, companies accounting for 95 per cent of Colombia's pipe manufacturing market signed an anti-bribery agreement in 2005 (see *Global Corruption Report 2008*).[6] The agreement includes a 'don't pay, don't offer, don't receive, don't request' stance against bribery, establishes mechanisms for fair pricing, and calls for measures to promote an anti-bribery culture within companies. To strengthen the agreement an ethics committee was formed, consisting of independent, third-party experts[7] tasked to monitor compliance and promote activities to prevent corruption risks.

The ethics committee's oversight capacity was tested for the first time in October 2007, when a signatory company submitted a complaint alleging questionable tendering practices. The complaint suggested that a publicly owned water supply and sewage company in the department of Bolívar had suspended a tendering process to select a pipe supplier for a water network, only to announce a new tender for the same project shortly thereafter. The material specifications in the second tender were altered in such a way that, for the same amount of pipe of the same diameter, the budget was almost doubled.[8] The

---

4 For a more detailed discussion of the law, see TI Colombia, 'Recomendaciones para la Reforma a la Ley 80 de 1993' (Bogotá: TI Colombia, 2007).

5 For example, see 'Escándalo en el Chocó es para Tapar lo de la "Parapolítica": Gobernador', *El País* (Colombia), 29 March 2007.

6 The signatory companies to the agreement are American Pipe and Construction SA, PVC Gerfor SA, Titán Manufacturas de Cemento SA, Durman Esquivel (Tubotec SA), Celta SA, Colombiana de Extrusión-Exrucol SA and Flowtite Andercol SA.

7 Committee members may not provide services to, or have labour ties or executive connections with, the agreement's members or with the sector's professional association.

8 The original tender information is available at www1.minambiente.gov.co/contratacion/cfp/2007/LP_000_07_agua_la_linea/index.htm; information on the second tender is available at www1.minambiente.gov.co/contratacion/CFP/2007/LPI_RLL_002_07/index.htm.

ethics committee undertook a detailed study, which drew on the technical expertise of the agreement's members. The committee's investigation concluded that justifications for the second tender 'dismis[sed] other materials available in the country and abroad that [were] perfect substitutes and that could even imply significant savings'.[9]

The committee further determined that, in the absence of a competitive bidding process, the tender was effectively biased towards a single bidder.[10] The committee formally requested that the procuring body suspend its tender process[11] and lodged a complaint with the superintendent of industry and trade. Adopting the role of a public watchdog, the committee drew media attention to the tender[12] and provided case details to the Ministry for the Environment, Dwellings and Territorial Development (MAVDT), as well as to the president's anti-corruption programme and the commission that regulates drinking water and basic sanitation.

The procuring body claimed that the tender was legitimate because it adhered to Law 142,[13] which regulates public services. The procuring body further stated that the World Bank, which provided funds for the procurement, made no objection to the process.[14] The ethics committee argued that, because the tender was partially funded by MAVDT, a government agency, the constitutional principles of transparency had to trump any less stringent procurement regulations. These findings were supported by TI Colombia and Transparency International, both of which brought the committee's investiga-

tion to the attention of World Bank officials. The World Bank examined this analysis and appointed an investigator to look more closely at the case. Conclusions should be forthcoming within a year.

For the pipe manufacturers, the ethics committee's actions mark a significant success. In evaluating the case, the committee seized opportunities for action and impact that have strengthened the pipe manufacturers' coalition and shaped public expectations. The committee alerted companies and third-party actors associated with the agreement to transparency threats in the sector. It likewise advised financial organisations about the risks that undermine their investments, while commanding the attention of Colombia's regulatory agencies. The committee's ability to draw media focus alerted the public to the need for improved contracting standards for both the Colombian government and multilateral lending agencies. Because of these actions the pipe manufacturers' agreement is stronger today. If private sector actors continue to play a proactive role in monitoring the public sector, the same might eventually be said for all public contracting in Colombia.

Industry joins with citizens to monitor distribution of energy royalties

Between 1994 and 2005 oil companies in Colombia paid approximately US$5.6 billion in operating royalties, equivalent to almost 1 per cent of Colombia's GDP for that period.[15] Despite these payments, in 2002 not one of the six provinces that received the most royalties

---

9 A. García, 'Pronunciamiento del comité de ética en el caso de Santa Rosa de Lima: Licitación No RLL 002/2007 - Santa Rosa de Lima - Bolívar, Colombia', 14 March 2008.

10 Ibid.

11 Ibid.

12 *El Universal* (Colombia), 14 March 2008; *Dinero* (Colombia), 15 February 2008.

13 Law 142 of 1994.

14 Response to the Ethics Committee from the contracting body, Empresa Intermunicipal de Servicios Públicos, 20 February 2008.

15 TI Colombia, *Informe Final de Ejecución de los Contratos para el Acompañamiento a los CSIR Sucre-Córdoba y Arauca* (Bogotá: TI Colombia, 2007).

had achieved minimum standards in health, education, basic sanitation or the provision of drinking water.[16]

In 2004 Colombia's general comptroller addressed this disparity by calling on the petroleum and hydrocarbon industries to fund the establishment of and participate in Royalties Control Committees (*Comités de Seguimiento y Evaluación a la Inversión de Regalías*, or CSIRs).[17] Each committee operates on a departmental level and relies on the joint efforts of the government, private sector associations, citizens and regulatory bodies to collectively monitor the department's use and administration of royalties.[18] Activities vary between committees but generally focus on furthering public knowledge and citizen participation. Members may evaluate resource distribution, inspect the quality of royalty-funded work, collect citizen complaints, organise accountability events or develop public bulletins.

The call for voluntary participation in CSIRs was initially met with little enthusiasm by companies, as they were concerned about adopting a monitoring role traditionally perceived as a state responsibility.[19] Companies also worried that participating in a CSIR could generate confrontations with local leaders with whom they have business relations.[20] Despite initial hesitation, positive experiences of corporate CSIR engagement in the departments of César and Guajira may have encouraged more companies to take part.[21] More than ten foreign and domestic companies are now members of CSIRs, contributing between US$75,000 and US$100,000 per committee.[22] Activities are increasing. Aided by funds from a participating company, a CSIR in the department of Córdoba was able to split and develop a new CSIR in the department of Sucre in the summer of 2008.[23] Meanwhile, a CSIR in the department of Huila organised a community forum to discuss how royalties could be used to improve the delivery of basic services.[24]

Corporate leadership has proven vital to CSIR success. In addition to providing logistical expertise, member companies attract local actors, who, in regions overrun by illegal armed groups, may previously have been hesitant to tackle local issues independently. In several cases corporate leadership has helped CSIRs gain the attention of local public agencies.

This model of corporate citizenship also carries benefits for extractive companies. In communities where CSIRs inform local citizens of the amount of royalties received from resident companies,[25] citizens may begin to demand services of their local government rather than businesses. This represents a stark contrast from just a few

---

16 J. Restrepo and A. Giraldo, '¿Para qué Han Servido las Regalías? Propuesta de Redistribución', Colección Análisis y de Políticas Públicas (Bogotá: Contraloría General de la República, 2002).

17 *El Universal* (Colombia), 31 July 2008.

18 TI Colombia, 'Primeras Notas sobre los Comités de Seguimiento a la Inversión de las Regalías' (Bogotá: TI Colombia, 2007).

19 Based on interviews with participating companies by A. González Espinosa from March to April 2007 in the cities of Bogotá, Sincelejo and Montería.

20 Ibid.

21 See www.anticorrupcion.gov.co/areas/estrategia_regional/convenios/CInterinstitucionalACP.pdf.

22 A. Maldonado, *Diagnóstico de los Comités de Seguimiento a la Inversión de las Regalías – CSIR – y Propuestas de Metodología para su Funcionamiento* (Bogotá: International Finance Corporation, 2007). As of April 2008 CSIRs had been established in the departments of Arauca, Sucre, Córdoba, Huila, César and Guajira, with hopes for new CSIRs in the departments of Santander, Bolívar, Meta and Casanare.

23 *El Universal* (Colombia), 31 July 2008.

24 *Diario del Huila* (Colombia), 1 September 2008.

25 Interviews by A. González Espinosa, 2007.

years earlier, when citizens may not have known the destination of royalties, or even realised their municipality received them.[26] As citizens begin to demand government accountability, less pressure may be placed on companies to foot the bill for infrastructure such as schools or health care centres.

Despite their benefits, CSIRs have limitations. While CSIRs can monitor government decisions, they have no mechanisms to examine industry behaviour. Nor have they methods to confront conflicts of interests experienced by industry members. For example, a participating company's desire to maintain good relationships with local authorities may undermine its capacity to monitor that same government objectively. Committees also risk being dominated by industry leadership. In many cases, industry officials have single-handedly selected a CSIR technical secretary and decided how resources were to be administered and allocated. These problems, paired with entrenched public mismanagement and uncertainties over the committees' long-term financial sustainability, threaten the success of CSIRs.

Even facing these challenges, CSIRs can assist in combating the misuse of royalties. Such help is overdue. In the first months of 2008 the national planning department received 5,800 files suggesting that royalties had been wasted on risky purchases, prohibited investments and flawed contracts.[27] While CSIRs have neither the legislative nor enforcement capacity to quash royalty misuse by themselves, they nevertheless have an important role to play. By promoting local democracy, bolstering citizen participation and furthering public access to information, over time CSIRs may help drive these numbers down.

Recent surveys

According to a recent survey on the implementation of bribery-prevention practices in Colombian businesses, 91 per cent of company managers or legal representatives said they believe that there are Colombian entrepreneurs who offer bribes in the course of their business.[28] The study, undertaken by TI Colombia and the Universidad Externado of Colombia, examined 537 companies representing the geographic spread of business in Colombia and covering enterprises of all sizes and sectors, including industry, trade, services and agriculture/mining.

The findings suggest that entrenched perceptions of public and private corruption in Colombia discourage companies from establishing measures to prevent bribery. Seventy-two per cent of those polled agreed that anti-bribery principles would be useful, yet most do not implement them because they are put off by suspicions of corruption in the public sector (47 per cent) or perceived corruption on the part of competitors (42 per cent). For some, it seems as though bribes make good business sense, with 54 per cent viewing bribery as a strategy to trump the competition.

Such attitudes offer little incentive for companies to implement anti-bribery measures. Indeed, only 11 per cent of responding enterprises said they have comprehensive programmes against bribery. Because it is large businesses that display the greatest progress in establishing measures to counter bribery, however, the researchers suggest that Colombia's biggest enterprises have a central role to play in making their anti-bribery expectations known to smaller suppliers. The researchers further conclude that

26 Ibid.
27 *El Tiempo* (Colombia), 28 February 2008.
28 TI Colombia and the Universidad Externado de Colombia, 'Primera Encuesta Nacional sobre Prácticas contra el Soborno en Empresas Colombianas' no. 15, Cuadernos de Transparencia (Bogotá: TI Colombia, Universidad Externado, 2008).

international monitoring mechanisms ought to demand higher standards from the anti-bribery policies of multinational companies, and that the Colombian market can create incentives for companies to establish counter-bribery mechanisms. Though many Colombian businesses believe that anti-corruption initiatives threaten profits, the collective reluctance to implement public and private anti-corruption measures is hurting business. In its 2007–2008 *Global Competitiveness Report*, the World Economic Forum found corruption to be the second most significant factor, after taxes, hampering business in Colombia.[29]

Alma Rocío Balcázar, in collaboration with Ana Carolina González Espinosa and Luz Ángela Díaz (TI Colombia)

Additional reading

A. Maldonado, *Diagnóstico de los Comités de Seguimiento a la Inversión de las Regalías – CSIR – y Propuestas de Metodología para su Funcionamiento* (Bogotá: International Finance Corporation, 2007).

TI Colombia, 'Contratación estatal: Transparencia y Eficiencia', *Revista Economía Colombiana*, no. 321 (Bogotá: Contraloría General de la República de Colombia, 2007)
    Mesas de Trabajo: Transparencia en la Contratación pública: Retos hacia el futuro (Bogotá: TI Colombia, 2007).

TI Colombia and Universidad Externado de Colombia, *Estudio sobre la Implementación de Prácticas contra el Soborno en Empresas Colombianas* (Bogotá: TI Colombia, Universidad Externado, 2007).

TI Colombia: www.transparenciacolombia.org.co.

---

29 It should be noted that corruption and political instability both rank as the second most problematic factor for business in Colombia. M. E. Porter and K. Schwab, *Global Competitiveness Report 2007–2008* (Geneva: Palgrave Macmillan, 2007).

Nicaragua

Corruption Perceptions Index 2008: 2.5 (134th out of 180 countries)

Conventions

OAS Inter-American Convention against Corruption (signed March 1996; ratified March 1999)
UN Convention against Corruption (signed December 2003; ratified February 2006)
UN Convention against Transnational Organized Crime (signed December 2000; ratified September 2002)

Legal and institutional changes

- The law of municipal procurements was enacted in September 2007,[1] granting municipalities autonomy in acquisition procedures and giving them the freedom to decide whether to offer a tender for the purchase of goods and services. The law does not apply to acquisitions financed with foreign cooperation. Procurement between municipalities or with state institutions is also excluded from the new legislation, falling instead under the state procurement law. Under the new law, public employees who receive benefits from a bidder, or who provide information that gives one bidder an advantage over competitors, can be found to have committed a serious offence, resulting in an investigation by the comptroller's office. Smaller infractions, such as failure to keep orderly records or improperly filing procurement documents, are considered minor offences punishable by the loss of fifteen days' salary.[2]

- Law 621, regarding access to public information, came into force in December 2007. The law guarantees the public's right to access information contained in state documents, databases and files. It also obliges institutions that administer or receive state funds in addition to private financing, including private companies and some civil society organisations, to make their documents publicly available. The new law represents the first successful access to information initiative in Nicaragua, and reflects the culmination of four years of legislative debate and judicial evaluation. A recent study of compliance with the law demonstrates that, of ten written requests for information sent to various public institutions, four received no response, two were refused, one response did not correspond to the information requested, and only three were answered correctly and in a timely manner.[3] Though limited in scope, the study suggests that public officials continue to use high levels of discretion

---

1 Law 622, 'Ley de Contrataciones Municipales'.
2 *La Prensa* (Nicaragua), 16 October 2007.
3 Only the National Assembly and the Ministry of Education provided the requested information in a timely fashion. Requests for access to information sent to the Ministry of Government and the Nicaraguan army were refused, while requests to the Council for Communication and Citizenship and the Ministry of Foreign Relations both went unanswered. The Nicaraguan Electric Company failed to answer a first request, and sent a response that did not correspond to the information petitioned in a second request. For further survey details, see www.violetachamorro.org.ni.

when responding to public requests for information.

Ortega government denies playing favourites to politically connected companies

In 2008 the government of Daniel Ortega came under criticism for failing to disclose publicly the tendering details and project costs in the development of an affordable housing project in Managua.[4] The case that eventually emerged revealed a problematic intersection of interests between members of political parties, public institutions and Nicaraguan business. The government initially claimed it had no oversight of the development of the complex, known as 'El Pueblo Presidente', because the project's funding was derived from the profits of ALBANISA,[5] the bi-national Nicaraguan and Venezuelan oil company.[6]

Local journalists reported that the Nicaraguan Social Security Institute (INSS), which is responsible for financing health services, providing social services and managing the pensions system, had lent US$190,000 to the company Tecnologías y Sistemas SA (Tecnosa) for the construction of the dwellings.[7] News sources revealed that, in addition to the first loan, the INSS provided a further loan of nearly US$2 million.[8] Granting loans, especially those that provide a social benefit, fall within the purview of the INSS. Journalists demonstrated, however, that the INSS funded the project even after its financial evaluation determined that doing so

would represent a substantial financial risk. In its report, the INSS justified the funding decision with the consideration that the project would benefit low-income families.[9]

Reporters questioned these motives, citing serious conflicts of interest stemming from personal relationships between executives of Tecnosa and the ruling Sandinista National Liberation Front (FSLN) government. Tecnosa was founded by immediate relatives of Francisco López,[10] president of the Nicaraguan oil company Petronic, vice-president of ALBANISA and treasurer of the FSLN.[11] López is also president of Tecnología Electromecánica SA (Tesa), a company for which Tecnosa is often a subcontractor. In this instance, Tecnosa was partnering with Tesa on the El Pueblo Presidente project. Reporters argued that, because of López's ranking in the FSLN and his position at ALBANISA, which was involved in the project, contracting with either Tecnosa or Tesa violated the state contracting law,[12] which prohibits a public official from participating in a tendering process in which he or she has a personal, familial or commercial interest. [13]

El Pueblo Presidente was not the only Tecnosa project that appeared to receive a leg-up from government officials. As the case developed, a Nicaraguan newspaper also learnt that, in late 2007, the Ministry of Education had successfully petitioned the comptroller's office for permission to offer Tecnosa a contract to build sixty-five classrooms without undertaking a competitive bidding process.[14] In addition to receiving the contract, Tecnosa was given tax exemptions

---

4 *El Nuevo Diario* (Nicaragua), 19 May 2008.
5 *El Nuevo Diario* (Nicaragua), 2 June 2008.
6 *El Nuevo Diario* (Nicaragua), 12 June 2008.
7 *El Nuevo Diario* (Nicaragua), 2 June 2008.
8 *La Prensa* (Nicaragua), 27 June 2008.
9 *El Nuevo Diario* (Nicaragua), 2 June, 2008.
10 *El Nuevo Diario* (Nicaragua), 5 June 2008.
11 *El Nuevo Diario* (Nicaragua), 2 June 2008.
12 Agencia Mexicana de Noticias (Mexico), 3 June 2008.
13 See article 13, Law 622; available at www.cesdepu.com/foro/nicaragua.htm.
14 *El Nuevo Diario* (Nicaragua), 23 May 2008.

amounting to NIO 1.9 million (approximately US$100,000).[15]

Both the INSS and the Ortega government defended the El Pueblo Presidente loans. An advisor to President Ortega argued that the loan was a short-term 'bridging-loan', offered just long enough for Tecnosa to collect funds from a Nicaraguan credit agency.[16] This explanation was rejected by journalists, who noted that the corresponding INSS documents made no mention of a short-term loan.[17] Reporters also questioned what assurances the INSS had sought in granting the loan. News reports stated that the INSS accepted as collateral a coffee farm that Tecnosa valued at US$1.8 million, without seeking appraisals to confirm the value.[18] The INSS's president denied this, citing that two independent appraisals had confirmed the value.[19]

Responding to the case, an FSLN legislator and member of the INSS's advisory council claimed that, regardless of the circumstances under which the loan was granted, the institution was meeting a basic need by providing housing to low-income individuals.[20] While few would take issue with the project's goals, however, some questioned the motivation for the loans. Alfonso Silva, head of an association of urban developers, claimed that, around the time the loan was made, his organisation had also asked the INSS to set aside funds for affordable housing. He was told that, due to bad past experiences, the INSS had no immediate plans to fund such projects.[21] Silva suggested that, although the motives may have been well intentioned, the INSS nevertheless should have been required to be more transparent in the criteria it applies when allocating project funding.[22]

This sentiment was echoed by a former vice superintendent of the pensions department, who suggested that the risky investment in Tecnosa was indicative of systemic failures at the INSS: 'What emerges from all of this is the need for a comprehensive reform of the INSS, because the mechanisms that are currently being used have always been criticised ... A transparent and highly monitored system must be created.'[23]

Responding to the concerns raised by members of the Nicaraguan media, the comptroller's office decided to undertake a preliminary investigation of all loans made by the INSS since Ortega assumed the presidency in January 2007.[24] The case took on a larger dimension still when an IMF official confirmed that, on an upcoming visit to Nicaragua, the organisation would also solicit information about the INSS's loan to Tecnosa.[25] The long-term impact of these investigations, and the reception of their findings among the Nicaraguan public, remain to be seen.

Grupo Cívico Ética y Transparencia (TI Nicaragua)

15 *El Nuevo Diario* (Nicaragua), 6 June 2008.
16 Agencia Mexicana de Noticias (Mexico), 3 June 2008.
17 I. Olivares, 'INSS-TECNOSA: Gobierno rectifica', *Confidencial*, no. 587, June 2008.
18 *El Nuevo Diario* (Nicaragua), 2 June 2008.
19 R. Cuadra, 'FSLN Triplicará Reservas INSS', *Pueblo Presidente!*, 12 June 2008.
20 *El Nuevo Diario* (Nicaragua), 2 June 2008.
21 Ibid.
22 Ibid.
23 *El Nuevo Diario* (Nicaragua), 6 June 2008.
24 *La Prensa* (Nicaragua), 27 June 2008.
25 *El Nuevo Diario* (Nicaragua), 5 June 2008.

Additional reading

K. González, *El Control de la Corrupción en Nicaragua* (Managua: Hagamos Democracia, 2007).

Grupo Cívico Ética y Transparencia (EyT), *Estudio Anti-corruption 2006* (Managua: EyT, 2006).
Grupo Cívico Ética y Transparencia: www.eyt. org.ni.

Paraguay

Corruption Perceptions Index 2008: 2.4 (138th out of 180 countries)

Conventions

OAS Inter-American Convention against Corruption (signed March 1996; ratified November 1996)
UN Convention against Corruption (signed December 2003; ratified June 2005)
UN Convention against Transnational Organized Crime (signed December 2000; ratified September 2004).

Legal and institutional changes

- In November 2007 the Ministry of Education, in conjunction with the Council for the National Integrity System (CISNI), proposed a national plan intended to develop a citizenry that is critical, capable of exercising its rights and active in issues of national interest. The project will reach out to all members of society, regardless of age, location or socio-economic status. In addition to planning activities for citizen participation and education, the plan promotes the development of codes of ethics for all educational institutions and, more broadly, all public institutions.[1]

- Law 3439, of December 2007, established the National Department of Public Procurement as an autonomous institution and a legal entity of public law. The department's objective is to design and issue general policies on public procurement and develop provisions for compliance with the new law.

- Under the 1992 national constitution, the president must obtain the Senate's approval for his/her appointments for the president and directors of Paraguay's Central Bank and for Paraguayan directors of bi-national entities. In order to avoid manipulation of the appointment process, Law 3186 of September 2007 now stipulates that the president must

---

1 D. Zarza, 'Paraguay: MEC y CISNI presentan "Plan Nacional de Integridad"' (Asunción: Mercosur Educacional, 2007).

present his/her candidate to the Senate within sixty days. If the Senate fails to approve the choice, the president will have an additional sixty days to propose a new candidate.

- In 2007 and 2008 the Supreme Court passed a series of agreements that aim to enhance internal control mechanisms within the judiciary. In 2007 Agreement 475/07 established a complaints office to monitor irregularities committed by magistrates, Justice Department officers and assistants. Agreement 478/08 created a department to oversee judicial management, and Agreement 472/07 mandated an office of institutional integrity. Agreements 516 and 521, which the court ordered in April and May 2008, respectively, clarified the system of expense reimbursement for magistrates and other court officials in order to increase transparency.[2]

Government takeover of Multibanco does little to improve its accountability

Financial institutions around the world are expected to play a crucial role in detecting and reporting suspicious transactions, as well as cooperating with investigations of possible illicit behaviour. A Paraguayan case that has now stretched over five years reflects the failure of both the private and the public sectors to ensure best practice in the banking industry, however.

In 2003 the Paraguayan central bank detected a US$10 million deficit at the Paraguayan bank Multibanco SA. When the central bank intervened it discovered that two Multibanco directors had transferred large sums of money to an offshore bank with fifty related fictitious companies, adding an additional US$11 million to the estimated deficit.[3] In the ensuing process

of liquidating Multibanco, the presiding judge decried the central bank's 'passive attitude' and suggested it had not done enough to monitor Multibanco in the lead-up to its bankruptcy.[4]

The central bank's subsequent takeover of Multibanco did little to improve its transparency. In 2006, during an investigation of then-President Nicanor Duarte Frutos, a prosecutor with the Public Ministry's Anti-corruption Unit requested from the Superintendent of Banks that all Paraguayan banking institutions report whether Duarte had held or operated any bank accounts during the previous ten years. The prosecutor further asked to be informed of any safe deposit boxes, credit cards or cash transfer operations in Duarte's name,[5] making it clear that the request also applied to banks that had had central bank intervention or been liquidated. According to the prosecutor's office, Multibanco, now under government control, did not contact the Public Ministry to report an account Duarte held with the bank. All other banks, including those that had been liquidated, did send pertinent account details.[6]

When it later became apparent that Duarte had held an account with the bank, speculation varied as to why details had not been forthcoming from Multibanco. Some observers hinted that information on Duarte's account had been withheld because the officers in charge of Multibanco's liquidation were appointed by a friend of the President.[7] Others pointed to a bureaucratic disagreement over which public agency was responsible for maintaining account details: the Superintendent of Banks, which managed the intervention of Multibanco for two years, or the General Receiver's Office, which took control of the bank in mid-2005.[8]

---

2 Agreements available at www.pj.gov.py/acordadas.asp.
3 *Business News Americas* (Chile), 22 July 2003.
4 *Business News Americas* (Chile), 17 November 2003.
5 *Última Hora* (Paraguay), 21 February 2008.
6 Ibid.
7 Ibid.
8 *Última Hora* (Paraguay), 6 March 2008.

Accountability at the bankrupt Multibanco appears not to have improved. In February 2008 Paraguay's prosecutor of economic crimes launched a formal money-laundering investigation related to the Multibanco account in Duarte's name. The prosecutor's office estimates that some US$1.3 million was funnelled through the account between its opening in March 2001 and its closure in early 2003.[9] Multibanco, which remains under the control of the General Receiver's Office, has done little to assist in the case. In February 2008 an official overseeing Multibanco for the General Receiver's Office announced that a comprehensive search of the Multibanco offices had uncovered no files related to Duarte's account.[10] When faced with a warrant a week later, the same official located pertinent documents. Nevertheless, upon examination of these materials, prosecutors determined that important documentation remained missing.[11]

While no conclusions are forthcoming about the legitimacy of Duarte's bank account, the outlook for Multibanco appears grim. After five years of poor management and lapses in regulatory oversight, the Multibanco case has revealed shortcomings in the ability of Paraguay's oversight bodies to implement higher standards of transparency and accountability in financial institutions.

Road project unearths a lack of public oversight on contracting of private companies

By shining a persistent spotlight on poor business practices and lax government oversight, journalists in Paraguay often take on a role that few others will. Adopting the responsibility of public watchdog, however, can come at a cost. In early 2008 three newspaper employees were brought to court for accusing two auditors and a former comptroller of knowingly approving the misspending of foreign funds allocated to a large-scale roads project.

The case began almost a decade earlier, when then minister of finance Federico Zayas had decried how a construction company that did shoddy and incomplete work nevertheless was overpaid by the Ministry of Public Works (MOPC).[12] A formal audit later undertaken by the comptroller's office found a slew of fraudulent activity related to the project. The MOPC's former head was roundly criticised in the report, which uncovered the granting of contracts without sufficient budget support, inflated overtime pay and pay for defective work.[13]

While fingers were pointed at the director of MOPC, journalists at the newspaper *ABC Color* also accused individuals in the comptroller's office of intentional wrongdoing. In their investigation, journalists suggested that, at the behest of the then-comptroller, two auditors produced a positive report on the construction project without having examined the work. According to *ABC Color*, this report was formulated after the comptroller had disregarded an earlier report from his office that pointed to irregularities.[14] The second report gave MOPC the green light it needed to pay the construction company.

In response to the newspaper's coverage, the auditors and the former comptroller brought defamation and slander charges against the two journalists and *ABC Color*'s director.[15] This action backfired. The journalists used their trial to call

---

9 Xinhua News (China), 29 February 2008.
10 *Última Hora* (Paraguay), 1 March 2008.
11 *Última Hora* (Paraguay), 6 March 2008.
12 *ABC Color* (Paraguay), 7 October 2005.
13 *ABC Color* (Paraguay), 29 April 2007.
14 *ABC Color* (Paraguay), 5 May 2008.
15 *ABC Color* (Paraguay, 21 April, 2007.

attention again to the poor quality of oversight afforded to the contracted companies. During the trial, *ABC Color*'s lawyer suggested that the prosecutor's office should consider undertaking a new investigation, either into fraud or dangerous construction activities, on the part of the project's contractors.[16]

Along with finding the newspaper staff innocent in May 2008, the presiding judge suggested that the public prosecutor should open a new investigation into the irregularities surrounding the roads project.[17] In addition to keeping the case on the public radar, the journalists offered real oversight of private businesses and government bodies when the public sector either could not or would not. The capacity of these efforts to effect real change seems limited, however: in late 2008 editors at *ABC Color* continued, though unsuccessfully, to push the comptroller's office for a rigorous investigation of the public and private dimensions of the case.[18] Nevertheless, the result of media coverage and a public trial

may contribute to changing public expectations for transparency and accountability.

María Celeste Jara, in collaboration with María del Pilar Callizo (Transparencia Paraguay)

Additional reading

M. Callizo and L. Fretes, *Encuesta Nacional sobre Corrupción 2008* (Asunción: Transparencia Paraguay, 2008).

Ministerio de Educación y Cultura (MEC), *Plan Nacional de Educación en Valores* (Asunción: MEC, 2007).

Monitoreo de Recomendaciones de la Contraloría (CGR) a Instituciones Públicas y al Ministerio de Obras Públicas; available at www.transparencia.org.py.

Transparencia Paraguay, *Indice de Transparencia, Integridad y Eficiencia 2006*; available at www.transparencia.org.py.

Transparencia Paraguay: www.transparencia.org.py.

---

16 *ABC Color* (Paraguay), 10 April 2008.
17 *ABC Color* (Paraguay), 1 May 2008.
18 *ABC Color* (Paraguay), 20 October 2008.

Trinidad and Tobago

Corruption Perceptions Index 2008: 3.6 (72nd out of 180 countries)

Conventions

OAS Inter-American Convention against Corruption (signed April 1998; ratified April 1998)

UN Convention against Corruption (signed December 2003; ratified May 2006)

UN Convention against Transnational Organized Crime (signed September 2001; ratified November 2007)

Legal and institutional changes

- In October 2007 the Trinidad and Tobago High Court ruled that judges and magistrates are not subject to the provisions of the Integrity in Public Life Act no. 83 of 2000 and the Integrity in Public Life (Amendment) Act no. 88 of 2000, which regulate the disclosure requirements and conduct of public officials.[1] The ruling relieves judges and magistrates of the obligation to file a declaration of their debts and assets, and to register their interests. To the extent that financial disclosure is an effective anti-corruption tool, the ruling could increase the risk of corruption in the judiciary. In practice, however, the decision may have little effect on a system that is already underperforming: of 726 declarations received by the Integrity Commission in 2005, only one had been certified by 31 December 2006.[2]
- The above ruling also confirmed that members of the boards of all statutory bodies and state enterprises, including those in which the state has a controlling interest, are subject to the acts. This was clarified in January 2008 to include members of boards of all private bodies incorporated under an act of parliament, such as charitable organisations and service clubs. This has considerably increased the number of organisations with members who are likely to be subject to the acts. With the capacity of the Integrity Commission already far from adequate, this larger reporting base will demand greater administrative resources to process declarations.[3] The government has signalled its intention to revise the legislation in order to narrow the reporting base.

Overlapping directorships: an invitation for conflicts of interest?

With a relatively small entrepreneurial pool operating in Trinidad and Tobago, it is not uncommon for individuals to serve simultaneously in multiple leadership positions at various

---

1 *Newsday* (Trinidad and Tobago), 8 January 2008.

2 Integrity Commission of Trinidad and Tobago, *19th Annual Report to Parliament by the Integrity Commission of Trinidad and Tobago on Its Activities for the Year 2006* (Port of Spain: Integrity Commission of Trinidad and Tobago, 2007).

3 *Newsday* (Trinidad and Tobago), 8 January 2008.

public and private institutions. While this is perhaps inevitable in a country with just over 1 million residents, a recent case highlights a growing concern that, when not properly regulated, overlapping directorships leave state resources and private shareholder equity vulnerable to allegations of manipulation and insider dealings.

In March 2007 the company Stone Street Capital paid TT$110 million (US$17.8 million)[4] for over 40 per cent of the shares of Home Mortgage Bank (HMB), which is partly owned by the state. At the time of the purchase, Stone Street Capital co-owner André Monteil was chairman of both HMB and the privately owned Colonial Life Insurance Company (CLICO) Investment Bank, which sold the HMB shares to Stone Street Capital.[5] The propriety of the purchase was called into question during a parliamentary debate in April 2007, when a member of the opposition questioned whether Monteil's leadership positions with all three companies involved created a conflict of interest or led to insider trading.[6] Monteil's role as treasurer of the ruling party, the People's National Movement (PNM), further called the ethics of the purchase into question.[7]

Whereas even a few years earlier the purchase might not have been legal, legislative changes in 2005 and 2007 paved the way for the sales. A 2005 amendment to the Home Mortgage Bank Act[8] removed restrictions on the owner-ship or transfer of shares at HMB. The 2007 amendment to the act gave the central bank regulatory responsibilities over HMB but did not allow the bank any oversight of share structure. Presumably, had the bank had such oversight powers, it could have prevented the sale. The prime minister, Patrick Manning, admitted that it was these legislative changes, passed by his government with the support of opposition members, that facilitated the sale.[9]

The case was further complicated by suggestions that financing for the private purchase of HMB shares was supported by public funds.[10] In 2007 a member of the opposition alleged that, in February of that year, CLICO Investment Bank accepted a deposit of TT$100 million (US$16.5 million) from the Housing Development Corporation (HDC). Monteil was chairman of both institutions.[11] Because the deposit occurred a matter of weeks before CLICO[12] sold HMB shares to Monteil's Stone Street Capital, some speculated that the HDC deposit to CLICO Investment Bank gave the bank sufficient liquidity to be able to lend Monteil's Stone Street Capital the money to pay for the HMB shares.[13]

Both events led to a review of the purchase by government oversight bodies, but little has been uncovered. The Ministry of Finance discovered no evidence of wrongdoing in the sale of the HMB shares[14] and the Trinidad and Tobago Securities and Exchange Commission found the

---

4 *Trinidad and Tobago Express,* 30 August 2007.
5 House of Representatives, Hansard, 17 August 2007. At the time of the sale, Monteil was also chairman of two other state-owned companies, the Housing Development Corporation (HDC) and the Educational Facilities Company Ltd (EFCL), positions from which he later resigned. He was also deputy chairman of the state-owned Mortgage Finance Company Ltd (MFCL).
6 House of Representatives, Hansard, 25 April 2007.
7 Ibid.
8 Act no. 17 of 2005, the Home Mortgage Bank (Amendment) Act, 2005; Act no. 1 of 2007, the Home Mortgage Bank (Amendment) Act, 2007.
9 House of Representatives, Hansard, 29 August 2007.
10 House of Representatives, Hansard, 25 May 2007.
11 House of Representatives, Hansard, 17 August 2007.
12 CLICO and CLICO Investment Bank are both subsidiaries of the holding company CL Financial Limited.
13 House of Representatives, Hansard, 25 May 2007.
14 *Trinidad and Tobago Express*, 16 May 2007.

sale did not violate the Securities Exchange Act, because HMB was not listed on the country's stock exchange.[15] Additionally, the central bank concluded that the trade met the conditions established by the revised Home Mortgage Bank Act. The prime minister brushed off suggestions of impropriety surrounding the HDC deposit to CLICO Investment Bank, stating that it was a short-term deposit of TT$60 million (US$9.8 million) made only to earn interest. Although no illegal activity was uncovered, leading PNM members conceded that the transaction undermined the integrity of the institutions concerned. The prime minister emphasised his displeasure with the purchase and noted that HMB, as an institution established by statute, had to meet higher standards of corporate governance and best-practice principles.[16]

Arguing that the original intention of the amendments to the Home Mortgage Bank Act to create wider public ownership of HMB had been undermined by Stone Street Capital's massive purchase of shares, Manning referred the case to the commissioner of police, the Integrity Commission and the director of public prosecutions. He further reassured parliament that the government, with the guidance of the central bank, would introduce legislation to 'ensure that the shares are re-transferred at the same price the shares were transferred in the first place'.[17] He also confirmed that legislation would be introduced to prohibit similar transactions from occurring again.

Although the prime minister assured lawmakers that revised legislation would be introduced before the November 2007 general election, it was only in November 2008 that the Financial Institutions Bill was brought before parliament.[18] In the same month the promised 're-transfer' of shares took place when HMB's board of directors approved the National Insurance Board's acquisition of 7 million HMB shares held by Stone Street Capital. Along with the re-transfer of the shares, HMB confirmed in a statement that Monteil had resigned as chairman and director of the bank. This news came as a surprise to the country, which had been led to believe that Monteil had resigned in May 2007.[19]

A junior finance minister claimed in the *Trinidad Guardian* that, even weeks after the initial sale of the shares, neither the government nor the HMB board of directors had been aware of the transaction.[20] Despite this lack of transparency, and allegations of insider trading, control bodies have declined to investigate the role of private sector actors in the transaction or are moving very slowly in the process. In June 2008 the police confirmed that the case remained under investigation by the Anti-corruption Investigations Bureau,[21] though no findings have been forthcoming. Such treatment gives credibility to the suggestions of one parliamentarian that Monteil's ranking among the ruling party effectively exempted him from government scrutiny.[22]

The case begs the question as to whether oversight bodies could have been more proactive in preventing the purchase. Using its 'Corporate Governance Guidelines', the central bank might have been able to push HMB to comply more strictly with requirements for transparent, fair and balanced relationships between board

15 *Trinidad and Tobago Express*, 21 May 2008.
16 House of Representatives, Hansard, 17 August 2007.
17 House of Representatives, Hansard, 29 August 2007.
18 See www.ttparliament.org/legislations/b2008h24.pdf.
19 *Trinidad Guardian*, 22 November 2008.
20 *Trinidad Guardian*, 4 May 2007.
21 NationNews.com (Barbados), 18 June 2008.
22 House of Representatives, Hansard, 25 April 2007.

members, regulators, shareholders and stake-holders.[23] The central bank might also have been able to demand greater transparency regarding the HDC deposit with CLICO Investment Bank. This failure to fully investigate potential con-flicts of interest or insider trading in a case in which one individual appears as a leading actor in all the enterprises involved would seem to be, at the very least, unfortunate. Moreover, even after the issue had been brought to the fore, the claim could be made that the central bank failed to follow effectively its own 'Fit and Proper Guideline',[24] as Monteil was allowed to retain his positions as chairman and director of the HMB for a period of fifteen months after its initial investigation and reporting on the matter.

The government's failure to address the implica-tions of highly overlapping directorships under-mines public trust and threatens the integrity of the state. If overlapping directorships continue to be a facet of Trinidad and Tobago's public and private enterprises, the door remains open for conflicts of interest to tempt those in posi-tions of power to abuse their status for personal gain. While closing that door could put to rest some public suspicions of executive misconduct, avoiding overlapping directorships may not be possible in a market as small as Trinidad and Tobago's. What is possible, however, is for the regulatory framework to be reformed to require enterprises with overlapping directorships to exercise much higher standards of transparency and accountability.

Trinidad and Tobago Transparency Institute

Additional reading

Integrity in Public Life Act no. 83 of 2000; avail-able at www.ttparliament.org/legislations/a2000-83.pdf.

Integrity in Public Life (Amendment) Act no. 88 of 2000; available at www.ttparliament.org/legislations/a2000-88.pdf.

Judgment in the High Court of Trinidad and Tobago, HCA 1735, 'In the matter of the Integrity in Public Life Act, 2000, as Amended and In the Matter of the Construction of Paragraphs 8 and 9 of the Schedule to the Integrity in Public Life Act 2000 as Amended', Delivered By the Hon J. Jones, 15 October 2007; available at www.webopac.ttlawcourts.org/LibraryJud/Judgments/HC/jones/2007/HCA_1735_05DD15Oct07.rtf; and the Addendum of 21 January 2008; available at www.webopac.ttlawcourts.org/LibraryJud/Judgments/HC/j_jones/2007/HCA_1735_05DD21Jan08.rtf.

Trinidad and Tobago Transparency Institute: www.transparency.org.tt.

---

23 Central Bank of Trinidad and Tobago, 'Corporate Governance Guidelines', revised May 2007.
24 Central Bank of Trinidad and Tobago, 'Fit and Proper Guideline', May 2005.

United States of America

Corruption Perceptions Index 2008: 7.3 (18th out of 180 countries)

Conventions

OAS Inter-American Convention against Corruption (signed June 1996; ratified September 2000)

OECD Convention on Combating Bribery of Foreign Public Officials (signed December 1997; ratified December 1998)

UN Convention against Corruption (signed December 2003; ratified October 2006)

UN Convention against Transnational Organized Crime (signed December 2000; ratified November 2005)

Legal and institutional changes

- The Honest Leadership and Open Government Act (HLOGA)[1] was signed into law in September 2007, significantly increasing public disclosure requirements for lobbyists registered under the Lobbying Disclosure Act (LDA), the principal federal lobbying disclosure law. The HLOGA reforms became effective on 1 January 2008, requiring quarterly reporting on lobbying activity and semi-annual reporting on political and certain other contributions (see *Global Corruption Report 2008*). Registered lobbyists made their first semi-annual political contribution filings in July 2008.
- In March 2008 an important reform not included in HLOGA was adopted by the House of Representatives. The reform establishes an independent ethics office to strengthen enforcement of congressional ethics rules. The new Office of Congressional Ethics and independent oversight board will oversee enforcement of financial disclosure, gifts and other rules governing members of the House. Eight former officials (four from each political party, including two alternates) were appointed to the board in July. As leading political reform groups have noted, when the oversight board and Ethics Office become operational (probably not before January 2009) this will mark the first time that private citizens have been entrusted with an active role in the congressional ethics enforcement process.[2]
- The Congress is considering legislation[3] that would require oil, gas and mining companies registered with the Securities and Exchange Commission to disclose revenues paid to foreign governments for natural resources. In July 2008 the bill was referred to the Senate Committee on Banking, Housing, and Urban Affairs.

---

1 Public Law no. 110-81.
2 See, for example, Common Cause, 'House Leaders Appoint Distinguished Panel to Lead New Ethics Office', press release, 24 July 2008.
3 H.R. 6066, S. 3389, 'Extractive Industries Transparency Disclosure Act'.

US attack on corporate corruption abroad intensifies

The 1977 US Foreign Corrupt Practices Act established the first comprehensive prohibition by any country against bribing foreign government officials for business purposes. The FCPA bans the use of bribery to obtain or retain business or to secure any other undue business advantage, and imposes strict record-keeping requirements for public companies. While enforcement in the early years was limited, it has increased markedly since the United States ratified the OECD Convention in 1998. From 2003 to 2007 the average number of new FCPA enforcement actions nearly tripled compared to the preceding five-year period.[4]

In 2007 the upward trend in FCPA enforcement accelerated, with a record number of investigations and prosecutions. New investigations involving twenty-nine corporations were launched in 2007, and by the end of the year all open investigations, including those continuing from previous years, were reported to involve a total of eighty-two corporations.[5] The number of cases prosecuted has also grown significantly, with thirty-eight cases brought by the US Department of Justice (DOJ) and the SEC in 2007, and another sixteen cases brought in the first six months of 2008.[6]

In April 2007 the DOJ and SEC announced the largest monetary fine for an FCPA violation to date, US$44 million against Baker Hughes and a related subsidiary.[7] Other notable settlements involved large criminal penalties (US$26 million for Vetco International[8] and US$27 million for Chevron[9]); high-profile cases implicating the UN Oil-for-Food Programme (Textron, York International, Flowserve, Volvo AB); a largely passive investment by a private investor group (Omega Advisors); and settlements with several foreign-based companies (Vetco International, Paradigm BV).

Many of the new cases were voluntarily reported by companies to federal authorities, following due diligence reviews or, in some cases, assessments to certify internal controls under the Sarbanes–Oxley Act. In a number of cases, companies received credit for disclosure, earning non-prosecution or deferred prosecution agreements, and reduced fines on the condition of continuing cooperation (US$500,000 in the case of Omega Advisors).[10] In other self-reported cases, however, companies with substantial internal control programmes were nevertheless heavily penalised because of repeat offences and/or inadequate implementation.

Recent cases highlight several other notable trends. The US authorities are requiring more companies to 'disgorge' profits associated with illicit payments (US$23 million in the case of Baker Hughes).[11] Increased cooperation among enforcement authorities has been specifically credited in several recent settlements. A much

---

4 D. Newcomb and P. Urofsky, 'Recent Trends and Patterns in FCPA Enforcement', in *FCPA Digest of Cases and Review Releases Relating to Bribes to Foreign Officials under the Foreign Corrupt Practices Act of 1977* (New York: Shearman & Sterling LLP, 2008).

5 Ibid. This figure excludes investigations that were terminated, converted to prosecutions or consolidated with other investigations.

6 Gibson, Dunn & Crutcher LLP, '2008 Mid-year FCPA Update', 7 July 2008.

7 'Baker Hughes Admits Kazakhstan Bribery', *Energy Daily*, vol. 35, no. 81 (2007).

8 See article starting on page 382; *International Herald Tribune* (US), 20 December 2007.

9 D. Newcomb and P. Urofsky, 2008.

10 US Attorney, Southern District of New York, 'US Announces Settlement with Hedge Fund Omega Advisors, Inc. in Connection with Omega's Investment in Privatization Program in Azerbaijan', press release, 6 July 2007.

11 SEC, 'SEC Charges Baker Hughes with Foreign Bribery and with Violating 2001 Commission Cease-and-Desist Order', press release, 26 April 2007.

broader range of violations is being investigated and prosecuted, extending beyond 'traditional' cases of large-scale bribery to include regulatory bribery (US$43,000 in customs bribes from Delta and Pine Land Company[12]), alternative business structures (hedge fund investors in Omega Advisors) and foreign-based companies (a UK-based parent company and subsidiaries in Vetco International).[13]

Criminal prosecution of individuals is also increasingly common. A recent survey of FCPA enforcement actions over the past decade reported that forty-six individuals had been charged criminally by the DOJ, most within the last three years.[14] Many were senior executives or high-ranking employees of major international companies. Over two-thirds of the forty-six indicted individuals (thirty-three people) had been convicted of at least one charge arising from participation in a foreign bribery scheme.[15] Most of those convicted, including twenty-eight who pleaded guilty, received substantial prison sentences. The conclusion drawn from this data was that 'senior executives and other high-ranking employees who are implicated in a foreign bribery scheme are likely to face at least some term of incarceration, even if they accept responsibility for their actions, plead guilty and agree to cooperate with any ongoing government investigation'.[16]

A further notable development in 2007/8 has been the growing attention to collateral private lawsuits against companies and individuals for alleged violations of the FCPA. Although the FCPA does not authorise enforcement by private persons, recent cases suggest several alternative grounds for seeking damages or equitable relief. In one case, a former customer relied on federal conspiracy (the Racketeer Influenced and Corrupt Organizations Act) and common-law fraud statutes in a complaint, alleging US$2 billion in bribe-induced overcharges over a fifteen-year period.[17] In another case, lawyers representing Iraq filed a multi-billion-dollar suit against ninety-three companies that had allegedly paid kickbacks to the former Hussein regime under the UN Oil-for-Food Programme. Although these legal theories have yet to be tested in the courts, there is a general expectation of more FCPA-based damages lawsuits in the future from a broader range of parties, including injured competitors and shareholders.

Proposed federal acquisition rules to expand compliance and reporting requirements

The US government is the largest purchaser of goods and services in the world, with a total annual budget of US$465 billion and more than 9 million procurement contract actions per year.[18] To regulate procurement, the United States has a comprehensive system of laws and implementing regulations, known as the Federal Acquisition Regulations, or FAR. These regulations apply throughout the government and address all aspects of procurement, including bids and solicitations, the qualification of bidders and offerers, the evaluation of proposals, types of contracts, awards, performance, cost and pricing considerations, modifications during performance and termination.

12 SEC, Litigation Release no. 20214, 26 July 2007.
13 D. Newcomb and P. Urofsky, 2008.
14 Bloomberg, *Law Reports: Risk & Compliance*, vol. 1, no. 6 (2008).
15 Of those not convicted, six individuals were currently awaiting trial, four were either fugitives or subject to pending extradition charges and three had been acquitted at trial or had charges dismissed.
16 Bloomberg, 2008.
17 *Alba* v. *Alcoa*, 2:0/08-CV-299 (27 February 2008).
18 See www.fpds.gov, 'Trending Analysis for the Last Five Years', for financial year 2007.

The FAR are issued and maintained by two inter-governmental agencies: the Civilian Agency Acquisition Council and the Defense Acquisition Regulation Council. A transparent process of public notice and comment rule-making is regularly employed to amend and update the FAR to address new legislative requirements, issues that arise in litigation, and policy initiatives from the executive branch or Congress.

In 2007 these two agencies issued a final rule amending the FAR to require most companies that obtain US government contracts to adopt policies and practices addressing corruption in procurement. Specifically, the rule requires contractors to:

- adopt written codes of business ethics and conduct;
- institute a business ethics training programme and an internal control system to promote compliance with the code (small businesses are exempt); and
- display posters promoting the Office of the Inspector General's fraud hotline unless they have instituted other mechanisms to encourage the reporting of suspected instances of improper conduct.

The rule applies not only to prime contractors but to subcontractors as well, and is a significant step towards raising the level of anti-corruption practice in the business community.

In addition to the exemption for small businesses, the new rule does not apply to contracts of less than US$5 million and with a performance period of less than 120 days, contracts for commercial items only,[19] or contracts that can be performed wholly outside the United States (although several of these provisions are

under review, as noted below). Even with these exemptions, the rule, which went into effect in December 2007, imposes significantly greater requirements on the private sector than had been contained in prior FAR regulations.

Even before the release of the final rule, there were calls, notably from Congress and the DOJ, to strengthen the rules related to contractor ethics. A new proposed rule was published in the US Federal Register for public comment in November 2007. If enacted, the rule would impose additional requirements on all companies that contract with the US government, including:

- requiring a compliance programme to help fulfil a contractor's obligation to develop a satisfactory record of integrity and business ethics (this would be a qualification standard for any contractor);
- requiring mandatory disclosure to the government when there is a 'reasonable basis' to suspect a violation of criminal law related to the award or performance of a contract or subcontract;
- establishing a cause for debarment or suspension for the 'knowing failure' to report contract overpayments or violations of federal criminal law related to the award or performance of the contract or subcontract;
- setting minimum standards – as a contractual obligation – for internal control systems, such as regular internal reviews to detect criminal conduct and regular assessments of the code's effectiveness;
- mandating 'full cooperation' with government audits, investigations and corrective action; and
- eliminating the exemption for contracts involving commercial items and contracts

---

19 The FAR define a 'commercial item' as any item that is 'customarily used for nongovernmental purchases' and that has also been made available to the public. This also includes items that are not yet available to the public marketplace but are intended to be so, and commercial items that undergo 'minor modifications' not available to the public.

that can be performed wholly outside the United States.[20]

As with the original rule, the proposed rule would apply to contracts with a value of more than US$5 million and a performance period of 120 days or more, and the small business exception from the training programme and internal control system requirement would remain. The proposal signals a continuing trend towards greater regulation and oversight of government contracts and raising standards among contractors.

While generally well received, one of the few contentious issues in the proposed rule is the affirmative obligation to report to the government when a contractor has a 'reasonable basis' to suspect a violation of criminal law and the attendant threat of suspension or debarment for a 'knowing failure' to do so. Some in the business and legal communities have expressed concern over the vagueness of the terms 'reasonable basis' and 'knowing failure', and the potential implementation problems these requirements, as currently worded, may cause. Concerns have also been raised about the possibility that companies could be required to divulge legal advice sought in an effort to comply with the rule, jeopardising the attorney–client privilege.[21] Companies argue that protections for attorney–client communications make it more likely that they will investigate past conduct to identify shortcomings and remedy problems. Lacking those protections, some argue that companies may be less likely to take a hard look at their anti-bribery programmes.

Some have also opined that the requirement for 'full cooperation' with government audits, investigations and corrective action could also be read to require waiver of the attorney–client privilege. Additional language has been proposed to make it clear that federal officials cannot pressure contractors into waiving the privilege.[22]

TI USA

Additional reading

N. Boswell, 'Prognosis for Progress on the Anti-corruption Agenda: The Role of International Organizations and Citizen Engagement', *Journal of Financial Crime*, vol. 15, no. 2 (2008).

A. Florini (ed.), *The Right to Know: Transparency in an Open World* (New York: Columbia University Press, 2007).

A. Fung, M. Graham and D. Weil, *Full Disclosure: The Perils and Promise of Transparency* (New York: Cambridge University Press, 2007).

B. Heinemann, *High Performance with High Integrity* (Cambridge, MA: Harvard Business Press, 2008).

B. Pagano and E. Pagano, *The Transparency Edge: How Credibility Can Make or Break You in Business* (New York: McGraw-Hill, 2004).

S. Rose-Ackerman, 'Corruption', in B. Lomborg, *Solutions for the World's Biggest Problems: Costs and Benefits* (New York: Cambridge University Press, 2007).

N. Shaxson, *Poisoned Wells: The Dirty Politics of American Oil* (New York: Palgrave Macmillan, 2007).

G. T. Ware, S. Moss, J. E. Campos and G. P. Noone, 'Corruption in Public Procurement: A Perennial Challenge', in J. E. Campos and S. Pradhan, *The Many Faces of Corruption: Tracking Vulnerabilities at the Sector Level* (Washington, DC: World Bank, 2007).

TI USA: www.transparency-usa.org.

---

20 For additional discussion, see PricewaterhouseCoopers, 'Aerospace & Defence Technical Alert: Contractor Code of Business Ethics and Conduct', 2008.

21 See, for example, the American Bar Association's comments to the proposed FAR rule, from June 2008; available at www.abanet.org/poladv/priorities/privilegewaiver/2008jun20_farcase_gsaltr.pdf.

22 Ibid.

Bolivarian Republic of Venezuela

Corruption Perceptions Index 2008: 1.9 (158th out of 180 countries)

Conventions

OAS Inter-American Convention against Corruption (signed March 1996; ratified May 1997)

UN Convention against Corruption (signed December 2003; not yet ratified)

UN Convention against Transnational Organized Crime (signed December 2000; ratified May 2002)

Legal and institutional changes

- Published on 31 October 2007, the Joint Resolution of the Finance Ministry, the Ministry of Light Industries and Trade (MILCO) and the Ministry of Energy and Petrol decreed that, effective January 2008, in order to strengthen national industry, the importation of vehicles would require an import licence issued by MILCO.[1] The resolution gives MILCO the exclusive power to set the maximum number of vehicles to be imported by each assembly plant or seller, according to its assessment of factors including national needs, production capacity, fuel efficiency and sales records. If the assessment criteria do not have sufficiently objective technical indicators the resolution could encourage automobile companies to rely on personal connections and informal channels to influence public officials responsible for licensing.

- In January 2008 the Commission for Foreign Exchange Administration (CADIVI) published Provision no. 085, which establishes requirements, controls and procedures for authorising the purchase of currency needed to buy imports.[2] The provision enhances the discretion that both the president and his ministers have over the distribution of foreign currency. Article 15 gives the president or ministers the power to exempt natural or legal persons from meeting the requirements to obtain 'preferential dollars'.[3]

- The new law of public contracting of March 2008 repeals by presidential decree the former procurement law. The new law excludes from current procurement requirements contracts that fall within the framework of international cooperation agreements between Venezuela and other states, including public–private enterprises (oil contracts, for example, would fall under this exemption). Beyond circumstances that traditionally call for exceptions from procurement regulations – defence and national security purchases, emergency procurement or the lack of multiple suppliers

---

1   *Venezuelan Official Gazette*, no. 38.800, 31 October 2007.

2   'Providencia mediante la cual se Establecen los Requisitos, Controles y Trámite para la Autorización de Adquisición de Divisas correspondientes a las Importaciones', *Venezuelan Official Gazette* no. 38.862, 31 January 2008.

3   The preferential dollar is the official value the Venezuelan government gives to the US dollar for currency operations. To obtain preferential dollars, one must complete a series of administrative procedures established by CADIVI.

– the law creates new exemptions for certain purchases and hiring, paving the way for more instances of direct procurement.

Red tape in currency system poses risk to transparency

In February 2003, when currency control was decreed in Venezuela, President Hugo Chávez announced, 'Not one dollar for the *coup*-mongers.'[4] Only a few months earlier Chávez had been briefly deposed during a failed coup attempt supported by many members of the Venezuelan business community.[5] Chávez's threat to withhold currency from '*coup*-mongers' reflected a continuing tension between his government and many private sector actors. Five years on, the government's management of foreign currencies continues to be a sticking point for many Venezuelan businesses.

With national levels of imports at historic highs,[6] access to international currency is vital. CADIVI's currency application process is characterised by strict ministerial, financial and customs controls, however, making access to foreign currency a cumbersome bureaucratic process. For example, companies seeking foreign currency are required first to obtain non-production certificates from MILCO, which demonstrate that the importation of a specified product will not damage the national manufacturing industry.[7] Observers have also noted that CADIVI enjoys considerable discretion in granting foreign currency;

although an applicant may meet all the requirements necessary to obtain dollars, there is no guarantee that the application process will be successful, and there is no appeals process.[8]

Businesses have been discouraged by recent delays in currency allocation, which have led some firms to make late payments to international suppliers of 160 days or more. A regional director of the Venezuelan Federation of the Chambers of Commerce stated, 'Many companies which have asked for our institution's help are on the point of receiving lawsuits (from suppliers) for not meeting foreign commitments.'[9] In May 2008 the president of the federation estimated that CADIVI had delayed the delivery of US$15 billion, with dire repercussions for all aspects of the economy.[10]

While officials attribute the delays to inefficiency caused by an influx of currency requests,[11] others suspect that red tape is hiding deliberate delays. One newspaper report alleged that CADIVI officials charged illegal commissions of up to 30 per cent of the total value of the currency request in order to accelerate processing time. The report found that under CADIVI's previous administration the processing time for currency requests averaged thirty days. Under the new administration the procedure was estimated to take between 120 and 180 days, 'unless payments of VEB 400 (US$0.19) are made to [a CADIVI lawyer] and her group of agents, for each preferential dollar [to be allocated]'. According

---

4 *El Universal* (Venezuela), 5 February 2003.
5 Most notably, Pedro Carmona Estanga, head of the Venezuelan Federation of Chambers of Commerce and Industry prior to the coup, was one of Chavez's most outspoken opponents, and was named interim leader of the government following Chavez's ousting. For further information about the tensions between the Chávez administration and business leaders in the lead-up to the 2002 coup attempt, see Human Rights Watch, *Human Rights Watch World Report 2003* (New York: Seven Stories Press, 2003).
6 Based on 2007 figures; see Venezuelan Central Bank, 'Exportaciones e Importaciones de Bienes y Servicios ségun Sectores', 2007; available at www.bcv.org.ve/excel/2_4_9.xls?id=325.
7 See www.unionradio.net/Noticias/Noticia.aspx?noticiaid=242852.
8 Baker & McKenzie, *Doing Business in Venezuela* (Caracas: Baker & McKenzie, 2004).
9 *El Carabobeño* (Venezuela), 28 May 2008.
10 See www.bancaynegocios.com/noticia_det.asp?id=10223.
11 See www.unionradio.net/Noticias/Noticia.aspx?noticiaid=242852.

to the report, over 80,000 requests for currency may have been held back for this reason.[12] All the same, there is reason to believe that the situation may be improving. In July 2008 the head of CADIVI announced a new electronic system to accelerate the processing of currency requests and bring the response time back to thirty days.[13]

These instruments may not solve deeper concerns about discrimination within the currency allocation system. A 2007 academic study suggested that the currency control system could be used as an instrument of political pressure to limit the economic capacity of private sector actors who oppose the Chávez government, while bolstering the economic activity of those favourable to him.[14] The study assessed the degree of economic damage experienced by businesses that identified with the opposition in Venezuela. The researchers based their study on the 'Maisanta list', which included the personal data of those who signed a recall referendum against Chávez. This list was circulated publicly and used to blacklist signatories from positions within government- and state-owned companies.[15] Although Chávez eventually came out publicly against the use of the list, much of the damage had already been done.

The study found that 'those signing have very low chances of being employed in the public sector, and much higher of ending up in the black economy. The firms whose boards signed against the president recorded lower profits than those who had a neutral or pro-Chávez board, suffered much higher tax pressure, and received fewer dollars from CADIVI.'[16] The study concluded that companies with boards of directors

that signed the petition against Chávez received approximately 50 per cent less foreign currency than firms where no board member signed the petition.[17] Firms whose boards signed in favour of the government received 55 per cent more official currency.[18]

Delays and discretion in currency allocation are fuelling feelings of mistrust and contributing to allegations of corruption and political discrimination. If mechanisms are not established to ensure that currency is allocated fairly, transparently and efficiently, Venezuelans can expect a downturn in national manufacturing capacity and continued animosity between members of the business community and the government.

Carry-on cash catches up with Venezuelan business

In late 2008 international media attention focused on a case that spanned three countries and muddied relations in business, politics and international diplomacy. PDVSA, Venezuela's state-owned oil and gas company, emerged as a central player in the case and raised doubts about the government's commitment to stopping corruption at state-owned enterprises.

On 4 August 2007 Venezuelan-American businessman Guido Alejandro Antonini Wilson was detained at Argentine customs. He had just arrived on a government-chartered flight from Venezuela, accompanied by Argentine government officials and PDVSA employees, when a customs official searched his bag and discovered US$800,000. Wilson was charged with a customs infraction and released from custody. Shortly

12 *6to Poder* (Venezuela), 9 April 2008.
13 Agencia Bolivariana de Noticias (Venezuela), 25 June 2008.
14 C.-T. Hsieh, D. Ortega, *The Price of Political Opposition: Evidence from Venezuela's Maisanta*, Working Paper no. 23 (Chicago: Booth School of Business, University of Chicago, 2007).
15 Bloomberg News (US), 17 April 2006.
16 *El Nacional* (Venezuela), 6 April 2008; C.-T. Hsieh, D. Ortega, *et al.*, 2007.
17 C.-T. Hsieh, E. Miguel and F. R. Rodriguez, *et. al.*, 2007.
18 *El Nacional* (Venezuela), 6 April, 2008.

after the incident, rumours hinted that the money had been intended for the presidential bid of Cristina Fernández de Kirchner in Argentina.

Within a few days of returning to his home in Florida, Wilson alerted officials from the Federal Bureau of Investigation that he was being pressured by representatives of the Venezuelan government and PDVSA to keep silent about the case.[19] The United States instigated an investigation and trial, on the grounds that five businessmen were acting as unauthorised agents of a foreign government within the United States.[20] Three agreed to cooperate with prosecutors, one contested the charges and another remained at large.

Moises Maionica, a lawyer who had been tapped by PDVSA to keep Wilson quiet, testified that the oil company offered him US$400,000 for his efforts.[21] Other testimony suggested that, when PDVSA officials were unable to orchestrate an effective cover-up, high-level officials, including Chávez's intelligence chief and Chávez himself, stepped in to ensure that Wilson would not talk.[22] In his testimony, Maionica further confirmed that PDVSA, using Wilson as a middleman, had sent the money as a contribution from the Venezuelan government to Fernández de Kirchner.[23] In later interviews with the media, Wilson supported this account.[24]

In addition to allegations that the company had facilitated the delivery of the US$800,000,

Wilson also stated his belief that from the same flight another US$4.2 million had passed through customs undetected.[25] A PDVSA vice-president whose son had been on the plane with Wilson was also heard voicing concerns about the whereabouts of these funds.[26] Following publicity surrounding his son's presence on the plane, the vice-president later resigned from his position at the oil company.[27]

Both Chávez and Kirchner denounced the US investigation as a politically motivated attempt to create conflict between Caracas and Buenos Aires.[28] Attorneys for the accused contended that the United States had pursued the case to embarrass the Chávez government.[29] These arguments notwithstanding, testimony from the case suggests that the Venezuelan government at once encouraged and facilitated the illicit behaviour of PDVSA. Should subsequent revelations prove beyond doubt that the government used PDVSA to fulfil political aims, the Chávez administration will have a hard time assuring citizens of its dedication to fighting corruption in either the public or private sectors.

Oscar Vallés (Universidad Metropolitana) and
Mercedes De Freitas (TI Venezuela)

Additional reading

G. Coronel, 'Corrupción, Administración deficiente y Abuso de Poder en la Venezuela de Hugo Chávez' (Washington, DC: Cato Institute, 2006).

19 *International Herald Tribune* (US), 10 September 2008.
20 *El País* (Spain), 8 July 2008.
21 Associated Press (US), 17 September 2008.
22 *New York Times* (US), 15 September 2008.
23 *New York Times* (US), 11 September 2008.
24 *El País* (Uruguay), 10 November 2008.
25 Ibid.
26 *La Nación* (Argentina), 14 September 2008; Associated Press (US), 24 September 2008.
27 Agencia EFE (Spain), 4 August 2008.
28 *International Herald Tribune* (US), 10 September 2008.
29 Associated Press (US), 2 July 2008.

H. Malavé Mata, *Los Extravíos del Poder: Euforia y Crisis del Populismo en Venezuela* (Caracas: Universidad Central de Venezuela, 1987).

H. Njam, *La Corrupción, un Problema de Estado* (Caracas: Universidad Metropolitana, 2008).

O. Ochoa, 'La Economía Venezolana 2006–2007: Crecimiento, Inflación y Corrupción', *Analítica*, vol. 12 (2006).

W. Pérez Parra, 'La Lucha contra la Corrupción en Venezuela: Balance y Perspectiva en el Marco de la nueva Administración pública', VII International Congress of CLAD on State Reform and Public Administration, Lisbon, 8–11 October 2002; available at www.unpan1.un.org/intradoc/groups/public/documents/CLAD/clad0044108.pdf.

TI Venezuela: www.transparencia.org.ve.

6.3 Asia and the Pacific

Bangladesh

Corruption Perceptions Index 2008: 2.1 (147th out of 180 countries)

Conventions
ADB–OECD Anti-Corruption Action Plan for Asia Pacific (endorsed November 2001)
UN Convention against Corruption (acceded February 2007)

Legal and institutional changes

- The Anti-Corruption Commission (Staffs) Service Rules 2008 were approved by the government and came into effect on 15 June 2007. They were prepared by the commission in order to impose these rules upon the commission staff, while earlier efforts by the previous government were considered by stakeholders including civil society organisations to be detrimental to their independence.[1]

- On 15 July 2007 the Public Procurement Act (Amendment) 2007 was passed. The amendment brings procurement for any foreign or development/cooperative organisation under the jurisdiction of the act. On 28 January 2008 the Public Procurement Rules 2008 were enacted to ensure the transparency and accountability of the process, including project tender and approval, the execution of work and civil servant duties.[2]

- The Local Government Commission

---

1 *Bangladesh Gazette*, SRO no. 147-Act/2008, 15 June 2008.
2 *Bangladesh Gazette*, SRO no. 21-Act/2008, 28 January 2008.

Ordinance 2008 was promulgated on 13 May 2008 in order to institutionalise the decentralisation and empowerment of local government.[3] The ordinance establishes a permanent local government commission to oversee the decentralisation process while ensuring accountability and transparency in local government institutions.

- The National Identity Registration Authority Ordinance 2008 was promulgated on 15 May 2008 to facilitate the establishment of the national identity registration authority.[4] The main objective of the national identity card is to establish a digital database for preparing a credible voter list, in order to eliminate false voting and track the records of criminal offences. The national identity card will also facilitate transparency in transactions for various utility services.
- On 16 June 2008 the government amended the Supreme Judicial Commission Ordinance 2008.[5] Some years earlier, on 2 December 1999, the Appellate Division of the Supreme Court had given twelve directives to the government in a landmark judgment in the Masdar Hossain case on the separation of the judiciary (see the *Global Corruption Report 2007* and *2008*). The previous two governments delayed implementing the directives as many as twenty-eight times. This development represents the most significant step towards achieving full independence of the judiciary.[6]
- On 11 June 2008 the Anti-Terrorism Ordinance 2008 was promulgated.[7] Under this ordinance a wide range of crimes, including money-laundering, arms-running and financing terror attacks, have been made non-bailable offences.[8]
- On 8 June 2008 the government promulgated the Truth and Accountability Commission Ordinance 2008.[9] The ordinance provides clemency for corrupt individuals on the basis of voluntary disclosure and confession of guilt, subject to the confiscation of illegally amassed wealth and property. Those granted clemency are to be barred from election to public office for five years. The ordinance will not apply to those already convicted.
- To ensure transparency and accountability in local government elections, the Election Commission approved the City Corporation (Election Ethics) Rules 2008 and the Powrasava (Election Ethics) Rules 2008 on 17 June 2008.[10] The rules include provisions to disclose basic general information regarding candidates, such as sources of income, assets and liabilities, election expenses and their source, and any criminal records.
- On 18 June 2008 the Council of Caretaker Advisors approved in principle the Right to Information Ordinance 2008.[11] This ordinance would mark a significant victory for civil society organisations in Bangladesh, which have long advocated such a law as a prerequisite for ensuring transparency, accountability and good governance. The draft law was circulated for public discourse and response – a unique move in the Bangladeshi context, as laws have traditionally been passed with no engagement with citizens.[12]
- The Money Laundering Prevention Ordinance 2008 provides that the courts will not take into consideration any money-laundering case

---

3 *Bangladesh Gazette*, Ordinance no. 15/2008, 13 May 2008.
4 *Bangladesh Gazette*, Ordinance no. 18/2008, 15 May 2008.
5 *Bangladesh Gazette*, Ordinance nos. 6/2008 and 29/2008, 16 June 2008.
6 *New Nation* (Bangladesh), 1 November 2007.
7 *Bangladesh Gazette*, Ordinance no. 28/2008, 11 June 2008; *Daily Star* (Bangladesh), 19 May 2008.
8 *Daily Star* (Bangladesh), 13 June 2008.
9 *Bangladesh Gazette*, Ordinance no. 27/2008, 8 June 2008.
10 Election Commission Secretariat, Government of Bangladesh, *Bangladesh Gazette*, 17 June 2008.
11 *Daily Star* (Bangladesh), 19 June 2008.
12 *Daily Star* (Bangladesh), 24 March 2008.

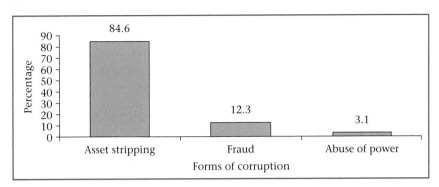

Figure 11: Forms of corruption in the private sector, 2007

without the sanction of the Anti-Corruption Commission. In addition, this ordinance will allow the Bangladesh Bank to seek cooperation with financial intelligence units of other countries or provide them with similar support.

Corruption in the private sector

Bangladesh's private sector is rapidly becoming a key source of economic growth and employment generation. In the fiscal year 2006/7 the private sector's share of investments in the economy was 23 per cent of a total Tk1137.3 crore.[13] The 2008/9 *Global Competitiveness Report* ranks Bangladesh 111th out of 134 countries, and 106th in terms of the efficiency of its market for goods.[14] The 2007 *Global Integrity Report* also ranks Bangladesh as being weak in business licensing and regulation.[15]

In common with every other sector, however, the private sector has been affected by widespread corruption. TI Bangladesh's Corruption Database illustrates the propensity of corruption in the private sector. In 2006 it was considered very corrupt, accounting for between 3.1 and 5 per cent of reported cases. In 2007 the private sector was a key actor in one-sixth of corruption reports published in the print media.[16] That year the most dominant form of private sector corruption was asset stripping (84.6 per cent), followed by fraud and abuse of power (see figure 11).

Despite the adoption of the Public Procurement Act 2006 and the Ordinance in 2007, the private sector has reportedly continued to engage in malpractices in the procurement process. According to the Planning Commission's Implementation, Monitoring and Evaluation Division, eighty-five contractors/companies/bidders faced punitive exclusion from the bidding process on account of fraudulent practices and collusive activities.[17]

In one case in 2008, a container handling contract was awarded at two container depots in Dhaka and Chittagong to a company favoured by politically powerful individuals, although

13 Ministry of Finance, *Bangladesh Economic Review 2007–08* (Dhaka: Ministry of Finance, 2007).
14 M. E. Porter and K. Schwab, *Global Competitiveness Report 2008–2009* (Geneva: World Economic Forum, 2008).
15 Global Integrity, *Global Integrity Report 2007* (Washington, DC: Global Integrity, 2008); available at report.global-integrity.org.
16 Other key actors were government officials in 58.6 per cent of cases, and NGOs and others in 7.8 per cent.
17 Central Procurement Technical Unit, www.cptu.gov.bd.

it lacked both the experience and skills to do the job. The allegations included the violation of tender conditions through the misuse of power.[18] In another such case, the Barapukuria coal mine operation contract was awarded to a Chinese company that allegedly engaged in collusive bidding with politically powerful individuals, involving a financial loss of Tk1.58 billion to the public exchequer.[19]

Exports and imports

Chittagong port is Bangladesh's main gateway for exports and imports, dealing with 65 to 70 per cent of the country's export/import trade. It is mandatory for importers to have their goods inspected by a pre-shipment inspection (PSI) agency before or at the time of shipment.

Outsourcing of the PSI system through privatisation was introduced in 2000/1 to help the National Board of Rèvenue maximise revenue collection and reduce corruption and other forms of harassment prevalent in the clearing of goods.[20] The main tasks of PSI agencies are to verify the description, quality and quantity of goods as per invoices and packing lists supplied by the exporters. This determines the correct HS (Harmonized System) codes[21] of the goods, attributes the correct values to imported items and ensures compliance with shipment procedures. There are currently four PSI companies: OMIC (Overseas Merchandise Inspection Co.) Ltd, SGS (Société Générale de Surveillance) Bangladesh Limited,

Bureau Veritas BIVAC (Bangladesh) Limited and Intertek Testing Limited. On 20 March 2008 the concerned port authority cancelled the agreement with Cotecna due to its involvement in 'massive irregularities'.[22]

Large-scale allegations of fraud and corruption by PSI companies have centred on allegations of incorrect declarations, under- and over-invoicing, the provision of HS codes for less than the valuation and the fraudulent certification of consignments.[23] In order to avoid higher tax liabilities, importers gain the assistance of PSI agencies to falsify the real value of imports by manipulating or hiding their real quality or quantity.[24] Between June and December 2007 the Customs Authority found that 7 per cent of the HS codes issued (out of 8,046) contained discrepancies.[25]

Problems arise because of the complex and time-consuming manual system of assessing imports and exports, shortcomings in the rules and regulations, the absence of a monitoring system of PSI activities, a weak inclination to investigate and penalise misdemeanours, and a poor auditing system.[26] In a system involving importers, clearing and forwarding agents, and PSI companies, all three parties take advantage by altering HS codes to their benefit, at the expense of government revenue.[27] Moreover, the penalty for PSI companies that violate the rules is nominal. The fines amount to merely Tk50,000 (US$715) to Tk100,000 (US$1,449), whereas anomalies in the Clean Report Finding

---

18 *Daily Star* (Bangladesh), 9 May 2008.
19 *Daily Star* (Bangladesh), 27 February 2008.
20 *Daily Star* (Bangladesh), 29 August 2008; 29 March 2005.
21 The six-digit HS code is part of the Harmonized Commodity Description and Coding System, which is maintained by the Customs Co-operation Council, an independent intergovernmental organisation based in Brussels with over 160 member countries.
22 *Daily Star* (Bangladesh), 29 August 2008; *Financial Express* (Bangladesh), 1 February 2008; *Daily Star* (Bangladesh), 29 April 2008.
23 *Financial Express* (Bangladesh), 1 February 2008.
24 TI Bangladesh, 'Study on Chittagong Customs', 21 June 2008; *Daily Star* (Bangladesh), 29 May 2008.
25 Chittagong Custom Authority; TI Bangladesh, 2008.
26 TI Bangladesh, 2008.
27 For example, see *Financial Express* (Bangladesh), 1 February 2008.

cost the government an average of Tk2.7 million (US$39,130) in revenue.[28]

Despite the fact that existing rules provide audit and monitoring systems to check irregularities, no audit of PSI companies has been conducted, nor has any specific monitoring activity taken place. For example, the government has not formed a central or local monitoring committee, as it has been mandated to do.

Corruption in private telecommunication through illegal VoIP

Telecommunication is a fast-growing sector in Bangladesh, the large investments it entails making a significant contribution to the country's economic development, and huge profits are generated. The revenue for private telecommunication service providers currently stands at approximately Tk15 billion each year.[29] With this growth, however, the revenues of the Bangladesh Telegraph and Telephone Board (BTTB) fell sharply from 2001/2 to 2005/6. In the fiscal year 2005/6 the BTTB recorded its lowest revenue in five years.[30] More importantly, the BTTB's earnings from international calls fell drastically from Tk3.79 billion in 2001/2 to Tk2.4 billion in 2005/6.[31] Among the reasons for this is the growth of illegal VoIP (Voice over Internet Protocol) operations by private cellphone operators, a trend facilitated

by deliberate inaction to regulate or legalise the VoIP business.[32] Although no authorisation was granted to any mobile phone operators, they have used their equipment for 'internet telephony' by terminating incoming international calls.[33]

In the past, governments have not controlled illegal VoIP or 'internet telephony', allegedly because the powerful VoIP operators influenced the government to delay the process of awarding licences and/or legalising VoIP operations. In late 2003 the Bangladesh Telecommunication Regulatory Commission (BTRC) announced that there would be an award of licences in January 2004, but three years later this had still not come into effect.[34]

According to the BTRC, 30 million international calls enter Bangladesh every day. Of these calls, 53.3 per cent are controlled by illegal VoIP operators.[35] As a result, the government loses about Tk12 billion in revenue each year.[36] After the caretaker government took over in January 2007, it was revealed that most private cellphone operators were involved in illegal VoIP business.[37] A huge amount of VoIP equipment was seized and many businesspeople involved in the illegal business were arrested.[38]

The caretaker government's drive against illegal VoIP operations revealed that many operators

---

28 TI Bangladesh, 2008.
29 BangladeshNews.com, 9 November 2007; Ministry of Finance, budget speech 2008/9, www.mof.gov.bd/mof2/budget/08_09/budget_speech/08_09_en.pdf.
30 BangladeshNews.com, 28 January 2007.
31 Ibid.
32 Ibid.
33 *Daily Star* (Bangladesh), 28 January 2008; BangladeshNews.com, 1 September 2007.
34 LIRNEasia, 'Bangladesh Illegal VoIP Operators Make Fortune as Govt. Stalls Licensing', 27 December 2005.
35 *Daily Star* (Bangladesh), 28 January 2008.
36 *Daily Star* (Bangladesh), 16 May 2008.
37 *Daily Star* (Bangladesh), 16 May 2008; 9 September 2007; VoIP Central, 'Bangladesh Seizes Illegal VoIP equipment', 30 September 2007.
38 The seized equipment includes GSM (Groupe Spécial Mobile) fixed terminals, fixed wireless terminals, wireless local loops, quantum gateway equipment, voice finder, V-sats (Very Small Aperture Terminal), computers, server, SIM (subscriber identity module) cards of different mobile operators, channel banks, ethernet converters. BangladeshNews.com, 14 January 2008.

were involved, including the four biggest mobile companies. For the involvement in illegal call termination through VoIP, the BTRC fined the four biggest mobile companies, GrameenPhone, City Cell, AKTEL and Banglalink, a total penalty of Tk8.38 billion.[39] The BTRC also filed legal cases against them. All four mobile companies paid the penalties.

Against this backdrop, the caretaker government has taken initiatives to legalise VoIP. An International Long Distance Telecommunication Services Policy has also been adopted, in order to issue licences to Bangladeshi entities.[40] Clearly, the caretaker government has been less swayed by private companies in terms of its policy formulation, and as a result government revenues began to increase again in 2007.

Iftekhar Zaman and Tanvir Mahmud (TI Bangladesh)

Additional reading

M. Ahmad and M. Farid, 'National Integrity Systems: Country Study Report, Bangladesh 2003' (Berlin: TI, 2004).

BRAC University, Institute of Governance Studies, 'The State of Governance in Bangladesh 2007' (Dhaka: BRAC University, 2008).

Global Integrity, *Global Integrity Report 2007* (Washington, DC: Global Integrity, 2008); available at report.globalintegrity.org.

Odhikar, 'Human Rights Concerns 2007' (Dhaka: Odhikar, 2008).

M. E. Porter and K. Schwab, *Global Competitiveness Report 2008–2009* (Geneva: World Economic Forum, 2008).

TI, *National Integrity Systems in South Asia* (Berlin: TI, 2006).

TI Bangladesh: www.ti-bangladesh.org.

---

39 *Daily Star* (Bangladesh), 10 October 2007; 15 January 2008; 15 August 2008.
40 *Daily Star* (Bangladesh), 1 September 2007.

People's Republic of China

Corruption Perceptions Index 2008: 3.6 (72nd out of 180 countries)

Conventions

ADB–OECD Anti-Corruption Action Plan for Asia-Pacific (endorsed April 2005)

UN Convention against Corruption (signed December 2003; ratified January 2006)

UN Convention against Transnational Organized Crime (signed December 2000; ratified September 2003)

Legal and institutional changes

- On 30 May 2007 the Central Government Anti-Business Bribery Leading Group, which has the responsibility for combating bribery under the Central Committee of the Communist Party of China (CPC), circulated a document entitled 'Suggestions on Deepening the Fight against Business Bribery'.[1] The document proposed intensifying inspections and speeding up the processing of business bribery cases, strengthening market monitoring and improving areas vulnerable to business bribery, such as construction projects, the grant of land use rights, the purchase of medical technology and medicines, and other forms of government procurement.

- On 8 June 2007 the Central Discipline Inspection Commission (CDIC) of the Communist Party of China circulated the 'Regulations on Prohibiting the Use of Official Positions for Unjust Gains'. The document defined some new types of corrupt activity, and required all CPC officials to carry out a self-evaluation and report to their supervisors within thirty days if they

had conducted any of those corrupt activities. The result of this measure has not been released yet.

- On 8 July 2007 the People's Supreme Court and the People's Supreme Procuratorate jointly issued the 'Suggestions on the Applicable Laws in Handling Some Bribery Cases'.[2] According to this new judicial interpretation, if any public servant takes advantage of his or her position to seek benefit for others or instructs others to give property to specified related parties (i.e. relatives, lovers, or those with whom he/she has a common interest), the person's activities shall be regarded as equivalent to accepting bribery. The document enlarges the scope of the individual by including the relatives and lovers of corrupt officials, not only corrupt officials and their spouses; provides a clearer definition of accepting bribes through intermediates; and closes the institutional loopholes created by the ambiguity of the criminal law in handling cases in which bribery has been accepted.

- Following four years' preparation, the National Bureau of Corruption Prevention (NBCP) was formally established on 13 September 2007.

---

1 *Procuratorial Daily* (China), 31 May 2007; www.jcrb.com/n1/jcrb1313/ca607979.htm.

2 Xinhua News Agency (China), 7 September 2007; www.lawinfochina.com/law/display.asp?id=6192&keyword=.

The vice-secretary of the CDIC and minister of supervision, Ma Wen, was selected as the director of the bureau.[3]

- On 6 November 2007 the 'Supplementary Regulations of the People's Supreme Court and the People's Supreme Procuratorate on Enforcing the Criminal Law and on the Determination of Some Criminal Terms' came into effect.[4] This judicial interpretation replaces the previous and out-of-date regulations on the 'crime of accepting bribery by company or enterprise staff' with the 'crime of accepting bribery by non-public official', and the 'crime of offering bribery by company or enterprise staff' with the 'crime of offering bribery by non-public official'. This represents a further improvement to the applicable scope of criminal sanctions with regard to bribery. As such, the crime of bribery is extended to all those with entrusted power.

- The State Council issued the 'Regulations on the Disclosure of Government Information' on 5 April 2008, which came into effect on 1 May 2008. The regulations set forth, among other things, the scope of the information to be disclosed, the forms and procedures for disclosure and the supervision mechanisms.

Corruption in the private sector: a new challenge for China

Corruption in the private sector in China has traditionally been severe and it remains one of the most commonly found forms of corruption. According to the statistics of the Ministry of Commerce, in the pharmaceutical industry, kickbacks for pharmaceuticals alone approach RMB772 million (US$110 million) of state

assets every year, an amount equivalent to approximately 16 per cent of the tax revenue for the whole pharmaceutical industry.[5]

In 2003 the US headquarters of Lucent Technologies Inc. dismissed four senior management staff of its company in China suspected of offering bribes in China.[6] In 2005 a public report by the US Department of Justice claimed that a Chinese subsidiary of US-based Diagnostic Products Corporation (DPC Tianjin) had paid approximately US$1.6 million in bribes in the form of illegal 'commissions' to physicians and laboratory staff employed by China's state-owned hospitals and was accused of violating the Foreign Corruption Practices Act of 1977.[7] Ultimately, DPC Tianjin paid a criminal penalty of US$2 million, and DPC paid approximately US$2.8 million, to the US Department of Justice and the US Securities and Exchange Commission, respectively.[8] These cases attracted wide media coverage in China.

Following such revelations, corruption in the private sector has gradually become better recognised as a challenge to the further development of China's economy. Previously, China put emphasis on fighting the demand side of corruption – generally public officials – while ignoring the role of suppliers, which were often private and multinational enterprises. As a result, corruption between actors in the private sector did not receive adequate attention. This pattern was exemplified by the rate of prosecutions between 1998 and 2002, when China's prosecution authorities placed 6,440 cases of bribery on file for investigation, far below the number of 207,103 crimes of 'taking advantage of duty' (such as accepting bribery and derelic-

3 China.com, 13 September 2007.
4 People's Supreme Procuratorate of China, 27 August 2007; www.spp.gov.cn/site2006/2008-06-21/0002419095.html.
5 *Beijing News* (China), 28 February 2006.
6 CFO.com (US), 7 April 2004.
7 US Department of Justice, press release, 20 May 2005.
8 Ibid.

tion of duty) subject to investigation.[9] Among all the cases of economic crime on file for investigation by the police, business bribery cases amounted to fewer than 1 per cent between 2000 and 2005.[10]

Outdated legislation constituted a barrier to anti-corruption activities in the private sector. Prior to 2005 the legal bases for investigating and punishing corruption in the private sector were mainly the Law against Unfair Competition 1993 and the Provisional Regulations on Prohibition of Business Bribery Activities 1996. Neither of these two laws authorised criminal sanctions for business bribery, however. The criminal law also defined the crime of accepting bribery narrowly, including only public officials. As such, private sector staff were not covered by the law, and there was no legal basis to impose criminal sanctions on them.

In November 2007 the judicial interpretation on offering bribes was changed to include non-public officials.[11] Despite this, the discovery and prosecution of private sector bribery is still insufficient. This reflects the fact that business bribery is often well hidden and difficult to detect by agencies, as the powers of investigation are dispersed among many government authorities and the provision of resources is limited. Business bribery is often disguised as, for example, technical service fees, consulting fees, trips and research. The coordination required between the People's Procuratorate, the public security authority, the People's Court, the administration for industry and commerce, the tax authority, the discipline supervision authority and the auditing authority further complicates matters.

China's progress against business bribery

Since March 2005 the Anti-Corruption and Governance Research Centre (ACGRC) at Tsinghua University has been promoting research into business bribery. With support from the China Society of Administrative Supervision (CSAS) and Transparency International, the ACGRC translated and published TI's 'Business Principles for Countering Bribery' into Chinese in 2005, which spearheaded the national anti-commercial bribery campaign in 2006.

In order to coordinate the nationwide anti-bribery work, involving various industries and sectors, a Central Anti-Business Bribery Leading Group was established with top leaders of twenty-two ministries. The group decided to focus on the areas most vulnerable to business bribery, such as construction projects, the grant of land use rights, the purchase of medical equipment and medicines, and government procurement.

Many ministries and provisional governments have followed the initiative of the group, by forming their own work plans to counter business bribery and facilitating anti-business bribery at various levels from policy to legislation to enforcement. The Ministry of Commerce established the United Supervision System on Business Credit. The State Administration for Industry and Commerce put its emphasis on business bribery in medicine procurement. The State Audit Office also prioritised business bribery in its annual audit work for 2006. All these have made business bribery a high-risk adventure. Given that, in the past, bribery receivers were subject to more stringent punishment than bribery suppliers,

---

9 Work Report by the Supreme People's Procuratorate to the tenth National People's Congress Standing Committee, March 2003; China.org, 11 March 2003.
10 *Beijing News* (China), 28 February 2006; www.bjreview.cn/EN/06-21-e/bus-1.htm.
11 See the legal and institutional changes section.

some local governments formulated their own blacklists for bribery suppliers.[12] Suppliers on the blacklists will be forbidden from participating in public bidding.

Since 1 January 2006 the database of crimes of bribery-offering, established by the procuratorate authorities, has been open to the public. Anyone can search the records of bribery-offering companies in the system.[13] The Bureau of Health in Beijing municipal government even established a system to denounce publicly those bribery suppliers in the course of medicine procurement, and as of 26 November 2007 twenty-one medical companies were blacklisted. For a period of two years those blacklisted medical companies would not be allowed to enter into the medicine procurement market in Beijing, and hospitals would not be able to purchase any products from them.[14]

Investigating and prosecuting business bribery cases has also become a focus for the discipline supervision authorities and the procuratorate authorities at all levels. The procuratorate authorities completed investigating over 31,119 business bribery cases, involving around US$7.08 billion, in the first eight months of 2007.[15]

Legislation applicable to business bribery has undergone continuous amendment. On 29 June 2006 the Standing Committee of the National People's Congress passed the 6th Amendment to the Criminal Law.[16] This amendment expanded the reach of the crime of business bribery from public official, company and enterprise staff to all people. On 6 November 2007 the 'Supplementary Regulations of the People's

Supreme Court and the People's Supreme Procuratorate on Enforcement of the Criminal Law on the Determination of Some Criminal Terms' came into effect.[17] This judicial interpretation replaces the 'crime of accepting bribery by company or enterprise staff' with the 'crime of accepting bribery by non-public official', and the 'crime of offering bribery by company or enterprise staff' with the 'crime of offering bribery by non-public official'. This represents a further improvement in the applicable scope of criminal sanctions regarding bribery. Those who can be accused of the crime of bribery are no longer limited to public officials, but all persons who may hold entrusted power.

China's anti-business bribery work shows that it has begun to fight against corruption from both the supply side and the demand side, and in a more balanced way. This new development has important strategic value for the prevention of corruption.

Integral social responsibilities as a common objective of Chinese enterprises

Fighting all forms of corruption (including extortion and bribery) is an important part of corporate social responsibility (CSR). In November 2005 the UN Global Compact summit was held in Shanghai. By 1 May 2008 ninety-one Chinese enterprises had signed the Global Compact, promising to fight against business bribery.[18] On 29 December 2007 the state-owned Asset Supervision and Administration Commission released the 'Guideline on Fulfilling Social Responsibility by Central Enterprises', requiring

---

12 Xinhuanet (China), 11 March 2006.
13 TI, 'National Integrity System Country Study Report: China' (Berlin: TI, 2006).
14 Jinghua Times (China), 27 November 2007; China.org, 29 November 2007.
15 *People's Daily* (China), 15 January 2008.
16 Xinhua News Agency (China), 29 June 2006.
17 People's Supreme Procuratorate of China, 27 August 2007; www.spp.gov.cn/site2006/2008-06-21/0002419095.html.
18 See http://gcp.cec-ceda.org.cn/joinin.html.

central government managing enterprises to take the lead in implementing their CSR, combating unfair competition and eliminating corrupt activities in business.[19]

On 16 May 2006 ACGRC and GE China hosted the Tsinghua/GE China Forum on Integrity Symposium on Controlling Business Bribery. The symposium addressed strategies for enterprises to combat business bribery and improvements to the relevant laws and regulations. The International Forum on China Corporation Social Responsibility has been held four times. In the third forum, on 16 January 2008, China Construction Bank, China Minmetals Corporation and Volkswagen Group (China) were named the Most Responsible Enterprises for 2007. The 2007 Golden Bee Ranking on Corporate Social Responsibility, which was organised by China Ocean Shipping (Group) Company (COSCO), BASF Corporation and *China WTO Tribune*, was released on 25 April 2008. Sixty of the 205 enterprises in the ranking stood out for their good quality.

One of the companies, COSCO, as a diversified cross-border service enterprise focusing mainly on shipping and modern logistics businesses, and one of the most responsible enterprises in China, took the position that fighting corruption would gain its customers' trust, contribute to a society with integrity and strengthen its employees' sense of belonging.[20] In 2005, COSCO joined the UN Global Compact and took various measures to prevent corruption. It established a department of supervision to strengthen administration over project evaluation, construction and public procurement. To create an integrity culture, COSCO kept a special anti-corruption volume on its website and invited the relatives of its middle-level management staff to join as 'part-time integrity supervisors'. The number of corruption cases discovered in COSCO decreased sharply, from 112 in 1997 to eleven in 2006.[21] This shows the impact of CSR on the creation of a society with integrity. With the deepening of China's economic reforms, more and more Chinese enterprises realise the importance of corporate social responsibility and, in particular, its role in the fight against corruption.

Guo Yong (ACGRC, Tsinghua University)

Additional reading

China Quarterly, 'Corruption in Transitional China: An Empirical Analysis', *China Quarterly*, vol. 194, no. 2 (2008).

Guo, Y., *Economic Transition, Institution and Corruption* (Beijing: Social Sciences Academic Press (China), 2007).

Ma, S. K., 'The Dual Nature of Anti-corruption Agencies in China', *Crime, Law and Social Change*, vol. 49, no. 2 (2008).

Ren, J., and Zhizhou, D., 'Institutionalized Corruption: Power Overconcentration of the First-in-Command in China', *Crime, Law and Social Change*, vol. 49, no. 1 (2008).

Ting, G., 'The Party Discipline Inspection in China: Its Evolving Trajectory and Embedded Dilemmas', *Crime, Law and Social Change*, vol. 49, no. 2 (2008).

Yan, S., 'Cadre Recruitment and Corruption: What Goes Wrong?', *Crime, Law and Social Change*, vol. 49, no. 1 (2008).

---

19 State Owned Assets Supervision and Administration Commission of the State Council, 29 December 2007.
20 *China WTO Tribune*, May 2007.
21 Ibid.

India

Corruption Perceptions Index 2008: 3.4 (85th out of 180 countries)

Conventions

ADB–OECD Anti-Corruption Action Plan for Asia-Pacific (endorsed November 2001)
UN Convention against Corruption (signed December 2005; not yet ratified)
UN Convention against Transnational Organized Crime (signed December 2002; not yet ratified)

Legal and institutional changes

- Although the Competition Act[1] was enacted by parliament in 2002, it remained largely a non-starter because of court cases filed by lawyers, mainly over the composition of the Competition Commission. The Supreme Court of India stayed the implementation of the provisions of the act in January 2005 and asked the government to amend the law. The government, after much deliberation and delay, amended the Competition Act in August 2007. With the passage of the amendments by parliament, it is expected that the commission will become fully operational by the end of 2008 or early 2009. In addition to its advocacy role,[2] which it already performs, the Competition Commission will be able to check corporate malpractice and abuse, the misuse of dominant positions and cartelisation. It will also have the power to enquire into mergers and acquisitions and prevent the formulation of conglomerates to the detriment of consumers. The act will assist the government in probing cartel-like behaviour.

It will put pressure on industry groups not to raise or lower prices for goods and services to their benefit in a pre-determined manner that incurs costs to consumer or user groups. The law will empower the government to refer complaints to the commission for enquiry and necessary action and it will have the power to investigate complaints, pass orders against companies and impose monetary penalties of up to Rs100 million (US$2.2 million). There is also a provision for three years in jail for offenders.

- In 2008 the country's central bank, the Reserve Bank of India (RBI), published guidelines for recovery agents.[3] They prescribe a code of conduct and procedure for recovery agents' training, and are intended to ensure that banks refrain from hiring disreputable people to recover debts and to prevent bad practice in the offering and management of loans by banks. They require the banks to follow the procedure prescribed by the law to recover loans and warn that, if the banks fail to mend their ways, the RBI as regulator will take action against the erring banks.

---

1 See www.cci.gov.in/.
2 As part of the advocacy role, the commission educates the stakeholders, including the federal government, states, corporations and chambers of commerce, about the provisions of law with regard to cartels, bid-rigging, intellectual property rights, abuse of dominance and compliance requirements for enterprises.
3 Circular on 24 April 2008; see www.rbi.org.

Stock market fraud: is SEBI consenting too freely?

India has witnessed stock market fraud by brokers in collusion with corporations that aim to cheat investors and circumvent the regulator, the Securities and Exchange Board of India (SEBI).

Two major securities scams have been publicised: the Harshad Mehta securities fraud and the Ketan Parekh scam.[4] Both scams were quite simple: brokers pushed up the prices of selected shares through artificial trade to attract retail investors and then suddenly withdrew from the trade. In several cases the share prices of bogus or paper companies were raised to very high levels.[5] Once the scandals had been exposed the share prices collapsed, resulting in huge losses to investors.

Another type of stock market fraud was exemplified by an initial public offering (IPO) scam. SEBI devised a formula for the allocation of shares, so as to encourage the participation of small investors in the market.[6] In order to corner the shares earmarked for small investors, however, some large companies and brokers opened fictitious bank accounts in large numbers and made applications through them.[7] SEBI enquired into the allocation of shares during IPOs, and a later formal investigation found that large numbers of multiple dematerialised accounts with common addresses had been opened in the name of *benami* (fictitious entities), with a view to taking the shares meant for smaller investors.[8]

On discovering the irregularities, the regulator passed an interim order in April 2006 directing the entities/persons who were alleged to have been responsible for the irregularities not to buy, sell or deal in the securities market, including in IPOs, directly or indirectly, until further notice. Through a consent order, however, the regulator dropped the proceedings against one financer after he had agreed to return the ill-gotten money and pay a consent fee of Rs100,000 (about US$2,200).[9]

Consent orders are one of the ways in which SEBI aims to tackle fraud and corruption. The consent order guidelines allow individuals, organisations and companies to pay monetary penalties for financial crimes, thus reducing SEBI's already strained workload. As such, consent orders achieve 'the twin goals of an appropriate sanction and deterrence without resorting to a long drawn litigation before SEBI/Tribunals/Courts. Passing of consent orders will also reduce regulatory costs and would save time and efforts taken in pursuing enforcement actions.'[10]

There is little inherent objection to the idea of SEBI deciding petty cases involving minor violations by means of consent orders. In theory, they would help the regulator to concentrate on bigger cases in which the violations are more serious. The reality is different, however. In some cases, it appears that SEBI has used its discretion to grant consent orders inappropriately.

For example, in the Ballarpur Industries Ltd scrip[11] case, SEBI passed a consent order in

---

4 D. Basu and S. Dalal, *From Harshad Mehta to Ketan Parekh: The Scam* (Mumbai: Kensource Information Services, 2005).
5 Meri News (India), 24 January 2008.
6 SEBI, 'Disclosure and Investor Protection Guidelines', 2000; available at www.sebi.gov.in.
7 *Hindu Business Line* (India), 13 January 2006. The findings of the investigation can be viewed at www.sebi.gov.in.
8 *Hindu Business Line* (India), 12 January 2006.
9 SEBI, consent order on the application submitted by M/s Pratik Pulp Pvt Ltd in the matter of irregularities relating to initial public offerings.
10 SEBI circular on consent orders, April 2007.
11 Scrip is a substitute for currency. It is not legal tender and is often a form of credit.

favour of a dealer of UTI Securities Ltd. The dealer was accused of 'passing on information to certain individuals regarding the impending large sales to be carried out by an institutional client. These individuals, in turn, short sold the scrip in large quantities prior to the large sale orders and bought them subsequently at lower prices.'[12] As a result of these serious accusations, in April 2008 the dealer was required to pay only Rs100,000 (US$2,200) for the consent order.[13]

Consent orders were also approved in cases involving the Adani Group. The gravity of the charges, which were washed away as a result of the consent order, can be ascertained from the order itself. According to the Securities Appellate Tribunal, which approved the consent order in the Adani case, '[I]nvestigations . . . revealed that there was an association between Ketan Parekh group of entities and Adani group . . . [T]here was a movement of shares from Adani Group to Ketan Parekh and vice versa and . . . there was also movement of funds from Adani Group of companies to Ketan Parekh entities.'[14] Furthermore, a detailed enquiry 'established that various market irregularities/illegalities had been committed during the course of the trading in the scrip of the company'.[15] On 25 May 2007 SEBI prohibited Adani Properties Ltd from accessing capital markets for two years. In May 2008, however, one appellant paid Rs1,050,000 (US$23,100) and others paid Rs750,000 (US$16,500) each to the regulator under the terms of the order. Since the Adani Group is a major consortium managed by a billionaire, Gautam Adani, the monetary penalties are not significant to the company.[16]

During the course of the last year SEBI has issued many consent orders. It is deciding cases pertaining to the Ketan Parekh securities scandal, the IPO scam and insider trading. According to the guidelines, consent orders should be reserved for cases that do not require fuller investigation and enforcement. It is questionable, however, whether all these cases fit this description.[17]

Stealing certificates: corruption in private education

Strong economic growth in recent years has resulted in the proliferation of institutions for technical education in India. Their conduct is not always above board, however. Some institutions, particularly those managed by private individuals or trusts, use the absence of adequate regulations in this area to exploit the situation of students by adopting unethical and coercive methods.

The problem with these institutions arises when they admit students to their courses well ahead of the beginning of the academic year and charge them the full tuition fee in advance. Students then may achieve better grades than predicted, thus entitling them to attend school elsewhere, or they may simply change their minds and wish to attend an alternative institution. In this case, the institutions are reluctant to refund the fees. Moreover, institutions often ask students to deposit their original educational certificates so as to prevent them from joining other institutions.[18]

As a result of such coercive actions, students are stuck with one institution. These prac-

---

12 Consent order, Ballarpur Industries Ltd, 17 April 2008. The consent order was submitted by Shri Raajeev Kasat.
13 Ibid.
14 *Adani Properties* v. *Securities and Exchange Board of India*, Securities Appellate Tribunal, Mumbai, 24 April 2008.
15 Ibid.
16 Draft Red Herring Prospectus (DRHP) filed by Adani Power Ltd with SEBI on 5 May 2008.
17 See www.sebi.gov.in/Index.jsp?contentDisp=WhatsNew. SEBI has laid down the procedure, but not the criteria, for the selection of cases in connection with the issuance of consent orders.
18 *The Hindu* (India), 30 June 2007.

tices amount to trapping students and making unlawful gains, as the students forfeit full course fees amounting to hundreds of thousands of rupees. In a recent case, for example, a student sought admission onto a course only to learn later that it was not recognised by the government. The student did have the fees refunded, however, after the case moved to the consumer court.[19]

In order to prevent the exploitation of students by technical institutes, the regulator, the All India Council for Technical Education (AICTE), issued a public notice asking institutes to refund fees if a student decides to leave an institution before beginning the course.[20] Similarly, the AICTE asked the institutes not to keep students' original certificates in order to 'force retention of admitted students'.[21]

The public notice, which was issued with a view to checking the commercial practices of technical education, would prevent institutions from adopting unethical methods to confiscate fees and force students to join a particular institute. Students already have the right to seek redress in court. Often it is not possible for students to seek legal recourse, however, as the process is cumbersome. Many students therefore forgo their claims, resulting in financial gains for the institutions.

TI India

Additional reading

S. K. Barua and J. R. Varma, *Great Indian Scam: Story of the Missing Rs4,000 Crore* (New Delhi: Vision Books, n.d.).

D. Basu and S. Dalal, *From Harshad Mehta to Ketan Parekh: The Scam* (Mumbai: Kensource Information Services, 2005).

K. N. Gupta, *Corruption in India* (New Delhi: Anmol Publications, 2001).

ICMR Center for Management Research, *The Ketan Parekh Scam: A Case Study* (Hyderabad: ICMR Center for Management Research, 2002).

S. M. Joshi, *Corruption in India: Ramifications and Remedies* (Mumbai: Popular Prakashan, 2005).

N. Vittal, *Corruption in India: The Roadblock to National Prosperity* (New Delhi: Academic Foundation, 2003).

TI India: www.tiindia.in.

---

19 *Hindustan Times* (India), 22 July 2007.
20 The public notice was issued on 14 September; see Indiaedunews.net, 14 September 2008.
21 *Hindustan Times* (India), 15 May 2008.

Indonesia

Corruption Perceptions Index 2008: 2.6 (126th out of 180 countries)

Conventions

ADB–OECD Anti-Corruption Action Plan for Asia-Pacific (endorsed November 2001)

UN Convention against Corruption (signed December 2003; ratified September 2006)

UN Convention against Transnational Organized Crime (signed December 2000; not yet ratified)

Legal and institutional changes

- With the 2009 general election in sight, a set of regulations is being developed to amend and regroup five different laws under a package law (paket UU Politik). The five laws relate to political parties (Law no. 31/2002), general elections (Law no. 12/2003), tools and procedures (Law no. 22/2003), presidential elections (Law no. 23/2003) and local government and local elections (Law no. 32/2004).[1] The House of Representatives (DPR) ratified the law on political parties on 19 January 2008.[2] Another law covering local and general elections was ratified on 31 March 2008.[3] The amendment of the law on local government and local elections was adopted by parliament in April 2008 and will take effect one month after it has been signed by the president.[4] The laws on presidential elections and on tools and procedures are currently being discussed in parliament.[5] Although such laws

are urgently needed to clarify election and political party regulations, several anti-corruption organisations have voiced concerns about the loophole left in political parties' financing.[6]

- The new law on political parties allows for increased individual and corporate contributions to political parties. Individuals are now allowed to donate up to R1 billion (over US$107,000), a tenfold increase from the previous limit. A significant increase was also approved for corporate contributions, from R750 million to R4 billion – R5 billion for a general election campaign. This is of particular concern, given that the law does not prevent different companies from the same group, or employees of the companies, from donating to political parties. Indeed, previous civil society monitoring initiatives revealed that the corporate financing of political parties through employees' accounts or through fictional companies set up by a holding company

---

1 Kompas (Indonesia), 'Paket UU Politik Jadi Prioritas Utama 2007', press release, 13 October 2006.

2 Law no. 2/2008 (UU no. 2 tahun 2008).

3 Law no. 10/2008 (UU no. 10 tahun 2008). The general election law covers the election of the National and Regional House of Representatives and the regional representative council (DPD).

4 *Tribun Jabar* (Indonesia), 2 April 2008.

5 Suara Karya Online (Indonesia), 28 October 2008.

6 Civil society coalition *Koalisi Ornop untuk Perubahan Paket UU Politik,* composed of PSHK-CETRO-LSPP-IPC-DEMOS-YAPPIKA-GPSP-PERLUDEM-ICW-TII-FORMAPPI-KRHNJPPR-LP3ES-DEL Inst.

was a common practice.[7] Donations by party members are unlimited, which some argue could have the effect of paving the way for seat-buying.[8]

- According to the same law, financial management and reporting procedures now depend on the parties' own internal regulations. An external audit by a public accountant is imposed only in the case of government funding to political parties, and does not cover private donations. The law on general elections requires all candidates and political parties to open a single account for donations within three days of their official nomination. Although political parties are obliged to submit a financial report to be audited by public accountants, there is no standard reporting format.[9] The lack of available accredited accountants, coupled with the absence of a standard reporting format, raises concerns about the capacity of the General Election Commission (KPU) to monitor and detect irregularities in political party financing efficiently.[10] Moreover, it is still unclear how donations made before the opening of the special account or outside the campaign period can be accounted for.

- The long-awaited law on freedom of information was ratified on 3 April 2008, almost five years after the first draft was submitted to parliament. This is the first comprehensive law regulating the public's right to information and outlining the obligations for public agencies in terms of information disclosure. The law regulates the kind of information to

be disclosed as well as the type of information that can be exempted and for how long. The law has institutionalised the Information Commission as an independent regulating agency mandated to handle disputes related to disclosure obligations defined by the law. Several limitations have been identified, however, including the fact that state-owned companies, notably national oil and mining companies, are not subject to the obligations. There is also an article on the criminalisation of misuse of public information that is perceived as an attempt to restrain the freedom of the media, as it does not clearly define what would constitute 'misuse'. Nevertheless, the law has set in motion moves towards increased transparency, and it also has a strategic role to play in complementing existing anti-corruption laws.

- A new Presidential Instruction was issued in December 2007, under Presidential Decree no. 80/2003 on public procurement, to establish an independent National Procurement Policies Office (NPPO). The NPPO is mandated to regulate public procurement and address inefficiency and under-spending of national and local budgets. According to the Commission for the Eradication of Corruption (KPK), around 30 per cent of the national procurement budget is lost to corruption each year,[11] while officials' lack of understanding of procurement regulations and tender procedures causes significant delays in budget implementation (20 per cent of 2007's national procurement budget

7 TI Indonesia, 'Laporan Studi: Standar Akuntansi Keuangan khusus partai politik' (Jakarta: TI Indonesia, 2003); TI Indonesia and Indonesia Corruption Watch (ICW), 'Modul Pemantauan Dana Kampanye' (Jakarta: TI Indonesia/Indonesia Corruption Watch, 2004). TI Indonesia and ICW found out about such irregularities while monitoring the 2004 elections.

8 T. Friend, 'History, Destiny, Ballots: Indonesia and East Timor', E-Notes July (Philadelphia: Foreign Policy Research Institute, 1999).

9 Article 39 of Law no. 2/2008 on political parties.

10 Indonesia Corruption Watch and Union of Indonesian Public Accountants (IAPI), 'Audit Dana Kampanye Rawan Pelanggaran', press release, 17 October 2008.

11 See www.majalahkonstan.com/index.php?option=com_content&task=view&id=844.

was still unspent by November 2007).[12] The National Development and Planning Agency expects that improved regulatory and supervisory frameworks could help curb corruption and increase the efficiency of public procurement by 30 to 40 per cent.[13] The NPPO, however, has not been granted the authority to handle complaints and arbitrate litigations. Complaints are instead submitted to the head of the relevant public department for arbitration. The National Ombudsman Office welcomes complaints, but can issue recommendations or report cases only to relevant authorities.

Corruption and environmental destruction

Indonesia is known as one of the most biodiverse countries in the world. Unfortunately, it also tops the list of the fastest destroyers of forests, clearing 1.87 million hectares of forest annually between 2000 and 2005. Indonesia has already lost more than 72 per cent of its intact forest and 40 per cent of its forests completely.[14] At the current deforestation rate, the lowland forests of Sumatra and Borneo will be virtually wiped out by 2022. Illegal logging takes place in thirty-seven out of forty-one national parks. In addition to the tremendous ecological cost, illegal logging costs the nation up to US$4 billion a year.[15]

In 2007 the national media were flooded with reports of corruption related to illegal logging or irregularities in the issuing of licenses and concessions. Numerous controversial court decisions in this area have also raised concerns about the integrity of the judiciary. The website illegal-logging.info reported in November 2007 that seven illegal logging cases were dismissed in West Sumatra in the previous year, fourteen suspects were freed in Papua and several others were acquitted in Aceh and West Kalimantan. In most instances, moreover, the suspects were freed by the courts despite what many officials said was 'compelling evidence they were involved in illegal logging'.[16]

On 5 November 2007 timber baron Adelin Lis was acquitted of corruption and illegal logging charges, despite 'a strong government case against him, including nearly forty eye-witnesses'.[17] This affair shed light on the links between environmental destruction, judicial corruption and political interference. In the case of Adelin, the controversy went as high as the forestry minister, M. S. Kaban, who issued a letter – later used by Adelin's defence team – stating that Adelin's activities were not a crime but an administrative error.[18]

Speculation about judicial corruption was fuelled by the Supreme Court's decision to promote four of the five judges who acquitted Adelin. Local media also reported that the police had been trying to work out why Adelin was released on the basis of an executive order dated 1 November, while the court did not hand down its judgment until four days later.[19] This early release allowed him to escape arrest on new charges of money laundering, scheduled for 6 November. Adelin

12 *Kontan* (Indonesia), 26 December 2007.

13 *Pikiran Rakyat*, 'LKPP Harus Jadi Alat Kontrol Jadi Acuan Daerah Dalam Tender Pembangunan', 2 January 2008.

14 Greenpeace Southeast Asia, 'Indonesia, a Great Country?', 30 August 2005; available at www.greenpeace.org/raw/content/seasia/en/press/reports/indonesian-deforestation-facts.pdf.

15 Telapak and Environmental Investigation Agency (EIA), 'The Thousand-headed Snake: Forest Crimes, Corruption and Injustice in Indonesia' (London/EIA: Telapak, 2007).

16 Illegal-logging.info, 'Red Faces over Lumber Boss' Acquittal', 16 November 2007.

17 *Jurnal Nasional* (Indonesia), 27 November 2007.

18 *Jakarta Post* (Indonesia), 19 July 2007.

19 Illegal-logging.info, 2007.

has since disappeared and is believed to have fled abroad.[20]

Political corruption in the issuing of licences and concessions for logging activities was also revealed after Bintan (Riau province) regency secretary Azirwan and House of Representatives lawmaker Al Amin Nasution were arrested by the KPK on 9 April 2008. Al Amin Nasution was caught receiving R4 million (US$430) from Azirwan, while R67 million (US$7,200) was seized from Nasution's car. Furthermore, KPK deputy chairman Mochammad Jasin said Azirwan promised Nasution an additional R3 billion (US$320,000) for a deal to convert about 200 hectares out of 7,300 hectares of conservation forest in Bintan, Riau Islands, into an administration office complex.[21] Nasution, a member of the House's Commission IV overseeing forestry, was being held and awaiting trial at the time of writing.

The building of political connections between illegal-logging syndicates and local officials has become obvious, highlighting the direct involvement of unscrupulous officials in the trade of illegal logs. The case of Marthen Rumadas in Papua is a telling example. Although he was removed from his position as senior local forestry official in Sorong, Papua, charged with the illegal smuggling of timber, Rumadas forged political alliances with powerful forces involved in creating the new province of Irian Jaya Barat. Despite being tried in another case of timber permit violation, he rose to the position of regional secretary, making him the third most powerful figure in the provincial government.[22]

Airline passengers' safety for sale

Deregulation of the airline sector in the late 1990s allowed a rapid expansion of the industry. The number of airline passengers tripled between 2000 and 2006, while the number of airlines increased from five to twenty-five. Such a rapid expansion generated many safety issues as well as opportunities for corrupt practices.[23]

According to official statistics, an aircraft incident was recorded in 2006 every nine to ten days in Indonesia, and the situation has not improved.[24] The crash of an Adam Air aeroplane in Batam on 10 March 2008 was the latest of a worrying series of incidents. Fourteen months earlier Adam Air flight 574 had crashed in the waters of Majene, West Sulawesi, killing eighty-five people.[25] An investigation then revealed serious deficiencies in maintenance and safety procedures, leading to a three-month suspension of the airline's licence. This had raised considerable public attention about the condition of the airline's fleet and irregularities in licensing, inspections and safety procedures in one of the fastest-growing aviation markets in the world.

The definition of a flightworthy airliner is not strictly regulated[26] and there is no minimum investment for starting up an airline company. Although the Civil Aviation Safety Regulations set minimum conditions, anyone can become the director of an airline.[27] According to a *Tempo* source, 'It is usually R500 million (US$53,000) per airline business license'.[28] As such, many directors lack experience, contributing to a situation in which, according to National Transportation

---

20 *Jurnal Nasional* (Indonesia), 27 November 2007.

21 Coordinating Ministry for Economic Affairs, *Trade and Investment News*, 14 April 2008.

22 Telapak and EIA, 2007.

23 *Tempo* (Indonesia), 1–7 April 2008.

24 BBC (UK), 18 January 2007.

25 *Tempo* (Indonesia), 1–7 April 2008.

26 Ibid.

27 Samudra Sukardi, former deputy chairman of the Indonesian National Air Carriers Association, quoted from *Tempo* (Indonesia), 2008.

28 *Tempo* (Indonesia), 2008.

Safety Committee member Captain Prita Wijaya, 60 to 70 percent of airline accidents are due to management's lack of attention.[29]

In a country in which about a half of the 262 airliners are at least twenty years old, maintenance and compliance checks with safety standards are critical. The National Transportation Safety Committee's investigation of the Majene tragedy revealed that the malfunction of a navigational instrument was one of the main causes of the accident. Records show that this device had malfunctioned 154 times in the previous three months, but there was no record of repairs or maintenance.[30]

Following the publication of the investigation report, several former Adam Air pilots reported being pressured by management to put safety considerations aside.[31] Airlines are responsible for the expenses related to inspections, 'including daily expenses, air tickets, and accommodation'[32] for the inspectors, which can potentially lead to conflicts of interest and put the quality of inspections in doubt. In addition, it is alleged that 'all matters regarding certificates, which include operating permits, pilot license extensions, increasing pilot ratings and even airplane flightworthiness, can be resolved by paying money. Even if all the conditions are met, you still have to fork over some money.'[33] The institutionalisation of such bribery acts as a disincentive to invest in maintenance and training costs, as money is needed regardless of standards in order to obtain licences.

The investigation also revealed insufficient pilot training. Even the testing and certification of graduating students appears subject to corruption. According to a *Tempo* source at the Inspectorate General of the Transportation Department, considerable amounts have to be paid for a pilot's licence: 'At the very least, be ready with R500,000. More, if he doesn't meet the requirements.'[34]

In order to address some of these issues, the director of the Air Transportation Department suggested establishing a non-tax state income to be paid by airlines or aviation factories.[35] This money would allow inspectors to be dispatched to validate newly acquired aeroplanes without the intrinsic relationship present when airlines pay for inspections directly. Furthermore, the withdrawal of Adam Air's licence is an encouraging sign that the authorities are taking a stricter stance towards enforcing air safety regulations. It is the first time the administrative sanction of Government Regulation no. 3 on Air Transport Security and Safety has actually been implemented for a major company.[36] Besides Adam Air, six other companies were listed in the same category in 2007.[37]

It can only be hoped that sanctioning Adam Air signals a government commitment to enforcing safety regulations more strictly, and that Indonesian airlines will realise it is in their best interest to invest in developing their human resources, maintenance and supervision procedures.

TI Indonesia

---

29 National Transportation Safety Committee member Captain Prita Wijaya.
30 National Transportation Safety Committee; www.dephub.go.id.
31 *Asia Times* (Hong Kong), 24 January 2007.
32 *Tempo* (Indonesia), 1–7 April 2008.
33 Ibid.
34 Ibid.
35 Ibid.
36 On 26 June 2007 the licence of Jatayu Airlines, a small airline operating domestic flights, was revoked.
37 ANTARA (Indonesia), 'Tak Satu Pun Maskapai Penuhi Syarat Keselamatan Penerbangan Sipil', 22 March 2007; 'Arisan Maut!', Edisi cetak harian Surya Surabaya, 23 March 2007. Besides Adam Air and Jatayu Airlines, all five other airlines listed in category III are still operating.

Additional reading

S. Davidsen, V. Juwono and D. G. Timberman, *Curbing Corruption in Indonesia, 2004–2006: A Survey of National Policies and Approaches* (Washington, DC: United States–Indonesia Society and Center for Strategic and International Studies, 2006).

ICW, *Corruption Assessment and Compliance – United Nations Convention against Corruption (UNCAC) 2003 in Indonesian Law* (Jakarta: ICW, 2008).

KPK, *Identification of Gaps between Laws/ Regulations of the Republic of Indonesia and the United Nations Convention against Corruption* (Jakarta: KPK, 2006).

Partnership for Governance Reform in Indonesia, *Fighting Corruption from Aceh to Papua* (Jakarta: Partnership for Governance Reform in Indonesia, 2006).

TI, *Corruption Perception Index* (Berlin: TI, 2006).

Curbing Corruption in Public Procurement: Experiences from Indonesia, Malaysia and Pakistan (Berlin: TI, 2006).

TI Indonesia: www.ti.or.id.

Japan

Corruption Perceptions Index 2008: 7.3 (18th out of 180 countries)

Conventions

ADB–OECD Anti-Corruption Action Plan for Asia-Pacific (endorsed November 2001)

OECD Convention on Combating Bribery of Foreign Public Officials (signed December 1997; ratified October 1998)

UN Convention against Corruption (signed December 2003; not yet ratified)

UN Convention against Transnational Organized Crime (signed December 2000; not yet ratified)

Legal and institutional changes

- The Act on Prevention of Transfer of Criminal Proceeds came into force partially in April 2007 and fully in March 2008. The act obliges financial institutions, leasing and real estate businesses, and other operators except for lawyers to ensure client identification and secure transaction records, as well as to report any suspicious transactions to the financial authorities.[1] Legal and accounting professionals are subject to the former obligations but not the latter. An original draft covered all these professions, but, faced with strong

---

[1] See www.npa.go.jp/sosikihanzai/jafic/horei/Lawptcp.pdf#search='Act on Prevention of Transfer of Criminal Proceeds' and www.mofa.go.jp/announce/announce/2008/4/1179305_1000.html.

opposition especially from bar associations, the Diet (parliament) enacted a final version that relieves legal and accounting professionals from the reporting obligations.[2] The legislation therefore is a step forward, even though the complicated issue of lawyer and accountant disclosure was not resolved.

- A bill for revising the Political Funds Control Law, aimed at increasing the transparency of funding flows to lawmakers, was enacted in January 2008. The amendment mainly addresses political organisations related to Diet members. The law as amended requires 'Diet member-related political organisations' to submit receipts for expenditures greater than ¥10,000 (US$100), along with a political funds report, to the Ministry of Internal Affairs and Communications and to prefectural election commissions. Beginning in 2009 those political organisations will be obliged to keep receipts for expenditures of ¥10,000 or less, and these receipts in principle are subject to disclosure if a request is filed. The law introduces an audit system for the financial reports of political organisations that will start in fiscal year 2009, and it sets up an expert committee to study and review the audit system.

Falsifying product quality

It was revealed in October 2007 that Nichias Corp. had fabricated data related to the performance of its fire-resistant construction material.[3] Despite an in-house inspection conducted a year earlier that detected the problem, Nichias's president ordered it to be covered up because of concerns that it would cause trouble for its clients, which are major housing builders.[4] Only after receiving an anonymous letter warning that the wrongdoing would be revealed unless it was appropriately addressed did the company feel compelled to report the data fabrication to the Ministry of Land, Infrastructure and Transport. The company admitted that the fabrication had begun in 2001, in order to gain a competitive edge against rival manufacturers by making it easier to pass fire resistance tests that the government had started in 2000.[5] The housing materials at issue are fire-resisting panels for the interior side of roofs. Nichias admitted it had subjected the materials to two to six times more water than normal in order to enhance the fire-resistant quality and pass the government's test.[6] There is no report on possible bribery or collusion between the company and the testing or inspecting company, but the fabrication continued for nearly fifteen years, leading to a loss of integrity and deceiving many clients and markets.

Nichias's announcement prompted another manufacturer to reveal its own data fabrication. Toyo Tire & Rubber Co. stated one day after the Nichias statement that it too had fabricated data concerning urethane fire-resistant panels used for housing walls and ceilings.[7] The panels, found to be three times more flammable than government certification allowed, were shipped to housing builders nationwide and used in at least 176 buildings across the country, including two public school buildings.[8]

Following these revelations the land ministry conducted a nationwide survey of building materials, covering some 14,000 items. The ministry announced in January 2008 that, among those checked, forty-five companies had submitted false specifications for government inspection

---

2 *Japan Times*, 7 March 2008.
3 *Nippon Keizai Shimbun* (Japan), 31 October 2007; 2–3 November 2007.
4 *Daily Yomiuri* (Japan), 1 November 2007.
5 *Kyodo News* (Japan), 2 November 2007.
6 *Daily Yomiuri* (Japan), 3 November 2007.
7 *Nippon Keizai Shimbun* (Japan), 6 November 2007; *Kyodo News* (Japan), 5 November 2007.
8 *Daily Yomiuri* (Japan), 7 November 2007.

or sold products that did not meet government certification, and three major building materials manufacturers sold products with substandard fireproof capabilities, leaving 786 houses in need of repair. Among the companies are three Tokyo-based construction material manufacturers: Nippon Light Metal Co., YKK AP Inc. and Nichibosai.[9] The findings resonated strongly in an earthquake-prone nation that still clearly remembers a 2005 case in which an architect and other collaborators fabricated earthquake-resistant data in building designs.[10]

Besides the fireproof scandals, early 2008 witnessed a different kind of product quality falsification. In January Nippon Paper Group Inc., the second largest paper manufacturer in Japan, revealed that it had sold recycled paper products containing smaller than the claimed amounts of used paper. Following the announcement, major manufacturers of electrical appliances, including Fuji Xerox Co., Konika Minolta Holdings Inc. and Ricoh Co., which Nippon Paper supplied with paper, announced that they would stop selling Nippon Paper's recycled copy and printer paper.[11] Suspicions had first been raised after recently privatised Japan Post Holdings Co. alleged that major paper manufacturer Oji Paper Co. misrepresented the amount of recycled paper in New Year's greeting cards.

Among paper products subject to the law requiring central and local governments to consider environmental protection when making purchases, the actual ratio of waste paper used by Nippon Paper was 59 per cent for copy paper, compared with the company's claim of 100 per cent; 35 per cent for notebook paper, against 80 per cent; and 50 per cent for printing paper, against 70 per cent.[12] The practice had started

in 1992, with the company explaining that it falsified used paper ratios to make the products look more environmentally friendly, since it was difficult to raise the ratios without hurting product quality.

Oji Paper, Japan's largest paper-maker, and three other major paper manufacturers admitted to similar falsifications.[13] Another paper manufacturer joined the group a few days later. Analysts say falsifications are a widespread practice in the industry, reflecting the fierce competition to produce higher-quality recycled products.[14]

These cases of fabrication and falsification indicate that some, though not all, Japanese businesses still exhibit a traditional convoy mentality, in which they do not feel safe unless they maintain equality with their competitors, leaving themselves insensitive to any harm they might cause their clients and consumers. One of the laws related to fireproofing fabrications is the Building Standards Act, though it does not impose a penalty on violators in such fire resistance quality cases. Amending legislation to introduce penalties could be effective if passed and relatively easy to realise, potentially preventing recurrences of similar wrongdoing.

Suspicions of foreign bribery

The Japanese government has been criticised by civil society for not putting enough energy into enforcing laws against foreign bribery, despite its ratification of the OECD Anti-Bribery Convention of 1997. Although there have been sporadic reports of Japanese companies' dubious transactions abroad, the law enforcement authorities have not taken enough action. Only in March 2007 did police bring one minor case of foreign

---

9 *Japan Times,* 26 January 2008.
10 *Nikkei* (Japan), 26 December 2005.
11 *Japan Times,* 18 January 2008.
12 Ibid.
13 *Japan Times,* 19 January 2008.
14 *Japan Times,* 21 January 2008.

bribery into summary court indictment. Officials of a subsidiary of a major power company in western Japan were charged with paying for Filipino public officials' golf sets in return for awarding a contract. The company officials were ordered to pay US$7,500 in fines.[15]

The tide began to turn in 2008. In February a major tyre manufacturer, Bridgestone Corp., admitted its involvement in improper payments to foreign agents, including foreign governmental officials,[16] and that it had set up an investigative committee including outside lawyers and experts. Analysts say that suspicions emerged during a Fair Trade Commission investigation into a cartel allegedly formed on sales of rubber marine hoses, and Bridgestone was one of the parties.[17] The company said that it has cooperated with the relevant authorities, including the US Department of Justice and the Japanese Public Prosecutor's Office. At the time of writing, no arrests or indictments had been reported.

Another allegation of a Japanese company involved in overseas bribery emerged in April 2008.[18] The case has been widely reported subsequently, and it could develop as the first major prosecution of foreign bribery in Japan. Suspicion reportedly surfaced with a confession by a former executive of construction consultancy Pacific Consultants International (PCI). Prosecutors were questioning him on suspicion of swindling the government out of hundreds of millions of yen by overcharging for a government project to dispose of chemical weapons abandoned by the Imperial Japanese Army in China at the end of World War II.[19] The former

executive reportedly told prosecutors that he bribed a Vietnamese official twice between 2003 and 2006 – under instructions from his superior, the company's then president – to get a contract for a government road construction project in Ho Chi Minh City.[20] The city undertook the project with financing from Japan's official development assistance. The bribes allegedly paid by the former PCI executive may have totalled about ¥90 million (US$870,000). Four former executives and PCI as a legal person were indicted in August 2008 on charges of foreign bribery under the Unfair Competition Prevention Act.[21]

The Japanese Ministry of Justice has asked the Vietnamese government for mutual legal assistance, but in vain to date.[22] The prosecutor's office tried to establish the case without obtaining confessions from the recipient side – an unusual step.

Toru Umeda (TI Japan)

Additional reading

N. Akiyama, *Bouei-Gigoku* [*Defence Ministry Scandals*] (Tokyo: Koudansha, 2008).

J. Kawada, *Oshoku/Fuhai/Kuraienterizumu-no-Seijigaku* [*Politics of Clientship*] (Kyoto: Minervashobo, 2008).

A. Wakabayashi, *Koumuin-no-Ijouna-Sekai* [*Unbelievable Stories of the Public Officials' World*] (Tokyo: Gentosha, 2008).

S. Yahagi, *Nippon: Fuhai-no-Ohkoku* [*Japan: The Kingdom of Corruption*] (Tokyo: Bungeisha, 2008).

TI Japan: www.ti-j.org.

---

15 *Japan Times*, 2 March 2007.
16 Bridgestone Corp., 'Investigations on Improper Payments to Foreign Agents and an Interim Report', press release, 23 May 2008.
17 *International Herald Tribune* (US), 12 February 2008.
18 *Japan Times*, 25 April 2008.
19 Japan Times Online, 16 May 2008.
20 *Japan Times* 16 May 2008; 26 August 2008.
21 *Japan Times*, 26 August 2008.
22 *Yomiuri Shimbun* (Japan), 26 August 2008.

Malaysia

Corruption Perceptions Index 2008: 5.1 (47th out of 180 countries)

Conventions

UN Convention against Corruption (signed December 2003; ratified September 2008)

Legal and institutional changes

- The twelfth general election in Malaysia, held on 8 March 2008, sent shock waves throughout the country.[1] For the first time since 1969 the ruling party, the Barisan Nasional (National Front) coalition, lost its two-thirds parliamentary majority. In addition, it lost four more states to the opposition compared to the 2004 election, to make it five in total. In 2004 the administration headed by Abdullah Ahmad Badawi had been voted in with the strongest ever mandate for an incumbent, specifically to clean up the decaying state of Malaysian institutions.[2] It has failed in many areas, however, especially in addressing corruption. The 2008 election results sent a very clear signal to the ruling party about the level of popular dissatisfaction with, among other things, the unbearable effects of corruption. The main opposition parties (which have subsequently restyled themselves as the Citizens' Coalition – Pakatan Rakyat)[3] ran on the platform of transparency, accountability and good governance and were able to capitalise on the discontent of the people.

- The Malaysian Anti-Corruption Academy (MACA) was launched by the prime minister on 12 April 2007. The MACA is intended to be the regional hub for anti-corruption capacity and capability building to fight corruption, by promoting best practices in investigation, monitoring and enforcement and by venturing into new areas such as forensic accounting and forensic engineering.[4]

- In a speech given at the ASEAN (Association of South East Asian Nations) Integrity Dialogue[5] on 21 April 2008, Badawi proposed the following measures to address public concerns. First, the Anti-Corruption Agency (ACA) would be restructured to become a fully fledged Malaysian Commission on Anti-Corruption (MCAC). The MCAC would report to a newly set up independent Corruption Prevention Advisory Board, to be appointed by the Supreme Ruler (head of state) on the advice of the prime minister. The board would advise the MCAC on administrative and operational matters. Second, the prime minister proposed setting up a Parliamentary Committee on the Prevention of Corruption. Finally, he introduced a proposal to protect whistleblowers

---

1 See www.asli.com.my/DOCUMENTS/An%20Analysis%20of%20Malaysia.pdf.
2 J. Liow, 'The Politics behind Malaysia's Eleventh General Election', *Asian Survey,* vol. 45, no. 6 (2005).
3 Global Information Network, 'Malaysia: Opposition Parties Form Formidable Coalition', 8 April 2008; accessed at www.proquest.com/ (accessed 9 October 2008).
4 See www.bpr.gov.my/maca/cda/m_about_us/about_maca.php.
5 See www3.pmo.gov.my/?menu=speech&page=1676&news_id=71&speech_cat=2.

and witnesses. All these reforms have yet to be implemented, however.

- The Malaysian Institute of Integrity (MII – Institut Integriti Malaysia) also stepped up its efforts when it launched two major publications, *National Integrity System: A Guiding Framework* and *Corporate Social Responsibility: Our First Look*.[6] This was part of its ongoing collaborative effort with UNDP Malaysia to develop the necessary human capital and knowledge resources within the institute.

- Penang state has introduced several measures to improve the regulatory environment with regard to government procurement,[7] in what is referred to as a CAT – a Competent, Accountable and Transparent – government. It is the first state government to implement the open tender system for government procurement and contracts. As an example, in civil works, contractors are able to bid in an open tender process and to review the successful contractors and object if they are not satisfied. Furthermore, the Penang government has issued a directive whereby all administrators and state executive councillors are not allowed to make any new land applications. It has also invited professionals to serve on various boards, such as the Penang State Appeals Board, and has established a Working Professional Committee comprising individuals from five different professional bodies to improve land procedures.

- The implementation of the watered-down Independent Police Complaints and Misconduct Commission (IPCMC) to a Special Complaints Commission (SCC) indicates the inability of the government to regulate gatekeepers.[8] The IPCMC, which was the recommendation of the 2005 Royal Commission, was diluted after open revolt[9] from the top brass of the Royal Malaysian Police. The bill that was subsequently produced prompted concerns that the recommendations of the Royal Commission were not adequately reflected, particularly with regard to the proposed SCC's independence and investigative powers. Not only did the bill grant the prime minister broad powers to appoint and dismiss commissioners, it also included the Inspector-General of Police as a permanent SCC member. In addition, the SCC did not have the power to oversee police investigation of complaints. The bill has yet to be debated, however, as it was deferred at the end of 2007 to the new parliamentary sitting.

Looks like me, talks like me, sounds like me

PEMUDAH, the government's special task force to facilitate business, citing a World Bank study, estimates that corruption could cost Malaysia as much as RM10 billion a year – an amount equivalent to 1 or 2 per cent of GDP. PEMUDAH also notes that the ACA investigated only 10.1 per cent, or just 7,223 cases, of the total 71,558 reported between 2000 and 2006. The number of people successfully convicted was only 0.7 per cent, or 524, of those suspected of corruption.[10]

PEMUDAH also notes that, per capita, Malaysia spends only RM5 (approximately US$1.5) on anti-corruption efforts.[11] This illustration of the Malaysian government's inaction in the light of the serious corruption allegations, along with its seeming inability to catch the

---

6 MII, 'Launching of 'National Integrity System & CSR: Our First Look'', press release, 8 May 2007.

7 'Reinventing Penang State Administration', summary of speech by Lim Guan Eng at the TI Occasional Talk in Corus Hotel, Kuala Lumpur, 11 September 2008.

8 Malaysiakini, 27 December 2007.

9 See www.jeffooi.com/2006/05/post_20.php.

10 Sun2Surf (Malaysia), 6 July 2008.

11 Ibid.

'big fish', instead focusing on the 'small fry', suggests that what anti-corruption efforts exist are mere tokens.

Weaknesses in the system for fighting corruption in all sectors were exemplified in 2007. The ACA came under fire when the director of Sabah ACA made a police report against the national director for corruption.[12] It was the first time in the ACA's forty-year history that the head of the agency itself had come under investigation. The prime minister refused to take any action until public pressure was put on him,[13] but the national director was subsequently investigated and cleared by a team from the ACA itself.[14]

The ACA rallied after the general election in early 2008, however, finally showing some effectiveness by smashing a long-standing corruption racket operated by staff of the privatised government agency tasked with ensuring the roadworthiness of vehicles.[15] More than thirty members of staff of Puspakom were arrested for accepting bribes in order to certify unworthy vehicles. It was a systematic operation in which junior and senior officers alike were involved, and it had a nationwide reach.[16]

Other failings in the system of gatekeeping were exposed by a Royal Commission[17] that had been set up at the end of 2007 to investigate alleged tampering in the appointment of judges. The V. K. Lingam case showed the extent of corruption, in which prominent businesspeople and their agents linked to political parties colluded to fix judicial appointments.

More startling, however, was the initial non-committal response from the government, even with audio-visual evidence.

Only after an extreme public outcry, as well as pressure from the opposition and the Malaysian Bar, did the government form the Royal Commission – and only then to verify the authenticity of the video. During the investigation by the commission, V. K. Lingam was quoted as saying of the character in the video that he '[l]ooks like me, talks like me, sounds like me, but it's not me'. The Royal Commission concluded that the video was authentic, however, and also recommended that appropriate action be taken.[18] Following this, the Malaysian Cabinet ordered the Attorney General to investigate[19] six of the prominent people in the case, including V. K. Lingam, two retired chief justices, Tun Mohd Eusoff Chin and Tun Ahmad Fairuz Sheikh Abdul Halim, and the former prime minister Tun Dr Mahathir Mohamad.[20] Importantly, however, as of November 2008 no formal criminal charges have been made.

While this case exposes severe flaws in the judicial system, including the inappropriate involvement of both politics and business in the judiciary, it also indicates the reluctance of the government to go after the 'top brass' when faced with corruption. It was only after being confronted with public pressure, and following disappointing results in the recent election, that there was any movement; and even then, with no convictions, it is difficult to see how justice will be served.

---

12 Bernama.com (Malaysia), 30 March 2007.

13 Malaysiakini, 21 April 2008.

14 Malaysiakini, 21 March 2007.

15 See www.nst.com.my/Current_News/NST/Friday/Frontpage/2335144/Article/index_html.

16 The Star Online (Malaysia), 28 August 2008.

17 Malaysiakini, 24 September 2007.

18 See www.malaysiakini.com/doc/lingam_tape_report.pdf.

19 Technically, this is not within the remit of the Cabinet, but in Malaysia the executive has sway over all other state apparatus. ABC (Australia); see www.radioaustralia.net.au/programguide/stories/200805/s2249493.htm.

20 Bernama Daily Malaysian News, 12 December 2008.

Revolving doors: the interrelationship between the government, the civil service and the private sector

A common thread running through politics, the civil service and the private sector is the revolving door, through which individuals move from government to business, or business to politics, and back again. In this way, significant government participation in the private sector and considerable business participation in politics means that the movement of gatekeepers to players and players to gatekeepers has a negative influence on the concept of checks and balances.

One of the biggest scandals of the year, was the fiasco involving the Port Klang Free Zone (PKFZ). This was a case involving politicians, government officials and businesspeople, and it resulted in a loss to taxpayers of RM4.6 billion.[21] The project was to have the following features: a 405-hectare facility comprising 512 warehouses, 2,000 covered parking bays, four office buildings, an exhibition centre and a four-star hotel.[22]

The project is owned by a government agency, the Port Klang Authority (PKA), and headed by O. C. Phang.[23] The land was bought by the PKA in 2002 for RM1.8 billion from Kuala Dimensi, which had bought the land in 1999 for RM95 million from Pulau Lumut Development Cooperative Bhd (PLDCB), a local cooperative of fishermen. The land price 'appreciated' more than nineteen times in three years.[24] Kuala

Dimensi was also the private company that was subsequently given the contract to develop the PKFZ.[25]

In 2006 enormous cost overruns were reported: the costs had risen from an estimated RM1.1 billion (US$315 million) to RM4.7 billion.[26] The extraordinary jump in the costs of the project was reported in a Cabinet meeting in July 2007, and it was found that the increased costs did not have the correct approval from government agencies.[27] The case involved 'serious regulatory and procedural lapses' – for example, Ministry of Finance procedures were bypassed when the Transport Ministry provided backing for the funds to buy the land from Kuala Dimensi, which was considered to be 'against normal government practice'.[28] There were also allegations that the political, government and business nexus was at fault.[29] Jafza, the operator of the Jebel Ali Free Zone, pulled out of a fifteen-year contract to manage the zone after claiming to have been constantly misled by PKA management, but the PKA claimed that the split had been amicable.[30]

Despite the debacle, the government decided to bail out the company to the tune of RM4.6 billion. Furthermore, there have been no criminal cases arising from this scandal, and no individual has been held accountable for the overrun in costs. There were calls for an investigation, and a report by PricewaterhouseCoopers is being prepared on the case, but the results are yet to be published.[31]

---

21 *Asia Times* (Thailand), 31 August 2007.
22 Malaysiakini, 25 June 2007.
23 The Star Online (Malaysia), 19 July 2007.
24 See www.parlimen.gov.my/hindex/pdf/DR-03092007.pdf (Hansard from the Malaysian parliament); see also *Asia Times* (Thailand), 31 August 2007.
25 *Asia Times* (Thailand), 31 August 2007.
26 Ibid.
27 Ibid.
28 The Malaysian Bar, quoting from *The Straits Times* (Singapore), 13 August 2007.
29 Malaysiakini, 15 August 2007.
30 Malaysiakini, 25 June 2007.
31 See *Daily Express* (Malaysia), 25 August 2007; *New Straits Times* (Malaysia), 22 December 2007; *Financial Express* (India), 7 September 2007.

What is interesting is the complex network of individuals involved, including politicians from the United Malay National Organisation (UMNO), officials at the Transport Ministry, Port Klang Authority officials and Kuala Dimensi.[32] Kuala Dimensi's chairperson is UMNO treasurer Azim Zabidi.[33] The legal firm that drafted the development agreement between the PKA and Kuala Dimensi is headed by the local UMNO branch vice-chief, Abdul Rashid Asari. Another local UMNO youth chief, Faizal Abdullah, is deputy CEO of the property development and investment firm behind the sale and development of the PKFZ. Faizal Abdullah's father-in-law, Onn Ismail, is the local UMNO branch permanent chairman as well as the former chairperson of the fishermen's cooperative that sold the land to Kuala Dimesi.

The complexity of the relationships between politics and the public and private sectors means that corruption may take place with impunity. Under the circumstances, therefore, the practice of revolving and rotating doors and active government participation in the economy creates an appearance of impropriety, and, with the weak oversight of public–private relationships, increases corruption risks. Until drastic action is taken to separate the cosy relationship between government, business and politics, the anti-corruption effort will remain no more than a token gesture.

Gregore Pio Lopez and TI Malaysia

Additional reading

E. T. Gomez, 'The State, Governance and Corruption in Malaysia', in N. Tarling (ed.), *Corruption and Good Governance in Asia* (London: Routledge, 2005).

E. T. Gomez and K. S. Jomo, *Malaysia's Political Economy: Politics, Patronage and Profits* (Cambridge: Cambridge University Press, 1997).

UNDP, *Tackling Corruption, Transforming Lives: Accelerating Human Development in Asia and the Pacific* (Delhi: Macmillan, 2008).

TI Malaysia: www.transparency.org.my.

---

32 *Asia Times* (Thailand), 31 August 2007.
33 The Malaysian Bar, quoting from *The Straits Times* (Singapore), 13 August 2007.

Nepal

Corruption Perceptions Index 2008: 2.7 (121st out of 180 countries)

Conventions

ADB–OECD Anti-Corruption Action Plan for Asia-Pacific (endorsed November 2001)
UN Convention against Corruption (signed December 2003; not yet ratified)
UN Convention against Transnational Organized Crime (signed December 2002; not yet ratified)

Legal and institutional changes

- The Right to Information Act 2007 seeks to give free public access to any information related to the public interest, thereby maintaining transparency, accountability and respect for the people's right to be informed. With the exception of information specifically categorised as confidential, all Nepalese are guaranteed free access to public information. Five categories of information are exempt from disclosure requirements: security and foreign policy, criminal investigations, commercial and banking privacy, ethnic or communal relations, and personal privacy (including that which threatens life, property, health and security).

- The Special Court in Nepal was established in 2002 to handle corruption cases. Due to the slow pace of legal proceedings, however, cases are piling up in the court. In order to speed up the process, amendments were made to the Special Court Act 2002 allowing the court to be flexible in determining the number of sitting judges required instead of being limited to the existing three.

- The Banking Offence Act 2007 was promulgated to control and mitigate the risks and impacts associated with, and to enhance public trust in, banking and financial trans-

actions. Offences punishable under the act include unauthorised involvement in banking transactions, fraud in electronic transactions, the misuse of bank loans and credits, tampering with accounting books, fraud in the valuation of assets, and irregularities in banking and financial transactions. Depending on the scale of the transaction, penalties range from three months' to four years' imprisonment.

- The Anti-Money Laundering Act 2008 was enacted in January 2008. The law opens up avenues to combat corruption cases involving property amassed through illegal means, including tax evasion, smuggling, investment in terrorist acts and other crimes punishable under international treaties and conventions signed by the government. The act lays the groundwork for ratifying the UNCAC. Nepal is a signatory to the UNCAC but ratification has been pending due to the country's political situation.

- The Good Governance Act 2008 was enacted in February 2008. The law's objective is to make public administration more people-oriented, accountable, transparent and participatory. Some of the good governance and anti-corruption clauses include the development of a code of conduct for public servants, methods for resolving conflicts of interest, mandatory public hearings and social audits, complaint-handling procedures and establishing Good Governance Units within each ministry.

- As provided for by the new Procurement Act 2007, the government has established a Public Procurement Monitoring Office (PPMO). The PPMO is a high-level policy-making body designed to streamline the public procurement system. Among several areas prone to corruption, public procurement is said to be the most susceptible. With a score of 2.8 on a scale of 1 to 7, Nepal ranks 116th among 125 countries assessed by the OECD for integrity in public procurement.[1]

- Despite several new good governance and anti-corruption laws, there have been many instances of indecision and setbacks. Initiatives not implemented or followed up include provisions in the interim constitution to broaden the mandate of the Commission for Investigation of the Abuse of Authority (CIAA) to cover corruption cases in the army and the judiciary, and the preventive and curative anti-corruption strategy mentioned in the Interim Development Plan (2008–2010). Other problems include: the operation of the CIAA without a chief commissioner since October 2006; the acquittal of high-profile corruption cases by the Special Court; a sharp drop in corruption complaints lodged at the CIAA (indicating fading public trust in the agency); the controversy over filing corruption charges against the central bank governor (on which the two remaining CIAA commissioners differed in their views); and donors shying away from investing in anti-corruption activities in Nepal.

Political transition affects anti-corruption activities

The nineteen-day-long political movement took down the royal government and reinstated

parliament in April 2006. It ended more than a decade of Maoist conflict and paved the way for elections to the Constituent Assembly (CA). The political changes took a toll on anti-corruption initiatives, however. Political parties were consumed with the election to the CA, which after a number of delays finally took place on 10 April 2008. Following the election, political parties concentrated on managing the political transition, resolving regional and ethnic conflicts, and maintaining law and order. As a result, the anti-corruption agenda could not become a priority issue, despite the fact that it had featured in all the major political parties' manifestos.[2] In the absence of effective political will to combat corruption, donors too shied away from supporting anti-corruption activities. With a weak and unstable coalition government in power, increased competition in the election to the CA and post-conflict spending imperatives, corruption opportunities must have increased in Nepal during the transition phase.

The private sector has also played a part, as both a cause and effect of corruption. The ever-oscillating positions of businesspeople in their attempts to build rapport with centres of power have cost them greatly in terms of donations and contributions to political parties and their sister organisations, such as trade unions, youth wings and student unions. Addressing the whole issue of how corruption is institutionalised in private business, *New Business Age* reported in 2004 that 'all the business houses or big companies have at least one person believed to have good contacts in the power centres whose only real job is to deal with the government bureaucracy'.[3]

The private sector had a rude awakening with the discovery of massive amounts of bank defaulting. In 2004 it was estimated that the loan defaulting exceeded Rs40 billion, representing

---

1 OECD, *Integrity in Public Procurement: Good Practice from A to Z* (Paris: OECD, 2007).
2 *Kathmandu Post* (Nepal), 22 March 2007.
3 *New Business Age* (Nepal), August 2004.

30 per cent of all credit flows into the country. Nepal's Credit Information Bureau still carries a list of 2,144 bank defaulters.[4] The massive bank defaulting is one among several factors that pushed the government to opt for foreign management contracts of the two state-owned commercial banks in Nepal. The recent promulgation of the Banking Offences Act, in 2007, is intended to improve the situation, as it is mainly directed at controlling the cases of bank fraud and the misuse of commercial loans.

State capture: business as politics and politics as business

Corruption can thrive at the nexus of the private sector, the bureaucracy and politicians. Politicians can provide security or camouflage for corrupt deals between private parties and bureaucrats. The spoils are shared among the three groups while the costs are passed on to the general public. Corruption in Nepal can be explained by looking into the behaviours and interrelationships among these three primary actors.

A 2006 study by TI Nepal found that the most profound influence of the private sector on government policy is in the realm of income tax. Other laws frequently amended to favour the private sector are those related to customs duties and budget provisions in fiscal acts.[5] While this is an extreme case of state capture and abuse of power for private gain, it is not the only one.

One of the biggest problems is that businesspeople can pay their way into politics by giving large donations to political parties.[6] Political donations became a major issue during the recent elections for the Constituent Assembly. In 2007 the Interim Parliament floated the idea of enacting a law on political party financing, but as the general election approached the scheme simply evaporated. Furthermore, the code of conduct prescribed by the Election Commission talks only of keeping limits on campaign expenditures. It is silent on the income side, leaving the door wide open for unlimited donations from powerful businesspeople. The July 2008 nomination of business tycoons by major political parties to the CA clearly signals the extent of the closed-door, hush-hush rapport between political parties and businesspeople in Nepal.[7] Once in positions of political power, businesspeople can influence decisions to their benefit, such as manipulating laws and interfering with the public procurement process.

Following five years of consultation, Nepal introduced a new public procurement law in 2007 that is in line with international standards and has provisions to combat corruption in public procurement. While the PPMO will assist in streamlining the public procurement system, the new law seeks to penalise active corruption, such as the offering of bribes. Nepal's previous law penalised only passive corruption, whereby public officials solicit or accept bribes.[8] The private sector's influence on public procurement is still strong, but the new law offers some reason for hope.

Nepal as a safe haven: corruption at the borders

Nepal has more than 1,700 kilometres of open and relatively unregulated borders with India. This stretch has long provided a safe haven for businesspeople engaged in illegal trade. There is limited regulation of the movement of people and goods over the border, which encompasses large amounts of informal trade not accounted

4 See www.cibnepal.org.np; see the blacklist; last accessed January 2009.
5 K. Subedi, *The Influence of the Private Sector on Policy Decisions of the Government* (Kathmandu: TI Nepal, 2006).
6 eKantipur.com (Nepal), 7 April 2008.
7 *Kathmandu Post* (Nepal), 5 July 2008.
8 *Kathmandu Post* (Nepal), 19 February 2008.

for in the official records of trade between the two countries.[9]

With increased globalisation and the opening of markets in China, illegal trading activities are also flourishing across the northern border with China. Not only are low-cost Chinese goods smuggled into Nepal and then India, contraband items are smuggled into China from Nepal.

Throughout 2007 the media in Nepal were rocked by regular news reports of the authorities confiscating truckloads of red sandalwood. International trade in this wood is banned under the Convention on International Trade in Endangered Species of Fauna and Flora (CITES), to which Nepal is a signatory. Much of the wood is smuggled more than 2,000 kilometres from southern India, unhindered despite the fact that there are numerous checkpoints along the way manned by the departments of forests, transport and trade tax. According to the World Wide Fund for Nature (WWF), more than 400 tonnes of red sandalwood logs were seized in Nepal in 2007 and 2008.[10] This is a lucrative business, as a kilogram of red sandalwood, worth about Rs300 (US$4) in Nepal, could easily fetch more than (Indian) Rs2,000 (US$45) in Tibet. Moreover, processed products such as a kilogram of sandalwood powder could sell for more than US$50 in European or US markets.

Many believe the discovery of this contraband is due to the regime change in 2006, as no such reports were made earlier. There are concerns that these reports are just the tip of the iceberg.

Narayan Manandhar (TI Nepal)

Additional reading

Kathmandu Frontier Associates, *A Study Report on the Effectiveness of CIAA* (Kathmandu: Kathmandu Frontier Associates, 2007 [in Nepali]).

N. Manandhar, *Corruption and Anti-corruption* (Kathmandu: TI Nepal, 2005).
   Corruption and Anti-corruption: Further Reading (Kathmandu: TI Nepal, 2006).
   Scripts on Corruption and Anti-corruption (Kathmandu: TI Nepal, 2008).

New Business Age (Kathmandu), 'Corruption: Supply Side Perspective' (August 2004).

D. R. Pandey, 'The "State for Sale" and the System of Reciprocal Exchanges: Contradictions and Challenges', paper prepared for the twelfth International Anti-Corruption Conference, Guatemala City, 13–18 November 2006.

TI Nepal: www.tinepal.org.

---

9 The amount of formal trade recorded in India (exports plus imports) is US$396 million, while informal trade is US$408 million. In Nepal, formal trade recorded is US$973 million, while informal trade is US$368 million. The discrepancy in the figures is due to differences in recording trade coverage in the two countries. B. K. Karmacharya, 2005.

10 *India Today*, 24 September 2008.

Pakistan

Corruption Perceptions Index 2008: 2.5 (134th out of 180 countries)

Conventions

ADB–OECD Anti-Corruption Action Plan for Asia-Pacific (endorsed November 2001)
UN Convention against Corruption (signed December 2003; ratified August 2007)

Legal and institutional changes

- In a meeting with a delegation of TI Pakistan on 17 July 2007, the former prime minister, Shaukat Aziz, gave assurance that the Public Procurement Rules of 2004 would be implemented in all the federal government ministries. He also claimed that transparency was the 'hallmark' of government policy and that the government was promoting e-governance as a tool for more openness and in order to make processes more efficient.[1] He claimed that the 'government had made it mandatory that integrity pacts are signed for all government contracts over Rs10 million'.[2] Moreover, the adoption of the rules 'minimises discretion, gives priority to technical competence and ensures that award of contract is on the basis of lowest evaluated responsive bidder in the shortest possible time'.[3] He also agreed with TI Pakistan that the Election Commission should 'hold the elections in the most transparent manner'.[4] These commitments were undermined after the departure of the former

prime minister in 2007. Under the caretaker government in 2008, complaints to the Public Procurement Regulatory Authority board were not acted upon.

- The former president, General Pervez Musharraf, issued the National Reconciliation Ordinance (NRO) on 5 October 2007, fifty-six days after the ratification of the UN Convention against Corruption.[5] In many ways this was a setback for anti-corruption measures in Pakistan, as all proceedings under investigation or pending in any court that had been initiated by or involved the National Accountability Bureau (NAB) prior to 12 October 1999 were withdrawn and terminated with immediate effect. The NRO also granted further protection to parliamentarians, as no sitting member of parliament or a provincial assembly can be arrested without taking into consideration the recommendations of the Special Parliamentary Committee on Ethics or the Special Committee of the Provincial Assembly on Ethics.[6]

---

1 *Business Recorder* (Pakistan), 19 July 2007; see www.transparency.org.pk/news/news.htm.
2 Associated Press of Pakistan, 19 July 2007; see www.transparency.org.pk/news/news.htm.
3 Ibid.
4 Ibid.
5 *Business Recorder* (Pakistan), 8 October 2007; see www.transparency.org.pk/news/news.htm.
6 Ibid.

Public ills, private woes: the survival of the private sector during political instability

Corruption is a serious problem in Pakistan, and this position is corroborated by a number of recent studies and reports. An assessment of Pakistan's infrastructure implementation capacity was carried out at the request of the government, and the resulting report was published in November 2007 jointly by the World Bank and the Planning Commission of Pakistan.[7] It states that approximately 15 per cent of the cost of corruption lies in procurement, costing the Pakistani development budget (2007/8) over Rs150 billion.[8] Furthermore, the World Bank's Control of Corruption Indicator in 2007 ranks Pakistan a mere 21.3 out of 100.[9]

In terms of the business sector, there are a number of measures that indicate that there is a serious issue of corruption. TI's Global Corruption Barometer 2006 reported that the impact of corruption on the private sector was perceived as almost equal to corruption in the public sector; and *The Global Competitiveness Report 2008–2009* ranked Pakistan 101st out of 130 countries and found that respondents pointed to corruption as the second most problematic factor for doing business in the country, after government instability.[10]

The instability of the political situation in Pakistan cannot be underestimated as a factor in permitting corruption in the private sector to flourish. Despite Musharraf's claim to be committed to fighting corruption, little headway has been made, and it is still considered to be 'pervasive and deeply entrenched'.[11] Musharraf relinquished military power in November 2007, and his supporters were defeated in the February 2008 general election by a coalition of the Pakistan People's Party and Nawaz Sharif's Muslim League. Musharraf resigned in August 2008, facing impeachment for alleged crimes including gross misconduct and violation of the constitution.[12]

The inauguration of the new president, Asif Ali Zardari, on 9 September 2008 ushers in a new era, but not one without challenges. The new democratically elected government will, therefore, require the immediate enforcement of good governance and transparency standards to counter the various dire problems facing Pakistan. There is an increased threat of terrorism, hyperinflation, a reduction in the Karachi Stock Exchange 100 Index, a sizeable depreciation of the currency,[13] a substantial reduction in foreign currency reserves[14] and a huge trade deficit inherited from the previous government.

Banking fines for cartels: the new Competition Commission

In Pakistan, monopolistic practices and cartels are perceived to hold sway in such businesses as banking, cement, sugar, automobiles, fertilisers and pharmaceuticals, to name a few. Although

---

7 World Bank, *Pakistan Infrastructure Implementation Capacity Assessment* (Washington, DC: World Bank, 2007).

8 *Business Recorder* (Pakistan), 24 September 2008; see www.transparency.org.pk/news/news.htm.

9 Control of corruption is one of the indicators used in compiling the Worldwide Governance Indicators (WGI) project. The indicator measures the extent to which public power is exercised for private gain, including petty and grand forms of corruption, as well as 'capture' of the state by elites and private interests. See http://info.world-bank.org/governance/wgi/sc_chart.asp#.

10 TI, 'Global Corruption Barometer 2006' (Berlin: TI, 2006); World Economic Forum, *The Global Competitiveness Report 2008–2009* (Geneva: World Economic Forum, 2008).

11 See www.business-anti-corruption.com/normal.asp?pageid=464.

12 Welt Online (Germany), 17 August 2008.

13 See www.fxstreet.com/fundamental/analysis-reports/emerging-markets-weekly/2008-11-17.html; 'Lost 23 Percent against the Dollar This Year as a Balance of Payments Crisis Developed'.

14 US$16.4 billion foreign country reserves for October 2007; see *The News* (Pakistan), 13 June 2008; US$4.7 billion for October 2008; see *Daily Telegraph* (UK), 14 October 2008.

cartels distort market prices, they also create other anomalies. Existing players in an industry may firmly block the entry of new entrepreneurs through cartels, in order to ensure their own market dominance. This practice acts as a clear disincentive for the much-needed expansion of Pakistan's industrial base.

In October 2007 a new Competition Commission was set up under the Competition Ordinance 2007, in order to 'provide for a legal framework to create a business environment based on healthy competition towards improving economic efficiency, developing competitiveness and protecting consumers from anti-competitive practices'.[15]

It was also meant to 'restrict the undue concentration of economic power, growth of unreasonable monopoly power and unreasonably restrictive trade practices', which are perceived to be 'injurious to the economic well-being, growth and development of Pakistan'.[16]

In one of its first initiatives, the Competition Commission challenged the Pakistan Banks Association (PBA) on its decision to 'collectively decide rates of profit and other terms and conditions regarding deposit accounts'.[17] The PBA is a membership association to which only banks in Pakistan can be affiliated, and it advertised its decision openly in a daily newspaper on 5 November 2007. The terms of the agreement included a number of its member banks imposing 'a 4 percent profit on Rs20,000 deposits and a Rs50 charge on less than a Rs5,000 balance' on bank accounts included in the new Enhanced Savings Account (ESA) scheme.[18] Furthermore, holders of basic accounts that met the criteria

would have their accounts changed to ESAs without the prior instruction or agreement of the account-holders.

The Competition Commission considered this move by the PBA to be in violation of section 4 of the Competition Ordinance 2007, and, moreover, in acting as a cartel, the banks were alleged to have behaved anti-competitively. The implications of the changes included customers with balances of less than Rs5,000 having to pay Rs50 each month and the transfer of accounts without the account-holders' prior permission. On 24 December a 'show cause' was issued to the PBA and the banks, and they were asked to provide justification of their behaviour to the commission by 10 January 2008.[19]

Both the PBA and the banks issued responses on 9 January, denying the charges of cartelisation, and on 28 February 2008 a further statement was issued, arguing that the commission did not have jurisdiction in this area and that, furthermore, the changes had been made 'at the behest of the regulator [the State Bank of Pakistan] in the larger public interest'.[20] The PBA also argued that it could not be considered to be stifling competition as the deposit amounts affected by the ESA scheme amounted to only 2.25 per cent. The commission found later, however, that in terms of the number of account-holders affected the impact was much higher, constituting 45.12 per cent.[21]

The final decision of the Competition Commission was made on 10 April 2008. The commission argued that the 'PBA has acted beyond its mandate . . . and has been instrumental in the formation of a cartel'.[22] As a

---

15 See www.mca.gov.pk/.
16 See www.mca.gov.pk/law.htm.
17 See www.mca.gov.pk/Downloads/Order_of_Banks.pdf
18 *Business Recorder* (Pakistan), 13 February 2008.
19 Competition Commission of Pakistan; see www.mca.gov.pk/Downloads/Order_of_Banks.pdf.
20 Ibid.
21 Ibid.
22 Ibid.

result, it had deprived small account-holders of the benefits they were otherwise earning on their savings accounts. The PBA and the culpable banks were ordered to discontinue the practice, not to repeat it and to pay considerable fines. The PBA was fined Rs30 million, and the seven banks involved were fined Rs25 million each.[23]

The penalised institutions did have recourse to appeal to the appellate bench of the Competition Commission, but they failed to do so within the stipulated time. On 27 May the PBA did, however, appeal against the decision of the commission with the Sindh High Court, which ordered the commission not to take any action against the PBA before the decision had been adjudicated in court.[24]

The commission appealed against the High Court's decision, and on 15 September 2008 the Supreme Court allowed the commission to proceed against the banks.[25] The Competition Commission's move against the banking cartel, as well as the support provided by the Supreme Court, is encouraging. It has sent the message that such practices by the private sector, including the maintenance of unreasonable power by monopolies and restrictive trade practices, will not be tolerated and that the institutions in charge of monitoring such practices have the power to act.

Privatisation: Pakistan Steel Mills

Corruption in privatisation in Pakistan is endemic: manipulation of the process can be found at all stages, from the evaluation of profits and assets of a company to the provision of kickbacks on completion of a settlement.

One of the most famous cases relating to privatisation involves the attempted privatisation of Pakistan Steel Mills. As Pakistan's largest and only integrated steel manufacturing plant, it is a private limited company, and 100 per cent of its equity is owned by the government.[26] The plant is the biggest producer of steel in Pakistan and was installed in 1981, with the collaboration of Russia, by the Ministry of Industries, Production and Special Initiatives. In 1997 the government of Pakistan decided to privatise it, and, following the rules, secured approval from the Council of Common Interests.[27]

In 1998 the privatisation of Pakistan Steel Mills was abandoned, and to make it profitable the labour force was reduced from 20,000 to 15,000. As the steel mill had been designed, constructed and fitted out entirely by the Soviet Union, in February 2003 General Musharraf visited Moscow and signed an agreement to expand production of the plant's steel from 1.1 million to 1.5 million tonnes. By December 2004, less than two years later, the privatisation of the plant was being discussed again, and by 10 February 2005 the decision to privatise the mill was taken by the government. The corporation, assessed at Rs72 billion, was sold to a consortium for Rs21.58 billion on 24 April 2006.[28]

On 23 June 2006 the Supreme Court ruled against the privatisation, and Chief Justice Chaudhry prevented the sale of the state monopoly to the

---

23 Ibid.
24 Dawn.com (Pakistan), 16 September 2008.
25 Ibid.
26 Judgment of the Supreme Court in Pakistan Steel Mills Privatisation Case, 9 August 2006; see www.dawn.com/2006/08/09/tab.pdf/.
27 This is a constitutional body, with a mandate for resolving inter-provincial inequalities and potential disagreements. The members are made up of the chief ministers of the provinces and a number of members nominated by the federal government. The council did not function between 1998 and 2006, when it resumed its work to decide on the privatisation of Pakistan Steel Mills.
28 *Business Recorder* (Pakistan), 18 August 2006.

private investors.[29] The Supreme Court concluded that approving the award of the contract reflected disregard for the mandatory rules, as well as the information necessary for arriving at a fair sale price.[30] The unexplained haste of the proceedings also cast reasonable doubt on the ethics of the whole exercise. While Chief Justice Chaudhry acknowledged that it was not the function of the court to interfere with the policy-making of the executive, the privatisation of the mills was 'vitiated by acts of omission' and violated the mandatory provisions of laws and rules.[31] The valuation of the project and the final terms offered to the consortium were not in accord with the initial public offering given through the advertisement.[32]

This case had implications that still resonate today, as it is considered one of the causes of the dismissal of Chief Justice Chaudhry in March 2007, who was not reinstated until July 2008. It is, therefore, partially responsible for a great civil society movement in Pakistan, which called for the restoration of an independent judiciary. There are also unanswered questions that still need resolution. In October 2006 a case was filed against the then prime minister, Shaukat Aziz, and ten other ministers, as well as the governor of the State Bank of Pakistan, alleging misuse of power – corruption as defined in section 9 of

the National Accountability Bureau Ordinance 1999, which covers corruption and corrupt practices.[33] If found guilty, they would be subject to punishment, up to fourteen years' imprisonment, under section 10 of the ordinance for their involvement in the attempted privatisation of Pakistan Steel Mills.[34] At the time of writing this report it was yet to be seen how the NAB, under the jurisdiction of the current government, will proceed with this case.[35]

Syed Adil Gilani (TI Pakistan)

Additional reading

Human Rights First, *Pakistan Courts and Constitution under Attack: Reversing the Damage* (New York: Human Rights First, 2008)

M. Iqbal, *Global Integrity Scorecard: Pakistan* (Washington, DC: Global Integrity, 2008).

S. Nishtar, *Pakistan's Health Sector: Does Corruption Lurk?* (Islamabad: Heartfile and TI, 2007).

M. Sohail and S. Cavill, 'Does Corruption Affect Construction?', paper presented at the Developing Countries International Symposium 'Construction in Developing Countries: Procurement, Ethics and Technology', Port of Spain, Trinidad and Tobago, 16 January 2008.

TI Pakistan: www.transparency.org.pk.

---

29 Ibid.
30 Judgment of the Supreme Court in Pakistan Steel Mills Privatisation Case, 9 August 2006; see www.dawn.com/2006/08/09/tab.pdf/.
31 Ibid.
32 Ibid.
33 See www.sbp.org.pk/l_frame/NAB_Ord_1999.pdf.
34 Ibid.
35 See www.ppp.org.pk/refs/ref0613.html. According to *The News* (Pakistan), 19 January 2009, the NAB will be replaced by a new independent accountability commission, which will pursue all cases filed with the NAB, including those relating to Pakistan Steel Mills. See also *The News* (Pakistan), 12 January 2009.

Papua New Guinea

> **Corruption Perceptions Index 2008: 2.0 (151st out of 180 countries)**
>
> **Conventions**
> ADB–OECD Anti-Corruption Action Plan for Asia-Pacific (endorsed November 2001)
> UN Convention against Corruption (signed December 2004; ratified July 2007)

Legal and institutional changes

- The police commissioner and the chief ombudsman signed an agreement in June 2007 to establish a police complaints ombudsman.[1] This gives the Ombudsman Commission (OC) oversight responsibility for high-profile cases. It will also shield police internal investigators from being influenced or interfered with and will ensure that officers comply with given actions. Under the agreement, the police will conduct investigations while OC officers will ensure that they are carried out professionally and transparently and that the process of dealing with police personnel is in accordance with the laws and police procedures. The agreement is being applied and is working.

- In October 2007 the Department of Personnel Management (DPM) delegated three key human resource management (HRM) powers to the heads of government departments, provincial administrations and government agencies.[2] The Public Services (Management) Act 1995 allows the department to delegate the powers of hiring, firing and the creation of new service positions.[3] The HRM Devolution Project was trialled through June 2008 with twenty-two sites. Following training and audits, most agencies have demonstrated the capacity to exercise the new powers, although in a few cases the DPM has revoked the powers after its audits showed non-compliance.[4] With regard to corruption, delegation provides the provincial and national agencies with the

---

1 Memorandum of Agreement between Commissioner of Police Gary Baki and Chief Ombudsman Ila Geno, Port Moresby, 1 June 2007.

2 Department of Personnel Management, Minute from Secretary Margaret Elias, Port Moresby, 5 October 2007. The powers and responsibilities of Part VII – Creation of Offices (sections 33, 34 and 35); Part IX – Recruitment (sections 36 and 37); and Part XII – Training (section 44) are those delegated. These powers have some limitations. First, they are limited to deputy secretary level; second, they must remain consistent with the parameters established in the new General Orders and Budgetary Ceilings; and, third, they must remain consistent with the provisions of the Public Services (Management) Act 1995.

3 The powers and responsibilities delegated are Part VII – Creation of Offices (sections 33, 34 and 35); Part IX – Recruitment (sections 36 and 37); and Part XII – Training (section 44). They are limited to deputy secretary level; they must remain consistent with the parameters established in the new General Orders and Budgetary Ceilings; and they must remain consistent with the provisions of the Public Services (Management) Act 1995.

4 Department of Personnel Management, 'HRM Devolution Project Post Implementation Review Report', Port Moresby, 21 May 2008.

power to sack dishonest or ghost staff more quickly. At the same time, however, these powers could be used for nepotism if not adequately monitored and audited by the DPM, and the payroll system's integrity could be at risk if it is not protected.

- In December 2007 parliament passed two sets of amendments to the Forestry Act 1991 without debate: the Forestry (Amendment) Act 2007 and the Forestry (Timber Permits Validation) Act 2007.[5] In the view of NGOs such as the Papua New Guinea Eco-Forestry Forum, this change legitimises illegal and unsustainable logging.[6] Non-governmental observers concur that the amendments were drafted without broad stakeholder consultation.[7] The legislation appears to serve the interests of the logging industry more than the community landowners (see below for further information).

- The Financial Intelligence Unit (FIU) was established in July 2007 and is working from the National Fraud and Anti-Corruption Directorate. The role of its team of specialists is to receive reports from financial institutions that handle cash transactions, identify and provide training to these cash dealers, analyse trends and statistics, and investigate financial crimes. The directorate can also arrest and charge offenders, as well as retain assets in collaboration with the Public Prosecutors' Office and issue guidelines to cash dealers, conduct on-site inspections and penalise cash dealers for non-compliance. In 2008 training on the Proceeds of Crimes Act 2005 was provided to police investigators and cash dealers. Suspicious Transactions Reports have been sent from commercial banks to the FIU since December 2007. The reports give the police a means to identify emerging trends and patterns associated with financial crimes, as well as the ability to initiate investigations or supplement criminal cases. The unit does not have the capacity to carry out all its responsibilities, however, due to a lack of resources, skills and manpower. For example, there is an acute lack of capacity in the area of forensic auditing. Australia's Anti-Money Laundering Assistance Team is providing training and support for the staff of the FIU, and is planning further assistance for prosecutors and the judiciary.[8] Over time, the FIU is expected to increase the police's capacity to prosecute increasingly complex financial crimes successfully.

- The Intergovernmental Financing Act is based on a proposal developed by the National Economic and Fiscal Commission (NEFC). A bill was tabled in the first half of 2008 and passed in July 2008.[9] The reform is based on extensive empirical research carried out by the NEFC in each province to calculate the actual cost to deliver services, taking into account factors such as the physical distance between administrative centres, schools and health clinics.[10] The new legislation lays out an intergovernmental financing system for recurrent goods and services budgets. The formula-based funding system is expected to increase accountability.[11]

---

5 Available at www.fiapng.com/fia_library_acts.html.

6 See, for example, the media release in *Eko-Forestri Nius*, vol. 9, no. 3/4 (2007), at www.ecoforestry.org.pg/ikoforestri/Vol.%209%20Iss.%203-4.pdf.

7 Personal communication by the author with staff from PNG environmental organisations, 17 October 2008.

8 See www.ag.gov.au/www/agd/agd.nsf/Page/InternationalDevelopmentAssistance_Anti-MoneyLaundering AssistanceTeam_Countryprojects#PapuaNewGuinea.

9 *Post-Courier* (Papua New Guinea), 17 July 2008.

10 National Economic and Fiscal Commission, 'It's More than Numbers', Port Moresby, September 2008.

11 National Economic and Fiscal Commission, 'Explanatory Memorandum for Organic Law on Provincial and Local-level Governments', Port Moresby, 2007.

Corruption and the private sector in Papua New Guinea

As reported daily in the media, corruption profoundly affects business operations, yet businesses are reluctant to speak out against it because of fear of losing state contracts or licences, or simply being shut down.[12] Overall, corruption in Papua New Guinea (PNG) is characterised as more political than bureaucratic in nature. That said, bureaucratic corruption is a significant concern to the private sector. Although businesses are not likely to find themselves paying small bribes on a daily basis, they may assume large entrance costs at the time of entering or expanding their operations in a given market, and may make side payments to bureaucrats to secure public contracts.[13]

Public–private partnerships

In late 2007 the government started working on a public–private partnerships (PPP) policy, which led to the formation of a PPP Task Force in June 2008.[14] The task force drafted a policy framework for the procurement and delivery of infrastructure and services of over K50 million through cooperation between public institutions and public enterprises.[15] While a positive development in principle, it raises concerns regarding how transparency in the tendering process will be monitored and ensured. In addition, the policy allows for the government to sound out the private sector for interest in certain projects, which may give consulted firms an unfair advantage in the eventual bidding process.

There is certainly reason for concern about the potential for corruption in the PPP projects, given instances of corruption in other public–private interactions. For example, in May 2008 an interim report by the Commission of Inquiry on the Department of Finance revealed that over US$100 million in public funds had disappeared between January 2000 and July 2006.[16] It is widely held that the missing funds have been paid to businesses and consultants holding bogus contracts with the state, but the final report is still pending. The on-again off-again inquiry was initiated in 2006, but its mandate and funding lapsed and were not renewed due to questions regarding the integrity of its members in May 2007.[17] It was reconstituted and relaunched by the prime minister in December 2007, and functioned through April 2008, when it lapsed again on account of a lack of funding and political will to pursue the inquiry.[18]

While the inquiry was taking place, civil servants as well as a prominent businessperson based in Port Moresby spoke publicly about the practice of bureaucrats and politicians extracting payments from businesses after a contract with the state has been awarded but before it is paid out.[19] Media reports suggest that parts of the private sector are complicit in an elaborate network within the bureaucracy, by which a percentage of some of the cheques produced by the Finance Department is taken out before payment is made to the private contractor.[20] Moreover, the private sector in collusion with the state may use

12 Based on comments by participants in the National Research Institute's Leadership Summit on Good Governance, Parliament House, Port Moresby, 12–28 August 2008.
13 Ibid.; *Post-Courier* (Papua New Guinea), 20 June 2007.
14 Public–Private Partnership Task Force, 'Draft National Public–Private Partnership Policy', Port Moresby, 2008.
15 Ibid.
16 *Post-Courier* (Papua New Guinea), 24 April 2008. The prime minister made some aspects of the report public on 13 May 2008.
17 *The National* (Papua New Guinea), 18 May 2007.
18 Prime Minister's Office, press release, December 2007.
19 *Post-Courier* (Papua New Guinea), 11 March 2008.
20 Doriga Henry, Finance Department deputy secretary, quoted in *The National* (Papua New Guinea), 19 November 2007; *Post-Courier* (Papua New Guinea), 11 March 2008.

litigation to extract out-of-court settlements for bogus claims.[21]

Forest governance

Forestry in Papua New Guinea has reached a critical juncture. The current levels of logging are said to be unsustainable, and the legality of many current concessions is in doubt. Although almost all operations have valid licences, logging is generally not considered by NGO watchdogs to be sustainable, and there are human rights abuses of the forest communities and local labour. A review of fourteen logging operations from 2001 to 2006 for instance, was highly critical of these, with the exception of the Japanese company that runs the Open Bay timber project.[22] Until recently, however, they were allowed by the government to continue, apparently with little oversight from public authorities.

In the first admission of its kind by a PNG government, the country's new forest minister, Belden Namah, told parliament in 2008 that logging companies routinely flouted the law with the help of corrupt officials.[23] He found that most of his departmental officers responsible for monitoring forestry operations had ignored the law and that many were 'in the pockets' of logging companies. The minister then suspended two forestry licences and announced that no permits are to be issued for log exports after 2010.[24]

More recently, the *Post-Courier* newspaper linked unnamed PNG politicians to US$45 million in a Singapore bank account, allegedly money earned through secret logging deals.[25]

By most accounts, this sad outcome has its roots in the convoluted system for forestry licences. In this view, the government's regulatory and taxing system for logging companies offers incentives and opportunities to bribe public officials to get logging licences and to undervalue logs for export. While current official log export prices suggest that the industry has been unprofitable for a number of years and therefore not economically viable, logging continues and companies still seek access to new forest areas.[26] This suggests that timber exports are grossly undervalued, and represent a significant loss of revenue for the government.[27]

The logging industry wields influence in Papua New Guinea through political donations, public sponsorship, lobbying and media ownership.[28] In other instances, companies simply 'buy' the rights to log outright from corrupt government officials.[29] Nonetheless, recently the courts seem to have become an effective vehicle for NGOs to challenge such corrupt practices. For example, in September 2007 the Supreme Court granted the Eco-Forestry Forum's application for an injunction to halt the Kamula Doso logging concession in Western Province pending judicial review of

---

21 *The National* (Papua New Guinea), 3 January 2007; *Post-Courier* (Papua New Guinea), 26 July 2006.

22 Forest Trends, *Logging, Legality and Livelihoods in Papua New Guinea: Synthesis of Official Assessments of the Large-scale Logging Industry*, vols. I, II and III (Washington, DC: Forest Trends, 2006).

23 *The Australian*, 23 April 2008.

24 Ibid.

25 *The Australian*, 20 August 2008.

26 Forest Trends, 'External Reviews Find Most Logging in Papua New Guinea Illegal, Unsustainable and Providing Little Benefit to the State and Forest Community', media release, 1 March 2006.

27 Overseas Development Institute (ODI), *Issues and Opportunities in the Forestry Sector in Papua New Guinea*, Papua New Guinea Forest Studies no. 3 (London: ODI, 2007).

28 Centre for Environmental Law and Community Rights and Australian Conservation Foundation, *Bulldozing Progress: Human Rights Abuses and Corruption in Papua New Guinea's Large-scale Logging Industry* (Carlton, Vic: Australian Conservation Foundation, 2006).

29 Ibid.

the case.[30] Kamula Doso contains 790,000 hectares of virgin rainforest.[31] In a not so distant past, similar forest settings around the country have disappeared through unsustainable logging activities.[32]

In an earlier decision, the Supreme Court in June 2007 also granted a stay on a decision of the National Court that had upheld the National Forestry Authority's agreement to grant logging rights in Kamula Doso to Wawoi Guavi Timbers, a subsidiary of Rimbunan Hijau. In granting the stay, the court argued that the National Forest Authority has a duty to comply with the requirements of the Forestry Act 1991.

Private sector action

To increase competitiveness in Papua New Guinea, small to medium-sized firms as well as large multinationals have an economic interest in taking collective action to reduce corruption. Some businesses have realised that it is in their interests to foster a more stable business environment, and on an individual basis have instituted business principles for countering bribery, including policies, strong internal controls and feedback mechanisms.

An example is NASFUND, the superannuation fund that was transformed from a corruption-ridden state enterprise to a highly profitable privately held one. Having inherited a debt of K 154 million, NASFUND assets have reached a record of K 1 billion (US$380 million), which its CEO attributes to finance sector reforms and a strong corporate governance platform.[33] Most public and private firms operating in the country have not been forced by crisis and public scrutiny to adopt similar corporate governance policies, however.

To their credit, businesses in Papua New Guinea have contributed financially to the work of non-profit organisations that fight corruption. A number of companies fielded teams of employees to participate in the Walk Against Corruption on 30 May 2008. Although individual firms are unlikely to speak out about corrupt practices and systems, the heads of chambers of commerce and business councils are in a safer position to make pointed public statements. To reduce the repercussions for firms for speaking out on such issues, business could take collective action through existing associations, such as the Port Moresby Chamber of Commerce, and business or industry councils.

Sarah Dix and Alphonse Gelu (National Research Institute)

Additional reading

A. Ayius, *Corruption in Papua New Guinea* (Boroko: National Research Institute, 2007).

A. Ayius and R. May (eds.), *Corruption in Papua New Guinea: Towards an Understanding of the Issues* (Boroko: National Research Institute, 2007).

C. Bowman, *Opportunities and Impediments to Private Sector Investment and Development in Papua New Guinea*, working paper (Canberra: Australian National University, 2005).

Forest Trends, *Logging, Legality and Livelihoods in Papua New Guinea: Synthesis of Official Assessments of the Large-scale Logging Industry*, vols. I, II, III (Washington, DC: Forest Trends, 2006).

TI Papua New Guinea: www.transparencypng. org.pg.

---

30 *Eko-Forestri Nius*, vol. 9, no. 3/4 (2007).
31 Figures from Papua New Guinea Forest Authority; see www.forestry.gov.pg/site/page.php?id=56.
32 *Eko-Forestri Nius*, vol. 9, no. 3/4 (2007).
33 T. Baeau, 'Interview: Rod Mitchell'; available at: www.islandsbusiness.com; Radio Australia, 11 September 2008.

Philippines

Corruption Perceptions Index 2008: 2.3 (141st out of 180 countries)

Conventions

ADB–OECD Anti-Corruption Action Plan for Asia-Pacific (endorsed November 2001)

UN Convention against Corruption (signed December 2003; ratified November 2006)

UN Convention against Transnational Organized Crime (signed December 2000; ratified May 2002)

Legal and institutional changes

- Several anti-corruption bills have been filed in the Philippine Congress. Among the notable are the following.[1]
  - An amendment to section 11 of Act 3019, otherwise known as the Anti-Graft and Corrupt Practices Act, to increase the pre-scription period for its violation from fifteen to thirty years.
  - An amendment to section 13 of Act 3019, on its non-application to impeachable public officers: officers, including those who can be removed only by impeachment, members of congress and members of the Supreme Court and appeals court, are now exempt from the Anti-Graft and Corrupt Practices Act.
  - An amendment to section 6 of Act 1379, otherwise known as the Forfeiture Law, allows 10 per cent of the value of forfeited properties in corruption cases to be allocated to the office of the ombudsman and for other purposes.
- In order to enhance transparency in public procurement, President Gloria Macapagal-

Arroyo signed Executive Order 662-A, amending Executive Order 662, to create the Procurement Transparency Group, headed by the Government Procurement Policy Board. The group will evaluate, comment on, record and monitor the procurement activities of national government agencies, government-owned and -controlled corporations, government financial institutions, state universities and colleges and local government. The group will be interested in the mode of procurement, budget, volume, susceptibility to problems or anomalies and the importance of the project to the development activities of the Philippines.[2]
- On 27 August 2008 a memorandum of under-standing was signed by the ombudsman, Meceditas Gutierrez, to establish a Center for Asian Integrity in the Philippines, the first of its kind in Asia.[3] The virtual academy will be incorporated into the Philippine Ombudsman Academy, which trains trainers, investigators and prosecutors about integrity. It will also incorporate a research programme to provide qualitative and quantitative research into corruption and include a virtual library to provide access to information on corruption

---

1 See www.senate.gov.ph/lis/leg_sys.aspx?congress=14&type=bill&p=1.
2 Executive Order no. 662-A.
3 *Philippine Daily Inquirer*, 27 August 2008; 9 September 2008.

and curricular support for the development of integrity courses to be accredited by the University of the Philippines. It will be funded by the Millennium Challenge Corporation – Philippine Threshold Programme through the Asia Foundation.

Corruption and the private sector in the Philippines

Graft and corruption are a fact of life in the Philippines; since liberation almost every administration has suffered its sensational graft cases.[4] Moreover, the private sector has cultivated various corrupt practices in order to obtain significant and continuing concessions and advance its private interests.

A recent study by the Social Weather Stations social research institution, based on its 2007 'Survey of Enterprises on Corruption', supplements anecdotal evidence and paints a picture of corruption through the eyes of private sector managers.[5] In terms of the extent of corruption in the sector, the survey found that three out of five managers saw 'a lot' of corruption in the public sector, compared to only one in twelve who saw 'a lot' of corruption in the private sector. Bribery was highlighted as a particular issue, with roughly half the managers revealing that 'most' or 'almost all' firms in their line of business give bribes to win government contracts, compared to only one-fifth giving bribes for private sector contracts.

The survey found that, while 'only a minority of companies follow the basic honest business practices of demanding and issuing receipts, keeping only one set of books, and paying taxes honestly', there was a willingness of managers to

contribute to the fight against corruption. The survey measured managers' readiness to donate money to an anti-corruption fund and found that, although in practice the amount donated has decreased in recent years, a half intended to donate for these purposes over the next two years.

Finally, the survey found that in the National Capital Region (Metro Manila) bribing for government contracts has declined and best practices in record-keeping have improved. It seems, therefore, that, while corruption in the private sector is still a big problem, the private sector is showing some willingness to become part of the solution.

Foreign-assisted projects: double standards and collusion

A big issue related to private sector corruption is the dynamic that is created when foreign investors and contractors enter the market. In February 2008 the issue was highlighted in an investigation by the Philippine Center for Investigative Journalism (PCIJ). According to the report, '[E]xcessive bids and cost overruns are quite common for projects funded by bilateral lenders – notably Japan, Korea, and China – that still tie up sizable portions of their foreign aid to the purchase of goods or services, including consultants, from companies based in their respective countries.'[6]

There is no ceiling or cap on costs for projects funded by foreign donors, leaving them open to collusion and bid-rigging. Although the Philippines sought to impose caps on bids, international financial institutions have 'insisted on exempting foreign-assisted projects from new

4 *Philippine Daily Inquirer*, 12 February 2008.
5 Social Weather Stations (SWS), 'Transparent Accountable Governance: The 2007 SWS Business Survey on Corruption', presentation to the Philippine Cabinet, 21 August 2007 (Quezon City: SWS, 2007).
6 R. Landingin, 'Bids Sans Caps, Tied Loans Favor Foreign Contractors' (part 2 of a three-part series on a PCIJ review of official documents covering seventy-one official development assistance (ODA) projects funded by the Philippines' biggest ODA lenders), 12 February 2008; available at www.pcij.org/stories/2008/oda5.html.

Philippine procurement rules that disallow bids above the so-called approved budget contract (ABC), an estimated cost that is calculated by third party consultants at considerable expense'.[7]

In its 2007 review of ODA, the National Economic and Development Authority (NEDA) reports that twenty-one of the 123 ongoing projects incurred cost overruns amounting to almost US$698 million.[8] While this had benefits for the contractors in terms of more lucrative contracts, it entailed considerable costs to the Philippines, as counterpart funding would have to be raised to pay back the loans.[9]

Collusion between foreign contractors has been seen in the multimillion-dollar foreign-funded infrastructure projects in Visayas and Mindanao. Large foreign contractors allegedly colluded with each other and rigged bidding processes, and, in doing so, dictated the terms of the bids in violation of 'government rules and policies'.[10] As such, it is clear that the recent slew of grand infrastructure projects involving foreign companies poses significant corruption risks. Furthermore, the involvement of foreign companies apparently decreases the access of Filipinos to information on the deals, while at the same time incurring potential loses to the state budget.

Broadband, deep pockets: China's funding of the national broadband network project

One of the most high-profile private sector corruption cases in 2007/8 involved the National Broadband Network (NBN) project. The NBN deal involved contracting a China-based telecommunications company to set up a broadband network connecting government offices throughout the country.[11] It was just one of many investments, however, that were agreed in a July 2006 memorandum of understanding between the Department of Trade and Industry and Zhong Xing Telecommunications Equipment International Investment Ltd (ZTE). On 21 April 2007 the US$329.5 million NBN contract was signed between the Department of Transportation and Communications and ZTE, funded by the Export-Import Bank of China.[12]

Controversy began to surface when Representative Carlos Padilla disclosed in a privilege speech on 29 August 2007 that the then chairman of the Commission on Elections, Benjamin Abalos, had allegedly served as a broker for the Chinese company, playing golf and meeting with ZTE executives several weeks before the NBN contract was signed in China. Abalos admitted to travelling to China and playing golf, but he denied playing middleman for the firm.[13]

On 5 September 2007 Senator Aquilino Pimentel filed a resolution calling for an investigation into the circumstances leading to the approval of the broadband contract with ZTE.[14] Moreover, on 10 September José de Venecia III, son of the House Speaker José de Venecia Jr., a majority shareholder in Amsterdam Holdings Inc. (AHI), one of the companies that stood against ZTE in the bid, claimed that he had overheard Abalos demand money from ZTE officials in China.[15]

7 Ibid.
8 NEDA, *Sixteenth Annual ODA Portfolio Review* (Pasig City: NEDA, 2007).
9 R. Landingin, 2008.
10 Ibid.
11 *Financial Times* (UK), 26 September 2008.
12 See www.newsflash.org/2004/02/pe/pe004246.htm.
13 Newsbreak Online (Philippines), 'Timeline: Exposing the ZTE Overprice', 8 February 2008.
14 Ibid.
15 Ibid.

The Senate investigated the charges of bribery. There were two Senate hearings, at which de Venecia III accused Abalos of offering him US$10 million to withdraw his bid, and claimed that the First Gentleman, José Miguel Arroyo, had personally told him to 'back off' from pursuing the NBN project.[16] The Supreme Court issued a temporary restraining order on the contract, and eleven days later, on 22 September, President Macapagal-Arroyo suspended the deal.

Despite the project's suspension, on 26 September 2007 Secretary Romulo Neri, the economic planning secretary at the time of the bidding, accused Abalos of offering him P200 million (US$4.36 million) for facilitating the approval of the project.[17] In a counter-attack, Abalos accused Neri of lying, and suggested that he might be in cahoots with José de Vencia III.[18] Neri later invoked executive privilege in response to questions regarding his conversations with President Macapagal-Arroyo on the bribe attempt.[19] In November the president cancelled the contract.[20]

In the meantime, the fallout from this case has been dramatic. In recognition of the growing public unease, in September the president set up the Chinese Projects Oversight Panel to oversee Chinese projects.[21] Nevertheless, in February, former Senator Jovito Salonga filed a criminal complaint against the president in relation to her involvement in the case.[22] This was only weeks after Macapagal-Arroyo had faced calls for her resignation, following testimony before the Senate that 'implicated former and current senior officials'.[23] In response, in February 2008, the president halted all 'fresh borrowings from China and other lenders of big infrastructure projects'.[24] As a result, alternative sources of funding would have to be sought for the eleven outstanding projects for which no contract had yet been signed.[25]

This case illustrates how the involvement of foreign companies, often supported by state loans and guarantees, can pose substantial corruption risks. Although it is encouraging that the Philippines has conducted extensive investigations into the allegations of bribery, it is disconcerting that the company at the centre of this debacle has not been held accountable for its part in the activities. When funding is sought from abroad and foreign companies are used in contracts, this apparently decreases the Philippines' ability to manage its affairs openly and transparently.

The Northrail Project: the corruption risks continue

The foreign assisted Northrail Project, also funded by the Export-Import Bank of China, threw up its own issues of corruption, including 'alleged onerous terms and conditions imposed upon the Philippine government in the contract'.[26]

During a December 2003 state visit to China, President Macapagal-Arroyo signed a memorandum of agreement between the North Luzon Railways Corporation and the China National Machinery and Equipment Corporation

16 *Financial Times* (UK), 26 September 2007.
17 *Financial Times* (UK), 19 February 2008.
18 Ibid.
19 Newsbreak Online (Philippines), 7 February 2008.
20 *Financial Times* (UK), 21 November 2007.
21 *Financial Times* (UK), 26 September 2008.
22 *Financial Times* (UK), 28 February 2008.
23 *Financial Times* (UK), 8 February 2008.
24 *Financial Times* (UK), 19 February 2008.
25 Ibid.
26 PinoyPress.com (Philippines), 21 November 2007.

(CNMEC). On 26 February 2004 a buyer credit loan agreement was made between the Export-Import Bank of China and the government, in order to fund the Northrail Project. The bank agreed to lend US$400 million of the total US$503 million, the remainder to be funded by the Philippine government.[27]

Allegations of corruption flew about the project, however. Protests began when it was found that the contract had been awarded without a competitive bidding process. In November 2007 Senator Aquilino Pimentel formally asked for the resumption of the Senate inquiry into the project, on the grounds that it was overpriced, it had been contracted without the approval of the monetary board and it burdened the Philippines with 'onerous conditions especially in case of default in the payment of the loan'.[28]

Notwithstanding the serious infirmities in the agreement, billions of pesos in public funds will be spent by the government pursuant to agreements in the contractual implementation of the Northrail Project when the project is resumed.[29] Meanwhile, the government continues to pay interest charges for the Northrail Project loans to the tune of P1 million (US$21,250) a day.[30] Despite these alarming issues, reasonable requests from media organisations such as the PCIJ for certified copies of the Northrail contract from the Philippine National Railways have been declined. Sadly, according to a PCIJ study, before scandals involving state projects began erupting late in 2006, the government seemed headed towards transparency;[31] this trend may be reversed by recent events.

Segundo Romero, Aileen Laus and Dolores Español
(TI Philippines)

Additional reading

P. Lacson, 'Legacy of Corruption', speech delivered before the Philippine Senate, 11 September 2007.

R. Landingin, 'Bids Sans Caps, Tied Loans Favor Foreign Contractors', 12 February 2008; available at www.pcij.org/stories/2008/oda5.html.

SWS, 'Transparent Accountable Governance: The 2007 SWS Business Survey on Corruption', presentation to the Philippine Cabinet, 21 August 2007 (Quezon City: SWS, 2007).

TI Philippines: www.transparencyintl.org.

---

27 Petition (For Certiorari and Prohibition with Prayer for the issuance of a Writ of Preliminary Injunction and/or Temporary Restraining Order) of the Northrail Contract. Supreme Court of the Philippines. Manila, Philippines.

28 PinoyPress.com (Philippines), 21 November 2007.

29 Senate of the Philippines, press release, 20 October 2008; see www.senate.gov.ph/press_release/2008/1020_pimentel2.asp.

30 Senate of the Philippines, press release, 14 July 2008; See www.senate.gov.ph/press_release/2008/0714_pimentel1.asp.

31 K. Ilagan, 'Government Curbs Access to Information Amid Senate Scrutiny of Projects', 30 March 2008; available at www.pcij.org/stories/2008/access-to-info.html.

South Korea

Corruption Perceptions Index 2008: 5.6 (40th out of 180 countries)

Conventions

ADB–OECD Anti-Corruption Action Plan for Asia-Pacific (endorsed November 2001)

OECD Convention on Combating Bribery of Public Foreign Officials (signed January 1999; ratified March 1999)

UN Convention against Corruption (signed December 2003; ratified March 2008)

UN Convention against Transnational Organized Crime (signed December 2000; not yet ratified)

Legal and institutional changes

- On 26 February 2008 the Special Act on Confiscation and Recovery of Corrupt Assets[1] was passed at the Assembly plenary session in order to implement the UNCAC. The law's essentials include international cooperation on corrupt crimes, special regulations on confiscation, and additional resources and staff focused on the recovery of corrupt assets. By incorporating the UNCAC into law, it is expected that international cooperation on corruption cases will be strengthened and more assets derived from corruption will be recovered from abroad. Nevertheless, the law has some shortcomings, including the lack of a comprehensive definition of corruption that covers, in particular, the private sector. Furthermore, it does not encourage the development of anti-corruption policies with the explicit involvement of civil society.
- Parallel to the ratification and implementation of the UNCAC, a contradictory and unconstructive law was passed on Anti-Corruption and the Establishment and Operation of the Anti-Corruption and Civil Rights Commission (ACRC).[2] This law aims to integrate three different government institutions: the Korean Independent Commission Against Corruption (KICAC), which is responsible for preventing corruption; the Ombudsman of Korea, which handles civil complaints; and the Administrative Appeals Commission, which is in charge of administrative adjudication. In addition to merging roles, which will affect the commission's ability to focus on corruption issues, the independence of the anti-corruption function of the new commission is seriously jeopardised. Whereas previously the KICAC was composed of nine commissioners recommended by the president, parliament and the Supreme Court, the new commission is almost entirely appointed by the president.[3] Moreover, although the KICAC was formerly

---

1 Act no. 8993, enacted on 28 March 2008, enumerates twenty-nine kinds of crimes regarded as corruption crimes from existing laws, but does not give any comprehensive definition on private corruption.

2 Act no. 8878.

3 Article 13 of Law on Anti-Corruption and the Establishment and Operation of the Anti-Corruption and Civil Rights Commission, enacted 29 February 2008.

under the auspices of the president, the ACRC is now under the control of the prime minister. A further indication of the commission's lack of commitment to corruption is that, while it calls itself the Anti-Corruption and Civil Rights Commission in English, the Korean name for the ACRC is simply Civil Rights Commission.[4]

- The Korean Pact on Anti-Corruption and Transparency (K-PACT) Council[5] is facing serious challenges. It made impressive developments as an active movement following its launch, spreading to several sectors including construction, education, social welfare, finance, forestry and health care, and also to several regions in South Korea. On 30 May 2008, however, the ACRC officially suspended the public sector's contribution to the K-PACT's expenses. The reasoning that was given included the need for the 'establishment of an efficient paradigm for government-civilian cooperation corresponding to the administrative philosophy of the new administration'.[6] Based on this decision, the public sector officially withdrew from the K-PACT, and as such the agreement on K-PACT between the four sectors (public, private, political and civil society) is facing crisis.

New government and pro-business policy

Following the introduction of a new government, South Korea is undergoing a change in policy that has influenced almost all fields related to corruption. Ten years of so-called 'left-wing' (progressive) government ended and power was moved to the 'right wing' (conservatives) at the end of 2007. Tackling the corruption problem should be an obligatory task for every government regardless of its leaning, but several examples illustrate what has become known as the 'setback' phenomenon, whereby the current government has introduced 'business-friendly' policies, sometimes at the expense of anti-corruption initiatives.

The new government's pro-business policy can be seen as reneging on previous governments' anti-corruption commitments and achievements. The closure of the KICAC, its merger with two other organisations (forming the ACRC) and the restructured composition of the new commission have undermined both the focus on corruption and the commission's independent decision-making processes. Now thirteen out of the fifteen commissioners are appointed by the president, making independent decision-making impossible.[7] Furthermore, the ACRC's subsequent withdrawal of funding to the K-PACT and its request to the Board of Audit and Inspection to assess the K-PACT Council's accounting records has further damaged this authority and questioned its ability to continue as a legitimate council.[8]

There has also been a setback directly related to the defence sector. In an attempt to reform the defence industry, former President Roh in 2003 organised a special committee under the prime minister to ensure transparency, fairness and efficiency. It proposed creating a new system of defence acquisition by establishing a

---

4 See www.acrc.go.kr/eng_index.jsp.

5 The Korean Pact on Anti-Corruption and Transparency is a voluntary agreement proposed by civil society and concluded on 9 March 2005 to form an anti-corruption system through alliances between public, political and private sectors and civil society. To support implementation and spread of K-PACT, each sector made an appointment to establish the K-PACT Council as the secretariat and has been submitting a share of expenses. See www. pact.or.kr/english/sub/menu_01_01.php.

6 *The Hankyoreh* (South Korea), 1 October 2008.

7 See footnote 3.

8 *The Hankyoreh* (South Korea), 1 October 2008

new national agency, the Defense Acquisition Program Administration (DAPA), which was set up in January 2006.[9] This new programme is facing crisis, however, as the Ministry of Defense contends that it undermines its decision-making power.[10] The provisional alternative proposed by the ministry is to return to it the main functions of DAPA related to strategic, medium- and long-term decision-making. As such, civil society has expressed deep concern this move could lead to a backward step for transparency.

Finally, in terms of monitoring private sector corruption and financial crimes, the system is likely to be further weakened. While the ACRC, as was the case for KICAC, covers only public sector corruption, the Fair Trade Commission has influence over the private sector, in terms of being able to restrict unfair transactions. While it focuses mainly on the transactions of conglomerates, it has the power to impact positively on anti-corruption efforts, as it has not only investigation rights but also exclusive accusation rights for law enforcement. There are concerns that this may change, however, because under the government's 'business-friendly' policies all previously enacted laws and ordinances are being amended under the new principle of easing regulations. The sanctions applying to the private sector do not constitute an adequate deterrent. The judiciary is widely considered to be generally lenient on white-collar crime, and the president, in celebration of Liberation Day in August 2008, granted an amnesty to 341,000 executives, politicians and bureaucrats convicted of crimes including fraud and embezzlement.[11]

As such, the new government's stand has damaged some of the most important anti-corruption institutions, on the premise that it desires a more business-friendly environment, thereby undermining the basic proposition that corruption harms business, and taking a step in the wrong direction in terms of fighting it.

Samsung, slush funds and succession

On 29 October 2007 former prosecutor and attorney Kim Yong-Chul, who had headed Samsung's legal advisory team, made a declaration of conscience to the Catholic Priests' Association for Justice in Korea[12] that Samsung had amassed a huge illegal slush fund and offered bribes to high-ranking officials.[13] The corruption scandal sent a shock wave through South Korean society.[14]

In his disclosure, Kim alleged that Samsung had amassed billions of won in slush funds by using borrowed bank accounts of company executives and employees. He also said that Samsung routinely offered bribes to high-ranking officials and public administration staff, including the public prosecutor-designate, the chairman of KICAC and the incoming head of the National Intelligence Service, all of whom were ex-prosecutors. He also said that Samsung

---

9 The committee also proposed many policies regarding enhancing competitiveness for the construction of a basis of self-reliance of national defence. The Defense Acquisition Program Act was enacted on 2 January 2006 (act no. 7845); see www.dapa.go.kr/eng/index.jsp.

10 The Ministry of National Defense (MND) is talking about closing DAPA but its real intent is to move the key functions of DAPA back to the MND, such as strategic, medium- and long-term decision-making, budget planning and questions relating to arms exports. The only acceptable reason for this trial is that, following the establishment of DAPA, the level of cooperation between each corps and DAPA has not been satisfactory. This objection pales into insignificance alongside the achievements of DAPA, however. Corruption cases numbered twenty-six in 2004 and sixteen in 2005, but after DAPA there were no corruption scandals in 2006 and 2007. See www.sisapress.com/news/articleView.html?idxno=46562 (Korean); *Korea Times*, 30 October 2008.

11 Reuters (UK), 11 August 2008.

12 This was one of the representative democratisation movement NGOs in the 1970s and 1980s.

13 'Whistle-blower lashes out at Samsung', Naver, 6 November 2007.

14 'Corruption charges', Naver, 7 November 2007.

had systematically and illegally transferred the right of management from chairman Lee Gun-Hee to his son Lee Jae-Yong, and that during this process many crimes had been committed, including huge amounts of tax evasion.

Despite the many political disputes, lawyer-turned-whistleblower Kim Yong-Chul made his disclosure in order to catalyse a special prosecutor to investigate the scandal. On 23 November 2007 the Assembly passed a special prosecutor law to investigate the Samsung scandal. A special prosecution team was formed, and investigations began on 10 January 2008. The three-month investigation included locating and seizing details of the borrowed bank accounts from Samsung's main building. On 17 April 2008 the special prosecutor announced that ten Samsung executives would be prosecuted, including the chairman and his son, yet no one was arrested. Five days later the chairman announced a reform plan, which included his resignation.[15]

The investigation found that a great deal of Kim Yong-Chul's disclosure was accurate.[16] The core of the case consisted of the illegal succession of the right to management from father to son and allegations of tax evasion. According to the investigation, the chairman's secretary's office had allowed affiliate companies of Samsung to issue convertible bonds and bonds with a warrant at a low price to the chairman's son. Through this process the son became Samsung's largest shareholder, and as such was assured his status as his father's successor. The investigation also revealed that slush funds of at least US$4.5 billion had been hidden by using 'borrowed name' bank accounts. Through the use of these 1,199 stock accounts the chairman is thought to have bought and sold the shares of Samsung group companies, including Samsung Electronics. By means of this process, it was alleged, he had made profits of US$564.3 million and evaded taxes to the tune of US$112.8 million.[17]

Disappointingly, from the perspective of anti-corruption efforts, the bribery allegations were not upheld by the public prosecutor. The reasons given included, in some cases, that there was not sufficient evidence to support bribery accusations and that the statute of limitation had expired.[18] In other cases, the prosecutor accepted the denial of the persons concerned. In October 2008 Lee Gun-Hee was convicted of evading a tax bill of only US$45.6 million related to the proceeds of covert stock trading using 'borrowed name' accounts.[19] Appeal judges dismissed the other charges related to the wealth transfer to his son.[20]

A number of lessons can be learnt from the Samsung case. First, it is significant that Kim Yong-Chul chose to bring his case to civil society rather than going down the official routes of the national audit or inspection institutions. This reveals a high level of distrust in national institutions and their ability to address issues of corruption.

The results of the official investigation were duly criticised by civil society.[21] Five important criticisms were raised in particular.

---

15 *Korea Times*, 10 July 2008.
16 The full text of the special prosecutor's investigation report can be downloaded in Korean at www.moneytoday.co.kr/view/mtview.php?type=1&no=2008041713484052141&outlink=1.
    See a brief report in English at www.koreatimes.co.kr/www/news/nation/2008/04/117_22685.html.
17 *Korea Times*, 17 April 2008.
18 *Economist* (UK), 26 April 2008.
19 Agence France-Presse, 10 October 2008.
20 Ibid.; *Jakarta Post* (Indonesia), 16 July 2008.
21 Through the temporary network organisation 'People's Actions for Investigation of Illegality of the Actions of Samsung and Lee Gun-Hee'.

- Through the low valuation of the convertible bonds, the valuation of the illegal profits and amount embezzled was too conservative.
- The special prosecutor reduced the amount of the illegal slush funds taken into account and did not uphold the accusation of fraudulent accounts.
- Although a witness to bribe-paying should be a high enough level of proof, the special prosecutor cleared high-ranking officials of the suspicion of bribe-paying, citing a lack of sufficient evidence.
- Despite there being a high risk of the suspected persons destroying evidence or fleeing the country, none of them were arrested.
- By clearing Lee Jae-Yong of any criminal involvement, the prosecutor legalised the succession of management rights from father to son.[22]

There are further concerns arising from the fact that just one large company could have routinely controlled so many of the most important national institutions and high-ranking officials. For the first time in South Korea's history, there was a real feeling this was a case of state capture. The problem of how to achieve the rule of law emerges as significant, as the judiciary has historically been lenient on the criminal activities of big conglomerates. In 2006, for example, Hyundai chairman Jung Mong-Gu was found guilty of retaining illegal slush funds of up to US$100 million and embezzling US$70 million, and former Daewoo chairman Kim Woo-Jung

was found guilty of keeping fraudulent accounts of up to US$23 billion.[23] Both were released or pardoned after very short terms in prison.[24]

While the Samsung case highlights serious deficiencies in the way corruption in large conglomerates is handled, there are also signs that the private sector in South Korea is beginning to address business ethics and starting to align with global standards of corporate social responsibility. Although it is clear that this is mainly due to civil society initiative and pressure, voluntary efforts are increasing. By July 2007 124 South Korean companies were participating in the UN Global Compact, and on 17 September 2007 the UN Global Compact Network Korea was established.[25]

Sung-Goo Kang (TI South Korea)

Additional reading

ACRC, *Anti-corruption Annual Report 2007* (Seoul: ACRC, 2008).

DAPA, *Pangwisaopch'ong kaech'ong paekseo* [*Defense Acquisition Program Administration Opening Report*] (Seoul: DAPA, 2005).

K-PACT Council, *A Precious Pact for a Beautiful Future: The K-PACT 2005–2008 Report* (Seoul: K-PACT Council, 2008).

J. Yi, *Naebu sin'go paekseo* [*White Paper of Whistleblowing*] (Seoul: KICAC/Friends of Whistleblowers, 2007).

TI Korea: www.ti.or.kr.

---

22 See blog.peoplepower21.org/Economy/23088 (in Korean); *Korea Times*, 18 April 2008.
23 *New York Times* (US), 31 May 2006.
24 Mr Jung Mong-Gu was sentenced on 28 April 2006; *International Herald Tribune* (US), 28 April 2006. Mr Kim Woo-Jung was sentenced on 30 May 2006; *Financial Times* (UK), 31 May 2006.
25 See www.unglobalcompact.kr/eng/index.php.

Sri Lanka

Corruption Perceptions Index 2008: 3.2 (92nd out of 180 countries)

Conventions

ADB–OECD Anti-Corruption Action Plan for Asia-Pacific (endorsed March 2006)

UN Convention against Corruption (signed March 2004; ratified March 2004)

UN Convention against Transnational Organized Crime (signed December 2000; ratified September 2006)

Legal and institutional changes

- The new Companies Act introduced in 2007 strengthens governance within companies. The act provides, *inter alia*, that directors must act in good faith and in the interests of the company and not in a manner that is reckless or grossly negligent. Furthermore, their interests should be registered in an Interests Register, and failure to register interests will result in a fine not exceeding Rs 200,000 (approximately US$1,800). Directors should also disclose their shares in the company, whether they are held directly or indirectly. The aim of the act is to codify directors' duties, create greater transparency and enable shareholders to compel the board to comply with the duties. Another unique feature in the act is that it has provisions for rewarding whistleblowers by entitling them to the reimbursement of legal expenses from the fines levied in the action.[1]
- In February 2008 the director general of the Commission to Investigate Allegations of Bribery or Corruption (CIABOC) was removed

and transferred to the Presidential Secretariat. By the time of writing of this report no permanent director general had been appointed, thus paralysing its work. In August 2008, in consultation with the CIABOC, the president directed the Attorney General's Department to take over all the 'important cases', and to set up a special Bribery Unit in its department. The huge stockpile of cases, incomplete investigations and failed prosecutions of CIABOC were given as justification for this transfer.[2]

- In March 2008 the National Public Procurement Agency (NPA) merged with the Treasury as the result of a presidential directive. This brought the plans of the previous government to establish the NPA as an independent body with powers to supervise all tender processes to the end. As the Treasury is under the purview of the Ministry of Finance, there will henceforth be no independent control of national procurement.[3]
- In May 2008 the president prorogued parliament, thus bringing all activities of parliamentary committees, including the Public Accounts Committee (PAC) and the then

---

1 Information provided by Dr Arittha Wickramanayake, attorney-at-law.
2 *Sunday Times* (Sri Lanka), 13 July 2008.
3 Interview with M. D. A. Harold, chairman of Transparency International Sri Lanka, 23 May 2008.

effective Committee on Public Enterprises (COPE), which had exposed large-scale corruption in 2007, to a halt. When parliament resumed work in July 2008, two government ministers were appointed to head these oversight committees. This was seen as a violation of democratic parliamentary norms and traditions of oversight committees being headed by members of the opposition, and an attempt to weaken the legislature further.[4]

- As of January 2008 a new Mandatory Code of Corporate Governance for Licensed Banks came into force.[5] The code was set up by the Central Bank of Sri Lanka. The implementation of the code is expected to improve the soundness of the banking system, which is vital to the maintenance of the financial system's stability.
- Following the passing of a new Prevention of Money Laundering Act in 2006, a separate Anti-Money Laundering Authority has been set up, and banks and financial institutions are required to report large-value transactions and adopt 'know your customer' rules[6] and best practices.
- The seventeenth amendment to the constitution, which was intended to re-establish an independent public service, continued to be ignored, leading to a further decline in public confidence in the rule of law and good governance.[7] Moreover, the Constitutional Council, a body created in 2001 to bring about transparency and accountability in public institutions, has not been appointed since its last term lapsed in March 2005. While

parliament finally nominated all appointed members to the Constitutional Council in February/March 2008, formal appointments had not been made by the president at the time of writing this report. In the absence of the Constitutional Council, appointments to key institutions are made by the president unilaterally without any scrutiny of the appointees.[8]

Defence sector corruption

Since the abrogation of the Norwegian-brokered ceasefire agreement between the Liberation Tigers of Tamil Eelam (LTTE) and the Sri Lankan government in January 2008, the civil war has intensified further and military spending has reached unprecedented levels. According to the budget proposal for 2009 presented by the president on 6 November 2008, 'security related expenditure to counter terrorism and protect public life and property' has increased from Rs 63 billion (US$500 million) in 2007 to Rs 117 billion (US$1 billion) in 2008.[9] Defence spending will increase again in 2009.[10]

Military expenses are not subject to control by the auditor general, and laws such as the Official Secrets Act of 1955 prevent any irregularities from being investigated. As a result of the existence of a mega-Cabinet (approximately a half of the Members of Parliament are in the Cabinet), effective parliamentary control of executive expenditure has become extremely weak. There is virtually no public oversight of

4 TI Sri Lanka, 'Resign from Chairmanship of COPE & PAC, Urges TSL', press release, 24 July 2008.
5 See www.cbsl.gov.lk/pics_n_docs/09_lr/_docs/directions/bsd/2007new/Direction_No_11_LCBs.pdf.
6 Government of Sri Lanka, 'Central Bank Warns against Unlawful Financial Transactions', press release, 19 February 2008.
7 For further discussion, see www.humanrightsinitiative.org/publications/nl/newsletter_summer_2006/article4.htm.
8 A detailed list of presidential appointments to high positions since 2006 is available in TI Sri Lanka, *The Forgotten Constitutional Council: An Analysis of Consequences of the Non-implementation of the 17th Amendment*, position paper (Colombo: TI Sri Lanka, 2008).
9 See www.treasury.gov.lk/docs/budget2008/speecheng.pdf.
10 Agence France-Presse, 4 November 2008.

military expenditure, and the media are systematically prevented from reporting on it.[11] There is a strong perception, however, that weapons deals are rigged, with key public figures playing a central role.[12]

The controversial multimillion-rupee Mikoyan MiG-27 deal was in the spotlight throughout 2007 and 2008. It involved the Sri Lanka Air Force (SLAF) and the Ukrainian company Ukrinmash, a subsidiary of the Ukrainian government-owned trading arm Ukrspetsexport.[13] The deal concerned the payment of US$14.6 million to offshore company Bellimissa Holdings Ltd, registered in London, for four old MiG-27 fighter jets and the overhaul of four others. The very same aircraft had been rejected by the SLAF in 2000, because of their age. In 2006, however, a much higher price was paid for the same jets, which by then were even older.[14]

Following revelations by the Sri Lankan *Sunday Times*, on 12 August 2007, the government announced the appointment of a parliamentary select committee to look into the deal.[15] With the prorogation of parliament in May 2008, however, the committee was dissolved, and the select committee has not been reappointed subsequently. The defence journalist who revealed the involvement in the deal of the then Sri Lankan ambassador to Moscow, a cousin of a powerful politician, received threats and subsequently withdrew from following up his investigation.[16] Investigations by the CIABOC were also halted in February 2008 with the removal of its director general.[17]

In a similar pattern, just a day before the MiG-27 deal was signed in July 2006, a state-owned company, Lanka Logistics & Technologies Ltd, was set up to procure all military goods and services. This arrangement allows the government to hold the monopoly over the procurement of all military hardware for the security forces and the police, and effectively debars the private sector from dealing with the government on any of the military items listed in the regulations.[18] In the absence of a tendering process and given the high secrecy for purchases, the final say on military procurement will remain in the realm of a select handful in the state-owned company. Allegations of corruption and fraud in connection with Lanka Logistics have contributed to the further erosion of public confidence in the government.[19]

VAT fraud

Tax fraud is widespread in Sri Lanka. Capacity problems in tax administration, the coexistence of parallel regimes and the existence of legal provisions enabling the Board of Investment (BOI) to override Inland Revenue and Customs laws in granting tax concessions provide an enabling environment for fraud and corruption at the expense of the Treasury.[20]

A highly publicised case in 2007 was the VAT (value added tax) scam, a blatant case of collusion between the private and public sectors. This scam, first revealed by Sri Lanka's auditor general in 2005, is Sri Lanka's – and probably Asia's – biggest alleged tax scandal, involving the loss

---

11 Independent reporting is discouraged by means of verbal threats and physical assault on journalists and their relatives. See www.rsf.org/print.php3?id_article=20798.
12 See www.business-anti-corruption.com/normal.asp?pageid=352.
13 *Sunday Times* (Sri Lanka), 12 August 2007.
14 *Sunday Times* (Sri Lanka), 19 August 2007.
15 Ibid.
16 See www.wsws.org/articles/2007/oct2007/sril-o08.shtml.
17 Sunday Times Online (Sri Lanka), 24 February 2008.
18 *Sunday Times* (Sri Lanka), 14 October 2007.
19 See www.indi.ca/2007/10/the-corruption-of-war/; *Sunday Times* (Sri Lanka) 6 May 2007.
20 See go.worldbank.org/T7A1VI8GH0.

of more than Rs 4 billion (approximately US$40 million) in taxes between 2002 and 2004.[21]

In January 2008 eleven leading Colombo businessmen, mostly involved in the garment trade, and two officers at the Income Tax Department were charged with the criminal misappropriation of Rs 4 billion accruing from VAT, by producing false documents.[22] In Sri Lanka, exporters can claim a VAT refund (12.5 per cent of the export value)[23] from the Inland Revenue Department (IRD) by proving costs of production and investment. A report by the former auditor general, Sarath Chandra Mayadunne, in August 2007 found that twenty companies had defrauded the IRD of Rs 3.6 billion,[24] using fictitious documents fabricated in support of non-existent exports. All the 235 refund cheques had been collected from the Tax Department by the same person, either on the day the cheques were written or a day or two afterwards. The cheque collector had also allegedly used thirteen National Identity Cards with different numbers, all of which were later found to be false. Of the companies indicted, sixteen were found to have declared exports valued at Rs 20.5 billion without having made any exports whatsoever. The four other companies had declared exports valued at Rs 5.6 billion, but the actual exports confirmed by the export entries amounted only to Rs 0.3 billion, or 6 per cent of the declared amount.[25]

A report by the Public Accounts Committee launched in November 2007 found that the IRD had also entertained VAT declarations from two bogus companies in 2004. The report noted that the computer system of the IRD had been manipulated so that two VAT assessments amounting to more than Rs 200 billion did not appear on the computer screen for control and audit. Furthermore, the report found that 183 out of 235 documents relevant to the refunds had gone missing.[26]

Finally, in January 2008 a presidential commission tasked to investigate the fraud discovered another large-scale VAT fraud, to the tune of Rs 50 million, committed by a polythene manufacturer. This company also submitted falsified documentation on export production to obtain VAT refunds.[27] While the court case continues, many important suspects and witnesses have left the country.[28]

Successful initiatives by the private sector

In January 2007 the Institute of Chartered Accountants of Sri Lanka (ICASL) and the Securities and Exchange Commission of Sri Lanka, in consultation with the Colombo Stock Exchange, started a joint initiative with a view to formulating standards on corporate governance for mandatory compliance by companies listed on the exchange.[29] These standards were incorporated into the 'Listing Rules' of the exchange in April 2007. The standards were formulated by a select committee, which took account of corporate governance standards in several jurisdictions, including the United Kingdom and

21 See asiatax.wordpress.com/2007/12/02/sri-lanka-billions-in-vat-frauds-pac/. While the auditor general's report of 2005 is not available electronically, the 2006 report can be downloaded at www.auditorgeneral.lk/reports/English/Annual%20Reports%20_2006_English.pdf.
22 *Sunday Times* (Sri Lanka), 27 January 2008.
23 Ibid.
24 *Daily News* (Sri Lanka), 30 November 2007.
25 Corruption Watch (Sri Lanka), 26 August 2007.
26 *Daily Mirror* (Sri Lanka), 30 November 2007.
27 *Lankanewspapers.com* (Sri Lanka), 26 January 2007.
28 Interview with J. C. Weliamuna, attorney-at-law and executive director of Transparency International, 16 June 2008.
29 See corruptionwatch.ard-acp.com/index.php?q=2&t=resource&id=82.

the United States. They relate to the minimum number of non-executive and independent directors, the basis for determining 'independence', disclosures required to be made by listed companies in respect of its directorate and the minimal requirements to be met by listed companies in respect of the audit committee and the remuneration committee.[30]

In December 2007, the Central Bank of Sri Lanka introduced a Mandatory Code of Corporate Governance for Licensed Banks in Sri Lanka.[31] The code has been designed as a series of rules based upon fundamental principles to promote a healthy risk management framework for banks, with accountability and transparency being achieved through the policies and oversight of the boards of directors. The code regulates the responsibilities of the board and its composition, and puts up criteria to assess the fitness and propriety of directors, appointment mechanisms for board committees and the disclosure of information.[32] Measures are also being taken by them to introduce a similar code for finance companies.

Bettina Meier (TI Sri Lanka)

Additional reading

Anti-Corruption Program (ACP), *Anti-Corruption Action Plan* (Colombo: ACP, 2007).

Associates in Rural Development (ARD), Inc., and USAID Sri Lanka, *Sri Lanka Anti-corruption Program: Final Project Completion Report* (Burlington, VT: ARD, Inc./USAID Sri Lanka, 2007).

CPA and TI Sri Lanka, *National Integrity Systems: Transparency International Country Study Report, Sri Lanka 2003* (Colombo: CPA/TI Sri Lanka, 2003).

K. M. de Silva, G. H. Peiris and S. W. R. de A. Samarasinghe (eds.), *Corruption in South Asia: India, Pakistan and Sri Lanka* (Kandy: International Centre for Ethnic Studies, 2002).

Global Integrity, *Sri Lanka Report* (Washington, DC: Global Integrity, 2007).

SI–CPA, *A Survey on Corruption in Sri Lanka 2007* (Colombo: SI–CPA, 2007).

USAID Sri Lanka, *Synopsis of Anticorruption and Related Laws* (Colombo: USAID Sri Lanka, 2007).

USAID Sri Lanka and SLEA, *The Impact of Corruption on Poverty and Economic Growth*, research paper (Colombo: USAID Sri Lanka/SLEA, 2007).

TI Sri Lanka: www.tisrilanka.org.

---

30 Listing Rules of Colombo Stock Exchange, available at www.cse.lk/270808/pdf/listing_rules/listing_rules_section_6_rules_on_corporate_governance.pdf. See also paper by G. Wickramashinghe, 'Recent Developments in Corporate Governance for Listed Companies in Sri Lanka', presented at the OECD Roundtable on Capital Market Reform in Asia, Tokyo, 12 October 2006.

31 See www.cbsl.gov.lk/info/09_lr/_popups/_2008_new.htm; Central Bank of Sri Lanka, Bank Supervision Department, 'Draft Mandatory Code of Corporate Governance for Licensed Banks in Sri Lanka', press release, 7 December 2007.

32 See www.cbsl.gov.lk/pics_n_docs/09_lr/_docs/directions/bsd/2007new/Direction_No_11_LCBs.pdf.

6.4 Europe and Central Asia

Armenia

Corruption Perceptions Index 2008: 2.9 (109th out of 180 countries)

Conventions

Council of Europe Civil Law Convention on Corruption (signed February 2004; ratified January 2005)

Council of Europe Criminal Law Convention on Corruption (signed May 2003; ratified January 2006)

UN Convention against Corruption (signed May 2005; ratified March 2007)

Legal and institutional changes

- In September 2007 the post of the head of the Anti-Corruption Strategy Monitoring Commission was filled after being vacant for three months. Gevorg Mheryan, assistant to the president, became chairman of the commission. At a 7 September meeting of the Anti-Corruption Council,[1] Mheryan stated that there was a need to develop a new strategy and action plan and that previous plans could be considered as having been completed based on reports by the commission and the protocols of the council. At the beginning of 2008 an expert group was set up consisting of local anti-corruption experts. Following terms of reference designed earlier, they set about developing a new strategy and presented the first chapter to civil society and international organisations for suggestions and feedback.

- In 2007 Armenia began implementing the Council of Europe's Group of States against Corruption (GRECO) recommendations. According to the report[2] submitted to GRECO in September that year, Armenia implemented ten recommendations completely, seven recommendations were implemented partially and seven were not implemented at all. Based on this information, GRECO experts prepared a compliance report, which was adopted at the thirty-eighth GRECO meeting in June 2008.

- In June 2007 a new constitutional provision came into effect, following amendments made during a referendum held on 27 November 2005.[3] The provision made the Control Chamber of the Republic of Armenia, the supreme audit institution, an

---

1 *Hayastani Hanrapetutyun* (Armenia), 8 September 2007.

2 At its twenty-seventh plenary meeting on 10 March 2006, GRECO officially submitted to the Armenian government twenty-four recommendations developed in the framework of the 'Joint First and Second Round Assessment Report' carried out by the GRECO evaluation team during its visit to Armenia in May–June 2005.

3 Article 83.4 of the constitution of the Republic of Armenia.

independent body; previously it had been under the authority of parliament. Parliament appointed the new chairman of the chamber on 5 November 2007.[4]

- In May 2007 the new Law on the Office of the Public Prosecutor brought several important changes related to corruption.[5] The changes include new procedures for appointing the prosecutor general and prosecutors, the establishment of a school for public prosecutors and a new system for sanctioning prosecutors. The law also establishes a new commission of ethics and a new system of remuneration for prosecutors and other employees working in the offices of public prosecutors. In addition, the prosecutor general will no longer be able to carry out pre-trial investigations. Formerly there had been opportunities for abuse of power, as the same body had been able simultaneously to conduct criminal investigations and oversee the legality of the investigations; these functions have now been separated.

- On 11 October 2007 a new Law on Securities Market Regulation was adopted.[6] The law protects the rights and lawful interests of investors, and promotes transparency and the sustainable and efficient development of the securities market, thus improving the reliability of the securities pricing system and the reduction of systemic risks in the securities market.

- On 22 October 2007 the Armenian parliament adopted the Law on Operational-Investigative Activities.[7] This law was included in the action plan of the first anti-corruption strategy. It defines the form of investigative activities carried out by government agencies, including their rights and duties, types of operative-investigative activities, and control and oversight. Civil society organisations have raised concerns that it might be used for political purposes. These fears were confirmed when law enforcement agencies were found tapping the conversations of opposition politicians during and immediately following the presidential election campaign.

- Several changes were implemented that could help in reducing corruption, including the Law on Fixed Payments (July 2007), the Law on the Organisation and Implementation of Inspections (11 October 2007), the Law on Simplified Tax (3 July 2007) and the Law on the Declaration of Property and Income of Physical Persons (18 December 2007).[8]

Company leadership in jail for revealing corruption in customs service

The customs system is considered to be one of the most corrupt services in Armenia. According to the results of a 2006 survey by the Transparency International Anti-corruption Center (TI AC; formerly CRD/TI Armenia), 85 per cent of respondents considered the customs system to be 'partially corrupt', 'corrupt' or 'very corrupt'.[9]

This perception was confirmed by President Serzh Sargsyan in his meeting with the State Customs Committee (SCC) on 17 April 2008,[10] when he drew attention to the extensive smuggling of goods by businesspeople who conspire with customs officers, as well as other attempts at evading customs duties. The presi-

---

4 *Official Bulletin of the Republic of Armenia*, vol. 55 (579), 14 November 2007.

5 *Official Bulletin of the Republic of Armenia*, vol. 19 (543), 11 April 2007.

6 *Official Bulletin of the Republic of Armenia*, vol. 53 (577), 31 October 2007.

7 *Official Bulletin of the Republic of Armenia*, vol. 59 (583), 28 November 2007.

8 All these laws are published in the *Official Bulletin of the Republic of Armenia*: volumes 37 (561), 2007; 54 (578), 2007; 37 (561), 2007; and 2 (592), 2008, respectively.

9 Center for Regional Development/Transparency International Armenia and UNDP, '2006 Corruption Perceptions in Armenia' (Yerevan: CRD/TI Armenia/UNDP, 2006).

10 Armenialiberty.org, 18 April 2008.

dent expressed concern about the State Customs Committee's (SCC's) unrestricted authority and ability to assess the value of imported commodities. Many journalists and experts,[11] however, have expressed scepticism concerning the existence of real political will to fight corruption, particularly considering that, in April 2008, President Sargsyan appointed Gagik Khachatryan as the new head of the office. Khachatryan had been directly involved in the following case.

On 26 July 2004 a press conference was held by Gagik Hakobyan, president of the Royal Armenia LLC joint venture (RA), and Aram Ghazaryan, RA's former managing director.[12] They claimed that, since the spring of 2003, the SCC had periodically discriminated against the company, which imports coffee (its share was 10 per cent of the total volume of coffee imports) and food into Armenia. The SCC was accused of ignoring company invoices and setting inflated customs prices for coffee, compared with other coffee importers. Based on comparable copies of customs declarations filed by RA and other importers, they demonstrated that at times they had paid 50 per cent more than other importers.[13]

Despite the RA filing suits against these actions, the SCC continued the same practice.[14] Hakobyan alleged that Khachatryan, SCC's deputy head at the time, and Surik Fahradyan, an SCC department head, had demanded that RA pay bribes for the shipments, but that the company had refused.[15] Hakobyan claimed

this refusal was the primary cause of the SCC's unlawful actions.

On 8 February 2005 the SCC filed a protocol against RA claiming that it had violated customs procedures, including misreporting the prices of coffee it imported – by both increasing and decreasing the official prices at different times.[16] Such changes were allegedly made by falsifying invoices received from its trade partner, American FIG LLC. The National Security Service filed a criminal case against RA and initiated a criminal investigation. Hakobyan and Ghazaryan were arrested and taken into custody.[17]

There were also accusations that RA did not qualify as a joint venture company and thus had unlawfully enjoyed the privileges that Armenian legislation gives to such entities for customs fees and profit taxes. As a result, the company illegally avoided paying a total of AMD 525 million (about US$1.7 million).[18] This accusation was based on the opinion that the foreign shareholder of the company had become a shareholder illegally.[19] At the press conference, RA management argued that the accusations were unfounded.

The trial in the Court of First Instance began in November 2006 and lasted until July 2007. Judge Pargev Ohanyan acquitted Hakobyan and Ghazaryan on 16 July, on the grounds that the argument presented was based on assumptions rather than evidence.[20] The Office of the Prosecutor General appealed to the review court, which reversed the initial verdict on 29

---

11 See, for example, www.armenialiberty.org/armeniareport/report/en/2008/04.
12 During the trial, Royal Armenia's lawyer submitted written materials on the case, including information about the press conference, to the representative of the Transparency International Anti-corruption Center.
13 Armenialiberty.org, 26 July 2004.
14 Ibid.
15 ArmeniaNow.com, 31 March 2006.
16 Ibid.
17 Ibid.
18 Ibid.
19 Ibid.
20 Armenialiberty.org, 16 July 2007.

November 2007 and sentenced the defendants to prison terms.[21]

This case is exceptional, because it demonstrates how businesspeople who consistently defended their rights and refused to submit to the illegal demands of the authorities were ultimately victimised and investigated on corruption grounds. Regardless of the RA's actual behaviour in this regard, the important conclusion is that the authorities appear to close their eyes to violations until the business in question 'sticks its head above the parapet' and makes life for the regime uncomfortable. Then, when the authorities do act, as in this case, the punishment can be as swift as it is severe.

An uncertain future for a private TV company

On 21 September 2007 Levon Ter-Petrosyan, the first president after Armenia's independence in 1991, delivered his first public speech since his resignation in 1998. He described the current regime as 'criminal and corrupt' and called for its ousting.[22] The speech was televised by two television stations; one of them a small, privately owned company, GALA.[23] It broadcast parts of the event on the same day in its evening news programme, and then on 14 October it broadcast Ter-Petrosyan's entire speech.

GALA's owner, Vahan Khachatryan, claimed that on 14 and 15 October he was approached by officials from the National Security Service, who advised him to stop reporting on politics. The authorities deny this claim.[24] On 17 October Grigor Amalyan, chairman of the National Commission on Television and Radio (NCTR), allegedly invited Khachatryan to his office in Yerevan and gave similar advice, warned him against airing the speech.[25] In all three cases, Khachatryan claims he rejected these 'requests' and insisted he would continue to provide impartial information to his audience.[26]

Allegedly, the authorities approached private businesses that advertised with GALA. GALA began losing its advertising contracts in October.[27] An official audit of the company began on 29 October, and on 14 November the State Tax Service submitted its final report, accusing Chap Ltd, the founder of GALA, of tax evasion due to underreporting advertising revenues.[28] It alleged that the company had avoided paying taxes worth AMD 26 million (US$78,000). There were also allegations that Chap Ltd manufactured fireworks without a government licence in 2001, a crime indeed admitted by Khachatryan.[29]

Chap Ltd objected to the tax evasion allegations, arguing that they were politically motivated and that the apparent inaccuracy arose from social

---

21 Hakobyan received six years in prison and Ghazaryan two years. Ghazaryan was freed in the courtroom immediately after the verdict was read because he had already spent nearly two years in prison, and Hakobyan's sentence was reduced by two years. The Office of the Prosecutor General demanded penalties milder than those it demanded when the case was tried in the Court of First Instance (twelve years for Hakobyan and eleven years for Ghazaryan).

22 Radio Liberty (Czech Republic), 21 September 2007.

23 Armenialiberty.org, 22 October 2007. Other Armenian TV stations did not broadcast that speech.

24 Armenialiberty.org, 31 October 2007; 12 November 2007; see also www.asparez.am.

25 Armenialiberty.org, 22 October 2007. Other Armenian TV stations did not broadcast the speech.

26 The 'Asparez' Journalists' Club NGO from Gyumri, actively involved in the support campaign of GALA, kindly submitted materials on this case to TI AC. These materials, as well as materials from www.armenialiberty.org, were used for the description of the case.

27 Armenialiberty.org, 31 October 2007; Armenia Observer Blog, 'Journalists from National Newspapers Visit Gyumri GALA TV in a Rare Act of Solidarity', 2 November 2007.

28 Armenialiberty.org, 31 October 2007.

29 Armenialiberty.org, 12 November 2007.

and self-made (individual) adverts that GALA broadcast for free.

On 26 November the State Tax Service asked the Economic Court to freeze the company's bank accounts and other assets amounting to the alleged tax shortfall, and on 3 December the court acceded to the demand.[30] The trial lasted until 19 March 2008, when the court upheld the accusations.[31] The cash-strapped TV company paid its fine after a week-long fundraising campaign that concluded on 1 April.[32]

In a parallel action, the mayor of Gyumri, where GALA is based, filed a suit in the Economic Court, requesting the removal of its transmitter from the TV tower located in the city, as the State Tax Service claimed it had been hosted there illegally.[33] On 29 February 2008 the court gave permission for the mayor's office to remove the transmitter.[34] GALA challenged this, and a delay was imposed on the removal, but on 14 April the Court of Appeal sustained the initial decision. As such, electricity was cut to the transmitter in order to force the company to dismantle it, but Khachatryan refused to do so and threatened to sue anyone who damaged his equipment. The company was finally granted a ten-day reprieve on dismantling the transmitter,[35] and at the time of writing the reprieve has been extended until negotiations between GALA and the Ministry of Transport and Communications on the use of the tower are completed.

As in the case of RA, it is difficult to assess whether the television company was truly guilty of the allegations levelled against it. The fact that the authorities started investigations after the broadcast of the political speech, however, has led many to see the investigations as political.

Varuzhan Hoktanyan (Transparency International Anti-corruption Center)

Additional reading

J. H. Anderson and C. W. Gray, *Anticorruption in Transition 3: Who Is Succeeding and Why?* (Washington, DC: World Bank, 2006).

CRD/TI Armenia and UNDP, *2006 Corruption Perceptions in Armenia* (Yerevan: CRD/TI Armenia/UNDP, 2006).

A. Kostanyan and V. Hoktanyan, *Anti-corruption Policy in Armenia* (Yerevan: TI AC, 2006), available at www.transparency.am/publication.php?id=24.

S. Rose-Ackerman, *Government and Corruption: Causes, Consequences, and Reform* (Cambridge: Cambridge University Press, 1999).

TI, *Global Corruption Report 2004* (Ann Arbor, MI: Pluto Press, 2004).

TI Armenia: www.transparency.am.

---

30 Armenialiberty.org, 4 December 2007.
31 Armenialiberty.org, 19 March 2008.
32 S. Vantsian, 'Gyumri TV Ends Fund-raising Campaign', Radio Liberty (Czech Republic), 1 April 2008.
33 Armenialiberty.org, 4 December 2007.
34 Armenialiberty.org, 25 March 2008.
35 S. Vantsian, 'Independent TV Granted 10-day Reprieve', Radio Liberty (Prague), 17 April 2008.

Austria

Corruption Perceptions Index 2008: 8.1 (12th out of 180 countries)

Conventions

Council of Europe Civil Law Convention on Corruption (signed October 2000; ratified August 2006)
Council of Europe Criminal Law Convention on Corruption (signed October 2000; not yet ratified)
OECD Convention on Combating Bribery of Foreign Public Officials (signed December 1997; ratified
  May 1999)
UN Convention against Corruption (signed December 2003; ratified January 2006)
UN Convention against Transnational Organized Crime (signed December 2000; ratified September
  2004)

Legal and institutional changes

- In December 2007 the Austrian parliament amended its anti-corruption legislation with new provisions to the penal code that came into force at the beginning of 2008.[1] These new provisions review active and passive bribery in the private sector;[2] increase the penalties for the active bribery of domestic and foreign public officials, including foreign and European parliamentarians; extend the provisions for the active and passive bribery of Austrian public officials; and cover the offer and acceptance of undue advantages in connection with carrying out official duties, without having to provide proof of the reciprocal act or omission of a public official. Unfortunately, because parliamentary members were less willing to introduce such rigorous rules for themselves, they are mostly excluded from the new provisions, which cover only the buying and selling of parliamentary votes in relation to parliamentarians. Accordingly, these provisions do not fully implement the UN Convention against Corruption or the Council of Europe Criminal Law Convention on Corruption.

- Parliament implemented plans for a public prosecutor's office to focus exclusively on corruption and exercise jurisdiction for the whole country.[3] In contrast to the Ministry of Justice's initial proposals in July 2007, the prosecutors will not be truly independent.[4] The ministry will be able to give instructions, but only in a transparent manner and in written form accompanied by reasons that

---

1 The Strafrechtsaenderungsgesetz 2008 (Penal Code Amendment Act 2008), *Federal Law Gazette* I 2007/109, article I.
2 The new sections of the Penal Code are 168c (acceptance of gifts by attendants or representatives) and 168d (bribery of attendants or representatives).
3 *Federal Law Gazette* I 2007/109, article II (footnote 1), and the Strafprozessreformbegleitgesetz II (Code of Criminal Procedure Reform Act II), *Federal Law Gazette* I 2007/112, article XI.
4 See 'Austria', in TI, *Global Corruption Report 2007* (Cambridge: Cambridge University Press, 2007).

will be accessible to all the parties to a lawsuit. The new prosecutor's office on corruption starts work on 1 January 2009.

- In July 2007 the Ministry of Justice proposed implementing a leniency programme in the field of corruption. Parliament postponed this discussion in December 2007, demanding an evaluation of the existing provisions (e.g. for combating organised crime) by the ministry, until September 2008.[5]
- In April 2008 the Ministry of the Interior proposed establishing a Federal Agency for the Fight against Corruption, with the aim of replacing the Bureau for Internal Affairs (BIA).[6] The new agency, as a specialised section of the police force, is to have jurisdiction to investigate all corruption cases (not only in the public sector, as was the case with the BIA) in close cooperation with the Public Prosecutor's Office. Because of the early termination of the legislature period of only two years, these plans were postponed to the period after the federal elections on 28 September 2008.

Corruption in the banking sector

Although corruption in the private sector is not considered a major issue in Austria, there were serious scandals in the banking sector in 2007/8 that received enormous public attention. The two most important cases, involving Meinl European Land (MEL) and BAWAG, shed light on major failings in the financial market supervisory system.

Following its foundation in 1997 and subsequent listing on the Vienna Stock Exchange in 2002, MEL, an investment company for real estate projects in eastern Europe, was highly criticised for how it advertised its purchase certificates as shares. Inexperienced investors were led to believe that these shares were absolutely safe (eligible for trusts). More than 150,000 small shareholders signed up.[7]

The share price fell dramatically in 2007, however, as a consequence of the international real estate crisis, from about €22 a share to €9 (US$32 to US$13). The situation worsened in November 2007, when MEL announced a share buy-back programme at prices far above market value, leading to an erosion of MEL's financial reserves.[8] While this kind of buy-back programme would usually require the consent of the general assembly, MEL is registered in Jersey, where such regulations do not exist.[9]

MEL was dismissed from the prime segment of the Vienna Stock Exchange[10] and became the subject of a number of court actions. The Chamber of Labour sued Meinl Bank, the market maker of MEL, and the Court of Commerce ruled that the original marketing material for the purchasing certificates was misleading. MEL appealed, arguing that the whole process was coordinated and agreed by the Austrian Financial Market Authority (FMA), including the approved market maker contract with Meinl Bank.[11] Nevertheless, the FMA fined board of management members €20,000 each (US$29,400) for misleading investors in a stock exchange announcement about the buy-back programme in July 2007. Again MEL appealed against this fine.

According to the magazine *Profil*,[12] the real scandal lies in the manner in which the Meinl

---

5 Stenografisches Protokoll des Nationalrats, XXIII; Gesetzgebungsperiode, December 2007.
6 See www.bmi.gv.at/begutachtungdownload/Korruptionsbek_Entwurf.pdf.
7 Verein für Konsumenteninformation; see www.verbraucherrecht.at.
8 Atrium European Real Estate Limited; see www.meinleuropeanland.com.
9 *Die Presse* (Austria), 31 August 2007; 14 July 2008.
10 This dismissal could have been avoided only by the promise of MEL to adhere to the regulations of the Austrian Stock Exchange in the future.
11 *Der Standard* (Austria), 9 April 2008.
12 'Julius im Plus', *Profil*, no. 14 (2008).

family allegedly enriched itself while small investors suffered significant losses. By various fee and management contracts, Meinl Bank earned about €360 million (US$530 million) from MEL for commissions and also for using the name 'Meinl'. The magazine also states that the contested buy-back programme was organised for the benefit of the Meinl family. As a 2007 capital increase in MEL was not successful, the unsold certificates were purchased secretly by Somal AVV – a company with relations to Meinl registered in the Netherlands Antilles. As the price of the MEL certificates continued to fall, the buy-back programme at prices far above market rates was launched, again without the knowledge of the investors and using a total amount of €1.8 billion (US$2.65 billion).

Following overwhelming criticism, the Meinl family stepped out of the management contracts with MEL. The transfer of these contracts to the Israeli Gazit Group provided Meinl with compensation of €280 million (US$412 million).[13] As of 1 August 2008 the company's name has been changed to Atrium European Real Estate Limited, and a new board of directors and a new CEO have been appointed. The existing arrangements with the managing company Meinl European Real Estate Limited (Meinl Bank) have been terminated.[14] Moreover, the shareholding structure has been changed as a consequence of the acquisition of 23.2 per cent of the voting

rights by CPI/Gazit Holdings Limited and Gazit Gaia Limited, also as of 1 August 2008.[15]

This affair is without comparison in Austrian capital market history.[16] Further legal action is proceeding and the Vienna Public Prosecutor's Office is investigating the suspected embezzlement and fraud. The current legal action is not final because of appeals, but, independently of legal qualifications, the MEL case may be seen as a 'misuse of entrusted power for private gain'.[17]

The BAWAG affair was highlighted in the *Global Corruption Report 2008*. Although the main issue relates to losses of more than €1.4 billion (US$2 billion) due to hazardous and uncontrolled financial speculations, this case is important from both a transparency perspective and a corruption perspective because of the close relationship between the bank, trade unions and political parties, and the corresponding corruption allegation. In a manner similar to the Meinl affair, the BAWAG case also revealed significant weaknesses in the Austrian bank supervisory system.

BAWAG, the Bank for Labour and Business, lost more than €1 billion (US$1.5 billion) in financial speculations in the late 1990s. The Austrian Trade Union Federation, as the majority shareholder until May 2007,[18] avoided bankruptcy for BAWAG by taking over liabilities and giving

---

13 *Die Presse* (Austria), 21 March 2008.

14 Atrium European Real Estate Limited, 'Investment and Restructuring Transaction Completes', ad hoc release, 1 August 2008.

15 Atrium European Real Estate Limited, 'Notice Pursuant to Sec 93 of the Austrian Stock Exchange Act to Be Distributed European wide', ad hoc release, 8 August 2008.

16 Further interesting reading on the influence of Meinl Bank on MEL as well as about the deficiencies of the Austrian capital market control are provided in the documentation of the discussions in the Austrian parliament; see www.parlament.gv.at/PG/DE/XXIII/J/J_01986/fname_091329.pdf.

17 A further disturbing aspect of the MEL case is the close relationship between banking and political institutions in Austria. The former finance minister, Karl-Heinz Grasser, is CEO and shareholder of MIP (Meinl International Power), another investment company of the Meinl Group. This has an informal influence on the way these investment companies are controlled by the respective organisations, because the actual system of the FMA was implemented in his term as a minister, and one of the two members of the executive board of the FMA is a former member of Grasser's Cabinet. *Die Presse* (Austria), 12 September 2007.

18 The bank was sold to a consortium led by Cerberus Capital Management, L.P., in May 2007.

guarantees in 2000. This was done in secret, however.

A parliamentary committee of inquiry, which worked from October 2006 until July 2007, could not agree on a common conclusion on the key issues of lack of control in the banking sector and the question of illegal party financing. Although no written report was published, this parliamentary inquiry enabled a clearer organisation and improved regulation of the banking supervisory system to be brought in. The previously poorly coordinated activities of the Austrian National Bank and the supervisory board of the FMA were amended by enforcing the role of the FMA. What remains to be scrutinised, however, is the appointment of FMA managers based on political considerations, thus reducing the independence and efficiency of this control body.

In July 2007 a criminal lawsuit was filed against seven former managers of the bank. One such manager is Wolfgang Flöttl, owner of the investment firms carrying out the financial speculations, son of a former BAWAG CEO (Walter Flöttl) and a partner of the external auditor, KPMG. The accusations of fraud and the falsification of financial statements involve a total amount of €1.44 billion (US$2.12 billion). This lawsuit is the largest economic court case in Austria's history, and it was still ongoing at the time of writing.[19]

One of the indicted managers, Johann Zwettler, a former BAWAG CEO, a former leading trade union manager and head of the BAWAG supervisory board, made a partial confession during the November 2007 trial regarding embezzlement and accounting fraud.[20] The allegations of party funding were reinforced by the opening of files found in the basement of another former BAWAG CEO, Walter Flöttl, in March 2008.[21] In two November 1989 letters addressed to Fritz Verzetnitsch (trade union president at that time), Flöttl revealed indirect financial support to BAWAG shareholders the Austrian Trade Union Federation (ÖGB) and Konsum Österreich, and the Social Democratic Party (SPÖ), which amounted to €95 million from 1972 to 1989.[22] BAWAG subsidised its shareholders as well as the SPÖ, for example by buying party-owned or union-owned enterprises for highly exaggerated prices and with extraordinarily good credit conditions.[23]

The cases of MEL and BAWAG demonstrate problems and inefficiencies in the Austrian banking control system, as well as the relationships between the banking sector and politics. Several other less spectacular cases, such as that of AMIS, a financial assets company, also reveal this fact. The traditional lack of coordination between ministries, the central bank and the control authorities has been improved, but the typical Austrian arrangement of close ties between representatives of these bodies and political parties still exists. The very complicated ownership structure of banks (including the central bank) and organisations with strong political influences can still lead to conflicts of interest.

TI Austria

Additional reading

I. Fellmann and F. Klug (eds.), *Vademecum der Korruptionsbekämpfung* (Linz: IKW Schriftenreihe, 2008).

---

19 Cf. E. A. Swietly and W. Okresek, *Der Bankkrach: Der große Absturz der Bawag* (Vienna: Edition Steinbauer, 2007); see diepresse.com/home/wirtschaft/economist/bawag/index.do.
20 *Die Presse* (Austria), 27 November 2007.
21 *Die Presse* (Austria), 11 March 2008.
22 The breakdown was as follows: €23 million to the SPÖ, €56 million to the ÖGB and €16 million to Konsum, the previous BAWAG shareholder.
23 *Die Presse* (Austria), 11 March 2008.

M. Kreutner (ed.), *The Corruption Monster: Ethik, Politik und Korruption* (Vienna: Czernin Verlag, 2006).

H. Sickinger, 'Korruption in Österreich: Verbreitung, ausgewaehlte Problembereiche, Reformbedarf', in Bundesministerium für Justiz, *35. Ottensteiner Fortbildungsseminar*

aus Strafrecht und Kriminologie (Vienna: Bundesministerium für Justiz, 2007).

E. A. Swietly and W. Okresek, *Der Bankkrach: Der große Absturz der Bawag* (Vienna: Edition Steinbauer, 2007).

TI Austria: www.ti-austria.at.

Bosnia and Herzegovina

Corruption Perceptions Index 2008: 3.2 (92nd out of 180 countries)

Conventions

Council of Europe Civil Law Convention on Corruption (signed March 2000; ratified January 2002)

Council of Europe Criminal Law Convention on Corruption (signed March 2000; ratified January 2002)

UN Convention against Corruption (signed September 2005; ratified October 2006)

UN Convention against Transnational Organized Crime (signed December 2000; ratified April 2002)

Legal and institutional changes

- A draft law giving legitimacy to an anti-corruption institution, as part of Bosnia and Herzegovina's (BiH's) obligation to the UN Convention against Corruption, was prepared in 2007 by a working group composed of representatives from relevant institutions.[1] It was supported by the American Bar Association's Rule of Law Initiative (ABA-ROLI).[2] According to the draft law, the institution's primary role would be, *inter alia*, to coordinate the activities of the financial police, customs and prosecutors' offices. The institution would also develop, coordinate and monitor an anti-corruption strategy and action plan, monitor the effects of laws and by-laws aimed at preventing corruption, cooperate with local and international institutions and organisations with similar objectives, and develop and supervise the implementation of anti-corruption education programmes. Unfortunately, because of administrative barriers in the BiH Council

---

1 Representatives from the following institutions participated in the working group: BiH Ministry of Security, BiH Ministry of Justice, BiH Central Electoral Commission, BiH Prosecutor's Office and Interpol. Unfortunately, the working group never received formal approval for their work from the BiH Council of Ministers.

2 TI Bosnia and Herzegovina, 'Strategiju mora usvojiti parlament', 10 December 2007.

of Ministers, the law has never come before parliament.

- The Law on Conflict of Interest was adopted at the state level in 2002, while the entities were obliged to adopt their respective laws within sixty days.[3] They have not done this, and so the BiH Central Election Commission is still in charge of preventing and punishing conflicts of interest, but it is questionable whether it has the necessary capacity to do so successfully. The Central Election Commission also lost credibility following the withdrawal of international members from its line-up. The commission's integrity was further put into question following its decision to stop implementing the law at the entity level, thereby leaving an enormous legal and institutional gap that it does not have the capacity to fill. Transparency International BiH sued the commission for the silence of the administration in a case of conflict of interest involving the FBiH prime minister. The court decided in favour of TI BiH and ordered the commission to make a formal decision on the case, as the institution in charge.

Opaque private negotiations in the privatisation process

While BiH's score of 3.3 in the Corruption Perceptions Index 2007 showed some improvement, anecdotal evidence from TI BiH's Advocacy and Legal Advice Centre (ALAC) provides a clearer picture of the spread of corruption. As of February 2008 8,500 private and legal entities reported corruption on the ALAC's toll-free hotline. Most frequent were reports on the work of the local government institutions, the education sector, public enterprises, privatisation, public procurement and the judi-

ciary. Furthermore, the Heritage Foundation's 2008 Index of Economic Freedom places BiH as one of the least free economies in the world, ranking 121st out of 162.[4] The size of the government, property rights and freedom from corruption are seen as the biggest problems.[5]

The privatisation of the Republika Srpska oil industry demonstrates how the government has taken a leading role in privatising the energy sector, but also how the process has been burdened by a lack of transparency. While this has had a strong impact on the process itself, it has also paved the way for similar practices in the future and sent a clear message to other potential investors on how to do business in BiH.

Republika Srpska's oil industry consists of an oil refinery in Bosanski Brod, a lubricant refinery in Modrica, and Petrol,[6] a company that distributes oil through a network of gas stations throughout the RS. All three companies have been state-owned by majority.

The Bosanski Brod oil refinery suffered a number of difficulties, including enormous debts to the state in the form of unpaid taxes and levies, unpaid salaries resulting in strikes, and outstanding payments to foreign companies delivering crude oil. According to the RS government's information on the privatisation of the oil industry, TI BiH estimated that by June 2008 the oil refinery in Bosanski Brod had accumulated debts of approximately BAM 300 million (US$250 million). In practice, the oil refinery was out of production for more than two years.[7]

Because of these difficulties, the RS government decided to privatise the oil industry, and began

---

3 BiH is constitutionally divided into two entities: the Federation of BiH (FBiH), which is largely Bosniak and Croat, and Republika Srpska (RS), which is primarily Serb.

4 The index covers 162 countries across ten specific freedoms, with 100 per cent being interpreted as totally free.

5 Heritage Foundation, '2008 Index of Economic Freedom' (Washington, DC: Heritage Foundation, 2008).

6 The names in Serbian are Rafinerija nafte a.d. Bosanski Brod, Rafinerija ulja a.d, Modriča and Petrol a.d. Banja Luka.

7 RS government, 'Information on privatisation of companies from the Republika Srpska oil industry', June 2008.

looking for a 'strategic partner'. According to government information from August 2006, the first step was to sign a protocol with the Russian state-owned oil company Zarubezneft and the Russian state-owned bank Vneshekonombank on their intention to participate in privatisation, reconstruction and management.[8] Using the method of direct selection, the RS government decided in December 2006 to sell its state-owned oil assets to the company Neftegazinkor, and the privatisation agreement was signed on 2 February 2007. There was public speculation that the selection process was highly influenced by improved relations between Serbia and Russia.[9] Zarubezneft owned 40 per cent of Neftegazinkor, while three limited companies each owned 20 per cent. The owners of these three companies remained unknown publicly.[10]

One of the most troubling aspects of the privatisation process was that the RS government, an exclusively political body, excluded the RS Directorate for Privatisation, the agency in charge of privatisation, and conducted the process autonomously. In order to do this legally, the government amended the privatisation law in order to enable it to carry out the privatisation of certain so-called 'strategic companies' directly.[11] Essentially, this law introduced a concept of privatisation that was completely new and radically different from the previous legislation. It gave the RS government exclusive power to search for potential buyers of state capital, negotiate with them, sign contracts and manage implementa-

tion of the contracts. In effect, the law retroactively legalised all the government's previous steps in this privatisation,[12] and abolished the role of the privatisation agency in privatising some of the most significant industries in the country.[13]

In reality, the whole privatisation process was a 'secret operation'. The final contract between the RS government and Neftegazinkor was marked as a classified document, and even members of the RS parliament had no insight into the main part of the agreement and its annexes.[14] After several months of public advocacy and a number of formal requests to the government, TI BiH in November 2007 succeeded in obtaining the main part of the agreement, though not the annexes. By May 2008 there was no reliable information about implementing contract clauses regarding the new owner's obligations. These include starting gas production based on Russian oil; investing an additional €100 million (US$150 million) over two years and building up a railroad whose value would be €45 million (US$70 million); and maintaining employment levels (i.e. not considering redundancies) for a determined period.

A final twist in the tale involved easing the burden of the company's debts on the new owner. The RS government postponed the company's debt payment for nine years with a four-year grace period and an additional five years free of interest. This is with over BAM 133

---

8 Ibid.

9 See www.vreme.com/cms/view.php?id=502846.

10 Conclusion of the BiH Concurrency Council, May 2007

11 Law on privatisation of the state-owned capital in enterprises (zakon o privatizaciji državnog kapitala u preduzećima), from 17 May 2006; law on amendments of the Law on privatisation of the state-owned capital in enterprises (zakon o izmjenama zakona o privatizaciji državnog kapitala u preduzećima), 11 January 2007.

12 The privatisation agreement with Neftegazinkor was signed on 2 February 2007, while the law that regulates specificities of the oil industry privatisation was adopted retroactively on 28 February 2007.

13 According to article 6 of the law, 'Companies from the fields of production and distribution of electric power, oil industry, rail transport, telecommunication, water supply industry, mining and forestry, public media, lottery, arms and munition production, and other companies of strategic interest, shall be privatised according to specific privatisation programmes enacted by the RS Government. . .'

14 See www.capital.ba/dodik-ugovor-o-prodaji-naftne-industrije-samo-pojedinacno-poslanicima/.

million (US$106 million) being owed to the state budget, and social and pension funds.[15] The price for 65 per cent of state-owned capital in the RS oil industry was approximately €110 million (US$172 million), plus bank guarantee costs of €20 million as a security for executing the contract's obligations.[16]

Independent experts[17] evaluating the privatisation contract concluded that it is not positive for, and is perhaps even harmful to, the RS budget and further development of the oil industry. They found that there is no balance between the contract price and the government's obligations: in effect, the two cancel each other out, since the government covers all the refinery's commercial debts, amounting to about €72 million (US$98.5 million). Moreover, the buyer of the oil industry lacks credibility in the current business environment (the company's estimated value was between BAM 3 and 6 million (US$2.4 and 4.8 million),[18] while the amount of all obligations originating from the main agreement exceeded €300 million (US$410 million), which is fifty times more than the company's value. Finally, it is considered that the contract may violate domestic rules on concessions, taxes, expropriations and competition by allowing a monopoly.[19]

Considering all the agreement's imperfections, including delays by the Russian partner in fulfilling its obligations and the RS government's unwillingness to justify all aspects of the agreement in a transparent manner, it is difficult to see how the economic interests of RS citizens

are being served. The extent of the damage remains immeasurable and the object of intense concern.

Political lobbies create concern

The company Aluminium Mostar is the biggest exporter in BiH. During the country's civil war in the 1990s the company was occupied by Bosnian Croat forces, and all Serb and Bosniak workers were fired. Since then the company has been under the control of Bosnian Croat interest groups and politicians.[20] Immediately following the war, the company was privatised. The Croatian company TML invested in the company and became a 12 per cent owner (about €10 million or US$13.7 million), while the other 88 per cent remained state-owned.[21]

After the adoption of privatisation laws in the Federation of BiH (the Bosniak- and Croat-dominated entity within BiH),[22] tough political negotiations commenced between politicians on how to divide the economic and political influence over the company. It was clear that it would be hard to satisfy Bosniaks' and Croats' interests by following the law's privatisation rules. Aluminium Mostar was granted preferential status by the FBiH government, which meant that the privatisation law was not applied to the company. As a result, the privatisation commenced (and is still in progress) based on a clear political consensus between two political parties and two dominant entities in FBiH.

15 Article 5 of the law on conditions for selling stocks of the companies from the Republika Srpska oil industry (zakon o uslovima prodaje akcija preduzeća iz oblasti naftne industrije republike Srpske), *Official Gazette of the Republika Srpska*, no. 20/07.

16 Article 3.1 of the RS oil industry privatisation agreement, 2 February 2007.

17 I.e. Svetlana Cenic, former RS minister of finance.

18 Decision of the BiH Competition Council, May 2007.

19 TI BiH, 'Analysis of Privatization Contract of the RS Oil Industry', www.ti-bih.org.

20 See http://ceemarketwatch.com/search.html?q=smelter&search_country=BA.

21 Tender provisions for the selling of 88 per cent of the state-owned capital in the aluminum company: FBiH Privatisation Agency and Aluminium JSC, March 2007, www.apf.com.ba/aktuelna-prod/tenderi/dokumentacija/aluminij/Pravila_tendera_Aluminij_Konacna_020307.pdf.

22 *Official Gazette of Federation BiH*, nos. 27/97, 8/99, 32/00, 45/00, 54/00, 61/01, 27/02, 33/02, 28/04, 44/04, 42/06.

To this end, an agreement was signed between the FBiH government and Aluminium Mostar management, and adopted (with amendments) in the FBiH parliament. It involved solving 'open questions' – namely, the strict legal rules and procedures on allowable privatisation methods, and ways to determine the company's ownership structure. This agreement established new rules on the structure of state-owned capital in the company and on the privatisation methodology. Once privatised, out of the 88 per cent of the state-owned capital subject to privatisation, 44 per cent of the selling price would be given to the employees made redundant, while the remainder would be retained by the company itself. The agreement introduced an ad hoc committee in charge of implementing the agreement. As a result of this negotiation, the rules differ substantially from the current Law on Privatisation in FBiH.[23]

This agreement has set a precedent, and illustrates how business and political lobbies can persuade governments to amend laws and allow privatisation. The general observation is that the company carried out the privatisation process itself, in contrast to other FBiH companies, and in a *sui generis* compromise with the FBiH

government. In correspondence with TI BiH's representatives, the FBiH prime minister, Nedžad Branković, admitted that the Aluminium Mostar privatisation was a clear political compromise between Bosniak and Croat politicians in the FBiH.[24]

Nebojša Milanović and Aleksandra Martinović (TI Bosnia and Herzegovina)

Additional reading

Centre for Investigative Journalism; www.cin. ba.

TI BiH, *Bosnia and Herzegovina at the Crossroads: EU Accession or a Failed State?* (Sarajevo: TI BiH, 2007).

Advancement of the National Integrity System: Suggestions for the BiH Anti-corruption Strategy (Sarajevo: TI BiH, 2007).

TI BiH and F. E. Stiftung, *Bosnia and Herzegovina 2008: Role and State of Media* (Sarajevo: TI BiH, 2008).

US Department of State, *Bosnia and Herzegovina: Country Report on Human Rights Practices – 2007* (Washington, DC: Department of State, 2008).

TI Bosnia and Herzegovina: www.ti-bih.org.

---

23 Official letter from the FBiH prime minister, Nedžad Branković, to TI BiH, 26 October 2007.
24 Branković, 2007.

Finland

Corruption Perceptions Index 2008: 9.0 (5th out of 180 countries)

Conventions

Council of Europe Civil Law Convention on Corruption (signed June 2000; ratified October 2001)

Council of Europe Criminal Law Convention on Corruption (signed January 1999; ratified October 2002)

OECD Convention on Combating Bribery of Foreign Public Officials (signed December 1998; ratified February 1999)

UN Convention against Corruption (signed December 2003; accepted June 2006)

UN Convention against Transnational Organized Crime (signed December 2000; ratified February 2004)

Legal and institutional changes

- On 12 December 2007 the Council of Europe's Group of States against Corruption (GRECO) gave its comments on the Finnish system of election and political financing. According to the report, the existing monitoring system for political finance lacks independence and the supervision of the accounts of political parties and candidates is 'purely formalistic'.[1] It also suggests that the reporting requirements concerning public financing are low and sanctions for breaches of the rules are inadequate. It urges the government 'to strengthen considerably the independence of monitoring of political funding at central and local level' and 'to review the sanctions available for the infringement of rules … and to ensure that these sanctions are effective, proportionate and dissuasive'. Recommendations were also made for improvement in reporting and auditing requirements to 'introduce a general ban on donations from donors whose identity is not known to the political party/candidate'; for the government 'to consider lowering the threshold of donations above which the identity of the donor is to be disclosed'; and to regulate donations more carefully by calling for this disclosure threshold to apply in cases where the same donor makes multiple donations during a calendar year. Finally, the report calls on the government to improve transparency in 'contributions by third parties' (e.g. interest groups or political education foundations) and 'to ensure proper substantial supervision … of the accounts of political parties and expenses linked to electoral campaigns'.

- The leaders of political parties represented in parliament agreed on 27 May 2008 that the threshold for declarations of election support

---

1 GRECO, *Evaluation Report on Finland on Transparency of Party Funding* (Strasbourg: GRECO, 2007).

would decrease from €1,700 to €1,000. They also agreed that the expenditures of electoral campaigns had to be specified.[2]

- The Ministry of Justice set up a committee on 30 May 2008 to 'renew financing of electoral candidates and political parties as well as legislation related to the oversight of the financing'. The committee is set to draft proposals in order to increase the transparency of political financing as well as to take into account the GRECO recommendations.

Survey findings: prevalence of corruption in Finland

According to a survey by Finland's Central Chamber of Commerce (Keskuskauppakamari) and the Helsinki Region Chamber of Commerce (Helsingin Seudun Kauppakamari), businesspeople in Finland find dealings with other businesspeople more prone to corruption than dealings with the authorities. The report identifies the construction and manufacturing sectors as being particularly problematic. Although the overall percentages were not especially high, it is notable that the private sector appeared to be much more prone to corruption than the public: only 1 per cent of respondents claimed to have faced bribery in dealings with the authorities, yet 8 per cent of business leaders from the construction sector and 5 per cent of business leaders from the manufacturing sector reported experiencing bribery in relations with other companies.[3]

Although, overall, 3 per cent of business leaders admitted that their company has faced bribery when dealing with other firms in Finland,[4] in recent years there have been no notable convictions for business-to-business bribery. A possible explanation for this is that the definition of bribery in the penal code uses the term 'undue benefit'[5] without further clarification as to what this means. The prosecution of bribery offences is therefore difficult. Although business leaders face situations they may perceive to be corrupt, it may be difficult for prosecutors to attain sufficient evidence that this indeed qualifies as 'undue benefit'. In relation to this, GRECO has called on the government 'to clarify in an appropriate manner what should be considered "due" and/or "undue" gifts/benefits, both in terms of material and immaterial advantages for all forms of bribery offences'.[6]

Alleged cases of corruption in the defence sector

A recent high-profile case of alleged private sector corruption is that of the Patria group of companies, which focus on aerospace and defence. The Finnish state owns a majority share in Patria.[7]

The Finnish National Bureau of Investigation (Keskusrikospoliisi) stated in a press release on 14 May 2008 that it had started two pre-trial investigations into suspected bribery in relation to arms sales by the Patria group.[8] According

---

2 Ministry of Justice, 'Oikeusministeriö Valmistelee Pikaisesti Ensimmäiset Muutokset Vaalirahoituslakiin Kunnallisvaaleihin', press release, 28 May 2008.

3 Survey, Keskuskauppakamari and Helsingin Seudun Kauppakamari, 'Yritysten Rikosturvallisuus 2008: Riskit ja niiden hallinta' (Helsinki: Keskuskauppakamari/Helsingin Seudun Kauppakamari, 2008). The survey consisted of the answers of 1,286 Finnish business leaders.

4 Ibid.

5 This translation of the Finnish/Swedish terms is provided by the GRECO Evaluation Team, which decided that the terms used in the official translation of the law – namely 'unjustified/unlawful benefit' – are slightly misleading. GRECO, *Evaluation Report on Finland on Incriminations (ETS 173 and 191, GPC 2)* (Strasbourg: GRECO, 2007).

6 Ibid.

7 Information provided on the Patria website at www.patria.fi/index.asp?id=AC8B6447C293481BA304C7328C3D4 594&tabletarget=&MENU_1_open=true.

8 Keskusrikospoliisi, 'Kaksi Esitutkintaa Lahjusepäilyistä Patria-konsernin Yhtiöissä', press release, 14 May 2008.

to the press release, one investigation is into whether employees of Patria Weapon Systems Ltd engaged in bribery when the construction technology of 155mm field artillery guns was sold to Egypt.[9] A second pre-trial investigation deals with suspected bribery in the sale of armoured moving vehicles by Patria Vehicles Ltd to Slovenia. According to the Finnish National Bureau of Investigation, two people were detained and multiple houses were searched on 13 May 2008. On 15 May one of the detainees was released and the other was arrested as a suspect.[10] A press release by Patria dated 14 May 2008 states that 'Patria's understanding is that its personnel have followed all relevant legislation both in Slovenia and Finland'.[11]

Two people from the Patria management were placed under pre-trial detention for suspected aggravated bribery and bribery in business operations by a decision of the Helsinki District Court on 13 November 2008.[12] According to press information, one of the detained persons was Jorma Wiitakorpi, who served as Patria CEO at the time of the sale of armoured moving vehicles, and the other a current Patria executive.[13] Wiitakorpi was released on 28 November 2008.[14]

In another case of suspected corruption in the defence sector, police investigated suspicions of bribery in a tender for the disposal of tanks. The tender was worth €7 million (approximately US$11 million).[15] The police interrogated three employees of Stena Metalli Ltd and an employee of the Finnish Defence Forces as suspects in the

case.[16] Two of the main suspects were arrested and kept in custody for two weeks in November 2007. The police investigated allegations including aggregated fraud, breach of official secrets and misuse of business secrets, as well as bribe-giving and taking.[17] According to a statement by a policeman, the case involved accommodation and services provided to a state official at training camps of the Finnish Defence Forces in Finnish Lapland.[18] The investigation into the case started after the Finnish Defence Forces filed a report to the police about their suspicions in September 2007.[19]

Although these cases may be isolated incidents, the government should seriously consider obliging state-owned companies to adopt and follow ethical codes of conduct, which is not currently the case. As many state-owned companies maintain monopolies and/or operate in sectors such as defence or energy that often have quite far-reaching secrecy clauses, they are not necessarily subjected to the peer scrutiny that other companies face. They may thus be more prone to unethical business practices, such as rigged tender procedures, trading in influence or bribery. Obligatory ethical codes of conduct for state-owned companies would safeguard these companies from unethical business procedures.

Official report on corruption in Finland

A review of corruption called *Korruptiotilannekuva 2008* (*A Snapshot of Corruption 2008*), published by the Finnish National Bureau of Investigation,

9 Ibid.
10 Keskusrikospoliisi, 'Yksi Vangittu Patrian Jutun Esitutkinnassa', press release, 20 May 2008.
11 Patria, 'Investigations Related to Patria's Vehicle Contract in Slovenia and Howitzer Contract in Egypt', press release, 14 May 2008.
12 Keskusrikospoliisi, 'Patria Vehicles Oy:n panssariajoneuvokaupan esitutkinta', press release, 14 November 2008.
13 *Ilta-Sanomat* (Finland), 13 November 2008
14 *Helsingin Sanomat* (Finland), 29 November 2008.
15 *Helsingin Sanomat* (Finland), 1 December 2007; *Ilta-Sanomat* (Finland), 30 November 2007.
16 *Ilta-Sanomat* (Finland), 30 November 2007.
17 Ibid.
18 Ibid.
19 Ibid.

is the first official review on corruption in Finland in recent years.[20] It is based on data from Finnish police records from the years 2002 to 2007. According to the review, organised crime groups, which rely on legal firms for their activities, provide a platform for the growth of corruption. The review suggests that organised crime groups transfer assets and activities to legal businesses, especially in the construction industry. The review indicates that there may be significant amounts of corruption in public procurement as yet undisclosed, especially in the case of municipalities. According to the review, there are particularly opportunities for corruption in the pre-bidding stage.

Currently, high-ranking civil servants have to declare their interests only to their employer, which makes control by the wider public and by their superiors very difficult. The review recommends further political research by a collaboration of research bodies, focusing on the basis on which pre-trial investigations or considerations of charges are given up or why prosecutors' demands are rejected in court.

Although a survey by the Central Chamber of Commerce and Helsinki Region Chamber of Commerce indicates that companies engage in bribery in some sectors of the economy,[21] the review's finding is that there have been no business prohibitions on the basis of bribery. There was some debate about why this may be through a discussion of the multiple types of corruption raised by the Swedish National Council for Crime Prevention (Brottsförebyggande rådet – Brå) in its report *Korruptionens Struktur i Sverige* (*The Structure of Corruption in Sweden*), and an assessment as to whether such types of corruption also occur in Finland.[22]

The review found few reports of the offence referred to as 'Entertainment', in which information about products offered for sale is presented to managers alongside offers of musical or VIP events. This is not surprising, however, as according to current Finnish legislation it is not a crime to offer reciprocal hospitality when nurturing long-term personal and community relations.

On the other hand, the type of corruption called 'Entrepreneur adapts rules of representation' was found to be very common. This type of corruption refers to cases in which 'representational gifts' by companies are handed out to buyers of services or products as a 'thank you' for purchasing from that company. These gifts often fall in the grey area between what is allowed and what is prohibited. The review states that in the Finnish police records there were thirteen reports of offences of this type. If the government were to respond to the GRECO recommendation to clarify the definitions of 'due' and 'undue' gifts, this grey area would be eliminated. This would also reduce uncertainty in the economy, as companies would know the parameters of acceptable hospitality better, creating a more level playing field between companies and reducing the corruption risks.

Finally, the review found that there have been press reports linking Finnish companies and their subsidiaries abroad to cases that could be labelled 'International corrupt trade worth billions'. The 'billions' are likely to refer to billions of Swedish krona, or more than US$170 million. This type of corruption refers to cases in which huge foreign investment is carried out with the help of intermediaries working in a target region.[23] The use of intermediaries makes the international money flow more difficult to

20 Keskusrikospoliisi, *Korruptiotilannekuva 2008* (Helsinki: Keskusrikospoliisi, 2008).
21 Survey, 'Keskuskauppamari', 2008.
22 Brå, *Korruptionens Struktur i Sverige* (Stockholm: Brå, 2007).
23 Keskusrikospoliisi, *Korruptiotilannekuva 2008*: p. 29.

track. They are often given the task of finding the right contact persons as well as providing legal advice.[24] Remuneration is often paid only after a positive decision about the trade has been made.[25] Pre-trial investigation in such cases is costly, as a great deal of the police work has to be done overseas.[26] The fact that the Finnish National Bureau of Investigation has committed the resources necessary to investigate the Patria case, however, indicates that such corruption is taken seriously.

In sum, while the report does not reveal a huge amount of corruption, there are certainly weaknesses and loopholes in Finnish legislation. While certain types of corruption are not made illegal and while grey areas in the law persist, it will be difficult to measure with any precision how common such practices really are. The three types of corruption identified above suggest that a three-pronged approach needs to be taken: the possible criminalisation of certain types of entertainment; clarification on the giving and receiving of 'undue' gifts; and the dedication of resources to investigate international corruption.

Santeri Eriksson (Transparency Finland)

Additional reading

GRECO, *Evaluation Report on Finland on Transparency of Party Funding* (Strasbourg: GRECO, 2007).

Evaluation Report on Finland on Incriminations (ETS 173 and 191, GPC 2) (Strasbourg: GRECO, 2007).

Keskuskauppakamari and Helsingin Seudun Kauppakamari, 'Yritysten Rikosturvallisuus 2008: Riskit ja niiden hallinta' (Helsinki: Keskuskauppakamari/Helsingin Seudun Kauppakamari, 2008).

Keskusrikospoliisi, *Korruptiotilannekuva 2008* (Helsinki: Keskusrikospoliisi, 2008).

TI Finland: www.transparency.fi.

---

24 Ibid.
25 Ibid.
26 Ibid.

France

Corruption Perceptions Index 2008: 6.9 (23rd out of 180 countries)

Conventions
Council of Europe Civil Law Convention on Corruption (signed November 1999; ratified April 2008)
Council of Europe Criminal Law Convention on Corruption (signed September 1999; ratified April 2008)
OECD Convention on Combating Bribery of Foreign Public Officials (signed July 2000; ratified September 2000)
UN Convention against Corruption (signed December 2003; ratified July 2005)
UN Convention against Transnational Organized Crime (signed December 2000; ratified October 2002)

Legal and institutional changes

- On 13 November 2007 a new law was passed to transpose the criminal provisions of the Council of Europe criminal and civil conventions, and the UN Convention against Corruption, into French law.[1] The new law is a step in the right direction towards reinforcing anti-corruption regulations. It should help facilitate the work of financial judges by creating new offences, extending the scope of existing offences and strengthening the means of detection and investigation. Other areas of progress include extending the offence of the bribery of foreign public officials beyond the scope of international trade; creating the offence of accepting bribes by public officials and elected representatives of other countries and officials of international organisations; creating the offence of influence peddling by officials in international organisations; excluding companies convicted of corruption

from public–private partnerships; and establishing legal protection for whistleblowers in the private sector. Despite these developments more guarantees must be provided to implement the system effectively.

- Strengthening resources for financial jurisdictions was discussed in a parliamentary debate on 10 October 2008 related to the law of 13 November 2007. Although the current number of specialist judges appears to be sufficient, it is essential to bolster their training and material resources, and the number of clerks and financial experts available to them. The minister of justice's statement to parliament to increase the number of 'experienced judges' and 'specialist assistants' in the Paris financial division will need to be monitored, while at the same time not neglecting the specialist regional jurisdictions.

- Also discussed in parliament on 10 October was the possibility that civil society organisations might be able to launch anti-corruption

---

1 Law no. 2007-1598 of 13 November 2007 on the fight against corruption; *Journal Officiel*, 14 November 2007.

proceedings in the future. Currently, certain associations are authorised to enter proceedings as plaintiffs in order to defend specified collective interests worthy of legal protection (anti-racism, the protection of minors, etc.). In order to strengthen the recognition and protection of corruption victims, the fight against corruption must be similarly enshrined as an interest for which specialist associations can bring legal proceedings. An amendment tabled by the law's sponsor at the National Assembly to allow anti-corruption associations to join criminal proceedings as plaintiffs was rejected by MPs.[2] The mere fact that it was discussed, however, is the first evidence that people's positions are changing on this matter.

Combating corruption in the private sector: current practices in France

As part of a huge game of poker being played by exporting nations that are signatories to the OECD Anti-Bribery Convention, there is uncertainty over which practices are really being implemented by French authorities and businesses and which are merely a bluff. Despite an international consensus on the need to combat corruption, countries such as France that have begun to respect their international obligations are still observing the behaviour of their main competitors extremely closely. Governments and policy-makers are careful not to go too far in imposing penalties for international corruption in order to prevent their domestic companies from suffering from 'ethical dumping'.[3] Such a situation is created when anti-corruption systems and policies vary between different countries, and governments are forced to arbitrate between

their desire to fight corruption and the need to preserve their economic interests. Governments are also keen to avoid, for example, the condemnation the United Kingdom suffered when it decided to bring down the curtain on an investigation into the role of its leading arms firm in an alleged corruption case involving Saudi Arabia.[4]

In France, the risks have moved

France's score in TI's Corruption Perceptions Index 2008 (6.9) is still mediocre compared to most other western European countries.[5] This score, which has not improved significantly over time, indicates that France still has much progress to make in terms of the integrity of relationships between public officials, politicians and businesspeople. For example, at the very beginning of his mandate President Nicolas Sarkozy accepted an invitation to spend his holidays on a yacht belonging to a French billionaire industrialist, Vincent Bollor, who also owns a number of press organisations.[6] This created an outcry in France and abroad.

Many observers would agree that corruption in public procurement in France has been reduced, following the politico-financial scandals of the 1990s and the adoption of a succession of laws designed to prevent corruption in public procurement and regulate the financing of politics more effectively.[7] Corinne Lepage – a lawyer, former environment minister and a TI France board member – shares this opinion with regard to the risky water and waste management sector.[8] She stresses, however, that the risks have changed. No longer is the issue necessarily traditional corruption in the form of bribery as defined by French

---

2 See www.assemblee-nationale.fr/13/cri/2007-2008/20080007.asp.
3 A number of MPs used this expression in the 13 November 2007 debate on the law on the fight against corruption. See www.assemblee-nationale.fr/13/cra/2007-2008/007-2.asp.
4 Radio France Internationale, 16 January 2007.
5 Other scores include 9.0 for Switzerland, 7.9 for Germany and 7.7 for the United Kingdom.
6 *Washington Post* (US), 10 May 2007.
7 See www.legifrance.gouv.fr/affichTexte.do?cidTexte=JORFTEXT000000186650&dateTexte=.
8 C. Lepage, *La Lettre de Transparence*, no. 36, March 2008.

law, but more a question of influence-peddling and lobbying – activities that are still not adequately regulated in France. Sponsoring symposia, financing study trips and recruiting relatives of public decision-makers are all common practices that, without being acts of corruption in the eyes of the law, are nevertheless instances of influence-peddling and the source of decisions that are not justified in terms of the public interest.

Internationally, French companies state that their situation is difficult

In public statements, French business organisations make no secret of the difficulties they face abroad in countries with weak governance. According to Jean Monville, chairman of construction company SPIE and of the Medef's internationalisation board,[9] companies are frequently put under pressure both before and during the contracting process.[10] The French Council of Investors in Africa (CIAN)[11] indicated that corruption increased worldwide from 1997 to 2007, and that the sums at stake are higher than ever before.[12] The CIAN, which has noted that a number of OECD companies are leaving countries due to weak governance, has also observed an increase in inappropriate solicitations during tax controls, customs procedures and other regulatory operations. Moreover, it observes that members in some countries that consider resisting are exposing themselves to the risk of major reprisals, including the seizure of bank assets, the placement of seals on company premises, the confiscation of passports, the refusal to renew residence permits and even physical threats.

The nineteen investigations undertaken in France against French companies for bribing foreign officials confirm this worrying picture.[13] It is worth noting that most of these proceedings target major groups, which are generally thought to have greater wherewithal than small and medium enterprises to resist inappropriate solicitations and bribery attempts.

A May 2008 survey by Ernst & Young[14] sheds a slightly different light on this issue. Somewhat surprisingly, managers of French companies who answered the survey believed that their companies are less exposed to fraudulent practices than other companies in the world.[15] Fewer of them had been involved in an act of corruption, had been approached to pay an unofficial commission or had lost out in a deal to a competitor who engaged in corruption. French business leaders tended to believe, more so than their counterparts in other countries, that legislation was more stringently applied than it was five years ago.

Penalties for corruption

French law currently has an extensive arsenal for fighting corruption in the private sector. The various forms of corruption (active and passive, public and private, domestic and foreign) are all specific offences that Law no. 2007-1598 of 13 November 2007 harmonised. The question, therefore, is to determine to what extent French courts actually apply these provisions. Once again, it is important to distinguish between acts committed in France and those committed overseas.

There are some doubts about the policy of recent governments towards penalising corruption

---

9 The Medef (Mouvement des Entreprises de France) is France's leading confederation of business leaders.

10 TI France Symposium 2007, 'What Rights for Victims of Corruption?', TI France/Sécure Finance/Graffic, 2008.

11 CIAN is an association of about 100 French companies that invest and specialise in Africa.

12 CIAN, 'Responses to the Consultation Paper on the Review of the OECD Anti-Bribery Instruments'.

13 See page 327.

14 Ernst & Young, *Corruption or Compliance – Weighing the Costs: 10th Global Fraud Survey* (London: Ernst & Young, 2008).

15 The survey included thirty-three countries in North America, Latin America, the Middle East, Europe, Africa, Asia and Oceania.

committed in France. It is difficult to assess how sanctions may have changed, however, as statistics are not collected. The only statistics available are global, and cover 'economic and financial offences', of which corruption is only a part. We can simply note that the number of offences brought before the courts relating to economic and financial crime increased between 2004 and 2006.[16]

One observation can be made. For the most part, the most important corruption cases to hit the headlines recently in France have concerned activities dating from the 1990s, such as fictional jobs at Paris City Hall[17] and public procurement contracts involving school construction in the Ile-de-France region.[18] It is unlikely, however, that this means corruption has declined, as this does not fit with the image portrayed by international business leaders and French citizens when they are interviewed.[19] An explanation for this finding may be weaknesses – deliberate or otherwise – in the detection system, which means that corruption cases no longer come before judges. Attention should also be given to the insufficient resources made available to investigators and magistrates to tackle white-collar crime.

Judge Isabelle Prevost-Desprez, vice-president to the Fifteenth Chamber (economic and financial crime) of Nanterre, attributes this situation to the reaction of elites after the wave of convictions of the 1990s.[20] In her view, political pressure on judges has increased, particularly since

2002. Moreover, most of the reforms of criminal proceedings have been dictated by the will of the elites to protect themselves from judges. Upon closer inspection, the recent procedural changes in fact target only white-collar crime. For example, the requirement since 1 July 2007 that investigating judges draft a mission statement before recruiting a financial expert – the draft and expert having to be approved by various stakeholders in the case – is a new source of potential slowdowns in procedures.

It should be noted, however, that 2007 saw the first formal indictment for 'corruption of a private official'. This offence has existed since 2005, when France incorporated the Council framework decision of the European Union on the issue into its domestic law.[21] This indictment concerns a journalist suspected of receiving bribes from a foreign businessman in exchange for a flattering portrait in a widely circulated weekly magazine.[22]

According to the 2008 TI progress report on the implementation of the OECD Convention on Combating Bribery of Foreign Public Officials, France was one of the signatory states that was most diligent in applying the convention.[23] Since July 2000, when the convention was incorporated into French national law, nineteen investigations have been started against French companies suspected of paying bribes to foreign public officials. According to press reports, some of these investigations are focused on major corporations, including Total,[24] Thales[25] and Alstom.[26]

---

16 8,172 in 2004, 9,391 in 2005 and 10,040 in 2006; Ministry of the Interior, Institut National des Hautes Etudes de Sécurité (National Institute for Further Studies in Security).
17 *Le Monde* (France), 20 February 2007.
18 *Le Monde* (France), 23 April 2005.
19 See TI's Corruption Perceptions Index and Global Corruption Barometer.
20 'Les moyens de la justice française face à la corruption', conference organised by TI France, 12 June 2007.
21 'Loi no. 2005-750 du 4 juillet 2005 portant diverses dispositions d'adaptation au droit communautaire dans le domaine de la justice'; www.legifrance.gouv.fr.
22 'Journalist Marc Francelet released', Nouvelobs.com, 13 June 2008.
23 F. Heimann and G. Dell, *Progress Report 2008: OECD Anti-Bribery Convention* (Berlin: TI, 2008).
24 *Le Figaro* (France), 15 October 2007.
25 *Le Monde* (France), 9 December 2005.
26 *Le Figaro* (France), 16 May 2008.

Nevertheless, sanctions for acts of corruption abroad have not been quite so clear-cut. The French government seems intent on retaining control over judicial processes in this field. The public prosecutor, who receives his instructions from the Ministry of Justice, has a monopoly on initiating proceedings relating to offences committed outside the European Union. The government justifies this[27] by its desire to prevent any attempt at manipulating the French justice system. For example, there may be a hypothetical situation in which a self-declared victim might be manipulated by a foreign company or state for the sole purpose of obtaining the indictment of a French company, thereby damaging its reputation. This public prosecutor monopoly creates a risk of interference in international corruption affairs, however. This risk has been highlighted by the OECD[28] and GRECO.[29]

There are other obstacles to the better implementation of the OECD convention in France. The OECD's most recent evaluation report[30] points to the statute of limitations of three years for corruption cases, which it views as too short. As previously noted, it is also essential to strengthen the training of specialised investigators and judges, and enhance the facilities available to them and the number of clerks and financial experts at their disposal. Some judges in the Paris financial division also believe they are not treated fairly by their management structure compared to their colleagues from other jurisdictions in terms of promotion and support for their investigations.[31] Finally, it is important to note that, despite the nineteen investigations that have been opened since 2000 on the basis of the OECD convention, no convictions have yet been made.

The prevention of corruption in business

Since 2003, when the tenth principle of the UN Global Compact on the fight against corruption and extortion was adopted, French companies have become increasingly aware of these issues. Specialist forums, studies, conferences and seminars aimed at the private sector have increased in recent years.[32] For example, Jean Monville believes that 'not to become involved in anticorruption may lead [companies] to run major risks'.[33]

As such, more large companies are declaring their intention to set up prevention policies and programmes, such as codes of conduct, compliance officers and training. This move was encouraged by the US Sarbanes–Oxley Act of 2002, which requires publicly traded companies to implement procedures relating to compliance (e.g. whistleblowing). In 2006 TI France produced a report on the anti-corruption policies and systems of large French companies.[34] Of the twenty-four firms that responded, twenty-two

---

27 In addition to the public prosecutor, generally any victim is authorised to bring public proceedings by registering an official complaint and petitioning to join the proceedings as a plaintiff.

28 OECD, *Country Reports on the Implementation of the OECD Anti-Bribery Convention and the 1997 Revised Recommendation* [*Phase 1 Report*, 2000; *Phase 2 Report*, 2004; *Phase 2 Follow-up Report*, 2006] (Paris: OECD).

29 Evaluation report September 2001, compliance report October 2003 and addendum to the compliance report June 2006.

30 OECD, 2004; 2006.

31 Anecdotal evidence, collected by the author.

32 One example is 'Anticorruption Symposium – Between the Desire to Regulate and the Reality on the Ground: The Actions of a Responsible Company in Ethical Globalisation', Medef, 7 December 2006. Participants included the World Bank chair, the OECD secretary general, the treasury director and TI's chair.

33 TI France/Sécure Finance/Graffic, 2008.

34 TI France, *Corruption Prevention: What Is the Situation among Major French Corporations? Assessment 2005/2006* (Paris: TI France, 2006).

stated they had a formal anti-corruption policy and seventeen said that they had set up procedures for prevention.

The Ernst & Young study shows a certain uniqueness in France.[35] French firms tended to regard internal audits focused on compliance and increased controls on high-risk financial exchanges as the most effective procedures for minimising exposure to corruption, whereas companies from other countries considered staff training to be the most effective deterrent. In contrast, very few French managers interviewed believed in the effectiveness of systems such as whistleblowing, while this procedure has frequently been cited with approval by companies from other countries. This can be explained by a cultural specificity, as denunciation is not well accepted culturally in France.

The margin for potential progress is greater still in raising awareness, as many managers are still unfamiliar with anti-corruption regulations and *a fortiori* in terms of prevention systems. Among the 512 French companies that have joined the UN Global Compact, only forty reported in 2008 having implemented good practice in applying their commitment to fighting corruption.[36] Moreover, when these statements are studied in detail, there is very little information on the good practices that are claimed to be implemented.

TI France offers assistance to French enterprises to establish or improve their anti-bribery devices, working, for example, with the Lafarge construction group from April 2004 to December 2005. The collaboration focused on analysing Lafarge's exposure to corruption and extortion risks. Based on the diagnosis, Lafarge has developed specific materials to raise local managers' awareness and help them handle ethical dilemmas.

Outlook and conclusion

While corruption in public procurement has apparently decreased at the national level, France still has to improve the integrity of relations between business and the political class. Lobbying, in particular, needs to be regulated swiftly. The government also needs to offer more guarantees of its willingness to punish white-collar crime by giving the justice system independence as well as the procedural and material means.

Regarding international corruption, France seems to be arbitrating between its seemingly genuine desire to help advance the fight against corruption across the world, for example by adopting a proactive policy to ensure that the UN Convention against Corruption is applied by all the signatory countries, and on the other hand defending French companies.

As for businesses, though much remains to be done, progress has been made in recent years in terms of awareness and prevention. This progress may be jeopardised, however, by the unfair competition that French companies regularly complain about. Companies are keeping a close watch on the developments of the Al Yamamah case in the United Kingdom. If BAe Systems is not brought to book in this case of alleged bribery of foreign officials, this is likely to lead to the general deterioration of corporate practices in the major exporting countries, including France.

The French business community has put forward a number of proposals to reduce imbalances in competition. The Medef suggests, for example, that Europe insert an anti-corruption and anti-money-laundering clause in all trade agreements to put pressure on countries such as China, Russia and South Korea.[37] Along with the CIAN,

---

35 Ernst & Young, 2008.
36 See www.institut-entreprise.fr/index.php?id=649.
37 TI France/Sécure Finance/Graffic, 2008.

the Medef also proposes extending the possibility of pre-trial guilty pleas to all corruption offences. In addition to speeding up judicial procedures, this would present many other advantages for French companies. It would level the playing field with US companies, because the negative reputational effects of a pre-trial procedure would be less than the indictments currently applied in France. French companies also argue that pre-trial guilty pleas, accompanied by corporate commitments to implement corrective actions, would encourage the development of prevention systems.

Daniel Lebègue and Julien Coll (TI France)

Additional reading

A. Dulin, 'Biens mal acquis … profitent trop souvent: La fortune des dictateurs et les complaisances', working document (Paris: Comité Catholique contre la Faim et pour le Développement, March 2007).

P. Montigny, 'L'entreprise face à la corruption internationale', press release, www.ethic-intelligence.com, 23 October 2006.

P. Montigny, Bernard Bertossa, Alexis Blois, David Martinez Madero, François Franchi and François Vincke, *La corruption, un risque actuel pour les entreprises* (Paris: Secure Finance, 2006).

OECD, *Phase 2 Follow-up Report on the Implementation of the Phase 2 Recommendations on the Application of the Convention and the 1997 Recommendation on Combating Bribery of Foreign Public Officials in International Business Transactions* (Paris: OECD, 2006).

TI France: www.transparence-france.org.

Germany

Corruption Perceptions Index 2008: 7.9 (14th out of 180 countries)

Conventions

Council of Europe Civil Law Convention on Corruption (signed November 1999; not yet
ratified)

Council of Europe Criminal Law Convention on Corruption (signed January 1999; not yet
ratified)

OECD Convention on Combating Bribery of Foreign Public Officials in International Business
Transactions (ratified September 1998)

UN Convention against Corruption (signed December 2003; not yet ratified)

UN Convention against Transnational Organized Crime (signed December 2000; ratified September
2005)

Legal and institutional changes

- The new Law on the Status of Civil Servants,
adopted on 17 June 2008,[1] implements a
whistleblower protection provision as per
article 9 of the Council of Europe Civil Law
Convention on Corruption.[2] Section 38 (2)
of the law provides that officials now have
the right to report suspicions of corruption
directly to the competent law enforcement
authorities without previously informing their
superiors. GRECO, the Council of Europe's
anti-corruption monitoring body, recommended twice in the past that disciplinary
measures should not apply to an official who
directly reports a grounded suspicion of corruption to the police or prosecutors.[3]

- In December 2007 the Bundestag (federal parliament) adopted the Law on Reform of the
Interception of Communications. The new
article 100a of the Criminal Procedure Code
allows communications to be intercepted in
cases of active and passive bribery of public
officials as well as serious bribery offences in
the private sector. This step was also recommended by GRECO.[4]

- The federal government introduced a bill in
October 2007 to implement the provisions of
the UN Convention against Corruption, the
Council of Europe Criminal Law Convention
on Corruption, the Additional Protocol to
the Criminal Law Convention on Corruption
and the EU Council Framework Decision on
Combating Corruption in the Private Sector.[5]

---

1 See www.bgblportal.de/BGBL/bgbl1f/bgbl108s1010.pdf.
2 Council of Europe Treaty Series no. 174.
3 GRECO, *First Evaluation Round: Evaluation Report on Germany* (Strasbourg: GRECO, 2002); *Second Evaluation Round: Evaluation Report on Germany* (Strasbourg: GRECO, 2005).
4 GRECO, 2002.
5 *Bundestags-Drucksache* 16/6558.

The draft law seeks, *inter alia*, to extend the scope of the offence of bribery involving foreign public officials (see below).

- Due to its weak criminal law provisions regarding bribery involving members of parliament (section 108e of the Penal Code), Germany has still not ratified the UN Convention against Corruption. Two opposition parties, the Greens (in 2007) and the Left (in 2008), have introduced bills recently to bring the respective German laws into compliance with international standards.[6]
- On 29 May 2008 the regional parliament of Sachsen-Anhalt adopted a freedom of information act. In addition to the Federal Law on Freedom of Information, there are currently freedom of information laws in nine out of the sixteen German *Länder,* and a draft law in one more.[7]

Siemens still an issue

The Siemens scandal still dominates the public discussion on corruption in Germany.[8] It is not surprising therefore that Germans today believe that, apart from political parties, no sector is more affected by corruption than the private sector.[9] In May 2007 Andreas Kley, a former finance chief of Siemens' power generation unit, and an ex-colleague were given suspended prison sentences for bribing two managers of the Italian energy company Enel from 1999 to 2002. Siemens was ordered to pay €38 million (US$52 million),[10] though the fine was thrown out on appeal.[11] In October 2007 Siemens was sentenced to pay €201 million (US$274 million) for corruption in its telecommunications branch.[12] In July 2008 former telephone division manager Reinhard Siekaczek was convicted of forty-nine counts of being a party to the misappropriation of corporate funds, fined €108,000 (US$135,000) and given two years' probation for his role in overseeing slush funds used to pay bribes.[13] With more prosecutions expected, Germany's largest post-war economic scandal is likely to dominate the news for the next few years.

The scandal and Siemens' extensive measures to prevent future corruption[14] have already triggered a boom in establishing and strengthening compliance mechanisms, and particularly anti-corruption controls, in German companies.[15] By contrast, the federal government thus far has not used the scandal as an opportunity to improve the legal framework for corruption prevention. Heinrich von Pierer, a former Siemens CEO accused of involvement in foreign bribery cases by a former top manager of the company, even continued as head of the government think tank Innovationsrat until officials decided to dissolve the institution in early 2008.[16] Only the opposition Green Party directly reacted to the Siemens scandal, by introducing a parliamentary motion calling for, *inter alia*, establishing a blacklist of corrupt companies and strengthening whistleblower protection in the private sector.[17]

---

6 *Bundestags-Drucksache* 16/6726, 16/8979.
7 For sources on all freedom of information acts in Germany and the draft law, see www.dgif.de/index.php?id=56&Fsize=0.
8 For an extensive analysis of the Siemens scandal, see H. Leyendecker, *Die große Gier* (Berlin: Rowohlt, 2007).
9 See TI's Global Corruption Barometer 2007.
10 *Süddeutsche Zeitung* (Germany), 14 June 2007.
11 *Der Spiegel* (Germany), 29 August 2008.
12 *Süddeutsche Zeitung* (Germany), 5 October 2007.
13 *Der Spiegel* (Germany), 28 July 2008.
14 *Die Welt* (Germany), 31 March 2008.
15 *Handelsblatt* (Germany), 26 February 2008.
16 *Die Welt* (Germany), 18 April 2008; 5 May 2008; *Frankfurter Allgemeine Zeitung* (Germany), 7 April 2008.
17 *Bundestags-Drucksache* 16/4459.

Currently, the criminal offence of corruption in the private sector applies only to active and passive bribery that distorts or may distort business competition. Most other legal systems prefer to protect individual companies (and thereby the economy) by focusing on breaches of duty within an intra-organisational principal–agent relationship. A bill introduced by the federal government in October 2007[18] aims to implement a respective provision of the EU Council Framework Decision on Combating Corruption in the Private Sector, suggesting that the definition of the offence be extended to corrupt practices involving a breach of duties by employees beyond business competition.[19] Thus, although parliament has not yet considered the bill, it is likely that the criminal law framework for combating corruption in the private sector will be improved sooner or later. Furthermore, the Federal Ministry of Food, Agriculture and Consumer Protection has announced recently that it is working on a draft law to improve consumer-related whistleblower protection in the private sector.[20]

Using the OECD Guidelines for Multinational Enterprises to tackle corporate corruption

TI Germany (TI-G) has used the OECD guidelines to lodge various complaints against corrupt business practices. The guidelines are a set of social, labour, environmental and anti-corruption standards developed by the OECD for transnational companies based in or operating from their territories.[21] Forty nations – thirty OECD members and ten non-member states – have endorsed the guidelines as a basic component of responsible corporate conduct. While the guidelines are voluntary for companies, they have been useful for promoting corporate accountability. Adhering countries are bound by intergovernmental agreement to set up a National Contact Point (NCP), whose functions include responding to complaints arising from alleged violations.

The objective in all cases raised by TI-G was to remind the German government of its responsibility to promote adherence to the guidelines' anti-corruption provisions and encourage companies that had failed to do so to improve their precautionary measures. With its June 2007 complaint against fifty-seven companies involved in the alleged manipulation of the UN Oil-for-Food Programme in Iraq, TI-G launched the most significant case in the history of the guidelines.

In October 2005 the Independent Inquiry Committee (IIC) into the UN Oil-for-Food Programme reported that 2,253 companies had paid a total of US$1.8 billion in kickbacks – illicit or disguised payments – to the Iraqi government to obtain contracts to supply food, medicine and other humanitarian goods to the country.[22] At least fifty-seven German companies, including Siemens, Linde, Daimler-Chrysler, Fresenius Medical Care, Schering and Braun Melsungen, were listed in the IIC report as having allegedly participated. According to the report, their cumulative kickback payments totalled US$12 million.

---

18 *Bundestags-Drucksache* 16/6558.
19 See S. Wolf, 'Modernization of the German Anti-corruption Criminal Law: The Next Steps', *German Law Journal*, vol. 8, no. 3 (2007). For a harsh critique of the draft law, see T. Rönnau and T. Golombek, 'Die Aufnahme des Geschäftsherrenmodells in den Straftatbestand des § 299: ein Systembruch im deutschen StGB', *Zeitschrift für Rechtspolitik*, vol. 40, no. 6 (2007).
20 *Frankfurter Allgemeine Zeitung* (Germany), 21 May 2008.
21 The complete text, including procedural guidance to the OECD Guidelines for Multinational Enterprises (Revision 2000), is available at www.oecd.org/dataoecd/56/36/1922428.pdf.
22 Independent Inquiry Committee into the UN Oil-for-Food Programme, 'Report on Programme Manipulation', 27 October 2005.

Based on evidence presented in the IIC report, TI-G filed a formal complaint with the German NCP requesting that it examine whether the German companies had breached the guidelines' anti-bribery provisions (chapter VI), and if so to ascertain whether they had subsequently introduced appropriate precautionary measures to prevent such breaches occurring in the future.[23] While acknowledging that initiating action against such a large group of companies was unprecedented, TI-G pointed out that nothing in the guidelines' procedures precludes it. Moreover, even though several years had elapsed since the alleged guideline breaches had occurred, TI-G was not aware of any evidence that the companies involved had installed precautionary measures to prevent the alleged misconduct from recurring.

The German NCP made its decision notwithstanding the evidence in the IIC report, dismissed the arguments put forward in TI-G's complaint and informed TI-G that its inquiry could not be accepted as falling under the OECD guidelines' complaint procedure. The NCP justified its rejection on the grounds that:

- the guidelines are part of the OECD Declaration on International Investment and Multinational Enterprises, and are thereby tied to foreign investment and not applicable to trade activities; and
- the German court system is already dealing with the issues, and the NCP cannot act parallel to the ongoing investigations.

OECD Watch commented in its April 2008 newsletter that these are 'familiar, threadbare excuses

for inaction', and that 'in very few circumstances would a specific action ever need to be dropped to avoid prejudicing criminal proceedings'.[24] The Trade Union Advisory Committee (TUAC) to the OECD seconds this assessment, saying that other proceedings – whether criminal, civil or administrative – can never determine compliance with the guidelines.[25]

By declaring the Oil-for-Food Programme complaint inadmissible, the German NCP, which already had a reputation for applying a highly qualified interpretation of the guidelines, went beyond its prior restrictiveness. Never before had the NCP invoked 'parallel procedures' as a basis for refusing to deal with a complaint. Furthermore, while it is possible that the danger of prejudicing ongoing legal proceedings could be invoked with regard to some companies, it is unlikely that this would be the case for all fifty-seven of them. Finally, the assertion that the guidelines cannot be applied to trade activities, while not new, remains unwarranted, as they do not differentiate between investment and trade activities. Similar concerns and aspirations have led national parliaments in the United Kingdom, Canada, the Netherlands and elsewhere to call for a variety of changes, and in some cases to produce significant reforms of NCPs' institutional arrangements, funding and operational procedures.[26]

Corruption and labour relations

In a recent corruption scandal involving Volkswagen (VW), an entire works council accepted immense bribes, including luxurious overseas trips, extra payments and invitations

---

23 TI-G's complaint against fifty-seven German companies is available from its website, www.transparency.de.
24 'Iraq Oil-for-Food Complaint Rejected: German NCP Misses Opportunity for Reinforcing Anti-bribery Message', *OECD Watch Newsletter*, April 2008.
25 'TUAC Submission on Cases Being Treated under Parallel Domestic Procedures', in OECD, *Annual Report on the OECD Guidelines for Multinational Enterprises 2004* (Paris: OECD, 2004); *Annual Report on the OECD Guidelines for Multinational Enterprises 2006* (Paris: OECD, 2006).
26 'The Model European National Contact Points', *OECD Watch*, September 2007.

to brothels.[27] Although these bribes were not directly based on services in return, they encouraged works council members to pursue employer-friendly policies. Beyond this, there seems to be a worrying new dimension of corruption in German labour relations, with companies funding or even establishing employer-friendly would-be unions to compete with and weaken traditional unions.[28]

The largest case so far is the scandal involving Wilhelm Schelsky, former head of the employer-friendly organisation Arbeitsgemeinschaft Unabhängiger Betriebsräte (AUB), and Johannes Feldmayer, a former Siemens board member.[29] Siemens secretly paid Schelsky more than €50 million (US$70 million), most of which was used to fund the AUB.[30] Schelsky funded AUB staff, rental fees, seminars, campaigns for works council elections and even summer camps for children of AUB members. As a result, the AUB was able to maintain offices throughout Germany, and played a significant role in the Siemens supervisory board despite its small membership and low membership fee. Schelsky admitted that the Siemens managing board explicitly wanted the AUB to weaken IG Metall, a traditional union.[31] It has recently become public that Aldi, Germany's largest supermarket chain, had also financed AUB.[32] In April 2008 both Ulrich Adam, a member of the Bundestag, and the Christian Democratic Union (CDU) in the state of Mecklenburg-West Pomerania admitted receiving thousands of euros from Schelsky.[33]

A second example is the Pin–GNBZ scandal. Pin, a private postal services company, paid more than €130,000 (US$200,000) to the Gewerkschaft der Neuen Brief- und Zustelldienste (GNBZ).[34] This organisation was established in October 2007, when the federal government considered introducing a minimum wage in the postal sector. Pin encouraged its workers to become GNBZ members. Then, only a couple of days before the statutory minimum wage went into force, Pin and GNBZ signed a wage agreement below the official minimum wage.[35] Verdi, the traditional union in the services sector, described GNBZ as a 'pseudo trade union' and brought a charge against it for being unduly financed by third parties.[36]

It is not clear whether current legislation is sufficient to deal with this new dimension of corruption in German labour relations. In the Siemens–AUB case, the relevant legislation seems to be section 119 of the Betriebsverfassungsgesetz prohibiting manipulation of works council elections,[37] as Siemens money was allegedly used to finance AUB election campaigns.[38] In the Pin–GNBZ case, however, this section is not relevant. Moreover, prosecutors have already stated the offence of bribery in the private sector does not apply since there was no business transaction between Pin and GNBZ.[39] In many cases

---

27 H. Leyendecker, 2007.
28 *Passauer Neue Presse* (Germany), 8 April 2008.
29 This case should not be confused with the Siemens bribery scandal.
30 *Süddeutsche Zeitung* (Germany), 16 April 2008.
31 S. Wolf, 'Die gekaufte Gewerkschaft. Anmerkungen zur Korruptionsaffäre Siemens-AUB', *Forum Recht*, vol. 26, no. 1 (2008).
32 *Süddeutsche Zeitung* (Germany), 7 April 2008.
33 *Ostsee-Zeitung* (Germany), 22 April 2008.
34 *Berliner Zeitung* (Germany), 26 March 2008.
35 Südwestdeutscher Rundfunk – SWR.de (Germany), 10 March 2008.
36 *Handelsblatt* (Germany), 20 March 2008.
37 *Süddeutsche Zeitung* (Germany), 16 April 2008.
38 Südwestdeutscher Rundfunk – Report Mainz (Germany), 19 March 2008.
39 *Focus* (Germany), 17 April 2008.

of private sector corruption, prosecutors apply the offence of misappropriation of property. This provision would also apply in the Siemens–AUB case. From an economic point of view, however, it is questionable whether companies paying huge bribes to works council members or employer-friendly trade unions really 'misappropriate' money. In the VW scandal, former general works council chairman Klaus Volkert argued that, despite the huge undue benefits he received from the company, his employer-friendly policies had saved VW at least €500,000 (US$600,000) per year.[40] The court did not follow this argument.[41] Nevertheless, the federal government should consider establishing a specific criminal offence concerning the bribery of trade unions and similar organisations.

Lobbyists in federal ministries

In Germany some employees of companies and interest groups also work in federal ministries and offices while retaining their private sector jobs.[42] They not only participate in all internal meetings but also represent government institutions without revealing the special employment conditions to which they are subject.[43] In April 2008 a scandal that had been smouldering for nearly five years hit the headlines.

In 2003 reports led to parliamentary inquiries into 'external employees' in federal ministries.[44] Between October 2006 and January 2007 the political TV programme *Monitor* investigated

and reported on dozens of lobbyists and conflicts of interests. Two opposition factions, the Greens and the Liberal Party (FDP), questioned the government in parliament. The government admitted that about 100 external employees from companies and interest groups were currently working or had been working for federal ministries in the previous four years.[45] This high number was due to a human resources exchange programme between the public and private sector initiated in 2004 by interior minister Otto Schily and an executive board member of Deutsche Bank, Tessen von Heydebreck.[46] After intensive investigations of federal ministries, the German Federal Court of Auditors published a report in April 2008 requesting major changes in this practice.[47]

Grand tax evasion

In February and March 2008 one of the most highly debated topics in Germany was grand tax evasion involving the well-known tax haven of Liechtenstein. The issue arose after Deutsche Post CEO Klaus Zumwinkel was arrested under suspicion of evading €1 million (US$1.5 million) in taxes. He resigned the next day.[48] The Federal Intelligence Service revealed that it had spent more than €4 million (US$6 million) to obtain information about large sums deposited by wealthy Germans in secret bank accounts in Liechtenstein.[49] The authorities announced hundreds of tax evasion investigations, from which they expect the public purse to receive

40 H. Leyendecker, 2007; *Der Spiegel* (Germany), 21 November 2006; *Wirtschaftswoche* (Germany), 22 February 2008.
41 Norddeutscher Rundfunk online (Germany), 22 February 2008.
42 K. Otto and S. Adamek, *Der gekaufte Staat* (Cologne: Kiepenheuer & Witsch, 2008).
43 *Monitor* (TV programme, Germany), 3 April 2008.
44 *Report Mainz* (TV programme, Germany), 6 October 2003; Response of Parliamentary Undersecretary of State Ute Voigt, 23 October 2003.
45 Response of the Federal Government on the Short Inquiry of the FDP Fraction, *Bundestags-Drucksache* 16/3395; Response of the Federal Government on the Short Inquiry of the Green Fraction, *Bundestags-Drucksache* 16/3727.
46 Hertie School of Governance, 'Evaluation Report on the HR Exchange Programme', 10 May 2006.
47 Tagesschau.de (Germany), 2 April 2008.
48 *Die Welt* (Germany), 15 February 2008.
49 Spiegel online (Germany), 18 February 2008.

several hundred million euros in additional tax payments. Meanwhile, the scandal led to an unprecedented diplomatic crisis between Germany and Liechtenstein, which accused the German authorities of buying stolen bank data and misusing their political power to extort a small country.[50] The German government claimed that it put pressure only on criminal Germans. Opposition parliamentarians in Liechtenstein argued that that country should revise its tax haven policy.[51]

Because certain states have high levels of bank secrecy, money laundering can still prosper despite huge efforts to eliminate it. These tax havens provide the conditions in which corrupt elites, often from developing countries, are able to hide their illegally acquired money.[52] Liechtenstein is not the only tax haven.[53] Moreover, German banks also offer possibilities for tax evasion, for instance for Swiss citizens.[54] While the European Union has failed so far to press Liechtenstein and Switzerland to adopt strict rules, the US authorities have been able to

obtain information on the high-interest earnings of US citizens in Switzerland and have received lump tax payments. Germany and the European Union should push Liechtenstein, Switzerland and other tax havens to reach such an agreement.[55]

Sebastian Wolf, Shirley van Buiren and Christian Humborg (TI Germany)

Additional reading

S. Adamek and K. Otto, *Der gekaufte Staat* (Cologne: Kiepenheuer & Witsch, 2008).
H. Leyendecker, *Die große Gier* (Berlin: Rowohlt, 2007).
OECD Watch Newsletter, 'Iraq Oil-for-Food Complaint Rejected: German NCP Misses Opportunity for Reinforcing Anti-bribery Message', *OECD Watch Newsletter*, April 2008.
S. Wolf, 'Modernization of the German Anti-corruption Criminal Law: The Next Steps', *German Law Journal*, vol. 8, no. 3 (2007).
TI Germany: www.transparency.de.

---

50 *Financial Times Deutschland*, 12 February 2008.
51 *Süddeutsche Zeitung* (Germany), 23 February 2008.
52 See UNCAC chapter V, articles 51–9.
53 Telepolis (Germany), 3 March 2008.
54 Zweites Deutsches Fernsehen – ZDF.de (Germany), 10 March 2008.
55 *Die Tageszeitung* (Germany), 20 February 2008.

Greece

Corruption Perceptions Index 2008: 4.7 (57th out of 180 countries)

Conventions

Council of Europe Civil Law Convention on Corruption (signed June 2000; ratified February 2002)
Council of Europe Criminal Law Convention on Corruption (signed January 1999; ratified July 2007)
OECD Convention on Combating Bribery of Foreign Public Officials (signed December 1997; ratified February 1999)
UN Convention against Corruption (signed December 2003; ratified May 2008)
UN Convention against Transnational Organized Crime (signed December 2000; not yet ratified)

Legal and institutional changes

- In May 2007 the Council of Europe's Criminal Law Convention on Corruption and its additional protocol were ratified with Law 3560/2007.[1] Consequently, felonies related to corruption are being tackled at an international level.
- Following the promises of the government and a wave of allegations over corruption scandals shaking the Greek political scene, the UN Convention against Corruption was ratified by parliament with a large majority in May 2008 and came into effect with Law 3666/2008.[2] The most important of the provisions are summarised in the following points.
  - The bribing of a civil servant will no longer be treated as a misdemeanour, but as a felony. More particularly, there is an upgrade of the wrongdoing of the passive as well as the

active bribery of public servants as well as of MPs and local and municipal council servants, foreign and national alike. The misdemeanours are converted automatically into felonies in those cases where the received benefits amount to or surpass the sum of €73,000. Up until now all such wrongdoings have been considered minor offences.

- In addition, all illegal acts in the private sector (including banks, large companies and public benefit institutes) are to also be converted from misdemeanours to felonies when the amount surpasses the total of €73,000.
- The ratification also introduced a new provision (part of the Law 366/2008) providing for the protection of corruption witnesses, similar to the protection envisaged for witnesses in cases of terrorism. In this way the legislator provides for the protection of the witness from intimidation or acts of

---

1 Law 3560/2007, 'Ratification and application of the Criminal Law Convention on Corruption and of its additional protocol', published in *Official Government Gazette* with ΦΕΚ Α΄103/14-5-2007. Ref. number 117 at the Ministry of Justice website: www.ministryofjustice.gr/modules.php?op=modload&name=Nomothetiko&file=page.
2 Law 3666/2008, 'Ratification of the UN Convention against Corruption and replacement of relative provisions of the Criminal Law', published in *Official Government Gazette* with ΦΕΚ Α΄ 105/10-6-2008. Ref. number 123 at the Ministry of Justice website: www.ministryofjustice.gr/modules.php?op=modload&name=Nomothetiko&file=page.

revenge while ensuring the highest level of protection (not previously legislated).

- Additionally, a specific provision has been set concerning the responsibility of legal entities and misdeeds that were committed for their benefit. For the time being, beyond the criminal responsibility of physical persons, the legislator envisages administrative sanctions when the offences were committed in favour of a legal entity. The existing legal order does not provide for the application of punitive sanctions against legal entities.

- Many ministries have undertaken initiatives against corruption in both the public and private sector. Specifically, the Ministry of the Interior proceeded at the beginning of 2007 with the creation of a special phone line, '1564', that all citizens can call in order to report, *inter alia*, cases of alleged corruption of pubic servants, thus bringing them to the attention of the relevant authorities.[3] Another example was a circular announced by the same ministry obliging all public sector services to make publicly available via the internet all their calls for tenders, procurements, and public contracts.[4] Likewise, the Ministry of Health set up a special committee for combating corruption in the process of procurement with annual funding of €500 million. In addition, it imposed an obligation upon all hospitals to establish an annual budget in line with current international standards. These examples provide evidence that, to some extent, efforts have been made to undertake initiatives and establish institutional changes and policies, with the ultimate aim of combating corruption.

Siemens causes political turbulence

On 1 July 2008 an Athens prosecutor filed charges of bribery and money-laundering, following a two-year investigation that had looked into deals involving the government and the Greek affiliate of Siemens AG.[5] The enquiry looked into contracts that had been won by Siemens in relation to 'an expensive security system for the 2004 Athens Olympics' and the supply of equipment for the Greek state-owned telecommunications operator OTE (Hellenic Telecommunications Organisation) in the 1990s.[6]

The investigation began after revelations in 2005 that Siemens had earmarked significant funds so as to ensure that it secured foreign contracts.[7] This was corroborated in an April 2008 report commissioned by Siemens, which found that 'domestic as well as foreign compliance regulations [had] been violated' between 1999 and 2006.[8] During the investigation, approximately 100 people testified to the Athens prosecutor, Panayiotis Athanassiou.[9]

Speculation in daily newspapers has estimated that Siemens officials set aside more that €12 million (US$19 million) for two of Greece's main political parties, Pasok and the ruling New Democracy (ND) conservatives, which took over from Pasok after the 2000 general election.[10] Accusations rocked the political scene as the media revealed that slush funds had been donated to political parties in exchange for contracts related to the 2004 Summer Olympic Games.[11] Theodoros Tsoukatos, close adviser to Costas Simitis, the former prime minister

3 Official site of the deputy minister of the interior, Apostolos Andreoulakos (retired): www.andreoulakos.gr/index. php?option=com_content&task=view&id=218&Itemid=2.

4 Ministry of the Interior circular of 21 February 2008: www.ypes.gr/ypes_po/detail.asp?docid=1740.

5 *International Herald Tribune* (US), 1 July 2008.

6 Deutsche Welle (Germany), 2 July 2008.

7 Ibid.

8 *International Herald Tribune* (US), 1 July 2008.

9 *Eleftherotypia* (Greece), 10 February 2008; Deutsche Welle (Germany), 2 July 2008.

10 *Kathimerini* (Greece), 1 July 2008.

11 *Athens News* (Greece), 8 February 2008.

and Pasok party deputy from 2000 to 2004, admitted that he had accepted DM1 million (approximately US$790,000) as a 'campaign contribution' to the Pasok party prior to the 2000 general election.[12] He claimed that the money was eventually passed on to Pasok in instalments, though Pasok treasury officials claimed that there was no evidence that the money ever reached the party.[13] The ruling party is also implicated, as, although most of the contracts were secured before it came to power in 2004, contracting did take place at the last minute and there were speculations that 'gifts' may have been offered 'to ND people to keep the wheels smooth'.[14]

There are also accusations that, during the 1990s, OTE staff had taken bribes to enable Siemens to win contracts in relation to modernising the telephone network in 1997.[15] In an interesting legal twist, OTE has reportedly pursued claims in both the Greek and Munich courts in relation to the alleged bribery and the slush funds that the German company has admitted operating. [16] Greek prosecutors have requested to have access to the confessions and statements of Siemens' employees.[17] The request has been made in order that the company can seek adequate compensation for damages caused to OTE as a result of the actions of Siemens and also in order to identify the employees involved in the affair.[18] In October 2008 Greek prosecutors questioned Reinhard Siekaczek, a former Siemens executive in Munich; the case is ongoing.[19]

Although there have not been any charges brought against any individual in Greece, the case has been able to progress as charges can be filed against 'all those responsible'. This allows an investigation to be conducted while charges are simultaneously filed against individuals who are considered suspects within the course of the investigation.[20] Meanwhile, Pasok has asked for a special parliamentary committee to look into the affair. The prime minister, Costas Karamanlis, has agreed to hold an all-party parliamentary committee investigation once the judicial proceedings have been completed, arguing that he would not wish to undermine or terminate the legal investigation.[21]

This is a landmark case for Greece, not only because of its links to one of Germany's largest ever corruption scandals, but also because of the implications for two of Greece's largest political parties. Furthermore, OTE's move to bring charges against Siemens in Germany is the first legal case taken by a foreign company against Siemens in relation to its operation of slush funds, and could set a precedent with wide repercussions, considering the extent of Siemens' alleged corruption overseas.[22]

Pension funds bond scandal: watershed in the Greek political scene

The relationship between the state and the investments that it has made in the private sector in relation to state-run pension funds have come under considerable criticism since March 2007.

---

12 Deutsche Welle (Germany), 2 July 2008; Athens News Agency (Greece), 11 April 2008.
13 Athens News Agency (Greece), 26 June 2008; 28 June 2008.
14 *Athens News* (Greece), 8 February 2008.
15 Associated Press (US), 13 December 2006.
16 Reuters (UK), 30 May 2008.
17 Agence France-Presse, 31 January 2008.
18 *Athens News* (Greece), 25 July 2008.
19 Agence France-Presse, 6 October 2008.
20 Reuters (UK), 2 July 2008.
21 *Kathimerini* (Greece), July 18, 2008.
22 Agence France-Presse, 2 August 2008.

Investments were made in structured bonds, which are a risky investment vehicle, and they have reportedly lost the state in excess of €20 million.[23] According to the press, the scandal resulted in the removal of Savvas Tsitouridis[24] from his post as minister of employment and social protection in April 2007, along with the special secretary for pension funds in the Ministry of Employment and Social Protection, Evgenios Papadopoulos.[25]

The case involved the €280 million sale of structured bonds, and sparked a wider investigation looking into investments made by state-run pension funds between 1999 and 2005. The bonds in question had been underwritten by J. P. Morgan and subsequently sold to North Asset Management, a British-based hedge fund, for just over 92 per cent of their nominal value.[26] They were then sold on to HypoVereinsbank in Germany and Acropolis Securities in Greece, before being sold on again to several state pension funds at inflated prices.[27] The purchase of these bonds incurred losses to the state. Nevertheless, in 2007 J. P. Morgan agreed to buy them back in order to make good the losses suffered by the pension funds.[28]

In June 2007 the Greek parliament launched an inquiry into the affair, during which J. P. Morgan claimed that it had entered into the transactions in good faith, but had been misled by a Greek government banker.[29] Despite this, a J. P. Morgan banker was dismissed following his testimony

in the parliamentary enquiry, as he had not 'promptly shared his knowledge'.[30] Furthermore, Greek unions, including the major civil service union, have requested regulators in the United States and the United Kingdom to investigate both J. P. Morgan and North Asset Management in relation to the case.[31] Neither the Serious Fraud Office nor the Financial Services Authority has yet provided any conclusions.

In August 2007 a report was drafted and sent to the authorities by the head of the Anti-laundering Unit, Giorgos Zorbas, who investigated the issue. The report was deemed inadmissible, however, due to technicalities in its drafting, and it was rendered not legally valid in September 2007.[32] The prosecutor, Georgios Koliocostas, sent back the report, but forwarded the evidence gathered by Zorbas to an investigating magistrate, not including his conclusions.[33] The report has not been made public, but purported extracts leaked to the press claimed that finance ministry officials knew the bonds would be sold and that some intermediaries had allegedly made excessive profits, which were given to an unnamed political party.[34] Nevertheless, when Zorbas testified before the Special Permanent Committee on Institutions and Transparency on 7 November 2007 he claimed that no political persons were involved.[35]

Koliocostas has pressed charges against more than sixty people: the crimes included money-laundering, tax evasion, breach of trust and

23 *Eleftherotypia* (Greece), 10 August 2008.
24 Economia Internet Portal, Business File Politics, December 2007.
25 *Kathimerini* (Greece), 5 May 2007; 30 April 2007.
26 *International Herald Tribune* (US), 12 June 2008.
27 Ibid.
28 Ibid.
29 *International Herald Tribune* (US), 13 June 2007.
30 Ibid.
31 Ibid.; Times Online (UK), 27 May 2008.
32 *Kathimerini* (Greece), 25 September 2007.
33 *Kathimerini* (Greece), 22 August 2007.
34 Economia Internet Portal, Business File Politics, December 2007.
35 *Kathimerini* (Greece), 8 November 2007.

membership in criminal organisations.[36] The names of those indicted were not released to the press – an eventuality catered for by existing Greek law, but one that is seldom invoked.[37] On 12 June 2008, however, Nikos Tsourakis, the former head of TAXY (the hotel workers' pension fund), became the first official to be indicted and detained on charges of corruption. The accusations against Tsourakis involve breach of faith over the purchase of three structured bonds from which TAXY allegedly lost €12 million (US$18.6 million) in 2005 and 2006.[38] The sentence Tsourakis faces if he is convicted is a minimum of ten years, but to date no trial has been set.

In June 2007 the scandal led to legislation being passed requiring all pension funds to have professional investment advisers in future.[39] It is to be hoped that this will ensure that future investments by the government are better managed and allow fewer opportunities for corruption.

The case illustrates how loopholes and complexity in private sector investment can have a negative impact on state investment practices, and in this case seriously impact on state pension holders. The positive response of the government in indicting the suspects and J.P. Morgan in making good the investments means that the public may not lose out.

Apostolos Dousias (TI Greece)

Additional reading

T. Konstantinopoulos, *Justice Being Accused* (Athens: Paraskinio Publications, 2000).

G. Lazos, *Corruption and Anticorruption* (Athens: Publications of the Library of Law, 2005).

D. Raikos, *Public Administration and Corruption* (Athens: Sakkoulas Publications, 2006).

H. Trova, *Authorities and Transparency* (Athens: Sakkoulas Publications, 2005).

TI Greece: www.transparency.gr.

---

36 *Eleftherotypia* (Greece), 27 June 2008; *Kathimerini* (Greece), 14 July 2007; *International Herald Tribune* (US), 12 June 2008.
37 *Kathimerini* (Greece), 26 June 2008.
38 *International Herald Tribune* (US), 12 June 2008.
39 Economia Internet Portal, Business File Politics, December 2007.

Hungary

Corruption Perceptions Index 2008: 5.1 (47th out of 180 countries)

Conventions

Council of Europe Civil Law Convention on Corruption (signed January 2003; ratified December 2003)

Council of Europe Criminal Law Convention on Corruption (signed April 1999; ratified November 2000)

OECD Convention on Combating Bribery of Foreign Public Officials (signed December 1998; ratified February 1999)

UN Convention against Corruption (signed December 2003; ratified April 2005)

UN Convention against Transnational Organized Crime (signed December 2000; ratified December 2006)

Legal and institutional changes

- On 1 October 2007 the government adopted a decree on a programme of 'New Order and Freedom'.[1] The decree lists the responsibilities of the commissioner for the new programme, which include, *inter alia*, coordinating the preparation of a bill on party financing, developing rules on salaries and allowances for MPs, fighting corruption and reforming the administration. A legislative change came out of this programme in April 2008 in the form of improvements to the transparency of public funds.[2] The law introduced stricter conflict of interest regulations so that, for example, chairs of the regional development councils are now excluded from making decisions concerning subsidy allocations. In effect, this stops them or their close relatives from filing allocations for subsidies to their own offices.

- In June 2008 the Competition Act 1996[3] was amended to introduce the 'substantial lessening of competition' model for testing trust requests. It also increases the influence of the Competition Authority to implement the leniency policy, which means that, if a member of a cartel denounces it to the authority, this party will be immune from sanctions. As such, it encourages the disclosure of cartel agreements.

- In April 2007 the State Audit Office announced proposals for public finance regulations aimed at establishing rules, institutions and technical solutions to make public finance more transparent, predictable and efficient at the central and local government levels as well as in public institutions.[4]

---

1 1074/2007. (X. 1.), government decree on the assignments of the governmental commissioner for the 'New Order and Freedom' programme.
2 Act CLXXXI of 2007, on 'Transparency of Subsidies Provided from Public Funds'.
3 Act LVII of 1996, on 'Prohibition of Unfair Market Behaviour and Limiting Competition'.
4 Theses on the Regulation of Public Finances; www.asz.hu/ASZ/www.nsf/publications_other.html.

- In order to transpose the new EU Money Laundering Directives into Hungarian legislation, parliament has adopted a law on the Prevention of Money Laundering and the Financing of Terrorism.[5] Now all types of financial crime will be reported to and investigated by the Customs and Finance Guard. Previously the tasks had been split between the police and the customs office.

- The government has set up the Anti-corruption Coordination Board (ACB), which started its work in August 2007.[6] The ACB has no investigative powers and is not authorised to examine individual cases. Moreover, it cannot issue any decision with public authority. Its main duties include reviving anti-corruption work and stressing supra-legal measures.[7] As such, it had a mandate to draft the government's anti-corruption strategy, which it completed in 2007. Despite both the strategy and a related action plan being prepared, the government had not begun implementing the strategy as of November 2008.

Extent of business crimes in Hungary

Sixty-two per cent of companies in Hungary have been victims of serious business crimes, according to PricewaterhouseCoopers' 2007 'Global Economic Crime Survey'.[8] The most frequent crimes were theft and the mismanagement of funds (48 per cent), crimes concerning intellectual property (26 per cent) and bribery and corruption (17 per cent). Interviews conducted

by TI Hungary for the National Integrity System country study[9] indicate that corruption in Hungary has been on the rise over the last five to ten years. Businesspeople estimated that corruption fees range between 3 and 25 per cent of the value of a given transaction.[10] A media content study of corruption cases between January 2006 and December 2007 identified 107 cases. Straightforward corruption represented 61.1 per cent of the cases and multi-player cases stood at 38 per cent. [11]

Public procurement: the intersection between the public and private spheres

This country report is based on a study of the corruption risks in the business sector in Hungary[12] as part of the National Integrity System survey. As well as some of the themes highlighted by the research, which was conducted during 2006 and 2007, it also provides illustrative case studies from 2007/8.

The ease with which companies can be set up and operated is often used as a signifier for whether or not corruption will thrive in the private sector. When running a business is perceived to be difficult, the danger is that companies may adopt alternative means to survive, or that the complex bureaucracy will provide opportunities for corruption to thrive. According to the World Bank's *Doing Business* study, Hungary ranked fifth among eastern European EU countries in 2008, behind Estonia, Latvia, Lithuania and

---

5 Act CXXXVI of 2007.

6 1037/2007. (VI. 18.), governmental decree on tasks concerning the fight against corruption.

7 Proposal of the Ministry of Justice for the 6 September 2007 meeting of the ACB.

8 PricewaterhouseCoopers, *Economic Crime: People, Culture and Controls*, Global Economic Crime Survey 2007 (London: PricewaterhouseCoopers, 2007).

9 E. Pálinkó, Z. Szántó and I. J. Tóth, 'Üzleti korrupció Magyarországon vállalatvezetők szemszögéből. Interjúelemzés', study prepared for TI Hungary, 2008.

10 These were the two extremes mentioned by interviewees on the rate of corruption. Interviews conducted by TI Hungary.

11 T. Cserpes, Z. Szántó and I. J. Tóth, 'Korrupciógyanús esetek a médiában', in background studies for *Corruption Risks in the Business Sector*, and TI Corvinus University, Budapest, 2008.

12 N. Alexa, R. Bárdos, Z. Szántó and I. J. Tóth (eds.), *Corruption Risks in the Business Sector*, *National Integrity System Country Study*, Part two (Budapest: TI Hungary, 2008).

Slovakia.[13] As a result, the administrative burden on companies is considered high: between 4.5 and 6.7 per cent of GDP, compared to an average of 3.5 per cent in the EU25.[14]

Hungary's small economy and flooded market leads to a lack of competition. The state's role in the economy also restricts the intensity of competition: a large percentage of businesses make their living either directly or indirectly through government orders or on state subsidies. As such, Hungary has a large black economy; according to various estimates, it may be equivalent to as much as 15 to 18 per cent of official GDP.[15]

Some businesspeople in Hungary appear to believe that corrupt practices are necessary for success.[16] It is not uncommon for corruption to emerge at the intersection between the public and private spheres when a state exercises significant regulatory control over the economy. The risks are exacerbated by a frequently changing legal environment; close personal links between the private sector, politicians and civil servants; the liquidity problems of local governments; and low wages in the public and political sectors.

Public tender transactions are some of the most vulnerable to corruption, and are cited as such by businesspeople.[17] Although there was a new Public Procurement Act in 2004 (PPA) that fulfils EU criteria, it is overcomplicated and has been modified several times. Inconsistencies in the application of the law, as well as serious defects in the party financing system, result in corrupt practices aimed at circumventing the regulations.

One of the most serious problems is when loopholes in the PPA are utilised to sign state or local government contracts without a public procurement procedure.[18] Since the law came into effect, the number of infringements has increased substantially from its first year: twelve cases in 2004, seven in 2005 and forty in 2007.[19]

One of the main complaints regarding public procurement is that often only one company can meet a bid's technical or formal specifications. While the institution calling for tenders can invite external experts to help in the specifications, and these experts must sign a 'no conflict of interest' declaration, conflicts arising between these experts and bidding companies cannot always be avoided and the specifications may still favour one bidder. Furthermore, the approval of tender documentation is generally made by a body, so no one individual bears personal responsibility. If the public procurement tender is found to contain irregularities and a court decides on a fine, the institution calling for the tender pays the fine from public funds.

One particular anomaly occurs when bidding coalitions are formed by the institutions calling for tenders. The future winner may be asked to provide at least two other bids that state a higher price, and simultaneously to include 'extra services' (serving private, party or community interests) in the bid. It is also not unusual for the institution calling for tenders to agree with the future winner on signing subcontracts with certain companies. The subcontractors may have personal connections to the person calling

---

13 World Bank, *Doing Business* (Washington, DC: World Bank, 2008).

14 See www.vg.hu/index.php?apps=cikk&cikk=195145.

15 Report of the Economy Whitening Committee, February 2007; www.feheredes.org/docs/2008februar.pdf.

16 N. Alexa, R. Bárdos, Z. Szántó and I. J. Tóth (eds.), 2008.

17 T. Cserpes, Z. Szántó and I. J. Tóth, 2008.

18 Report of the Public Procurement Council to parliament on the experience of the fairness and transparency of public procurements and on the activities carried out between 1 January and 31 December 2006, Public Procurement Council, July 2007: www.kozbeszerzes.hu/index.php?akt_menu=280&details=846.

19 T. Cserpes, Z. Szántó and I. J. Tóth, 2008.

for tenders and reward the order by providing favours to the representative of the institution or his/her party.

In July 2007 a bid for a tender in the municipality of Kistokaj Község illustrated some of the irregularities that may occur during the bidding process. The municipality published a call for tenders to build 1,440 metres of covered rainwater trenches and gates. The call was sent out to ten potential applicants on 31 July 2007. The evaluation criteria included the bidding price, the financial stability of the applicant, work references, the guarantee and the most favourable bid overall. The authority modified the evaluation criteria and weighted them based on bidding price (10), guarantee and insurance (5), deadline (5) and work references (5).

Seven bids were submitted (one of which was not valid). In response to the municipality's final decision, one of the rejected bidders appealed against the decision on the grounds that the municipality did not follow the evaluation method in the original tender documentation. As a consequence, the procurement was annulled.[20]

Although the municipality's motives in changing the criteria are not clear (whether it was inefficiency or dishonest manipulation), what is clear is that it did not adhere to the procurement rules. Such deviations from procurement rules increase the risk of corrupt practices entering the process. It is particularly important that deviations from procurement rules be avoided, because many such instances do not come to light; losing bidders often do not challenge such occurrences, partially out of concerns that, once they are considered troublemakers by the authorities, they will lose future opportunities to win tenders.

On the other hand, the tendering process can also be manipulated by the private sector. This can come in the form of cartels set up by private companies bidding for the same government contract. In practice, these companies agree on which one will win the contract and at what price. The Competition Authority, which investigates these practices, produces evidence of collusion in every tenth reasonably suspicious case, leading to three to five cartel cases per year.[21] Fines for such behaviour do not provide an adequate deterrent, however, and often fall far short of the claim for damages made by the institution calling for tenders.

In November 2007 the Competition Authority revealed a cartel agreement between the Hungarian Post Office and the Hungarian Newspaper Distribution Company to divide the market for the distribution of different types of newspapers and journals from 2001 to 2007. The sanction for each cartel member was Ft 468 million (US$2.34 million).[22] The office also fined the Kortex Engineering Office Ft 77 million (US$380,000) for signing a contract with another company to become the exclusive subcontractor during a public procurement procedure.[23] Although the Competition Authority is strict enough in imposing fines and successful in revealing cartel agreements, it does not have enough capacity to investigate smaller-scale cartels involving small and medium-sized enterprises.

As can be seen, the public procurement system has high corruption risks for both the authorities and the companies taking part. The ongoing modification and focus on the Public Procurement Act is a step in the right direction, but it is not likely to prevent corruption based on the network of mutual favours formed from personal connections. While the legislation is adequate and the legal sanctions on business

---

20 Decision D. 543/9 /2007. of the Public Procurement Arbitration Board, 24 October 2007.
21 Statistical Data of the Competition Office.
22 Decision Vj-140/2006/69. of the Competition Council, 8 November 2007.
23 Decision Vj-81/2006/74. of the Competition Council, 18 December 2007.

crime and crimes against fair administration have become stricter, the systems for detecting such crimes are inefficient and the enforcement of the law is problematic. Court rulings based on inadequately prepared investigation documents impose sanctions that do not have a deterrent effect. The perception of the general public is that violating the law has no serious consequences, because of the inextricable and never-ending nature of court cases.[24]

Obstacles to fighting corruption

The political elite and the government have a decisive role to play in the fight against corruption. Countering corruption in the business sector cannot be successful without a real commitment from the political elite, however, and without placing business ethics at the forefront of business thinking.

Ninety-nine per cent of companies in Hungary are small or medium enterprises (SMEs).[25] Such companies, with little capital, are characterised by 'subsistence' corruption, most typically illegal employment, tax fraud, fake invoice transactions, kickbacks on orders and cartel agreements. Issues abound for SMEs that are unable to make enough profit to pay high taxes and social contributions. As a result, they may become involved in corrupt activities in a bid to stay in business. A consideration in developing legislation and regulations to fight this type of corruption is that, without reforming the tax system, cleaning up the sector may result in SMEs being forced to close due to insolvency and the inability to continue business.

In the end, although corruption in the private sector is acknowledged, it is difficult to tackle effectively. Indeed, according to the prime minister, Ferenc Gyurcsány, 'Business players are inclined to limit competition, to seek agreements for setting prices above the market and to realise extra profit under non-market conditions.'[26]

Noémi Alexa (TI Hungary)

Additional reading

N. Alexa, R. Bárdos, Z. Szántó and I. J. Tóth (eds.), *Corruption Risks in the Business Sector, National Integrity System Country Study, Part two* (Budapest: TI Hungary, 2008).

G. Báger, L. Hamza and R. Kovács, *A köz- és magánszféra együttműködésével kapcsolatos nemzetközi és hazai tapasztalatok* (Budapest: State Audit Office, 2007).

P. Hack and B. Garai (eds.), *Az igazságszolgáltatási rendszerek átláthatósága* (Budapest: TI Hungary, 2008).

E. Kósa and N. Alexa (eds.), *Corruption Risks in Hungary, National Integrity System Country Study, Part one* (Budapest: TI Hungary, 2007).

J. Krekó and G. P. Kiss, *Adóelkerülés és a magyar adórendszer*, Discussion Paper no. 65 (Budapest: Hungarian National Bank, 2007).

Open Society Institute, 'Corruption and Anti-corruption Policy in Hungary' (New York: Open Society Institute, 2002).

PricewaterhouseCoopers, *Economic Crime: People, Culture and Controls, Global Economic Crime Survey* 2007 (London: Pricewaterhouse Coopers, 2007).

Z. Szente (ed.), *Korrupciós jelenségek az önkormányzati közigazgatásban* (Közigazgatási Intézet, 2007).

Z. É. Nagy, Z. Szántó and I. J. Tóth, *Kutatási eredmények a magyarországi korrupcióról: A szakirodalom áttekintése* (Budapest: TI Hungary, 2008).

TI Hungary: www.transparency.hu.

---

24 *Heti* Vilaggazdasag, 'Peaks of White-collar Crime', September 2008; available at www.hvg.hu/itthon/20080831_fehergalleros_bunozes_iteletek.aspx.
25 Hungarian Statistics Office.
26 Opening speech of the prime minister, Ferenc Gyurcsány, at the International Cartel Conference, 2007.

Israel

> **Corruption Perceptions Index 2008: 6.0 (33rd out of 180 countries)**
>
> **Conventions**
>
> UN Convention against Corruption (signed November 2005; not yet ratified)
>
> UN Convention against Transnational Organized Crime (signed December 2000; ratified December 2006)

Legal and institutional changes

- Israel has not ratified the United Nations Convention against Corruption (UNCAC), mainly because of the absence of a law declaring the bribery of foreign public officials and officials of public international organisations a criminal offence. On 8 February 2008, however, a precedent was set by Judge Altuvia Magen at the Tel Aviv-Jaffa District Court, when he stated that bribery payments of foreign officials are not tax-deductible.[1] It had been suggested that the Israeli national tax authorities acknowledge the payments of bribery abroad and consider them 'commission expenses'.[2] In his arguments, the judge referred to the argument raised by the plaintiff: that at the time the offence of paying a bribe was committed Israel had not ratified the UNCAC, but that in signing the UNCAC

the country was making a statement about the way it views the issue of bribe-paying abroad, and that this applied even prior to its actual ratification. On 7 April 2008 the Ministry of Justice issued a memorandum[3] that included an amendment to the Penal Code to include measures to counter the bribery of foreign public officials and officials of public international organisations; the Knesset (parliament) approved the amendment to the Penal Code[4] on 14 July 2008. It is hoped that, now there are no obstacles to the ratification of the UNCAC, Israel will ratify it by the end of 2008.

- On 1 April 2008 Shlomo Benizri, a former minister and still an MP, was convicted[5] of bribery, fraud and breach of trust, committed during his tenure as labour and welfare minister. Benizri was sentenced[6] by the district court to eighteen months' imprisonment, with eight months suspended and a

1 Censored (company and individual names) v. *Natanya Income Tax Assessor*, 1015/03 Tel Aviv-Jaffa District Court; http://info1.court.gov.il/Prod03/ManamHTML4.nsf/93D55D7E07D40647422573EB00554640/$FILE/2B60AA9FC AC685BC422573E9001F895E.html?OpenElement.

2 In a panel conducted by TI Israel in 2007, statement made by a well-known accountant in Israel; see www.ti-israel. org/Index.asp?ArticleID=648&CategoryID=80&Page=1.

3 see www.justice.gov.il/NR/rdonlyres/45B9A973-96AD-4304-8D2E-5862FF16267D/0/onshinshohad.pdf.

4 see www.knesset.gov.il/privatelaw/Plaw_display.asp?lawtp=2.

5 YNetNews.com (Israel), 4 January 2008.

6 *Israel State* v. *Benizri & Elbaz* 2062/06, Jerusalem District Court; see info1.court.gov.il/Prod03/ManamHTML4.nsf/ CD8E2F1A677B15A6422574380055952A/$FILE/28AC5E37EA433F854225742A00241885.html?OpenElement.

fine of NIS80,000 (approximately US$24,000). Benizri was suspended from the Knesset only after his conviction and a legal opinion passed by the Knesset that his acts bore moral turpitude.[7] An amendment made to the 'Basic Law: Knesset' on 21 March 2007[8] rules that an MP is suspended as soon as he or she is convicted for a moral turpitude even if he or she still intends to file an appeal. Prior to this amendment, any wrongdoing by an MP had to be raised as an issue by another member, and the offence was decided upon by the Knesset Committee; this had the potential to allow decisions to be influenced by politics.[9]

- On 25 July 2007 an amendment to the Freedom of Information (FOI) Law redefined its application to public authorities. Previously, the FOI Act had been applied only to public authorities for which the minister of justice had issued a specific warrant stating that the FOI Act applied to them. The act now applies to all public authorities, except those excluded by the minister of justice with the approval of the Constitution Committee of the Knesset. This leaves the onus on the minister and the committee to justify why certain information cannot be disclosed.
- On 9 October 2007 the Planning and Construction Act was amended with regard to the transparency of its committees. The amendment mandates the recording of all meetings of the committees and the publishing of a written protocol that reflects the meeting.
- On 2 April 2008 the Knesset approved the Lobbyists' Act, which defines a lobbyist, defines the registration procedures and regulates lobbyists' work at the Knesset. Lobbyists have to declare who they are representing, wear a lobbyist tag and commit themselves to behaving according to the law. Moreover, the Knesset has published lobbyists' details on its website.

- On 17 July 2007 an amendment to the Promotion of Sound Governance Act was passed obliging the authorities to notify whistleblowers of their right to receive a certificate of findings. All complaints should be reported to the internal controller, who is obliged to report annually to the Public Complaints Committee at the Ombudsman's Office. As Barak Calev[10], head of the legal department at the Movement for Quality Government in Israel, emphasises, this should generate a positive incentive to 'blow the whistle', and might serve as a 'shield' against retaliation that could help whistleblowers to defend themselves.
- On 21 December 2006[11] the Jerusalem District Court grappled with an issue that might assist in the redefinition of outsourced employees working in the public sector. The court found a security guard at the interior ministry office in eastern Jerusalem guilty of bribery and the improper use of power of office. He was accused of having received money and sexual benefit in return for line advancement. In his appeal,[12] on 19 November 2007, three judges of the Supreme Court found him guilty of bribery but not of improper use of the power of office. An appeal by the state attorney, which will be deliberated in front of a panel of nine Supreme Court judges, will try to answer the question of the definition of a 'public official' and whether this definition applies to an outsourced employee.

---

7   YNetNews.com (Israel), 28 April 2008.
8   See www.knesset.gov.il/laws/special/heb/yesod2.htm.
9   See www.knesset.gov.il/laws/special/eng/basic2_eng.htm.
10 Interview by author, 14 April 2008.
11 *Israel State* v. *Barak Cohen & Jamal HiJazi* 242/03, Jerusalem District Court; see www.nevo.co.il/Psika_word/mechozi/m03000242-371.doc.
12 *Barak Cohen & Jamal HiJazi* v. *Israel State* 766/07, Supreme Court; see http://elyon1.court.gov.il/files/07/660/007/S03/07007660.s03.htm.

Siemens Israel

Siemens Israel is the local branch of the international Siemens enterprise in Israel.[13] Siemens Israel comprises four divisions: energy, mobility, automation and drives, and health care, of which the first two constitute its main business in Israel. Siemens owns 75 per cent of Siemens Israel Ltd, and the remaining 25 per cent is held by Zingler Engineering, which is partially owned by the Ahronson family.[14]

In the last few years Siemens International has been investigating its representatives around the world, as there have been a number of cases in which Siemens employees have been found to be working unethically.[15] On 6 September 2007 a magistrates' court revealed[16] that Siemens Israel was suspected of alleged bribery involving millions of shekels. The allegations involve a former district judge, Dan Cohen, who was director and chair of the assets committee at the Israeli Electricity Company (IEC). This alleged bribe was given to Cohen to promote the purchase of two turbines without a tender. The purchase of the two followed a purchase of three turbines via a tender won by Siemens in 2002.[17] At a cost of approximately €100 million each (approximately US$126 million), the two additional turbines were represented to the board as an 'urgency to prevent serious damage'. At the time of writing, however, these turbines were still at the storage depot of the IEC. The IEC claims that the turbines were ordered in response to a government request; it declared that it has acted according to the tender law,

and that any misbehaviour of its management will be taken care of.[18]

On 9 September 2007 the court allowed the publication of information revealing that Oren Ahronson, the CEO of Siemens Israel, was the main suspect[19] in the alleged bribery of Cohen. On 17 March 2008[20] Siemens decided to send Ahronson on a leave of absence (vacation),[21] but Ahronson claims he was fired.[22] This started a 'war' between Ahronson and Siemens in which the former claims he is a scapegoat; the disagreement is still ongoing in court. Meanwhile, Cohen, who fled to Peru a few years ago, received threats to his life should he agree to be a state witness and expose the way the system works.[23]

The questions that this case raises are many, including whether this is just a case of widespread misconduct in one organisation or whether bribe-paying is the norm in the industry as a whole and considered a 'necessary evil' for doing business and winning tenders. Whatever the answer, the extensive and international nature of the wrongdoings at Siemens have shone a spotlight on corruption in this form, and the role of multinational companies in ensuring that their governance and ethical standards are both high and consistent.

An emerging trend or one step forward in fighting organisational corruption?

In the past three to four years anecdotal evidence has suggested that corporate social responsibility (CSR) is becoming a buzzword for many Israeli

13 See www.siemens.co.il/.
14 Marker Online (Israel), 27 March 2008.
15 *Der Spiegel* (Germany), 17 November 2006.
16 Marker Online (Israel), 9 September 2007.
17 *Ha'aretz* (Israel), 7 September 2007.
18 Marker Online (Israel), 6 September 2007.
19 *Ha'aretz* (Israel), 10 September 2007.
20 *Ha'aretz* (Israel), 19 March 2008.
21 Marker Online (Israel), 27 March 2008.
22 Ibid.
23 Marker Online (Israel), 10 April 2008.

companies. This has resulted in an increase in companies adopting codes of ethics and ethics programmes. Other developments that act as incentives encouraging this move include international trends, particularly the influence of US changes on the Israeli market as a result of companies trading with the United States, and the actions of the regulators of banks and insurance industries as they react to international changes.

The main components of an effective ethics programme include an organisational code of ethics, the appointment of an ethics officer (and/or an ethics committee), the implementation of the code in daily organisational life and an effective reporting system of misconduct. Much research has been carried out in the United States on the effectiveness of ethics programmes.[24]

In 2008, according to the Maala Corporate Social Responsibility ranking of Israeli companies,[25] 88 per cent of the sixty companies[26] checked (of which thirty-nine were public and twenty-one private) had a code of ethics, compared to only 69 per cent in 2006. Of the companies that had a code, 69 per cent also had an ethics programme (in different stages). There are no official statistics on the companies not included in the index, but it can be considered that the sample represents a noticeable trend towards having a code of ethics in many parts of the private sector.

Israeli companies that trade on the NASDAQ are obliged by the US Securities and Exchange Commission to include information on their code of ethics in their financial reporting. As such, incentives for adopting such ethical programmes have increased. There are other incentives for engaging in ethics programmes in Israel, such as the rankings composed by the Maala Index[27] a CSR index, of which 21 per cent of its ranking in 2008 included having a code of ethics (9 per cent) and an internal system for implementing the code (12 per cent). In addition, in March 2008, following the second of the Basel II Accords, the banking supervision office issued a draft on strengthening corporate governance in banking corporations that requires banks to have a code of ethics and implement it.[28] Furthermore, the inspector of insurance companies issued a draft memorandum[29] for the board of directors' reports, to include whether a company has a code of ethics, its contents, whether the organisation implements the code, the ethical behaviour of the management and employees and changes to be made to the code.

There are other signs of a changing attitude. The Goshen Committee, nominated by the Israeli Securities Authority (ISA) to submit recommendations on corporate governance in Israel, did so on 12 December 2006.[30] Although these recommendations have not been implemented, in January 2008 Professor Zohar Goshen was nominated as the head of the ISA, which, it is hoped, will be a first step towards adopting the recommendations.

It is too soon to tell whether the codes of ethics will be effective. It does seem, however, that practices are changing in Israel. The influence of the international scene and the activities of

---

24 For more information, see www.ethics.org and chapter 8 of the US Federal Sentencing Guidelines, which outlines its criteria for measuring the effectiveness of an ethics programme.
25 See www.maala.org.il.
26 The ranking includes companies that apply and qualify in respect of one of the criteria: membership of the TA-100 index (the top 100 companies listed on the Tel Aviv Stock Exchange) or a company with more than US$100 million income.
27 See www.maala.org.il.
28 See www.bankisrael.gov.il/deptdata/pikuah/basel2/hasdara_30032008.pdf.
29 See www.mof.gov.il/hon/2001/general/t_hozrim.asp?a.
30 See www.isa.gov.il/Download/IsaFile_45.pdf.

global and international companies contribute to this trend. While Israel still has a long way to go and is still at an early stage, it is moving in the right direction.

Susanne Tam (TI Israel)

Additional reading

E. Bukspan and A Kasher, 'Ethics in Business Organizations: Legal and Moral Considerations', *IDC Law Review*, vol. 2, no. 2 (2005).

J. Cory, *Selected Issues in Business Ethics and Social Responsibility* [in Hebrew] (Jerusalem: Magnes, 2008).

D. Navot (supervised by Mordechai Kremnitzer), *Political Corruption*, vol. I, *A History of a Controversial Concept* [in Hebrew] (Jerusalem: Israel Democracy Institute, 2008).

R. Wolf, *Ethics is Good for Business* (Jerusalem: Rubin Mass Ltd, 2008).

TI Israel: www.ti-israel.org.

Lithuania

Corruption Perceptions Index 2008: 4.6 (58th out of 180 countries)

Conventions

Council of Europe Civil Law Convention on Corruption (signed April 2002; ratified January 2003)

Council of Europe Criminal Law Convention on Corruption (signed January 1999; ratified March 2002)

UN Convention against Corruption (signed December 2003; ratified December 2006)

UN Convention against Transnational Organized Crime (signed December 2000; ratified May 2002)

Legal and institutional changes

- In July 2008 the government submitted a new National Anti-corruption Programme[1] for 2008–2013 for consideration in parliament.[2] Following a largely ineffective previous National Anti-corruption Programme, the new document is a welcome development.[3] It remains to be seen what changes parliament will make and how effective they will be, but there are a number of visible shortcomings. In its current form, the programme

---

1 Lithuanian News Agency, 15 April 2008.
2 See www.lrv.lt/teises_aktai/files/2008/07/11081.doc.
3 In spring 2008 TI Lithuania organised a public discussion regarding the draft National Anti-corruption Programme.

does not include the concept of private corruption, nor does it pay sufficient attention to the active implementation of freedom of information provisions, the role of electronic governance or the encouragement and protection of whistleblowers. There is also a lack of emphasis on the use of cost-benefit analysis to ensure the accountability of larger initiatives or the assessment of the public's experience of corruption, as opposed to its perceptions.

- In June 2008 parliament passed amendments to article 18 of the Law on Funding of Political Parties and Political Campaigns and on the Control of this Funding.[4] The amendments prohibit certain political advertising through 'audio and visual production (advertising clips, films) on radio and television'. The amendments also lay down provisions for uniform advertising fees for all political parties and the advertisement of all political parties and their candidates on a proportional basis, so that parties with the most votes in the previous election will receive more airtime, except on Lithuanian national radio and television.

- In 2008 a new draft law was proposed on the financing of political parties and political campaigns, and changes to financing controls.[5] The law intends to abolish party donations by legal persons and limit the venues for campaigning and means of political advertising. While positive, these changes do not strike at the root of the problem of reducing the costs of political campaigning.

Private sector transparency and business ethics initiatives in Lithuania

The concept of private-to-private corruption is a new one in Lithuania. Although there has been relatively little research regarding the actual perception and experience of ethical business practice, a survey in 2005 found that 67 per cent of Lithuanians claimed they had never heard of socially responsible business.[6] Furthermore, it appears that Lithuanian businesses tend to view socially responsible behaviour as a luxury. In a 2005 report businesspeople claimed they could see no incentives for behaving responsibly and that they lack government support to do so.[7]

Despite this, there have been some private sector integrity initiatives in recent years, including the UN Global Compact and Baltoji Banga (White Wave).[8] The UN Global Compact was established in Lithuania in 2005 and includes forty organisations, while the Baltoji Banga initiative started in 2007 in the aftermath of a whistleblower scandal involving an employee of a company belonging to a prominent politician.[9] Baltoji Banga promotes transparent business practices and unites thirty-one businesses.[10]

Mass media

According to the Lithuanian Map of Corruption of 2007, only 8 per cent of surveyed business people believed the media not to be corrupt, while 51 and 32 per cent believed the media

---

4 The current Law on Funding of Political Parties and Political Campaigns and on the Control of this Funding (Law no. IX-2428) was passed on 23 August 2004. See www3.lrs.lt/pls/inter3/dokpaieska.showdoc_l?p_id=323445.

5 Draft Law no. XP-2662; see www3.lrs.lt/pls/inter3/dokpaieska.showdoc_l?p_id=308370&p_query=&p_tr2=.

6 Spinter Tyrimai, 'Social Responsibility as People See It: Civil Value or Western Trinket?', April 2008.

7 'What Does Business Think about Corporate Social Responsibility?: Part 1. Attitudes and Practices in Estonia, Latvia and Lithuania', prepared within the 'Enabling a Better Environment for Corporate Social Responsibility – Diagnostics' project, 2005.

8 See www.baltojibanga.lt.

9 The worker spoke publicly of illegal practices at the 'Krekenavos agrofirma' and was subsequently fired by the company. The company was found guilty of illegal firing of the whistleblower in question. The court also found the company guilty of fraudulent accounting, tax evasion and illegal payment with produce. The company and its management were obliged to pay a variety of fines.

10 For the list of companies supporting the initiative, see www.baltojibanga.lt/?Nariai.

to be either 'partially corrupt' or 'very corrupt', respectively.[11] This was an increase in the perception of corruption since the 2005 study, which appears consistent with the widespread allegations and anecdotal evidence of slander campaigns, the prevalent use of 'advertorials' (editorials paid for by a business) and general disregard and perceived unawareness of journalistic ethics that seem to be characteristic of a number of leading Lithuanian dailies.

TI Lithuania's 2007 media transparency survey 'Promoting Media Transparency' aimed to understand the trends in the Lithuanian media and their relationship to other business sectors. It also sought to promote more transparent media practices.[12] According to the results, an overwhelming number of representatives from medium and large businesses believe that the media are so powerful that they can influence the success or failure of a business or individual. In particular, a high percentage of people believed (62 per cent) or were likely to believe (29 per cent) that unfavourable media coverage could destroy both people and companies. More importantly, however, over half the businesspeople who had contact with the media understood that, in exchange for advertising in a particular outlet, they were assured positive coverage. Such an 'understanding' was most frequent in contacts with representatives of weekly magazines, with regional television and the national press coming in second and third, respectively.

There is plenty of anecdotal evidence of the media trading in influence, but direct accounts are difficult to come by. Understandably, both parties are low-key about this illicit behaviour. A rare public acknowledgement of such widespread practices did arise, however, in an interview with the head of leading energy company Dujotekana. In a television interview on Lithuanian Television's (LTV's) weekly programme Savaitė,[13] Rimandas Stonys commented that 'the majority of main country newspapers do not dare to offer your opinion, if you do not offer it as an advertorial. You pay and then you have a right to say what you think. This is why I regard it as an absolutely natural practice.'[14]

While this seems to indicate that corruption in the media is ingrained, businesspeople claim that they are quite confident at recognising it. Some 24 per cent say they can 'easily' spot a hidden advertorial, while another 40 per cent say they would be able to spot one with 'relative ease'. Such advertorials are rarely marked as public relations pieces, with the names of their 'authors' changed or completely unavailable.

Further concerns about the media include the lack of separation between owners and editors of newspapers, with many owners *de facto* acting or serving as chief editors.[15] A large number of media outlets also appear to lack codes of conduct and ethics, essential in establishing clear-cut rules of procedure and the journalistic

11 The Lithuanian Map of Corruption 2007 was commissioned by the Special Investigation Service of the Republic of Lithuania and conducted by the TNS Gallup sociological company in October to November 2007; see www.transparency.lt/new/images/lkz_2007_galutine.pdf.

12 The project was funded by the Nordic Council of Ministers Office in Lithuania and featured cooperation with TI chapters in Sweden and Latvia. For the survey, 502 business leaders of companies with ten or more employees were interviewed. The survey methodology was developed with the help of a focus group and three working groups with media representatives, sociologists and board members of TI Lithuania.

13 LTV weekly broadcast Savaitė, November 2006.

14 See, for instance, R. Juozapavičius, 'Stonys demaskuoja žiniasklaid' ['Stonys exposes mass media'], at www.alfa.lt/straipsnis/c10312, 17 November 2006; R. Sakadolskis, 'Kaip kritiškai skaityti laikraštĈr kam to reikia?' ['How to read a newspaper critically and why would you need that?'], in a 2007 TI publication.

15 L. Meier and S. Turpin, 'Goodbye media transparency? Lithuania's corrupt press corps', *Café Babel*, 31 October 2007.

practice of a company.[16] This creates opportunities for the abuse of power entrusted to the mass media and leads to the damaging effect of imposing a profit-seeking mindset on quality and integrity standards.

Solutions to the lack of transparency in the media are difficult to come by, but popular answers according to businesspeople include publishing information related to financing; more effective monitoring of the media; establishing effective reactions to violations by outlets; and more open discussions about the role of the media. To this end, TI Lithuania in spring 2008 began working with journalists in providing ethical media training in order to introduce them to concepts of journalistic integrity and sound journalistic practices. A further civil society initiative,[17] aimed at preparing for the October 2008 general election, provided media representatives with guidelines on how to report fairly and effectively.[18] At the time of writing, however, it remained to be seen whether they would make use of these recommendations and to what extent.

Pharmaceutical sector

According to the Lithuanian Map of Corruption 2007, the health and pharmaceutical sector is considered to be the most corrupt field of activity by 66 per cent of Lithuanians and 52 per cent of businesspeople.[19] An in-depth study conducted in the spring of that year for the first time gathered data on the relationship between medical practitioners and companies.[20] The survey found that medical practitioners receive gifts and other tokens from pharmaceutical companies' representatives who meet with them regularly. Almost two-thirds of the practitioners claimed that they received a visit between one and five times a month, while 27 per cent admitted doing so more frequently: between six and twenty-five times each month.

In terms of the gifts received, 85 per cent of doctors claimed that they were given inexpensive representational gifts not worth more than LTL 35 (US$14). In addition, 74 per cent received academic medical literature, 22 per cent received financial support for travel to academic seminars and conferences, and 13 per cent received funding for training and the writing of academic articles. Such practices were viewed positively by many doctors, who claimed that they were not overly influenced by the gifts, which played only a secondary role in their decision-making when prescribing drugs. Doctors also downplayed the importance of 'wining and dining' in their relationships with medical company representatives. They claimed that the manner in which pharmaceutical companies presented merchandise to them was a much more important factor in deciding what to prescribe.

Medical practitioners were not in general agreement about the level of transparency in their relations with pharmaceutical companies. Some 44 per cent considered their dealings with them

---

16 TI Lithuania is currently involved in a second media transparency project funded by the Nordic Council of Ministers. The aim of this project is to analyse the ethical practices of the Lithuanian, Latvian and Swedish media regarding corrections, ownership, staff policies, reporting policies and interactivity. The project will be concluded in early 2009.

17 The initiative 'Rinkis Rimtai!' [Cast a Well-thought Vote!] is led by an informal umbrella network 'Piliečių Santalka' [Citizens' Union].

18 For a list of guidelines, see www.transparency.lt/new/images/santalka_10_pasiulymu_2008-6.pdf.

19 'The Lithuanian Map of Corruption 2007'; www.transparency.lt/new/images/lkz_2007_galutine.pdf.

20 TI Lithuania together with the Association of Ethical Pharmaceutical Companies, the Association of Drug Producers, the Ministry of Health of Lithuania and the Union of Lithuanian Doctors launched the project 'Greater Integrity in Medical Treatment'. The project featured a survey of medical practitioners commissioned by TI Lithuania and carried out by the TNS Gallup sociological company; 402 doctors representing ten different professional fields were interviewed in March 2007.

to be transparent, while 36 per cent did not. Over a half of the practitioners agreed, however, that such companies usually chose to deal with more influential doctors and that in some cases there was a distortion in the market whereby cheaper drugs that could compete with more expensive medication did not make it onto the market. Of more concern to the medical practitioners was the impact that non-transparent practices can have on public perceptions. They also disclosed that their reason for participating in such practices is the unreasonably low remuneration they receive for their work.

Taking into consideration the views expressed by medical practitioners in the survey, some civil society actions have been taken to address the problems. TI Lithuania has developed six recommendations that aim to improve transparency in the sector:

- implementing more transparent policies for including drugs on the list of state-financed medication;
- adopting a revised code of conduct for medical practitioners that would be more detailed and have a broader scope that the current code;
- publishing any support that doctors receive from medical companies;
- increasing the control of professional medical organisations;
- implementing more effectively the Code of Drug Marketing adopted by the Association of Ethical Pharmaceutical Companies; and
- promoting widespread discussion and debates on the integrity of medical practices.

In autumn 2008 the Association of Ethical Pharmaceutical Companies will start using a newly adopted Code of Pharmaceutical Marketing Practices. It remains to be seen whether the current version of the code will become a more effective instrument than the last version in ensuring the greater accountability and integrity standards some association members appear to seek.

Sergej Muravjov (TI Lithuania)

Additional reading

EKT Group, *Mainstreaming CSR among SMEs in the Baltic States: Quantitative Research Final Report Lithuania* (Vilnius: EKT Group, 2007).

R. Juozapavičius (ed.), *Žiniasklaidos Skaidrumas* [*Mass Media Transparency*] (Vilnius: Eugrimas and TI Lithuania, 2007).

P. Mazurkiewicz, R. Crown and V. Bartelli, *What Does Business Think about Corporate Social Responsibility?*, Part one, *Attitudes and Practices in Estonia, Latvia and Lithuania* [report prepared for 'Enabling a Better Environment for CSR in CEE Countries' project] (Washington, DC: 2005).

UNDP Lithuania, 'Baseline Study on CSR Practices in the New EU Member States and Candidate Countries' (Vilnius: UNDP Lithuania, 2007).

Baseline Study on Corporate Social Responsibility Practices in Lithuania (Vilnius: UNDP Lithuania, 2007).

TI Lithuania: www.transparency.lt

Poland

Corruption Perceptions Index 2008: 4.6 (58th out of 180 countries)

Conventions

Council of Europe Civil Law Convention on Corruption (signed April 2001; ratified September 2002)

Council of Europe Criminal Law Convention on Corruption (signed January 1999; ratified December 2002)

OECD Convention on Combating Bribery of Foreign Public Officials (signed December 1997; ratified September 2000)

UN Convention against Corruption (signed December 2003; ratified September 2006)

UN Convention against Transnational Organized Crime (signed December 2000; ratified November 2001)

Legal and institutional changes

- The government appointed Julia Pitera (a member of Transparency International from 1998 to 2007 and a member of the board from 2001 to 2005) as the government plenipotentiary for the struggle against corruption. Her main task will be to create proposals for changing legislation and transforming the Anticorruption Bureau (CBA). According to the prime minister, there should be an analysis of the laws and regulations, to see which have been successful and which have not.

- An amendment to the Public Procurement Law became effective on 11 June 2007.[1] This amendment will help 'speed up and simplify the utilisation of . . . EU funding'. The amendment places limitations and restrictions on the appeals process for companies when there are potential violations of the procurement law. In particular, there are changes to the minimum values of the contracts that can be appealed against: from €60,000 to €137,000 or €211,000 (depending on the legal status of a company). This has liberalised the system, in the sense that for contacts lower than these amounts there is very little oversight and there is no right to appeal against the issuing of such a contract.

- On 11 May 2008 the Polish Football Association (PZPN) passed a resolution to create the position of a disciplinary proceedings representative.[2] As per the resolution, this position should be filled by a successful lawyer, with a good reputation, who does not already work in the football industry. The main tasks of the new spokesperson will include dealing with issues of 'corruption, doping, racism, xenophobia and hooliganism'.[3] All PZPN parties are obligated to help the new spokesperson meet the challenges.

---

1 See www.funduszestrukturalne.gov.pl/NR/rdonlyres/DAB3615A-E6B1-455E-9673-186DC707299B/34136/u_pzp82 _561.pdf.

2 See www.pzpn.pl/a/uchwala_walne_maj2008.pdf.

3 Ibid.

Corruption within social housing societies

According to EU legislation[4] and the Polish equivalent, contained in article 296a of the Penal Code, every individual holding a management position in a company is liable to criminal sanctions for activities that lead to or cause corruption. Based on news and press releases from the police, a wide range of discussions on social housing societies (TBSs) has evolved on the subject.[5]

A TBS is a privately owned company (although often the county government is among the shareholders) that builds and provides housing for low-income residents. It has a special status in Poland, as tenants may sign a lifelong lease, but never become owners. Currently there are about 385 TBSs that have an approved statute or contract, but only 230 of these have built flats. The Ministry of Infrastructure estimates that, across the country, there is a need for about 300,000 flats, whereas, during the twelve years of its existence, the TBS programme has built only 76,300.[6]

Any person who meets the criteria has the right to an apartment and is placed on a waiting list; these criteria are generally related to income. Flats should be allocated to those who need them most, for example those who live in municipal flats, buildings that will be demolished or those who are threatened with eviction.

If a tenant exceeds the income threshold, becomes an owner of a flat in the same community or does not submit an income declaration, the TBS may terminate the part of the contract relating to the amount of monthly rent and demand the market value.[7] A tenant may also choose to leave the contract, whenever he or she likes. On termination of the contract the investor (usually the tenant) may obtain permission from the TBS to transfer the rights of the flat to someone else, but this is usually not granted unless the resident has lived in the apartment for more than one year. If no new tenant is designated, the TBS selects a tenant from the waiting list; people on the basic waiting list may wait as long as two years before being assigned a flat.[8]

There are opportunities for corruption in this process, however, resulting from attempts to bypass the formal procedures. In effect, tenants may 'sell' their flats to new tenants by taking a certain sum in order to designate their flat to the 'buyer'.[9] This practice is not illegal but, rather, uses a loophole in the TBS rules. A further complexity, however, is that, when the TBS agrees to the termination of a contract, at times 'administrative problems' are created by TBS representatives in order to extract money from the tenants.[10] It has been suggested that those demanding the fees could include TBS board members, proxies or anyone else in a position of power in a TBS.[11] In effect, if the former tenant pays the bribe and the 'buyer' moves in, all parties have something to gain. The consequence of this is that administrative procedures are circumvented and low-income families waiting for their turn on the waiting list may never get the accommodation to which they are entitled.

---

4 EU Council Framework Decision 2003/568/GHA, 22 July 2003, on combating corruption in the private sector; Dziennik Ustaw 1997 no. 88 poz. 553, Kodeks karny z dnia 6 czerwca 1997.

5 Policija.pl, press release, 8 June 2007; *Gazeta* (Poland), 6 November 2003; Epoznan.pl, 5 June 2006; Money.pl, 21 April 2008; *Gorzow* (Poland), 26 July 2008.

6 See www.mieszkaniowy.com/wyboista_droga_do_wlasnosci_w_tbs-nieruchomosci1616.html (last accessed 20 January 2009).

7 *Gazeta Podatkowa* (Poland), 18 February 2005.

8 *Gazeta Wroclawska* (Poland), 11 July 2008.

9 Ibid.

10 Policja.pl, 30 April 2008.

11 Prokuratura Okregowa w Poznaniu, press release, 7 May 2008; see www.poznan.po.gov.pl/index.php?idt=230.

The authorities acknowledge this corruption in the TBS system. The Highest Inspection Chamber has pointed out many irregularities in the functioning of TBSs, and there have been numerous investigations and arrests. Furthermore, according to press releases, as well as board members and officials, politicians have been involved in the corruption.[12] There have been investigations in Poznan, Białystok, Warsaw and Gliwice. In Poznan, for example, corruption flourished because the city council did not play the proper supervisory role over the TBS, despite being the main shareholder (owning 99 per cent). As a result, decisions were made by the minority shareholder Unia Wspólnego Inwestowania (Joint Investment Union) and Poznan TBS lost approximately zł2 million (US$523,711).[13]

According to reports from the police headquarters on 2 May 2008, a member of the Poznan TBS was arrested for accepting illegal money from a tenant who wanted to bribe him to transfer the right illegally to someone else.[14] On 29 April 2008 officers of the Anti-Corruption Bureau entered the office of the accused, Radosław M., just as he received the money and was ready to put it into his drawer.[15] Radosław is facing a possible five years in prison for bribery.[16] Subsequent investigations led to other persons involved in corruption being arrested. Currently, Radosław R., Emil D., Adrian P., Jędrzej P. and Daniel S. have been detained and accused of bribery in managerial positions.[17]

These cases have created a lot of heat and concern about the way TBSs function and operate. The Anti-Corruption Division has recently stated that there will be more detentions in the near future.[18]

Football poker: redefining the rules of the game

Corruption in football teams and involving the Polish Football Association is a major issue in Poland. Every sports club that wants to take part in the games is obliged to be a member of the PZPN, which is also responsible for appointing referees for each game. The PZPN has the power to discipline either a sports club or an individual associated with the club. Clubs may be disciplined when they do not respect the statutes and rules of the International Federation of Football Associations (FIFA), the Union of European Football Associations (UEFA) or the PZPN, or in which the principle of fair play is violated according to the criteria of the PZPN.[19]

Most sports clubs are joint-stock companies and, as such, they are subject to the provisions of the Polish Code of Commercial Companies. As a commercial entity, a club has freedom to create its legal form and is not subject to the public procurement law, and clubs can be taken over simply by buying a controlling stake in the company. This results in great efficiency, but is also a potential source of corruption. Allegations of corruption in football have been rife for a few years, but, with the prospect of Poland hosting the Euro 2012 finals alongside Ukraine, there are efforts to clean up the sport.

The so-called 'Polars' affair in 2005 highlighted the issue of corruption in football, sparking a

---

12 *Epoznan* (Poland), 5 June 2006.
13 See www.bip.nik.gov.pl/pl/bip/wyniki_kontroli_wstep/inform2006/2006142.
14 Policija.pl press release, 2 May 2008.
15 Ibid.; Prokuratura Okręgowa w Poznaniu, press release, 7 May; Policija.pl, press release, 30 April 2008.
16 Policija.pl, press release, 30 April 2008.
17 Prokuratura Okręgowa w Poznaniu, press release, 7 May 2008.
18 Policija.pl, press release, 30 April 2008.
19 See www.pzpn.pl/statut_pzpn.php; article 4, part 2.

large-scale investigation that was finally handled by the Public Prosecutor's Office of Appeal in Wrocław in 2007.[20] Officials of two football clubs – Polar Wrocław and Zagłebie Lubin – were accused of match-fixing. In May 2005 the chairman of Górniczy Klub Sportowy Katowice, Piotr Dziurowicz, cooperated with the police and revealed further corruption, resulting in the successful arrest of a referee from the First League.[21] In the subsequent months the investigation intensified, and among the arrested people were not only referees and PZPN observers but also other high-ranking officials. These included a First League referee and the chairman of the referees' board in the Silesian PZPN, who were detained after provocation in which they were handed a bribe.[22]

In June 2006, as the investigation continued, Ryszard Forbrich (nickname: Fryzjer) was arrested. The prosecutor's office in the city of Wrocław eventually impeached him, with over fifty accusations against him, including setting up and leading a criminal organisation since 2000 that had been involved in match-fixing practices on a very wide scale.[23] In most cases, the criminal activity consisted of bribing the PZPN referees and observers. There were also suspicions that Fryzjer could have been influencing decisions concerning the appointment of referees to each match.[24] In August 2006 the magazine *Sports Review* published a so-called 'Fryzjer's list' that gave the names of over twenty football referees who were supposedly cooperating with him.[25]

As the investigation intensified, it became clear that the scale of corruption was enormous.

In January 2007, after the imprisonment of a member of the PZPN board, the minister of sport appointed a temporary officer for the PZPN, thus suspending the board. The reaction of FIFA and UEFA was unambiguous: a few days after the appointment they made a statement claiming that the only body recognised as a representative of Polish football would be the PZPN executive committee. There was concern that Poland would be suspended from member privileges in UEFA and FIFA, and thus excluded from European and international games. UEFA and FIFA did not carry out those threats, however, and Poland's probationary status was lifted in March 2007.[26]

One of the latest examples of corruption detection and its punishment is the case of the Widzew Łódź sports club. On 28 November 2007 a former stockholder and member of the Widzew Łódź board, Wojciech Szymański, was arrested and charged with corruption.[27] In December 2007 the PZPN discipline department, on the basis of sources obtained from the prosecutor's office in Wrocław, accused the club of fixing twelve matches in the 2004/5 sports season. The department imposed the punishment of relegation to a lower league and a fine of zł35,000 (US$14,525). Widzew Łódź made an appeal to the tribunal of the PZPN, but the latter upheld the decision of the discipline department. The question was brought by Widzew Łódź to the Arbitration Tribunal of the Polish Olympic Committee, which cancelled the decision regarding relegation and discontinued the proceedings on 23 July 2008. Afterwards, the PZPN decided to file an appeal in the Supreme Court, as it found the

---

20 tvn24.pl, 29 November 2007; Gazeta (Poland), 13 May 2004.
21 *Dziennik Sport* (Poland), 14 December 2007.
22 *Wprost24* (Poland), 2005.
23 Dziennik.pl, 8 January 2008.
24 *Gazeta* (Poland), 18 November 2006.
25 *Sports Review* (Poland), 26–7 August 2006; see www.files.e-grajewo.pl/pdf/wydanie.pdf.
26 Uefa.com, press release, 22 January 2007.
27 TVN24 (Poland), 29 November 2007; *Gazeta Wyborcza* (Poland), 30 November 2007.

evidence of corrupt practices in Widzew Łódź to be clear.[28]

Interestingly, the Widzew Łódź club is implementing an anti-corruption strategy within the field of its operations and has begun cooperating with Transparency International Poland. The priority of this partnership is the creation of a code of ethics to prevent irregularities and anomalies in the area of sports club activities. The cooperation between TI and Widzew Łódź has begun with an anti-corruption audit of the club.

During its convention, in May, the PZPN adopted a resolution. The resolution states that relegation for corruption prior to 30 June 2005 will cease from 1 July 2009. The document also calls for loss of benefits such as premiums and point standings and appoints the disciplinary spokesperson described above. All these provisions were made as a response to corruption, which is common in Polish football. As the verdict of the Arbitration Tribunal of the Polish Olympic Committee shows, however, measures attempting to fight against criminal practices still come up against hard obstacles in football circles. Thus, in order to prevent these new institutions from becoming just an artificial creation and to improve the current situation, the full engagement of the sports clubs themselves is necessary, as well as of the members of the PZPN and other officials.

TI Poland

TI Poland: www.transparency.pl.

---

28 Sport.pl, 23 July 2008; Polish Olympic Committee Decision of the Arbitration Tribunal; see www.pkol.pl/pl/pages/display/15580.

Romania

Corruption Perceptions Index 2008: 3.8 (70th out of 180 countries)

Conventions

Council of Europe Civil Law Convention on Corruption (signed November 1999; ratified April 2002)
Council of Europe Criminal Law Convention on Corruption (signed January 1999; ratified July 2002)
UN Convention against Corruption (signed December 2003; ratified November 2004)
UN Convention against Transnational Organized Crime (signed December 2000; ratified December 2002)

Legal and institutional changes

- In November 2007 the provisions related to the organisation and functioning of disciplinary commissions within public institutions and authorities were modified by Government Decision no. 1344/2007.[1] The decision's main shortcoming is related to the character of the meetings organised by the disciplinary commissions, which are no longer public. Formerly these meetings were generally held in public, except in cases in which civil servants were being investigated or the president of the commission requested the contrary.[2] The new decision limits this framework and states that sessions should be public 'only at the request of, or with the written consent of the person under investigation'. Consequently, the general character of these meetings is secret. This is a significant backwards step in the field of transparency and may well diminish the accountability of these disciplinary forums.

- Law no. 268/2007 introduced new amendments to Law no. 182/2002,[3] related to access to classified information. Under the amendments, five categories of public officers – president, prime minister, ministers, senators and members of the Chamber of Deputies – can gain access to classified information without being required to comply with the otherwise generally applicable verification procedure.[4] This system creates a premise for discriminatory situations, enabling unwarranted access to confidential information.

- In 2007 the law relating to ministerial responsibilities, Law no. 115/1999,[5] was modified by a set of amendments and decisions of the Constitutional Court.[6] The only concrete result, however, was a set of disparate, heavy-

---

1 For the text of the government decision, see www.anfp.gov.ro/oip/doc/publicare/propuneri%20legislative/30627ABCDEFhg%20modif%20HG%201344.doc.

2 Government Decision no. 1210/2003, *Official Journal*, no. 757, 29 October 2003.

3 Law no. 268/2007, *Official Journal*, 1 October 2007.

4 See www.cdep.ro/proiecte/2006/900/20/0/leg_pl920_06.pdf.

5 *Official Journal*, Part I, no. 200, 23 March 2007.

6 Law no. 115/1999 underwent three amendments in 2007: Decision 665/2007 of the Constitutional Court, Emergency Ordinance 95/2007 and Decision 1133/2007 of the Constitutional Court. See also TI Romania, 2008.

handed and virtually inapplicable regulations. The Constitutional Court passed Decision no. 665/2007[7] declaring parts of Article 24 of Law no. 115/1999 unconstitutional. This article, through amendments made in 2005, had provided common law procedures regarding the criminal trials of former members of the government for crimes committed during their time in office. The court's decision to declare this article unconstitutional was justified by the lack of consistency between the modifications in 2005 and the court's jurisprudence. Although the decision was made on the correct basis, it has led to dissatisfaction and criticism, particularly as it has generated questions about notorious and large-scale corruption cases that had already been completed.[8]

- Decision no. 1133/2007 of the Constitutional Court declared unconstitutional any extra-judicial organisation set up to investigate and enact criminal prosecutions. The decision is an important step ahead, as establishing a special commission was an opportunity to breach the principle of equality before the law and represented a supplementary filter in the activity of prosecutors. At the same time, the decision produced some misunderstanding with regard to procedures to be followed and the institutional competencies regarding the criminal investigation of ministers who are also MPs. The solution came with Decision no. 270/2008, which determines an extension of the parliamentary immunity beyond the limits of the constitutional text.

- The Government Emergency Ordinance no. 82/2007 brought new amendments to the law relating to legal persons, Law no. 31/1990, and supplemented the extensive reforms of corporate law made in 2006. The amendments aim to align the Romanian business environment with European standards in the field of share-based companies. The law provides a set of professional disqualifications that prohibit from founding a company any persons lacking legal capacity or people who had been convicted of fraudulent management, breach of trust, forgery, the use of forgeries, cheating, embezzlement, perjury or corruption.[9] The ordinance also adds money-laundering to the list of criminal offences. Notwithstanding such improvement, the respective provisions apply only to company founders, not managers.

Pre- and post-accession Romania: the impact on corruption

Romania joined the European Union on 1 January 2007. This change in status had a massive impact on the country. In particular, there was a major concern over corruption, which the European Commission (EC) had identified as an issue prior to Romania's accession. A June 2007 EC report assessed Romania's progress on corruption issues and found that, while the government had successfully achieved the effective drafting of laws, action plans and programmes, little real change had been achieved in practice.[10]

This assessment was backed up in relation to corruption in the private sector, as the 2007 Global Corruption Barometer found that 25 per cent of Romanians polled perceived the private sector as extremely corrupt, compared to only 3 per cent who did not see it as at all corrupt.[11] As such, despite efforts to align domestic legislation to

---

7 For the text of the Constitutional Court decision, see www.ccr.ro/decisions/pdf/ro/2007/D665_07.pdf.

8 TI Romania's *National Corruption Report 2008* offers an in-depth analysis of the amendments brought to Law no. 115/1999.

9 Law no. 31/1990, which specifies such provisions in title II, chapter 1, article 6, was published in the *Official Journal*, no. 1066, 17 November 2004.

10 EC, *Report on Romania's Progress on Accompanying Measures Following Accession* (Brussels: EC, 2007).

11 Global Corruption Barometer 2007; www.transparency.org.ro/politici_si_studii/indici/bgc/2007/GCBsurvey Romania.pdf.

the *acquis communautaire*,[12] there is clearly still a lot of room for improvement.

Recent concerns on the part of international actors[13] have highlighted a series of legislative and practical vulnerabilities that are generating some reconsideration of the risks that might occur at the nexus between the public and private spheres. As an example of this anxiety, the Bucharest Chamber of Commerce and Industry (CCIB) addressed a letter to both the president and prime minister highlighting the impact of the high level of corruption and the influence of interest groups on overall economic activity. The CCIB still considers corruption one of the major obstacles to economic development, particularly in the tourism and food industries. The CCIB did not approach the relevant authorities that work on corruption issues, however, and, as such, its impact is likely to be limited.[14]

While business representatives claim that the phenomenon has become a general trend exacerbated by bureaucracy and technological shortcomings, a former CCIB president said the private sector is affected by the intrusion of politics in the same way that politics is unduly influenced and corrupted by business figures.[15]

Some of the main weaknesses of Romanian legislation, according to a 2005 Group of States against Corruption (GRECO) evaluation, are the lack of legal accountability for individuals committing corrupt acts on behalf of legal persons (for example, a company); shortcomings in regulations concerning professional disqualifications for misconduct and other accounting obligations; and miscommunication between authorities involved in preventing and detecting corruption.[16] Moreover, the EC expressed its concern regarding the transposition of the 2003 Council Framework Decision on combating corruption in the private sector into domestic legislation. This decision addresses active and passive corruption in the private sector and makes legal persons (companies/firms/non-governmental organisations) liable for the corrupt behaviour of their staff.[17]

The Romanian authorities have responded to these challenges in several ways. First, in 2006, the government amended the Criminal Code.[18] Coming into force in 2007, it made legal persons liable for the corruption of their staff. While this did not mitigate the individual liability of staff members, this is the first time that criminal liability has been incurred on legal persons, serving as an incentive for companies to ensure that corruption is not a practice tolerated within their organisations.[19] Sanctions faced by legal persons include dissolution, suspension of activity and bans on participating

---

12 The total body of EU law accumulated so far.

13 Group of States against Corruption in the Evaluation Report on Romania, Second Evaluation Round adopted in October 2005, and the European Commission, which emphasised the importance of ensuring 'that both active and passive corruption in the private sector are criminal offences in all Member States and that legal persons may be held responsible for such offences and that all these offences incur effective, proportionate and dissuasive penalties' in its Report to the Council released on 18 June 2007; see http://ec.europa.eu/justice_home/doc_centre/crime/economic/doc/com_2007_328_en.pdf.

14 See www.bursa.ro/on-line/?s=print&sr=articol&id_articol=23205.

15 Ibid.

16 Evaluation Report on Romania, Second Evaluation Round, adopted by Group of States against Corruption at its twenty-fifth plenary meeting, October 2005.

17 Report from the Commission to the Council based on article 9 of the Council Framework Decision 2003/568/JHA of 22 July on combating corruption in the private sector; http://ec.europa.eu/justice_home/doc_centre/crime/economic/doc/com_2007_328_en.pdf.

18 Law no. 278/2006, *Official Journal*, no. 601, 12 July 2006.

19 TI Romania's *National Corruption Report 2007* analyses the modifications brought to the Penal Code, including the impact of Law no. 278/2006.

in public procurement procedures for one to three years.[20]

Preventing private sector corruption is also an objective of the National Anti-corruption Strategy for 2005 to 2007.[21] Law no. 31/1990,[22] which regulates commercial companies, has specified a series of offences to restrict people convicted of certain crimes from founding commercial companies. Following GRECO's recommendations, the law was amended by Emergency Ordinance 82/2007,[23] which added money-laundering to the previous list of criminal offences. Despite these improvements, the law is restricted to the founders of companies and does not extend to managers.

Other measures established as of 2007 include new rules to verify the function of companies during and after registration to ensure that they are legitimate entities.[24] This was linked to ensuring that registration was effective, and new protocols were established in relation to the National Trade Register Office to have access to the trade register database.[25]

Privatisation after accession to the European Union

Public sector contracts, concessions and privatisations are common vehicles for corruption in many countries.[26] Privatisation is a particular problem in Romania, given changing privatisation practices, the endemic nature of corruption and the fragile enforcement capacity of anti-corruption bodies.

Since 2002 major institutional and legislative developments have transformed Romania's mass privatisation model of manager–employee buyout schemes. The former privatisation model gave priority to insiders rather than foreign investors, as employees of state-owned companies were offered preferential treatment when it came to buying shares.[27]

The inflow of foreign direct investment (FDI) through privatisation has contributed massively to economic growth in recent years. Although the upward trend appeared to slow during 2007, privatisation-related FDI still reached approximately €1.7 billion (US$2.2 billion).[28] One of the major factors responsible for this slowdown was the decelerating privatisation of state-owned enterprises. Consequently, this trend is reflected in investments, with the FDI portion of external net borrowing dropping from 89 per cent in 2006 to 44 per cent in 2007.[29]

Many large industries in Romania have already been privatised, including oil, banking and energy, implying that future investments are likely to be in the so-called 'greenfield' sector.[30] Despite this trend, a relatively large number of

20 Law no. 278/2006, *Official Journal*, no. 601, 12 July 2006.
21 The National Anti-corruption Strategy 2005–2007; see www.guv.ro/obiective/200504/050401-strategie-anticorup-tie.pdf.
22 Law no. 31/1990 specifies such provisions in title II, chapter I, article 6; it was published in the *Official Journal*, no. 1066, 17 November 2004.
23 Emergency Ordinance no. 82/2007, *Official Journal*, 29 June 2007.
24 Second Evaluation Round, Evaluation Report on Romania, adopted by GRECO in October 2005; see www.coe.int/t/dg1/greco/evaluations/round2/GrecoEval2(2005)1_Romania_EN.pdf.
25 GRECO, *Compliance Report for Romania, Second Evaluation Round* (Strasbourg: GRECO, 2007), adopted by GRECO in December 2007.
26 D. Hall, 'Privatizations, Multinationals and Corruption', *Development in Practice*, vol. 9, no. 5 (1999).
27 G. Laurentiu, 'Privatisation, Institutional Culture and Corruption in Romania', paper presented at the 10th International Anti-corruption Conference, Prague, 10 October 2001.
28 'Investitii straine de 1,7 miliarde de euro din privatizari in 2007'; see www.standard.ro, 31 May 2007.
29 Ibid.
30 See www.standard.ro, 2007.

companies (367) are still listed by the Authority for State Assets Recovery (AVAS) for the 2007 privatisation portfolio. Among them were seventy-three in which the state was the major shareholder, but only twenty-six were considered to be large companies.[31]

In 2007 moves were made to reform and simplify the privatisation process. From 1 January that year AVAS integrated into its structure the Office for State Participation and Privatisation in the Industrial Sector.[32] Other companies, formally under the Ministry of Economy and Finance, were also transferred to AVAS.[33]

A further step was to modify the law related to free access to public information.[34] A 2007 amendment obliges public institutions and authorities to make available privatisation contracts that were concluded after the law came into force on 22 December 2001. The context in which the amendment was made raises a few questions, however. The new provision is likely to have a limited impact, as the privatisation process is coming to an end and the big privatisation contracts are already finalised. Furthermore, there are a number of 'exceptions' in the law that prohibit information regarding commercial or financial activities from being made public if doing so would conflict with the right to intellectual or industrial ownership, or with the principle of fair competition. As such, these legal provisions establishing legal exceptions may seriously limit access to information with regard to the privatisation process.[35]

AVAS's 2007 privatisation plan underlines the importance of initiating a normative act regulating the privatisation process in Romania.[36] It also cites the European Union's recommendation for a legislative framework to encompass privatisation and the restructuring of trade companies. Along these lines, AVAS proposed a law to harmonise domestic legislation to EU standards.[37] The new normative act intends to establish clear rules to accelerate privatisation based on transparency, establish an equitable price according to supply and demand, and guarantee equality among bidders. The proposed law also provides regulations regarding subsidy regimes, eliminating clauses that represent obstacles to freedom of information and limiting government interference in social protection matters and investment ensured by the buyer.[38]

Despite these efforts, Romania faced an EC investigation into possible aid granted during the privatisation of several state-owned companies: SC Tractorul SA, SC Automobile Craiova SA and SC Petrotub SA.[39] The case of Automobile Craiova is by far the most significant in terms of media coverage and, consequently, its impact on the privatisation process.

The formal investigation involving Automobile Craiova was initiated in October 2007 and considered the privatisation process involving the sale of the state-run company to the Ford Motor Company a month earlier. Saying that it 'had doubts whether the tender itself was open,

---

31 AVAS, 'Activity Report 2007' (Bucharest: AVAS, 2007); available at www.avas.gov.ro/upload/RAPORT%20DE%20 ACTIVITATE%202007.pdf.
32 Emergency Ordinance no. 101/2006, *Official Journal*, no. 1015, 20 December 2006.
33 Government Decision no. 1103/2007, *Official Journal*, no. 640, 19 September 2007.
34 Law no. 188/2007, which modifies Law 544/2001. Law no. 544/2001 was published in the *Official Journal*, Part I, no. 663, 23 October 2001.
35 TI Romania, 2008.
36 AVAS, 'Privatization Plan 2007'; see www.primet.ro/col_docs/doc_479.pdf.
37 Draft Law for the approval of Emergency Ordinance no. 3/2007; see www.cdep.ro/pls/proiecte/upl_pck. proiect?idp=8260.
38 AVAS, 'Privatization Plan 2007'.
39 European Commission, press releases, 25 September 2007; 26 September 2007; 27 February 2008.

transparent and non-discriminatory',[40] the European Union suspended the granting of any unlawful aid until a decision on its appropriateness was reached.[41]

AVAS announced in May 2007 the sale of its 72.4 per cent share in Automobile Craiova. It established specific conditions for the privatisation, namely producing at least 200,000 cars in the fourth year after privatisation, continuing the current activity for four years, and maintaining the 3,900 former employees of Automobile Craiova and Daewoo Romania.[42] The only company to propose an offer was Ford, which won the tender for €57 million (US$72 million).[43]

The EU investigation raised a number of concerns. It said that conditions attached to the bid may have resulted in a lower sales price and, as such, the government incurred costs – in essence, government aid – to facilitate the sale. The money forgone by the government could then be used by the winning company to meet the conditions imposed. Second, the Romanian government had seen fit to impose a special law[44] accompanying the sale that led to the wholesale write-off of considerable debts and a guarantee of the payment of debts of former Daewoo subsidiaries.[45] In contrast to the conditions of the contract advertised as part of the bid, the incentives in terms of the debt relief were not offered to other potential bidders.[46]

The investigation concluded that the imposition of conditions on the bid had indeed lowered the sale price, thus constituting state aid. While this is not necessarily illegal, the Automobile Craiova privatisation did not meet the criteria for 'compatible restructuring aid or compatible regional aid', and as such was incompatible with a single market and constituted a distortion in competition in providing an 'economic advantage' to Automobile Craiova and Daewoo Romania.[47]

The estimated value of the state's 72.4 per cent stake in the company was €84 million (US$106 million), and therefore it had relinquished €27 million (US$34 million) in the sale. In February 2008 the European Union directed Romania to recoup the full amount.[48] With regard to the waiving of debt by Romania, the European Union's concerns were allayed. In particular, Romania surrendered an outstanding customs claim amounting to €800 million (US$1 billion). This case had previously been annulled by a Romanian court, and as such the European Union agreed that the waiving of debts did not constitute granting of new aid.[49] While this case does not constitute corruption *per se*, it is clear evidence of the complexity of the privatisation process and the necessity of having clear guidelines and transparent practices.

Victor Alistar, Alina Lungu and Florentina Nastase
(TI Romania)

---

40 See http://ec.europa.eu/comm/competition/state_aid/register/ii/doc/C-46-2007-WLWL-en-27.02.2008.pdf.
41 European Union, 'State Aid: Commission Opens In-depth Investigation into Possible Aid in Privatisation of Romanian Car Producer Automobile Craiova', press release, 10 October 2007.
42 Ibid.
43 Ibid.
44 Law no. 36/2008, *Official Journal*, 17 March 2008, regarding some measures on the privatisation of Automobile Craiova.
45 European Union, 2007.
46 Ibid.; 'Great Privatization Cases Turned into Investigations in Brussels', *Gardianul* (Romania), 24 December 2007.
47 European Union, 'State Aid: Commission Requests Romania to Recover €27 million Unlawful Aid from Automobile Craiova', press release, 27 February 2008.
48 Ibid.
49 See http://ec.europa.eu/comm/competition/state_aid/register/ii/doc/C-46-2007-WLWL-en-27.02.2008.pdf.

Additional reading

AVAS, *Activity Report 2007* (Bucharest: AVAS, 2007).

I. Coşpănaru, M. Loftis and A. Nastase (V. Alistar, coordinator), *National Corruption Report 2007* (Bucharest: TI Romania, 2007).

National Corruption Report 2008 (Bucharest: TI Romania, 2008).

EC, 'Spring Economic Forecasts 2008–2009', *European Economy*, no. 3 (2008).

TI Romania: www.transparency.ro.

Russian Federation

Corruption Perceptions Index 2008: 2.1 (147th out of 180 countries)

Conventions

Council of Europe Criminal Law Convention on Corruption (signed January 1999; ratified October 2006)

UN Convention against Corruption (signed December 2003; ratified May 2006)

UN Convention against Transnational Organized Crime (signed December 2000; ratified May 2004)

Legal and institutional changes

- In July 2007 the Governmental Commission on Administrative Reform adopted programmes against corruption that were to act as models for the regions and the federal governmental bodies to develop their own anti-corruption programmes. They were developed according to the provisions of the October 2005 Concept of the Administrative Reform in order to implement the institutional anti-corruption policy. Accordingly, all federal governmental bodies and regions should develop and adopt anti-corruption programmes by the end of 2008; at the time of writing the process was ongoing.

- In August 2007 the prosecutor general established a special department in charge of measures against corruption in the Prosecutor General's Office. Such departments will also be established in the regional offices. Their main task will be to oversee the implementation of the legal norms against corruption, to provide special oversight to the legal cases related to corruption offences and to foster an anti-corruption environment in the sphere of state and municipal public service.

- On 19 May 2008, almost immediately after his inauguration, President Dmitry Medvedev signed Presidential Decree 815 on Measures against Corruption. In his key electoral speech, in February 2008, he had announced that an anti-corruption policy would be one of the top priorities of his presidential programme. The decree created the Presidential Council for Combating Corruption, with the president at its head.[1] The main tasks assigned to the council are the development of a national anti-corruption policy and plan as well as relevant legislative proposals and the coordination of the efforts of the federal, regional and local executive and legislature against corruption. Among the members of the council there are the heads of the Constitutional, Supreme and Supreme Arbitrage Courts, the prosecutor general, the auditor general, the minister of the interior, the minister of economic development and other senior officials. The Presidium of the Council (the executive body of the council) is chaired by the head of the presidential administration, Sergei Naryshkin.

- On 25 June 2008 Naryshkin presented the draft of the National Anti-corruption Plan (NAP) to the president.[2] The NAP provides the general strategic outline of the national anti-corruption policy and prioritises the implementation of anti-corruption measures. The NAP establishes the following major spheres of anti-corruption efforts: legislative actions, including the drafting and adoption of the federal law against corruption; measures on corruption prevention in public service; measures on the improvement of public governance and governmental institutions; and measures on the enhancement of legal and anti-corruption education. The plan was signed by the president on 31 July 2008. According to the plan, twenty-five laws should be submitted to the State Duma no later than October 2008. Furthermore, all government departments and all regions should have adopted their own anti-corruption plans by 1 October 2008.

- The majority of the measures proposed in the National Anti-corruption Plan were formalised in draft laws submitted by the president to the State Duma in October 2008.[3] He requested that it review, discuss and adopt the proposed legislative drafts in an expeditious manner in order to have operational and applicable anti-corruption legislation by January 2009. The package includes the Basic Law against Corruption and three draft amendments to existing acts to align them with the Basic Law against Corruption, the UN Convention against Corruption and the Council of Europe Criminal Law Convention on Corruption. The Basic Law against Corruption is the main measure in the package, and it defines corruption as a social and legal phenomenon; a corruption offence as a manifestation of corruption entailing disciplinary, administrative, criminal and other liabilities; and countermeasures against corruption as the coordinated work of federal, regional and local executive bodies, civil society and individuals to prevent corruption, initiate criminal prosecution of perpetrators and minimise and/or eliminate its consequences.[4] The draft laws established measures to prevent corruption, including special requirements for those applying for public office; oversight of the income, property and liabilities of public officials; the development of institutions for public and parliamentary oversight; and the improvement of anti-corruption expertise in regulatory acts.[5] In order for this to be carried out in a coordinated way, the draft provides for special coordinating bodies to work at the federal, regional and local executive

---

1　President of Russia's official website, 19 May 2008.
2　National Anti-corruption Plan, 31 July 2008.
3　Federal law 'On Counteracting Corruption'.
4　This summary is based on the Explanatory Memorandum to the Draft of the Federal Law 'On Counteracting Corruption'; see www.kremlin.ru/eng/articles/corruption2.shtml.
5　Ibid.

institutions. Their structure, manner of formation and powers are not defined, however, and the bodies are to be formed at the discretion of the president. There should also be coordination between the prosecutor general and other prosecutors to counter corruption, including identifying, preventing, suppressing, exposing and investigating offences.

A new era of anti-corruption reforms in the private sector too?

Newly elected President Medvedev has declared corruption to be a key threat to Russian modernisation and social stability. In one of his first speeches following his election, at the State Council on 27 March 2008, he called for protection for small businesses. In particular, he addressed the issue of arbitrary inspections by officials – from firemen to the police – as potential opportunities for extorting bribes from small firms.[6] At the same meeting, he 'ordered the government to review legislation to protect small companies from being forced to enter dubious contracts with officials'.[7] He added, 'It is clear this is a legalised bribe, which was formally passed on in an envelope and now dressed up in a perfectly respectable form.'

Medvedev's engagement with the issue of corruption represents a departure from the previous ten years, during which the government had been almost silent on the subject. On the one hand, the continuing and systemic nature of corruption ensured that it was always at the centre of the ongoing public and media debate, but, on the other, the government, public institutions and civil society had never before been so active

in acknowledging the problem or taking significant measures to research and tackle corruption systematically.

Needless to say, such measures had long been awaited by Russian society. According to research in September 2008, 74 per cent of the population believed that the level of corruption in Russia was either 'high' or 'very high'.[8] The institutions perceived to be the most corrupt were the traffic police (33 per cent), municipal bodies (28 per cent) and the police (26 per cent), the overall figure being 23 per cent. According to the same research, 43 per cent did not consider the government's anti-corruption activities in the previous year to have been efficient, and, moreover, 10 per cent believed that corruption had actually increased in the previous twelve months. Other research during the same time period showed that 29 per cent of citizens and 56 per cent of businesspeople had paid a bribe.[9] Respondents to this survey were also very sceptical of Russia's capacity to fight corruption: 56 per cent of businesspeople and 58 per cent of citizens stated that it was 'hardly possible'.

It is difficult to blame people for such scepticism, given that this has been the rhetoric, even of senior government officials, in recent years. According to the head of the Investigations Committee of the Prosecutor General's Office, the number of bribery offences is continuing to grow: although some 6,700 offences were recorded in the last six months of 2007, this rose to 8,000 such offences in the first six months of 2008.[10] Furthermore, more than 500 cases of bribery of senior officials were submitted to the courts in 2007.[11]

---

6 Reuters (UK), 27 March 2008.
7 Ibid.
8 'Prichiny korruptsii i kak s nimi borotsya?' ['Causes of Corruption and What to Do against Them'], Russian Public Opinion Research Centre (VCIOM), press release no. 1048, 17 September 2008.
9 'Socialnye resursy preodoleniya korruptsii' ['Social Resources for Tackling Corruption'], Public Opinion Foundation (FOM), 22 September 2008.
10 See www.gzt.ru/society/2008/08/07/223011.html.
11 See www.rg.ru/2008/06/07/bastrikin.html.

Often, when there is bribery involving high-level government officials and civil servants, the private sector also has a role to play: altogether, the Investigations Committee of the Prosecutor General's Office estimates that businesses in Russia pay up to US$33.5 billion each year in bribes and kickbacks.[12] One of the most notable cases in 2008 was that of a former senator of the Council of Federation, Levon Chakhmakhchan, who was sentenced to nine years in prison for extorting US$1.5 million from the air company Transaero.[13] Another case involved the deputy head of the Audit Chamber, Vasily Koryagin, and the head of inspection of federal property, Sergei Klimantov, who extorted a bribe worth US$120,000 from one of the top oil refineries. Finally, the Moscow City district prosecutor, Vladimir Samoilov, as well as several other top prosecutors were found to have falsified cases against private companies and illegally confiscated their property; the value of the property was estimated to be as much as US$22 million.[14]

Shortly after arriving in office, Medvedev set to work to address some of these problems. Following his formal inauguration on 7 May 2008, the president called a governmental meeting on corruption. He claimed: 'Corruption became a systemic problem and we have to confront this problem with systemic actions.'[15] On 19 May 2008 the presidential decree 'On the Measures against Corruption' was introduced and plans were announced to set up a National Anti-corruption Plan within one month.[16] While the measures are broad and deal with corruption in all sectors (see above), there are some that relate to the private sector. In particular, the second part of the plan covers the improvement of state management: it 'entails the withdrawal of officials from the boards of directors of state corporations and includes new rules on conflicts of interest'.[17] There are also measures for the creation of a system of public legal and anti-corruption education programmes, including a specific programme for lawyers and others within the legal profession, which should improve general awareness within the public and private sector on what constitutes corruption.[18] Moreover, the plan changes twenty-five existing laws, including a law to ensure that all public officials, civil servants, the police and judges submit asset declarations, which will reduce the opportunities for them to take or extort bribes. Commissions set up in each department will check the asset declarations.

Importantly, there will be a new mechanism for ensuring the liability of legal entities, including foreign entities. The draft establishes a general rule, in accordance with which, when a bribe is offered, or commercial bribery takes place, the legal entity, not just the individuals involved, will be held liable. In particular, there are provisions for warnings and administrative fines for legal entities. This requirement will be developed through an amendment to the Code of the Russian Federation on administrative offences.[19]

It is important to stress that the majority of the regulations, measures and provisions of the draft

---

12 Discussed in an interview with the deputy head of the Investigations Committee of the Prosecutor General's Office, Vasily Piskarev, in *Rossiiskaya Gazeta*, 19 June 2008.

13 See www.aif.ru/society/article/19661.

14 Discussed in an interview with the head of the Investigations Committee of the Prosecutor General's Office, Alexander Bastrykin, in *Argumenty i Fakty* (Russia); see www.aif.ru/society/article/19411.

15 See www.newsru.com/russia/19may2008/corrupt.html.

16 Decree on the Measures against Corruption 815, 19 May 2008.

17 *Kommersant* (Russia), 3 July 2008.

18 National Anti-corruption Plan, 31 July 2008.

19 This summary is based on the Explanatory Memorandum to the Draft of the Federal Law 'On Counteracting Corruption'; see www.kremlin.ru/eng/articles/corruption2.shtml.

legislative package constitute an absolutely new legal framework for the fight against corruption in Russia. The introduction of these drafts is clearly a conceptual breakthrough in Russia's approach to anti-corruption reforms. Despite this, questions and doubts abound about the complexity of such an approach, especially considering that they are being implemented without much publicity and in an environment that lacks transparency. Furthermore, the effectiveness of the reforms will hinge on the implementation of the law. As stated by the famous Russian writer Mikhail Saltykov-Shchedrin, 'The severity of Russian laws is balanced by the fact that *their enforcement is optional*' (emphasis added). Whether the country is genuinely

committed to a sustained attack on corruption will be seen only if it becomes clear that enforcement and implementation are rigorous. The initiatives of 2008 created no more than the framework for the change, and the applicability and efficiency of this framework still have to be tested in the realities of Russia's systemic corruption. Nonetheless, it remains the case that the preparation and announcement of President Medvedev's reforms constitute the most significant feature of the Russian anti-corruption landscape of the last decade.

Elena Panfilova (TI Russia)

TI Russia: www.transparency.org.ru.

Spain

Corruption Perceptions Index 2008: 6.5 (28th out of 180 countries)

Conventions

Council of Europe Civil Law Convention on Corruption (signed May 2005; not yet ratified)

Council of Europe Criminal Law Convention on Corruption (signed May 2005; not yet ratified)

OECD Convention on Combating Bribery of Foreign Public Officials (signed December 1997; ratified January 2000)

UN Convention against Corruption (signed September 2005; ratified June 2006)

UN Convention against Transnational Organized Crime (signed December 2000; ratified March 2002)

Legal and institutional changes

- A new Political Parties Funding Law (Ley Orgánica 8/2007) was passed on 4 July 2007. Despite some steps forward, such as prohibiting anonymous donations, this new law has

major drawbacks. The accounts of local organisations, companies and foundations of parties are still not sufficiently integrated into the central parties' accountancy books. Although private donations are limited, there is no limit on donations of real state goods. The cancellation of political parties' debts and the provision of credit at below-market rates are still permitted. The free provision of professional services to parties is allowed. Moreover, funds provided by autonomous communities and local governments to parties have been legalised without specifying how the funds should be distributed among the different parties.

- A new Public Sector Procurements Law (Ley 30/2007) was passed on 30 October 2007. The new act takes advantage of the need to incorporate European Parliament and Council Directive 2004/18/CE (on procedures for awarding public works, public supply and public service contracts) to carry out a global reform of traditional Spanish legislation on public procurement. One of the law's novelties is the introduction of a physical or legal person who is 'responsible for the contract'. This person is charged with monitoring the entire life of the contract to guarantee that deviations from the initial conditions are minimised and sensibly founded. This person cannot belong to the contracting commission or body, or be linked to it in a contractual arrangement.
- A specialised unit on land-planning crimes at the operative central unit of the Guardia Civil began work in autumn 2007. Two hundred agents compose the unit, which in its first six months was very active: eighty operations were still open, twenty-six were completed, fifty-seven people were arrested and 126 were prosecuted.[1] About twenty of these cases are clearly related to corruption at the local level.

Evaluation of the institutional framework to fight against corruption in the private sector

Spain has improved its legal capacity to fight corruption, thanks in part to its international commitments, namely ratification of the OECD Convention on Combating Bribery of Foreign Public Officials and the UN Convention against Corruption. Spain has not ratified the Council of Europe's civil and criminal conventions on corruption, however.

Although these two ratified conventions deal with corruption in the private sector, Spain has not developed adequate legislation in this regard. A proposed January 2007 amendment to the criminal code contained a number of offences that would have improved regulation in the private sector, such as introducing the crime of bribing company managers and the liability of legal entities, but the amendment failed to secure enough support. The foundering of this legislation illustrates the lack of commitment by politicians to fight private sector corruption. Even in the face of the countless local scandals in recent years, corruption seems not to have become a top issue on the public agenda. The Centro de Investigaciones Sociológicas (CIS) Barometers of 2007 and 2008 show that fewer than 3 per cent of people mentioned corruption as one of Spain's main problems.[2] This is in clear contrast to the government's reaction in the mid-1990s, when corruption was the most highly ranked problem on the public agenda as measured by polls.

Operation Hidalgo: using lawyers to launder money

Corruption in the private sector is rarely the act of an individual but, instead, part of a network involving a number of actors. Operation Hidalgo, which uncovered extensive money-laundering associated with illegal activity, is illustrative of networks involving not only the private sector but also lawyers and the judiciary. Operation Hidalgo was similar to previous operations, such

---

1 *El País* (Spain), 19 November 2007.
2 Barometers are surveys conducted monthly by the Centro de Investigaciones Sociológicas to measure public opinion on Spain's political and economic situation and future development perspectives; see www.cis.es.

as Operation Ballena Blanca or certain aspects of Operation Malaya, that have exposed the extent of money-laundering in Spain and the central role of some law firms.[3]

Operation Hidalgo broke on the Costa del Sol in April 2007, with more than twenty arrests in Málaga and Marbella. The suspects included three notaries, two of whom were also implicated in the Ballena Blanca and Malaya corruption cases, although the cases against all of them were dropped. Four lawyers from the offices of Rafael Cruz Conde in Marbella were also arrested. Property was searched in a number of Spanish provinces, but most attention was focused on the Rafael Cruz Conde offices, considered to be at the centre of the scandal.[4] The anti-corruption prosecutor believes it is linked to 800 ghost companies set up to launder money obtained from 'all types of criminal activity', including drug-trafficking.[5]

The first judge in charge of the judicial investigation was taken off the case in July 2007, as he was under investigation himself following the Malaya case for corruption on the Marbella town council.[6] He was also suspected of taking bribes from some of the Hidalgo suspects to get them out of jail.[7] He was sentenced to two years in prison in August 2008 for bribery and prevarication in relation to his involvement in the Malaya case, but is also under investigation in relation to Hidalgo.[8] Although the implication of this judge appears to be an isolated case, it suggests the strength, reach and capability of the criminal networks on the Costa del Sol.

In November 2007 the investigative judge from the Marbella Court of First Instance fixed the civil liability of the top 10 people involved at €520 million (US$730 million), which is three times the amount they are thought to have defrauded.[9] Although judges generally have some room to manoeuvre when fixing these liabilities, the decision to fix a quantity so high shows a clear concern for the seriousness of the crime.

In some positive developments following this string of cases, *El País* reported that the executive service of Bank of Spain's (the central bank's) Commission for the Prevention of Money Laundering and Monetary Offences (SEPBLAC) was taking a tougher stand with law firms to improve their cooperation in pursuing this kind of crime. According to the SEPBLAC, while notaries, real estate agencies and tax consultants have notably improved their cooperation in the fight against money-laundering, this is not the case with lawyers. Although the former are now communicating to authorities many more suspicious operations of money-laundering than in previous years, lawyers still resist this duty and tend to overprotect their clients. The SEPBLAC wrote a letter to ten distinguished Spanish law firms in December 2007 asking for their cooperation and warning them about possible future inspections if the information received was not adequate.[10]

While it is clear that there are still considerable factors in Spain that draw legitimate business into the criminal realm, it is encouraging that not only have severe civil liabilities been assigned

---

3 See Organización Profesional de Inspectores de Hacienda del Estado, 'Fraude, corrupción y blanqueo de capitales en España' ('Fraud, Corruption and Money-laundering in Spain') (Madrid: Organización Profesional de Inspectores de Hacienda del Estado, 2007). This report discusses the difficulties in investigating these crimes and the limited willingness of political authorities to develop a tougher policy.

4 *El País* (Spain), 17 April 2007; 20 December 2007.

5 *Cinco Días* (Spain), 18 April 2007

6 *El País* (Spain), 5 July 2007.

7 *El País* (Spain), 5 March 2008.

8 *Sur* (Spain), 8 August 2008.

9 See a general overview of the case in *El País* (Spain), 9 February 2008.

10 *El País* (Spain), 24 February 2008.

in the Hidalgo case, but that the authorities are beginning to work in a proactive manner.[11] As law enforcement has traditionally been one of the weakest points in the fight against corruption in Spain, successful court cases and clear sanctions for these deeds would demonstrate potential for improving anti-corruption activities.

The Gescartera affair: linking politics, banks and the private sector

The Gescartera affair, which broke in 2001, finally reached a resolution in court in March 2008. The affair illustrates the 'old boy network' at the heart of the Spanish establishment,[12] as well as the complicity of banks in the scandal. The affair concerned the collapse of the Gescartera brokerage house after investors had been swindled out of €88 million (US$120 million). In July 2001 its main shareholder, Antonio Camacho, was imprisoned.[13]

Camacho was an influential investment consultant and promised his investors record returns, and in the process raised a substantial personal fortune. As a result of his aggressive marketing he gained some extremely high-profile clients, including senior Church officials, welfare funds such as the naval pension fund, and large charities such as the police orphans fund and ONCE, a charity for the blind.[14] Gescartera was accused of transferring clients' money to offshore havens with the assistance of bank managers in order to cover up discrepancies between assets and liabilities.[15]

Once the company's unsustainable situation had become known, allegations were aired that Camacho's privileged connections with senior authorities linked to the Popular Party in the Ministry for the Economy and in the stock market regulator, CNMV (National Commission for the Stock Market), allowed him to hide irregularities in the firm's books. He had allegedly given gifts and jobs to CNMV and hired the sister of the junior finance minister, Enrique Giménez-Reyna (who resigned in the first weeks of the scandal) as managing director.[16]

In March 2008 the Court of First Instance in Madrid sentenced the firm's main directors to prison. Camacho received eleven years for embezzlement and forging public documents.[17] Also sentenced were two employees of two important Spanish savings banks, Caja Madrid Bolsa and La Caixa. This led the court to find the two banks, as necessary collaborators in the affair, civilly liable for the €88 million that had disappeared. The banks have appealed against the decision to the Supreme Court, arguing that their behaviour was not irregular, and that they respected the law and did not harm Gescartera's clients.[18]

This unusual decision, if upheld, will allow the swindled clients to recover their money, while serving as an important warning to all banks to be much more careful with the accounts they maintain. Although it seems that justice eventually will be served, one of the lessons of this case is the delay in the court's decision. Though laws are generally appropriate to address such

---

11 There has been a very important strengthening of the police corps dealing with money-laundering in the last two years. See L. Gómez, '130 investigaciones policiales ponen cerco al lavado de dinero negro', *El País* (Spain), 15 July 2007.
12 BBC News (UK), 21 September 2001.
13 Ibid. Camacho served three years in prison, was paroled in July 2004 and sent back to prison in March 2008.
14 Ibid.
15 Tax-news.com (Tortola, British Virgin Islands), 15 November 2002.
16 For a complete dossier on the Gescartera affair, see www.elpais.com/todo-sobre/tema/caso/Gescartera/53/.
17 *El País* (Spain), 27 March 2008
18 *El País* (Spain), 28 March 2008; *Agencia EFE* (Spain), 1 June 2008.

violations, Spain's judicial system is frequently very slow, ultimately hindering the effective resolution of corruption cases.

Self-regulation in the business sector

A very important element in the fight against corruption is the self-regulation of major actors in the business sector. ECODES (Foundation for Ecology and Development) and the Carolina Foundation recently published a report on the role of Spanish companies in the fight against corruption.[19] The report analyses the corporate integrity systems of Spanish firms with a high risk of exposure to corrupt practices in comparison with similar firms elsewhere in Europe. The integrity systems of Spanish firms were found to be less satisfactory than other European companies: 93 per cent of Spanish firms in the sample have an anti-corruption policy, but none have an advanced or good one. Among other European companies, 1 per cent have a good policy and 17 per cent have an advanced one. Furthermore, while 87 per cent of European companies have an anti-corruption system in place, only 71 per cent of Spanish firms do so.

The report also looks at the corporate integrity systems of the thirty-five Spanish companies on the IBEX 35,[20] the key index of the Madrid stock exchange. Compared to 2005, the 2007 report found substantial progress in the anti-corruption systems of these companies. There was a notable increase in the number of companies with both a clear anti-corruption policy and a managerial system to prevent and control corruption. There were no significant changes in the area of transparency of information, however, as fewer than 10 per cent of these

companies in each year provided information about their employee training programmes or mechanisms for the anonymous reporting of wrongdoing.

This improved performance of Spanish companies indicates a new and promising step forward in the field of self-regulation. Moreover, on 9 April 2008 the first Spanish sustainability index, FTSE4Good IBEX, was founded. Twenty-seven companies out of eighty-two candidates have joined the index, which requires member companies to take steps to counter bribery.

Such indices work on the assumption that companies that fight corruption can also be more effective financially. They can be a helpful tool for investors to identify companies with good practices in corporate social responsibility. It is to be hoped that these indices will promote healthy competition among companies to improve social and ethical standards, and serve as a deterrent to corrupt activities.

Fernando Jiménez (University of Murcia and an individual member of TI Spain)

Additional reading

J. Estefanía (ed.), *Informe sobre la democracia en España 2008* (Madrid: Fundación Alternativas, 2008).

E. García Viñuela, 'Los partidos se hacen una ley de financiación "a su medida"', *El Mundo*, 11 October 2007.

F. Iglesias (ed.), *Urbanismo y democracia: Alternativas para evitar la corrupción* (Madrid: Fundación Alternativas, 2007).

J. A. Rodríguez, 'El grupo policial contra delitos

---

19 Fundación Ecología y Desarrollo and Fundación Carolina, 'Negocios limpios, desarrollo global: El rol de las empresas en la lucha internacional contra la corrupción. Avances de las empresas españolas del IBEX35 2005–2007' ['Clean business, global development: The companies' role in the international fight against corruption. Steps forward of Spanish companies in the IBEX35 2005–2007'] (Zaragoza: ECODES, 2008). See www.ecodes.org/pages/publicaciones/archivos/Negocios_Limpios.pdf.

20 The IBEX 35 is composed of thirty-five representative securities from the four Spanish stock markets. Its composition is revised every six months.

urbanísticos se estrena con 100 operaciones y 57 arrestos', *El País*, 19 November 2007.

M. Villoria, 'Las nuevas medidas al servicio de la transparencia, la participación y el control en

el gobierno local en la Ley del Suelo', *Ciudad y Territorio: Estudios Territoriales*, vol. 29, nos. 152–3 (2007).

TI Spain: www.transparencia.org.es.

Switzerland

Corruption Perceptions Index 2008: 9.0 (5th out of 180 countries)

Conventions

Council of Europe Criminal Law Convention on Corruption (signed February 2001; ratified March 2006)

OECD Convention on Combating Bribery of Foreign Public Officials (signed December 1997; ratified May 2000)

UN Convention against Corruption (signed December 2003; not yet ratified)

UN Convention against Transnational Organized Crime (signed December 2000; ratified October 2006)

Legal and institutional changes

- At its plenary meeting in April 2008 the Council of Europe's Group of States against Corruption adopted its first evaluation report on Switzerland, assessing the quality of its implementation of the Council of Europe Criminal Law Convention on Corruption and its Additional Protocol. It found Switzerland to have made significant efforts to combat corruption, but also issued thirteen recommendations to improve the convention's implementation. Switzerland will have to report on its implementation of the recommendations by 31 October 2009.[1]

- After the elaboration of a draft for the Company and Accounting Law Reform by the FDJP[2], the Federal Council recommended that parliament accept the reform.[3] The bill improves, *inter alia*, corporate governance and the legal status of shareholders and replaces outdated accounting legislation. Furthermore,

---

1 Federal Department of Justice and Police (FDJP), 'Further Action Recommended to Combat Corruption', press release, 2 June 2008.
2 TI, *Global Corruption Report 2008* (Cambridge: Cambridge University Press, 2008).
3 Botschaft zur Änderung des Obligationenrechts (Opinion of the Federal Council for changing the Code of Obligations), 21 December 2007:

the regulations of the board of directors were tightened to require members to stand for election each year. Under the reform, shareholders will have the right of information about compensation paid to top company managers.[4] The Council of States will open the voting on the bill in spring 2009.

- Although Switzerland signed the UN Convention against Corruption in 2003, no action was taken until September 2007, when the Federal Council requested the National Council to ratify the UNCAC.[5] The National Council's expert commission for legal affairs agreed on 19 June 2008 to approve the Federal Council's recommendation and to open voting in parliament.[6] The National Council adopted the recommendation in December 2008. The Council of States will take its decision in spring 2009.[7] The federal administration highlights that Switzerland already meets the convention's legal requirements, because the country has adopted the Council of Europe Criminal Law Convention on Corruption, its Additional Protocol and the OECD Convention on Combating Bribery of Foreign Public Officials.[8]

The deals involving sports-marketing company ISMM and FIFA

On 11 March 2008 a remarkable legal proceeding was opened in Zug, Switzerland. The sports-marketing company International Sports, Media and Marketing (ISMM)[9] declared bankruptcy, leading to an investigation that uncovered an extensive series of bribes.

ISMM is a Swiss company founded by Horst Dassler, the son of the founder of Adidas. After Dassler's death in 1987, Jean-Marie Weber became responsible for networking at ISMM.[10] ISMM had a successful track record in sports marketing and gained the broadcasting rights for major sporting events such as the Olympics, the World Cup and the track and field world championships.[11] The sale of these rights is one of the largest sources of revenue for sports organisations such as the Fédération Internationale de Football Association (FIFA) and the International Olympic Committee (IOC).

Bribery seems to have been introduced in the process of awarding of sports broadcasting rights in the early 1990s, when ISMM lost its monopolistic position. With other companies bidding more for broadcasting rights, ISMM for the first time ever failed in 1996 to win the television rights for the Olympics. Nevertheless, ISMM continued buying the television rights for some of the most popular sporting events. In 1998 it held the rights for the world volleyball, swimming and gymnastics championships, as well as the US CART auto-racing series. In 1999 it signed the largest ever marketing and television contract in tennis with the Association of Tennis Professionals, securing rights worth US$1.2 billion over ten years. Analysts suggest that this contract was the beginning of ISMM's

4 FDJP, 'Company Law to Be Modernized', press release, 21 December 2007.

5 Botschaft zum UNO-Übereinkommen gegen Korruption (Opinion of the Federal Council Regarding the UN Convention against Corruption), 21 September 2007.

6 Anträge der Kommission für Rechtsfragen des Nationalrats (Request of the Commission for Legal Affairs of the National Council), 19 June 2008.

7 Author's information, received from the federal administration via e-mail.

8 FDJP, 'Globale Bekämpfung der Korruption wird verstärkt', press release, 21 September 2007.

9 In combination with the ISMM case, the name ILS (International Sports and Leisure), an ISMM subsidiary, appears regularly. This article mentions only ISMM.

10 Dassler was a personal assistant and financial expert. Weber's position at the time of ISMM's bankruptcy was chair of the board. B. Smit, *Drei Streifen gegen Puma. Zwei verfeindete Brüder im Kampf um die Weltmarktführerschaft* (Frankfurt/New York: Campus Verlag, 2005).

11 J. Staun, 'The Fall of the ISL', *Play the Game*, 2 June 2006.

collapse, as it was not successful in selling the broadcast time it had acquired at such a high price.[12] While contracts for the World Cup in 2002 and 2006[13] somewhat alleviated the liquidity troubles, it seems that they were too little too late. ISMM declared bankruptcy in 2001, with total debts of more than US$300 million.[14]

FIFA immediately initiated legal action against ISMM, claiming that ISMM had failed to make a previously agreed payment to FIFA of US$60 million, which represented 75 per cent of the income ISMM received from selling television rights for the 2002 and 2006 World Cups to Brazil and Japan.[15] During the investigations concerning the money owed to FIFA, allegations of widespread bribery on the part of ISMM emerged. FIFA withdrew its lawsuit and decided not to press charges, perhaps to quell the bribery scandal, which involved FIFA itself.[16]

The public prosecutor, Thomas Hildbrand, who investigated FIFA's original legal action, continued his investigation into the alleged financial crimes, including examining the offices of Joseph Blatter, the FIFA general secretary.[17] Hildbrand questioned the fact that FIFA had consistently granted broadcasting rights to ISMM.[18] According to the court, ISMM transferred approximately Fr138 million (US$166 million) in bribes to sports organisations and individual sports officials between 1989 and 2001.[19]

ISMM negotiated contracts worth billions of dollars, gaining the broadcasting rights from the IOC, FIFA, International Association of Athletics Federations, International Organization for Swimmers, International Basketball Federation, Confederation of African Football, Union of European Football Associations, Olympic Council of Asia, Association of Tennis Professionals and others.[20] Investigators discovered that between 1989 and 2001 US$21 million was transferred to persons who had a direct or indirect connection to contracts with ISMM.[21] The primary suspect, Jean-Marie Weber, remains silent on the beneficiaries of these payments. Nevertheless, the liquidator, Thomas Bauer, has revealed a few names.[22] Nicolas Leoz of Paraguay, a member of FIFA's managing committee and president of the South American Football Association, allegedly received US$250,000.[23] His former colleague on the FIFA managing committee, Muhidin Ndolanga of Tanzania, allegedly received US$20,000.[24] The former secretary general of the Olympic Council of Asia, Abdul Muttaleb of Kuwait, is alleged to have gained US$6 million.[25]

Around US$3 million went to a company named Renford Investment Ltd, owned by former FIFA

---

12 Ibid.
13 *Süddeutsche Zeitung* (Germany), 13 March 2008.
14 J. Staun, 2006.
15 *Der Bund* (Switzerland), 1 April 2008; *SonntagsZeitung* (Switzerland), 20 January 2008.
16 *NZZ Folio* (Switzerland), May 2006; *Der Bund* (Switzerland), 31 March 2008; *Neue Zürcher Zeitung* (Switzerland), 25 November 2008.
17 swissinfo, 11 March 2008; J. Staun, 'The Globo Money that Never Showed up', *Play the Game*, 2 June 2006.
18 *NZZ Folio* (Switzerland), May 2006.
19 J. Weinreich, 'Swiss Judge Reveals Sport's Largest Corruption Scandal Ever in Trial against FIFA Partners', *Play the Game*, 13 March 2008
20 *Berliner Zeitung* (Germany), 13 March 2008.
21 *Der Spiegel* (Germany), 23 February 2008; *Der Speigel* (Germany), 12 March 2008.
22 *Die Weltwoche* (Switzerland), 27 March 2008; Spiegel Online (Germany), 2 September 2008.
23 *Der Spiegel* (Germany), 12 March 2008.
24 *Der Spiegel* (Germany), 29 February 2008.
25 *Der Spiegel* (Germany), 12 March 2008.

president, João Havelange, and his former son-in-law, Ricardo Teixeira. Renford was ostensibly a transport company but, in fact, it was a front firm.[26] Havelange tried to appoint Teixeira as president of FIFA.[27] Teixeira was the president of the Brazilian Football Confederation and already had a position in the FIFA committee. In an unrelated case, he was accused by the board of inquiry of the National Congress in Brazil of money-laundering and tax evasion.[28]

Six ISMM managers were ultimately charged. One of them, former ISMM chief executive officer Christoph Malms, holds that bribery was necessary and not uncommon in the sports business.[29] Without these payments, he said, ISMM's existence would not have been secure. According to Malms, seeking preferential treatment from sports officials was a common practice right from the first days of ISMM. Malms also claims that more people should be held accountable in the case; he alleges that a lawyer's office in Zurich knew about the two foundations, Nunca and Sunbow, and that the federal tax authorities gave their consent.[30]

The prosecution requested imprisonment of up to four and a half years for the six ISMM managers on charges of embezzlement, fraud, the preferential treatment of a creditor, harming creditors and fraudulent bankruptcy.[31] The court acquitted the six managers of most of the charges, clearing three of all charges. The remaining defendants received moderate fines. Two managers were fined Fr30,000 and Fr12,000 for false certification. Weber, the main defendant, was fined Fr84,000 for embezzlement. One of the main accusations against ISMM, however, is that of the illegal payments accorded to different sports officials.[32] As expected, the payment of these bribes remained without criminal consequences for either ISMM or the bribe recipients.[33] Moreover, the six accused received a total compensation of Fr604,000.[34] Ironically, they earned a healthy profit.

Why private sector bribery needs stronger punishment in Switzerland

The legal treatment of corruption has intensified in Switzerland in recent years. The legal framework for addressing private-to-private corruption differs from public sector corruption in many respects, however. Public sector corruption is addressed by the Swiss Criminal Code, while private sector corruption is taken up by the Act against Unfair Practices of 1986. While the Criminal Code allows in the case of corruption for investigations by the public prosecutor,[35] private corruption cases must be initiated by a private individual in order for the bribe-giver or bribe-taker to face legal consequences.[36] The problem with this arrangement is that often no specific individuals are directly injured or aware

26 *Die Weltwoche* (Switzerland), 27 March 2008.
27 *NZZ Folio* (Switzerland), May 2006.
28 Ibid.
29 *Der Spiegel* (Germany), 12 March 2008.
30 *Berliner Zeitung* (Germany), 13 March 2008; *Der Spiegel* (Germany), 12 March 2008.
31 *Der Spiegel* (Germany), 29 February 2008.
32 J. Weinreich,'Krumme Geschäfte mit dem Sport', Deutschlandfunk (Germany), 2 July 2008.
33 Act against Unfair Practices, 19 December 1986, article 4a. This article was added in 2005 in the course of approving legislation of the Europe Council's Criminal Law Convention on Corruption and its Additional Protocol. This article prohibits private bribes. As the article was adopted in 2005, it was not yet valid in the ISMM case, in which bribes were paid until 2001.
34 *NZZ Folio* (Switzerland), 3 July 2008.
35 Swiss Criminal Code, 21 December 1937, article 322 (iii) to (viii).
36 Act against Unfair Practices, 19 December 1986, article 23, which defines private corruption as an offence that requires a report.

of its damage. Therefore, in many cases no investigation is initiated.

In the ISMM case, there was no plaintiff to denounce the bribe payments. Instead, the federal court found a creative way to address the bribery by arguing that contracts negotiated as a result of bribery are immoral and thus void by law.[37] In its relevant precedent ruling[38] from 1993, however, the federal court makes an important distinction between the negotiation and the content of a contract. Only contracts that purport bribe transfers are immoral and therefore void by law; negotiation due to bribe transfers is not.[39] Under this logic, the US$166 million that ISMM transferred through contracts to sports organisations and officials was completely legal. The court in Zug followed this logic, as the bribe payments were mentioned in the final judgment but were not part of the sentence. The judge's justification was that ISMM declared the bribes as costs for the acquisition of contracts and essential for the company's survival. Immoral contracts are not always compelling or damaging.[40]

The complicated cash flow that ISMM used to pay sports officials cannot be considered money-laundering in Switzerland, because the Swiss Criminal Code says that laundered money must be derived from criminal acts. Since private corruption is not labelled as a major crime but as a misdemeanour, the criteria for money-laundering are not met.[41]

There is a question about the legal treatment of FIFA as a bribe-taker. At the time, passive corruption was not illegal, as Switzerland did not implement the Council of Europe Criminal Law Convention on Corruption until 2006. Because the bribery occurred before this, it was not illegal. FIFA had to assume a share of the investigation costs, however, because it triggered the prosecution against ISMM.[42]

The ISMM case shows that private corruption is still a problem in Switzerland because the legal foundations are insufficient. Even though the Council of Europe Criminal Law Convention has been adopted, private corruption is not being treated as an official crime. Until it is, it is likely that only a few, if any, sentences for private corruption will be handed down in Switzerland. To change this situation, Swiss lawmakers should declare private corruption an official crime to be prosecuted by the authorities. Private corruption should also be defined as a major crime instead of a misdemeanour in order to meet the qualifications for money-laundering.

Carla Gasser (TI Switzerland)

Additional reading

N. Giannakopoulos, *Criminalité organisée et corruption en Suisse* (Berne: Verlag Paul Haupt, 2001).

J. Jessel and P. Mendelewitsch, *La face cachée du foot business* (Paris: Flammarion, 2007).

N. Queloz, *Processus de corruption en Suisse: Résultats de recherche, analyse critique du cadre légal et de sa mise en œuvre, stratégie de prévention et de riposte* (Basel: Helbing & Lichtenhahn, 2000).

J. Weinreich, *Korruption im Sport: Mafiose Dribblings, organisiertes Schweigen* (Leipzig: Forum Verlag, 2006).

TI Switzerland: www.transparency.ch.

---

37 *Der Bund* (Switzerland), 1 April 2008; Bill of Indictment.
38 Federal Court decision BGE 119 II 380 (consideration 4b&c).
39 Federal Court decision BGE 119 II 380 (consideration 4c).
40 Author's notes from the pronouncement of judgment on 2 July 2008.
41 TI, *Global Corruption Report 2006* (London: Pluto Press, 2005).
42 NZZ online (Switzerland), 2 July 2008.

United Kingdom

Corruption Perceptions Index 2008: 7.7 (16th out of 180 countries)

Conventions

Council of Europe Civil Law Convention on Corruption (signed June 2000; not yet ratified)

Council of Europe Criminal Law Convention on Corruption (signed January 1999; ratified December 2003)

OECD Convention on Combating Bribery of Foreign Public Officials (signed December 1997; ratified December 1998)

UN Convention against Corruption (signed December 2003; ratified February 2006)

UN Convention against Transnational Organized Crime (signed December 2000, ratified February 2006)

Legal and institutional changes

- In July 2007 the prime minister, Gordon Brown, appointed John Hutton, secretary of state for business, enterprise and regulatory reform, as the ministerial anti-corruption champion. Hutton's mandate is to work with other UK ministers to deliver the United Kingdom's 2007/8 Anti-Corruption Action Plan, focusing on improving the effectiveness of mechanisms, domestically and abroad, to counter international corruption.
- In November 2007 the Law Commission published a consultation paper that proposes a new offence of bribery, criminalising both active and passive bribery, and making no distinction between private sector and public sector bribery. The proposal would apply to acts abroad by UK nationals and foreign nationals living in England and Wales. The commission invited comments by March 2008 and will publish its final report and draft bill in autumn 2008.
- The government's Constitutional Renewal White Paper and Draft Bill removes the need

for the attorney general (AG) to consent to the prosecution of corruption offences. It also contains a disturbing new power for the AG to intervene in investigations and prosecutions of foreign bribery to safeguard 'national security', however. A certificate signed by a single minister confirming that the AG's intervention is necessary for this purpose would be regarded as sufficient justification. In July 2007 a Joint Parliamentary Committee report recommended that the AG should retain the power to give a direction in relation to any individual case, including cases relating to national security, on a non-statutory basis, and that the government should establish a procedure for the AG to report to parliament when he or she gives a direction in relation to an individual case. The committee took the view that, if the government decided to remove the AG's power to give a direction in an individual case, the AG should retain the power to intervene for the purpose of safeguarding national security, subject to the requirement to report to parliament.

- Granted royal assent in May 2008, the Criminal Justice and Immigration Act 2008 extends the Serious Fraud Office's (SFO's) powers to compel the production of documents and explanations of them during the vetting stage of foreign bribery cases. It is hoped that these powers, which came into effect in summer 2008, will make it easier for the SFO to determine whether investigations should be opened.

Corruption and the private sector in the United Kingdom

While not a widespread concern in the country, domestic corruption in the private sector is not unheard of. In March 2008 the police investigated allegations that a senior manager of transportation contractor Metronet awarded contracts worth £850,000 (US$1.26 million) to a company with which he had close business links and which appeared to be totally unqualified to undertake a project to refurbish London's Oxford Circus subway station.[1]

Surveys have highlighted concerns about corruption in specific industry sectors. For example, a 2006 survey of corruption in the UK construction industry undertaken by the Chartered Institute of Building (CIOB) revealed that:[2]

- 41 per cent of respondents had been offered a bribe at least once;
- 41 per cent of 335 construction professionals think corruption is widespread;
- 56 and 57 per cent of respondents feel bribery to obtain planning permission and contracts, respectively, are serious problems;

- more than two-thirds feel the UK construction industry is not doing enough to tackle corruption; and
- three-quarters do not feel the UK government is doing enough to tackle the problem.

Turning to the problem of foreign bribery, recent surveys indicate varying levels of awareness and attitudes in the UK business community towards corruption. KPMG's 2007 *Overseas Bribery and Corruption Survey* reveals that a large majority of respondents were aware that, under the UK Anti-Terrorism, Crime and Security Act, UK citizens can be prosecuted for an act of bribery committed wholly overseas. Of these respondents, however, almost a third said they had taken no action to communicate this to their employees. A half of these respondents said they 'did not think it was relevant to their business'.[3]

Surveys by Control Risks and Simmons & Simmons[4] show that awareness of UK laws against foreign bribery may be decreasing over time. In 2002, the year the act came into force, 68 per cent of respondents said they were familiar with its main points. By 2006 only 28 per cent said they had detailed knowledge of the law, and 48 per cent were totally ignorant of it. According to the same survey, about 90 per cent of UK respondents had adopted codes explicitly addressing bribery and facilitation payments. A survey by PricewaterhouseCoopers[5] found a similar incidence of anti-bribery codes in UK companies, but it also found that fewer than a quarter of respondents were confident these codes significantly mitigate corruption risks.

---

1 *Daily Mail* (UK), 13 March 2008.
2 CIOB, *Corruption in the UK Construction Industry: Survey 2006* (Ascot, UK: CIOB, 2006).
3 KPMG, *Overseas Bribery and Corruption Survey* (London: KPMG, 2007).
4 Control Risks and Simmons & Simmons, *International Business Attitudes to Corruption – Survey 2006* (London: Control Risks/Simmons & Simmons, 2006); Control Risks, *International Business Attitudes to Corruption – Survey 2002* (London: Control Risks, 2002).
5 PricewaterhouseCoopers, *Confronting Corruption: The Business Case for an Effective Anti-corruption Programme* (London: PricewaterhouseCoopers, 2008).

Ernst & Young's 2008 global fraud survey found that 13 per cent of UK respondents had experienced at least one incident of bribery or corruption in the previous two years (compared to 16 per cent in Germany, 6 in France and 24 globally).[6] Eleven per cent of UK respondents admitted that their company had been asked to pay a bribe to retain or win business in the previous two years, compared to 16 per cent in Germany, 13 in the United States and 10 in France.

TI's 2006 Bribe Payers Index ranked the United Kingdom sixth, implying that UK companies have a lower propensity to bribe than twenty-four of the thirty leading exporting countries covered in the survey.[7]

The case of BAe Systems

One of the most prominent and controversial corruption cases involves UK defence company British Aerospace Systems. In December 2006 the United Kingdom's Serious Fraud Office terminated its investigation into BAe Systems' involvement in the 'al-Yamamah' ('the dove') defence contract with Saudi Arabia, claiming that this was necessary to safeguard national and international security. In a deal called 'al-Salam' ('peace'), BAe Systems agreed to sell a reported £20 billion (US$30 billion) worth of combat aircraft to the Saudi air force.[8]

The SFO's investigation, which began in November 2004, focused on suspected false accounting in the 1985 al-Yamamah defence contract, which provided for the sale of combat aircraft and related equipment and services worth some £43 billion (US$64 billion).[9] The media reported the existence of a secret fund established by BAe Systems to channel benefits to Saudi agents in the contract.[10] In 2006 Saudi-owned Swiss bank accounts were said to be under investigation.[11] A year later the UK media alleged that payments exceeding £1 billion (US$1.5 billion) had been paid to a senior Saudi official in connection with the contract, and that these payments had been channelled through a mechanism set up by the UK Ministry of Defence.[12]

BAe Systems has repeatedly denied any wrongdoing.[13] In early 2007 the US Department of Justice (DOJ) started its own investigation into whether BAe Systems had violated the US Foreign Corrupt Practices Act.[14] As of August 2008 the UK government had yet to respond to a DOJ request for mutual legal assistance.[15] The SFO continued its investigations of bribery allegations in defence deals involving BAe Systems in the Czech Republic, Romania, South Africa and Tanzania.[16] In April 2008 the Administrative Court ruled that the SFO had failed in its responsibility. In July 2008 the House of Lords upheld the SFO's appeal and overturned the court's ruling.[17]

The al-Yamamah decision was heavily criticised both within and outside the United Kingdom, notably by prominent UK fund managers. In a

---

6 Ernst & Young, *Corruption or Compliance – Weighing the Costs: 10th Global Fraud Survey* (London: Ernst & Young, 2008).
7 TI, Bribe Payers Index, 2006.
8 Times Online (UK), 19 August 2006; 7 September 2007.
9 *Guardian* (UK), 'Secrets of al-Yamamah'.
10 *Guardian* (UK), 11 September 2003.
11 *Guardian* (UK), 29 November 2006.
12 BBC News (UK), 7 June 2007; 11 June 2007.
13 Ibid.
14 *Guardian* (UK), 14 June 2007; 26 June 2007.
15 *Corporate Counsel Magazine* (US), 20 November 2008.
16 *Daily Telegraph* (UK), 28 November 2008.
17 Associated Press (US), 30 July 2008.

letter to the UK defence procurement minister, F&C Asset Management, which has more than £100 billion (US$150 billion) under management, noted that, while the decision had provided a short-term boost to BAe Systems' share price, 'for long-term investors, bribery and corruption distort and destabilise markets, expose companies to legal liabilities, disadvantage non-corrupt companies and reduce transparency for investors seeking investment opportunities'.[18] In a letter to the then prime minister, Tony Blair, Hermes Pensions Management Ltd said, 'The decision will have a high cost to business and investment ... Further, lack of credibility in the regulation of one company can spread to the rest of the stock market, creating higher risk premiums and cost of capital for all market participants.'[19]

The case of Vetco International

In another prominent case, three subsidiaries of US-based oil and gas company Vetco International Ltd were caught up in an international bribery scheme. In February 2006 Vetco Gray Controls Inc., Vetco Gray Controls Ltd and Vetco Gray UK Ltd pleaded guilty to foreign bribery and were fined US$26 million under a deferred prosecution agreement following their cooperation with the US DOJ. At the time, the fine was the largest criminal fine ever in a DOJ prosecution of an FCPA case.[20]

The three companies admitted that they had violated and conspired to violate the FCPA. At least from September 2002 to April 2005, the companies hired a major international freight-forwarding and customs-clearing company to make at least 378 corrupt payments totalling about US$2.1

million to Nigerian Customs Service officials. The payments were meant to induce them to give the companies 'preferential treatment' during the customs clearance process.[21] Vetco Gray UK had already pleaded guilty in 2004 to violating the FCPA in connection with payments of over US$1 million in bribes to Nigerian officials who were evaluating bids for contracts on Nigerian oil exploration projects.[22]

Under their 2007 plea agreements with the DOJ, the companies agreed to hire an independent monitor to oversee a robust compliance programme, investigate their conduct in various other countries and ensure that, if any of the companies were sold, the purchaser would be bound to these obligations.[23]

Corporate responses

Changes in the UK and international regulatory environment, increasing concerns about reputational risks related to corruption and bribery, and the inclusion of corruption and bribery in corporate social responsibility reporting are eliciting responses within the UK corporate world.

In the defence sector, TI UK has helped encourage dialogue among major western European and North American defence companies on anti-corruption standards. In 2006 major UK companies formed the UK Defence Anti-Corruption Forum, and the AeroSpace and Defence Industries Association of Europe (ASD) established an Ethics and Anti-Corruption Working Group. After almost two years of negotiations, all thirty European defence industry associations agreed in 2008 to a common set of anti-bribery standards – the Common Industry Standards

---

18 *Guardian* (UK), 22 December 2006.
19 Letter from Mark Anson, chief executive of Hermes, to Tony Blair, 22 December 2006.
20 DOJ, 'Three Vetco International Ltd Subsidiaries Plead Guilty to Foreign Bribery and Agree to Pay $26 Million in Criminal Fines', press release, 6 February 2007.
21 Ibid.
22 Ibid.
23 DOJ, press release, 6 February 2007.

(CIS).[24] It is hoped that this will stimulate the development of a robust set of standards for the global defence industry. The UK Defence Manufacturers Association (DMA) and the Society of British Aerospace Companies (SBAC) have published a practical toolkit to explain the significance of the CIS, why defence companies should adopt them and how companies can implement them effectively.[25]

The al-Yamamah investigation may have been a major factor leading BAe Systems' board in 2007 to establish an independent external committee chaired by Lord Woolf, former Lord Chief Justice of England and Wales, to report publicly on the company's ethical policies and processes. In May 2008 the Woolf Committee made twenty-three recommendations to strengthen BAe Systems' ethical standards, including:

- adopting a global code of ethical business conduct, applied throughout the company regardless of location, unless local laws require a higher standard;
- appointing a senior executive responsible for implementing the code, reporting to the CEO and with direct access to the chair of the corporate responsibility committee; and
- regular assessments of business conduct, practice and progress by external auditors.[26]

If implemented and monitored rigorously and consistently, the Woolf recommendations would go a long way towards reducing the company's vulnerability to corruption. Given the gravity of the al-Yamamah case and its damage to both BAe Systems and the United Kingdom, however, it was disappointing that the committee did not recommend that BAe Systems

(as well as the UK and Saudi governments) specifically confirm that the new al-Salam contract was based on currently recognised principles of corporate integrity.

UK companies still have a long way to go to increase their awareness and adopt robust anti-bribery compliance programmes. Sectoral approaches that encourage companies to take industry-wide initiatives may be more successful, as creating a level playing field within a sector leaves companies less afraid of being at a competitive disadvantage.

Since the OECD Anti-Bribery Convention entered into force, the United States has brought 103 cases, Germany more than forty and France nineteen.[27] The United Kingdom has brought just one case. In light of the al-Yamamah fallout, it is essential for the government to improve its enforcement of the convention and bring more cases to court. The government and companies need to raise their game. Otherwise, the United Kingdom will be perceived as a country that is not serious about fighting international corruption.

TI UK

Additional reading

L. Cockcroft, *Corporate Corruption: Challenges in a Changing World* (London: ICC Commercial Crime Services, 2008).

M. Pyman, P. Foot and P. Fluri (eds.), *Building Transparency and Reducing Corruption in Defence* (Geneva: TI UK, Geneva Centre for Security Policy and Geneva Centre for the Democratic Control of Armed Forces, 2008).

---

24 ASD, 'Common Industry Standards for European Aerospace and Defence' (Brussels: ASD, 2007).
25 DMA and SBAC, 'Tools to Grow Your Business in a Changing Ethical Environment' (London: DMA/SBAC, 2008).
26 Woolf Committee, *Ethical Business Conduct in BAE Systems plc – The Way Forward* (London: Woolf Committee, 2008).
27 See F. Heimann and G. Dell, *Progress Report 2008: Enforcement of the OECD Convention on Combating Bribery of Foreign Public Officials in International Business Transactions* (Berlin: TI, 2008).

M. Pyman, D. Scott, A. Waldron and I. Voika, 'Building Integrity and Reducing Corruption Risk in Defense Establishments', *Connections*, vol. 7, no. 2 (2008).

UK Anti-Corruption Forum, *Fair and Efficient Debarment Procedures* (London: UK Anti-Corruption Forum, 2007).

Preventing Corruption: Guidance for Professional Bodies (London: UK Anti-Corruption Forum, 2008).

TI UK: www.transparency.org.uk.

Part three
Research

Introduction

Robin Hodess[1]

The focus on corruption and bribery continues to drive a number of academic research agendas, spanning legal studies, economics and the social sciences, as part of a quest to enhance our understanding of policy drivers, governance and growth. As the analysis of corruption and bribery diversify, so too do the strands of knowledge about this wide-reaching phenomenon, leading to a more subtle understanding of how, when and where our efforts to address it might best be placed. In the *Global Corruption Report 2009*, the research articles selected for publication add to our knowledge bank in a number of areas: from corruption's impact on macroeconomic variables to the critical role of resources in enforcing anti-corruption legislation. Several articles reflect new research into the private sector's role in fighting corruption, in line with the overall thematic focus of this volume.

In his annual review of the Transparency International Corruption Perceptions Index, Johann Graf Lambsdorff underlines the value added of the CPI in its multi-survey approach, as well as the high correlation of views from both in-country and non-local experts about the countries ranked. Lambsdorff also reflects at a broader level about perceived levels of corruption and their impact on economic growth, above all on per capita income, and reports that an improvement in the CPI by one index point would be associated with an increase in income of almost 4 per cent. This demonstrates clearly the devastating impact of corruption on the livelihoods of ordinary people.

Susan Rose-Ackerman takes up the important topic of how to lay the foundations for a low-corruption environment and put countries in the process of institution-building on a path to public accountability. In a comparative analysis of political settlements and institution-building in five post-crisis countries, Angola, Burundi, Guatemala, Kosovo and Mozambique, she finds that anti-corruption measures need to be considered early on and be built into the peace-building process. Rose-Ackerman also emphasises that investors, donors and the international community more broadly can provide important incentives to discourage corruption and help countries build accountable institutions.

Beyond this focus on broad patterns of corruption and their impact on the stability of income and institutions, a number of research articles that follow evaluate the role and views of companies vis-à-vis corruption and bribery. The first of these, reporting on TI's 2008 Bribe Payers Index (BPI), takes stock of expert opinion about corruption that is exported abroad, from the world's most influential economies. Transparency International's Juanita Riaño writes that no country has companies that are viewed as completely clean in terms of bribery abroad – and,

---

1 Robin Hodess is the director of policy and research at Transparency International.

moreover, in some emerging economies, such as India, Mexico, China and Russia, the view of company performance is rather poor. Business leaders indicate that corruption extends beyond companies paying a bribe to 'get the deal' and includes practices of state capture at worrying levels in a number of countries.

Control Risks also assesses senior business people's views on and experiences of corruption and bribery, focusing on central and south-east Europe. In this particular survey, Kristóf Gosztonyi and John Bray find that corruption was viewed as a much larger problem by business leaders in Bulgaria, Romania and Serbia than in central European countries. In Bulgaria, in particular, the experience of corruption in public sector contracts was at a high level. The overall results of the poll show that 'hearsay' or media-driven knowledge of corruption in public sector contracts far exceeded that of contracts awarded in the private sector, with actual experience of corruption at comparable levels across both types of contracts in the countries evaluated. This points to a potential oversight gap in the awarding of private sector contracts, which may need closer scrutiny if all forms of bribery and corruption are to be addressed.

The specific characteristics of African economies, including the rapid rises in investment in some countries and the significance of informal economic activity, make them an interesting setting in which to examine the issue of private sector corruption. Emmanuelle Lavallée and François Roubaud use survey research to analyse the informal economy in sub-Saharan Africa, evaluating the role of corruption therein. Although they conclude that the widespread lack of business registration is due more to weak law enforcement than corruption, they also report that a high proportion (more than one-third) of businesspeople in contact with public agents actually engage in bribery, indicating that bribery is a regular means of dispute settlement with public officials in the informal economy. Clara Delavallade carries out econometric research using survey data on north African firms and shows a link between fiscal evasion at low to medium levels (up to 55 per cent of undeclared sales) and administrative corruption. In countries in which hiding revenue payments is more complete, she points out, firms are less likely to resort to petty bribery, because of the high stakes of the evasion. Delavallade also points to strong evidence that state capture features when firms from the north African region do not have clear property rights, and that low competitiveness and low profitability are both strong drivers of corruption.

A second group of studies complements the analysis of the scale, scope and mechanisms of corruption relevant to the private sector and examines the use and efficacy of integrity and enforcement measures.

Susan Côte-Freeman focuses on company disclosure of anti-corruption efforts and reports on a Transparency International survey, called Transparency in Reporting on Anti-Corruption (TRAC), of 500 leading firms. TRAC evaluates companies' public reporting on anti-corruption strategies, policies and management systems. While recognising that non-financial reporting is relatively new and that the criteria for anti-corruption reporting are not yet standardised, the results of TRAC nevertheless reflect weak reporting by many of the world's largest companies, with an average score of just 17 out of a possible 50. Canadian and US companies report more than most, while firms from a number of critical emerging markets, such as Russia and China, show weak reporting practices. Although TRAC does not report on corruption per se, its focus on disclosure highlights the important role that reporting has in strengthening corporate governance and sustainable business practices.

In a similar study on reporting practices, TI focused on the oil and gas sector and on the critical role of transparency in revenue payments as a means of reversing the 'resource curse', whereby many resource-rich countries stubbornly remain some of the poorest in the world. Reflecting on the results of this study, which examined the reporting practices of forty-two oil and gas companies in twenty-one countries of operation, Juanita Olaya points out that transparency in revenue payments is not yet the norm in the industry. Wide variation in company practices indicates that the standard could be raised, however. Home-country regulation of companies, as well as stock market listing, seem to have a strong effect on reporting practices, with the upshot that both companies and governments need to do more to turn the tide towards greater transparency in the sector. As with the TRAC study, the results suggest that clear and widely-adopted standards for anti-corruption reporting would aid in these corporate efforts to reduce corruption's ill effects on business.

Most of the above research reflects on company practices with regard to corruption – practices that are often dependent on the enabling environment and the capacity of regulation to create a level playing field for firms. What emerges clearly is that addressing the role of companies in bribery and corruption requires strong effort by the entire spectrum of stakeholders, especially by governments.

For the past several years Transparency International has carried out assessments of the progress of OECD countries in implementing the OECD Convention on Combating Bribery of Foreign Public Officials in International Business Transactions, frequently called the OECD Anti-Bribery Convention. Utilising expert assessment, TI provides a benchmark of OECD implementation by looking at a number of indicators, from the number of cases brought under the convention, the institutional set-ups – such as for whistleblower protection – that are critical for implementation and the legal hindrances to enforcement. In 2008 thirty-four countries were included in the TI Progress Report. The findings are mixed: while enforcement has grown in some OECD countries, such as France, Germany and the United States, there remains little or no enforcement in others, such as Canada, Japan and the United Kingdom. A parallel finding with the research on company disclosure, presented above, is the weak provision for access to information in twenty-four of the thirty-four countries reviewed.

The call for more effective implementation of the OECD Anti-Bribery Convention is also supported by another research article: Alvaro Cuervo-Cazurra finds that implementation of laws against foreign bribery stand the best chance of demonstrating success if they are coordinated across countries. Using foreign direct investment flows, he establishes that investors from countries that have implemented laws against foreign bribery show signs of greater sensitivity towards – as evidenced by less investment in – countries reputed for their high corruption risks. These findings also point to the influential role that a key stakeholder – investors – may be playing in the fight against corruption.

Howell Jackson and Mark Roe show that the public enforcement of securities laws can be as powerful as private enforcement, with the latter most often achieved though lawsuits. This dispels the myth that regulatory agencies can have only a limited impact on financial markets. Two important and often overlooked factors for the success of public enforcement of rules, say Jackson and Roe, are staffing and budgets. Moreover, strong public enforcement is overwhelmingly reflected in better market outcomes. This finding offers important lessons for developing countries, where fundamental decisions taken regarding institutional development need to be linked to resourcing them adequately.

John Coffee brings together the strands of analysis of the previous articles – on the implementation of laws and financial market valuation – in his review of US and UK enforcement intensity and style. In so doing, he demonstrates again that budgets, staffing and modalities of enforcement are all crucial aspects of understanding whether securities regulation is effective. The lesson here is clear. If the regulation of markets is to increase in the coming years, to respond to investor and societal demand for greater transparency and stronger controls of corruption, then adequate resources must be available for new laws to be effective.

Finally, Alexander Dyck, Natalya Volchkova and Luigi Zingales shine the spotlight on the power of another anti-corruption stakeholder, the news media, in a unique study of the Russian market in the late 1990s. By assessing the strategy and impact of a leading investment fund, the authors determine that appeals to the international, above all English-language, financial news media effected significant impact on the willingness of Russian companies to redress alleged corporate governance violations. Media attention seemed to prompt interest and intervention from regulators and other political actors, indicating that public scrutiny *does* have a correcting effect on alleged corporate wrongdoing. This is encouraging for the fight against corruption, from a number of perspectives, since it underlines the crucial role of the free press and again emphasises the need for dramatic improvements, by companies and governments alike, in disclosing information about their efforts to curb corrupt practices. Public awareness, combined with activism, constitutes a powerful antidote to the secrecy in which corruption thrives.

7 Macro-perspective and micro-insights into the scale of corruption: focus on business

Corruption Perceptions Index 2008
Johann Graf Lambsdorff[1]

The Corruption Perceptions Index (CPI), now in its fourteenth year, ranks countries in terms of the degree to which businesspeople and country analysts perceive corruption to exist among public officials and politicians. The CPI ranks 180 countries. It draws on thirteen different polls and surveys from eleven independent institutions, using data published or compiled between 2007 and 2008. The data sources include the Asian Development Bank, the African Development Bank, the Bertelsmann Transformation Index, the World Bank's Country Policy and Institutional Assessment, the Economist Intelligence Unit, Freedom House's Nations in Transit, Global Insight, IMD International World Competitiveness Center, Merchant International Group, Political and Economic Risk Consultancy and the World Economic Forum. The statistical work is carried out at the University of Passau, and the CPI 2008 was published by Transparency International in September 2008.

The strength of the CPI lies in its combination of multiple data sources in a single index, so that erratic findings from one source can be balanced by at least two other sources. This reduces the probability of misrepresenting a country's perceived level of corruption. Involving local businesspeople and country analysts alongside non-resident experts is also an advantage. It makes it possible to recognise the specificities of local customs through the views of local experts, while at the same time enhancing the consistency of judgment across countries by involving non-residents. The high correlation between the different sources used in the CPI indicates that methodological differences between sources have only a minor impact on the findings. In an area in which objective data is not available, such an approach helps our understanding of real levels of corruption.

Poverty and corruption

A simple plot reveals a close association between a good performance in the CPI 2008 and income per head. This is in line with academic research.[2] Estimates suggest that an

---

1 Johann Graf Lambsdorff holds the chair in economic theory at the University of Passau, Germany, and is a senior research adviser for Transparency International.

2 For an overview of related contributions, see J. Lambsdorff, *The Institutional Economics of Corruption and Reform: Theory, Policy and Evidence* [paperback version] (Cambridge: Cambridge University Press, 2008).

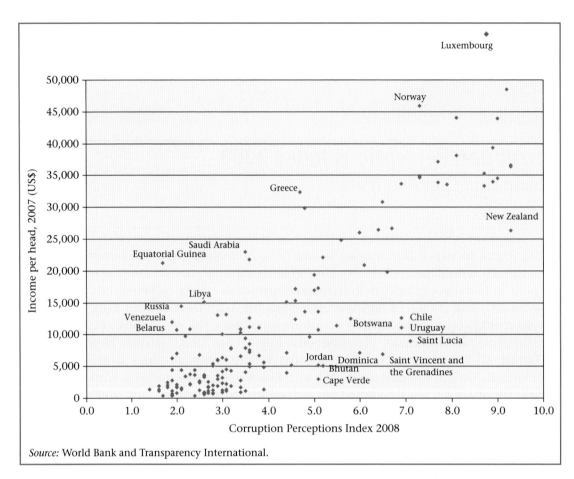

Figure 12: Corruption and poverty

improvement in the CPI by one index point (out of ten) is associated with higher productivity, a growth in capital inflows equivalent to 0.8 per cent of a country's GDP and an increase in average income by almost 4 per cent. These figures can help each country assess the annual losses that arise due to corruption.

Poverty does not necessarily need to entrap a country in a downward spiral of bad governance and economic deprivation, however. As highlighted in figure 12, countries such as Bhutan, Botswana, Cape Verde, Chile, Jordan, Uruguay and some Caribbean islands continue to exhibit relatively low levels of perceived corruption despite being relatively low-income. Some of these countries can thus provide inspiration for reform. At the same time, several countries rich in natural resources perform particularly badly. This provides a graphic demonstration of the well-known resource curse.

A more detailed description of the methodology and related research is available at www.transparency.org and at www.icgg.org.

Table 13: Corruption Perceptions Index 2008

Country rank	Country/territory	2008 CPI score[a]	Surveys used[b]	Confidence range[c]
1	Denmark	9.3	6	9.1–9.4
	New Zealand	9.3	6	9.2–9.5
	Sweden	9.3	6	9.2–9.4
4	Singapore	9.2	9	9.0–9.3
5	Finland	9.0	6	8.4–9.4
	Switzerland	9.0	6	8.7–9.2
7	Iceland	8.9	5	8.1–9.4
	Netherlands	8.9	6	8.5–9.1
9	Australia	8.7	8	8.2–9.1
	Canada	8.7	6	8.4–9.1
11	Luxembourg	8.3	6	7.8–8.8
12	Austria	8.1	6	7.6–8.6
	Hong Kong	8.1	8	7.5–8.6
14	Germany	7.9	6	7.5–8.2
	Norway	7.9	6	7.5–8.3
16	Ireland	7.7	6	7.5–7.9
	United Kingdom	7.7	6	7.2–8.1
18	Belgium	7.3	6	7.2–7.4
	Japan	7.3	8	7.0–7.6
	United States	7.3	8	6.7–7.7
21	Saint Lucia	7.1	3	6.6–7.3
22	Barbados	7.0	4	6.5–7.3
23	Chile	6.9	7	6.5–7.2
	France	6.9	6	6.5–7.3
	Uruguay	6.9	5	6.5–7.2
26	Slovenia	6.7	8	6.5–7.0
27	Estonia	6.6	8	6.2–6.9
28	Qatar	6.5	4	5.6–7.0
	Saint Vincent and the Grenadines	6.5	3	4.7–7.3
	Spain	6.5	6	5.7–6.9
31	Cyprus	6.4	3	5.9–6.8
32	Portugal	6.1	6	5.6–6.7
33	Dominica	6.0	3	4.7–6.8

Table 13 (continued)

Country rank	Country/territory	2008 CPI score[a]	Surveys used[b]	Confidence range[c]
	Israel	6.0	6	5.6–6.3
35	United Arab Emirates	5.9	5	4.8–6.8
36	Botswana	5.8	6	5.2–6.4
	Malta	5.8	4	5.3–6.3
	Puerto Rico	5.8	4	5.0–6.6
39	Taiwan	5.7	9	5.4–6.0
40	South Korea	5.6	9	5.1–6.3
41	Mauritius	5.5	5	4.9–6.4
	Oman	5.5	5	4.5–6.4
43	Bahrain	5.4	5	4.3–5.9
	Macao	5.4	4	3.9–6.2
45	Bhutan	5.2	5	4.5–5.9
	Czech Republic	5.2	8	4.8–5.9
47	Cape Verde	5.1	3	3.4–5.6
	Costa Rica	5.1	5	4.8–5.3
	Hungary	5.1	8	4.8–5.4
	Jordan	5.1	7	4.0–6.2
	Malaysia	5.1	9	4.5–5.7
52	Latvia	5.0	6	4.8–5.2
	Slovakia	5.0	8	4.5–5.3
54	South Africa	4.9	8	4.5–5.1
55	Italy	4.8	6	4.0–5.5
	Seychelles	4.8	4	3.7–5.9
57	Greece	4.7	6	4.2–5.0
58	Lithuania	4.6	8	4.1–5.2
	Poland	4.6	8	4.0–5.2
	Turkey	4.6	7	4.1–5.1
61	Namibia	4.5	6	3.8–5.1
62	Croatia	4.4	8	4.0–4.8
	Samoa	4.4	3	3.4–4.8
	Tunisia	4.4	6	3.5–5.5
65	Cuba	4.3	4	3.6–4.8
	Kuwait	4.3	5	3.3–5.2

Table 13 (continued)

Country rank	Country/territory	2008 CPI score[a]	Surveys used[b]	Confidence range[c]
67	El Salvador	3.9	5	3.2–4.5
	Georgia	3.9	7	3.2–4.6
	Ghana	3.9	6	3.4–4.5
70	Colombia	3.8	7	3.3–4.5
	Romania	3.8	8	3.4–4.2
72	Bulgaria	3.6	8	3.0–4.3
	China	3.6	9	3.1–4.3
	Macedonia	3.6	6	2.9–4.3
	Mexico	3.6	7	3.4–3.9
	Peru	3.6	6	3.4–4.1
	Suriname	3.6	4	3.3–4.0
	Swaziland	3.6	4	2.9–4.3
	Trinidad and Tobago	3.6	4	3.1–4.0
80	Brazil	3.5	7	3.2–4.0
	Burkina Faso	3.5	7	2.9–4.2
	Morocco	3.5	6	3.0–4.0
	Saudi Arabia	3.5	5	3.0–3.9
	Thailand	3.5	9	3.0–3.9
85	Albania	3.4	5	3.3–3.4
	India	3.4	10	3.2–3.6
	Madagascar	3.4	7	2.8–4.0
	Montenegro	3.4	5	2.5–4.0
	Panama	3.4	5	2.8–3.7
	Senegal	3.4	7	2.9–4.0
	Serbia	3.4	6	3.0–4.0
92	Algeria	3.2	6	2.9–3.4
	Bosnia and Herzegovina	3.2	7	2.9–3.5
	Lesotho	3.2	5	2.3–3.8
	Sri Lanka	3.2	7	2.9–3.5
96	Benin	3.1	6	2.8–3.4
	Gabon	3.1	4	2.8–3.3
	Guatemala	3.1	5	2.3–4.0
	Jamaica	3.1	5	2.8–3.3

Table 13 (continued)

Country rank	Country/territory	2008 CPI score[a]	Surveys used[b]	Confidence range[c]
	Kiribati	3.1	3	2.5–3.4
	Mali	3.1	6	2.8–3.3
102	Bolivia	3.0	6	2.8–3.2
	Djibouti	3.0	4	2.2–3.3
	Dominican Republic	3.0	5	2.7–3.2
	Lebanon	3.0	4	2.2–3.6
	Mongolia	3.0	7	2.6–3.3
	Rwanda	3.0	5	2.7–3.2
	Tanzania	3.0	7	2.5–3.3
109	Argentina	2.9	7	2.5–3.3
	Armenia	2.9	7	2.6–3.1
	Belize	2.9	3	1.8–3.7
	Moldova	2.9	7	2.4–3.7
	Solomon Islands	2.9	3	2.5–3.2
	Vanuatu	2.9	3	2.5–3.2
115	Egypt	2.8	6	2.4–3.2
	Malawi	2.8	6	2.4–3.1
	Maldives	2.8	4	1.7–4.3
	Mauritania	2.8	7	2.2–3.7
	Niger	2.8	6	2.4–3.0
	Zambia	2.8	7	2.5–3.0
121	Nepal	2.7	6	2.4–3.0
	Nigeria	2.7	7	2.3–3.0
	São Tomé and Principe	2.7	3	2.1–3.1
	Togo	2.7	6	1.9–3.7
	Vietnam	2.7	9	2.4–3.1
126	Eritrea	2.6	5	1.7–3.6
	Ethiopia	2.6	7	2.2–2.9
	Guyana	2.6	4	2.4–2.7
	Honduras	2.6	6	2.3–2.9
	Indonesia	2.6	10	2.3–2.9
	Libya	2.6	5	2.2–3.0
	Mozambique	2.6	7	2.4–2.9

Table 13 (continued)

Country rank	Country/territory	2008 CPI score[a]	Surveys used[b]	Confidence range[c]
	Uganda	2.6	7	2.2–3.0
134	Comoros	2.5	3	1.9–3.0
	Nicaragua	2.5	6	2.2–2.7
	Pakistan	2.5	7	2.0–2.8
	Ukraine	2.5	8	2.2–2.8
138	Liberia	2.4	4	1.8–2.8
	Paraguay	2.4	5	2.0–2.7
	Tonga	2.4	3	1.9–2.6
141	Cameroon	2.3	7	2.0–2.7
	Iran	2.3	4	1.9–2.5
	Philippines	2.3	9	2.1–2.5
	Yemen	2.3	5	1.9–2.8
145	Kazakhstan	2.2	6	1.8–2.7
	Timor-Leste	2.2	4	1.8–2.5
147	Bangladesh	2.1	7	1.7–2.4
	Kenya	2.1	7	1.9–2.4
	Russia	2.1	8	1.9–2.5
	Syria	2.1	5	1.6–2.4
151	Belarus	2.0	5	1.6–2.5
	Central African Republic	2.0	5	1.9–2.2
	Côte d´Ivoire	2.0	6	1.7–2.5
	Ecuador	2.0	5	1.8–2.2
	Laos	2.0	6	1.6–2.3
	Papua New Guinea	2.0	6	1.6–2.3
	Tajikistan	2.0	8	1.7–2.3
158	Angola	1.9	6	1.5–2.2
	Azerbaijan	1.9	8	1.7–2.1
	Burundi	1.9	6	1.5–2.3
	Congo, Republic	1.9	6	1.8–2.0
	Gambia	1.9	5	1.5–2.4
	Guinea-Bissau	1.9	3	1.8–2.0
	Sierra Leone	1.9	5	1.8–2.0
	Venezuela	1.9	7	1.8–2.0

Table 13 (continued)

Country rank	Country/territory	2008 CPI score[a]	Surveys used[b]	Confidence range[c]
166	Cambodia	1.8	7	1.7–1.9
	Kyrgyzstan	1.8	7	1.7–1.9
	Turkmenistan	1.8	5	1.5–2.2
	Uzbekistan	1.8	8	1.5–2.2
	Zimbabwe	1.8	7	1.5–2.1
171	Congo, Democratic Republic	1.7	6	1.6–1.9
	Equatorial Guinea	1.7	4	1.5–1.8
173	Chad	1.6	6	1.5–1.7
	Guinea	1.6	6	1.3–1.9
	Sudan	1.6	6	1.5–1.7
176	Afghanistan	1.5	4	1.1–1.6
177	Haiti	1.4	4	1.1–1.7
178	Iraq	1.3	4	1.1–1.6
	Myanmar	1.3	4	1.0–1.5
180	Somalia	1.0	4	0.5–1.4

[a] '2008 CPI Score' relates to perceptions of the degree of corruption as seen by businesspeople and country analysts, and ranges between 10 (highly clean) and 0 (highly corrupt).
[b] 'Surveys used' refers to the number of surveys that assessed a country's performance. Overall, thirteen surveys and expert assessments were used, and at least three were required for a country to be included in the CPI.
[c] 'Confidence range' provides a range of possible values of the CPI score. This reflects how a country's score may vary, depending on the measurement precision. Nominally, with 5 per cent probability the score is above this range and with another 5 per cent it is below. Particularly when only a few sources are available, however, an unbiased estimate of the mean coverage probability is lower than the nominal value of 90 per cent.

Bribe Payers Index 2008[1]

Juanita Riaño[2]

The Bribe Payers Index 2008 (BPI 2008) ranks twenty-two of the world's most economically influential countries according to the likelihood of their firms to bribe abroad. Transparency International uses this index, with its focus on the supply side of corruption, to complement the

---

1 This section draws on Transparency International's Bribe Payers Index 2008. To download the full report, visit http://transparency.org/policy_research/surveys_indices/bpi.
2 Juanita Riaño coordinates the Bribe Payers Index at Transparency International's Secretariat in Berlin.

findings of the Corruption Perceptions Index, which focuses on the demand side of corruption and records the perception of public sector bribery and bribe-takers. The CPI routinely shows developing countries – those with the greatest economic and governance challenges – performing poorly. The BPI shifts the focus to the international dimension of corruption, looking at the extent to which companies from the industrialised world are viewed as bribing abroad. The results of the BPI indicate the urgent need for those engaged in the fight against corruption to concentrate on the role and responsibility of the private sector in order to stop the flow of corrupt money.

Data sources and methodology

The BPI 2008 is constructed from responses to a survey of 2,742 senior business executives. A minimum of 100 senior business executives were interviewed in twenty-six countries that are important recipients of foreign direct investment (FDI).[3] The businesspeople were selected through a stratification process that took into consideration the size of firms, their sector and their location.

To calculate the BPI 2008, senior business executives who had indicated that they had business relationships with companies headquartered in one of the twenty-two countries to be ranked were asked to score each selected country on a five-point scale system (from 1 = never to 5 = almost always) when answering the question 'How often do firms headquartered in (country name) engage in bribery in this country?'.

The results of these questions provide an informed assessment of the views held by senior business executives on the prevalence of bribery 'exported' from many of the world's strongest economies. To facilitate the creation of the index, the five-point scale is then converted into a ten-point scale system. Since the BPI is meant to reflect views on foreign bribery, assessments of a respondent's own country were not included. The countries are then ranked based on the mean scores obtained for each country.

Results

Table 14 shows the BPI 2008 results. The higher the score for a country the lower the likelihood of companies from this country engaging in bribery when doing business abroad.

Companies from Belgium and Canada are regarded as the least likely to engage in bribery when operating abroad. These two countries are followed closely by the Netherlands and Switzerland. At the other end of the spectrum, respondents ranked companies from Russia and China as those most likely to engage in foreign bribery.

---

3 Argentina, Brazil, Chile, the Czech Republic, Egypt, France, Germany, Ghana, Hungary, India, Indonesia, Japan, Malaysia, Mexico, Morocco, Nigeria, Pakistan, the Philippines, Poland, Russia, Senegal, Singapore, South Africa, South Korea, the United Kingdom and the United States. These countries were selected on the basis of their trade and FDI flows. The combined global imports of goods and services and inflows of foreign direct investment of the twenty-six countries represented 54 per cent of the world total in 2006 (UNCTAD, *Handbook of Statistics* (Geneva: UNCTAD, 2008). See also www.unctad.org/Templates/Page.asp?intItemID=1890&lang=1.

Table 14: Bribe Payers Index 2008

Rank	Country/territory	BPI 2008	Standard deviation	Confidence interval 95%	
				Lower bound	Upper bound
1	Belgium	8.8	2.00	8.5	9.0
1	Canada	8.8	1.80	8.5	9.0
3	Netherlands	8.7	1.98	8.4	8.9
3	Switzerland	8.7	1.98	8.4	8.9
5	Germany	8.6	2.14	8.4	8.8
5	Japan	8.6	2.11	8.3	8.8
5	United Kingdom	8.6	2.10	8.4	8.7
8	Australia	8.5	2.23	8.2	8.7
9	France	8.1	2.48	7.9	8.3
9	Singapore	8.1	2.60	7.8	8.4
9	United States	8.1	2.43	7.9	8.3
12	Spain	7.9	2.49	7.6	8.1
13	Hong Kong	7.6	2.67	7.3	7.9
14	South Africa	7.5	2.78	7.1	8.0
14	South Korea	7.5	2.79	7.1	7.8
14	Taiwan	7.5	2.76	7.1	7.8
17	Brazil	7.4	2.78	7.0	7.7
17	Italy	7.4	2.89	7.1	7.7
19	India	6.8	3.31	6.4	7.3
20	Mexico	6.6	2.97	6.1	7.2
21	China	6.5	3.35	6.2	6.8
22	Russia	5.9	3.66	5.2	6.6

Source: TI Bribe Payers Survey 2008.

It is important to note that no country receives a score of 9 or 10, indicating that all the world's most influential economies were viewed, to some degree, as exporting corruption. As such, all countries need to improve their enforcement of anti-corruption legislation governing the private sector, and no company can be complacent about the strength of its anti-corruption systems along its entire supply chain.

Types of bribery

Other questions in the survey, which was carried out for TI by Gallup International, examine the frequency of three different types of corruption used by companies when operating abroad:

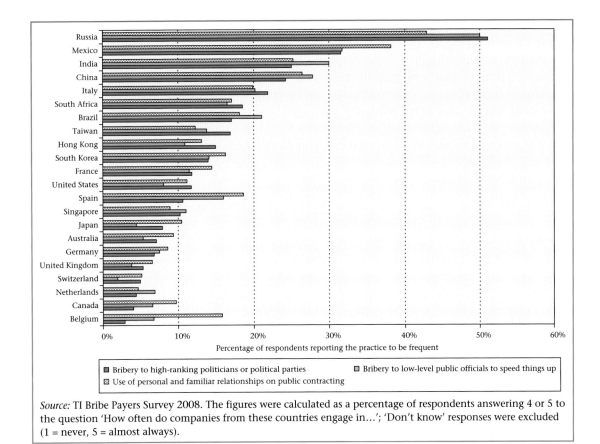

Source: TI Bribe Payers Survey 2008. The figures were calculated as a percentage of respondents answering 4 or 5 to the question 'How often do companies from these countries engage in...'; 'Don't know' responses were excluded (1 = never, 5 = almost always).

Figure 13: Types of foreign bribery

- the bribery of high-ranking politicians or political parties;
- the bribery of low-level public officials to 'speed things up'; and
- the use of personal or familiar relationships to win public contracts.

To evaluate these types of corruption, senior business executives were asked how often companies that they were familiar with and that were headquartered in one of the twenty-two ranked countries engaged in each form of bribery.[4] Figure 13 depicts the results.

Overall, the results from this analysis are consistent with the findings from the BPI 2008. Companies from Russia, Mexico, India and China were reported by respondents to engage most often in the three practices, but to exhibit different patterns of corruption. Examples include the following.

---

4 From the BPI 2008 list of twenty-two countries, business executives from the twenty-six countries surveyed were asked to select up to five countries with which they had had the most business contact when working in their region during the past five years. Only these countries were then evaluated. 0.6 per cent of respondents answered the question for more than five countries, and their responses were also used for the analysis as they did not alter the results.

- About a half of the respondents reported that companies from Russia often bribe high-level politicians and political parties and engage in the bribery of low-level public officials, while somewhat fewer considered it common practice for Russian companies to use personal and familiar relationships to win public contracts.
- Companies from Mexico were reported by 38 per cent of respondents to be likely to use personal and familiar relationships to win public contracts, but only by 32 per cent to bribe high-level politicians, political parties or low-level public officials.
- 30 per cent of respondents indicated that companies from India are likely to bribe low-level public officials to 'speed things up', which was a higher result than the other two types of foreign bribery assessed.

Even top BPI 2008 performers were reported to perform rather poorly in some areas.

- 16 per cent of respondents considered that Belgian companies 'often' or 'almost always' use familiar or personal relationships to win public contracts.
- 10 per cent reported that the use of familiar or personal relationships is 'often' engaged in by Canadian companies when operating abroad.
- 7 per cent of respondents reported that companies headquartered in the Netherlands 'often' engage in bribery to low-level public officials to 'speed things up' when operating abroad.
- 5 per cent of respondents reported that Swiss companies 'often' engage in the bribery of high-ranking politicians or political parties or use personal and familiar relationships to obtain public contracts.

The findings of the 2008 BPI show that many of the world's most influential economies continue to be viewed as greatly compromised by foreign corruption. As a result of these findings, TI therefore calls on governments and the private sector to renew their efforts to curb the supply side of corruption.

Corruption and post-conflict peace-building
Susan Rose-Ackerman[1]

States emerging from conflict are particularly susceptible to corruption. Many of the factors that create corrupt incentives in any society are likely to be simultaneously present in post-conflict environments.

Although corruption is a potential problem in all post-conflict states, the relative importance of the different types of corruption that emerge is shaped by the nature of the conflict and the specific conditions under which the conflict ended.

---

1 Susan Rose-Ackerman is the Henry R. Luce Professor of Law and Political Science at Yale University. This summary draws on S. Rose-Ackerman, 'Corruption and Government', *Journal of International Peacekeeping*, vol. 15, no. 3 (2008); 'Corruption and Post-conflict Peace-building', *Ohio Northern University Law Review*, vol. 34, no. 2 (2008); and 'Corruption in the Wake of Domestic Conflict', in R. Rotberg (ed.), *Corruption and Conflict* (forthcoming 2009).

Several of the following risk factors are likely to be present in post-conflict states:

- weak state institutions operating with unclear and poorly enforced rules;
- large, unique construction projects, often implemented quickly and without strong financial controls following the destruction of infrastructure during the conflict;
- the availability of substantial public resources that do not depend on taxation, especially emergency relief and aid funds, but also including natural resource rents in some cases; and
- the existence of entrenched, organised crime groups, which may have thrived on the arms trade or smuggling during the conflict and may be keen to consolidate their power in post-conflict situations through corruption or state capture.

The character of corruption in post-conflict states

Based on the review of the character and extent of corruption following conflicts in Angola, Burundi, Guatemala, Kosovo and Mozambique, several dimensions emerge as especially important: the nature of the government in power during the conflict; the level of destruction and displacement caused by the conflict; the form of the peace deal; the underlying economic and social conditions; and the role of outsiders, including other states, international institutions and organised crime groups.

These disparate but related cases shed some light on the difficulties of controlling corruption in states emerging from domestic conflict. Peace-building strategies must avoid triggering vicious spirals. Jump-starting the economy by giving monopoly powers to a few prominent people may produce a society that is both lacking in competition and unequal. Decisions taken in the early stages can lock in the power of a small elite, whose vested interests then hold back efforts to increase competition and enhance fairness.

In Angola, Mozambique and Guatemala, the old elites remained in power after the conflict ended. In Angola and Guatemala they were widely perceived as corrupt during the conflict, and in the case of Guatemala they also benefited from links to organised crime, mainly involving the drug trade. The wealth of the elite in Angola came from oil and, to a lesser extent, diamonds. In both countries, these sources of prosperity helped to keep entrenched networks alive, limiting the development not just of competitive politics but also of transparent and effective oversight and law enforcement institutions.

In contrast, levels of corruption in Mozambique increased once peace had been achieved, but this was not the result of the prior corruption of those in power. On the contrary, the end of hostilities provided increased corruption opportunities, through the development of a market economy in the context of a weak state. In addition, international donors allocated funds to pay off former rebels and ease their transition into political parties. Although this may have been an effective way to end the violence, it may also have limited the credibility of anti-corruption efforts.

The situation in Burundi and Kosovo was somewhat different. Former fighters against the previous regime gained control of the government. In Burundi this resulted in a formal power-sharing agreement; in Kosovo it led to Albanian dominance. Burundi became a weak state with widespread competition for illicit gain. Kosovo is beginning to move towards a somewhat more competitive politics, with the ability to penalise corrupt officials at the polls. Unfortunately, the delay in shifting from United Nations to European Union oversight may have limited Kosovo's progress.

Although corruption remains part of the post-conflict environment in all cases, two distinct situations are most troubling. First, corruption can accompany the entrenchment in power of old elites with access to significant rents, from crime or natural resources, as in the cases of Angola and Guatemala. Second, formal power-sharing deals, as in Burundi, can institutionalise corruption. Corruption within one group with a guaranteed share of power may simply encourage other groups, as part of the brokered peace deal, to seek personal enrichment as well.

In Mozambique and Kosovo the outlook is more hopeful. In the former, corruption appears to be a feature of transition, and reformers must ensure that the country does not descend into a vicious spiral. In the latter, despite high-level corruption scandals, corruption appears to be of both political and public salience, with competitive elections providing a check on malfeasance.

Lessons learnt

These cases, despite their variety, provide some general lessons.

Peace agreements following a conflict should incorporate measures to limit corruption. At this point in the process, negotiators might have the necessary leverage to push through anti-corruption reforms that may not be feasible later. These might include measures to ensure transparency and accountability, including free media, to establish an honest, well-paid civil service and to ensure competitive contracting. Furthermore, peace negotiations should not be viewed as a way to divide the rents under state control between different factions. Although transitional governments often have to reach a compromise between different groups, rigid power-sharing can entrench or create corrupt structures.

Anti-corruption efforts need some early and visible victories that fit the capacity of the country. International aid requires careful control and auditing to avoid its misuse. One option is to use trust funds to administer aid programmes, with the ultimate goal of turning over the monitoring to the government. For example, in Mozambique a trust fund to aid political parties accepted foreign donations. In some cases, such as in Mozambique, outside aid can help to incorporate rebel leaders and their followers into the new state as legitimate political actors. Alternatively, outsiders can arrange exile for former leaders: deeply corrupt leaders should be banished, not incorporated into the government.

International donors can review the training and integrity of law enforcement officers, military personnel, judges and prosecutors. International aid can also help integrate former rank and file combatants using financial aid and training. The armed forces and other security services should not be allowed to participate in businesses, either legal or illegal, and kickbacks should be outlawed. Oversight institutions need strengthening in most post-conflict states, but this may be a challenging task if trained personnel are in short supply.

Finally, at the global level, international organisations should work to develop stronger cross-border controls on money-laundering so as to make it difficult to export corrupt gains. Similarly, voluntary international initiatives, such as the Extractive Industries Transparency Initiative, appear to be making a promising start. Even in a resource-rich country such as Angola, these initiatives may have an effect, if supported by multinational investors.

Post-conflict states need strong leadership from the top if they are to move towards the goal of a more legitimate and better-functioning government and if they are to sideline those who have used the state for private gain. International assistance, in principle, can help, but donors need to tailor their assistance in order to avoid exacerbating the underlying problems created by the mixture of corruption and threats of violence from those inside and outside the government.

Public and private sector corruption in central and south-east Europe
Kristóf Gosztonyi and John Bray[1]

The post-socialist transition process in central and south-east Europe has been accompanied by widespread allegations of corruption and economic crime. In recent years, however, considerable progress has been made in the Czech Republic, Hungary and Poland, all of which joined the European Union in 2004. The European Commission issued two reports in July 2008 criticising Romania and – to a greater degree – Bulgaria, however, both of which joined in 2007 but failed to implement adequate institutional reforms to combat economic crime.[2] Meanwhile, questions remain about Serbia, whose new government has now formally expressed its desire to enter the European Union, but which has a long-standing record of corruption and organised crime.

The public debate on these issues raises questions about the impact on business. To what degree do corruption and crime impede economic development? What are companies doing to resist corruption? What should they do?

To find out, Control Risks commissioned a survey in 2007 of 244 international companies operating in six countries: Bulgaria, the Czech Republic, Hungary, Poland, Romania and

---

1 Kristóf Gosztonyi is a senior consultant at the Berlin office of Control Risks. John Bray is director (analysis) at the Tokyo office of Control Risks. Full survey results, published as *Business, Corruption and Economic Crime in Central and South-east Europe*, are available at www.control-risks.com.
2 See Associated Press, 'EU Criticizes Romania and Bulgaria over Lack of Justice Reforms', 4 February 2008.

Serbia.[3] The respondents were mainly senior managers of international companies, including both locals and expatriates.

A distinctive feature of the survey is that respondents were asked both about their *perceptions* of the scale of corruption and about their *concrete knowledge* of particular cases. The latter was defined as 'knowledge from your own experience or from the experience of reliable sources such as friends or colleagues', as distinct from 'media or hearsay' in the case of the former.

Research highlights

One of the most striking features of the responses was the sharp regional divide between central and south-east Europe. South-east European respondents were far more likely to say that corruption was 'very relevant' or 'highly relevant' to their business (see figure 14).

Bulgaria stands out as the country in which respondents were most likely to report first-hand experience of corruption in public sector contracts, as well as demands for bribes to speed up official government transactions.

With regard to competition for public sector contracts, 40.4 per cent of all respondents said that corruption occurs 'often' or 'always' in this context. Respondents in the Czech Republic and Bulgaria were most likely to express this view (see figure 15). A closer examination, however, shows that the number of respondents with concrete knowledge of public sector corruption was significantly higher in Bulgaria. By contrast, 42.5 per cent of Czech respond-

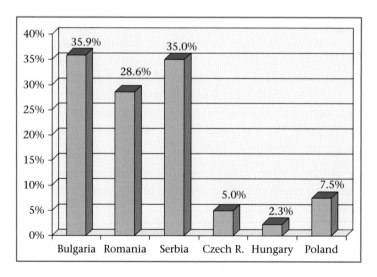

Figure 14: Respondents stating that corruption was 'very relevant' or 'highly relevant' to their business

3 In this study, Bulgaria, Romania and Serbia are considered south-eastern, and the Czech Republic, Hungary and Poland are considered central.

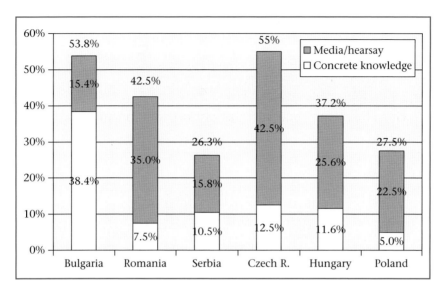

Figure 15: Percentage of respondents from each country stating that corruption took place 'often' and 'always' when companies compete for public sector contracts

ents reported that their knowledge came from the media or hearsay. There was a similar tendency for perception to outweigh concrete experience in the other four countries.

Compared with the results for public sector corruption, a much lower percentage – only 14.6 per cent – reported that private sector corruption occurred 'often' or 'always'. Again, Bulgaria stands out as the country with the highest percentages, indicating widespread perception and experience of corruption (see figure 16).

The greatest contrast with the public sector results is the much lower percentage of respondents reporting high levels of private sector corruption on the basis of 'the media or hearsay'. The most likely explanation is that media and academic attention has focused more on public sector corruption than on private sector bribery. People tend to give higher estimates of public sector corruption because they are more sensitised to the issue, even if it falls outside their direct experience. Concrete knowledge of specific cases was roughly comparable for competition for contracts in both the public and private sectors, however.

Policy implications

Until now, the main international anti-corruption initiatives have concentrated on public rather than private sector corruption. For example, the OECD focuses specifically on the bribery of public officials, in its Convention on Combating Bribery of Foreign Public Officials in International Business Transactions. This is justified, because public sector corruption often involves large amounts of money in connection with major projects financed by taxpayers.

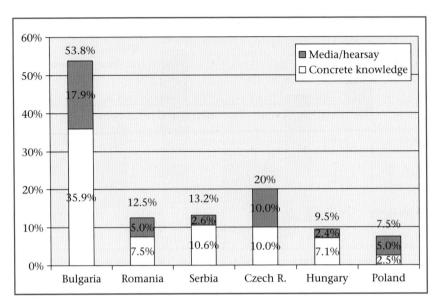

Figure 16: Percentage of respondents from each country stating that corruption took place 'often' and 'always' when companies compete for private sector contracts

Nevertheless, from a business perspective, there is a danger that companies may underestimate the legal and commercial risks associated with corruption in private sector contracts. Both kinds of corruption are socially and economically damaging and demand the attention of policy-makers.

Corruption and the informal sector in sub-Saharan Africa
Emmanuelle Lavallée and François Roubaud[1]

In sub-Saharan Africa (SSA), the informal sector is a major engine for employment, entrepreneurship and growth.[2] It operates in an environment that is characterised by a high incidence of corruption. According to Transparency International's Corruption Perception Index 2007,

---

1 Emmanuelle Lavallée is an Assistant Professor at University Paris Dauphine and associate researcher at DIAL. François Roubaud is a senior research fellow at IRD and DIAL.

2 The size of the sector is estimated to account on average for 42 per cent of GDP in Africa in 2000. See F. Schneider, *Size and Measurement of the Informal Economy in 110 Countries around the World*, discussion paper (Washington, DC: World Bank, 2002). According to a 2002 report by the International Labour Organization (ILO), the share of informal sector employment varies from nearly 20 per cent in Botswana to over 90 per cent in Mali. See ILO, *ILO Compendium of Official Statistics on Employment in the Informal Sector*, STAT Working Paper no. 1 (Geneva: ILO, 2002)).

almost 70 per cent of SSA countries scored below 3 out of a possible 10, indicating that corruption is perceived as rampant.[3]

From an analysis of previous research, it appears that, while the corruption and informal sector nexus has been explored in eastern Europe and the former Soviet Union countries, it has not been studied in a comprehensive empirical fashion in sub-Saharan Africa. In eastern Europe the research was into the growth of unofficial activities coinciding with the transition from communism to free markets,[4] but the SSA context is completely different. In sub-Saharan Africa, operating in the informal sector is the rule rather than the exception and is not the result of recent systemic change. As such, the concepts used to analyse the informal sector elsewhere are not necessarily applicable to the region.

This study makes use of a unique data set, called *1-2-3 surveys*,[5] to analyse the links between corruption and the informal sector in seven major cities in the Western African Economic and Monetary Union (WAEMU).[6] More precisely, it uses phase 2 of these surveys, which includes interviews with heads of informal production units (IPUs)[7] and assesses their principal economic and productive characteristics (production, value added, investment, financing), their difficulties and their demands for public support. A detailed analysis of this data leads to three conclusions.

The informal economy is more related to weak law enforcement than to corruption

In all WAEMU capital cities there are at least four types of registration that a fully law-abiding firm should undertake: fiscal, licensing, trade and social security (for IPUs with employees). The data shows, however, that, in WAEMU capital cities, fewer than 20 per cent of IPUs register with at least one of these registers, while this drops to less than 10 per cent in Dakar and Lomé. In almost 60 per cent of the cases it appears that non-registration is due to ignorance of the law: 39 per cent of IPUs considered registration to be non-compulsory and 21 per cent did not know if they were required to do so or not. The survey results clearly suggest that there is

---

3 In comparison, this proportion is about 33 per cent in the Americas, 43 per cent in the Asia-Pacific region and 55 per cent in eastern Europe and central Asia.

4 Estimating the share of the unofficial economy in total GDP using the consumption-based methodology, Johnson, Kaufmann and Shleifer find that the average unofficial share in east European countries starts in 1989 at 16.6 per cent, peaks at 21.3 per cent in 1992 and falls to 19 per cent by 1995, whereas in the former Soviet Union it starts at 12 per cent and rises to 32.6 per cent and 34 per cent, respectively. See S. Johnson, D. Kaufmann and A. Shleifer, 'The Unofficial Economy in Transition', *Brookings Papers on Economic Activity*, no. 2 (1997).

5 The *1-2-3 Survey* is a three-phase survey, the basic rationale of which is the following. The first phase is a labour force survey. In the second phase of the survey, a sample of the heads of the informal production units identified in the first phase are interviewed. Finally, in the third phase, a sub-sample of households, selected from phase 1, is administered a specific income/expenditure survey.

6 The *1-2-3 Surveys* are an original series of urban household surveys conducted in seven major WAEMU cities (Abidjan, Bamako, Cotonou, Dakar, Lomé, Niamey and Ouagadougou) from 2001 to 2003 by the countries' national statistics institutes (NSIs), AFRISTAT and DIAL as part of the PARSTAT Project – i.e. the Regional Statistical Assistance Programme for multilateral monitoring sponsored by the WAEMU Commission.

7 An IPU is defined as a production unit with no fiscal registration number and no formal written bookkeeping.

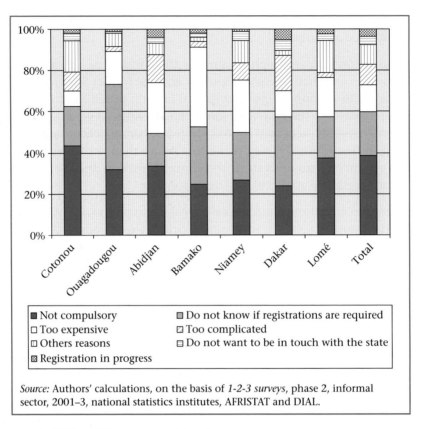

Source: Authors' calculations, on the basis of *1-2-3 surveys*, phase 2, informal sector, 2001–3, national statistics institutes, AFRISTAT and DIAL.

Figure 17: Reasons why IPUs' activities are not registered

no effective enforcement of registration requirements. Overall, only 6.2 per cent of the heads of IPUs claimed to have had problems with public agents in the previous year, ranging from 4 per cent in Bamako to 9 per cent in Dakar.

As a consequence, only a minority of IPUs (4.2 per cent) declared that they had had to pay bribes in the previous year. Nevertheless, taking into account only the IPUs that did have contact with the state in the previous year, the proportion paying bribes rises to 37 per cent, indicating that bribery is a significant means for settling disputes with public agents.

Although the incidence of corruption varies dramatically from city to city, it is particularly high in Lomé (47 per cent), Abidjan (45 per cent) and Bamako (40 per cent). Moreover, IPUs' responses suggest that the value of bribes paid is low, representing a minor part of the value added. It is possible, however, that IPUs' experience with corruption may reduce their propensity to register.

The phase 2 surveys also asked questions about the willingness of IPU heads to register their activities officially. Only 35 per cent of the IPU heads declared that they were willing to register their activities: variations in responses ranged from 21 per cent who were willing to do so in Lomé to 44 per cent in Dakar. The survey also found that the IPUs that

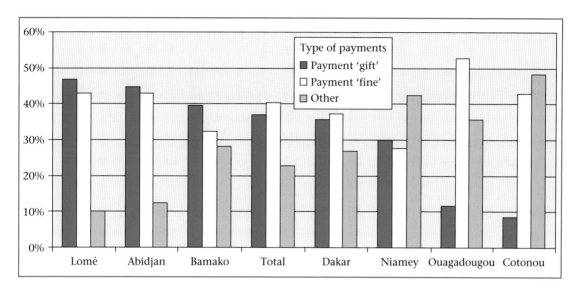

Figure 18: Proportion of IPUs that were in contact with public agents and made payments to them

Table 15: Predicted probability of the willingness to register according to the types of contact with public agents

Ideal type	Probability of willingness to register	95% confidence interval
An 'average' IPU that had no problem with public agents	0.30	0.28–0.33
An 'average' IPU that had to pay a bribe	0.36	0.27–0.46
An 'average' IPU that had to pay a fine	0.46	0.36–0.58
An 'average' IPU that used other means to settle its dispute with public agents	0.48	0.36–0.60

Source: Authors' estimations on the basis of *1-2-3 surveys*, phase 2, informal sector, 2001–3, national statistics institutes, AFRISTAT and DIAL.

Note: These predicted probabilities are computed on the basis of a probit model explaining the head of IPUs' willingness to register officially their activities. The values of the other independent variables (turnover, size, educational level, etc.) are held at their mean.

had come into contact with public agents and had experienced trouble with them were more likely to register their activities. It appears that contact with public agents helps to spread knowledge of the law, and that, once the sanctions for non-compliance are known, they are sufficiently dissuasive to encourage firms to register. On the other hand, corruption appears to have no such effect: the experience of paying bribes does not lead to a higher willingness to register activities than is the case for IPUs that had no problems with public agents.

Institutional determinants of corruption by Maghrebian firms

Clara Delavallade[1]

Although firms often pay large amounts of bribes, very few empirical studies have investigated the specific reasons why they are involved in corruption and how their involvement interacts with regulatory structures. An analysis of the corruption behaviour of north African firms contradicts the theoretical prediction that corruption increases with a firm's profitability and competitiveness[2] and sheds new light on the link between fiscal evasion and corruption.

Research scope and method

The business environment in north Africa has changed considerably over the last few years: foreign direct investment has risen and competition has increased, with more open borders both within the region and beyond. Firms have had to adapt their behaviour to this changing and more competitive environment, which may influence their approach to corruption.

This analysis focuses on three main determinants of a firm's bribe-paying activities: the extent of the firm's fiscal evasion, the security of its property rights and its competitiveness. The study examines these potential determinants in relation to two types of bribe-paying: 'administrative corruption', aimed at modifying the *application* of laws and regulations, and 'state capture', aimed at altering the *formulation* of laws and regulations.

The study relies on an econometric analysis of survey data from a random sample of 581 Algerian, Moroccan and Tunisian firms collected by the University of Paris Sorbonne in 2005. Ordered probit estimations were used to identify the motivations for state capture and administrative corruption in north Africa and then to compare these results with findings from Uganda[3] and transition countries.[4] The analysis is robust in the context of applying binomial and multinomial choice models, as well as when controlling for endogeneity and selection bias.

Research results

Fiscal evasion

The relationship between administrative corruption and fiscal evasion follows an inverted 'U' shape. When fiscal evasion is low, increasing it leads the firm to pay bribes more frequently, in

1 Clara Delavallade is a researcher at University Paris 1, Panthéon Sorbonne.
2 See C. J. Bliss and R. Di Tella, 'Does Competition Kill Corruption?', *Journal of Public Economy*, vol. 105 (1997).
3 J. Svensson, 'Who Must Pay Bribes and How Much? Evidence from a Cross-section of Firms', *Quarterly Journal of Economics*, vol. 118, no. 1 (2003).
4 J. S. Hellman, G. Jones and D. Kaufmann, *Seize the State, Seize the Day: State Capture, Corruption, and Influence in Transition*, Policy Research Working Paper no. 2444 (Washington, DC: World Bank, 2000).

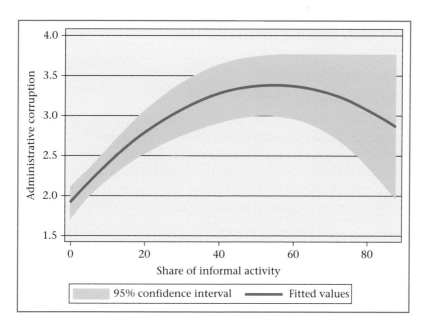

Figure 19: Administrative corruption and degree of informal activity

order to 'buy' controls and inspections; fiscal evasion and administrative corruption therefore go hand in hand. In contrast to what studies on transition countries have revealed, this is true only up to a certain point in north Africa. Above a certain threshold, hiding more revenues from tax payments reduces the likelihood that the firm practices frequent administrative corruption. For large-scale fiscal evasion, concealment by administrative corruption is ineffective, too risky or too expensive. Figure 19 presents this relationship. It suggests that the threshold lies at about 55 per cent of undeclared sales.

Security of property rights

Do state capture and administrative corruption increase in north Africa with the insecurity of a firm's property rights, expressed by the failure of courts to implement the law? This relationship was, for example, observed in the former Soviet Union countries.[5]

For north Africa, this seems to be the case only for state capture: firms that face a failing legal system resort more often to state capture, but not to administrative corruption – i.e. they try to have a direct influence on the formulation of laws, but do not significantly expand their efforts to use administrative corruption.

It appears, therefore, that attempts to influence the content of laws through bribes are rather driven by the insecurity of property rights due to a failing legal system, whereas administrative

---

5 See S. Johnson, D. Kaufmann and P. Zoido-Lobaton, 'Regulatory Discretion and the Unofficial Economy', *American Economic Review*, vol. 88, no. 2 (1998); J. S. Hellman, G. Jones and D. Kaufmann, 2000.

corruption is favoured by firms that try to keep some of their activities hidden (up to a certain threshold of undeclared sales).

Competitiveness

The data also indicate that both state capture and administrative corruption appear to be used to help compensate for poor competitiveness and low profitability. Our results show that north African firms that engage in more corruption are not the most profitable ones, as other research has suggested for Ugandan firms,[6] but the ones threatened most by competition. Low competitiveness encourages firms to turn to bribery to influence the content or application of laws and regulations in order to gain an unfair advantage over their competitors.

These findings are in line with the implications of a frequently referenced theoretical model proposed by Christopher Bliss and Rafael Di Tella, who argue that increasing competition may not reduce overall corruption.[7] They suggest that this may be due to the fact that the more profitable firms end up paying higher bribes once the less profitable firms are forced out of the market. In contrast, the findings for north Africa suggest that the underlying mechanism is related to the least profitable ones engaging in more corruption, in order to not be pushed out of the market. This conclusion also contrasts with previous studies on transition countries, which have found that the competitive position of firms does not explain the supply of corruption.[8]

With these contrasting findings, the study on north Africa highlights a new and different set of mechanisms through which institutions and a changing economic environment affect the level of corruption among firms.

---

6 See J. Svensson, 2003.
7 C. J. E. Bliss and R. Di Tella, 1997.
8 See J. S. Hellman, G. Jones and D. Kaufmann, 2000.

8 Strengthening corporate integrity: empirical studies of disclosure, rule diffusion and enforcement

Transparency in reporting on anti-corruption measures: a survey of corporate practices

Susan Côté-Freeman[1]

A stricter regulatory environment and a series of high-profile corruption scandals in the past decade are prompting companies to consider more seriously the risks that bribery and corruption pose to their businesses. Although surveys and anecdotal evidence point to a growing adoption of anti-corruption codes and measures by companies, little is known about the scope of these commitments. Moreover, public reporting by companies on anti-bribery and corruption measures appears uneven at best.

To shed some light on this issue, Transparency International commissioned research assessing company reporting based on the Transparency in Reporting on Anti-Corruption (TRAC) criteria. TRAC examines the extent to which 500 leading public companies from thirty-two countries/territories reported, as of July 2007, that they had in place strategies, policies and management systems for combating bribery and corruption. The data was gathered from publicly available sources, such as the annual reports, sustainability reports and websites of companies. TRAC's primary intent is to help improve and standardise corporate reporting on anti-bribery measures.

TRAC is based on a review of individual companies with results aggregated by country/ territory and sectors. TI has deliberately refrained from publishing a company ranking in this first edition of the survey so as to acknowledge that anti-corruption reporting remains a nascent practice. It was deemed more appropriate at this initial stage to communicate the criteria for reporting and highlight examples of best practice.

---

1 Susan Côté-Freeman is programme manager with Transparency International's private sector programme.

Box 6 Information sought on corporate anti-bribery efforts for TRAC survey

Strategy (maximum 10 points)

- An overall code of conduct or statement of principles, including a reference to anti-bribery (2)
- membership in key multi-stakeholder initiatives with an anti-corruption component (Global Compact, the World Economic Forum's Partnership Against Corruption Initiative (PACI), various sectoral initiatives, etc.) (3)
- a specific corporate anti-bribery or anti-corruption policy (2)
- the extent to which this policy is applied to employees, business partners and others (3)

Policy (maximum 15 points) – The extent and depth of the company's:

- anti-bribery policy commitment (5)
- prohibition of facilitation payments (3.5)
- regulation of inappropriate giving and receiving of gifts by employees (2.5)
- regulation and transparency of political contributions (2)
- commitment to making its lobbying activities transparent (2)

Management systems (maximum 25 points) – The extent to which the company:

- requires business partners to comply with its anti-corruption approach, including due diligence and training of partners, as appropriate (5)
- provides training to employees and agents, and clearly communicates its policies, including in indigenous languages, as appropriate (5)
- has a whistleblowing and employee help/guidance system in place, including non-victimisation provisions (5)
- has review and verification systems in place to monitor corruption-related issues and breaches, and act against employees involved, and has its systems externally verified/audited (5)
- reports relevant key performance indicators (KPIs), including the number and nature of complaints, the number of disciplinary actions for corruption and bribery, and the extent of bribery-related training (5)

TRAC's scoring system

The 500 companies selected for the TRAC survey were analysed to determine what publicly disclosed information existed for each element outlined in the box above. Every company was then given a numerical score for each of the three categories – 'Strategy', 'Policy' and 'Management systems' – as well as a total score. The total score was converted into a number of stars from one to

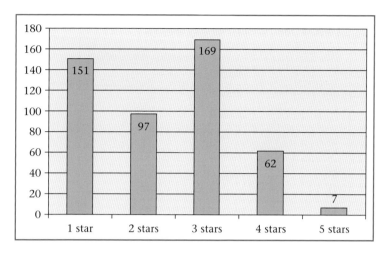

Figure 20: Number of companies by rating category

five, with a five-star score being the highest.[2] No company achieved the maximum possible score of 50; seventy-five companies scored zero points and were awarded the minimum of one star.

Survey highlights

The results demonstrate that, on average, leading companies fail to report convincingly on how they are embedding anti-corruption practices in their organisations. The average score was only 17 out of a possible 50. Only seven companies achieved a five-star score, with another sixty-two receiving four stars. While companies were often seen to adopt high-level strategic commitments of zero tolerance to bribery and corruption, these were not always complemented by an equivalent reporting of supporting systems.

TRAC also analysed the average scores of companies from a range of countries/territories, many of which represent major world economies. The average score for Canadian and US companies places them in the highest category, albeit with a three-star ranking that leaves much room for improvement, alongside the Netherlands and Switzerland. The countries/territories with the weakest averages were Russia, Taiwan, China, Belgium and Japan.

Rankings by industry sector also spanned a wide range. The oil and gas, and aerospace and defence, sectors were among the best performers. Although these sectors have long been viewed as prone to corruption, the results imply that some of the leading companies in these fields have developed more extensive disclosure practices, perhaps in reaction to high-profile scandals and greater stakeholder expectations. Construction and major engineering firms have considerably lower average scores, suggesting that they are failing to communicate publicly the measures they may be putting in place to manage the risk of corruption.

---

2 0–9.9 points = 1 star, 10–19.9 points = 2 stars, 20–29.9 points = 3 stars, 30–39.9 points = 4 stars, 40–50 points = 5 stars.

| Table 16: TRAC country/territory rankings ||
Stars	Country/territory
*	Russia
*	Taiwan
*	China
*	Belgium
*	Japan
**	Hong Kong
**	South Korea
**	France
**	Sweden
**	Germany
**	Italy
**	Spain
***	United Kingdom
***	Netherlands
***	Switzerland
***	United States
***	Canada

Note: Only countries/territories with more than ten companies in the sample are included in the ranking.

It is important to note that TRAC does not attempt to measure the extent to which companies may be corrupt. It also does not assume that companies with high scores are not involved in corrupt practices, or, conversely, that companies with low scores are resorting to corrupt practices. Nevertheless, the very poor reporting performance of some countries/territories and industry sectors raises concerns that their companies have not established policies and systems to prevent bribery.

TI believes that the risks and responsibilities associated with bribery and corruption demand a greater level of transparency by companies. TRAC is a first attempt by TI to capture the extent and quality of company disclosure of their systems to prevent bribery and corruption. The results demonstrate that much improvement is needed, and TI intends to assist in this area by producing anti-corruption reporting guidance. In the meantime, it is hoped that companies will take note of TRAC's assessment criteria to focus their anti-bribery disclosure practices, and that existing reporting initiatives will also consider TRAC to develop their criteria on bribery and corruption further.

Revenue transparency of oil and gas companies
Juanita Olaya[1]

Transparency International's *Promoting Revenue Transparency: 2008 Report on Revenue Transparency of Oil and Gas Companies*[2] evaluates forty-two leading oil and gas companies[3] on their current policies, management systems and performance in areas relevant to revenue transparency in their upstream operations. The origins of this report lie in the global movement to combat the 'resource curse', whereby the great wealth generated by extractive industries has the potential to undermine a country's economic growth and social development. Poorly managing extractive revenues can heighten corruption in the public and private sectors, or even fuel conflict. The resulting poverty, instability and weakening of the rule of law carry repercussions that extend beyond the local people; they can also damage company reputations and generate lower returns to investors.[4]

Enhancing the quality of resource governance is the key to transforming this curse into a blessing. A crucial step is the strengthening of the accountability of the decision-makers who control extractive resources and revenues. To ensure accountability, adequate information is needed about the resources being extracted, the revenues generated and where these funds flow. This information must be provided by companies and governments alike in order to allow cross-verification and in-depth monitoring by civil society.

Research design

Revenue transparency in the TI report considers three areas of corporate action in which disclosure can contribute to improved accountability in the management of extractive revenues: payments to host governments, operations and corporate anti-corruption programmes. Each area is examined across three levels of implementation: policy, management systems and performance. The companies are evaluated in a total of twenty-one countries of operation, based on information made publicly available by the companies.

Although the revenue-reporting practices of oil and gas companies are the primary focus, the analysis reflects the fact that companies act in a complex regulatory environment requiring the supportive participation of host and home governments. As a result, the methodology was designed to focus on the companies' roles, but not to hold them accountable or responsible for host- or home-government obligations.

---

1 Juanita Olaya was formerly the programme manager for the Promoting Revenue Transparency project at Transparency International.
2 The full report is available online in several languages at www.transparency.org/policy_research/surveys_indices/ promoting_revenue_transparency.
3 The companies in this report were chosen for their relevance, geographic spread and size, and are not a representative sample of all oil and gas extraction companies. It includes nineteen private international oil companies (IOCs) and twenty-three national oil companies (NOCs).
4 See article starting on page 54.

A participatory approach was adopted in researching and drafting the report. A variety of stakeholders, most notably the companies themselves, were engaged during the research design and data review process. Several companies used the opportunity to review their own data and provide feedback; regrettably, and despite all efforts to engage them, about thirty companies did not take this opportunity. The hope is that, in future iterations of the report, more companies will welcome the prospect of reviewing their data. The report-drafting process benefited from the input of a multi-stakeholder group.

Findings

The results of the report produce five primary findings.

- *Revenue transparency is not yet a common practice in the industry*. Two-thirds of the companies evaluated fall into the middle- or low-performance categories. Most of the evaluated companies provide insufficient reports on their payments to host governments (see figure 21).
- *Wide variation exists in company practice*. Leading IOCs and NOCs demonstrate that revenue transparency is possible and that proactive company efforts can make a difference. This information could be useful to encourage companies to exert peer pressure on their competitors to set a common high standard. Working to achieve such a standard is an imperative.
- *Good practice in revenue transparency starts at home*, where national regulations have a strong influence on current company revenue transparency practices.
- *Regulatory approaches produce systematic impacts*. Two main types of regulation currently have some limited impact and have the potential to level the playing field even further:
  - regulations with a multi-country impact, such as stock exchange listing regulations and accounting standards; and
  - host-government reforms along the lines of the Extractive Industries Transparency Initiative (EITI).[5]
- *Disclosure of information on revenue transparency is hindered* by diverse reporting formats that are difficult to obtain, interpret and compare between companies and countries.

Based on these key findings, the report introduces four main recommendations to improve revenue transparency.

First, oil and gas companies should proactively report in all areas relevant to revenue transparency on a country-by-country basis. They should also discourage governments from including in their contracts confidentiality clauses that obstruct revenue transparency. Companies that have already started to disclose information in some countries should extend their reporting to all countries in which they operate.

Second, home governments and the appropriate regulatory agencies should urgently consider introducing mandatory revenue transparency reporting for the operations of companies at

---

5   EITI is a voluntary initiative under which host governments and extractive companies agree to disclose company payments for extractive activities and government receipts, respectively. The two data sets then undergo a process of independent reconciliation.

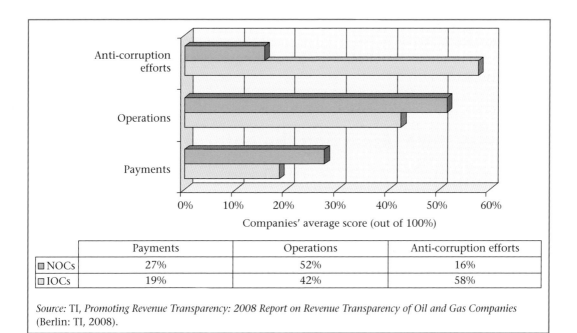

	Payments	Operations	Anti-corruption efforts
■ NOCs	27%	52%	16%
□ IOCs	19%	42%	58%

Source: TI, *Promoting Revenue Transparency: 2008 Report on Revenue Transparency of Oil and Gas Companies* (Berlin: TI, 2008).

Figure 21: IOC and NOC average results, by areas of revenue transparency

home and abroad. This would help to overcome confidentiality restrictions in host countries, hold host governments accountable and encourage a level playing field that achieves a higher degree of transparency. Based on these goals, the following actions are recommended:

- home governments should require revenue transparency from their companies;
- home governments should ensure that their NOCs operate under the highest standards of transparency in their operations at home and abroad; and
- when revenue transparency does not become mandatory by law, stock exchange listing regulations and international accounting standards should be adapted to encourage revenue transparency disclosure.

Third, governments of oil- and gas-producing countries should urgently consider introducing regulations that require all companies operating in their territories to make public all information relevant to revenue transparency. More host countries should fully implement EITI and introduce measures that will set the highest standards for revenue transparency in their territories. Countries already taking steps in this direction should ensure that regulations are implemented effectively. This includes disclosure by their own NOCs and other state-owned enterprises related to the industry. Along these lines, host countries are encouraged to eliminate aspects of confidentiality clauses that depart from legally protected information and prevent full revenue transparency in their territories.

Fourth, regulatory agencies and companies should improve the accessibility, comprehensiveness and comparability of reporting in all areas of revenue transparency by adopting a uniform global reporting standard. Efforts to introduce uniform standards (e.g. international accounting standards, stock exchange listing requirements) should receive full support. Regulatory initiatives need to address the characteristics and the quality of reporting when establishing reporting templates.

A mixed picture: assessing the enforcement of the OECD Anti-Bribery Convention
Gillian Dell[1]

The adoption of the OECD Convention on Combating Bribery of Foreign Public Officials in International Business Transactions (OECD Anti-Bribery Convention) in 1997 was a landmark event in the fight against international corruption: a collective commitment by governments of the leading industrialised states to address the supply side of corruption and ban foreign bribery. Because most major multinational companies are based in OECD countries, the convention was hailed as the key to overcoming the damaging effects of foreign bribery on democratic institutions, development programmes and business competition. There are now thirty-seven countries that are party to the convention and subject to the requirement to criminalise foreign bribery.

Monitoring enforcement of the convention is essential, in order to gauge its effectiveness and identify gaps that require further action by national policy-makers.

Methodology

Transparency International has developed a methodology to assess country-by-country progress in implementing the convention. TI's *OECD Anti-Bribery Convention Progress Report 2008*, the fourth in an annual series,[2] is based on information provided by national experts selected by TI national chapters in each country. These experts assess progress with a semi-structured questionnaire that addresses thirteen specific issue clusters, ranging from the number of cases and investigations brought to important related institutional features such as whistleblower protection, complaints procedures and legal obstacles. The number of investigations was difficult to obtain in many countries and was recorded only for the year covered to avoid the double-counting of investigations that turned into prosecutions. The inclusion in the progress report of key domestic cases concerning bribery by foreign companies or subsidiaries of such companies gives additional insights into how bribery affects OECD countries themselves and is addressed by those countries.

---

1 Gillian Dell is a programme manager at Transparency International.
2 TI, *OECD Anti-Bribery Convention Progress Report 2008* (Berlin: TI, 2008).

A glass still more than half empty

The findings highlight that significant enforcement is present in only sixteen out of thirty-four countries, with little or no enforcement in the others. This lack of enforcement on a significant scale creates a real risk of backsliding, including by strong enforcers that may be discouraged by the lack of collective progress. Against this backdrop, the United Kingdom's termination of its investigation into bribery allegations against BAe Systems in December 2006 was a particularly damaging setback for the convention.

Table 17 shows that enforcement has increased substantially in three G7 countries: France, Germany and the United States. It also shows there is still little or no enforcement in three other G7 countries: Canada, Japan and the United Kingdom.

With regard to transparency issues, experts in twenty-four of the countries reported a lack of access to information about cases and/or investigations.

The analysis also highlights the fact that the status of related legislation and enforcement systems is still far from adequate in many countries. Statutory obstacles were reported for eighteen countries, while enforcement is hampered by a lack of centralised coordination (in fourteen countries), a lack of adequate complaints procedures (in thirteen) and deficiencies in whistleblower protection in as many as twenty-six countries.

Sustaining the momentum for stronger enforcement will require continuing the rigorous monitoring under the auspices of the OECD Working Group on Bribery, and should include country visits, regular meetings with prosecutors and the publication of an annual report on foreign bribery prosecutions and investigations.

Table 17: Foreign bribery cases and investigations

	Country	Enforcement				Share of world exports (%) for 2007 (UNCTAD, 2007)
		Cases		Investigations		
		2008	2007	2008	2007	
1	Argentina	1	0	0	0	0.36
2	Australia	1 (1)	u	s (s)	4 (1)	1.06
3	Austria	0	0	2	0	1.25
4	Belgium	4	4	s	s	2.90
5	Brazil	u	0	s (s)	1	1.06
6	Bulgaria	3	3	0	0	0.14
7	Canada	1	1	s	s	3.14
8	Chile	0	0	0	0	0.45
9	Czech Republic	0	0	1	0	0.73
10	Denmark	17 (17)	1	0	21 (21)	0.97

Table 17 (continued)

	Country	Enforcement				Share of world exports (%) for 2007 (UNCTAD, 2007)
		Cases		Investigations		
		2008	2007	2008	2007	
11	Estonia	0	0	0	0	0.09
12	Finland	1	0	3	1	0.64
13	France	19	9	16	u	4.11
14	Germany	43+	+4	>88	>83 (63)	8.80
15	Greece	0	u	1 or 0	u	0.38
16	Hungary	23	18	1	27	0.58
17	Ireland	0	u	3 (3)	3 (3)	1.23
18	Italy	2	2	3	1	3.44
19	Japan	1	1	u	u	5.15
20	Mexico	0	0	0	0	1.80
21	Netherlands	7 (7)	0	3	8 (7)	3.69
22	New Zealand	0	0	s (s)	2 (2)	0.20
23	Norway	4	2	u	u	1.04
24	Poland	0	0	0	0	0.88
25	Portugal	u	0	u	2	0.41
26	Slovakia	0	0	0	0	0.32
27	Slovenia	0	0	0	0	0.17
28	South Korea	5	5	1	2	2.20
29	Spain	2	2	0	1	2.11
30	Sweden	1	1	15 (12)	14 (12)	1.34
31	Switzerland	16 (14)	1	36	23 (17)	1.31
32	Turkey	0	0	1	0	0.72
33	United Kingdom	0	0	20	15	4.56
34	United States	103	67	69	60	9.84

Source: Adapted from TI, 2008.

Note: ( ) = oil for food cases, some not bribery; u = unknown; s = some.

Laws against bribery abroad are effective in deterring investments in corrupt countries

Alvaro Cuervo-Cazurra[1]

In order to combat corruption, countries have laws to punish bribery and reduce demands for bribes by politicians and government officials. Such legislation may not be effective in all countries, however, as a judge may accept a bribe not to enforce the law, or a government official demanding a bribe may be a politician with the power to alter legislation or affect its implementation.

Another important strategy is thus to reduce the supply of bribes by foreign investors, by strengthening laws against bribery abroad in the countries from which foreign investments originate. Such laws reduce incentives for corruption by increasing the risks of detection for multinational companies that pay bribes to foreign government officials. Since the largest foreign investors tend to come from countries with relatively effective judicial systems, this may be a promising strategy for curbing corruption abroad.

There are doubts about the effectiveness of such laws, however. Investors from the United States have been bound by the Foreign Corrupt Practices Act since 1977, but studies have shown that US investors do not appear to be less likely to invest in corrupt countries than other investors.

This study argues, therefore, that countries need not only to implement laws against bribery abroad but also to coordinate their implementation with other countries, in order to effect sensitivity towards corruption in foreign investors in host countries. If anti-bribery laws are implemented by only one country, a corrupt government official can easily demand a bribe from competitors from other countries that do not have legal constraints on overseas bribery. This can put pressure on firms from the country with anti-corruption laws to remain competitive. When all competing companies are bound by similar laws, a level playing field will have been created on which companies will be able to compete abroad with integrity.

Research design

This idea was tested by analysing the effectiveness of the OECD Convention on Combating Bribery of Foreign Public Officials in International Business Transactions. The thirty members of the OECD and six other non-member countries[2] agreed in 1997 to change their national laws to prohibit bribes to foreign officials and to officials of international institutions. The convention was ratified in 1999, and it has resulted in the progressive change of national

---

1 Alvaro Cuervo-Cazurra is Assistant Professor at the Moore School of Business, University of South Carolina.
2 Argentina, Brazil, Bulgaria, Chile, Estonia and Slovenia.

legislation to outlaw the payment of bribes abroad. Additionally, the convention entails a periodic review process, which is meant to ensure that laws are not only altered but also implemented, and that the payment of bribes abroad is effectively prosecuted.

To test the impact of the convention, the study examines foreign direct investment inflows to 103 host economies for the period 1996 to 2002, with 1999, the year the convention was ratified, as the midpoint. The analysis focuses on whether investors from countries that introduced laws against bribery abroad as a result of the OECD convention became more sensitive to corruption in host countries and further reduced their investments in countries perceived as corrupt beyond the general reduction in FDI that corruption generates.[3] A series of econometric models, including so-called differences-in-differences estimations, was used to examine this question, while controlling for several standard determinants of foreign investment flows, such as country size, geographic distance and cultural similarities.

Results

The analysis reveals that investors from countries that have implemented laws against bribery abroad have become more sensitive to host-country corruption. These investors reduced their FDI in countries perceived as corrupt after their home countries had implemented laws against bribery abroad.

The study also specifically examines the behaviour of US investors before and after the ratification of the OECD convention. It finds that US investors may no longer have an incentive to bypass the FCPA when other leading foreign investors are bound by similar laws. US investors became more sensitive to host-country corruption and reduced their FDI in countries perceived as corrupt once the OECD convention had been ratified.

The implications of these findings suggest that laws against bribery abroad appear to be effective, but only when the legislation in place is coordinated in multiple countries. The study illustrates how the creation and implementation of laws against bribery abroad can be effective in influencing the behaviour of investors, thereby highlighting the benefits of cross-country collaboration and the value added by international institutions.

---

3 For the full study, see A. Cuervo-Cazurra, 'The Effectiveness of Laws against Bribery Abroad', *Journal of International Business Studies*, vol. 39, no. 4 (2008).

Public and private enforcement of securities laws: resource-based evidence

Howell E. Jackson and Mark J. Roe[1]

What governance mechanisms are most effective in supporting the development of financial markets? Private enforcement, for example though lawsuits brought by defrauded investors, or public enforcement through regulatory agencies?

So far, influential empirical studies have suggested that private enforcement is more effective and has helped shape the policy agenda accordingly.[2] Their assessment of public enforcement has focused largely on assessing the rules on the books and the structural design of regulatory oversight, however. Actual resources – staffing and budgets – have not been considered.

This study claims that taking into account these two resource-related variables produces a very different picture, with important implications for financial market development. Drawing on data for regulatory budgets and staffing levels in more than forty-five countries, public enforcement is shown to be at least as important as private enforcement in explaining financial market outcomes around the world. Intense public enforcement correlates with more robust financial outcomes.[3]

Research design

The study constructs two categories of resource-based public enforcement of securities regulations: one with regulatory budgets scaled to the nation's GDP and another with regulatory staffing scaled to its population.

The full sample to explore the importance of these categories consists of information on staffing numbers for fifty-three countries and territories and budget information for forty-six.

A series of econometric tests are performed to examine the role of these indicators in determining several parameters of financial market development and to compare the importance of *enforcement resources* relative to *private enforcement* and parameters of *formal enforcement*, such as laws and regulations or the structural design of regulatory institutions.

A very diverse picture

Countries in the study allocate very different resource levels to financial oversight. Canada, for example, reports nearly thirty-nine securities regulators per million of the population,

---

1 Howell E. Jackson and Mark J. Roe are Professors of Law at Harvard University. This paper is forthcoming in the *Journal of Financial Economics*; it is also available at ssrn.com/abstract=100086.
2 See, for example, R. La Porta, F. Lopez-de-Silanes and A. Shleifer, 'What Works in Securities Laws?', *Journal of Finance*, vol. 61, no. 1 (2006).
3 For the full study, see H. E. Jackson and M. J. Roe, *Public and Private Enforcement of Securities Laws: Resource-based Evidence*, Working Paper no. 08-28 (Cambridge, MA: Harvard Law School, 2007).

Table 18: Resources for public enforcement in securities regulation, selected countries

	Staff per million of population	Budget in US$ per billion US$ GDP
Argentina	3.46	15,984
Brazil	2.68	35,260
Canada	38.98	83,932
France	5.93	29,205
Germany	4.43	13,527
India	0.43	n/a
Indonesia	1.97	5,571
Japan	4.61	17,000
Netherlands	23.52	138,785
South Africa	3.82	118,453
South Korea	13.15	95,147
Turkey	6.18	45,417
United Kingdom	19.05	81,709
United States	23.29	76,459

whereas Spain, with a comparable GDP, reports only slightly more than seven staff per million of the population. The level of public resources devoted to financial regulation is typically higher in common law jurisdictions than civil law countries.

Strong rules on the books are not always matched by plentiful resources to enforce them. France illustrates this phenomenon: although the French securities regulators' formal powers and independence are high, the country allocates only some US$29,205 per billion of GDP to enforcement. The Netherlands, in contrast, has slightly below-average formal enforcement powers, but in terms of resources for measuring public enforcement ranks well above the mean.

Resources matter – public enforcement matters

The econometric analysis of the data set shows that budgetary resources and the staffing of regulatory agencies are significantly associated with standard measures of stock market development (stock market capitalisation, trading volume, the number of domestic firms, and the number of initial public offerings). More intense public enforcement is linked to better financial market outcomes, even when controlling for the strength of formal rules and regulatory structures. The resources earmarked for public enforcement can indicate the degree to which a public authority is able to conduct market surveillance, investigate individual firms for violations, bring enforcement actions and revise improved regulatory rules.

The research also found that public enforcement and private enforcement perform to similar levels, when taking into account the actual resources devoted to public enforcement. Public enforcement can invoke sharp criminal, financial and reputational penalties in order to deter wrongdoing. On the other hand, private enforcement can benefit from actors who are the best informed and close to the transactions concerned.

At the same time, neither public nor private enforcement is flawless. Public actors may have mixed and weak incentives to perform well and lack information about general market and specific firm conditions. Private enforcement may suffer from collective action and free-rider problems, as well as slow and inaccurate judiciaries, lawyers' rent-seeking and the inability of private actors to inflict severe monetary penalties on wrongdoers.

Implications for developing financial markets in weak governance contexts

This evidence sheds new light on issues associated with public enforcement in states with weak governance structures. It is currently assumed that private enforcement is preferable in such a setting, when corruption risks are high, and regulatory agencies and thus public enforcement are particularly vulnerable to capture by corrupt politicians and bureaucrats.

Even in this context, however, there is little reason to believe that private litigation is necessarily structurally more efficacious. Litigation depends on the functioning of a public governance mechanism, the judiciary, which *a priori* cannot be assumed to be less prone to corruption than regulatory agencies. On the contrary, it may prove more feasible *in the short term* to strengthen public enforcement and focus on reforming specialised regulators rather than promoting comprehensive judiciary reform to improve the prospects for private enforcement.

Law and the market: the impact of enforcement
John C. Coffee, Jr.[1]

Assessing the impact of laws and regulations on financial development is an important area of scholarly enquiry that provides vital input to the design of related governance frameworks. Much of the attention has so far focused on mapping substantive differences in legislation (the laws on the books) and linking these differences to the respective performance profiles of financial markets. Such a narrow approach may yield incomplete and at times misleading conclusions, however, since it leaves out an important dimension: the intensity of enforcement – that is, the extent to which enacted laws are put into practice.

A first crop of studies on enforcement intensity has begun to shed some light on the inputs for enforcement – e.g. the budgets and staff numbers of regulatory agencies. This study builds on

---

1 John C. Coffee, Jr., is Adolf A. Berle Professor of Law at Columbia University Law School, New York.

this body of work and extends the analysis to the enforcement outputs of the United Kingdom and the United States, such as the number of enforcement actions brought or the type and severity of penalties levied. The empirical results summarised here are part of a larger enquiry into the role of enforcement intensity in explaining financial development.[2] The numbers presented are meant only to flag some pertinent findings with regard to empirical differences in enforcement intensities and some challenges when comparing them.

Towards a nuanced picture of the rules and their efficacy: from laws to enforcement intensity and style

As figure 22 shows, the financial penalties imposed by securities regulators in the United Kingdom (the Financial Services Authority – FSA) and the United States (the Securities and Exchange Commission – SEC) vary significantly.

These disparities remain very significant when controlling for the different size of the stock markets in both countries.

At first sight, overall budget allocations may not appear to provide much of an explanation for these differences. The United States does not expend more than other countries on enforcement if one takes market size and GDP into consideration.

A closer look, however, reveals widely different approaches in how budgetary resources are allocated. The US SEC dedicated between 37 and 41 per cent of its total budget to enforcement activities between 2004 and 2007, while the UK FSA by comparison devotes only around a third – between 12 and 13 per cent – to the same activities.

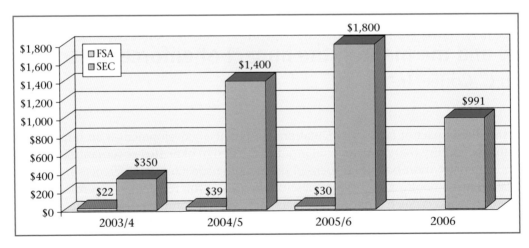

Figure 22: Financial penalties collected annually: SEC compared to FSA (US$ millions)

2 For the full study, see J. C. Coffee, Jr., 'Law and the Market: The Impact of Enforcement', *University of Pennsylvania Law Review*, vol. 156, no. 2 (2007).

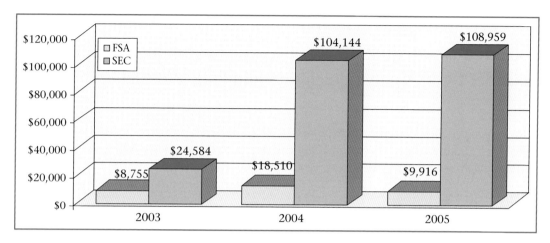

Figure 23: Financial penalties collected annually (US$ per billion dollars market capitalisation)

These figures reflect differences in enforcement styles. Even independently of the budgetary resources available to them, regulators can behave very differently. Some may advise, request and even admonish but be slow to punish. Others may believe that punitive fines generate a desirable general deterrent effect and that the great danger lies in levying overly mild penalties that can be easily absorbed as a cost of business. In this regard, the FSA and the SEC appear to be located at opposite ends of the continuum.

These empirical insights highlight the fact that enforcement intensity and style can and do vary widely between countries, and that these dimensions of enforcement need to be taken into account when assessing the efficacy and impact of particular laws and regulations.

Enforcement intensity and style matter. Ignoring budgetary resources, staffing numbers, output and the style of enforcement yields a distorted picture of what does and does not work in securities regulation.[3]

---

3 The full study takes these findings as a point of departure to re-examine claims about the efficacy of common versus civil law jurisdictions in supporting the developments of financial markets.

The corporate governance role of the media: evidence from Russia

Alexander Dyck, Natalya Volchkova and Luigi Zingales[1]

> Our basic approach is to thoroughly research and understand where the corporate malfeasance is taking place... We then share the stories to the press. By doing so we want to inflict real consequences – business, reputational and financial.
>
> Bill Browder, chairman of the Hermitage Fund

Hedge funds are among the most powerful players in corporate governance. Seeking to obtain the highest level of returns, fund managers have an interest in seeing the companies in which they invest operate according to governance standards that ensure the highest possible profit and stability.

One tactic for achieving this has been to draw public attention to corporate wrongdoing in order to foster change in company policy or leadership. Can hedge funds effectively encourage the media to report on misbehaving companies, however, and does coverage translate into real changes in company policy?

The business landscape of Russia in the late 1990s offers a unique set of conditions that allow these questions to be tested. During that period corporate governance violations in Russia were significant, common and visible. Because mechanisms to redress these violations were either ineffective or non-existent, it became possible to measure the effect that media coverage had on corporate governance outcomes. The presence of the Hermitage Fund in Russia offered a second advantage. An investment fund with low portfolio turnover, Hermitage adopted an aggressive media strategy in 1998 that shone a spotlight on corporate wrongdoing and sought to shame chief executive officers into better behaviour.

Research design

Between 1998 and 2002 the Russian investment bank Troika Dialog produced a weekly publication that highlighted all corporate actions that threatened the rights of outside investors. From this publication, ninety-eight serious governance violations were identified and grouped into seven categories, including corporate strategies to disenfranchise shareholders and methods to dilute returns to minority shareholders.

To measure the capacity of media coverage to spark action against poor corporate decisions, the outcomes of each of the ninety-eight events were examined and coded according to whether there was a significant change in corporate behaviour, a partial change or no change

---

1 Alexander Dyck is Associate Professor at the University of Toronto, Natalya Volchkova is an economist at the Center for Economic and Financial Research in Moscow and Luigi Zingales is Professor of Finance at the University of Chicago.

at all. The related media coverage was classified according to whether coverage came from the Russian media in the Russian language, the foreign media in the Russian language or the Anglo-American media in English.

Because one expects a relationship between levels of press coverage and the likelihood of redress in corporate governance violations (new coverage naturally gears towards scandals, scandals naturally demand redress), the study also examined the significance of a company belonging to the Hermitage portfolio, an exogenous component in news coverage. Hermitage's portfolio composition in 1998 was used to ensure that the hedge fund was not simply buying into companies that were highly visible or that it knew were about to receive increased media attention.

Research findings

The findings suggest that Hermitage's outreach to news media paid off. The hedge fund's position as a shareholder in the company increased the amount of media coverage that a corporate governance violation received, regardless of either the magnitude of the violation[2] or the general newsworthiness of the company in question. Although 47 per cent of media attention was determined by the size of the firm and its natural newsworthiness, 53 per cent was accounted for by Hermitage ownership.

Access to the international media proved to be a key source of leverage. Coverage of an event in the Anglo-American media significantly prompted redress of decisions that negatively affected outside investors. Violations reported by the international media, such as *The Wall Street Journal* and the *Financial Times*, were reversed 59 per cent of the time. In comparison, corporate actions that received no international media coverage were reversed only 22 per cent of the time.

Revelations in the local press had little impact. *Vedomosti*, a Russian-language paper produced by *The Wall Street Journal* and the *Financial Times* and distributed only in Russia, demonstrated no significant effect on corporate outcomes. This suggests that the reputational threat to companies was greatest when coverage came from the Anglo-American media.

In approximately a half of the cases, media pressure and the threat of a damaged reputation vis-à-vis foreign investors and policy-makers prompted a regulator or politician to intervene for at least partial resolution of the case. In 29 per cent of violations, press coverage that built on pre-existing opposition led to positive resolution of the case. Twenty-one per cent of instances were resolved by what appeared to be voluntary changes by the company, making it difficult to gauge the role of press coverage in this context.

Policy implications

The Hermitage strategy for using the media may be less important for hedge funds operating in other contexts. In the United States and most parts of Europe, hedge funds can adopt legal actions to address grievances over violations in corporate governance. While the situation in

---

2 Measured as the greatest potential loss that a violation might cause to minority shareholders.

Russia in the late 1990s carried unique conditions for study, general lessons can nonetheless be extrapolated.

Hermitage's communication efforts also demonstrate that media coverage does not depend solely on the newsworthiness of any given event. Interested parties can be effective in influencing media coverage and cause real consequences for corporate governance.

Index